Secrets
from the
Southern Living®
Test Kitchens

Oxmoor House®

© 2002 by Oxmoor House, Inc.
Book Division of Southern Progress Corporation
P. O. Box 2463
Birmingham, Alabama 35201

Library of Congress Catalog Number:
    2002105069
ISBN: 0-8487-2507-7

Printed in the United States of America
Second printing 2002

To order additional publications, call
    1-800-633-4910.

For more books to enrich your life, visit
oxmoorhouse.com

Southern Living®

Executive Foods Editor: Susan Dosier
Foods Editors: Andria Scott Hurst, Scott Jones
Associate Foods Editor: Shirley Harrington
Assistant Foods Editors: Cynthia Briscoe,
    Cybil A. Brown, Kate Nicholson,
    Shannon Sliter Satterwhite, Joy E. Zacharia
Test Kitchens Directors: Margaret Monroe Dickey,
    Lyda H. Jones
Recipe Development Director: Mary Allen Perry
Test Kitchens Staff: Rebecca Kracke Gordon,
    Vanessa A. McNeil, Jan Moon, James Schend,
    Vie Warshaw
Editorial Assistant: Vicki Poellnitz

Oxmoor House, Inc.

Editor-in-Chief: Nancy Fitzpatrick Wyatt
Executive Editor: Susan Carlisle Payne
Art Director: Cynthia R. Cooper
Copy Chief: Catherine Ritter Scholl

Secrets from the Southern Living® Test Kitchens

Copy Editor: Donna Baldone
Editorial Assistants: Suzanne Powell,
    McCharen Pratt
Assistant Research Writer: Heather Averett
Director, Production and Distribution: Phillip Lee
Books Production Manager: Larry Hunter
Production Assistant: Faye Porter Bonner

Contributing Staff

Editor: Margaret Chason Agnew
Designer: Nancy Johnson
Illustrator: Connie Formby
Indexer: Mary Ann Laurens

Contents

FOREWARD

When I first joined the *Southern Living* Foods staff in 1986, I was single and had just earned my B.S. degree in home economics with a focus on writing. I understood food from a scientific angle, but I had much to learn about "real" food preparation and the demands of cooking for a family. Wisely, I attached myself to our Test Kitchens staff watching, learning, and imitating their tricks.

Secrets from the Southern Living® Test Kitchens is a collection of hints, tips, and explanations that capture our Test Kitchens staff's experience at the stove, the oven, and the grill. The staff of 2002 is only slightly different than the one I came to love in 1986. Our knowledge base is further expanded by the addition of men and women with formal restaurant and culinary training.

This book compiles that remarkable cooking knowledge amassed during the nearly 40-year history of *Southern Living*. In 2001, then-Executive Editor for Foods Kaye Mabry Adams and Assistant Foods Editor Kate Nicholson began work on this collection alongside Oxmoor House Executive Editor Susan Carlisle Payne and former *Southern Living* Associate Foods Editor Margaret Chason Agnew.

First, Margaret delved through stacks of back issues of *Southern Living* magazine, organizing valuable nuggets of information into manageable files. As the book came together, the entire Foods staff—food editors and Test Kitchens experts as well as then-Associate Foods Editors Patty Vann and Peggy Smith—contributed. Text boxes scattered throughout the book expanded our dictionary definitions with timesaving tips, facts about health matters called "Lite Bites," and foodways unique to the South that became "Southernisms." Our current Test Kitchens staff reviewed the ideas and notes of those who came before, added any new revelations, and signed off on the copy.

In addition, we searched our files to find our top-rated recipes. We took special care selecting the Southern recipe entries dear to our hearts, and we even threw in a few "nonsouthern" recipes to help define terms you'll see in restaurants and in your travels. In these pages, you'll learn how to make biscuits, barbecue sauce, and pound cake—among hundreds of other great recipes.

As always, our readers play a significant role, and you'll see their kitchen-tested tips throughout the book as well as the results of a tip contest we sponsored for visitors to our Web site (page 8). I thank each of you who have ever written or called with a question or suggestion. You'll see the fruits of our combined labors here, so keep those tips and questions coming.

I learn something every time I sit down with this book. I hope you will, too. May your kitchen be a place of delicious discovery.

Susan Dosier
Executive Foods Editor

HOW TO USE THIS BOOK

Owning a copy of *Secrets from the Southern Living® Test Kitchens* is like having a round-the-clock hot line directly to our Test Kitchens staff! From now on, every time you use a cookbook, read a food magazine, or try a new recipe, this book will better explain how ingredients work and fill in the missing details that some recipes don't share. As a result, we hope you can cook more confidently and find more enjoyment in your culinary creations. We organized this book with a format that's easy to use. Look for these features scattered throughout to help answer your food-related questions:

• **Alphabetized Entries:** For easy reference, this book is organized from A to Z; each entry, (éclair, for instance), begins with a description, and if needed, the pronunciation (ay KLAIR). Within each entry, you'll find storage instructions and, when appropriate, charts, illustrations, and step-by-step photographs plus cross-reference suggestions that direct you to related entries.

• **Recipes:** You'll find more than 300 kitchen-tested recipes, each chosen because we consider it to be an outstanding example of that particular food topic.

• **Test Kitchens Secrets:** You'll be intrigued by the keen knowledge of Test Kitchens staffers as they share secrets about ingredients or recipes. For example, Vanessa McNeil shares her secret for making a thick gumbo (page 246).

• **Southernisms:** Southern cooking has played a vital role in our nation's heritage, and we're proud to share food facts and folklore about regional specialties such as Brunswick stew (page 67).

• **Reader Tips:** Over the years, our readers have taught us a great deal about their hard-learned food tips, the best of which we've included among these pages. Read about how one reader improvised a rolling pin (page 28).

• **Q & A Boxes:** Questions abound about certain topics, so we've repeated many questions you've asked us through the years in "question and answer" boxes. For example, you'll never again wonder if it's necessary to sift flour before making a cake (page 205).

• **Rescue for…:** When you think you've ruined a recipe, don't despair. You'll find ways throughout the book to rescue less-than-perfect results. For example, you'll know just what to do if you brown the biscuits a bit too much (page 46).

• **Timesaving Tips:** For all who are busy—and who isn't?—we share timesaving tips that deliver results fast. Don't miss our fast frosting for bar cookies (page 32).

• **Lite Bites:** If you count calories and fat grams, you'll appreciate these facts about easy ways to eat more healthfully. For example, discover why Southern-grown avocados should be your pick if you're counting fat grams (page 22).

Whether you're just learning your way around the kitchen or you're a seasoned cook, we hope you'll find joy, answers, and a helping hand in this exciting new resource. Keep it in a special place so you can refer to it often.

15 Facts

You Should Know About
Our Testing Procedures

In our Test Kitchens, we try many outstanding reader recipes. Of course, all that work is for naught unless the recipe works for the reader at home. Here, we give you the inside scoop on exactly how we test. Follow our tips in your kitchen for foolproof recipes every time.

❶ Measure dry ingredients correctly. To measure dry ingredients of any kind, we spoon them into a dry measuring cup, then we level the top with a knife. Unless we specifically call for sifted flour (or biscuit mix, cake flour, or powdered sugar) we don't sift it.

❷ You're all wet. For liquid ingredients, we measure in a liquid measuring cup—usually made of glass or plastic—with a spout. Unless you have a new kind of liquid measuring cup that's accurately read while standing, read liquid measures at eye level with the cup on a flat surface.

❸ Make the grade. We always test with white, Grade A large eggs. We also use top-quality ingredients that are fresh, blemish-free, and not overly ripe (unless we specify, such as bananas for banana bread).

❹ "Grease" demystified. When we say to "grease" a pan or baking dish, we use vegetable shortening, such as Crisco, or butter. When we "lightly grease," we spray the baking dish, pan, or baking sheet with vegetable cooking spray.

❺ Butter up. We test with salted butter and edit for "butter or margarine," which comes in sticks. Don't use whipped butter, butter spread, or light butter unless we call for it. To soften butter, we place it on the counter for 30 minutes at room temperature.

❻ Undercover cooking. We tell you to cover a casserole if we covered it in testing; we use either aluminum foil or a lid that comes with the dish. If we don't say, we didn't cover it.

❼ Don't get "mixed" up! If we say "mix," look for instructions about using an electric mixer. Normally we use a regular stand electric mixer; if we specify "heavy-duty" electric mixer, we use at least a 300-watt KitchenAid mixer. If we use a hand mixer, we call for a hand mixer.

❽ Whisk like Julia Child. If we say "whisk," we really use a whisk. It creates better texture and results than a spoon, fork, or spatula. We always use nonmetal utensils on nonstick finishes.

❾ Get that temperature right. We frequently calibrate our ovens to ensure the correct temperature and baking time. To make sure your oven heats correctly, place an oven thermometer inside. Turn the oven on and set it to the desired temperature. When the oven has preheated, check your thermometer. Is it in sync with the temperature you set? If not, adjust baking times accordingly. In our kitchens, we begin checking for doneness before a recipe says it should be done—just in case.

❿ Check the dates. Call us compulsive, but we check the dates on baking powder and baking soda. If it's even a day off, we throw it out. In addition, smell oils to be sure they haven't turned rancid. And replenish dried spices and herbs after a year to be sure they're still pungent and hard-working.

⓫ Turn away from the dark side. We test on metal baking pans and in clear glass baking dishes. We don't use dark pans, baking sheets, or brown-colored glass. Dark finishes change the baking time of the items that bake on or in them.

⓬ On the rise. Our recipes tell you to let yeast rise in a warm spot, about 85°. Here's what we do: Place an 8- or 9-inch square dish of hot tap water on the lower oven rack. Place the bowl of yeast dough, covered with a clean kitchen towel, on the oven rack above it, to rise until doubled. Close the oven door to keep the interior temperature very close to 85°. But please—no accidents—remember to remove the dough before preheating the oven!

⓭ Beat the heat. We preheat our ovens for 10 minutes before baking anything. That's about how long it takes for the oven to heat to the selected temperature. If you don't preheat, you may have to bake things a little longer.

⓮ Watch commas carefully! Where we place them in the ingredient list tells you the order we did things. For example "1 pound fresh shrimp, cooked and peeled" means we started with shrimp in the shell and cooked and peeled it ourselves; however, "1 pound cooked and peeled fresh shrimp" means we bought the pricey product at the market to save time. The difference is about ½ pound of cooked shrimp, which is significant if you don't interpret the shrimp directions the way we tested the recipe.

⓯ Nonstick know-how. Many of our recipes tell you to coat a nonstick skillet with vegetable cooking spray. We've recently learned that the newer nonstick coatings actually work better without cooking spray. If you've been doing this for a long time, you may already have buildup on your finish, and it may not matter. For the new cookware, however, check the instruction manual. See, even we're still learning!

Top 10
Secrets
from Savvy Cooks

*It's obvious these cooks know their way around the kitchen.
Here we share the prizewinning cooking secrets from our readers.*

While compiling this book, we asked the visitors to our *Southern Living* Web site to enter a contest sharing with us their best tips and secrets in the kitchen. After reviewing hundreds of entries, we selected these top 10 tips to share with you. As you'll see, our focus all comes down to a matter of cooking smarter and faster!

1 If there's only one or two of you and you want to save money by buying in bulk, here's a tip for pork chops from Vicki Dudai of Grovetown, Georgia.
Buy the cost-saving family-size package of pork chops. Rinse the chops, and pat dry. Place chops on a baking sheet coated with cooking spray, and freeze about an hour. When partially frozen, transfer the chops from the baking sheet to a large heavy-duty zip-top plastic bag, and refreeze. Then you can easily remove individually frozen chops as you're ready to cook them.

2 Nona Ware of Clinton, Mississippi, shares a smart tip for chocolate candy makers who don't have a double boiler.
To keep chocolate warm for dipping candy, melt dipping chocolate in a heavy saucepan over low heat. Then place saucepan in an electric skillet with temperature set at 150° (or at "warm" setting) and filled with 1 inch of water. Chocolate will stay at a warm temperature for dipping candy perfectly every time. If you don't have an electric skillet, fill a large skillet with 1 inch of water, and heat to just below simmering (about 150°). Place saucepan of melted chocolate in skillet of hot water to keep chocolate warm while dipping.

3 C.E. Aupperle from Apex, North Carolina, has a suggestion that will make grilling marinated meats a cinch.
To prepare meats and their marinades up to a month in advance of grilling, combine them in a large heavy-duty zip-top plastic bag, and freeze. When the mood strikes to grill, simply place the bag in the refrigerator to thaw. The meat marinates as it thaws, so you're ready to grill in no time, and cleanup is a breeze—just throw away the empty bag.

4 Joan Vogan of Sugar Land, Texas, minimizes her time over a hot stove with this handy tip.
Whenever I make a white sauce, a roux, gravy, or anything that requires adding a liquid to a butter and flour (or fat and flour) mixture and stirring over heat until thickened, I always microwave the liquid 30 to 45 seconds first. This makes the process quicker and easier and shortens the time I spend stirring over a hot stove.

5 How sweet it is! Martha Helton of Conway, Arkansas, shares her secret for subtly flavoring sugar.
I keep a whole vanilla bean in my sugar container. The bean adds a subtle vanilla flavor and a taste surprise when you use the sugar to sweeten your coffee or in your favorite recipe.

6 Necessity was the mother of invention for caterer Patricia Haydel from Hammond, Louisiana. She discovered this idea in a pinch getting ready for a party.
Lemon-lime soft drink, such as Sprite or 7UP, does double-duty as a food preservative. To prevent apples or other fruit from turning brown after slicing, just pour the drink (or diet drink) over the sliced fruit if you're out of lemon juice. You can even add a few ice cubes to help keep the fruit crunchy. The carbonated drink doesn't affect the taste of the fruit.

7 Vickie Maxwell of Cary, North Carolina, shares a tip that will help you frost a beautiful cake with no messy crumbs in the frosting.
Before frosting a layer cake, freeze the layers 30 minutes to 1 hour. Any loose crumbs brush off easily and frosting goes on smoothly without any crumbs in the frosting.

8 Longtime recipe contributor Carol Noble of Burgaw, North Carolina, shares a clever tip for keeping her bakeware as good as new.
If you have problems with your cookie sheets, cakepans, or baking pans rusting, wash them in hot, soapy water after using, and return them to the oven still warm from baking to dry them completely. "I've never 'lost' one to rust since I began doing this years ago," says Carol.

9 Casey Bordovsky of Austin, Texas, shares a timesaving tip for cookie lovers everywhere!
Everyone loves warm homemade cookies, but who has time to make them? Next time you make a drop cookie dough, such as chocolate chip, double the batch. Drop uncooked cookie dough by teaspoonfuls onto baking sheets, and freeze until firm. After they're frozen, place them in a large heavy-duty zip-top plastic bag. When you have guests coming or just have a cookie craving, simply place the frozen cookie dough on a baking sheet, bake, and enjoy!

10 Marilou Robinson from Portland, Oregon, really "uses her marbles" when she's cooking. We enjoyed her practical idea for simplifying a common cooking procedure.
Drop 3 or 4 marbles or several dried beans into a double boiler or steamer pan to alert you if the liquid in the pan gets too low during cooking. If this happens, the marbles or beans will rattle, alerting you to add more liquid to the pan to avoid burning the food.

acid A sour substance that imparts one of the four basic flavors of food. Many natural foods are acids, such as vinegar (acetic acid), lemon juice (citric acid), and wine (tartaric acid). Because acids break down proteins, they're often used in cooking as a tenderizer for meats and fish. Acids can also be diluted with water (1 tablespoon lemon juice per 1 cup water) to prevent the browning of fruits that darken when sliced. (*see also* **flavor** *and* **meat tenderizer**)

acini de pepe (ah CHEE nee dee PEE pee) Italian term for peppercorns; it's also a type of small rice-shaped pasta. (*see also* **pasta** *and* **peppercorn**)

acorn squash A small- to medium-sized acorn-shaped winter squash with a dark green fluted shell and pale orange flesh. The easiest way to prepare this slightly sweet nutty-flavored squash is to cut it in half, remove the seeds, and bake. Select firm, unblemished squash that feel heavy for their size. **Storage:** Cut acorn squash will keep in the refrigerator for about 1 week; uncut can be kept for 1 month in a cool, dark place. (*see also* **squash**)

GRILLED ACORN SQUASH WITH ROSEMARY

2 tablespoons olive oil, divided	4 garlic cloves, pressed
¼ cup white wine vinegar	2 pounds acorn squash,
1 tablespoon fresh rosemary	thinly sliced
½ teaspoon salt	Garnish: fresh rosemary sprigs

• Combine 1 tablespoon oil, vinegar, and next 3 ingredients in a large heavy duty zip-top plastic bag; add squash. Seal and turn to coat. Marinate in refrigerator 2 hours.
• Remove squash from marinade, reserving marinade. Brush squash with remaining tablespoon oil.
• Cook squash, covered with grill lid, over medium-high heat (350° to 400°) about 10 minutes on each side. Place on a serving dish, and drizzle with reserved marinade. Cover and let stand 10 minutes. Garnish, if desired. Yield: 8 servings.

adobo sauce (ah DOH bo) A Mexican seasoning paste or sauce made from ground sesame seeds, chiles, herbs, and vinegar. Find it in the Mexican foods section of your grocery. (*see also* **sesame seed**)

aïoli (ay OH lee) A garlic mayonnaise originating from France's Provence region. It's typically served as a spread or as a condiment with poached vegetables, fish, or chicken. (*see also* **condiment** *and* **mayonnaise**)

à la king (ah lah KING) Diced or shredded chicken in a cream sauce with mushrooms, pimientos, green bell pepper, and possibly sherry.

à la mode (ah lah MOHD) A French term that has been "Americanized" to mean pie topped with ice cream.

albacore (AL bah kohr) One of the most prized species of tuna. The meat is light in color and is often used for canned tuna. (*see also* **tuna**)

alcohol A liquid, suitable for drinking, that's made by distilling the fermented juice of fruits or grains. Pure ethyl alcohol is clear, flammable, and caustic, so water must be added to reduce its potency. In the United States, the average amount of alcohol in distilled spirits is 40 percent or 80 proof. (*see also* **liqueur, liquor, proof,** *and* **wine**)

Q **When alcohol is used in a recipe that's cooked, does the alcohol cook out?**

A The amount of alcohol that remains depends on the type of liquor and the cooking time. If you add liquor to a dish just before serving it, 85 percent of the alcohol remains. When you cook the dish 20 minutes, about 35 percent remains. If you use wine in a slow-cooked stew, only about 5 percent of the alcohol remains, but all of the flavor is there. If you choose not to use alcohol, substitute an equal amount of another liquid such as fruit juice or broth.

ALCOHOL SUBSTITUTION CHART

ALCOHOL	SUBSTITUTION
Amaretto, 2 tablespoons	¼ to ½ teaspoon almond extract*
Bourbon or sherry, 2 tablespoons	1 to 2 teaspoons vanilla extract*
Brandy, fruit-flavored liqueur, port wine, rum, or sweet sherry: ¼ cup or more	Equal amount of unsweetened orange or apple juice plus 1 teaspoon vanilla extract or corresponding flavor
Brandy or rum, 2 tablespoons	½ to 1 teaspoon brandy or rum extract*
Grand Marnier or other orange-flavored liqueur, 2 tablespoons	2 tablespoons unsweetened orange juice concentrate or 2 tablespoons orange juice and ½ teaspoon orange extract
Kahlúa or other coffee- or chocolate-flavored liqueur, 2 tablespoons	½ to 1 teaspoon chocolate extract plus ½ to 1 teaspoon instant coffee dissolved in 2 tablespoons water
Marsala, ¼ cup	¼ cup white grape juice or ¼ cup dry white wine plus 1 teaspoon brandy
Wine, red, ¼ cup or more	Equal measure of red grape juice or cranberry juice
Wine, white, ¼ cup or more	Equal measure of white grape juice or apple juice or chicken broth

*Add water or apple juice to get the specified amount of liquid (when the liquid amount is crucial).

al dente (al DEN tay) Italian expression that means "to the tooth"; describes pasta cooked just until pliable but still firm to the bite and no longer starchy. (*see also* **pasta**)

TEST KITCHEN SECRET

Cooked pasta can be easily reheated. Just drop the cooked pasta into boiling water that has been removed from the heat and let it stand for 1 to 2 minutes. This is handy when you've cooked pasta ahead for company. VIE WARSHAW

ale (AYL) An alcoholic beverage brewed from malt and hops. It resembles beer, but is stronger. The color varies from light to dark brown. Its bold flavor makes it excellent for making beer bread. (*see also* **beer**)

Alfredo sauce Sauce made with butter, cream, and Parmesan cheese and often served over fettuccine. (*see also* **fettuccine** *and* **pasta**)

allspice The berry of an evergreen tree of the myrtle family widely grown in Jamaica. The dried dark brown berries are available whole or ground and taste like a combination of cloves, cinnamon, and nutmeg. Allspice is used in sweet and savory foods. (*see also* **spice**)

almond The edible kernel of the almond tree that's grown in California and the Mediterranean. The smooth white nut has a thin brown skin and a pitted tan shell. The prized nuts can be roasted, toasted, or used raw in cooking and baking. They're available chopped, sliced, slivered, or whole as well as smoked, blanched, or with skins. They're often sold in vacuum-sealed bags or containers because their high fat content makes them perishable. Almonds are processed to manufacture extract, oil, paste, and liqueur. **Storage:** Store almonds in the shell in an airtight container in a cool place up to 6 months. Refrigerate shelled nuts up to 4 months or freeze up to 8 months. (*see also* **nuts**)

Q **Why do recipes often call for toasted almonds, and how do I toast them?**

A Toasting brings out the maximum flavor of the nut. If toasting a small amount, place the almonds in a small skillet and cook over medium heat, stirring often for 5 to 7 minutes or until golden. Larger amounts are best toasted in a shallow pan at 350° for 5 to 8 minutes or until lightly browned, stirring every few minutes. Always watch closely as you toast almonds because they go from light gold to blackened in a flash, and can continue browning a little after removing from heat.

almond extract A concentrated flavoring made from almond oil and alcohol. The flavor is intense so it should be used sparingly. Almond extract is used in pastries, baked goods, and occasionally beverages. (*see also* **extracts**)

almond paste A firm but pliable paste made mostly of ground blanched almonds and sugar and used to flavor pastries. It's similar to marzipan, but coarser and not as sweet. (*see also* **marzipan**)

alum (AL um) A mineral salt once widely used as a preservative to ensure crispness in home-canned pickles, but not used as often today because it can cause digestive problems. Due to modern canning methods, it's no longer needed.

amandine (AH mahn deen) A French term for a dish garnished with almonds.

CLASSIC TROUT AMANDINE

2 cups milk	1¼ cups butter or margarine, divided
2 teaspoons salt, divided	1 tablespoon olive oil
2 dashes of hot sauce	½ cup sliced almonds
6 trout fillets	2 tablespoons lemon juice
¾ cup all-purpose flour	2 teaspoons Worcestershire sauce
½ teaspoon pepper	¼ cup chopped fresh parsley

• Combine milk, 1 teaspoon salt, and hot sauce in a 13- x 9-inch baking dish; add fillets, turning to coat. Cover and chill 2 hours. Drain, discarding marinade. Combine flour and pepper in a shallow dish.
• Melt ¼ cup butter in a large skillet over medium heat; add oil. Dredge fillets in flour mixture; add to skillet, and cook 2 to 3 minutes on each side or until golden, in batches if necessary. Remove to a serving platter; keep warm.
• Combine remaining 1 cup butter and almonds in a saucepan; cook over medium heat until lightly browned. Add lemon juice, Worcestershire sauce, and remaining 1 teaspoon salt; cook 2 minutes. Remove from heat; stir in parsley. Pour over fillets, and serve immediately. Yield: 6 servings.

amaretti (am ah REHT tee) Crisp, airy Italian macaroon cookies made with bitter almond or apricot-kernel paste for eating out-of-hand or ground to make pastry shells. (*see also* **macaroon**)

amaretto (am ah REHT toh) Amber-colored almond liqueur.

amberjack Also known as "yellowtail," this lean, mild-flavored fish swims the waters of the Gulf of Mexico and the West Indies. Cook it shortly after catching or freeze for later use. It's best prepared as fillets or steaks, and baked or coated with breadcrumbs or cornmeal and fried. (*see also* **fish**)

ambrosia (am BROH zhah) In Greek mythology, ambrosia was the food of the gods on Mt. Olympus, but we know it as a dessert or side dish of orange sections, coconut, sugar or honey, and sometimes pineapple and cherries. Southerners traditionally serve this sweet, simple fruit dish as a light dessert after Christmas dinner or as a side dish. (*see also* **section**)

AMBROSIA

8 medium navel oranges	1 cup whipping cream
1 (8-ounce) can crushed	2 tablespoons powdered sugar
pineapple, drained	Maraschino cherries
½ cup flaked coconut	

• Peel and section oranges over a bowl, reserving any juice. Stir together orange sections, juice, pineapple, and coconut. Cover and chill 8 hours.
• Beat whipping cream until foamy; gradually add powdered sugar, beating until soft peaks form. Spoon fruit mixture into individual dishes; top each with whipped cream and a cherry. Yield: 4 to 6 servings.

American cheese Any of a group of cheeses made with emulsifiers to increase smoothness and pasteurized milk to increase storage life. Cheeses labeled "spreads" or "foods" contain liquid added to make them soft and spreadable. According to government standards, only 51% of the final weight must be cheese. Processed cheeses keep well and melt smoothly, but lack the distinctive texture and flavor of natural cheeses. (*see also* **cheese**)

Anaheim chile pepper (AN uh hym) A long, tapered chile pepper with a pale to medium green color and a mild flavor. Named for the California city where it was first grown commercially, this pepper is available fresh, canned, or roasted. Anaheim peppers are often dried and used to make the decorative "ristra," a long string or wreath of chile peppers. (*see also* **chile pepper** *and* **peppers**)

ancho chile pepper (AHN choh) A dried, deep reddish-brown poblano chile pepper that's broad at the stem end and tapers to a rounded tip. Its flavor ranges from mild to pungent. (*see also* **peppers**)

anchovy (AN choh vee) A member of the herring family, this small silvery fish is found in the Mediterranean and off the coast of southern Europe. The fish are typically filleted, salt-cured, and then canned in oil. They're most often used to flavor sauces, dressings, or appetizers, but use them sparingly because they're very salty; when cooked, they virtually dissolve, leaving only a subtle, salty, nonfishy flavor. (*see also* **anchovy paste**)

> **TIMESAVING TIP**
> It's quicker and easier to mince anchovies with a fork than with a knife.

anchovy paste Pounded anchovies mixed with vinegar and spices and usually sold in a tube. Refrigerate leftover anchovy paste up to a month. (*see also* **anchovy**)

> Q **How much anchovy paste equals 1 anchovy fillet?**
> A Use ½ teaspoon paste for 1 anchovy fillet.

andouille sausage (an DOO ee) A spicy, smoked pork, French country sausage traditionally used in Cajun cooking. It's a good spicy choice for any recipe that calls for smoked sausage. (*see also* **Cajun cooking** *and* **sausage**)

Southernism

Andouille is popular with New Orleans cooks, particularly those specializing in flavorful Cajun dishes such as jambalaya and gumbo.

angel food cake A light, frothy white cake made without egg yolks or other fats and leavened with stiffly beaten egg whites and air. It's traditionally baked in a tube pan with legs on which to invert the pan while the cake cools. If your tube pan doesn't have legs to rest the inverted cake on while cooling, then invert the pan onto an inverted metal funnel or a glass soft drink bottle. This allows air to circulate thoroughly around the pan and gives the cake a chance to stretch and set. The cake will collapse if cooled upright or if removed while still warm. (*see also* **cake**)

Q **Why don't angel food cake recipes call for greasing the pan like most cakes?**

A This fragile, foamy batter shouldn't come into contact with any fat because it will cause the beaten egg whites to deflate. When heated, the air within the beaten whites expands and forces the batter to climb the sides of the ungreased pan. If the pan was greased, the batter would slip down the sides and not rise as high.

LEMON ANGEL CAKE

12 **egg whites**	1 **tablespoon grated lemon rind**
1 **teaspoon cream of tartar**	3 **tablespoons fresh lemon juice**
¼ **teaspoon salt**	¼ **teaspoon vanilla extract**
1¼ **cups sifted powdered sugar, divided**	1 **cup sifted cake flour**

• Beat first 3 ingredients at high speed with an electric mixer until foamy. Add ¾ cup powdered sugar, 1 tablespoon at a time; beat until stiff peaks form. Fold in lemon rind, lemon juice, and vanilla.

• Combine remaining ½ cup powdered sugar and cake flour; gradually fold into egg white mixture. Spoon batter into a 10-inch tube pan.

• Bake at 375° for 35 to 40 minutes or until golden. Invert pan onto a wire rack; cool cake completely. Yield: 1 (10-inch) cake.

TEST KITCHEN SECRET

There are several secrets to making angel food cakes. First, don't let even a trace of yolk get into the whites. Also, use a very clean glass or metal bowl for beating, and be sure not to overbeat; stop when the foam slips just a tad when the bowl is tilted. Vanessa McNeil

angelica (an JEHL ih cah) A sweet herb that's a member of the parsley family. Its pale green celery-like stalks are often candied and used to decorate desserts. Angelica commonly flavors liqueurs, confections, and sweet wines. (*see also* **herbs**)

angostura bitters (ang uh STOOR ah) (*see* **bitters**)

anise (AN ihs) A member of the carrot family that has bright green leaves and a distinctive licorice flavor. The leaves are considered an herb, and the seeds a spice. Anise extract and anise oil are also available. (*see also* **spice**)

READER TIP

"We grow anise in our garden every year to use in fruit salads. Sometimes we even toss the fresh leaves into mixed green salads." M.M., Memphis, TN

anisette (AN ih seht) A clear licorice-flavored French liqueur made from anise seeds. (*see also* **anise** *and* **liqueur**)

annatto (un NAH toh) This paste and powder come from the seeds of a tropical tree of the same name and are used to color butter, margarine, cheese, and to spice many Caribbean dishes. Annatto oil and lard are also made from parts of the seed.

antipasto (ahn tee PAHS toe) Literally meaning "before the pasta" in Italian, this appetizer course may be hot or cold, and usually includes simple foods such as cheese, hams, salami, sausages, olives, and marinated vegetables.

apéritif (ah pear uh TEEF) The French equivalent of the cocktail. It's a beverage, usually alcoholic, served before a meal to stimulate and whet the appetite. It might be champagne, dry sherry, or dry white wine.

appetizer A finger food served before a meal to soothe, and at the same time, whet the appetite. Sometimes it's served as a seated, first course of the meal and may then be referred to as the "starter."

apple Perhaps the most common tree fruit, apples are round or tapered, have a thin skin, and a core. They're red, yellow, or green; tart or sweet; crisp, juicy, or mealy. While apples are available year-round, they're at their peak September through November. Look for apples that have smooth skins without bruises. The apple variety you choose should depend on what you'll use it for (see Apple Selection Chart on the following page). Apples can be eaten or made into apple juice, apple cider, applejack, applesauce, apple pie filling, apple butter, jams and jellies; they can also be canned or dried, and sliced or chopped.

LITE BITE
You can boil down apple juice or cider to a thick syrup and use it as a low-calorie alternative to jams.

Q How many apples do I buy?

A
1 pound = 4 small
= 3 medium
= 2 large

2 medium = 1 cup grated apple

About 2 pounds are needed for 1 (9-inch) pie

1 pound = 3 cups diced
= 2¾ cups sliced

1 bushel = about 42 pounds
= 16 to 20 quarts of slices

Varieties: There are some 7,000 known apple varieties in the world today. Of course, only a few of these are available to most shoppers. The ones shown in the chart are the most popular.

Storage: Apples ripen very quickly at room temperature, so refrigerate them in the cold drawer of your refrigerator. If you plan to eat them soon after purchase, store at room temperature.

Preparing: Peel apples with a sharp paring knife or vegetable peeler. Special apple corers are available to smoothly remove the core.

APPLE SELECTION CHART

TYPE	APPEARANCE	FLAVOR	USES
Braeburn	Red with yellow-green overtone	Tart-sweet	All-purpose
Cortland	Large, red with greenish-yellow highlights	Pleasing tartness	All-purpose
Empire	Red	Tart-sweet	All-purpose
Fuji	Yellowish-green	Sweet-slightly spicy	All-purpose
Gala	Red with golden overtone	Sweet	Eating
Golden Delicious	Yellow with a faint pink blush	Sweet	All-purpose
Granny Smith	Bright green	Tart	All-purpose
Jonathan	Bright red	Slightly tart	All-purpose
McIntosh	Red with green overtone	Tart-sweet	All-purpose
Pippin	Pale yellowish-green	Slightly tart	All-purpose
Red Delicious	Red; elongated body	Sweet	Eating
Rome	Deep red	Tart-sweet	Cooking
Stayman	Dull red	Tart	All-purpose
Winesap	Dark red	Tangy-winy	All-purpose
York	Red with yellowish overtone	Slightly tart	Cooking

GRANNY SMITH APPLE PIE

1½ (15-ounce) packages
    refrigerated piecrusts, divided
6 medium Granny Smith apples,
    peeled and sliced
1½ tablespoons lemon juice

¾ cup brown sugar
½ cup sugar
⅓ cup all-purpose flour
1 teaspoon ground cinnamon
½ teaspoon ground nutmeg

• Stack 2 piecrusts; gently roll or press together. Fit pastry into a 9-inch deep-dish pieplate.
• Toss together apple and lemon juice in a large bowl. Combine brown sugar and remaining 4 ingredients; sprinkle over apple mixture, and toss to coat. Spoon into prepared piecrust.
• Roll remaining piecrust to press out fold lines; place over filling. Fold edges under, and crimp; cut slits in top for steam to escape. Bake at 450° for 15 minutes. Reduce oven temperature to 350°, and bake 35 minutes. Yield: 1 (9-inch) pie.

TEST KITCHEN SECRET

Once cut, apples turn brown, so we dip them in pineapple juice or a mixture of lemon juice and water. MARGARET MONROE DICKEY

apple butter A thick, sweet spread made by cooking apples, sugar, spices, and sometimes cider. Southerners slather apple butter on pancakes and hot biscuits. How long to cook it is important. "When done, the brown mixture should cling to the spoon, although this depends on how juicy your apples are," says Mark Sohn, author of *Hearty Country Cooking*. (*see recipe on the following page*)

OVEN APPLE BUTTER

8 Granny Smith apples, peeled   1 cup sugar
  and diced   1 teaspoon ground cinnamon
1 cup apple juice

• Cook apple and juice in a Dutch oven over medium heat 30 minutes or until apple is tender. Stir until apple is mashed. Stir in sugar and cinnamon.
• Pour apple mixture into a lightly greased 11- x 7-inch baking dish.
• Bake, uncovered, at 275° for 4½ hours, stirring every hour, or until spreading consistency. Cover and chill. Yield: 3 cups.

applejack An apple brandy made from ground and pressed apples, which are fermented into cider and distilled. Calvados, one of the best-known brands, is made in France. (*see also* **brandy** *and* **Calvados**)

applesauce A mixture of apples, sugar, and sometimes spices cooked to a smooth or chunky puree. When making applesauce, select tart, juicy all-purpose apples, such as the Cortland, Empire, Granny Smith, and McIntosh. (*see also* **apple**)

TEST KITCHEN SECRET

If you want to end up with chunky applesauce, add the sugar before the apples are cooked. Adding the sugar after the apples are cooked and mashed yields a smoother sauce. JAN MOON

LITE BITE

For a simple fat substitute in baked goods, use applesauce measure for measure to replace oil.

apricot A small fruit that resembles a peach, only smaller. It has pale yellow to deep burnt-orange skin, a golden meaty flesh, and an almond-shaped pit. The flavor is similar to a peach, but has a hint of lemon. Fresh apricots are most plentiful in June and July. Canned and dried apricots and apricot nectar are always available.
Storage: Fresh apricots are highly perishable, so eat them as soon as possible, or store them in the refrigerator up to 2 days.

Arborio rice (ar BOH ree oh) An Italian-grown rice that's shorter and plumper than most short-grain rice. It's the rice of choice for risotto because its higher starch content gives risotto a creamy texture when cooked. (*see also* **rice** *and* **risotto**)

arrowroot A starchy, flavorless white powder made from dried roots of the tropical arrowroot plant and used as a thickener, though not as often now as in the past. It thickens sauces and leaves them crystal clear. For best results, mix arrowroot with a little cold water before cooking it, and boil it to ensure proper thickening. (*see also* **thickening agent**)

Q **If I don't have arrowroot in my pantry, what can I substitute?**

A An equal amount of cornstarch or twice as much flour.

artichoke The bud of a plant from the thistle family; has gray-green, petal-shaped leaves with soft flesh that can be dipped in a sauce, and an inedible choke cloaking the tender center (heart) that's considered the prize of the artichoke. Fresh artichokes are available year-round, but the peak season for fresh artichokes is spring. Artichoke hearts and bottoms are available canned; the hearts are also available frozen.

Selection: Look for heavy, compact artichokes that have deep green, tight leaves.

Q **How do you eat an artichoke?**

A Cook just until tender (recipe below). Then pull off the leaves 1 at a time. Dip the base of each leaf into a sauce or melted butter, and then remove the sweet flesh from the bottom of each leaf by drawing or scraping it between your teeth. Discard the upper portion of the leaf. When all the leaves are gone, with a spoon, scoop out and discard the fuzzy choke. Then quarter the artichoke heart, and enjoy eating it.

Storage: Store artichokes in a plastic bag in the refrigerator up to 1 week.

Southernism

A Carolina favorite, "harty choaks" were popular from 1811 and were cheap enough in those days that only the bottoms were used, never the leaves.

WHOLE COOKED ARTICHOKES

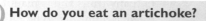

4 large artichokes   3 tablespoons lemon juice
Lemon wedge

• Hold artichokes by stem, and wash by plunging them up and down in cold water. Cut off stem ends, and trim about ½ inch from top of each artichoke. Remove any loose bottom leaves. With scissors, trim approximately one-fourth off the top of each outer leaf, and rub top and edges of leaves with lemon wedge to prevent discoloration.

• Place artichokes in a large stainless steel Dutch oven; cover with water, and add lemon juice.

• Bring to a boil; cover, reduce heat, and simmer 35 minutes or until lower leaves pull out easily. Drain and serve with desired sauce. Yield: 4 servings.

TEST KITCHEN SECRET

Cooked artichoke leaves are soft and sweet, and deep inside the jagged exterior lies a soft heart with a nutty sweetness. When cooking, use stainless steel cookware and add a little lemon juice to the water to keep the leaves from darkening. But don't worry too much about discoloration—it doesn't affect the flavor. JAMES SCHEND

arugula (ah ROO guh lah) A tangy salad green with dark green, spiky, dandelion-like leaves and a mustard-like flavor. Arugula also has a peppery flavor that makes a pleasantly assertive accent when mixed with other salad greens. **Storage:** Arugula is highly perishable. Wrap a moist paper towel around the bunch and store up to 2 days. Dirt particles cling tightly to the leaves, so wash them well just before using. (*see also* **lettuce**)

ascorbic acid The scientific name for vitamin C. It's present naturally in many fruits and is manufactured as a powder to be mixed with water to prevent peeled or cut fruits from darkening when exposed to air.

Q **Where do I purchase ascorbic acid?**

A Ascorbic acid can usually be found in the supermarket by canning and freezing supplies.

Asian noodle Many different types of noodles are popular in Asian cooking: China's cellophane noodles, egg noodles, rice flour noodles, and Japan's harusame, ramen, and soba. Most Asian noodles are sold fresh or dried in markets. They can be eaten hot or cold; some require steaming, while others are stir-fried. (*see also* **cellophane noodles, harusame, ramen,** *and* **soba**)

TEST KITCHEN SECRET

To perfectly cook Japanese noodles and keep starchy foam from forming, use the 'add water' technique. For 1 pound dried noodles, bring 4 quarts salted water to a boil; add noodles. When the water returns to a boil, stir in 1 cup cold water, and return to a boil. Repeat procedure 3 times. Rinse cooked noodles to remove excess starch. MARY ALLEN PERRY

asparagus Long vegetable spears that are most often green, but sometimes white, with slightly pinkish buds on the tips. Asparagus has a mild flavor and delicate texture that becomes tougher as it ages. **Varieties:** Most asparagus sold in the United States is green, but Europeans love white asparagus, which has been kept covered underground while growing and therefore doesn't turn green. **Selection:** During peak season, February through June, pencil-thin spears are plentiful. Later, the spears generally become thicker and aren't as tender when cooked. Asparagus is sold fresh, frozen, and canned. For fresh, choose firm ½-inch-thick stalks with tightly closed tips. Stalks that are too thick can be tough and somewhat bitter. **Storage:** Use fresh asparagus as soon as possible. Store stalk side down in a glass of water; cover with plastic wrap, and refrigerate. (*see also* **vegetables**)

TEST KITCHEN SECRET

It's best to remove and discard the tough ends of asparagus spears before cooking. The easiest way to do this is to bend each end until it snaps. It will snap where the most tender part begins. VIE WARSHAW

aspartame (ah SPAHR taym) An artificial no-calorie sweetener that is about 200 times sweeter than sugar (although in some bulk forms it can measure cup for cup and spoon for spoon just like sugar). Aspartame breaks down when heated, therefore it may lose sweetness in prolonged heating applications requiring modifications to recipes. Aspartame is excellent as a sweetener for cold dishes. Common brand names are Equal® and NutraSweet®. (*see also* **sugar substitute** *and Sugar Substitute Guide, page 565*)

aspic (AS pihk) A clear savory jelly made from meat, fish, herb, or vegetable stock and gelatin and used to glaze cold foods. The term also refers to opaque aspic made with tomato juice and gelatin and eaten as a salad.

au gratin (oh GRAH tan) A French term to describe a dish with a topping of breadcrumbs mixed with butter or cheese and browned in the oven or under a broiler until golden and crispy.

au jus (oh ZHEW) A French term for meat served with its unthickened natural juices. Roasted meat, poultry, and wild game are often served au jus.

au lait (oh LAY) A French term that refers to foods or beverages that are served with milk. (*see also* **café au lait**)

aux champignons (oh sham pee NYOHN) A French term indicating a dish that is prepared with mushrooms. Aux champignons dishes might include pastas, sauces, crêpes, and soups. (*see also* **mushroom**)

avocado (a voh CAH doh) A tropical fruit grown mostly in Florida and California that's round or pear-shaped, has green to dark purplish skin, buttery-smooth yellow to green meat, and a large pit. This fruit is known for its lush, buttery texture and mild, nutlike flavor. It's served peeled, sliced, or pureed in salads and dips.
Varieties: The oval-shaped, almost black Hass variety can be identified by its rough skin and has a rich flavor and texture, while larger Florida varieties have smooth skin and a mild flavor. California varieties are available year-round; Florida varieties are in markets June through December.
Storage: Some avocados are rock hard when purchased. Place these in a paper bag and leave at room temperature; they'll soften in 2 to 5 days. Refrigerate ripe avocados and use within a few days. Avocados don't freeze well.
(*continued on the following page*)

RESCUE for surface browning:
Cut avocados are quick to turn brown, and there's no fool-proof way to prevent this, but brushing with lemon juice or ascorbic acid helps. Also, if you're going to use just half of the avocado, store the remaining half with the pit still in it; wrap it tightly with plastic wrap and place in the refrigerator. The pit will help protect at least some of the cut surface from exposure to air.

Ripeness: Ripe avocados will yield to gentle pressure, but a soft avocado is sometimes bruised rather than truly ripe. To be sure, try to flick the small stem off; if it comes off easily, and you can see green underneath, it's ripe and ready to eat. If the stem doesn't come off or if you see brown underneath, the avocado isn't ripe.

baba (BAH bah) Also called "baba au rhum," this rich yeast cake is studded with raisins and soaked in rum syrup. The classic dessert is baked in a tall, cylindrical mold. When baked in a large ring, it's called "savarin." (*see also* **savarin**)

bacon Cured and smoked meat cut from the side or belly of a hog. Bacon is generally about 50 percent fat, although leaner versions can be as low as 33 percent fat. Bacon is available either thickly or thinly sliced, in a slab, and may be sugar cured, maple cured, or hickory cured. Bacon bits are crisp pieces of bacon that are preserved and dried. Bacon can be fried or cooked in the microwave oven; it can also be broiled or baked.

Storage: Refrigerate in original packaging up to 2 weeks or freeze up to 1 month. Cooked bacon can be frozen in a zip-top plastic bag. (*see also* **pork**)

bagel (BAY guhl) A dense, unsweetened doughnut-shaped yeast roll that's cooked in boiling water and then baked, giving it a shiny glaze and chewy texture. Traditional Jewish bagels are made without eggs or added fat. Egg-enriched bagels are not as chewy.

baguette (bag EHT) A long, thin loaf of French bread, typically only 2 or 3 inches wide, with a fairly hard, crisp crust, and a soft, chewy interior. It can be served as a dinner bread or thinly sliced and toasted to make crostini. (*see also* **crostini**)

baguette pan This pan is used for proofing and baking baguettes. It's made of 2 long, metal, half-cylinders joined together side-by-side.

bain-marie (bane mah REE) A French cooking vessel, often called a water bath, used to gently cook delicate food, such as custards, or to keep cooked food, such as sauces, hot. The food sits on a tray inside the bain-marie, and hot or simmering water is added so that it comes no more than halfway up the side of the food container and provides gentle heat. (*see also* **water bath**)

bake To cook food in the dry, indirect heat of an oven. Breads, cakes, pies, and cookies are all baked; when we refer to cooking meat or poultry in the oven, we talk of roasting, but it's actually baking. To bake successfully, make sure your oven has an accurate temperature gauge or thermometer. (*see also* **roast**)

RESCUE for improperly heated ovens: Ovens can develop hot spots and fail to cook at the correct temperature. To determine your oven's accuracy, buy an oven thermometer to leave in the oven. If the thermometer reads the same as the temperature you set it for, you're fine. If there's a discrepancy, go with the thermometer reading. In the future, set the dial higher or lower to compensate. You could also have the oven professionally calibrated by an appliance service company.

baked Alaska A dessert of a single cake layer topped with a rounded mound of ice cream and coated with sweetened Italian meringue. This impressive dessert is baked in a hot oven for about 5 minutes just before serving so the meringue lightly browns. (*see also* **meringue**)

B

baking dishes and pans The bakeware you use plays a big role in the taste and texture of baked goods. You'll want dishes and pans that cook food evenly, brown it nicely, and resist sticking or burning. Baking dishes are glass or ceramic and round, square, or rectangular; most are microwave-safe. Pans also come in a variety of sizes and shapes, but since pans are made of metal, never use them in the microwave oven.

Bakeware Materials

You'll find dishes and pans made from different materials, each with advantages and disadvantages.

• *Aluminum* is a good heat conductor; it heats and browns evenly. Anodized aluminum has been treated to make it harder and more durable. Insulated aluminum is also good because it heats more slowly to help avoid burnt bottoms, which is important for baked goods. Lightweight aluminum tends to warp. Aluminum isn't good for cooking acidic foods such as tomato sauce because of a chemical reaction that gives certain foods a metallic taste.

• *Cast iron* is not only durable, but it conducts heat evenly and turns out delicate muffins and corn sticks with fine, thin crusts and moist interiors. The natural nonstick surface of a seasoned cast-iron skillet cooks food quickly and evenly. (*see also* **cast-iron cookware**)

• *Glass and ceramics* are used mainly for baking dishes and pieplates, because they encourage even browning and retain heat better. This means food bakes quickly in glass and ceramic dishes.

• *Nonstick* coating means less sticking and easier cleanup. Nonstick aluminum is a good heat conductor, but is not as sturdy as nonstick heavy-gauge steel. Look for a double-layer nonstick coating, and use wooden or plastic utensils so you won't scratch the surface.

• *Stainless steel* is sturdy and easy to clean. The shiny surface of tinned steel prevents overbrowning. Dark steel pans are excellent at absorbing heat and distributing it evenly, but can easily overbrown baked goods if you don't watch carefully.

Bakeware Options

Here's what you'll need for a well-stocked kitchen. It's expensive to purchase good-quality cookware all at once, so add to your collection over the years.

TEST KITCHEN SECRET

Buy the heaviest gauge bakeware you can afford. It'll cook more evenly and hold up longer. LYDA JONES

• *Baking dishes and pans:* The most common are a 13- x 9-inch rectangular and an 8- or 9-inch square. Pay close attention to whether our recipes call for a baking "dish," which is glass, or "pan," which is metal, because that indicates what we tested with. Food bakes quicker in dishes (glass) and browns more in pans (metal). So if you use a piece of equipment different from what a recipe specifies, you may not get the same results. If a recipe calls for a pan and you only have a dish in that size, reduce the oven temperature 25°.

• *Baking sheet or cookie sheet:* You'll need at least 2 cookie sheets for making batches of cookies. This flat pan usually has no rim on one or two ends and is designed for sliding cookies onto a cooking rack. Avoid dark sheets because these will cause cookies to burn on the bottom. Nonstick sheets work well, as do insulated sheets. However, insulated sheets protect cookies from intense heat and sometimes bake cookies slower, so don't use these when you want thin, crisp cookies.

• *Bundt pan:* This pan has a central tube, fluted sides, a fixed bottom, and no feet. Be sure to grease and flour the crevices of the pan well so the cake releases without tearing the edges. Let Bundt cakes cool in the pan 10 to 15 minutes before inverting for best results.

• *Cakepans:* You need at least 2 round cakepans 8 or 9 inches in diameter. Square and rectangular cakepans are also handy.

• *Jellyroll pan:* This flat rectangular pan has shallow sides and is used to make sponge cakes that are filled and rolled. It's also handy for baking rolls and roasting veggies or small cuts of meat. The size jellyroll pan we most commonly use is 15 x 10 inches.

• *Loafpan:* A standard metal loafpan is 9 x 5 inches and is used for baking bread and meat loaf. Glass dishes come in the same size. Smaller loafpans bake gift-size loaves.

• *Muffin pan:* Most muffin or cupcake pans have 6 or 12 cups. Jumbo and miniature muffin pans are also available. These can be lined with paper liners or greased before they're filled. Most muffin pans are made of aluminum or steel; cast iron and nonstick pans are also available.

• *Pieplate:* Glass, ceramic, and metal piepans are available in 9- and 10-inch sizes. You'll want at least one of each size as well as a deep-dish pieplate if possible. We bake the majority of our pies in glass pieplates as we prefer the nice, even browning they provide. Glass pieplates also let you see how the bottom crust is browning.

• *Popover pan:* This pan has extradeep cups that allow popovers to rise high. It's typically made of cast iron or black steel. If you don't have a popover pan, you can bake popovers in muffin pans, but they won't hold as much batter; custard cups can also be used, but the popovers won't rise as high.

• *Springform pan:* This deep, round metal pan has sides that clamp shut for baking and expand when the clamp is released. This makes it easy to remove a cheesecake. The most common sizes are 9 inches and 10 inches. Some people serve the dessert on the bottom pan, but we like to carefully transfer the dessert to a serving plate if the crust is sturdy enough.

(continued on the following page)

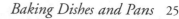

- *Tart pan:* Tart pans are shallow and usually have fluted sides. They sometimes have removable bottoms. The most common sizes are 10 inches and 11 inches.
- *Tube pan:* This pan has a central tube and straight sides; those designed for angel food cakes have removable bottoms and small feet for the inverted pan to rest on. Choose light rather than dark pans for best browning results.

baking powder A leavening agent made of baking soda, an acid, and a starch. When mixed with a liquid, the baking powder immediately reacts with the acid and produces carbon dioxide gas bubbles that, in turn, cause baked products to rise. There are two main types of baking powder. Most all baking powder today is *double-acting,* which releases some gas when it gets wet and more gas when heated. Older recipes probably used *single-acting* baking powder, which is triggered immediately when mixed with a liquid. So if you prepare your grandmother's old biscuit recipe with double-acting baking powder, your biscuits might rise a little higher than hers used to. Baking powder is best stored in its original airtight can. (*see also* **leavening agent**)

> **Q** How long can I keep baking powder?
>
> **A** Baking powder weakens after about 6 months, so always check the expiration date on the can. If uncertain as to the strength of your baking powder, you can do this test: Mix 2 teaspoons of baking powder with 1 cup of hot tap water. If there's an immediate fizzing and foaming, the powder is fine. If the reaction is delayed or weak, get a fresh can.

baking soda Also known as bicarbonate of soda, baking soda is an alkaline compound used to make baked goods rise. When combined with moisture and an acid, such as buttermilk, yogurt, or molasses, it produces carbon dioxide gas bubbles that cause doughs or batters to rise. Baking soda is also a necessary ingredient in baking powder. Store the baking soda box inside a zip-top plastic bag to keep it airtight. Also check for an expiration date because it starts to weaken after 6 months. To test for freshness, stir 1 teaspoon into ¼ cup vinegar. An immediate fizz means it's still strong. (*see also* **leavening agent**)

TEST KITCHEN SECRET

> *"We're all familiar with placing an open box of baking soda in the refrigerator to absorb odors, but soda is also useful in removing built-up coffee oils and tea stains from coffee pots and tea cups. And if you have a grease fire on your cooktop, douse the flames with baking soda."* LYDA JONES

baking stone A heavy round or rectangular ceramic or stone plate used instead of a baking sheet for pizza and breads because it produces especially crisp crusts. Food is baked directly on the stone.

baking tools The right tools make baking easier, more fun, and more successful. Purchase as many of the following tools as you can now, and acquire the remainder as your budget allows.

• **Dough scraper:** This flat-ended tool lifts dough as you work it and scrapes the dough and flour from work surfaces. It's also handy for dividing pastry or dough into portions. It's usually made of stainless steel, but plastic scrapers are available.

• **Cooling rack:** These wire racks allow air to circulate evenly on all sides of freshly baked cakes, cookies, pies, and breads. They can be square, rectangular, or round, and have small feet to elevate them above the countertop. It's handy to have 2 or 3 cooling racks, especially when making cookies or multiple cake layers.

• **Measuring cups:** You'll need 2 types of measuring cups. A clear glass (at right) or plastic cup with a pour spout marked in fluid ounces to measure liquids; common sizes are 1 quart, 1 pint, and 1 cup. Dry ingredients are measured using a set of graduated cups (at left) ranging from ⅛ or ¼ cup to 1 cup; they're usually made of plastic or metal.

• **Metal spatula:** This long, flat metal utensil has a slender, flexible, 6- to 12-inch blade without a sharp edge. It's helpful for frosting cakes and spreading butter.

• **Mixing bowls:** Having several bowls in a range of sizes and materials is helpful. Bowl selection may not be as simple as you think. You'll probably want a variety. Here's help:

  • Ceramic bowls change temperature slowly, keeping hot ingredients warm and cold ones cool.
  • Copper is ideal for beating egg whites, but it produces flavor changes with acidic ingredients. *(continued on the following page)*

(continued on the following page)

SIZING UP BAKING DISHES AND PANS

If a recipe calls for a specific size dish or pan and you don't have it, consult this chart for substitutes of similar sizes. But remember: When you substitute a pan that holds the same amount but is a different shape, the recipe's cooking time will vary.

13- x 9-inch baking dish	12 to 15 cups
10- x 4-inch tube pan	16 cups
10- x 3½-inch Bundt pan	12 cups
9- x 3-inch tube pan	9 cups
9- x 3-inch Bundt pan	9 cups
11- x 7-inch baking dish	8 cups
8-inch square baking dish	8 cups
9- x 5-inch loafpan	8 cups
9-inch deep-dish pieplate	6 to 8 cups
9- x 1½-inch cakepan	6 cups
7½- x 3-inch Bundt pan	6 cups
9- x 1½-inch pieplate	5 cups
8- x 1½-inch cakepan	4 to 5 cups
8- x 4-inch loafpan	4 cups

- Glass bowls are attractive for serving but can be heavy and fragile and their slippery surface can prevent egg whites from properly foaming.
- Plastic bowls are light and useful for storing and transporting. Avoid mixing delicate batters in plastic bowls because they can retain odors and oil and prevent egg whites from foaming.
- Stainless steel bowls are light and durable and won't react with food as does aluminum.

- **Mixing spoons:** Wooden mixing spoons are popular, and there's stainless steel or plastic spoons. Keep a mix of sizes on hand for different tasks.

- **Pastry blender:** This tool helps cut the fat into the flour when making pastry dough. It should have a sturdy handle which anchors several rows of steel wires formed into a U-shape.

- **Pastry brush:** At least 2 separate brushes are needed: one for brushing water, egg washes, melted butter, or glazes on pastry; the other to baste meats and poultry as they cook.

- **Rolling pin:** Used for rolling out pastry and other types of dough as well as crushing crackers and flattening meat. You might prefer a heavy, smooth wooden pin or a French-style pin without handles. Marble or stainless steel pins stay cool when rolling dough for delicate pastry.

- **Sifter:** Sifters are handy for blending ingredients, sifting cake flour, and removing lumps from powdered sugar. Sifters are usually made of metal or plastic and fitted with 1 or 2 mesh screens and a handle that rotates a blade, which forces ingredients through the screens.

- **Whisk:** You'll want varying sizes and shapes of this tool. Sauce whisks are long and thin with stiff wires to mix ingredients without adding excess air. Balloon whisks have rounded heads and thinner gauge wires that help incorporate air into egg whites and cream. Flat whisks that help you get into the corners of a pan are used for making gravies and sauces.

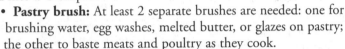

baklava (BAHK lah vah) A Middle Eastern dessert pastry made of many layers of flaky phyllo dough, chopped nuts, and spices. It's traditionally cut into diamond-shaped pieces after baking.

BAKLAVA

1 (16-ounce) package frozen
  phyllo pastry, thawed
1 cup butter, melted
3 cups finely chopped pecans
  or walnuts

¼ cup sugar
1½ teaspoons ground cinnamon
½ teaspoon ground nutmeg
Syrup

• Butter a 13- x 9-inch pan. Set aside.
• Cut phyllo in half crosswise, and cut each half to fit prepared pan; discard trimmings. Cover remaining phyllo with a slightly damp towel. Layer 10 sheets of phyllo in pan, brushing each sheet with melted butter. Set aside.
• Combine nuts and next 3 ingredients; stir well. Sprinkle one-third of nut mixture over phyllo in pan; lightly drizzle with melted butter.
• Top nut mixture with 11 sheets of phyllo, brushing each sheet with melted butter. Repeat procedure twice with remaining nut mixture, phyllo, and butter, ending with buttered phyllo.
• Cut stack into diamond shapes, using a sharp knife. Bake at 350° for 45 minutes or until golden. Cool completely. Drizzle Syrup over Baklava. Cover and let stand at room temperature 24 hours. Yield: 3 dozen.

SYRUP

1 cup sugar
½ cup water

¼ cup honey

• Combine all ingredients in a medium saucepan, and bring to a boil. Reduce heat, and simmer, uncovered, 4 minutes. Yield: 1¼ cups.

balsamic vinegar (bal SAH mihk) A traditionally dark, aged Italian vinegar with a pungent-sweet flavor. It's made from concentrated white grape juice fermented and aged for 15 to 20 years. Light-colored balsamic vinegar can be found in many markets. (*see also* **vinegar**)

bamboo shoot The tender sprouts of a young bamboo plant commonly used in Chinese cooking to give sweetness and crunch to soups and stir-fried dishes. Canned bamboo shoots come whole or sliced and are best used right away because they become tasteless and limp if kept too long after opening the can. Occasionally, fresh shoots can be found in special Chinese markets, but they need to be parboiled before they're eaten.

banana A crescent-shaped tropical fruit. Most bananas have a yellow peel with black or greenish tips, but some peels are rosy red. The peel encases white, pulpy meat with tiny edible black seeds; it has a distinctive sweet flavor and aroma. Fresh bananas are available year-round in the produce section of your market; they can also be purchased dried in slices or pieces.
Varieties: The main commercial varieties of the banana are:
Cavendish: The most familiar and most available. Has a yellow peel and is firm but moist and sweet. (*continued on the following page*)

Dwarf or finger: A shorter, plumper banana with yellow peel and black spots. Meat is tart and slightly crunchy with a strawberry-like flavor.

Plantain: Large, firm, and usually has a greener peel. It's popular in Latin American countries, where it's used for cooking much like a squash.

Red: Shorter than the Cavendish and has a red peel that turns reddish-black when ripe. The meat has pink overtones with a sweet flavor.

Storage: Store at room temperature until ripe; then refrigerate. The peel will turn black once refrigerated, but the meat will remain firm and white for several days.

RESCUE for overripe bananas: Don't throw them away. Peel them, and place them in a zip-top plastic bag, and freeze. You can add more bananas to the bag, and when you have enough, thaw at room temperature until softened, and make banana bread. Or whirl the frozen fruit in the blender to thicken fruit drinks.

LITE BITE
Substitute mashed banana for oil when baking breads, cookies, or muffins in which a hint of banana would be flavorful.

Q How can I prevent sliced bananas from turning brown?

A Toss the slices in a mixture of 1 tablespoon of lemon juice to 1 cup of water or in an ascorbic acid mixture prepared according to package directions to keep them from turning brown.

banana pepper A yellow-green, banana-shaped chile pepper with a mild flavor. It can be stuffed, pickled, or used in salads. (*see also* **peppers**)

bananas Foster A dessert of sliced bananas sautéed in butter, rum, and sugar, then flambéed and spooned over ice cream. It's often cooked table side. (*see also* **flambé**)

Southernism

Bananas Foster was first made in the 1950s in New Orleans at Brennan's Restaurant. The Brennan family named the recipe for Richard Foster, a favorite customer, and it's still one of their most requested desserts.

barbecue Below the Mason-Dixon line, the definition means to cook meat outdoors in a closed grill or pit by indirect heat, which cooks the meat slowly without burning or drying out. The process makes even tough cuts of meat so tender they literally fall off the bones. Historically, barbecuing is as much a social event as it is a way to cook. Throughout the South, basting sauces and serving sauces define the barbecue as much as the technique itself. (*see also* **barbecue sauce** *and* **grilling**)

Southernism

Barbecue is big business in the South. There are almost as many opinions of what constitutes good 'cue as there are barbecue restaurants dotting roadsides. Hundreds of thousands of individuals cook it for fund-raisers or for just plain good eating. Depending on where you were raised in the South, you may prefer beef, pork, or chicken barbecue. And sauce secrets, especially those of competitive barbecue contestants, are guarded like gold.

Barbecuing Tips
- Soak chunks of hardwood, such as hickory or mesquite, in water for 1 hour. Have ready to add to fire for smoky flavor.
- Resist peeking. This causes heat loss and slows down the cooking process.
- Build an auxiliary fire in a bucket, charcoal chimney starter, or extra grill.
- Keep adding coals and wood chunks on a regular basis to maintain the correct temperature.
- Place additional briquets on already burning coals in small piles on either side of the grill.
- Wear heavy-duty rubber gloves to test hot cooked meat. (Pork should be done if you feel it give beneath your fingers and a meat thermometer registers 160°.)

barbecue sauce Distinctions and preferences for the flavor of barbecue sauce used to baste and to accompany barbecued meats and poultry vary from region to region. In fact, you can travel from the East Coast to Texas and find 4 distinct kinds. Tennessee and most of Texas claim bragging rights for their thick tomato-based sauces. North Carolina is known for pungent vinegar-pepper-based sauces and ketchup is added in the western part of the state. South Carolina boasts all these types as well as a mustard-flavored one. Mayonnaise-based and other variations pop up in small pockets throughout the South, too. (*see also* **barbecue** *and two more recipes on the following page*)

EAST CAROLINA PEPPERY VINEGAR SAUCE

1 quart cider vinegar	1 tablespoon salt
1 tablespoon dried crushed red pepper	1½ teaspoons pepper

- Stir together all ingredients, blending well. Yield: 4 cups.

WEST CAROLINA CIDER VINEGAR BARBECUE SAUCE

1½ cups cider vinegar	½ teaspoon salt
⅓ cup firmly packed brown sugar	½ teaspoon onion powder
¼ cup ketchup	½ teaspoon pepper
1 tablespoon hot sauce	½ teaspoon Worcestershire sauce
1 teaspoon browning and seasoning sauce	

- Stir together all ingredients in a medium saucepan; cook over medium heat, stirring constantly, 7 minutes or until sugar dissolves. Cover and chill until ready to serve. Yield: 2 cups.

Note: For testing purposes only, we used Texas Pete Hot Sauce and Kitchen Bouquet Browning & Seasoning Sauce.

TEXAS BARBECUE SAUCE

2 cups ketchup
½ cup white vinegar
½ cup honey
½ cup water
2 teaspoons dried crushed
green pepper

1 tablespoon minced onion
2 tablespoons Worcestershire
sauce
¼ teaspoon ground black pepper
Dash of garlic powder
Dash of ground red pepper

• Bring all ingredients to a boil in a large saucepan over medium-high heat, stirring often. Cover and chill until ready to serve. Yield: 3½ cups.

SPICY MUSTARD BARBECUE SAUCE

1½ quarts ketchup
½ cup cider
½ cup light corn syrup
½ cup prepared mustard
⅓ cup Worcestershire sauce
1 tablespoon salt

1½ teaspoons garlic powder
1 to 1½ teaspoons ground
cinnamon
1 to 1½ teaspoons celery seeds
1½ teaspoons black pepper
1 teaspoon ground red pepper

• Combine all ingredients in a Dutch oven; cook over low heat until thoroughly heated, stirring often. Chill until ready to serve. Yield: 2 quarts.

bar cookie A type of cookie made from a batter or soft dough that has been baked in a pan or baking dish with sides. After baking, the cookies are cooled and cut into individual bars or squares. (*see also* **cookie**)

TEST KITCHEN SECRET

We line the baking pan with aluminum foil, allowing several inches to extend over sides; lightly grease the foil. Spread the batter in pan; bake and cool. Lift from pan using foil; press foil sides down, and cut the cookies into desired size and shape. Mary Allen Perry

TIMESAVING TIP

An easy way to give bar cookies a sweet chocolate topping without having to mix a frosting is to crumble a large chocolate bar, and scatter the pieces directly on top of the hot bar cookies when they come out of the oven. Cover the pan with aluminum foil for a minute or two. As the chocolate bar softens, use a table knife to spread it evenly over the entire top. Cool the bar cookies, and allow the quick topping to firm.

barding Wrapping a thin sheet of fatback or bacon around roasted meats to keep them moist or to prevent overcooking. Barding fat is often added to small birds such as quail, dove, or Cornish hens.

barley A small, spherical grain with a mild, starchy flavor and chewy texture. It's one of the oldest known grains and is used in a variety of dishes, including cereals, breads, and soups. Pearl barley, the outer hull of which has been removed and steamed and polished (or pearled), is the most popular barley for cooking. It's sold in regular- and quick-cooking forms. Scotch barley is sometimes available in health food stores, but since it's less processed, it requires a much longer soaking time. You may also find barley grits and barley flour in supermarkets. Barley is also used for animal fodder and for making malt for beer, ale, and whiskey. (*see also* **grain**)

basil (BAY zihl) A member of the mint family, this easy-to-grow herb has a strong, pungent, peppery flavor reminiscent of licorice and cloves. Its color can vary from shades of green to purple, and it's available fresh or dried. It's key in Mediterranean cooking and is grown widely in the South. It's the basis for pesto. This herb is also known as sweet basil. (*see also* **herbs** and **pesto**)

TIMESAVING TIP

Make quick work of slicing fresh basil by rolling up a small bunch of leaves and snipping it into shreds with kitchen shears. To chop it, snip the shreds crosswise.

TEST KITCHEN SECRET

Fresh basil is easy to grow, so if you have a bumper crop, I'd suggest making pesto. It can be tossed with hot pasta, spread on toasted French bread, or added as a topping to pizza. LYDA JONES

---

basmati (bahs MAT tee) An aromatic long-grain rice sometimes aged to decrease its water content. It has a creamy yellow color and a distinctive perfumy, nutlike flavor and aroma. It's often used in pilafs and Indian cuisine. (*see also* **pilaf** *and* **rice**)

bass A general name given to a variety of fresh and saltwater fish with spiny fins and rough scales. Bass are lean fish with a delicate to mild flavor. Bass are excellent fried, broiled, baked, and grilled. (*see also* **fish** *and* **striped bass**)

baste To spoon or brush a liquid over food during cooking in order to moisten it and add flavor. The liquid can range from pan juices to melted butter, wine, fruit juices, or a special basting sauce.

batter A semiliquid mixture, usually made of flour, eggs, and milk or another liquid, used to coat foods for frying or for making cakes, muffins, pancakes, or other bread products. It may be thick or thin, but it should always be fluid enough to pour or drop easily from a spoon.

batter bread A simple-to-make yeast bread that doesn't require kneading. It's made with a very thick batter that may include extra yeast. The texture of batter bread is slightly coarser than bread that has been kneaded.

Bavarian cream A chilled dessert of egg custard thickened with gelatin and lightened with whipped cream. It's typically flavored with fruit, liqueur, or chocolate and spooned into stemmed glasses or molded into a decorative shape. (*see also* **custard**)

bay leaf The firm laurel leaf of the evergreen bay laurel tree. The leaves are used as an herb to impart a lemon-nutmeg flavor to soups, stews, vegetables, fish, and meats. They're usually removed from the cooked dish before being served because the leaf itself actually tastes bitter and can be a choking hazard if swallowed. As a general rule when cooking, add 1 bay leaf per quart of liquid. (*see also* **herbs**)

bean curd A custardlike product made from curdled soy milk from which some of the water has been removed. Commonly referred to as tofu, it may be soft, firm, or extra-firm depending on how much water is removed. It has a white color and slightly nutty, bland flavor that absorbs other flavors when cooked. It's usually formed into a cube and packed in a brine of water, and often is referred to as Chinese cheese. It can be sliced, diced, or mashed in a variety of dishes such as sauces, soups, casseroles, and stir-fries. (*see also* **soybean, soy milk,** *and* **tofu**)

LITE BITE
Bean curd is easy to digest, low in calories, high in protein, and cholesterol-free. It's no wonder many Americans are trying to add it to their diet.

beans, dried Any of several varieties of seeds in the legume family that are left in the bean pod until mature and then shelled and dried. Dried beans are very nutritious and are rich in protein, fiber, folate, calcium, phosphorus, and iron.

Selection: Buy dried beans in a clear package so you can examine them for color/size and uniformity (so they'll cook evenly) and visible defects. Cracked seeds, pinholes, and foreign material are signs of low quality. Discard those with imperfections before soaking.

Soaking: Dried beans require soaking before cooking, but dried peas and lentils do not. *For quick soaking,* add 6 to 8 cups water to 1 pound dried beans and bring to a boil. Cover and cook 2 minutes; remove from heat, and let stand 1 hour. Then rinse and drain, and cook by package directions. *For overnight soaking,* add 6 cups water to 1 pound dried beans. Let stand 8 hours at room temperature. Then cook according to package directions. *Beans soaked this way retain their shape better and cook faster.*

TIMESAVING TIP
Canned beans can be substituted for dried beans. When deciding how much, use this rule of thumb: 1 (15-ounce) can beans yields 1¾ cups drained and 1 pound (about 2 cups) dried beans yields 5½ to 6½ cups cooked. For best results, drain the canned beans in a colander and rinse thoroughly with tap water before using.

LITE BITE
Some old recipes add baking soda to the soaking water, but today we know that reduces the nutritional value. Skip the soda.

Cooking: Cooking time varies depending on the age of the peas and beans. Most beans cook in 1 to 2½ hours. Split peas and lentils usually cook in 45 minutes to 1 hour. Check the package for more specifics. Simmer them gently to prevent skins from bursting, and stir occasionally to prevent sticking.

Storage: Store dried beans at room temperature in tightly covered containers up to 1 year or freeze 2 years. (*see also* **fava bean, great Northern beans, legume, lentil, lima bean, navy bean, pea bean, pinto bean,** *and* **soybean**)

Q Is there any way to keep dried beans from being ... well ... gassy?

A Not totally, but if you change the soaking water several times and then cook the beans in fresh water, it will definitely reduce the effect. Also, remember that the longer the beans are soaked and the slower they're cooked, the easier they are to digest.

beans, fresh

There are 2 main categories of fresh beans: pod beans and shell beans. Pod beans, such as green beans, are eaten whole, in the pod. But only the inner seeds of shell beans, such as lima beans or fava beans,

can be eaten, and the pod is discarded. When 1 pound of fresh green beans are cut into 1-inch pieces and cooked, the yield will be about 2½ cups.

LITE BITE
The sooner you cook fresh beans, the more nutrients they'll have. So, start snapping!

Selection: Look for small, tender, crisp pod beans with bright color. The best beans are usually found at the bottom of the bin, because they haven't been picked over. If they're fresh, you'll hear the snap when you bend pod beans.

Varieties: The main commercial varieties of fresh beans are:

Chinese Long: A slender green pod, up to 2 feet long; sold mainly in Asian markets.

Fava: Also called broad bean; has soft, pale green plump pods packed with pale green beans. The pods are shelled and discarded, and the beans are cooked.

Green: Also called snap bean or bush bean and pole bean or string bean; has a rounded green pod that's several inches long.

Haricot Verts: Also called French green beans; has a green, pencil-thin, tender pod that's considered a delicacy and priced accordingly. (*continued on the following page*)

Chinese long

green

Italian Green: Has a wide, flat, green pod.
Lima: Also called butter bean; has a broad, flat, green pod filled with green-white beans. The pods are shelled and discarded, and the beans are cooked.
Purple: Has a small purple pod that turns green when cooked.
Wax: Has a slender yellow pod.

Italian

Storage: Fresh beans should be washed before being stored in the refrigerator in plastic bags up to 3 or 4 days. (*see also* **fava bean, green bean, haricot verts, lima bean,** *and* **vegetables**)

Southernism

"The green beans of my childhood were cooked long and slow with ham or bacon. Crisp wasn't a suitable adjective for these beans, nor was bright green an acceptable color. Today I've discovered that green beans actually cook quickly, and partner well with a variety of herbs." Donna Florio

bean sprouts The tender, young shoots of germinated seeds from the mung bean, alfalfa seed, soybean, or wheat berry. The pale shoots are crisp and have a nutlike flavor. They're generally eaten fresh in salads and sandwiches sprinkled over dishes, or stir-fried. Choose sprouts that look and smell fresh, and avoid those beginning to turn dark or slimy. Canned bean sprouts are available, but lack the texture and flavor of fresh sprouts.
Storage: Sturdy sprouts, such as mung sprouts, should be rinsed, patted dry, and refrigerated in a plastic bag for no more than 3 days. Delicate sprouts, such as alfalfa sprouts, should be refrigerated up to 2 days in the ventilated plastic containers in which they're sold. Be sure to wash them before eating.

béarnaise sauce (bair NAYZ) A classic French sauce made with butter, vinegar, egg yolks, shallots, and tarragon and served with meat, seafood, eggs, and vegetables. (*see also* **mother sauces** *and* **sauce**)

BÉARNAISE SAUCE

¼ cup tarragon vinegar or white wine vinegar
¼ cup dry white wine
¼ cup finely chopped shallot
3 egg yolks, lightly beaten
2 tablespoons chopped fresh tarragon or 1 teaspoon dried tarragon
½ cup butter or margarine, cut into pieces

• Combine first 3 ingredients in a saucepan; bring to a boil over medium heat. Reduce heat to low, and simmer until liquid reduces to 1 tablespoon (about 10 minutes). Pour through a wire-mesh strainer, reserving liquid and discarding solids. Cool liquid slightly.
• Combine reserved liquid, egg yolks, and 2 tablespoons tarragon in a small, heavy saucepan. Cook over low heat, stirring constantly with a wire whisk until mixture thickens. Immediately add one-third of butter; cook over low heat, stirring constantly with a wire whisk, until butter melts.
• Add another third of butter, stirring constantly; as butter melts, stir in remaining butter. Cook, stirring constantly, until smooth and thickened. Serve immediately. Yield: about ¾ cup.

beat To mix by stirring vigorously in a circular motion using a spoon, wire whisk, rotary beater, or electric mixer. (*see also* **mixer** and **rotary beater**)

beaten biscuit A traditional Southern, hard, crisp biscuit that dates back to the 1800s. The characteristic texture is created by beating the dough with something heavy such as a rolling pin, as long as 45 minutes until it's smooth and elastic. After the dough is beaten, it's rolled out, cut into small circles, and pricked with the tines of a fork before baking.

Southernism

Beat the dough 300 times for family, 500 times for company—that was the rule when it came to preparing beaten biscuits a century ago. They were irresistible doused with syrup or sliced open and piled high with slivers of country ham. Today, these time-consuming biscuits are rarely made.

Beaujolais wine (boh zhoh LAY) A light, fruity red wine made from the Gamay grape in the southern Burgundy region of France. Beaujolais Nouveau, wine bottled after fermentation but not aged, is light and fruity. It's released every November just in time for Thanksgiving and is best served slightly chilled and within a few months of the vintage date. (*see also* **wine**)

béchamel sauce (bay shah MELL) A white sauce, classified as one of the French mother sauces, made with milk and thickened with a roux. This sauce, named for its creator, Louis XIV's steward, Louis de Béchamel, is the base for other sauces. (see also **mother sauces, roux,** and **sauce**)

beef The red meat that comes from cattle when they are older than a year. Beef is one of the most popular meats in America and a leading source of protein. From pricey tenderloins to economical ground chuck, there's something for every appetite and occasion. The USDA has a grading system for beef based on the proportion of meat to bone, fat to lean, and overall quality. These grades are found at retail:

Prime: The highest grade and the most expensive; is well-marbled with fat.

Choice: The most popular grade; it has less marbling than prime, but contains enough fat to be cooked with dry heat and still be tender.

Select: The least expensive grade; contains the least marbling and often is sold as a house brand.

Selection: Look for beef with a bright to deep red color, a moderate amount of marbling, and very little fat on the edge. Most meat should be trimmed so fat is less than ¼ to ⅛ inch wide. (*continued on the following page*)

STORAGE FOR BEEF

TYPE OF BEEF	REFRIGERATOR	FREEZER
Fresh steaks, roasts	3 to 4 days	6 to 12 months
Fresh ground beef	1 to 2 days	3 to 4 months
Leftover cooked beef (all types)	3 to 4 days	2 to 3 months

It's helpful to know the location the cut comes from because this tells you how tender it will be. Tender cuts come from the lightly used muscles along the upper back of the animal; less tender cuts come from heavily used muscles near the front and back end. Less tender cuts require longer cooking times or other tenderizing methods, such as marinating or pounding.

Handy test for doneness Chef Richard Chamberlain of Chamberlain's Prime Chop House in Dallas, Texas, has an unusual technique for testing doneness: Compare pressure points on your hand to the firmness of the cooked meat. Here's how it works: Turn your palm up, spreading fingers far apart. Press the center of your palm—that's what a medium to well-done steak should feel like. Below your index finger feels like a medium steak, below your thumb is medium-rare, and beneath your little finger is rare. If you're uncomfortable with the hand method, cut into the steak for a quick look at the interior. Here's how to tell when a ¾-inch-thick steak grilled over hot coals, covered with a grill lid, is done:

Medium rare: Center is very pink, slightly brown toward the exterior; cook 5 to 6 minutes per side.

Medium: Center is light pink, outer portion is brown; cook 7 to 8 minutes per side.

Well done: Meat is uniformly brown throughout; cook 9 to 10 minutes per side. (*see also* **kobe beef** *and* **veal**)

TIMETABLE FOR ROASTING BEEF

CUT	APPROXIMATE WEIGHT IN POUNDS	INTERNAL TEMPERATURE	APPROXIMATE TOTAL COOKING TIMES IN HOURS AT 325°
Rib roast, bone-in	4	145° (medium rare)	1½
		160° (medium)	1¾
		170° (well done)	2
	6	145° (medium rare)	2
		160° (medium)	2½
		170° (well done)	3
Rib roast, boneless rolled	4	145° (medium rare)	1¾
		160° (medium)	2
		170° (well done)	2½
	6	145° (medium rare)	2¾
		160° (medium)	3
		170° (well done)	3½
Tenderloin, whole	4 to 6	145° (medium rare)	¾ to 1*
half	2 to 3	145° (medium rare)	½ to ¾*
Rolled rump	5	145° (medium rare)	2¼
		160° (medium)	3
		170° (well done)	3¼
Sirloin tip	3	145° (medium rare)	1½
		160° (medium)	2
		170° (well done)	2¼

*Roast at 425°

BEEF CUTS

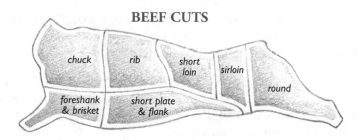

Familiarizing yourself with the large sections of beef from which retail cuts are taken will make shopping and cooking easier for you. The main sections are the:

chuck roast

• **Chuck:** The shoulder section from which flavorful, but tough, cuts are taken. It's the source of the chuck roast, blade roast, and short ribs, all of which benefit *short ribs* from moist cooking methods such as braising. Chuck roast makes a flavorful pot roast; ground chuck makes juicy hamburgers; and short ribs can be simmered in a spicy sauce.

• **Rib:** This rib and backbone section produces cuts that are flavorful, juicy, and tender. They include the standing rib roast, rib-eye steak, and back ribs. *standing rib roast* Rib roasts are ideal for oven roasting; rib-eye steaks can be broiled or pan-fried; and back ribs, sometimes known as country-style ribs, can be braised or roasted.

• **Short loin:** The front portion of the beef loin is the source of the *T-bone* very tender, most prized loin eye muscle and short tenderloin. Among the cuts it produces are the T-bone steak, tenderloin, and tenderloin *tenderloin and medaillon* roast, all of which can be grilled, roasted, broiled, or pan-fried.

• **Sirloin:** This section contains a portion of the backbone and hip bone as well as a portion of the tenderloin muscle. Cuts from this section are tender and flavorful, but not as tender as those from the short loin; the sirloin section is the source of sirloin steak, which can be broiled, roasted, or pan-fried.

• **Round:** This section from the animal's hind leg *round steak* or rump produces fairly tender and flavorful cuts such as round *eye round roast* steak and eye round roast. Round steak can be tenderized by cubing, pounding, marinating, or cutting across the grain into thin strips; however, even without this, it's tender enough to be braised or pan-fried. Eye round roasts should be braised or roasted.

• **Short plate and flank:** These sections produce cuts that are flavorful but tough. The flank is the source of lean flank steak, which can be tenderized by marinating it *flank* before it's braised, grilled, or broiled; cut it diagonally across the grain into thin slices for serving.

• **Foreshank and brisket:** This front limb and breast section yields tough, but flavorful, cuts. The most familiar cut from this section is the brisket, which can be braised, but *brisket* is often cured in a seasoned brine and served as corned beef.

beefsteak tomato Largest of all tomatoes identified by its ribbed sides. It's ideal to eat fresh because 1 slice covers an entire sandwich. (*see also* **tomato**)

beef stroganoff Russian in origin, this dish calls for thin strips of beef (usually top loin or tenderloin), onions, and mushrooms browned quickly in butter and combined with a sour cream sauce. It's served over noodles or rice. (*see also* **beef** *and* **sour cream**)

beef Wellington A roasted filet of beef spread with goose liver pâté or a seasoned mushroom spread, then wrapped in pastry and baked until golden.

> **TIMESAVING TIP**
> Fresh pastry is wonderful for Wellington, but when pressed for time, substitute refrigerated piecrust pastry or frozen phyllo pastry sheets. Thaw phyllo pastry sheets at room temperature 30 minutes before using.

beer A low-alcohol beverage made by brewing malted grains mixed with yeast and flavored with hops. The alcohol content of beer brewed in the United States is typically 5 percent. In fact, water makes up about 90 percent of beer's volume and plays a major role in the beer's taste; beer made in different regions of the country will vary in flavor and character due to the water used in brewing.

Types: Different types of beer are distinguished by the type of yeast used and the brewing process. Most beer sold in the United States is pale, light bodied, mellow lager beer. Ale has a sharp flavor, more body, and its color ranges from pale gold to amber. Porter beers are dark and heavy with a strong, sweet flavor of hops. Stout is a very dark porter.

> **LITE BITE**
> Light beer is the same as lager beer, but has fewer calories and usually less alcohol. Be sure to check labels. Most light beer supplies only about ⅓ fewer calories than traditional counterparts, so they're not as light as you think.

BEER-PAIRING GUIDE

With so many types of beer available, finding what you like can be overwhelming. When tasting, move from light to dark. Remember, food brings out the flavor in beer rather than the other way around.

TYPE BEER	SERVING SUGGESTIONS
Golden or blond ale	Spicy foods
American wheat ale	Spicy foods
Amber ale	All-purpose for any food that isn't sweet. Complements soups, pizzas, sandwiches, and barbecue
American brown ale	Hamburgers and sausages
Cream, sweet, or imperial stout	After-dinner beer made for chocolate and fruit desserts.
Pilsner or pale lager	Sausage, spicy foods, German foods
Dark lager or bock (German beers)	Robust menus or German foods
Sweet lambics (Belgian beers)	Desserts

Beer can be an important ingredient in many recipes. It adds bold flavor to soups and stews and chili, and can be found in recipes for breads and batters for deep-frying. Sometimes it's also added to the water for cooking rice. (*see also* **hops** *and* **yeast**)

beet This firm, round root vegetable ranges in color from white to deep red, and has a large leafy top. When cooked, it has a sweet, earthy flavor and tender texture. Fresh beets are available year-round, but are most abundant March through July. Most are marketed with their edible green tops still attached. Canned beets come whole, diced, sliced, and in julienne strips. Jars of pickled beets are also available. Beets are often used in salads, pickles, and the bright pink soup known as borscht. The beet flavor pairs wells with ingredients such as orange juice, vinegar, and wine.

LITE BITE
When cooking fresh beets, leave about 1 inch of stem attached to prevent loss of nutrients and color.

Selection: Look for small to medium well-shaped beets with smooth skins. Very large beets may be tough. If leaves are attached, they should be crisp and bright green.

RESCUE for beet stains:
When cut, beets stain everything they touch, including hands and cutting boards. To help remove these stains, sprinkle stained area with salt; then rinse, and scrub with soap. Wear disposable gloves to keep fresh beets from staining your hands.

Storage: Cut the greens from the roots before storing them, leaving about 1-inch of stem attached during cooking. Store beets in a plastic bag in the refrigerator up to 2 weeks. Beet greens are highly perishable so use within a day. Just before cooking, gently wash the beets, being careful not to pierce the skins. Use your fingers to slip off the skins after cooking. (*see also* **borscht, greens, Harvard beets,** *and* **vegetables**)

beignet (ben YAY) A French fritter, similar to a yeast doughnut, that's deep-fried until crisp, puffy, and golden. It's typically served hot with a generous dusting of powdered sugar. Savory beignets, filled with herbs or crabmeat, are also popular. (*see recipe on the following page*)

Southernism
Puffy doughnut pillows under a blanket of powdered sugar, warm beignets are a sweet invitation to Southern Louisiana. The word "beignet" is French for "fritter," and in New Orleans, these concoctions come light, yeasty, and without holes.

BEIGNETS

...nce) envelope active	¼ cup shortening
yeast	1 teaspoon salt
...espoons warm water	1 large egg, lightly beaten
...00° to 110°)	3 cups all-purpose flour
...p milk	2½ to 3 quarts vegetable oil
... cup sugar	Powdered sugar

Combine yeast and 3 tablespoons warm water in a large bowl; let mixture stand 5 minutes.

• Heat milk in a small saucepan over medium heat (do not boil). Stir in sugar, shortening, and salt. Cool to lukewarm (100° to 110°).

• Add milk mixture, egg, and 2 cups flour to yeast mixture, stirring well. Gradually stir in enough remaining flour to make a soft dough.

• Turn dough out onto a floured surface; knead 8 to 10 minutes or until dough is smooth and elastic. Place in a well-greased bowl, turning to grease top. Cover and let rise in a warm place (85°), free from drafts, 1 hour or until doubled in bulk.

• Punch dough down, and turn it out onto a floured surface. Roll dough into a 12- x 10-inch rectangle; cut into 2-inch squares. Place on a floured surface; cover and let rise in a warm place (85°), free from drafts, 30 minutes or until doubled in bulk.

• Pour oil to a depth of 2 to 3 inches into a Dutch oven; heat to 375°. Fry beignets, in batches, 1 minute on each side or until golden. Drain on paper towels; sprinkle with powdered sugar while still hot. Yield: 2½ dozen.

Note: To make ahead, turn dough out onto a floured surface; knead 8 to 10 minutes or until smooth and elastic. Place in a well-greased bowl, turning to grease top. Cover and refrigerate overnight. Punch dough down, and follow directions above.

TEST KITCHEN SECRET

This easy dough can be made ahead and stored in the refrigerator overnight. Maintain the oil temperature at 375° and gently lower (don't drop) beignets into the oil using a spatula. REBECCA KRACKE GORDON

Belgian endive (EN dyv) A member of the chicory family, this small cigar-shaped head of compact, pointed leaves is grown in complete darkness to prevent it from turning green. The leaves are creamy white with pale yellow-green tips. The slightly bitter flavor of Belgian endive is ideal for adding to mixed greens in a salad. Also known as French endive and witloof (white leaf), it's available from September through May with its peak months between November and April.

Storage: Wrap Belgian endive in a damp towel and refrigerate up to 3 days. (*see also* **endive** *and* **lettuce**)

bell pepper A large, fresh sweet pepper with a bell-like shape, thick juicy flesh, and a mild sweet flavor. Bell peppers come in a variety of colors: green, yellow, orange, red, purple, and brown, though the most common are bright green. Red bell peppers are vine-ripened green peppers, which have become even sweeter during their longer ripening time. Bell peppers are available throughout the year; they're also available chopped and frozen, as dehydrated flakes, and roasted in jars. Sometimes bell peppers are called "sweet" peppers.

Storage: Cover and store fresh peppers in your refrigerator up to 2 weeks. They can be sliced or chopped and frozen in freezer bags up to 6 months. (*see also* **peppers**)

> ### TEST KITCHEN SECRET
>
> *"The best way to stem and seed a bell pepper is to slice about ⅛ inch from the bottom of the pepper and set it upright; then slice downward from stem to tip, following the shape of the pepper, to slice the sides off the core. Trim any strips of white membrane from the interior of the pepper and discard the core and seeds."* VANESSA MCNEIL

Q How do I roast bell peppers?

A Cut the peppers in half crosswise; discard seeds and membranes. Place the peppers, skin side up, on a lightly greased jellyroll pan; flatten with palm of hand. Broil peppers 3 inches from heat for 15 minutes or until charred and bubbly. Place the peppers in a heavy-duty zip-top plastic bag or small paper bag; seal and let stand 10 minutes to loosen skins. Peel the skin with your fingers or the edge of a knife. You can also use the microwave to roast peppers: Rub 2 medium peppers with vegetable oil; pierce each with a fork and arrange stems facing out in a 9-inch pieplate in the microwave. Cover with a paper towel. Microwave at HIGH 3 to 4 minutes. Turn peppers over; cover and rotate pieplate. Microwave at HIGH 6 to 8 minutes or until skins look blistered.

bellini (behl LEE nee) A cocktail made of sparkling wine or champagne and peach nectar or peach brandy. Sometimes pureed peaches and grenadine are stirred into this drink mixture.

> ### TEST KITCHEN SECRET
>
> *"Bellinis are a perfect drink for a brunch in place of mimosas. Their peach inspiration makes them especially Southern."* MARGARET MONROE DICKEY

Bénédictine (ben eh DIHK teen) Possibly one of the oldest known liqueurs, this light brown liquid is believed to have been developed in 1510 by monks in Normandy. Though the recipe is a secret, it's supposedly made from herbs, honey, dried fruit skins, and brandy. Another use of the term refers to a specialty of Louisville, Kentucky, named after its creator, caterer Jennie Benedict; it's a spread made of cream cheese, cucumber, dill, and green food coloring. (*see also* **brandy**)

eds (BEHN ee) (*see* **sesame seed** *and* **benne seed wafers**)

eed wafers An old Southern recipe, these thin, crisp, cookie-'s are made of butter, flour, brown or white sugar, and toasted

eeds. You can
e sesame seeds
skillet or the
; just be sure to
atch them closely
because they brown
quickly.

Southernism

South Carolinians have referred to sesame seeds as benne seeds since the seventeenth century when Africans first brought the seeds to this country. Though cooks in South Carolina use benne seeds in a variety of recipes, the most popular use is in benne seed wafers.

BENNE SEED WAFERS

½ cup sesame seeds (about 2½ ounces)
½ cup butter or margarine, softened
1 cup sugar
1 large egg

½ teaspoon vanilla extract
1¾ cups all-purpose flour
2 teaspoons baking powder
½ teaspoon baking soda
½ teaspoon salt

• Cook sesame seeds in a heavy skillet over medium heat 5 minutes or until toasted, stirring often.
• Beat butter at medium speed with an electric mixer until creamy; gradually add sugar, beating well. Stir in sesame seeds, egg, and vanilla.
• Combine flour and remaining 3 ingredients; stir into butter mixture. Cover and chill at least 1 hour.
• Shape dough into ½-inch balls, and place on lightly greased baking sheets. Flatten to ¹⁄₁₆-inch thickness with floured fingers or a flat-bottomed glass.
• Bake at 325° for 10 minutes or until lightly browned. Immediately transfer to wire racks to cool. Yield: 10 dozen.

berry A small, juicy fruit that grows on a vine or bush and is usually soft and highly perishable. Berry flavors range from sweet to tart.
Storage: Store berries in a single layer on paper towel-lined shallow pans, lightly covered, in your refrigerator, and use within 3 days. Blueberries aren't as perishable as other berries and will keep about a week. Wash berries just before using. Freeze berries by removing stems and placing berries in a single layer on a baking sheet; place in freezer until solid, then quickly transfer to a plastic freezer bag or container, and keep in the freezer up to 9 months. (*see also individual berries*)

Q How can I prevent berries from sinking to the bottom of baked products?

A To keep berries from sinking, toss them with flour, coating well, before adding to the batter.

SELECTING BERRIES

There are many varieties of berries, some of which are sold at the market, and some of which must be hand-picked or purchased from roadside stands.

TYPE BERRY	APPEARANCE	FLAVOR
Blackberry	Purplish-black	Sweet, tangy
Blueberry	Purplish-blue	Mildly sweet
Boysenberry	Purplish-black	Sweet, tangy
Cranberry	Shiny burgundy red	Tart
Currant	Red, white, or black	Tart, tangy
Gooseberry	Pale green	Tart
Huckleberry	Blue or black	Mildly sweet
Ligonberry	Dark red	Very tart
Loganberry	Purplish-red	Tart
Mulberry	Bluish-purple, red, or almost white	Mildly sweet to sour
Raspberry	Red or golden	Mildly sweet
Strawberry	Bright red	Sweet

TEST KITCHEN SECRET

Don't wash berries until you're ready to use them, and wash them before removing the stem. Added moisture will hasten the growth of mold. Washing blueberries before freezing toughens their skin. Jan Moon

betty A simple pudding made by alternating sweetened spiced fruit and buttered breadcrumbs in a baking dish. The most popular is apple brown betty.

beurre blanc (burr BLAHN) This classic French sauce is made by cooking a mixture of wine, vinegar, and shallots until it's reduced. Chunks of cold butter are then whisked into the mixture until thickened and smooth. Serve the sauce with poultry, seafood, and vegetables. (*see also* **sauce**)

beverage A general term for any drinkable liquid; it can be hot or cold, alcoholic or nonalcoholic, carbonated or noncarbonated.

Setting up a bar: When planning a basic bar, include Scotch, vodka, bourbon, gin, and rum; fruit juices, carbonated beverages, sparkling water, wine, and beer. To calculate how much to buy, consider the number of guests, how long the party will last, and what other beverages, such as punch, will be available. For each guest, estimate 1 drink, 1 beer, or 2 glasses of wine per hour; for each guest that doesn't drink alcoholic beverages, have cans of cola or sparkling water available. Plan 10 ounces of mixer, 2 to 3 glasses, and ½ pound of ice per person.

TIMESAVING TIP
If you need to chill champagne quickly, submerge the bubbly in a mixture of half ice, half tap water. This chills it quicker than ice alone.

Alcohol mathematics: It's also helpful to know that 1 (750-milliliter) bottle of liquor equals 17 (1½-ounce) jiggers, or 1 (1-liter) bottle liquor equals 22 (1½-ounce) jiggers, and 1 (750-milliliter) bottle champagne equals 6 (4-ounce) servings. (*see also* **alcohol, coffee, jigger, liqueur, liquor, tea,** *and* **wine**)

B

biscotti (bee SKAWT tee) Twice-baked Italian-style cookies made by baking dough as a loaf, and then slicing the loaf and baking the slices. The cookies are very crunchy, which makes them perfect for dipping into coffee.

COCOA-ALMOND BISCOTTI

½ cup butter, softened	2¼ cups all-purpose flour
1 cup sugar	1½ teaspoons baking powder
2 large eggs	¼ teaspoon salt
1½ tablespoons coffee liqueur	1½ tablespoons cocoa
or chocolate syrup	1 (6-ounce) can whole almonds

• Combine butter and sugar in a large bowl; beat at medium speed with an electric mixer until light and fluffy. Add eggs, beating well. Mix in liqueur.
• Combine flour and next 3 ingredients; add to butter mixture, beating well. Stir in almonds. Divide dough in half; shape each portion into a 9- x 2-inch log on a lightly greased baking sheet. Bake at 350° for 30 minutes or until firm. Cool on baking sheet 5 minutes. Remove to wire racks to cool.
• Cut each log diagonally into ½-inch-thick slices with a serrated knife, using a gentle sawing motion. Place on ungreased baking sheets.
• Bake at 350° for 5 to 7 minutes. Turn cookies over, and bake 5 to 7 more minutes. Remove to wire racks to cool. Yield: 2½ dozen.

biscuit (BIHS kit) This term refers to a small, flaky quick bread, leavened with baking soda or baking powder that has a light, tender texture. Most Southerners pat the biscuits into little circles, but they can be rolled and cut with a biscuit cutter or dropped from a spoon before baking. Tender biscuits are delicious split and spread with butter, honey, and jam, or filled with slivers of ham or steak. In the South, some cooks swear soft wheat flour makes the most tender, flaky biscuits. White Lily and Martha White are the most popular brands of soft wheat flour in the South. If they aren't available in your area, use equal amounts of all-purpose and cake flour. Mix only until the ingredients just hold together. Overmixing the dough will develop the gluten in the flour and toughen the biscuits.

Storage: Wrap leftover biscuits in foil, place in a plastic zip-lock bag, and freeze up to 3 months. To serve, thaw and heat foil-wrapped biscuits in a 300° oven for several minutes or until heated. (*see also* **baking powder** *and* **baking soda**)

RESCUE for overbrowned biscuits: Forget and leave the biscuits in the oven too long? Gently scrape the flat burned undersides against a fine-toothed grater to remove most of the mistake. Do this over the sink; it's messy.

TIMESAVING TIP
Try making biscuit dough in your food processor. Combine dry ingredients in the processor bowl; add the fat, and pulse 6 or 7 times, until the mixture resembles coarse meal. Slowly add the liquid through the food chute, with the processor running, just until the dough forms a ball and leaves the sides of the bowl. The processor can easily overwork the dough, so watch it closely. Then shape the biscuits.

LIGHTER-THAN-AIR BUTTERMILK BISCUITS

⅓ cup butter or margarine, cut up   ¾ cup buttermilk
2 cups self-rising soft wheat flour   Butter or margarine, melted

• Cut ⅓ cup butter into flour with a pastry blender until crumbly (photo 1); add buttermilk, stirring just until dry ingredients are moistened.

• Turn dough out onto a lightly floured surface; knead 3 or 4 times (photo 2).

• Pat or roll dough to ¾-inch thickness; cut with a 2½-inch round cutter (photo 3), and place on a lightly greased baking sheet.

• Bake at 425° for 12 to 14 minutes. Brush biscuits with melted butter. Yield: 8 biscuits.
Note: For testing purposes only, we used White Lily Self-Rising Soft Wheat Flour.

READER TIP
"I've found that sticky, slightly wet dough makes the best biscuits. I keep the damp dough from sticking to my hands by kneading with a metal dough scraper. The scraper lets me lift the dough and fold it over on a floured surface. Once it becomes less sticky, I knead by hand." M.E.J., Decatur, AL

TEST KITCHEN SECRET
If you like biscuits with crusty sides, place them 1-inch apart on a shiny baking sheet. For soft sides, arrange them close together in a shallow baking dish or pan. JAN MOON

1. Cut butter or shortening into dry ingredients until crumbly.

2. Knead dough lightly with heel of your hand.

3. Punch out biscuits with a 2½-inch cutter.

bisque (BIHSK) A thick, smooth cream soup usually made with shrimp or other shellfish, but also prepared with vegetables, such as tomato.

bistro (BEES troh) A small, casual café that serves simple food and wine.

bitters A flavoring agent, usually quite bitter and pungent, distilled from herbs, leaves, roots, or fruit rinds. Bitters are consumed plain or with water or in drinks, especially alcoholic drinks. They're also used as a home remedy for fevers, as a digestive aid, or as an appetite stimulant. Angostura bitters is the trade name for a well-known brand of bitters.

black beans Sometimes called turtle beans these small, shiny black beans have a cream-colored flesh and sweet flavor and are used in soups and dips. (*see also* **beans, dried**)

TIMESAVING TIP
Canned black beans are a good substitute for dried beans. Two (15-ounce) cans of black beans equals about ½ pound (1 cup) dried beans cooked.

blackberry Purplish-black in color, the plump blackberry ranges from ½- to 1-inch long and has a sweet, tangy flavor when ripe. Blackberries are widely cultivated in the United States, and are sometimes called bramble berries because they grow wild on bramble vines along rural roadsides from May through August. Blackberries can be eaten out-of-hand, in pies, or topped with sweetened whipped cream. Blackberries are also available canned and frozen. The only drawback to the blackberry is its fairly large, crunchy seeds. When pureeing blackberries, press them through a sieve to remove the seeds and pulp. (*see also* **berry**)

black bottom pie A rich custard pie traditionally made with a layer of dark chocolate filling on the bottom, topped with a layer of white rum filling, and garnished with whipped cream and chocolate shavings. (*see also* **pie**)

blackened A Cajun cooking method in which food, usually meat or fish, is rubbed with a spice mixture and cooked in a very hot cast-iron skillet, giving the food a charred, extra-crisp crust. Blackened redfish first prompted the interest in blackened dishes, but it's now commonly used for other more available fish such as catfish, pompano, or tilefish. If these aren't available, substitute salmon steaks or red snapper fillets. (*see also* **Cajun cooking**)

Southernism

Paul Prudhomme, the chef of K-Paul's Louisiana Kitchen in the French Quarter of New Orleans, popularized spicy blackened recipes with his famous blackened redfish. Now the dish is so well known nationwide that it has made redfish an endangered species.

BLACKENED CATFISH

2 tablespoons paprika	1½ teaspoons ground red pepper
2½ teaspoons salt	1 teaspoon onion powder
2 teaspoons lemon pepper	1 teaspoon dried thyme
1½ teaspoons garlic powder	4 farm-raised catfish fillets
1½ teaspoons dried basil, crushed	1 cup unsalted butter, melted

• Combine first 8 ingredients in a large shallow dish. Dip fish in butter; dredge in paprika mixture. Place on wax paper.

• Heat a large cast-iron or heavy aluminum skillet over medium-high heat 10 minutes.

• Cook fish, 2 at a time, 2 to 3 minutes on each side or until fish is blackened and flakes easily with a fork. Yield: 4 servings.

TEST KITCHEN SECRET

Making blackened recipes is not for everyone because you must have a very strong exhaust fan to remove all the smoke that's produced. If you don't have a heavy-duty exhaust fan, we suggest blackening recipes outdoors by placing your skillet directly on top of hot coals in your grill. LYDA JONES

black-eyed pea A small, oval, cream-colored legume with a black oval eye that has a cream-colored dot in the center. Also known as the cowpea, black-eyes are the main ingredient in the traditional New Year's Day dish, Hoppin' John. The peas are available fresh, dried, or canned. (*see also* **hoppin' John**)

Southernism

Black-eyed peas have been a staple in the South for more than three centuries. It's believed their introduction in the United States coincided with the African slave trade. Over the years, the peas have become part of Southern folklore, and many believe that eating black-eyes on New Year's Day will bring good luck all year long.

Black Forest cake This German cake is created by layering chocolate cake flavored with kirsch (cherry liqueur), a sweet cherry mixture, and Kirsch-laced whipped cream. The cake is finished with a generous coating of whipped cream and a top layer of cherries. (*see also* **liqueur**)

blanc (BLAHN) A term used to describe champagne or white wine made exclusively from the white Chardonnay grape. It's also the French word for white. (*see also* **Chardonnay**)

blanch To cook food briefly in boiling water or steam. The food is plunged into boiling water and then into cold water to stop the cooking process. Blanching is generally done as part of the preparation of fruits and vegetables for freezing. It's also done to remove the skins of some foods, such as tomatoes, peaches, and almonds, or to quickly cook green beans, broccoli, and cauliflower and soften their fibers before baking, frying, or sautéing.

TIMESAVING TIP
When blanching vegetables, blanch them in a strainer, then put into a large bowl of ice water. With this method, there's no fishing around for vegetables when they're cool. Simply lift the strainer and let the water drain back into the bowl.

TEST KITCHEN SECRET
If faced with peeling a bushel of tomatoes for canning or making relish, we dip the tomatoes into boiling water for 30 seconds to 1 minute; then we plunge them into cold water. The skins will slip off easily. JAMES SCHEND

blend To combine 2 or more ingredients until they're smooth and uniform in texture, flavor, and color. This procedure can be done by hand, with an electric mixer, or a blender. (*see also* **beat**)

blender An electrical appliance that has a tall, narrow container and short, rotating blades that chop, blend, puree, and liquefy foods. However, a blender doesn't whip egg whites or cream since its design doesn't allow for the incorporation of air into food. Blenders are useful for making soups, purees, sauces, and milk shakes.

blintz (BLIHNTS) A very thin pancake rolled around a filling, typically of cottage or ricotta cheese and fruit. The filled blintz is baked or sautéed and served with a topping of sour cream.

blood orange This sweet-tart orange is originally from Sicily and has a blood-red flesh. It's typically eaten out-of-hand or sliced for salads or desserts. It's available during the winter months. (*see also* **orange**)

bloody Mary A popular alcoholic cocktail made with tomato juice, vodka, Worcestershire sauce, hot sauce, and lemon juice. It's often served with a celery rib as a swizzle stick. A virgin Mary contains no alcohol. (*see also* **liquor** *and* **Worcestershire sauce**)

bloom A dull gray film that sometimes appears on chocolate. This occurs if the chocolate is stored in too warm of an environment. Bloom on chocolate doesn't affect flavor. (*see also* **chocolate**)

blueberry A tiny, round, deep purplish-blue berry with a tiny star-shaped cap. The delicate orbs have a refreshing, frosty appearance, and a mild, sweet flavor. Blueberries are grown on bushes in Canada and in the northern United States. They're packed with vitamins A and C and may be eaten out-of-hand, in pies, pancakes, salads, jams and jellies, or with a topping of whipped cream. They're also available canned or frozen. (*see also* **berry**)

blue cheese The name given to several varieties of blue-veined cheeses treated with molds that form blue or green veins throughout. The molds give these cheeses their characteristic strong flavors and aromas. Aging is an important part of the manufacturing of blue cheese; the longer it's aged, the stronger the flavor. Some of the blue cheeses available in the market include: Danablu, Gorgonzola, Roquefort, and Stilton. Blue cheese is often added to green salads or used to make blue cheese dressing. (*see also* **cheese**)

blue crab Gulf and Atlantic coast crabs named because of their blue claws and dark blue-green shell. Before they mature they shed their hard shells and are sometimes sold as soft-shell crabs. Soft-shell crabs are available in spring and summer and are eaten shell and all.
Storage: Leftover cooked crabmeat stores well: Put it in a heavy duty zip-top plastic bag, add milk (to prevent freezer burn), carefully squeeze out the air, close, and freeze. It keeps in a refrigerator freezer 2 months or in a deep freezer for 6 months. Thaw in the refrigerator overnight; drain off milk before using. (*see also* **crab**)

Southernism

Southerners passionately pursue these live crustaceans using simple, time-honored methods: suspending metal crab traps from a dock, lowering a baited drop net, or luring crabs into a dip net using a chicken neck tied to a string. All the while, Southerners can escape from their hurried days to peaceful places, where life ebbs and flows with the tides, and where a chicken neck is the most lethal weapon—in the secret, watery world of the blue crab.

TEST KITCHEN SECRET

Keep crabs cool and moist until you're ready to cook them. They travel well in an ice chest, but should be used the day they're caught. Don't add water or they'll drown. Never cook a dead crab. JAN MOON

blush wine A term that refers to rosé wines that range in color from pink to pale orange to light red. The flavors of blush wines range from dry to sweet. Serve them chilled with lightly flavored foods. (*see also* **wine**)

Boboli (BOH boh lee) A brand name for Italian bread that's shaped into large or small flat rounds. It can be eaten as a snack, made into sandwiches, served with soups, or topped with pizzalike ingredients and baked.

body A term used to describe the flavor, feel, texture, and weight of a food or beverage on the palate. For example, a full-bodied wine or a full-bodied coffee has a flavor that lingers in the mouth.

boeuf (BEUF) The French term for beef.

boil Heating a liquid to a boil or until bubbles break the surface. Boiling is a moist-heat cooking method. A full rolling boil means the bubbles cannot be interrupted by stirring; they rise in a steady pattern, breaking on the surface. Since liquids evaporate more rapidly at high elevations, the boiling point will decrease the higher the altitude. At sea level, water boils at 212°; at 2,000 feet, the boiling point is 208°; at 5,000 feet, 203°; at 10,000 feet, 194°. (*see also* **high altitude**)

TIMESAVING TIP
In a hurry for the water to boil? Place the saucepan over high heat and cover with a lid. This will cause a quicker buildup of steam and pressure, resulting in a faster boil.

boiled icing A fluffy white cake frosting or Italian meringue made by gradually pouring hot sugar syrup over beaten egg whites and beating constantly until the mixture is smooth, satiny, and stiff enough to spread. (*see also* **frosting**)

BOILED ICING

1 ½ **cups sugar**	⅛ **teaspoon salt**
½ **cup water**	4 **egg whites**
½ **teaspoon cream of tartar**	½ **teaspoon almond extract**

• Combine first 4 ingredients in a heavy saucepan. Cook over medium heat, stirring constantly, until mixture is clear. Cook, without stirring, until mixture reaches soft ball stage or candy thermometer registers 240°.
• While syrup cooks, beat egg whites at high speed with an electric mixer until soft peaks form; continue to beat egg whites, adding the hot syrup mixture in a heavy stream.
• Add almond extract. Beat until stiff peaks form and icing is thick enough to spread. Yield: 7 cups.

boiling water bath A special cooking container that's used during the canning process to preserve high-acid foods such as fruit, pickles, and tomatoes. It's a large, deep vessel that allows water to cover the tops and sides of canning jars. It should have a tight-fitting lid and contain a rack to keep the jars in place and off the bottom of the container. (*see also* **bain-marie, canning,** *and* **water bath**)

Southernism

Don't let the procedure of a boiling-water bath scare you. Preserving is an old Southern art easily mastered once you know the rules. Think of the water bath as a way of safely tucking your produce in for a long nap.

TEST KITCHEN SECRET

If you don't have a boiling-water bath container, place filled jars on a rack in a large Dutch oven or kettle so water flows evenly around them. Add hot water to reach 1 to 2 inches above jar lids. Cover and set timer for processing time after water comes to a boil. VIE WARSHAW

bok choy (bahk CHOY) A mild-flavored Chinese cabbage with large, crunchy white stalks and tender, dark green leaves. Bok choy looks somewhat like a big bunch of celery with long, full leaves and can be eaten raw or cooked.
Storage: Store bok choy in a plastic bag in the refrigerator and use within a few days. (*see also* **cabbage** *and* **Chinese cabbage**)

bologna (bah LOW nyah) Highly seasoned, precooked sausage, often called baloney, made from pork, beef, and veal, and named after Bologna, Italy. It's typically sliced and served as a luncheon meat or cold cut. Italian bologna sausage is called mortadella. (*see also* **sausage**)

bolognese (boh loh NEESE *or* boh loh NEEZ) A thick Italian sauce for pasta made from ground meat, tomatoes, celery, carrots, sometimes bacon, and seasoned with garlic, herbs, and olive oil. Also refers to foods prepared in the cooking style of Bologna, Italy. (*see also* **pasta**)

bombe (BAHM) A frozen French dessert made of layers of ice cream or sherbet. Softened ice cream is packed into a mold, one layer at a time, and frozen. To serve, the bombe is unmolded, sometimes decorated, and often accompanied with a sweet sauce.

bon appétit (bahn nah pay TEE) French for "good appetite"; it means to have a good meal or to enjoy your meal.

bonbon (BAHN bahn) French for a bite-sized piece of candy, confection, or sweetmeat. Bonbons are typically a small piece of candy, usually chocolate-dipped fondant that's sometimes mixed with nuts or fruits.

bone To remove the bones from meat, fish, or poultry.

TIMESAVING TIP
Use kitchen tweezers to pull tiny bones from fish.

boniato (bou nee AH tou) Often referred to as a Cuban sweet potato, the boniato has a thick light yellow skin and pale yellow mealy flesh. The boniato becomes dry and fluffy when cooked. It's not as sweet as a sweet potato. (*see also* **sweet potato**)

Bordeaux wine (bore DOH) These elegant, rich, and fragrant red and white wines take their name from the region of France where they're produced. Bordeaux is the largest fine-wine district in the world. More than 75 percent of the wine produced in the region is red (Cabernet Sauvignon and Merlot are king). Most of the white wine is Sauternes, the world-famous white dessert wine. (*see also* **wine**)

bordelaise sauce (bohr duh LAYZ) A dark, flavorful French sauce made from wine, brown stock, shallots or onions, parsley, and herbs, and traditionally, bone marrow. It's typically served with beef or pork. (*see also* **sauce** *and recipe on the following page*)

BORDELAISE SAUCE

4 thin slices onion	⅔ cup water
1½ tablespoons butter or	⅓ cup dry red wine
margarine, melted	¾ teaspoon dried parsley flakes
1½ tablespoons all-purpose flour	¼ teaspoon dried thyme
1 teaspoon beef bouillon granules	¼ teaspoon pepper

• Sauté onion in butter in a heavy skillet until onion is tender; discard onion. Cook butter over low heat until it begins to brown. Add flour, stirring until smooth. Cook 1 minute, stirring constantly. Add bouillon granules, and gradually stir in water and wine. Cook over medium heat, stirring constantly, until thickened and bubbly. Stir in parsley flakes, thyme, and pepper. Yield: 1 cup.

borscht (BOHR sht) A Polish or Russian soup made with fresh beets. It sometimes includes other vegetables and/or meat. It can be served hot or cold. Always garnish the ruby red soup with a dollop of sour cream. (*see also* **beet**)

Boston baked beans A hearty, slow-cooked casserole of pea beans or navy beans flavored with salt pork and molasses. It takes its name from Puritan women in Boston, who cooked a pot of the beans for Saturday dinner with the plan of serving leftovers the next day since cooking was forbidden on the Sabbath. Boston brown bread often accompanies the beans. (*see also* **Boston brown bread, navy bean,** *and* **pea bean**)

Boston brown bread A dark, sweet steamed bread that's the traditional accompaniment to Boston baked beans. It's made with rye and wheat flour, cornmeal, molasses, and often raisins. (*see also* **Boston baked beans**)

Boston cream pie Actually a cake rather than a pie, this dessert is made of 2 layers of sponge cake filled with thick vanilla custard and topped with chocolate glaze. Sometimes the pie is made from a single layer of cake that's split horizontally.

botulism A severe form of food poisoning that can lead to paralysis and even death. Foods most susceptible to this poison are home-canned foods, such as peas and beans if canned improperly, and commercially canned foods if damaged, such as tuna. The best prevention is to use only reliable recipes when canning at home and to throw away any canned goods, either home-canned or store-bought with cloudy liquids, loose lids, spurting liquid, or cracked jars. (*see also* **food safety**)

TEST KITCHEN SECRET

We have a saying in our Test Kitchens and, that's 'When in doubt, throw it out.' Though botulism is very rare, it can be deadly, and you don't want to take a chance. LYDA JONES

boudin (boo DAHN) A spicy-Cajun link sausage of pork and rice that originated from the frugality of stretching the meat with rice. Its broad popularity today in Louisiana defies its humble beginnings. Boudin blanc refers to a white sausage made of pork, chicken, fat, eggs, cream, breadcrumbs, and seasonings; boudin rouge is a blood-filled sausage now only available homemade

Southernism

Ubiquitous signs dot roadsides throughout South Louisiana proclaiming "Hot Boudin" for sale. The regional "fast food" simmers in slow cookers at peoples' homes, gas stations, and corner stores.

because the U.S. Department of Agriculture outlawed commercial sales for food safety reasons. (*see also* **Cajun cooking** *and* **sausage**)

bouillabaisse (BOOL yuh BAYZ) A French seafood stew made from a variety of fish and shellfish, tomatoes, white wine, garlic, saffron, and herbs, and served over thick slices of crusty French bread. The following version *sans* saffron is authentic "N'awlins" style, according to Acadian culinary folklorist Marcelle Bienenu.

MARCELLE'S BOUILLABAISSE

1 **pound unpeeled, medium-size fresh shrimp**	2 **celery ribs, chopped**
2½ **pounds trout or redfish fillets**	3 **garlic cloves, minced**
1 **teaspoon salt, divided**	½ **cup butter**
1 **teaspoon ground red pepper, divided**	2 **(28-ounce) cans crushed tomatoes**
3 **medium-size yellow onions, coarsely chopped**	4 **bay leaves**
2 **medium-size green bell peppers, coarsely chopped**	½ **cup dry white wine**
	2 **tablespoons chopped fresh parsley**

• Peel shrimp, and devein, if desired. Set aside.
• Sprinkle fillets with ½ teaspoon salt and ½ teaspoon red pepper; set aside.
• Toss together remaining ½ teaspoon salt, remaining ½ teaspoon red pepper, onion, and next 3 ingredients.
• Melt butter in a 6-quart Dutch oven over medium heat, and remove from heat.
• Arrange half of fish fillets in Dutch oven; layer with half of vegetable mixture, half of tomatoes, and 2 bay leaves. Repeat procedure with remaining fish fillets, vegetable mixture, tomatoes, and bay leaves. Arrange shrimp on top; add wine.
• Bring mixture to a boil. Cover, reduce heat, and cook 1 hour. (Do not remove cover.) Sprinkle each serving with chopped parsley. Discard bay leaves. Yield: 12 cups.

bouillon (BOOL yahn) A broth made by simmering meat, poultry, fish, or vegetables in water. The solids are strained out and discarded, leaving the clear bouillon for use as a base for soups, sauces, or poaching. For convenience, substitute instant bouillon granules, bouillon cubes, and canned broth. (*see also* **broth** *and* **consommé**)

> ♡ **LITE BITE**
> Removing the surface fat from homemade bouillon makes it healthier. The easiest way to do this is to refrigerate the mixture overnight and then lift the congealed layer of fat from the surface. For a quicker technique, try wrapping an ice cube in cheesecloth and skimming it over the surface of the soup, or add ice cubes directly to the mixture. The fat will congeal on contact with the ice, and then it can be easily removed.

bouquet (boo KAY) The complex aroma that wine develops after aging in a barrel or bottle. (*see also* **wine**)

bouquet garni (boo KAY gahr NEE) French culinary term for a bundle of herbs, usually parsley, thyme, and bay leaf. Sprigs of the herbs are tied together or placed in a cheesecloth bag and used to flavor sauces, soups, and stews. Bundling the herbs makes removal easy.

bourbon A popular whiskey that's distilled from fermented grain. If called "straight" bourbon, it has been distilled from a mash of at least 51 percent corn; if "blended," it contains no less than 51 percent straight bourbon; and "sour mash" bourbon is made by adding a portion of old mash to help start fermentation in a new batch. Southerners savor the liquor on the rocks, blended into mint juleps, and even stirred into sweet potatoes and batters for breads and cakes. (*see also* **liquor**)

Southernism

According to legend, a Baptist preacher named Elijah Craig is credited as the originator of bourbon whiskey in what was then Bourbon County of the Kentucky territory. However, Craig's 1789 corn liquor was most certainly not the first distillery, as property inventories show that there were about 2,000 stills in the state by 1811. During pre-Prohibition, the South lead the nation in bourbon manufacturing, and even today, some of our region's famous whiskeys are legally manufactured in counties where their sale is prohibited by law.

Boursin® (boor SAHN) A white, buttery textured, triple cream cheese flavored with herbs, garlic, or cracked pepper. It pairs well with dry white or fruity red wines. (*see also* **cheese**)

boysenberry A blackberry, loganberry, and raspberry hybrid that's shaped like a large raspberry and looks like a blackberry with a purplish-black color. In taste, the boysenberry resembles both the raspberry and the blackberry, and can be used in the same ways as either one. (*see also* **berry**)

braise (BRAYZ) A moist-heat method of browning or searing meat in hot oil, then covering and simmering in a small amount of liquid over low heat on the cooktop or in the oven. The long, slow cooking method is ideal for tough cuts of meat because it tenderizes them. A tight lid is important to prevent liquid from evaporating. Check the liquid from time to time to ensure enough remains to not only do the job, but also to allow for a gravy to go with the meat. (*see also* **beef**)

bran The coarse outer layer of a grain kernel that's removed during milling. Bran is a good source of fiber and B vitamins and is sometimes added to enrich baked goods and cereals.
Storage: Store bran in an airtight container in a cool, dry place up to 1 month. Refrigerate bran up to 3 months, or freeze it up to 1 year. (*see also* **fiber, grain, oat, rice,** *and* **wheat**)

Q Are all types of fiber the same?

A Definitely not. Corn bran provides the highest amount of fiber, most of which is insoluble. Rice bran and wheat bran also contain a high amount of insoluble fiber. Oat bran is high in soluble fiber. It's believed that insoluble fiber helps reduce the risk of colon cancer. Soluble fiber may help reduce LDL (bad) cholesterol and may help control blood sugar levels in people with diabetes.

brandy A liquor distilled from wine or other fermented fruit juice and aged in wood casks. The color, flavor, and aroma depend on the type of wine or juice used and the length of time it ages in the cask. (*see also* **liquor**)

bratwurst (BRAHT wurst) A German link sausage made of pork or veal and seasoned with herbs and spices. (*see also* **sausage**)

braunschweiger (BROWN shwi ger) A soft, spreadable German smoked liverwurst sausage enriched with eggs and milk. (*see also* **sausage**)

Brazil nut The seeds of a tree grown in the Amazon; the 3-sided nuts grow in clusters inside 3- to 4-pound coconut-like pods. The nuts have a very hard, dark brown triangular shell. The nut is high in fat.
Storage: Keep unshelled nuts in a cool, dry place up to 6 months. Refrigerate shelled nuts and use within 3 months; freeze up to 8 months. (*see also* **nuts**)

Q What is the easiest way to crack Brazil nuts?

A These nuts are hard to crack unless they're steamed or boiled for a few minutes. Place them in a saucepan, cover with water, and bring to a boil. Boil for 3 to 4 minutes, and then drain. Cover the nuts with cold water and let stand 1 minute. Then shell with a handheld nutcracker.

bread A food staple baked from a dough or batter made with flour or meal, water or other liquid, and usually a leavener. Bread can be baked, cooked on a griddle, fried, or steamed. All breads fall into 4 categories: yeast breads, which require kneading; batter breads, which are vigorously stirred instead of kneaded; quick breads, which use baking soda, baking powder, or eggs for rising; and unleavened breads, which remain flat. (*see also* **batter bread, leaven, quick bread,** *and* **yeast**)

Q What's the secret to getting neat slices from a fresh loaf of bread?

A Use a long serrated-edged bread knife. However, even a bread knife sometime fails to cut through the thick bottom crust. To solve this, turn the loaf on its side so that you're cutting through the top and bottom crusts at the same time.

RESCUE for stale bread:
If bread becomes stale, refresh it with one of these two tricks. First, sprinkle the stale bread with water; wrap it in aluminum foil, and bake at 350° until it's warm and soft. Or, place individual slices of bread on a splatter screen and hold them over a pan of simmering water for a minute or two.

bread-and-butter pickles Sweet cucumber pickles flavored with onions, mustard, celery seeds, cloves, and sometimes turmeric. (*see also* **pickle**)

breadcrumbs Small bits of bread used as a coating for fried foods or as a filler or topping for casseroles. There are 2 types of breadcrumbs: dry and fresh. Dry breadcrumbs are usually commercially prepared and seasoned or plain; they can also be made from fresh breadcrumbs that have been oven-dried. Fresh breadcrumbs are homemade and soft. These 2 types of breadcrumbs usually aren't interchangeable in recipes.
Storage: Store breadcrumbs in the refrigerator in a tightly sealed container for 1 week, or freeze up to 6 months.

breading A coating of breadcrumbs, cracker crumbs, cornmeal, flour, or other dry meal applied to foods to be fried or baked. As part of this process, the meat, poultry, fish, or vegetables are generally dipped in beaten egg, egg white, milk, or buttermilk first, to help the breading adhere.

TEST KITCHEN SECRET

The secret to making sure that breading sticks to the food is to start with food completely dry. First coat it with flour, then dip it in beaten egg or milk, and then flour, or apply other coating. After it's dipped and coated, let it sit on a rack and dry for 15 minutes or so before cooking. VANESSA MCNEIL

TIMESAVING TIP
The easiest way to coat food with a breading is to use a zip-top plastic bag. Place the breading mixture in the bag, and add the food to be cooked, a few pieces at a time. Close the top of the bag, and shake well.

bread machine An appliance that mixes, kneads, proofs, and bakes a small loaf of bread. Directions for brands vary, so be sure to read the instructions that came with your model. Be sure to measure ingredients carefully. Bread machines are not as forgiving as the traditional bread-making method.

COUNTRY WHITE BREAD

1 cup plus 2 tablespoons water	2 tablespoons instant dry milk
1¼ teaspoons salt	powder
1½ tablespoons butter	2 tablespoons sugar
3 cups bread flour or all-purpose	2 teaspoons bread-machine
flour	yeast

• Combine all ingredients in bread machine according to manufacturer's instructions. Select bake cycle; start machine. When machine cuts off, remove bread from pan; cool on wire rack. Yield: 1 (1½-pound) loaf.

bread pudding A baked dessert made with stale French bread cubes or slices that have been soaked in a mixture of eggs, milk, sugar, and flavorings. Chopped fruits or nuts are sometimes added. The pudding may be served hot or cold and is often drenched with whiskey sauce. The bread pudding we know today is derived from England's famous hasty pudding made from flour, milk, eggs, butter, and spices. Today's Southern bread puddings often show up as savory dishes with cheese, onion, garlic, and other herbs. (*see also* **French bread, hasty pudding,** *and* **pudding**)

BREAD PUDDING WITH CUSTARD-WHISKEY SAUCE

8 large day-old croissants, torn into small pieces*	1 cup pecans, toasted
	1½ tablespoons vanilla extract
4 cups milk	1 teaspoon ground cinnamon
3 large eggs, lightly beaten	½ teaspoon ground nutmeg
2 cups sugar	Custard-Whiskey Sauce

• Place bread in a lightly greased 13- x 9-inch pan.
• Pour milk over bread, and let stand 10 minutes. Blend mixture well, using hands. Stir eggs and next 5 ingredients into bread mixture. Bake at 325° for 40 to 45 minutes or until firm. Serve with custard sauce. Yield: 15 servings.

CUSTARD-WHISKEY SAUCE

1 cup sugar	2 tablespoons whiskey or
½ cup butter or margarine	½ teaspoon vanilla extract
½ cup half-and-half	

• Bring first 3 ingredients to a boil in a heavy saucepan over medium heat, stirring until sugar dissolves. Reduce heat, and simmer 5 minutes. Cool; stir in whiskey or vanilla. Yield: 1½ cups.

* Substitute 1 (16-ounce) loaf French bread for croissants, if desired. Bake at 325° for 55 minutes or until firm.

breads, quick These breads get their name because they require no kneading or rising time, and use baking powder, baking soda, or eggs as a leavening agent instead of yeast. Avoid overmixing the dough because this toughens the bread. Stir just until the liquid and dry ingredients blend, and then start shaping.

Storage: Store most quick breads in a plastic bag at room temperature up to 3 days. Wrap breads tightly in heavy foil or freezer bags and freeze up to 3 months. (*see also* **biscuit, muffin, pancake, popover, scone,** *and* **waffle**)

TIMESAVING TIP

For fresh muffins or biscuits for breakfast, measure the ingredients the night before. Put the dry ingredients in a bowl on the counter and chill the wet ingredients. Preheat the oven the next morning while you stir up the batter.

TEST KITCHEN SECRET

"To test a loaf-type quick bread for doneness, insert a wooden pick into the thickest part of the bread; it should come out clean and free of crumbs when done." Jan Moon

breads, yeast Baked breads that use yeast as a leavener to make them rise. These breads have a wide variety of textures and shapes, but all require kneading or beating to develop gluten (an elastic protein in flour that gives yeast bread its structure). The yeast produces carbon dioxide gas bubbles, which become trapped in the gluten, causing the bread to expand and rise.

RESCUE for overrisen dough: Punch the dough back down and let it rise again. The texture may be a little denser but the flavor won't be affected.

There are 2 main types of yeast bread: kneaded and batter. In kneaded yeast breads, the dough must be worked by hand or machine to develop the gluten. Kneading is vital to developing the gluten in the dough as well as to incorporate air into the dough. The kneading process gives the bread a finer grain or texture. Batter breads typically use a little less flour and are beaten by hand or mixer to help develop the gluten. Batter bread dough, which is stirred vigorously instead of kneaded, is stickier than kneaded dough and has a coarser texture after baking.

TIMESAVING TIP

Give store-bought frozen yeast dough a try. It's great for pizza dough and quick rolls. Thaw the dough overnight in the refrigerator. It rises as it thaws and will be ready to bake.

Storage: Once cooled, wrap fresh-baked yeast bread in foil, plastic wrap, or place in a zip-top plastic bag. Store it in a cool, dry place up to 3 days. To freeze, place the bread in a freezer bag or wrap tightly in heavy-duty aluminum foil, and freeze up to 3 months. Thaw frozen bread at room temperature for 1 hour or wrap it in foil and heat at 300° for 15 to 20 minutes.

Working with Yeast: Most of our recipes call for dissolving the yeast in warm water (100° to 110°) before adding other ingredients (photo 1, opposite page), and the temperature of the water is critical. Water that's too hot will kill the yeast; water that's too cool inhibits rising.

1. Dissolve yeast in warm water.

2. Knead dough to develop gluten.

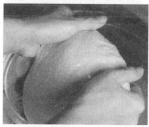
3. Place in greased bowl, turning to grease top.

Kneading Dough: Turn dough out onto a smooth, floured surface. With floured hands, lift the edge of the dough farthest from you and fold it toward you. Using the heel of 1 or both hands, press down into the dough and away from you (photo 2). Give dough a quarter turn. Fold the dough toward you again, and repeat the kneading procedure until the dough begins to feel smooth and elastic—an ultimate goal that ensures good texture for all yeast breads. Continue kneading in small amounts of flour until dough loses its stickiness; on humid days dough will absorb more flour. The process can take up to 10 minutes.

Proofing Dough: After kneading, place dough in a greased bowl, turning it to coat the top (photo 3). Cover bowl with a barely damp kitchen towel or lightly greased plastic wrap. The ideal rising temperature for yeast bread is 85°. An oven with a pan of very hot water placed on the rack under the dough should provide this temperature (photo 4). Rising is complete when the dough has doubled. To test the dough, press 2 fingers ½ inch into the dough (photo 5). If the indentation remains, the dough has risen enough.

Shaping Dough: Punch the dough down in the center with your fist (photo 6), and fold edges to the center. Turn the dough over, and place it on a lightly floured surface. Divide the dough according to your recipe, and form 1 portion into a ball. (Dough dries out quickly, so cover and store excess in the refrigerator until needed.) Cover the dough, and let it rest 5 to 10 minutes. This makes the dough less elastic and easier to handle. Individual recipes give specific directions for shaping the dough. After shaping, place the dough in a prepared loafpan or on a baking sheet, and allow it to rise again, according to directions. When the shaped dough is double in size, press 2 fingers against the edge of the loaf. If the indentation remains, the dough has risen enough. (*continued on the following page*)

4. Cover and let rise in warm place.

5. Test to see if rising is complete.

6. Punch dough down.

Baking Bread: Bake the bread in a preheated oven, unless the recipe specifies otherwise. Place the pan in the center of the oven to make sure your bread bakes evenly. If you're baking more than 1 pan in the same oven, leave some space around each pan so heat can circulate freely.

Outward appearance doesn't always indicate doneness. Tap the loaf lightly and listen for a hollow sound. Turn it on its side; it should easily fall out of the pan. If it's still soft and not hollow, return it to the oven. Remove bread from pans immediately after baking. Cool completely on a wire rack before wrapping in foil or plastic wrap. (*see also* **batter bread, knead,** *and* **yeast**)

brew To prepare tea, herb tea, or coffee by steeping the tea leaves or coffee grounds in hot water to extract flavor. This can also refer to the process of brewing beer. (*see also* **beer, coffee, infusion, steep, tea,** *and* **tisane**)

Brie cheese (BREE) A creamy cow's milk cheese, originally produced in France, that has a buttery-soft interior, soft white edible rind, and nutty flavor. Brie is usually sold in rounds or wedges that have been cut from rounds. Brie has a fairly short life, so use it within a few days. Avoid buying Brie that smells of ammonia because it may be overripe. (*see also* **cheese**)

TEST KITCHEN SECRET

To keep Brie fresher longer, wrap it in parchment or wax paper, and refrigerate. Plastic wrap hastens its demise. JAMES SCHEND

brine A strong salt and water solution used for pickling, preserving, or flavoring foods. Sometimes, especially when smoking fish, herbs, spices, or a sweetener such as brown sugar are added to the brine. Brining poultry or meat to enhance flavor and juiciness is an old-fashioned technique that's becoming popular again. See what it does to fried chicken in the recipe below.

OUR BEST SOUTHERN FRIED CHICKEN

3 quarts water	1 teaspoon pepper, divided
1 tablespoon salt	1 cup all-purpose flour
1 (2- to 2½-pound) whole chicken, cut up	2 cups vegetable oil
	¼ cup bacon drippings
1 teaspoon salt, divided	

• Combine 3 quarts water and 1 tablespoon salt in a large bowl; add chicken. Cover and chill 8 hours.
• Drain chicken; rinse with cold water, and pat dry.
• Sprinkle ½ teaspoon salt and ½ teaspoon pepper over chicken. Combine flour and remaining ½ teaspoon salt and remaining ½ teaspoon pepper in a large heavy duty zip-top plastic bag.
• Place 2 pieces of chicken in a bag; seal and shake to coat. Remove chicken, and repeat procedure with remaining pieces.
• Combine oil and bacon drippings in an electric frying pan or a large deep skillet; heat to 360°.

- Add chicken, a few pieces at a time, skin side down. Cover and cook 6 minutes; uncover and cook 9 more minutes. Turn chicken pieces; cover and cook 6 minutes. Uncover and cook 5 to 9 more minutes, turning pieces during the last 3 minutes for even browning, if necessary. Drain on paper towels; keep warm. Yield: 4 servings.

brioche (BREE ohssh) A tender French yeast bread enriched with eggs and butter, which give it a light yellow color. The classic brioche is baked in special fluted molds or brioche pans and topped with a small ball of dough, which creates a top knot after baking. However, large round loaves can also be baked with brioche dough.

MORRISON HOUSE BRIOCHE

Don't limit this buttery bread to breakfast, although it is a signature item at Morrison House, a bed-and-breakfast establishment in Alexandria, Virginia. It's also delicious as a sandwich or dinner roll.

4⅓ cups all-purpose flour	2 teaspoons salt
2 tablespoons sugar	8 large eggs
½ package active dry yeast (1½ teaspoons)	1¼ cups unsalted butter, chilled and cut into pieces
¼ cup warm water (100° to 110°)	1 large egg, lightly beaten

- Combine flour and sugar in a large mixing bowl. Make a well in center of mixture; add yeast and water in center. Let stand 5 minutes.
- Add salt and eggs; beat at low speed with an electric mixer until blended. Add butter gradually, beating well (small bits of butter will be visible). Cover and chill at least 8 hours (dough will be sticky).
- Divide dough into 12 portions; pinch off a 1-inch ball of dough from each portion, and set aside.
- Roll larger pieces into balls on a lightly floured surface; place in well-greased individual brioche molds or a muffin pan on a baking sheet.
- Make a well in center of each ball. Shape remaining dough pieces into balls. Shape a slight "V" on 1 side of balls, and insert "V" into wells.
- Brush brioche with beaten egg; let stand 30 minutes.
- Bake at 350° for 30 minutes. Cool in molds 10 minutes; remove from molds. Yield: 1 dozen.

TEST KITCHEN SECRET

If you don't have brioche pans, you can substitute muffin pans.

Mary Allen Perry

brisket (BRIHS kiht) A cut of beef from the foreshank and brisket section, beneath the first 5 ribs. It usually requires long, slow cooking such as braising or smoking, as in Texas barbecue. Corned beef is made from the brisket. (*see also* **beef** *and* **corned beef**)

LITE BITE

"Flat-cut brisket" is lower in fat than many cuts of beef, so consider it if you're looking for leaner cuts of beef.

brittle A hard, flat, irregularly shaped candy made by mixing nuts into caramelized sugar. Peanuts and pecans make popular Southern brittles. (*see also* **candy** *and* **caramel**)

PEANUT BRITTLE

2 cups sugar	3 tablespoons butter or margarine
1 cup light corn syrup	1 teaspoon vanilla extract
¾ cup water	1 teaspoon baking soda
2 cups raw peanuts	¼ teaspoon salt

• Combine first 3 ingredients in a heavy 3-quart saucepan. Cook over medium-low heat, stirring constantly, until sugar dissolves.

• Cover and cook over medium heat 2 to 3 minutes to wash down sugar crystals from sides of pan. Add peanuts; cook until a candy thermometer registers 300° (hard crack stage), stirring occasionally. Remove from heat. Stir in butter and remaining ingredients. (Candy will foam as baking soda is added due to a chemical reaction. This makes the brittle porous.)

• Working quickly, pour candy mixture into a well-buttered 15- x 10-inch jellyroll pan; spread to edges of pan. Cool completely; break into pieces. Store in an airtight container. Yield: 15 servings (2 pounds).

broccoflower (BROH koh flowr) A light green cauliflower that's a cross between broccoli and cauliflower, but has a milder flavor than either vegetable. Use it just like regular cauliflower. (*see also* **cauliflower**)

broccoli A green vegetable with rigid, thick stalks topped with tightly packed florets. Fresh broccoli is available year-round with its peak from October through April.

Selection: Look for firm stalks with tightly bunched heads. If the heads show signs of buds beginning to turn yellow, it's over the hill.

Storage: Refrigerate fresh broccoli in a plastic bag up to 4 days. To revive limp broccoli, trim ½ inch from the base of the stalk and set the head in a glass of cold water in refrigerator overnight.

TEST KITCHEN SECRET

Don't throw away the leaves and tough stalks of broccoli. Dice or shred them for salads and stir-fries. LYDA JONES

TIMESAVING TIP

When you're in a hurry stand a bunch of fresh broccoli upside down, and use a chef's knife to trim the florets into bite-sized pieces. These tender crowns steam in about 5 minutes. Precut florets are available in the produce section of many markets.

broccoli raab (BROH klee RAH beh) A vegetable related to the cabbage and turnip families with a tall, leafy green stalk with scattered clusters of tiny broccoli-like florets and a pleasantly bitter flavor. It's a newcomer to Southern markets, but it's a staple in Italy. Sauté or steam it to serve alone or to toss into pastas or toppings, or use it raw in salads. (*see also* **greens** *and* **rape**)

brochette (broh SHEHT) A French word that refers to cooking food on a skewer. Most brochettes are composed of meat, poultry, or seafood that's grilled or broiled.

broil To cook food directly under a dry, direct heat source, usually in the oven but sometimes in a separate unit. When broiling, food is often placed on a broiler pan, which has a perforated upper pan or rack that allows the fat to drip into the lower, deeper pan. Broil essentially means grilling in the oven with the heat element located above the meat. Broiling is best used with naturally tender cuts of meat. Broiled meats, chicken, and seafood tend to take on a smoky, somewhat charred flavor as the juices and fats are released.

broiler-fryer (*see* **chicken** and **poultry**)

broth A liquid resulting from cooking meat, poultry, fish, or vegetables in water, usually with seasoning. Prepared broths are available canned, and broths can be made from bouillon cubes or granules. Some commercial broths are condensed and must be diluted with water, but all broth products can be used as a base for soups, sauces, stews, and gravies. With commercial products readily available, homemaking broth is becoming a lost art. But don't ignore the personal satisfaction and fresh flavor gained from simmering a homemade broth from the holiday carcass, especially for making soups and gumbos. After broth is cooked, let it cool, and then refrigerate. The fat will rise to the top and can be skimmed off easily and discarded. (*see also* **bouillon, consommé,** *and* **skim**)

brown To cook food quickly over high heat in a skillet, broiler, or oven in order to develop an appealing color and to seal in flavor and juices. Sometimes meats and poultry are dredged in flour and seasonings before they're browned to maximize the color and flavor.

For the best browning, three things are essential: Make sure the oil is hot enough to make an immediate sizzle when you add the food. Cook in batches rather than overcrowding the pan; otherwise you'll steam the food and it won't brown well. And for the best color, don't turn or move the food around often; just leave it to sizzle. VIE WARSHAW

brown butter Butter that has been cooked over low heat to a light pecan color. It's sometimes flavored with vinegar or lemon juice, capers, and parsley, and is often served over fish, eggs, or vegetables.

brownie A rich bar cookie, usually made with chocolate, but can also be vanilla or butterscotch. Some brownies also include nuts or chocolate morsels; the texture can range from cakelike to dense and chewy.

Storage: When fully cooled, transfer brownies to an airtight container and store at room temperature up to 3 days. Freeze brownies up to 3 months. For individual immediate chocolate cravings; wrap individually or in small stacks in plastic wrap. Pack the wrapped cookies in plastic containers or in zip-top plastic bags, and freeze. Thaw at room temperature. (*see also* **bar cookie**)

Q **What makes the texture of some brownies cakelike and others dense and chewy?**

A This depends on the recipe—the proportion of fat to flour and the number of eggs used. Baking time also plays a role; the longer you bake them, the more dry and cakelike they'll be.

READER TIP
"My family loves fudgy brownies, but I don't like how they stick to the pan. So I've started lining my pans with heavy-duty foil. First, I coat the pan with cooking spray. Then I line the pan crosswise and lengthwise with foil, making sure the foil overhangs a bit on the sides; then I add the batter. After baking, I can lift the foil and brownies from the pan in a single piece." D.C., Bainbridge, GA

Note from the Test Kitchen: *D.C. will be happy to know that Reynolds makes a new "quick release" foil that requires no cooking spray.*

brown sauce Known as Espagnole sauce in France, where it's esteemed as one of the mother sauces used as a base for other sauces. It's made with a rich brown meat stock to which a roux is added, sometimes along with vegetables, herbs, and tomato paste. (*see also* **mother sauces** *and* **sauce**)

brown sugar White sugar with molasses added to soften its texture. Light brown sugar has less molasses flavor, while dark brown sugar has more. Granulated brown sugar is great for sprinkling because it's dry and doesn't clump. It's not a substitute for regular white or brown sugar in recipes. Be sure to seal brown sugar in an airtight bag to keep it soft and fresh. (*see also* **sugar**)

Q **How do I measure brown sugar?**

A Pack it into a dry measuring cup so that it keeps its shape when unmolded. That's why we call for firmly packed brown sugar in our recipes.

RESCUE for hardened brown sugar:
If brown sugar becomes hard, microwave it at MEDIUM LOW (30% power) until soft, usually 1 to 2 minutes. Or, if you don't need the sugar right away, place an apple wedge in the bag, and seal overnight.

bruise (BROOZ) To partially crush an ingredient, such as an herb or a clove of garlic, to release its flavor and aromatic oils.

brûlé (broo LAY) French for burned; often used to describe the browning of a food by direct, intense heat, as is done in preparing crème brûlée. The browning is traditionally done under the broiler, but you can use a chef's cooking torch or salamander to help you caramelize the perfect sugar cap. (*see also* **crème brûlée** *and* **salamander**)

brunch An informal, late-morning meal combining breakfast and lunch. It's usually served between 11 a.m. and 3 p.m. Weekend brunches are popular in the South at home and in restaurants.

brunoise (broo NWAHZ) Finely diced or shredded vegetables (⅛- x ⅛- x ⅛-inch). (*see also* **chop** *and* **dice**)

Brunswick stew A sturdy, long-cooking concoction of chicken (and sometimes pork), tomatoes, corn, onion, and sometimes butter beans and okra. (*see also* **burgoo** *and recipe on the following page*)

Southernism

Where Brunswick stew originated causes heated discussions in the South. Depending on which story you accept, it was created either in Brunswick County, Virginia, in 1828, or on St. Simons Island, Georgia, in 1898. Supporters on both sides hotly dispute which state possesses bragging rights. In Virginia, the basic ingredients are boiled chicken, potatoes, onions, butterbeans, corn, and tomatoes. Huge batches simmer for hours, resulting in a thick stew that's eaten with a fork. Virginians serve it as a main dish with bread on the side. In Georgia, the stew is more tomato- and barbecue-based, and usually includes barbecued pork and chicken. There, it's a prized side dish of the best barbecue joints, and real aficionados order it by the bowlful. Most Georgians laugh at the Virginia version that adds butter beans.

BRUNSWICK STEW

Hickory wood chunks
2 (2½-pound) whole chickens*
1 (3-pound) Boston butt
   pork roast*
3 (14½-ounce) cans diced
   tomatoes
2 (16-ounce) packages frozen
   whole kernel yellow corn
2 (16-ounce) packages frozen
   butterbeans, thawed

2 medium onions, chopped
1 (32-ounce) container chicken
   broth
1 (24-ounce) bottle ketchup
½ cup white vinegar
½ cup Worcestershire sauce
¼ cup firmly packed brown sugar
1 tablespoon salt
1 tablespoon pepper
2 tablespoons hot sauce

• Soak wood chunks in water at least 1 hour. Prepare charcoal fire in smoker; let burn 15 to 20 minutes. Drain wood chunks, and place on coals. Place water pan in smoker; add water to depth of fill line.

• Remove and discard giblets from chicken. Tuck wings under; tie legs with string, if desired. Place chicken and pork on lower food rack; cover with smoker lid. Cook chicken 2½ hours; cook pork 6 hours or until a meat thermometer inserted into thickest portion registers 160°. Cool. Remove chicken from bone. Chop chicken and pork.

• Stir together chicken, pork, tomatoes, and remaining ingredients in a 6-quart Dutch oven. Cover and simmer over low heat, stirring occasionally, 2½ to 3 hours. Yield: 28 cups.

*Substitute 2 pounds smoked, cooked chicken and 2½ pounds smoked, cooked pork for whole chickens and pork roast.

bruschetta (broo SHEH tah) An Italian appetizer of sliced, toasted bread rubbed with garlic and drizzled with olive oil. Sometimes, bruschetta is topped with chopped tomatoes and fresh basil leaves. Bruschetta is similar to, but sliced thicker than, crostini. (*see also* **crostini**)

Brussels sprouts A green vegetable that's a member of the cabbage family and, in fact, looks like a tiny compact cabbage, and even tastes like it. Smaller brussels sprouts have a milder flavor; older, larger sprouts are prone to have a bitter flavor. They're in season in fall and winter.
Selection: Look for sprouts that are heavy for their size and have compact bright green leaves. Avoid soft heads and loose leaves.
Storage: Refrigerate unwashed brussels sprouts in a plastic bag up to 3 days. (*see also* **vegetables**)

TIMESAVING TIP
Whole brussels sprouts cook quicker and more evenly if you cut a tiny "X" into the stem end before cooking.

TEST KITCHEN SECRET

Our favorite way to prepare brussels sprouts is to cut them in half; cut each half crosswise into thin slices, and sauté until tender. VANESSA MCNEIL

brut (BROOT) A term meaning the driest (the least sweet) champagne or sparkling wine. (*see also* **champagne** *and* **wine**)

bûche de Noël (BOOSH duh noh EHL) A traditional French Christmas cake made to resemble a yule log. It's made from a thin sheet cake that's spread with buttercream frosting, rolled up, and frosted with chocolate frosting. The surface is ridged (made by fork tines pulled through frosting) to look like tree bark.

buckwheat A plant that produces triangular seeds that are ground into flour and used for pancakes or added to baked goods. Though buckwheat is used as flour, it's botanically a fruit. It has a strong, earthy flavor. Buckwheat groats are the hulled and crushed kernels that are commonly cooked like rice.
Storage: Store buckwheat in an airtight container in a cool, dry place up to 3 months. It can be refrigerated up to 6 months or frozen up to 1 year. (*see also* **grain** *and* **kasha**)

LITE BITE
Buckwheat is gluten free, so it's suitable for people allergic to protein, since gluten is a protein substance.

Buffalo wings Deep-fried or roasted chicken wings served in a spicy red sauce and usually accompanied by blue cheese or Ranch dressing. Usually served as an appetizer, this finger food originated in a bar in Buffalo, New York.

buffet Any type of meal where guests serve themselves to foods arranged on a table or sideboard. Seating is not always provided. Buffets offer a quick and convenient way to serve a large crowd.

READER TIP
"Guests find it easier to serve themselves from a buffet if most of the food is precut or sliced. To keep things moving, I put silverware and the beverage on a separate table." B.R., Montgomery, AL

bulghur (BUHL guhr) Wheat kernels that have been steamed, dried, and ground into various degrees of coarseness. Bulghur wheat, a Middle Eastern staple, has a nutty flavor, a tender but chewy texture, a golden brown color, and is often cooked like rice or incorporated into stews, pilafs, or salads such as tabbouleh.

TEST KITCHEN SECRET
Bulghur is often confused with cracked wheat, but cracked wheat hasn't been steamed. MARY ALLEN PERRY

Storage: Store bulghur in an airtight container in a cool, dry place up to 6 months, or freeze indefinitely. (*see also* **grain, kibbe, pilaf,** *and* **tabbouleh**)

Bundt pan (*see* **baking dishes and pans**)

buñuelo (boo NWAY loh) A light, hollow, deep-fried Mexican pastry that's dusted with cinnamon-sugar.

burgoo (bur GOO) A thick, savory tomato-based stew similar to Brunswick stew with several kinds of meats and vegetables. The name originated in the seventeenth century and refers to a thick porridge that was a staple on the high seas. As it came to America and settled in Kentucky, the stew got even thicker with the addition of pork, chicken, beef, lamb, and even squirrel and possum. Today, exact ingredients vary and usually depend on what happens to be in the refrigerator. The only consistency in the recipe is the underlying notion that the longer you cook burgoo, the better it tastes. (*see also* **Brunswick stew**)

Southernism

No one quite knows where burgoo originated, how it got its name, or how it found its way to western Kentucky. But what is known is that burgoo, a close cousin of Brunswick stew, enjoys close ties to Kentucky's barbecue heritage and a tradition founded on hospitality, good food, and lots of it, writes Southern food historian John Egerton in Southern Food.

KENTUCKY BURGOO

1 (3- to 4-pound) whole chicken	2 cups frozen whole kernel corn
1 (2-pound) beef chuck roast	1 cup frozen baby lima beans
2 pounds pork loin chops, trimmed	1 cup frozen English peas
5 quarts water	3 garlic cloves, minced
1 dressed rabbit (optional)	2 quarts beef broth
1 pound tomatoes	1 (32-ounce) bottle ketchup
5 potatoes, peeled	2 cups dry red wine
5 celery ribs	1 (10-ounce) bottle Worcestershire sauce
4 carrots, scraped	¼ cup white vinegar
2 onions	1 tablespoon salt
2 green bell peppers	1 tablespoon pepper
1 small cabbage	1 tablespoon dried thyme

• Bring first 4 ingredients and, if desired, rabbit to a boil in a large heavy stockpot. Cover, reduce heat, and simmer 1 hour or until tender.

• Remove meat from stockpot, reserving liquid in pot. Skin, bone, and shred meat; return shredded meat to pot.

• Chop tomatoes and next 5 ingredients; shred cabbage. Add chopped vegetables, corn, and remaining ingredients to meat; cook over low heat, stirring often, 4 hours. Yield: 6 quarts.

Burgundy wines
A group of dry red and white wines produced in the Burgundy region of eastern France. Four times the amount of red wine is produced than white, most often using Pinot Noir or Gamay grapes. The whites are typically made from Chardonnay grapes. (*see also* **wine**)

burnet
(BUR niht) A green herb that has a sharp, nutty, cucumber-like flavor and aroma. The tiny leaves are used in salads and soups, or to flavor drinks such as tea. (*see also* **herbs**)

burnt sugar (*see* **caramelize**)

burrito (bur EE toh) A Mexican or Tex-Mex specialty consisting of a flour tortilla folded and rolled around savory fillings such as shredded meat, refried beans, grated cheese, lettuce, tomatoes, and sour cream. (*see also* **Tex-Mex**)

butter A dairy product made by churning cream until it reaches a semi-solid state. Real butter contains at least 80% milk fat. Butter is available plain (sometimes called sweet butter) or salted, whipped, and as light butter, and a butter-margarine blend. Whipped products have air and sometimes water incorporated to make them more spreadable, so never substitute whipped butter for regular when preparing baked goods. **Storage:** Refrigerate butter as soon as possible after purchase. Store it near the center of the refrigerator, near the back, and away from the door. Keep unused portions in a covered container so they won't absorb odors of other foods. Store salted butter up to 3 weeks in the refrigerator and unsalted up to 2 weeks; or they can both be frozen up to 9 months. (*see also* **clarified butter, fats and oils,** *and* **margarine**)

Q Should I use plain or salted butter?

A A safe guide is to use what your recipe calls for. Our recipes specify unsalted butter if that's what we tested with. But there are other factors you can consider. Many people prefer unsalted butter for baked goods and for spreading because it's perceived to be fresher. Salt is added to butter as a preservative, so salted butter is generally stored longer and perceived not to be as fresh. Others prefer unsalted because it's lower in sodium. Try both of them, and use what you prefer.

LITE BITE

Light butter has half the fat and calories of real butter, so it's a great-tasting alternative to real butter for spreading on baked goods and seasoning veggies. Water is added to the butter to lighten it, so it's not a good substitute for real butter in baked goods.

TEST KITCHEN SECRET

We all like to save a few calories when we can, but when it comes to baking cakes and cookies, go ahead and use real butter; it's worth it.

MARY ALLEN PERRY

butterbean (*see* **beans, dried; beans, fresh;** *and* **lima bean**)

B

buttercream A smooth, fluffy frosting or filling for cakes and pastries made of butter, powdered sugar, milk or cream, and flavoring. (*see also* **frosting**)

butter curler A tool with a curved serrated blade that's used to make shell-like curls of butter when it's pulled across solid butter. The trick to making pretty butter curls is to dip the curler in warm to hot water before pulling it across the top of a slightly softened stick of butter. Transfer the curls with a wooden pick so the heat of your hand doesn't melt them. Drop them in a bowl of ice water to keep them hard until ready to serve.

buttermilk A tangy liquid that, when stirred into quick breads and cake batters, adds tenderness and flavor usually expected only in scratch cooking. In days past, "real" buttermilk was the butter-flecked liquid left after hours of churning butter. Today's refrigerated versions—both full fat and fat free—are made thick and tart by special cultures added to milk. Dry buttermilk powder also is available. Buttermilk will separate and break down when heated to a near boil, so it's used mostly in baking or in cold soups, smoothies, or ice cream. (*see also* **milk**)

Southernism

Buttermilk upholds not only a long, special status as a homestead beverage, but also as a key ingredient in traditional Southern baked goods such as buttermilk biscuits, pancakes, and crumb and layer cakes. Folklore proclaims that buttermilk immunizes against such toxins as poison oak and ivy. And many a pioneer woman used a buttermilk facial wash to create a flawless, creamy, butter-like complexion.

READER TIP

"I always try to keep buttermilk on hand—mostly for making my mother's cornbread. When I buy a carton of buttermilk, I use a cup to make the cornbread, and I pour the rest into ice cube trays. Once frozen, the cubes go into a heavy duty zip-top plastic freezer bag. Next time I need buttermilk, I just drop eight cubes (which equals a cup) into a glass measuring cup and defrost them in the microwave." N.H., Mobile, AL

 TIMESAVING TIP
If you need buttermilk in a hurry but don't have any on hand, add 1 tablespoon lemon juice or white vinegar in a liquid measuring cup to enough milk to make 1 cup liquid. Stir well, and let stand 5 minutes before using. When the milk curdles, it's ready to use.

buttermilk pie An old Southern specialty, this custard pie is made with buttermilk, egg yolks, sugar, cornstarch, butter, and lemon juice. It can be baked with or without a meringue topping. It's similar to chess pie, only tangier. (*see also* **chess pie**)

butterscotch A sweet flavor created by cooking brown sugar and butter together. It's used to make cookies, candies, sauces, and frostings.

cabbage A vegetable having a firm head of tightly packed waxy leaves. Cabbages range in color from almost white to green to red, and their shapes vary from elongated to round. Cabbage can be eaten raw or cooked and is the staple ingredient of coleslaw. (*see also* **coleslaw** *and* **vegetables**)

> ### ⏱ TIMESAVING TIP
> To shred quickly, cut the cabbage into small wedges to fit the feed tube of a food processor after cutting away the hard core. Use a slicing blade to make large shreds or the shredding blade for finer shreds. No processor? No problem. Just quarter the cabbage, cut away the core, and thinly slice the cabbage into shreds.

Common types:
Green: Round with light green leaves; delicate flavor when raw, but stronger flavor and aroma when cooked.
Red: Round with reddish-purple leaves; tastes similar to green cabbage.
Chinese: A name given to several Oriental cabbages, including *bok choy,* which grows in bunches like Swiss chard, and *napa* cabbage, which grows in dense oblong heads.
(*see also* **Chinese cabbage**)
Savoy: Round with dark green ruffled and veined leaves. Savoy is milder and not as firm as green cabbage.
Storage: Refrigerate cabbage, wrapped in plastic wrap, up to 1 week. Don't cut or shred it until ready to use to maximize freshness, color, and nutrients.

green cabbage

red cabbage

bok choy

napa

savoy

> ### ♡ LITE BITE
> Cabbage rivals citrus fruit as a source of vitamin C, and it contains other antioxidants thought to prevent certain cancers. It's high in fiber, vitamins, and minerals.

Cabernet Sauvignon (cab air NAY soh vihn YOHN) The premier red wine grown in California and the Bordeaux area of France. Wines from these grapes are full bodied and fruity. (*see also* **wine**)

cacciatore (kah chuh TOR ee) Italian for "hunter," cacciatore is a stew-like dish flavored with onions, herbs, mushrooms, tomatoes, and sometimes wine. Chicken cacciatore is the most popular dish that's prepared "hunter" style.

cactus The pear-shaped, fleshy leaves of the prickly pear cactus are pale to dark green and have a delicate, slightly tart, green-bean flavor. Though fresh cactus is available year-round in Mexican markets, it's at its most tender and juicy in the spring. Before using cactus leaves, remove the thorns using a vegetable peeler or paring knife. Cut the flesh into small pieces or strips, simmer in water until tender, and use in salads and soups.
Storage: Refrigerate cactus leaves in a plastic bag up to 1 week.

Caesar salad (SEE zer) A salad traditionally made of Romaine lettuce, tossed with a garlicky vinaigrette flavored with Worcestershire sauce, lemon juice, coddled eggs, and sometimes anchovies. The salad is typically finished with croutons and freshly grated Parmesan cheese. Today's Caesar salads omit the coddled eggs or call for egg substitute instead because it's not safe to eat uncooked eggs. (*see also* **lettuce** *and* **vinaigrette**)

CAESAR SALAD

1 garlic clove, halved	¼ cup red wine vinegar
2 heads romaine lettuce, torn	2 garlic cloves, minced
1 (6-ounce) package seasoned croutons	1 tablespoon Worcestershire sauce
½ cup extra-virgin olive oil	½ cup grated Parmesan cheese
¼ cup egg substitute	1 (2-ounce) can anchovies, drained

• Rub sides of a wooden salad bowl with garlic halves. Add lettuce and croutons, tossing well.
• Process oil and remaining 6 ingredients in a blender until smooth, stopping to scrape down sides. Pour over lettuce mixture, tossing to coat. Yield: 6 to 8 servings.

café au lait (ka FAY oh LAY) French for coffee with hot milk; beverage of equal parts hot, strong coffee and hot milk.

café brûlot (ka FAY broo LOW) A traditional New Orleans drink of dark coffee and brandy, flavored with citrus rind. It's a dramatic finale to an evening meal because it's generally prepared table side with flaming brandy.

café latte (ka FAY LAH tay) An Italian coffee drink made from espresso and foamy steamed milk.

caffeine (kaf FEEN) An odorless, colorless, somewhat bitter substance found in coffee, tea, chocolate, and cola. Caffeine acts as a natural stimulant on the central nervous system. It also acts as a diuretic, causing the body to lose fluids.

LITE BITE
Because caffeine acts as a diuretic, drink beverages with caffeine in moderation.

Cajun cooking (KAY juhn) A style of cooking, made famous by the French Acadians (Cajuns), now living in Louisiana, who used what nature provided and added their joy for life to the pot. Cajuns used fresh ingredients locally obtained so literally, that Cajun cooking near the Mississippi River area differs from that on the prairies of southwest Louisiana. The common thread in all types is the cook's ability to adapt to what foods are available and the delicious outcome of the effort. Cajun cooking is noted for pungent, peppery dishes that often feature a thick, dark roux. Cajun dishes include étouffée and gumbo. (*see also* **Cajun seasoning, Creole cooking, étouffée, filé powder,** *and* **gumbo**)

Q **What's the difference between Cajun cooking and Creole cooking?**

A Cajun cooking is simpler, heavier, spicier, and more robust than Creole cooking, which places its emphasis on butter, cream, and tomatoes. Both styles of cooking use lots of filé powder and base many foods on what they call their "holy trinity" of chopped peppers, onions, and celery.

Southernism
Cajun cooking came out of the rural swamplands and bayous of south Louisiana, where it remained until improved transportation and communications ushered in the restaurant age after World War II. Today, Cajun food remains a distinctive cuisine, and many of its traditional dishes can be enjoyed in New Orleans' restaurants.

Cajun popcorn An appetizer of shelled, battered, and deep-fried crawfish tails made famous in Louisiana.

Cajun seasoning A spicy blend of herbs, onion, chiles, and salt that can be purchased or made at home to season Cajun dishes.

cake A sweet dessert made from a batter that's baked. Cake usually contains flour, sugar, flavoring, eggs, and baking powder or baking soda. There are 2 main categories of cakes: Shortening or butter cakes depend on shortening, butter, margarine, or oil, and baking powder or soda for their fine texture; they have a variety of flavors, such as white, yellow, chocolate, and spice. Pound cakes and fruitcakes are included in this category. Foam cakes include angel food, chiffon, and sponge cakes; these depend on air beaten into eggs for their airy texture.
Storage: Cool cakes completely before storing them, even the unfrosted ones. (*continued on the following page*)

RESCUE for sticky cakepans:
If company's coming and your cake layers come out of the pan in pieces, don't panic. Pull out your parfait glasses, cut cake into cubes, and layer it with whipped cream, sliced fruit, and sprinkles of liqueur, if desired.

TEST KITCHEN SECRET
Even though I grease and flour my cakepans for layer cakes, I line them with wax paper for added insurance so that they'll come out of the pans beautifully. MARY ALLEN PERRY

If covered while still warm, cakes may become sticky on top. Store unfrosted cakes and those with a creamy frosting under a cake dome. Covering a frosted cake with plastic wrap also will work, but first insert wooden picks into the cake in several places to keep the wrap from touching the frosting. Cakes with fluffy meringue frosting are best eaten the day they're made; meringue frosting gradually disintegrates when stored several days. Always store cakes with cream filling or frosting in the refrigerator. Most cakes freeze well for 2 to 3 months. If frozen longer than that, they take on a taste of the freezer. As soon as the layers are cool, wrap them in plastic wrap and put them in the freezer. To freeze a frosted cake, place it uncovered in the freezer just until frozen, then loosely, but thoroughly, wrap and return it to the freezer. It should keep up to 3 months. Before serving, unwrap frozen cakes, and thaw at room temperature for several hours.

CAKE TROUBLESHOOTING

Since cake baking requires precise measuring, mixing, and baking procedures, it's only natural that things can go wrong. Use the following chart to help correct problems.

If batter overflows:	• Overmixing • Too much batter in pan
If cake falls:	• Oven not hot enough; opening oven door during baking • Undermixing • Insufficient baking • Too much baking powder, baking soda, liquid, or sugar
If cake peaks in center:	• Oven too hot at start of baking • Too much flour or not enough liquid • Batter overmixed
If crust is sticky:	• Insufficient baking or oven not hot enough • Too much sugar
If cake sticks to pan:	• Cake cooling in pan too long • Pan not properly greased and floured
If cake cracks and falls apart:	• Removing from pan too soon • Too much shortening, baking powder, soda, or sugar
If texture is heavy:	• Overmixing when adding flour and liquid • Oven temperature too low • Too much shortening, sugar, or liquid
If texture is coarse:	• Inadequate mixing • Oven temperature too low • Too much baking powder or baking soda
If texture is dry:	• Overbaking • Overbeating egg whites • Too much flour, baking powder, or baking soda • Not enough shortening or sugar • Pan too large

Ingredients and Preparation:
• Use the freshest ingredients you can find, and let butter, milk, and eggs sit at room temperature 20 minutes before mixing. (Or take the chill off refrigerated eggs by running them, still in the shell, briefly under warm water.)
• There's no substitute for real eggs, butter, or stick margarine when making a cake. Light butter or margarine, whipped butter or margarine, and egg

substitutes are not intended for classic baking.
• An accurate oven is a must. Always preheat your oven 10 minutes.
• Use the correct pan size, measuring it across the top. An incorrect pan size can cause a cake to be flat and shrunken or rise to a peak and fall.
• Use only shortening to grease cakepans. Oil, butter, or margarine may cause cakes to stick or burn. Dust greased cakepans with flour, tilting the pans to coat bottoms and sides. If baking a chocolate cake, dust greased pans lightly with cocoa instead of flour.
• All-purpose flour is presifted, so there's no need to sift it unless the recipe specifies. But always sift cake flour before measuring.
• Substitute all-purpose flour for cake flour by using 2 tablespoons less per cup.

Measuring:
• Measure flour by spooning it lightly into a dry measuring cup, letting it mound slightly. Then level it off with a straight-edged spatula or knife.
• Measure liquids in glass or clear plastic-spouted measuring cups. Measure dry ingredients in nested metal or plastic "dry" measuring cups (those intended for dry ingredients).

Mixing:
• Beat softened butter and sugar thoroughly—5 minutes with a heavy-duty mixer, 6 minutes with a standard mixer, and 7 minutes with a hand mixer.
• Add only 1 egg at a time to batter, and beat until blended after each addition. Do not overbeat.
• Add dry and liquid ingredients alternately to beaten mixture in about 4 portions. Gently beat after each addition just until batter is smooth. Use a rubber spatula to scrape sides of bowl often during beating.
• Unless your recipe specifies otherwise, fill cakepans half-full with batter.

Baking and Cooling:
• Bake layers on the center oven rack, and stagger pans for even baking, being careful not to let pan sides touch.
• Keep oven door closed until the minimum baking time has elapsed.

To test for doneness: Insert wooden pick in center of cake; if pick comes out clean, cake's done.

• Test cake for doneness before removing it from the oven. Cake is done when a wooden pick inserted in center comes out clean. (Underbaking can cause a cake to fall.)
• Let layer cakes cool in pans 10 minutes and let tube cakes cool in pan 15 minutes. Then invert cakes onto wire racks to cool completely.
• Let cake layers cool completely before adding filling and frosting. Gently brush away loose crumbs before frosting a cake. (*see also* **high altitude**)

To cool cakes: Invert cake onto a wire rack to cool completely.

Cake 77

cake comb A small, triangular-shaped tool of hard plastic or stainless steel with serrated edges of different sizes on 3 sides. The comb makes a decorative swirled pattern when pulled across the frosting on a cake.

cake decorating To add special flair to cakes and cupcakes with frosting and other trimmings, sometimes for a special occasion. Simple decorations include sifted powdered sugar, small candies, tinted coconut, nuts, and packaged decorations. Piped frosting borders, leaves, flowers, and writing require the use of a piping bag and decorating tips.

Decorative Touches: With practice, you can garnish cakes using a decorating bag and a variety of metal tips. The cone-shaped decorating or pastry bag can be cloth or plastic,

> ### TEST KITCHEN SECRET
>
> *We often make a quick, disposable piping bag from a heavy-duty zip-top plastic bag. Just snip a small hole in a corner of the bag, and place the tip in the bag so that it pokes out of the hole. Add frosting, seal the bag, and decorate. Even faster, if you simply want a plain drizzle, skip the metal tip, snip a tiny hole in a corner of the bag, and drizzle directly from the bag.* JAN MOON

> ### TIMESAVING TIP
>
> When you want to write a chocolate message on top of a frosted cake, put semisweet chocolate in a zip-top plastic bag, seal, and drop bag into a bowl of very hot water. Remove after a few minutes, cool to the touch, and gently knead with your fingers to finish the melting. Make a tiny snip across 1 corner of the bag with scissors. Hold the bag in 1 hand, and gently squeeze chocolate out of the hole as you write.

and comes in a range of sizes. The metal decorating tips come in 5 basic groups—drop flower, star, round, leaf, and rose—determined by the size and shape of the tips' openings. Before actually decorating, practice piping designs on an inverted cakepan placed on a turntable or on top of an inverted stockpot for some height. Pipe the practice designs, and then just wipe off the frosting and use it again. You can practice over and over with the same frosting. (*see also* **pastry bag**)

calabaza (kah lah BAH sah) A large, spherical or pear-shaped squash with a firm orange-colored flesh and pumpkin flavor. The skin color can range from green to tan to red-orange.

calamari (kal uh MAHR ee) Italian name for squid. Fried calamari is a popular appetizer on restaurant menus. (*see also* **squid**)

Calvados (KAL vah dohs) A dry apple brandy distilled from a mash of sour apples and made in Calvados, the Normandy region of France. A good substitute is applejack. (*see also* **applejack** *and* **brandy**)

calzone (kal ZOH nay) A savory turnover eaten as a sandwich. Calzone is filled with meats, vegetables, and cheeses, and then baked or fried.

CALZONES WITH PASTA SAUCE

1 cup small-curd cottage cheese
3 tablespoons grated Parmesan cheese
1 large egg
1 tablespoon chopped fresh or 1 teaspoon dried parsley
½ teaspoon garlic powder

1 (3.5-ounce) package pepperoni slices, chopped
4 Monterey Jack cheese slices, chopped
2 (10-ounce) cans refrigerated pizza crusts
2 cups pasta sauce

• Stir together first 5 ingredients until blended. Stir in pepperoni and chopped cheese slices. Divide each pizza crust into 2 portions. Roll each dough portion into a 7-inch circle.

• Spoon ½ cup cottage cheese mixture in center of each circle. Fold dough over filling, pressing edges to seal; place on a lightly greased aluminum foil-lined baking sheet. Prick dough several times with a fork.

• Bake at 375° for 20 to 25 minutes or until golden. Let stand 5 minutes. Serve calzones with warm pasta sauce. Yield: 4 servings.

Camembert (KAM uhm behr) Made of cow's milk, this soft, creamy French cheese has a white rind. It's often confused with Brie. However, Camembert comes in smaller rounds and has a stronger flavor than Brie. When perfectly ripe, the soft interior should ooze thickly; if overripe, it becomes runny and bitter and has a strong ammonia odor. (*see also* **Brie cheese** *and* **cheese**)

Canadian bacon A cured and smoked pork loin that's more like ham than bacon. It comes in a cylindrical shape and is leaner and tastier than regular bacon and costs more. It can be fried, baked, grilled, or used cold on sandwiches or in salads.
Storage: Refrigerate Canadian bacon in its original packaging or wrapped in plastic wrap until ready to cook. Sliced bacon will keep for 3 to 4 days; unsliced, about a week. Freeze bacon up to 2 months. (*see also* **pork**)

canapé (KAN uh pay) French for "couch," a canapé is an appetizer consisting of a small open-face sandwich cut into a decorative shape and topped with a savory spread. It's served as an appetizer. Crackers can also be used as a canapé base. (*see also* **appetizer**)

C

candy A confection made principally of sugar and flavorings. Candy may be soft, chewy, or hard, depending on the preparation of ingredients and length of cooking time. Flavors and fillings might include chocolate, nuts, peanut butter, fruits, and nougat.

Storage: Store all candies in airtight containers layered between sheets of wax paper as soon as they're cool; this prevents them from picking up moisture from the air. Most candies will stay fresh up to 1 week; fudge-type candies will keep up to 1 to 2 weeks if properly stored. (*see also* **fudge**)

Equipment needed to make candy:

Saucepans: You'll need several sizes of heavy saucepans. Candy mixtures usually triple in volume as they cook, so you'll need pans large enough to allow the candy mixtures to boil without boiling over. Aluminum pans are a good choice because they conduct heat more evenly than stainless steel.

Stirring Equipment: Long-handled wooden spoons are preferred because wooden spoons don't hold heat like metal spoons. A sturdy, free-standing electric mixer is handy for beating divinity and nougat mixtures, though they're not recommended for stirring or beating most other candy mixtures.

Candy Thermometer: You can test for the correct candy temperature by using the cold-water test (see chart below), but a candy thermometer is almost a necessity because it allows you to cook to a precise temperature and doneness stage. Buy one that's clearly marked and has an adjustable clip so it can be attached to the side of the pan. (*see also* **thermometer**)

TESTS FOR CANDY STAGES

These simple tests of dropping the candy mixture into cold water help determine doneness when you don't have a candy thermometer.

STAGE	TEMPERATURE	TEST
Thread Stage	223° to 234°	Syrup spins a 2-inch thread when dropped from a metal spoon.
Soft Ball Stage	234° to 240°	In cold water, syrup forms a soft ball that flattens when removed from water.
Firm Ball Stage	242° to 248°	In cold water, syrup forms a firm ball that doesn't flatten when removed from water.
Hard Ball Stage	250° to 268°	Syrup forms a hard, yet pliable, ball when removed from cold water.
Soft Crack Stage	270° to 290°	When dropped into cold water, syrup separates into threads that are hard but not brittle.
Hard Crack Stage	300° to 310°	When dropped into cold water, syrup separates into threads that are hard and brittle.
Caramel Stage	310° to 340°	Syrup will be honey-colored when spooned onto a white plate. The longer it cooks, the darker it becomes.

Test Kitchen Candy Tips:

• Plan to make candy on a dry, sunny day. If you must make it on a humid or rainy day, cook the candy until the thermometer registers 1 to 2 degrees higher than the recipe specifies.

• Measure ingredients and assemble equipment before you start cooking because you may not have time once the process begins.

• When cooking candy, it's important to control the formation of sugar crystals. We recommend buttering the sides of the saucepan as an initial way to prevent crystals. Also, stir the candy gently until it comes to a boil and the sugar dissolves.

• Cover the pan and cook over medium heat for 2 to 3 minutes to wash down any sugar crystals that form. Then remove the lid and continue cooking. Avoid stirring after this unless the recipe specifies.

Q **My candy thermometer is old. Is there a way I can test it to make sure it's still accurate?**

A Test the accuracy of your thermometer before cooking by letting it stand in boiling water for 10 minutes. If the thermometer registers 212°, it's in mint condition. If it measures above or below 212°, allow for the inaccuracy when cooking.

TEST KITCHEN SECRET

"When using your candy thermometer, make sure the bulb is in the boiling mixture, but not touching the bottom of the pan. We've found that it's crucial to watch the thermometer carefully as the candy nears doneness because the temperature often rises very quickly. Also, remember to read the thermometer at eye level." REBECCA KRACKE GORDON

• Avoid doubling a candy recipe. It's safer to make a second batch.

• Some recipes call for candy mixtures to cool in the pan until lukewarm or 110°. If so, let the pan sit undisturbed during this cooling period; don't stir unless instructed to, or the candy will be grainy.

• When the mixture is ready for pouring, do so quickly, and take care not to scrape the sides of the pan since this may add sugar crystals to the candy. Let it cool completely before cutting or storing.

candy coating A general term used for a variety of confectionary products used for making and dipping candy because it melts easily and firms up without being soft or tacky at room temperature. It's called almond bark coating, chocolate bark coating, or vanilla bark coating, and is available in packages, blocks, or round disks. Find candy coating on the grocery aisle with the baking supplies and at cake-decorating supplies stores.

candy thermometer A kitchen thermometer used to make candy that gauges critical temperatures of 100° to 400°. (*see also* **candy** *and* **thermometer**)

cane syrup Made from sugar cane, this thick, sweet syrup is used to top pancakes and waffles. (*see also* **syrup**)

cannellini beans (kan eh LEE nee) Large, white Italian kidney beans available dry and canned. They're often used in soups and salads and may be referred to as white kidney beans. (*see also* **beans, dried**)

cannelloni (kan eh LOH nee) Large tubes of pasta that are boiled, stuffed with meat or cheese, and baked in a sauce. (*see also* **pasta**)

canning Preserving food by heating jars of food hot enough and long enough, and, with some types of food, under enough pressure to keep food from spoiling. Canning makes it possible to capture seasonal produce to enjoy in homemade condiments and other canned goods throughout the year. There are two basic methods of home canning, and the type of food you want to can determines the method to use. The **boiling water bath method** is for high-acid foods such as fruits, tomatoes, and pickles; it processes the food in a water bath canner at 212°. The **pressure method** is used for low-acid foods like most vegetables, meats, poultry, and seafood; it processes food in a pressure canner at 240°. It's essential to follow the latest standard canning procedures recommended by the USDA; our recipes follow these guidelines.

Q **How do I know if my home-canned jars have sealed properly?**

A Once jars have been processed, carefully remove them with tongs and place right side up on a cloth towel or wire rack to cool for 12 to 24 hours. As the jars cool, you should hear loud pops indicating the vacuum seal has occurred. When jars are completely cooled, remove the metal bands only, and check lids for a proper seal. The center of the lid should dip downward. Press down on the center of the lid; it should not spring back when released. Wipe the lids and seal clean, and reattach the bands.

TEST KITCHEN SECRET

Always label and date your home-canned products before storing in a cool, dry place. And don't assume they'll keep for 4 or 5 years; most canned products are good for about a year. Always throw it out if you're not positive it's still good. We've got a saying in the Test Kitchens ... 'If in doubt, throw it out.' MARGARET MONROE DICKEY

For recipes in question, check with the county Cooperative Extension System in your state for information concerning processing times, pressures to use, headspace, and altitude adjustments. Or go to **homecanning.com** on the Web for the latest, up-to-date canning recommendations. (*see also* **boiling water bath** *and* **pressure cooker**)

Equipment for Canning:
Boiling Water Bath Canner: A boiling water bath canner has a tight-fitting lid and a metal rack to hold the jars. If you don't have a canner, you

can use any big metal stock pot or kettle that's deep and large enough to submerge the jars. Be sure to place a wire rack in the bottom of the pot to keep jars from sitting directly on the bottom of the pot.

Pressure Canner: More elaborate than a boiling-water bath, this consists of a large kettle with a rack to hold jars, a locking lid with a seal, a pressure lock, and a dial or weighted gauge.

RESCUE for lid-sealing problems:
If a lid fails to seal, the food should be repacked and reprocessed in hot jars within 24 hours with new, properly prepared lids. Or, if you don't have time to reprocess, store the food in the refrigerator. Length of storage will depend on the type of food.

Jars and Lids: Use only standard canning jars and lids with screw-on bands; leftover food jars aren't safe to use. Make sure the lids have sealed properly before storing canned food.

Jar-Lifting Tongs: These enable you to safely lift hot jars from a canner.

cannoli (kan OH lee) An Italian dessert; tubular or horn-shaped pastry that has been deep-fried and filled with sweetened ricotta mixed with chocolate, candied citron, or nuts. (*see also* **ricotta cheese**)

canola oil (kan OH luh) An oil made from rapeseeds. Canola oil is low in saturated fats and contains omega-3 fatty acids that are believed to lower cholesterol and triglycerides. It has a bland flavor suitable for salad dressings and cooking. (*see also* **fats and oils** *and* **rapeseed oil**)

cantaloupe (KAN teh lohp) A muskmelon that has a smooth grayish-tan skin with a raised netting. Cantaloupe has a sweet refreshing flavor, pale orange flesh, a cavity full of nonedible seeds, and a distinctively sweet aroma. To pick the best melon, shake melon, and listen for the rattle of seeds. Pick a melon with a soft stem end. Look for a light yellow ridged or smooth outer shell. Avoid cantaloupe with a green cast.
Storage: Store unripe cantaloupes at room temperature and ripe melons in the refrigerator for 1 to 2 days. (*see also* **melon**)

capellini (kahp payl LEE nee) An extremely thin spaghetti. It's sometimes referred to as angel hair pasta. (*see also* **pasta**)

caper (KAY per) The tiny unopened flower bud of the caper shrub that's native to the Mediterranean region. Capers, often used to garnish and season food, are cured in salted white vinegar and have a sharp, salty-sour flavor.

caponata (kap oh NAH tah) A Sicilian side dish, salad, or relish made with eggplant, onions, tomatoes, anchovies, olives, and pine nuts flavored with vinegar and capers and cooked in olive oil. (*see also* **eggplant** *and recipe on the following page*)

CAPONATA

1 eggplant, unpeeled and diced	1 (6-ounce) can tomato paste
1 medium onion, coarsely chopped	¾ cup pitted ripe olives, sliced
1 medium-size green bell pepper, chopped	½ cup salad olives, chopped
½ cup chopped celery	1 to 2 tablespoons sugar
2 garlic cloves, minced	2½ tablespoons vinegar
¼ cup olive oil	Dash of hot sauce
1 (8-ounce) can tomato sauce	⅛ teaspoon dried oregano
	¼ teaspoon salt
	¼ teaspoon pepper

• Sauté eggplant, onion, bell pepper, celery, and garlic in oil in a large skillet. Add tomato sauce, tomato paste, olives, sugar, and vinegar; cover, reduce heat, and simmer 30 minutes, stirring often. Stir in hot sauce, oregano, salt, and pepper; chill 24 hours. Serve with crackers. Yield: 4½ cups.

cappuccino (kap poo CHEE noh) An Italian coffee beverage made from equal parts espresso, steamed milk, and foamy milk. Sometimes cappuccino is sprinkled with sweetened cocoa powder or ground cinnamon. (*see also* **coffee** *and* **espresso**)

capsaicin (kap SAY ih sihn) The compound that gives some peppers their fiery heat. Most of the capsaicin is found in the membranes and seeds of peppers, so if you're sensitive to the heat of peppers, remove the seeds and membranes before chopping. (*see also* **peppers**)

TEST KITCHEN SECRET

The oils in hot peppers can severely irritate skin and eyes. We wear rubber gloves when handling potent peppers. LYDA JONES

carambola (kair ahm BOH lah) Often referred to as star fruit because its small oval body has 5 deep, lengthwise grooves running its length; when cut crosswise, it looks like a star. The tropical carambola has a waxy, bright yellow skin, and sweet to tart yellow flesh that tastes like a combination of lemon, pineapple, and apple. When ripe, the carambola is juicy and fragrant. Choose carambola that are firm to the touch and have an even golden color. Avoid those with green on the ribs.

Q How do I eat a carambola?

A They don't have to be peeled. Just rinse and slice to use in desserts or salads, or as a garnish.

caramel (KAIR ah mehl) The liquid produced by cooking sugar until it melts; its color ranges from pale golden to dark brown. Caramel can be used for coloring and flavoring desserts and sauces. When it cools, caramel cracks easily and is the hard candy part of peanut brittle. Soft caramel is a chewy candy made with caramelized sugar, butter, and milk.

CARAMEL SAUCE

2 cups whipping cream
¼ cup butter
½ teaspoon baking soda

2 cups sugar
½ cup water
2 teaspoons lemon juice

- Cook first 3 ingredients in a Dutch oven over medium heat, stirring occasionally, until butter melts; remove mixture from heat.
- Bring sugar, water, and lemon juice to a boil in Dutch oven over high heat, stirring occasionally. Reduce heat to medium-high, and boil, stirring occasionally, 8 minutes or until mixture begins to brown. Reduce heat to medium, and cook, stirring occasionally, 5 minutes or until caramel colored.
- Pour sugar mixture gradually into whipping cream mixture. Remove from heat; let stand 1 minute. Whisk until smooth.
- Cook over medium-low heat, stirring occasionally, until a candy thermometer registers 230° (thread stage); cool. Yield: 2½ cups.

caramelize (KAIR ah meh lyz) A process of heating sugar until it develops into a syrup ranging in color from pale golden to dark brown. Granulated or brown sugar can be caramelized by sprinkling on top of food and placing under the broiler or other heat source; crème brûlée is a popular dessert finished with this method. Caramelized sugar is also referred to as burnt sugar. Caramelize also can refer to the process of natural sugars in some produce browning when cooked. Onions caramelize when slowly cooked on the cooktop; vegetables such as potatoes, squash, and peppers caramelize as they roast. (*see also* **burnt sugar** *and* **crème brûlée**)

TEST KITCHEN SECRET

It's tough to clean up a skillet and spoon used to caramelize sugar. The easiest way is to fill the skillet with water and gently heat it, along with the spoon, until the hardened syrup dissolves. Then pour the liquid down the drain. Vie Warshaw

caraway seeds (KAIR uh way) Small, crescent-shaped brown seeds of the caraway plant. They have a distinct aniselike taste and frequently flavor rye bread, cheese, soups, and some sausages. (*see also* **spice**)

carbohydrates A group of foods essential to a balanced diet, including sugars, starches, and certain food fibers. Carbohydrates mostly come from plant sources such as fruits, vegetables, and grains and also are found in milk and other foods of animal origin. They are excellent sources of energy. (*see also* **fats and oils** *and* **proteins**)

LITE BITE

Contrary to popular opinion, low-carbohydrate, high-protein diets can be damaging long-term. These diets stress the kidneys and heart and omit important nutrients. We recommend that 55 percent to 60 percent of your daily calories come from carbohydrates.

cardamom (KAR duh muhm) A member of the ginger family, cardamom is a pungent, aromatic spice with an exotic sweet flavor. It's used in Middle Eastern dishes, particularly in Indian curries; it's also used to flavor teas, coffees, liqueurs, and pastries. Cardamom comes in pods, but is most available in seeds and ground seeds. If using whole pods, gently crush them before adding; the shell will disintegrate while the dish cooks. (*see also* **spice**)

carob (KAIR uhb) Sometimes called the locust bean, carob is made from the pods and seeds of the tropical carob tree. The seeds and pods are dried, roasted, and ground into powder and used to flavor baked goods and candies. Because carob is sweet and tastes similar to chocolate, it's often used as a chocolate substitute. Look for it in health food stores.

carpaccio (kahr PAH chee oh) An Italian dish of thinly sliced raw beef fillet drizzled with olive oil and lemon juice. The dish is often garnished with capers and onions and served as an appetizer.

carrot A member of the parsley family with long green lacy foliage and an edible long orange root that has a mild, sweet flavor and crunchy texture. Carrots are sold fresh with or without their green tops; they come frozen and canned as well as conveniently pre-washed, cleaned, and shredded. Baby carrots, already cleaned and packaged, have become popular in recent years as an easy snack food. Carrot juice, a healthy beverage, is also available.

TIMESAVING TIP
When cooking carrots, remember that baby carrots will cook faster. Regular carrots also will cook faster if first cut into strips or slices.

RESCUE for limp carrots: Revive carrots limp from long storage by soaking them in ice water for 20 to 30 minutes.

Storage: Remove carrot tops if attached; place carrots in plastic bags, and refrigerate up to 2 weeks. (*see also* **vegetables**)

BROWN SUGAR-GLAZED CARROTS

1 pound medium carrots	½ cup minced onion
¾ teaspoon salt	1½ tablespoons dark brown sugar
2 tablespoons butter or margarine	⅔ cup apple juice
	¼ teaspoon pepper

• Cut carrots diagonally into ¼-inch-thick slices. Cook in boiling water to cover with ½ teaspoon salt 5 minutes or until crisp-tender. Drain and rinse with cold water. Pat dry with paper towels.

• Melt butter in a large skillet over low heat; add onion, and cook, stirring constantly, 10 minutes. Add brown sugar; cook, stirring constantly, 5 minutes. Add apple juice; cook, stirring occasionally, 10 minutes. Stir in carrot, remaining ¼ teaspoon salt, and pepper. Yield: 6 servings.

carving Cutting or slicing cooked meat or poultry into serving-size portions. To properly carve, use a long, sharp carving knife or an electric knife. A dishwasher-safe cutting board is also needed. (*see also* **turkey**)

casaba (kah SAH bah) A muskmelon, this globe-shaped fruit has a yellow-green rind that wrinkles at its tapered end. The creamy white flesh is juicy and has a mild, cucumber-like flavor.

casein (KAY seen) A milk protein that works with rennet to solidify milk into cheese. People with lactose intolerance should avoid foods with casein and other milk derivatives. (*see also* **lactose**)

cashew Native to Brazil, India, and the West Indies, the kidney-shaped cashew nut is found within a shell that grows from the bottom of the cashew apple. The shell is highly toxic, so care is taken in removing, cleaning, and polishing the nut. Cashews are prized for their rich, buttery flavor. **Storage:** Cashew nuts are high in fat and can easily become rancid; store them in the refrigerator in an airtight container. Refrigerated, the nuts will keep up to 6 months; in the freezer, up to 1 year. (*see also* **nuts**)

cassava (kuh SAH vuh) A large, long starchy root with a tough brown skin which, when peeled, reveals crisp, white flesh. Cassava is a staple in South American and Latin American cuisines, where it's also known as yuca. The cassava root is used in making tapioca, breads, stews, and as a substitute for rice.

casserole A round, oval, or rectangular baking dish intended for oven cooking; it can be made of any material that will hold and diffuse heat, and customarily has two small handles and a lid. A casserole is also the general name of any recipe made with meat, poultry, fish, shellfish, pasta, and/or vegetables; they are typically bound with a sauce and topped with breadcrumbs or cheese, and cooked in a casserole dish. Casseroles are a favorite at family reunions and church socials. They also fit the needs of today's busy families as hearty weeknight meals that can be made ahead, frozen, and reheated as hectic schedules dictate.

> ### TEST KITCHEN SECRET
>
> *Use the correct size dish when preparing a casserole. Casserole dishes are sometimes measured by volume or quarts, rather than in inches, so if you're not sure of the size, just measure the amount of water it holds. You might also keep in mind that if you use a deeper casserole dish, the food will take longer to cook than if you put the same mixture in a shallow casserole dish.* JAN MOON

Casserole dinners make cleanup a breeze. Toss a bag of salad greens with your favorite dressing, and supper's on the table.

Storage: Most main-dish casseroles can be frozen up to 3 months; however, recipes containing creamed cottage cheese, hard-cooked eggs, cheese, and mayonnaise do not always freeze well. Before reheating a frozen casserole, thaw it in the refrigerator overnight or in the microwave.

TIMESAVING TIP

Though casseroles are among the easiest recipes to double and freeze, they do take up lots of space. If you want to save space in the freezer, line the casserole with heavy-duty aluminum foil or plastic wrap, leaving a generous overhang on all four sides. Add the casserole mixture, and freeze until solid. Remove the foil liner, and wrap the food, using the overhangs, or seal it in a freezer bag. Label the food package, and return it to the freezer. When ready to serve, remove wrapping, and return food to the dish to thaw and to reheat.

cassis (kah SEES) A reddish-purple liqueur made from black currants. (*see also* **currant** *and* **liqueur**)

cassoulet (ka soo LAY) A French stew of white beans, sausages, pork, and goose or duck cooked in a casserole; the ingredient combination varies according to regional preference. A cassoulet is covered and cooked slowly to harmonize the flavors.

cast-iron cookware Heavy cookware made from iron or cast iron, sometimes coated with enamel. This type of cookware distributes heat evenly and retains high temperatures. Old-fashioned unseasoned iron pots and pans must be seasoned before using to prevent sticking. The purpose of seasoning cast iron is to smooth out the microscopic roughness that might cause foods to stick to the surface. (*see also* **cookware**)

Q **How do I season my new cast-iron skillet?**

A First scrub with steel wool soap pads and hot water; then hand-wash with a mild detergent and dry thoroughly. Iron left uncoated will rust, so immediately spread shortening on the inside, including the underside of the lid. Place the pan in a 250° oven for 15 minutes; remove from the oven and wipe any excess grease around the interior to evenly coat the surface. Return to the oven, and bake 1½ to 2 more hours. Remove from the oven, and let cool to room temperature. Repeat the greasing and baking procedure two or three times. The finished product will be dark with a nice sheen. Continued use, gentle cleaning with hot water, and wiping it dry immediately will improve the seasoning. Never wash cast iron in a dishwasher.

catfish Its long whiskers give this fish its name. Catfish are generally thought of as a freshwater fish, though they are also plentiful in saltwater. However, the majority of catfish sold at market are farm-raised, and only these and freshwater catfish are recommended for eating. Catfish don't have scales; instead, they have a tough skin that must be removed before fish are cooked. The flesh is firm and mild in flavor, making catfish good for frying, poaching, steaming, baking, or grilling. (*see also* **fish**)

Southernism

There was a time in the South when you didn't have catfish on the table unless you spent a hot afternoon dangling a cane pole from a riverbank. But all that has changed due to catfish farms. The rank of the lowly catfish has been elevated to that of an important crop in the South, now that it's available in markets across the country. One thing hasn't changed—we still love our catfish, and it's a favorite at fish fries and the dinner table.

CLASSIC FRIED CATFISH

¾ cup yellow cornmeal
¼ cup all-purpose flour
2 teaspoons salt
1 teaspoon ground red pepper
¼ teaspoon garlic powder

6 (4- to 6-ounce) farm-raised
   catfish fillets
¼ teaspoon salt
Vegetable oil

• Combine first 5 ingredients in a large shallow dish. Sprinkle fish with ¼ teaspoon salt; dredge in cornmeal mixture, coating evenly.
• Pour oil to a depth of 1½ inches into a deep cast-iron skillet; heat to 350°. Fry fish, in batches, 5 to 6 minutes or until golden; drain on paper towels. Yield: 6 servings.

catsup (*see* **ketchup**)

cauliflower (KAWL ih flow uhr) This member of the cabbage family has a fairly round head of tightly packed white florets that are partially covered at the stem end with large, waxy, pale green leaves. Besides the white variety, you'll occasionally find a purple or greenish variety. When cooked, cauliflower has a mild cabbagelike flavor and aroma. It can be cooked in a number of ways including boiling, baking, and sautéing; the whole cauliflower head may be cooked in one piece and topped with a sauce.

Storage: Wrap fresh cauliflower in plastic wrap, and refrigerate 3 to 5 days. Once cooked, it can be refrigerated 1 to 3 days. (*see also* **vegetables**)

caviar (KA vee ahr) Lightly salted sturgeon fish roe (eggs), though other less expensive fish sometime borrow its name. The best and most expensive caviar is from the beluga sturgeon; it's prized for its soft, large pea-size eggs, which range in color from pale silver-gray to black. Caviar is extremely perishable so it must be kept very cold. It's best served in a bowl placed inside another container of finely crushed ice. Spread caviar over toast points.

cayenne pepper (KI yen) A hot, pungent powder made from various ground dried hot chiles. It has a bright orange-red color and is often referred to as ground red pepper. (*see also* **chile pepper, peppers,** *and* **red pepper**)

celeriac (seh LER ee ak) Also called celery root, this is a small to medium-sized brown knobby vegetable that's the root of a specially bred celery plant. Before using, it's a good idea to peel and soak it briefly in lemon juice and water to prevent discoloration. Its flavor is a cross between strong celery and parsley with a turniplike texture; it can be grated or shredded and eaten raw in salads, or cooked in soups and stews. It can also be boiled, sautéed, or baked.
Storage: Refrigerate celeriac in a plastic bag for 7 to 10 days.

celery (SELL er ree) A popular green vegetable that grows in bunches of long stalks or ribs surrounding a tender heart and joined at the base. Enjoy it raw in salads, stuffed as an appetizer, or cooked in soups and casseroles.

TIMESAVING TIP
Recipes often call for a small amount of chopped celery. Rather than breaking off one or more ribs and ending up with too much, try chopping the entire bunch across the top. It's easier to get just the amount you need, and the whole bunch gets shorter as you use it, so it's easier to store.

Storage: Store celery in a plastic bag in the refrigerator, leaving the ribs attached to the stalk until ready to use. It will typically keep up to a couple of weeks. To restore crispness to fresh celery, trim the ribs and soak them in ice water 15 minutes. (*see also* **vegetables**)

celery root (*see* **celeriac**)

celery salt A seasoning blend of ground celery seeds and salt. It's used to season soups, salads, meats, fish, and vegetables.

celery seed Small brown seeds of a wild celery called lovage that are typically used in pickles, salad dressings, and coleslaw, and as a flavoring for meat, fish, and vegetables. (*see also* **lovage** *and* **spice**)

cellophane noodles (SEHL uh fayn) Very thin, flavorless, translucent Asian noodles, made from the starch of mung bean flour. The noodles are sold dried and must be soaked briefly in hot water before using in most dishes. They can be purchased in the ethnic section of many markets and in Asian grocery stores. (*see also* **Asian noodle**)

Celsius (SEHL see uhs) Also known as centigrade, Celsius is a temperature scale with 0° as the freezing point of water and 100° as its boiling point. To convert Celsius to Fahrenheit, multiply the Celsius temperature by 9, divide by 5, and add 32.

cèpe (SEHP) This delicious earthy wild mushroom is also known in Italy as a porcini mushroom. The mushrooms range in color from white to dark brown and can weigh from an ounce up to a pound. Their caps can be large—up to 10 inches in diameter, and they have a meaty texture and a pungent, woodsy flavor and aroma. The dried form of this mushroom is more available, but they must be soaked in hot water for about 20 minutes before using. (*see also* **mushroom**)

cereal grains Any plant from the grass family that yields an edible grain or seed. Popular grains are barley, corn, millet, oats, quinoa, rice, rye, sorghum, triticale, wheat, and wild rice. Cereals are a readily available source of protein and fiber and contain more carbohydrates than most other foods; they're a staple throughout the world. (*see also* **grain**)

ceviche (*see* **seviche**)

Chablis (sha BLEE) Considered one of the world's great wines, true Chablis is a white burgundy wine made from Chardonnay grapes from the village of Chablis in northern Burgundy, France. Chablis is generally crisp and dry, a pale straw color, and can be thin and tart or rich and full. In the United States and Australia, the term Chablis is sometimes used to describe any inexpensive and not necessarily dry white wine. (*see also* **wine**)

chafing dish (CHAYF ing) A deep metal dish, with or without a water basin underneath, used to warm or cook food. A chafing dish consists of a container with a heat source, usually a candle or solid fuel (Sterno), directly beneath it. A chafing dish might be used when entertaining buffet-style to keep foods, such as creamed chicken, warm.

challah (KHAH lah) A tender, rich Jewish yeast bread usually made with eggs, butter, and honey, and shaped into a braided loaf. It's typically served on the Sabbath, on holidays, and other ceremonial occasions as well as for everyday. (*see also* **yeast**)

chalupa (chah LOO pah) Spanish for "boat," the food term describes a corn tortilla formed into the shape of a boat and fried. Popular in Mexican cuisine, the fried chalupa is filled with shredded beef, pork, chicken, vegetables, or cheese. (*see also* **tortilla**)

champagne (sham PAYN) The world's most famous sparkling wine; the supreme wine for celebrations. The saying goes, "All champagne is sparkling wine, but not all sparkling wine is champagne." Sparkling wines are made all over the world, but only that which is produced in the Champagne region in France can be truly called champagne. Champagne is produced using a specific blend (or cuvée) of Pinot Noir, Chardonnay, and Pinot Meunier grapes and a unique bottling and fermentation process.

Q **How should champagne be opened?**

A Carefully! Keep your palm over the top of the bottle while removing the foil and wire cage. Then firmly hold your palm over the top of the cork, while holding the bottle at a 45-degree angle away from you or guests. With your other hand, twist the bottle; as the cork begins to loosen, grasp the cork.

The most popular variety of champagne is Brut, with almost all of it designated as Nonvintage (NV). Champagne producers work hard to establish a particular "house" style that will remain consistent year after year. In doing so, producers blend wines (from their own cellars) that have been stored for at least 2 years to achieve this signature cuvée. Only in exceptional years will champagne have a vintage date.

Champagne ranges in color from pale gold to blush, and the flavor ranges from toasty to yeasty, and from dry with no added sugar, to sweet. The label indicates the level of dryness or sweetness: brut is very dry; extra dry is also very dry; sec is slightly sweet; demi-sec is sweet; and doux is very sweet. Demi-sec and doux are served as dessert wines. (*see also* **wine**)

champignon (sham pee NYOHN) The French word for small common cultivated mushrooms usually called button mushrooms. (*see also* **mushroom**)

chanterelle (shan tuh REHL) A trumpet-shaped wild mushroom that has a bright yellow to orange color, a slightly chewy texture, and a fruity, nutty flavor. Chanterelles are generally imported from Europe and are found dried or canned in most markets, though they're also grown on the West Coast and East Coast. Select those that are plump and spongy; they can be cooked as a side dish or added to other foods. Since they cook quickly, it's best to add them toward the end of the cooking time. (*see also* **mushroom**)

chantilly (shan TIHL lee) A French term that describes a sweet or savory, hot or cold sauce to which whipped cream has been added. Crème chantilly is a lightly sweetened whipped cream sometimes flavored with vanilla and used as a dessert topping. (*see also* **cream**)

chapon (shah POHN) A piece of bread that's been rubbed with garlic or doused with garlic-flavored olive oil and used to garnish a salad or a soup, or to rub the inside of a salad bowl to impart a hint of garlic to the greens.

chard Also referred to as Swiss chard, this member of the beet family has crinkly dark green leaves and silvery, celery-like stalks. There's also a variety with dark green leaves and reddish stalks that resembles rhubarb. Chard leaves are prepared like spinach and have a similar flavor. The stalks are prepared like asparagus and have a tart, slightly bitter flavor. It's available only in the summer.

Storage: Store chard in a plastic bag in the refrigerator up to 3 days.

> **TEST KITCHEN SECRET**
>
> *Mild greens, such as Swiss chard, retain their flavor better when cooked quickly, just until tender.*
>
> LYDA JONES

Chardonnay (shar duh NAY) The classic grape of France's famous white-wine producing regions of Burgundy and Chablis. Styles of Chardonnay can vary widely—from the dry and delicate, as in Chablis, to big and oaky examples from California and Australia. However, despite the particular flavor components and region variations, Chardonnay is usually made in a medium- to full-bodied style, and has the distinctive aroma and flavor of green apples. Chardonnay is generally a deep golden color, which hints that it has been aged in oak barrels. (*see also* **wine**)

charlotte (SHAR luht) A dessert in which a mold is lined with a shell of ladyfingers, sponge cake, or bread; these are sometimes sprinkled or soaked with rum or liqueur. The shell is then filled with a mixture of fruit and custard or whipped cream strengthened with gelatin; the charlotte is chilled thoroughly and unmolded before serving. Charlotte russe is the most familiar of these desserts. The charlotte originated in France, but it's as Southern as ambrosia. (*see recipe on the following page*)

CHARLOTTE RUSSE WITH STRAWBERRY SAUCE

2 envelopes unflavored gelatin
¼ cup cold water
⅔ cup sugar
4 egg yolks
1⅓ cups milk
1 teaspoon vanilla extract
½ cup sour cream
⅓ cup chopped almonds, toasted
1 cup whipping cream, whipped
16 ladyfingers, split
Strawberry Sauce
Garnish: fresh strawberries

• Sprinkle gelatin over cold water; let stand 1 minute. Set aside.
• Combine sugar and egg yolks in a heavy saucepan; beat at medium speed with an electric mixer until thick and pale. Add milk; cook over medium heat, stirring constantly, until thermometer reaches 160° (about 5 minutes). Add gelatin mixture, stirring until gelatin dissolves. Stir in vanilla, sour cream, and almonds; cool to room temperature. Fold in whipped cream.
• Line a 2-quart mold with enough 20- x 2-inch strips of wax paper to cover mold, slightly overlapping. Line sides and bottom of mold with ladyfingers. Spoon cream mixture over ladyfingers. Arrange remaining ladyfingers over cream mixture. Chill at least 8 hours. Invert mold; remove dessert. Carefully peel off wax paper. Serve dessert with Strawberry Sauce, and garnish, if desired. Yield: 8 to 10 servings.

STRAWBERRY SAUCE

1 pint fresh strawberries
1 tablespoon lemon juice
½ cup sugar
2 tablespoons framboise or other raspberry brandy*

• Wash and hull strawberries. Process strawberries and remaining ingredients in a blender until smooth. Yield: 1⅓ cups.

* Black raspberry schnapps may be substituted for framboise.

Châteaubriand (sha toh bree AHN) A thick beef filet steak, large enough to serve two, cut from the center of the tenderloin. The meat is usually grilled or broiled and served with béarnaise sauce and sautéed potatoes. (*see also* **béarnaise sauce**)

chayote (chy OH tay) Often called a mirliton, the chayote is a squash about the size and shape of a large pear. It has a delicate green skin, a rather bland white flesh, and a soft seed. Chayotes can be prepared as any summer squash, or they can be stuffed and baked. **Storage:** Chayotes can be refrigerated in a plastic bag up to 1 month. (*see also* **squash**)

Southernism

Unadorned, chayote squash has the crisp flesh of a cucumber and the subtle flavor of yellow squash. In Louisiana, it's called mirliton, but in other locales, it's referred to as vegetable pear, mango squash, or chayote.

Cheddar A firm-textured cow's milk cheese that originated in the village of Cheddar in England. It ranges in flavor from mild to extra sharp, and from white to bright orange in color. It's available in chunks, shredded, or in wheels. (*see also* **cheese**)

cheese Dairy products made from heated milk treated with an enzyme such as rennet to form creamy curds and watery whey. There are two categories of natural cheese: fresh and ripened or aged. Most fresh cheeses are curds separated from their whey and pressed into shapes, while ripened cheeses undergo aging or curing to develop a variety of textures and flavors. The longer a cheese ages, the drier and more flavorful it becomes.

Natural cheese is categorized by degree of hardness, ranging from soft and semisoft, to hard, very hard, and blue-veined. Within the soft category there are soft, fresh cheeses and soft-ripened cheeses. Soft, fresh cheeses such as cottage cheese and cream cheese have a high moisture level, delicate flavor, and are the most perishable. Soft-ripened cheeses such as Brie and Camembert ripen inside a powdery white rind. Gouda and Monterey Jack are common semisoft cheeses and are good for shredding and melting. Hard cheeses contain less moisture and have a firmer shape; Cheddar and Swiss are good examples. Very hard cheeses such as Parmesan are best grated and will keep for a long time. Blue-veined cheeses are sprayed with spores of special molds and aged to develop their characteristic earthy flavors.

Processed cheese is made from natural cheese that has been pasteurized, and sometimes other ingredients are added for flavoring and to give it a softer texture and a longer shelf life. These include pasteurized process cheese, process cheese food, and process cheese spread. Process cheese is often too soft to shred or grate; however it melts nicely and doesn't become tough when heated. **Storage:** Keep all natural cheese covered in plastic wrap and stored in the refrigerator. In general, the softer the cheese, the shorter the storage life; cottage and ricotta should be stored no longer than a week after purchase. If a soft cheese develops mold, it should be thrown away. Firm and hard cheeses can be stored for as long as several months; if they develop mold, just cut it off. Freezing is not the best method of storage for cheese, but it can be done. You can freeze most cheese up to 6 weeks; thawed cheese is better for cooking than just eating. (*continued on the following page*)

> ## TEST KITCHEN SECRET
>
> *When we add cheese as a topping for casseroles, we like to shred or cut it into small pieces, and add it during the last 5 minutes of baking time; that way the cheese won't toughen and harden. Also, when adding it to a sauce, we like to grate or shred it first so that it will melt and blend quickly.* JAN MOON

Q **What is imitation cheese?**

A Imitation cheese is a product that doesn't meet government standards of the product it's imitating. It generally consists of tofu, rice starch, calcium caseinate, lecithin, and various additives.

SELECTING NATURAL CHEESES

Familiar cheese such as Cheddar and Parmesan are easily recognizable. Enjoy these other varieties we describe below as you taste and explore the many selections available in the cheese section of the supermarket.

Soft Cheeses

Boursin (boor SAHN): Brand name for a triple cream cheese with a buttery texture. It's often flavored with garlic, herbs, or pepper. Good appetizer cheese; pair with dry white wine or fruity red wine.

Brie: A soft-ripened cheese that's known for its oozing, buttery interior and snow-white edible rind. Once ripe, Brie has a short shelf life, so use it within a few days. It's a popular appetizer wrapped in pastry and baked.

Crème fraîche (krehm FRESH): A specialty hailing from France, this is a very rich, thickened cream. Its silky texture and pleasing sour, nutty flavor make it similar to sour cream, but with a sweeter, slightly tangy flavor. Spoon it over fresh fruit or warm cobbler for dessert. (*see also* **crème fraîche**)

Farmer cheese: A form of cottage cheese but with no curds. Instead, it's pressed into a block that can be sliced. It's available fresh or very dry. A delightful country cheese. Firm; pleasantly mild. An all-purpose cheese for eating and cooking; good on dark bread or with fruit and a light wine.

Feta (FEHT uh): The classic Greek cheese. It's salty and sharp, firm and crumbly. Feta is usually sold pressed into a square cake and packed in brine. It's great crumbled over a salad or on pizza. Though traditionally made from sheep's milk, some American-made feta comes from cow's milk.

Goat cheese: The French call this pure white goat's milk cheese chèvre (SHEV ruh). It's sold in many shapes, though logs are most common. It has a distinct tart flavor and is sometimes coated in edible ash, herbs, or pepper. Store up to 2 weeks in the refrigerator. (*see also* **chèvre**)

READER TIP

To quickly and easily slice a log of soft goat cheese, slide a long piece of dental floss under it, cross the ends of the floss above, and pull the floss through the cheese. You'll have neat slices, and no messy knives. Also, fresh mozzarella cheese can be easily sliced with an egg slicer; close the slicer to cut through the cheese, and then separate the individual slices. C.C., Athens, GA

Mascarpone (mas cahr POHN ay): A soft and fresh triple cream dessert cheese with fluffy texture. Often sold in plastic tubs, mascarpone is best known for its use in tiramisù, which combines this sweet cheese with ladyfingers soaked in espresso. (*see also* **tiramisù**)

Semisoft Cheeses

Cream Havarti: Mild and buttery; slightly sweet with a smooth, supple texture. A favorite for snacking or for sandwiches. Excellent for slicing or melting.

Fontina: One of Italy's great cheeses with a pronounced flavor and smooth, creamy texture. A superb melting cheese. A Swedish-style fontina is also available; it's firm and mild-flavored.

Gouda: America's favorite Dutch cheese with a buttery, nutlike flavor. Enjoy it cubed as a snack or in a salad or sandwich. Its smoked version is also popular. Gouda's a good match for beer and dark bread.

Pepper Jack: A creamy, smooth, and pliable version of Monterey Jack cheese flecked with bits of chile peppers. Slices well; melts readily. It's used often in Mexican dishes.

Port Salut: This buttery semisoft cheese was first made by Trappist monks at the Monastery of Port du Salut in France. Made from cow's milk, it has a mild flavor, satiny-smooth texture, and is covered with an orange rind. It highlights fruit platters, salads, and is used in cooking.

Provolone: A firm, golden cheese with a slightly smoky tang. It's similar to mozzarella. As provolone ripens, the color becomes a richer yellow and the flavor sharpens. It's ideal for snacks and appetizers, and is an excellent cooking cheese, particularly in lasagna or ravioli.

String Mozzarella: A type of mozzarella shaped into ropes or sticks that "string" when pulled apart. Great pizza cheese.

TIMESAVING TIP

If you get tired of dirtying the grater when a recipe calls for only a half cup of shredded cheese, then shred an entire pound at one time; use what's needed, and refrigerate or freeze the rest. If you use a hand grater, spray it with vegetable cooking spray before shredding to keep the cheese from sticking to the surface.

Hard or Firm Cheeses

Asiago (ah SYAH goh): A popular pale yellow Italian cheese with rich, nutty flavor. A great snack cheese when young accompanied with beer or a full-bodied red wine; good for grating when aged over a year.

Emmentaler (EM en tahl er): Named for Switzerland's Emmental valley, this cheese is the king of Swiss cheeses. It has a nutty-sweet, mellow flavor; firm texture with dime-size holes called "eyes." Traditionally used in fondue.

Gruyère (groo YAIR): A rich, sweet, nutty-flavored Swiss that's typically aged for 1 year. It has a firm, pale yellow interior. A rich cooking cheese that's often used in fondue or atop French onion soup. (*see also* **fondue**)

Jarlsberg: A buttery rich cheese from Norway with a creamy texture and mellow, nutty flavor. It's good for salads, snacking, and cooking.

Raclette: Swiss cow's milk cheese, similar to Gruyère; it's used for fondue and in sauces. Piquantly mild with a nutlike goodness.

Smoked Cheddar: A deep golden Cheddar with an edible brown rind; creamy, nutty smoked flavor with a smooth, firm texture.

Vermont white Cheddar: A rich, aged, creamy Cheddar that remains undyed. It's an excellent cheese for sauce making.

Very Hard Cheeses

Parmesan: A hard, dry grating cheese made from cow's skim milk; has a rich, sharp flavor and a pale yellow color with a golden rind.

Parmigiano-Reggiano: Italy's luxurious hard grating cheese that's typically aged at least 2 years. With a prized granular texture (from aging) and complex sharp flavor, this cheese is best eaten unadorned and with fresh fruit.

Romano: A sharp and tangy, slightly salty, hard cheese. Available as pepato with black peppercorns throughout its white interior. A good cheese for grating for the same uses as Parmesan. (*continued on the following page*)

Blue-Veined Cheeses

Gorgonzola: An aged, distinctively sharp semisoft cheese with a creamy interior streaked with blue-green veins. Excellent for dessert, in salads, or tasting with a full-bodied red wine. It teams naturally with pears and walnuts. When aged over 6 months, Gorgonzola takes on a strong (some would say offensive) aroma.

Maytag blue: Best-known American blue cheese (made by the same Maytags who make washing machines). Ivory-colored blue cheese marbled with blue-gray veins. It has a tangy, slightly sweet flavor with a firm, crumbly texture.

> **Q Is there a difference between blue cheese and Roquefort cheese?**
>
> **A** Roquefort is actually a type of blue cheese made from sheep's milk near the French village of Roquefort. True Roquefort comes in a foil wrapper marked with an emblem of a red sheep and is the only type of blue cheese that can carry the name "Roquefort." It's wonderful in salad dressings or served at the end of a meal with a dessert wine.

Stilton: A blue cheese first sold in the small village of Stilton in Huntingdonshire, England. Stilton is made from whole cow's milk and is allowed to ripen 4 to 6 months. It has a creamy blue-green veined interior that's slightly crumbly. It's a rich, creamy cheese with a pungent bite. Best enjoyed with a glass of port or full-bodied red wine.

cheesecake A rich, smooth dessert made by blending cream cheese and ricotta or cottage cheese with sugar, eggs, flavoring, and sometimes sour cream. The mixture is baked in a springform pan that's lined with a crumbled cookie or ground nut crust. After baking, the dessert is chilled and often topped with sour cream or fruit. Cheesecakes also have evolved from dessert to appetizer and entrée selections that mingle seafood, poultry, veggies, and herbs among the creamy cheese base.

Storage: Cheesecake is a great dessert choice because it can be made ahead and chilled. Just leave it in the springform pan until time to unmold and serve. Cheesecakes can also be frozen up to 1 month; remove the pan, place cake on a cardboard circle, and wrap in heavy-duty aluminum foil. Thaw in refrigerator.

cheesecloth Lightweight, loosely woven cotton cloth available in large grocery stores and used in many tasks, such as making bouquet garni, straining liquids, and lining cheese and dessert molds. (*see also* **bouquet garni**)

cheese straws Often served at Southern showers, weddings, and events such as Derby parties, these are little strips of baked cheese dough spiked with ground red pepper for punch and baked until crisp and golden. They may be pressed through a cookie press or shaped by hand. Store them in an airtight container between wax paper up to a week. (*see also* **cookie press**)

SALLY'S CHEESE STRAWS

1 pound sharp Cheddar cheese, shredded and softened	¼ cup butter, softened
	1 teaspoon salt
1½ cups all-purpose flour	¼ teaspoon ground red pepper

• Process all ingredients in a food processor about 30 seconds or until mixture forms a ball.
• Use a cookie press fitted with a star-shaped disc to shape mixture into straws, following manufacturer's instructions, on ungreased baking sheets.
• Bake at 375° for 8 to 10 minutes or until lightly browned. Transfer to wire racks to cool. Yield: about 8 dozen.

chef's salad A salad of tossed greens topped with julienne strips of cold ham, chicken or turkey, cheese, sliced vegetables, and hard-cooked eggs. The salad can be topped with any choice of salad dressings.

Chenin Blanc (SHEN ihn BLAHN) A white wine grape grown in California and France's Loire Valley. This grape makes wine that has an intense, spicy, and slightly sweet flavor. (*see also* **wine**)

cherimoya (chair uh MOY ah) Also called "custard apples," this tropical fruit is heart-shaped with pale green, leathery, scalelike skin. The custardy flesh is creamy white with large shiny black seeds. When ripe, the cherimoya tastes like a sweet combination of pineapple, mango, and strawberries. The best way to enjoy the fruit is to cut it in half, remove the seeds, and scoop out the flesh with a spoon.
Storage: Store at room temperature until ripe, then refrigerate, wrapped in plastic, up to 4 days.

cherries jubilee A dessert made by combining dark pitted cherries, sugar, and kirsch or brandy; the mixture is sautéed, flamed, and spooned over vanilla ice cream. The cherries are usually prepared and flambéed tableside in a chafing dish.

CHERRIES JUBILEE

1 pound frozen sweet cherries	½ cup orange juice
3 tablespoons sugar	½ cup water
1 tablespoon cornstarch	½ cup brandy
½ teaspoon grated orange rind	Vanilla ice cream

• Partially thaw cherries; set aside. Combine sugar, cornstarch, and orange rind in a saucepan. Stir in orange juice and water; bring to a boil, stirring constantly. Add cherries; reduce heat, and simmer 10 minutes, stirring gently. Transfer cherry sauce to a chafing dish or flambé pan, and keep warm.
• Place brandy in a small, long-handled saucepan; heat until warm (do not boil). Remove from heat. Ignite with a long match; pour over cherries. Stir until flames die down. Serve immediately over ice cream. Yield: 4 to 6 servings.

cherry A small, round, plump fruit with a pit, a light golden to deep red shiny, smooth skin, and a long, slender stem. The fruit inside clings to the pit and has a juicy texture and sweet-to-sour flavor. Cherries are available fresh, but you can also find them frozen, canned, candied, and dried. Maraschino cherries have been preserved and dyed with food coloring and flavored with almond (for red cherries) and mint (for green cherries).

TIMESAVING TIP

The quickest way to pit fresh cherries is with a cherry pitter, but if you don't have one, try these techniques: Push the cherry firmly down onto the pointed, jagged end of a pastry bag tip or, push a drinking straw through the bottom of the cherry, forcing the pit up and out through the stem end.

There are two main groups of cherries: Sweet, which are eaten plain or cooked, and sour, which are used for cooking or canning.
• *Sweet:* These include the black Bing, Lambert, and Tartarian to the golden, red Royal cherries.
• *Sour:* These are the bright red Early Richmond and Montmorency, and the dark red Morello.
Storage: Fresh cherries should be eaten as soon as possible; they can be covered and refrigerated up to 4 days. After opening canned cherries, store in an airtight container in the refrigerator up to 1 week. Maraschino cherries last up to 6 months in the refrigerator.

TEST KITCHEN SECRET

Cherry pits have an almond flavor, which explains why cherry recipes are often flavored with almond extract. We've found that just a drop of almond extract added to cherry pie or cobbler or a cherry dessert sauce will actually enhance the cherry flavor. REBECCA KRACKE GORDON

chervil (CHER vuhl) A mild-flavored herb that resembles parsley; its dark green leaves have a sweet, anise flavor. Chervil is available fresh or dried and is generally used like parsley. (*see also* **herbs**)

chess pie A single-crust pie that has a simple filling of eggs, sugar, and butter plus small amounts of vinegar and cornmeal or flour. When baked, the filling becomes dense and translucent with a thin, crusty top.

Southernism

This pie has always been a favorite with Southerners, but no one seems to know exactly where it got its name. It's believed that at first it was called jelly pie or Jefferson Davis pie, and later became known as chess pie because of the pie chest in which it was typically stored. In any event, we probably have chess pie to thank for the eventual creation of the even more popular pecan pie.

chestnut This sweet, edible nut is the fruit of the chestnut tree. Once peeled of their hard, dark brown outer shells and bitter inner skins, chestnuts can be roasted, boiled, pureed, preserved, and candied; they're used in desserts or served as a savory main-dish accompaniment. The golden nuts have a sweet, starchy flavor and a moist, crumbly texture. They're available fresh only during winter months, but they can also be purchased canned or dried.

Q **I've always heard about roasting chestnuts on an open fire. How is this done?**

A First, cut an "X" on the flat side of each chestnut. Then place them in a skillet with a perforated bottom, and put the skillet over the coals of an outdoor fire or a fire in a fireplace. It will generally take about 15 to 20 minutes of heating and shaking the chestnuts for them to roast; they will pop open when done. An easier way to roast them is in a shallow baking pan at 400° for 15 minutes.

Storage: Fresh chestnuts are perishable, so they should be kept unshelled in the refrigerator in a plastic bag no longer than 2 weeks; they may be frozen several months. Dried chestnuts will keep indefinitely in an airtight container in the refrigerator or freezer. (*see also* **water chestnut**)

chèvre (SHEHV ruh) This pure white goat's milk cheese has a deliciously tart flavor. Chèvre ranges in texture from moist and creamy to dry and semifirm, and comes in a number of shapes, such as logs and cones. It's available plain or coated with edible ash, herbs or crushed pepper.
Storage: Wrap chèvre in plastic and refrigerate up to 2 weeks. (*see also* **cheese**)

Chianti (kee AHN tee) A sturdy, dry red wine made in Tuscany, Italy. This wine was once recognized by its squatty, straw-covered bottles; it's now more often found in the traditional Bordeaux-type bottle. Chianti's bold flavor pairs nicely with highly seasoned or Italian foods. (*see also* **wine**)

chicken A domestic bird recognized by the USDA as a principal kind of poultry that provides meat and eggs. Chicken is known for being a high-protein, low-fat food; it's available either fresh or frozen, and whole or cut into parts. This versatile bird can be prepared in almost any way: baking, broiling, boiling, roasting, frying, braising, barbecuing, and stewing. (*continued on the following page*)

TIMESAVING TIP
A whole, small chicken takes about an hour to roast, but if you're in a hurry, butterfly the chicken and save at least 20 minutes. With poultry shears, cut through the bones on either side of the backbone, which you then remove and discard; turn the chicken over, and use the heel of your hand to flatten the breastbone.

Types: The common types of chicken you can buy at your local market:

• *Petit Poussin* is French for a very young, small chicken weighing no more than 1½ pounds. It's best grilled or broiled.

• The *broiler-fryer* is the most commonly purchased whole bird, ranging from 2 to 4 pounds. This economi-

cal all-purpose bird can be cooked by just about any method, from roasting or grilling to stewing. A 3-pound broiler-fryer yields four to six servings or about 3 cups chopped, cooked chicken.

• *Roasters* are slightly larger than broiler-fryers; they weigh from 4 to 6 pounds. They are higher in fat than fryers, too, which makes them ideal for oven roasting and rotisserie cooking. The cooked chicken is flavorful in salads, soups, and casseroles.

• *Hens* or stewing chickens range from 3 to 8 pounds. They're flavorful mature birds, but less tender. Moist-heat cooking such as stewing or braising suits these tougher birds.

• A *capon* is a rooster that has been castrated while very young. It weighs from 4 to 10 pounds and is full-breasted with flavorful meat particularly suited to roasting.

• *Free-range chickens* are not necessarily organic chickens (free of chemicals or additives), but they can be. They're fed a special vegetarian diet, and they have more

Q **Is it really more economical to purchase a whole chicken and cut it up myself, or am I better off buying it already cut up?**

A You can buy a whole chicken for a lot less per pound, cut it up in 10 to 15 minutes, serve three extra pieces, counting wings and wishbone, and make stock for the freezer with the giblets and back. Or, you can spend more per pound for a cut-up chicken and lots more per pound for a package of pick-of-the-chick pieces (breasts, legs, and thighs). Cutting up a chicken may seem tricky, but once you've done it several times, it becomes easier on you and your pocketbook. Here's how:

1. Remove leg-thigh portion by cutting between thigh and body. Twist thigh to break hip joint. Cut through joint.

2. Separate drumstick and thigh by cutting through meat at knee joint; break joint, and cut two pieces apart.

3. Remove wings by cutting through skin and joint on inside of wings.

4. Using poultry shears, cut through rib cage along backbone. Reserve bony back portion for broth, if desired.

5. Split breast into two breast halves by cutting along breastbone.

6. Cutting up your own chicken gives you these 8 pieces—2 breasts, 2 thighs, 2 drumsticks, and 2 wings.

freedom of movement than chickens that are mass produced. As a result, free-range birds cost more. They weigh 4 to 5 pounds typically.

Storage: Fresh chicken is highly perishable. As soon as you arrive home from the market, wrap chicken in plastic wrap and store in the coldest part of your refrigerator up to 2 days. For longer storage, you can freeze properly packaged chicken parts up to 9 months, and whole chickens up to 1 year. Most cooked chicken can be refrigerated up to 4 days after preparation; however, use cooked ground chicken and chicken in gravy within 2 days. To save money, buy bone-in breasts and debone them yourself. Just split the breast in half lengthwise, place the split breast bone side down, and starting at the breastbone side of the chicken, slice the meat away from the bone, cutting as close as possible to the bone.

Safety Tips:
• Never leave a package of chicken sitting on the counter to thaw because bacteria thrive at room temperature.
• The most accurate way to determine doneness of chicken is to use a meat thermometer; dark meat should register 180° and breast meat, 170°. This is most easily done with an instant-read thermometer.
• Never place cooked chicken on the same platter that held the uncooked meat; this could occur when grilling. Example: The chicken is taken to the grill on one platter; that platter should be thoroughly cleaned or replaced before bringing in the grilled chicken.
• Never refrigerate a raw or cooked whole chicken with stuffing inside the body because of the risk of increased bacterial growth. Store the bird and stuffing separately. (*see also* **brine** *and* **poultry**)

TEST KITCHEN SECRET

"When we cut up raw chicken, we use a plastic cutting board, because it's easier to clean than a wooden one. We suggest washing the plastic boards in hot, soapy water, or running them through the dishwasher to disinfect after coming in contact with raw chicken. And don't forget to wipe off the kitchen counter where you were working with a disinfectant." JAMES SCHEND

Q **What can I use to disinfect the kitchen counter after I've been handling raw chicken?**

A You can purchase a disinfectant or you can try this solution: The Disney Institute Cooking School teaches students to keep cutting boards, work surfaces, and utensils clean with a squirt of a sanitary solution made of one part bleach to six parts water. The mixture is stored in a small spray bottle and kept nearby during food preparation and cleanup for easy spray and wipe.

chicken-fried steak A dish that's popular in the South and Midwest. This comfort food refers to a thin, inexpensive cut of steak that has been tenderized by pounding. It's dipped into a batter of milk, egg, and seasoned flour, then deep-fried like chicken until crisp, and served with a rich and creamy seasoned country gravy. This dish is definitely not suitable for a low-fat diet. "I don't see too many people

Southernism

Whether it's called country-fried steak, smothered steak, or chicken-fried steak, one thing is certain: Southerners have grown up loving this cast-iron comfort food beef dish. It's a supper menu we all like: deliciously crisp and tender chicken-fried steak, green beans, mashed potatoes, and, of course, creamy country gravy.

worrying about it—they just don't eat it every day," says Eddie Wilson, owner of Threadgill's in Austin, Texas, the legendary mecca for chicken-fry fans. "Fifteen years ago we sold so much chicken-fried steak it was almost sinful. Now folks eat more of that chicken-fried *chicken*, which to me, is a lot like drinking a bourbon and Diet Coke." (*see also* **country gravy**)

CHICKEN-FRIED STEAK

¼ teaspoon salt
¼ teaspoon pepper
4 (4-ounce) cube steaks
38 saltine crackers (1 sleeve), crushed
1¼ cups all-purpose flour, divided
½ teaspoon baking powder

2 teaspoons salt, divided
1½ teaspoons ground black pepper, divided
½ teaspoon ground red pepper
4¾ cups milk, divided
2 large eggs
3½ cups peanut oil

• Sprinkle salt and pepper evenly over steaks. Set aside.
• Combine cracker crumbs, 1 cup flour, baking powder, 1 teaspoon salt, ½ teaspoon black pepper, and red pepper.
• Whisk together ¾ cup milk and eggs. Dredge steaks in cracker crumb mixture; dip in milk mixture, and dredge in cracker mixture again.
• Pour oil into a 12-inch skillet; heat to 360°. (Do not use a nonstick skillet.) Fry steaks 10 minutes. Turn and fry 4 to 5 more minutes or until golden brown. Remove to a wire rack on a jellyroll pan. Keep steaks warm in a 225° oven. Carefully drain hot oil, reserving cooked bits and 1 tablespoon drippings in skillet.
• Whisk together remaining ¼ cup flour, 1 teaspoon salt, 1 teaspoon black pepper, and 4 cups milk. Pour mixture into reserved drippings in skillet; cook over medium-high heat, whisking constantly, 10 to 12 minutes or until thickened. Serve gravy with steaks and mashed potatoes. Yield: 4 servings.

chicken Kiev (kee EHV) A boneless chicken breast wrapped around a cold piece of herbed butter and secured tightly with wooden picks. The chicken packet is breaded and fried until crisp on the outside. When served and sliced open, the chicken oozes fragrant butter.

chickpea These round, irregular-shaped buff-colored legumes have a firm texture and mild, nutlike flavor. Also called garbanzo beans, chickpeas are used frequently in Mediterranean and Middle Eastern cuisines, especially for soups, stews, and salads. Chickpeas are readily available canned or dried.

chicory (CHIHK uh ree) A salad green that's also called "curly endive"; it forms a head with crisp, frilly, dark green leaves. Chicory has a pleasantly bitter tang and a prickly texture. Radicchio is a red variety of chicory. Chicory roots can be ground into a coffee enhancer, which also is called chicory. (*see also* **curly endive, endive, lettuce,** *and* **radicchio**)

> ### TEST KITCHEN SECRET
>
> *We never see salad recipes that call for just chicory because they would be way too bitter. Instead, we frequently mix it in with milder lettuces, such as Bibb or Boston lettuce. It's also good mixed in salads that contain nuts and fruits.* VANESSA MCNEIL

chiffonade (shihf uh NAHD) Finely sliced or shredded greens or herbs used as a garnish. This term can also refer to a salad dressing that has been embellished with shredded hard-cooked egg, herbs, beets, or onions.

> ### TIMESAVING TIP
>
> To quickly make a chiffonade, tightly roll up leaves of basil or lettuce, and slice thinly with a knife or kitchen shears to make long shreds.

chiffon cake A light sponge cake, similar to angel food cake, it depends on beaten egg whites for its airy texture. It's richer than angel food cake because it includes oil, egg yolks, and leavening. (*see also* **cake**)

CHIFFON CAKE

1 cup all-purpose flour
1½ teaspoons baking powder
¼ teaspoon salt
1 cup sugar, divided
¼ cup vegetable oil
4 large eggs, separated
¼ cup water
1 teaspoon vanilla extract
½ teaspoon cream of tartar

• Sift together flour, baking powder, salt, and ½ cup sugar in a large mixing bowl. Make a well in center; add oil, egg yolks, water, and vanilla. Beat at high speed with an electric mixer about 5 minutes or until satiny smooth.
• Beat egg whites and cream of tartar in a large mixing bowl at high speed until soft peaks form. Add remaining ½ cup sugar, 2 tablespoons at a time, beating until stiff peaks form. Pour egg yolk mixture in a thin, steady stream over entire surface of egg whites; gently fold whites into yolk mixture.
• Pour batter into an ungreased 10-inch tube pan, spreading evenly with a spatula. Bake at 325° for 1 hour or until cake springs back when lightly touched. Invert pan; cool 40 minutes. Loosen cake from sides of pan, using a narrow metal spatula; remove from pan. Yield: 1 (10-inch) cake.

chiffon pie A single-crust pie with a fluffy sweet cream or custard filling that's lightened with stiffly beaten egg whites and sometimes gelatin.

chile bean paste A paste made from fermented fava beans, flour, red chiles, and sometimes garlic. It's used as a flavoring in Chinese cuisines, particularly Szechuan-style dishes, and is available in Asian markets and large supermarkets. (*see also* **fava bean**)

chile oil Vegetable oil that contains whole or ground bits of dried red chiles steeped in the oil to impart flavor and color. Chile oil typically has a reddish color and is used as a cooking oil and flavoring in Asian cuisine.

chile pepper A smooth-skinned pod of the Capsicum family. These peppers range in flavor from mild to fiery hot and vary in color from yellow to red or green. They vary in size from long and narrow to plump and round. Some varieties of chile peppers are eaten fresh, and other are used dried; some are also available canned. Chile peppers are also used to make chile paste, hot sauce, ground red pepper, and dried red pepper flakes. **Storage:** Fresh chiles can be stored in the vegetable drawer of the refrigerator. (*see also* **Anaheim chile pepper, chipotle chile pepper, habanero chile pepper,** *and* **peppers**)

RESCUE for working with hot peppers: After working with chile peppers, it's important to wash your hands thoroughly to avoid accidentally burning the eyes or skin. Wearing rubber gloves when preparing chile peppers will remedy this.

chiles rellenos (CHEE leh rreh YEH nohs) A Mexican dish of mild roasted chiles stuffed with cheese, then dipped in an egg batter and fried.

chili con carne (CHIHL ee kon KAHR nay) This hearty dish is a mixture of cubed or ground beef and chile peppers or chili powder. The stewlike mixture originated in Texas, where it's often referred to as a bowl of red. In Texas, they don't add beans to the mixture. But in may other parts of the country, beans are considered necessary, as are tomatoes or tomato sauce, and onions. Just as the ingredients vary, so does the flavor; it can range from hot to mild, depending on the amount and type of peppers.

chili powder A powdered seasoning mixture of dried chiles, garlic, oregano, cumin, coriander, and cloves. It's used most often in Southwestern and Mexican dishes. (*see also* **spice**)

chili sauce A spicy ketchup-like sauce made from tomatoes, chile peppers or chili powder, onions, green peppers, vinegar, sugar, and spices.

chill To cool to below room temperature in the refrigerator or over ice.

chimichanga (chee mee CHAN gah) A Mexican deep-fried burrito filled with chicken, beef, or pork, refried beans, and cheese, and garnished with sour cream, salsa, pico de gallo, guacamole, and shredded cheese.

Chinese cabbage This is a name given to a variety of Asian cabbages. Chinese cabbages are not at all like head cabbages; they're more like a cross between celery and lettuce with crinkly, thickly veined leaves, and they're generally crisp with a mild flavor. They can be eaten raw, sautéed, baked, or braised. Purchase them at most Asian markets and large supermarkets. There are two basic kinds:
- **bok choy,** an elongated cabbage with long, white, celery-like stalks and large deep green leaves. Bok choy has a sweet, mild, cabbage-like flavor.
- **napa,** an elongated, tightly curled cabbage with white ribs and frilly pale green tips. It's crunchy and slightly sweeter than regular head cabbage.
Storage: Refrigerate all Chinese cabbage in plastic wrap up to a week. (*see also* **cabbage** *and* **bok choy**)

> ### TEST KITCHEN SECRET
>
> *We've seen a growing use of Chinese cabbages in Asian stir-fries, salads, and as fillings for egg rolls, spring rolls, and won tons. If you can't find bok choy or napa, substitute regular head cabbage.* MARGARET MONROE DICKEY

Chinese cuisine The various cuisines of China are noted for their great contribution to the world of food. The cuisine has been divided into five cooking styles based on the different regions of China:
- **Szechuan** cooking from the western part of China features hot, spicy dishes.
- **Cantonese** cooking from the southeastern coast of China is famous for its roasting and grilling meat and also for fried rice.
- **Fukien** cooking from the east coast is noted for soups and seafood dishes.
- **Peking** cooking from the Yellow River basin in the northernmost part of China is famous for Peking duck, dumplings, and pancakes.
- **Honan** cooking from the central area and lower plains of the Yangtze; is the home of sweet-and-sour cooking.

These different regional cuisines share a common base of procedures and techniques that are perceived as being Chinese, and three aromatic flavoring ingredients that are indispensable to all the cuisines: fresh ginger, soy sauce, and green onions.

Chinese noodle A variety of noodles used in Asian cooking such as:
- **cellophane:** Thin, transparent flavorless noodles made from ground mung beans. They're cooked in a liquid or deep-fried. They might also be called bean threads or bean noodles.
- **Chinese egg:** Very fine noodles that taste and look like regular noodles; they're made from wheat flour.
- **rice sticks:** Transparent, flavorless rice flour noodles similar to cellophane.
(*see also* **Asian noodle, cellophane noodles, noodle,** *and* **rice sticks**)

chipotle chile pepper (chih POHT lay) A smoked jalapeño pepper available dried, canned, and pickled. If dried, it has a dark red color with a wrinkled skin and a smoky, slightly sweet, hot flavor. They're typically canned in adobo sauce, which can be used as a seasoning along with the chipotles. Chipotles are added to stews and sauces; the pickled variety often is eaten as appetizers. (*see also* **adobo sauce, chile pepper,** *and* **peppers**)

chips The British word for what's known in America as French fries. British potato chips are called crisps.

chitterlings The small intestines of freshly slaughtered pigs or hogs; chitterlings are cleaned and simmered until tender. Then they can be battered and fried or cooked in cornbread.

Southernism

Farm cooks in the Old South considered it necessary to use every part of the animals they butchered for food. The making of chitterlings (chitlin' or chitling as they're called in the South) were simply part of the process. One of the South's many food festivals, the Chitlin' Strut, is held in late November in Salley, South Carolina.

chive A member of the onion and leek family, this fragrant herb has slender green, hollow stems and blooms a purple flower. Chives have a mild onion flavor, and they're generally used fresh, although chopped chives are available frozen and freeze-dried. Fresh chives can be snipped with kitchen shears to the desired length, and are delicious in many cooked dishes as well as cold salads. **Storage:** Store fresh chives in a plastic bag in the refrigerator up to a week.

chocolate We revere chocolate for its crisp snap when we bite into it, and savor the melt-on-the-tongue texture when we don't. How is this flavorful tantalizing treat made? Cacao beans are roasted, ground, and refined to make pure chocolate. Pure chocolate is about 50 percent cocoa butter, which gives chocolate its smooth texture. When most of the cocoa butter is removed from pure chocolate, the remaining product is cocoa powder. Chocolate is available in squares, chunks, and morsels as well as candies, syrup, ice cream toppings, and chocolate milk.

There are many different types of choco-

Q **Can I make a substitution if I don't have the kind of chocolate that my recipe calls for?**

A Our recipes specify the type chocolate we used, but if you need to make a substitution, here's a guide:
• For every 1-ounce square of unsweetened chocolate, you can substitute 3 tablespoons cocoa plus 1 tablespoon of shortening.
• For 1 cup semisweet chocolate morsels or for 6 ounces semisweet chocolate squares, you can substitute 2 ounces unsweetened chocolate, ½ cup sugar, and 2 tablespoons of shortening.
• For one 4-ounce bar sweet baking chocolate, you can substitute ¼ cup cocoa, ⅓ cup sugar, and 3 tablespoons shortening.

late and chocolate products. Among them:

- **Sweet chocolate:** Made of at least 15 percent pure chocolate, extra cocoa butter, and sugar. Includes sweet and dark chocolate.
- **Milk chocolate:** Made of at least 10 percent pure chocolate, extra cocoa butter, sugar, and milk solids. Its most popular form is the candy bar.
- **Semisweet chocolate:** Made of at least 35 percent pure chocolate, extra cocoa butter, and sugar. It includes bittersweet chocolate and chocolate morsels.
- **Unsweetened chocolate:** Made of pure chocolate with no sugar or flavoring. It includes baking chocolate, bitter chocolate, and plain chocolate; it's used only for baking and cooking.
- **Couverture chocolate:** A professional quality chocolate that contains at least 32 percent cocoa butter. It's usually available in special candy-making shops.
- **Chocolate products:** Not made from chocolate and contain oil rather than cocoa butter. Includes chocolate-flavored bark coating.
- **White chocolate:** Contains no cocoa solids and is not really a chocolate. It's a blend of vegetable fat, sugar, dry milk solids, vanilla, and cocoa butter.

Q Sometimes my chocolate looks gray. Can I still use it?

A This gray covering is called "bloom" and does not affect the taste or cooking quality; it will disappear when the chocolate is heated. Bloom develops when chocolate is stored in warm or humid conditions.

TIMESAVING TIP
For quick, velvety melted chocolate, put squares or morsels into a heavy-duty zip-top plastic bag, and drop the bag into a small bowl. Pour very hot tap water or boiling water over the bag, and let it sit a few minutes until the chocolate melts. Then, if desired, you can snip a tiny hole in one corner of the bag with scissors, and squirt the chocolate decoratively onto dessert plates, over ice cream, or into a recipe that calls for melted chocolate.

Storage: Store tightly covered in a cool, dry place. In hot weather, you may want to refrigerate chocolate, but wrap it in foil and seal in a plastic bag so it won't absorb odors from other foods. When bringing refrigerated chocolate to room temperature, leave it wrapped so moisture doesn't condense on it; moisture will cause it to lump or seize if |melted.

Hints for Melting:
Chocolate can be melted in a heavy pan over low heat on the cooktop or in a microwave-safe container in the microwave oven. Be sure all utensils are very dry because even a little water will cause the chocolate to stiffen and become lumpy or seize. To melt in the microwave oven, place 1 cup chocolate pieces or

RESCUE for seized chocolate:
If chocolate seizes while melting, try stirring a tablespoon of vegetable oil or shortening (per 6 ounces chocolate) into the lumpy mixture and keep cooking over low heat. Sometimes the extra fat will smooth out things.

6 (1-ounce) squares of chocolate in a microwave-safe measuring cup or custard cup, and microwave, uncovered, at MEDIUM (50% power) for 2 to 3 minutes or until soft enough to stir smooth. (*see also* **cocoa**)

cholesterol (koh LESS ter all) A complex fatty alcohol, essential for the proper working of the digestive and nervous systems, found in foods of animal origin or saturated fats. There are many kinds of cholesterol; the main two are LDL or low density lipoprotein, and HDL or high density lipoprotein. LDL comes from foods high in saturated fat and cholesterol and is considered "bad cholesterol" because it clogs arteries with fatty deposits. HDL is beneficial and helps keep arteries clear; it's not affected by the type of fats you eat, but by weight, exercise, and smoking. (*see also* **fats and oils**)

chop A small cut of meat taken from the rib section that includes part of the rib. Pork, veal, and lamb chops are the most popular.

chopping Cutting food with a knife or cleaver into small, irregular pieces. A food processor may also be used to chop food. Cutting boards and sharp knives are crucial for quicker chopping. Many professionals suggest quickly sharpening knives with a sharpening steel after each use. A chef's knife or a mezzaluna (a curved blade with a wooden handle at each end) can also make quick work of chopping. (*see also* **brunoise, concassé, cube, dice, julienne, knife, mince,** *and* **mirepoix**)

Q **Is there really a difference between chopping, mincing, cubing, and dicing?**

A Yes! *Chopping* refers to cutting food into irregular pieces about the size of peas. *Mincing* is chopping food into tiny irregular pieces. *Cubing* is cutting food into uniform, same-size pieces, usually about ½ inch large. And *dicing* is similar to cubing, except the pieces are ⅛ to ¼ inch on each side. Chefs sometimes use these terms to designate the differences in chopping: brunoise, concassé, julienne, and mirepoix.

READER TIP
"I use my food processor all the time; it makes it easy to chop onion, nuts, breadcrumbs, and parsley. I like to chop them ahead of time and keep them on hand in the freezer. It makes cooking quicker." A.H., Macon, GA

chopsticks A pair of slender, cylindrical, and slightly pointed sticks made of ivory, plastic, wood, or metal. The sticks are held between the thumb and fingers of one hand and used to move food during eating or cooking. They are mainly used in Asian countries.

chop suey (chop SOO ee) An Asian-American dish of stir-fried beef, pork, chicken, or shrimp combined with bean sprouts, mushrooms, water chestnuts, bamboo shoots, and onions in a starchy sauce served over rice.

chorizo (chor EE zoh) A ground pork sausage flavored with garlic, chili powder, and other spices, often used in Mexican and Spanish cuisines. Mexican chorizo is made with fresh pork, while the Spanish version uses smoked pork. The casing is usually removed before sausage is cooked. (*see also* **sausage**)

choux pastry (SHOO) A classic French pastry dough used to make éclairs, and cream puffs. The unique, sticky, pastelike dough is made with boiling water, milk, butter, flour, and eggs. The mixture bakes into pastry with a hard, crisp exterior and a nearly hollow interior. After baking, choux puffs may be split and filled with custard or whipped cream. (*see also* **cream puff** *and* **éclair**)

chowchow A zesty mustard-flavored vegetable and pickle relish. It's typically made of cabbage, hot and sweet peppers, cucumbers, and onions in a sugar and vinegar brine. Chowchow is served as a condiment with meats and cooked vegetables.

Southernism

This vegetable relish has appeared in many early Southern cookbooks as "piccalilli" and "Indian pickle." The vegetables were chopped, cooked, seasoned, and put up in jars to be enjoyed year round.

chowder A thick, hearty soup generally made from fish and shellfish, and often vegetables, usually potatoes. Clam chowder is one of the most well-known chowders. (*see also* **clam chowder**)

Q **What's the difference between New England-style and Manhattan-style chowder?**

A The New England chowder is made with milk or cream, and the Manhattan chowder is made with tomatoes.

chow mein (chow MAYN) An Asian-American dish that contains meat, poultry, or shrimp, and crisp-tender bean sprouts, water chestnuts, bamboo shoots, mushrooms, and onions. The dish is served over fried noodles or crisp chow mein noodles, which are available in cans or packages.

chuck An inexpensive cut of beef taken from the area between the neck and shoulder blade. The most popular cuts of chuck are roasts, cubed steaks, and ground chuck. Since this is a tougher cut of meat, it must be cooked slowly by stewing or braising. (*see also* **beef**)

chutney (CHUHT nee) A spicy East Indian relish that generally contains fruit, vinegar, sugar, and spices, although it can also contain vegetables. The texture can range from smooth to chunky, and the flavor can be sweet to tart and fiery. Chutney might include mangoes, raisins, tomatoes, apples, peaches, and other ingredients. It's usually served with cheese or curried dishes, or as a condiment for cooked vegetables or meats.

cider Made by pressing juice from apples. Before being fermented, it's sweet cider; after fermentation it's hard cider. Apple cider is also used to make vinegar and applejack brandy. (*see also* **applejack** *and* **cider vinegar**)

cider vinegar Vinegar made from apple cider. It has a pale brown color and a strong, some say harsh flavor. (*see also* **vinegar**)

cilantro (sih LAHN troh) The fresh, bright green lacy leaves from the coriander plant that have a pungent fragrance and taste. It's also known as Chinese parsley. Many describe the flavor as (pleasantly) soapy tasting. Cilantro is definitely an acquired taste, and strong opinions prevail; people either love it or loathe it. Cilantro is widely used in Mexican, Asian, and Caribbean cuisines. Find it year-round in most supermarkets. Refrigerate it up to 1 week in a plastic bag. (*see also* **coriander** *and* **herbs**)

cinnamon The inner bark of a tropical evergreen tree. The bark is harvested, dried, and sold as cinnamon sticks or ground into powder. The spice has a dark, reddish brown color with a strong, spicy-sweet flavor and aroma. In addition to ground and stick, oil of cinnamon is available. (*see also* **spice**)

Q **How can I use cinnamon sticks for baking? Also, how do I use oil of cinnamon?**

A Cinnamon sticks can be grated with a grater that has small, fine holes and used as ground cinnamon. The sticks are also nice used as swizzle sticks in hot beverages, especially hot apple cider. Oil of cinnamon is used to flavor hard candies.

cioppino (chuh PEE noh) A stew made with tomatoes and a variety of fish and shellfish. It's popular in the San Francisco area, where Italian immigrants are credited with creating the dish.

citric acid (SIHT richk) This white powder is extracted from citrus and other acidic fruits. It has a strong, tart taste and is used as a preservative and flavoring agent in foods and beverages. Citric acid can be found in health food stores, in the canning section of large supermarkets, or it's available online at **americanspice.com** if difficult to find. Sometimes it's labeled "sour salt" and found with kosher foods. (*see also* **acid**)

citron (SIHT ron) A semitropical citrus fruit that's similar to a large lemon and has a thick, yellow-green rind. Citron flesh is very sour and not suitable for eating raw; instead, the thick peel is candied and marketed during the holiday season to use in fruitcake. It can be purchased in pieces, diced, and as part of mixed candied fruits. For maximum freshness, freeze in an airtight freezer bag.

citrus fruit Tropical fruits that are high in vitamin C, including citron, grapefruit, kumquats, lemons, limes, oranges, and tangerines. The fruits generally range in flavor from tart to sweet, and in color from orange and yellow to green.

Storage: Store for 2 or 3 weeks in the crisper drawer of the refrigerator.

TIMESAVING TIP

To get more juice when squeezing your own citrus, start with fruits that are heavy for their size; they contain more juice. Leave the fruit out at room temperature before juicing, and roll it on the counter under the palm of your hand a few seconds before you start. You can also consider using the microwave oven to warm the fruit; microwave it on HIGH for 15 to 30 seconds before juicing.

citrus stripper A special kitchen tool that uses a metal notched edge to cut ⅛-inch-wide strips from the rind of citrus fruits.

citrus zester This tool is similar to a citrus stripper, except the cutting edge of the zester has five very tiny holes which, when pulled across the surface of a lemon or orange, makes threadlike strips of peel or zest.

clafouti (kla foo TEE) A country-French dessert consisting of fruit, usually cherries, and a cake or custardlike topping.

clam This bivalve mollusk, found in coastal saltwater, has either a hard or soft back-hinged shell. The meat inside the shell is pinkish-tan to gray in color, often chewy, and has a mild to sweet flavor. Clams are sold live in the shell, fresh shucked, canned, and smoked. Live hard-shell clams should have shells that are moist and tightly closed or that snap close when tapped. Lightly touch the protruding neck of a soft-shell clam; if it moves, it's alive. If it doesn't move, the clam is probably not safe to eat. Discard suspicious clams, and never harvest them in areas of contaminated water. Fresh, shucked clams should be plump with clear liquid. For best taste and texture, gently steam or bake fresh clams. Hard-shell clams found on the East Coast come in three shell diameter sizes: littleneck, which is less than 2 inches; cherrystone, about 2½ inches; and chowder, about 3 inches. Soft shell clams have thin, brittle shells and don't completely close because they have necks that stick out between the shells. The most common East Coast soft-shell clam is the steamer clam.

Q **How do I shuck fresh hard-shell clams?**

A Start by cleaning the shells with a vegetable brush under cold running water; then soak the clams in a mixture of ⅓ cup salt per gallon of water for 15 minutes, discarding any clams that do not sink to the bottom. Drain and rinse the clams with cool water. Next, hold the clam with the hinged back against a heavy cloth in the palm of your hand; working over a plate to catch the juices, insert a sturdy blunt-tipped knife between the shell halves. Move the blade around the clam, cutting the muscles that hold the shell together. Twist the knife slightly to pry open the shell. Then cut the meat from the shell, saving the meat and juice.

TEST KITCHEN SECRET

Clams are delicate, so cook them gently. When baking shucked clams, they're done when the edges become firm, but the centers are still soft. Steamed clams are done when their shells open. VANESSA MCNEIL

TIMESAVING TIP Chill live clams before shucking to make them easier to open.

Storage: Cover live clams with a moist cloth and refrigerate up to 2 days. Shucked clams will keep in the refrigerator up to 4 days, or they may be frozen in their liquid up to 3 months. (*see also* **mollusk**)

clam chowder A hearty soup or stew made with fresh or canned clams. There are two main types: Manhattan style, which is tomato-based, and New England style, which is milk or cream-based. (*see also* **chowder**)

MANHATTAN CLAM CHOWDER

4 slices bacon, coarsely chopped	2 cups diced potatoes
1 onion, chopped	½ teaspoon salt
2 celery ribs, chopped	¼ teaspoon dried thyme
1 garlic clove, minced	2 (6½-ounce) cans minced
2 cups water	clams, undrained
1 (28-ounce) can whole tomatoes,	2 tablespoons cornstarch
undrained and chopped	

• Cook bacon in a Dutch oven until lightly browned. Add onion, celery, and garlic; sauté until tender. Add water and next 4 ingredients. Cook, covered, over medium heat 20 minutes or until potatoes are tender.
• Drain clams; reserve liquid. Add cornstarch to liquid; stir until smooth. Stir clams and liquid into vegetable mixture. Bring to a boil over medium heat, stirring constantly; cook 1 minute or until slightly thickened. Yield: 10 cups.

claret (KLAR iht) A term used in the United States to describe a light, red table wine made from red wine grapes. In England, claret refers to any red wine from the Bordeaux region of France. (*see also* **wine**)

clarified butter (KLAIR ih fyd) Also known as "drawn" butter, this is unsalted butter that has been slowly melted, allowing most of the water to evaporate and the milk solids to separate and sink to the bottom of the pan, leaving golden clarified butter on top. Clarified butter has a high smoke point, which makes it ideal for sautéing at high temperatures. It's also a simple classic accompaniment for dipping lobster. The traditional way to clarify butter is to melt it over low heat; the fat rises to the top and the milk solids sink to the bottom. Skim off the white froth that appears on top, and strain off the clear, yellow butter, keeping back the sediment of milk solids. (*see also* **butter**)

TIMESAVING TIP

A quick way to clarify butter is to put the unmelted butter into a fat separator cup. Microwave the butter briefly until melted. The milky layer will pour out through the spout, leaving you with clarified butter in a hurry. Clarified butter may be chilled until ready to use, then reheated; or you can freeze it up to 2 months.

clarify (KLAIR ih fy) To clear a cloudy liquid such as broth by removing suspended particles and sediment. One way to clarify is to add egg whites or egg shells to a liquid and simmer for 10 to 15 minutes; then cool for about an hour, and pour the mixture through cheesecloth or a sieve to strain residue.

clay pot Unglazed, clay cooking pots are porous and promote slow, moist, even cooking. The most popular food cooked in clay pots is chicken, though meats, fish, and vegetables are also suitable. Clay pots are meant for oven cooking and most are microwave safe. They should be soaked in cold water before every use; when heated, steam from the wet clay helps cook the food. Most clay pots are not dishwasher-safe. To clean, scrub with a nylon pad; if needed, soak overnight in water. Store with the top inverted in the pot.

cleaver A large, heavy, almost rectangular knife often used by butchers and Chinese cooks. Its flat side powerfully pounds meats or crushes garlic, while its sharp blade cuts though bones and chops vegetables with finesse.

clementine (KLEHM uhn tyn) (*see* **mandarin orange**)

clotted cream A thick cream, also known as "Devonshire" cream, made from unpasteurized milk gently heated until a semisolid layer of cream forms on top. After cooling, the thickened cream can be spread on scones or bread or served over fresh fruit. To store, cover and chill up to 4 days.

clove A dark reddish brown, nail-shaped, pungent-sweet spice. Cloves are the dried unopened flower bud of the tropical evergreen clove tree. Purchase whole or ground cloves to flavor a variety of dishes, from desserts to meats to pickles. This term also refers to a segment of a bulb of garlic. (*see also* **spice**)

club sandwich A double-decker sandwich made of 3 slices of toasted or untoasted bread layered with chicken or turkey, lettuce, tomato, and bacon. They're often sliced into triangles before serving, to show off the layers.

CLASSY CLUB SANDWICHES

1 (8-ounce) carton sour cream	4 slices Swiss cheese
2 tablespoons prepared horseradish	8 lettuce leaves
2 teaspoons honey mustard	¾ pound thinly sliced turkey
¼ teaspoon garlic salt	8 tomato slices
⅛ teaspoon white pepper	4 bacon slices
¾ pound thinly sliced ham	16 pitted ripe olives
12 slices whole wheat bread, toasted	16 pimiento-stuffed olives

• Combine first 5 ingredients; stir well. Place 3 ounces of ham on each of 4 slices of bread. Top each with 1 to 2 teaspoons spread, 1 slice cheese, a lettuce leaf, and another slice of bread. Place 3 ounces of turkey on each slice, and add 1 teaspoon spread, lettuce leaf, 2 slices tomato, and 1 slice bacon. Top with the remaining slices of bread.
• Skewer olives on each of 16 wooden picks. Cut each sandwich into 4 triangles, and secure each quarter with a pick. Chill leftover sour cream mixture to serve with roast beef or other sandwiches. Yield: 4 servings.

coagulate To transform a food from a liquid or semiliquid state to a drier, more solid state. For example, when an egg is heated, it changes from semiliquid to semisolid.

coat To cover a food with an outer coating. This process usually involves dipping the food into beaten eggs or milk before dredging in breadcrumbs, flour, seasonings, or a batter. The food is usually fried or baked. Sweets may also be coated with chocolate or various glazes. (*see also* **breading** *and* **dredge**)

cobbler A deep-dish baked dessert made with a fruit filling and a top crust of biscuit-like dough or pastry, which can be a single layer, strips, or cut into individual biscuits or "cobbles."

Southernism

Summer is cobbler time in the South. According to the cooks at Peach Park, off Interstate 65 in Chilton County Alabama, customers stand in line with spoons and bowls ready, waiting to devour their choice of syrupy-sweet peach, blueberry, or blackberry cobbler. Remember, cobblers are homey desserts that don't have to look picture-perfect.

OLD-FASHIONED BLACKBERRY COBBLER

4 cups fresh blackberries	1 tablespoon lemon juice
or 2 (16-ounce) packages	Pastry
frozen blackberries, thawed	2 tablespoons butter or mar-
¾ cup sugar	garine, melted
3 tablespoons all-purpose flour	Whipping cream
1½ cups water	Sugar

• Place berries in a lightly greased 2-quart baking dish. Combine ¾ cup sugar and flour; add water and lemon juice, mixing well. Pour sugar mixture over berries; bake at 350° for 15 minutes. Place Pastry over hot berries; brush with butter.

• Bake at 425° for 20 minutes or until Pastry is golden. Serve warm with whipping cream, and sprinkle each serving with sugar. Yield: 8 servings.

READER TIP

"My mother always said to get the cobbler filling hot and bubbly before adding the pastry. I think the heat from the hot fruit helps cook the topping more evenly." V.L.M., Atlanta, GA

PASTRY

1¾ cups all-purpose flour	¼ cup shortening
2 to 3 tablespoons sugar	⅓ cup whipping cream
2 teaspoons baking powder	⅓ cup buttermilk
1 teaspoon salt	

• Combine first 4 ingredients; cut in shortening with a pastry blender until mixture is crumbly; stir in whipping cream and buttermilk. Knead dough 4 or 5 times; roll to ¼-inch thickness on a lightly floured surface. Cut dough to fit baking dish. Yield: pastry for 1 cobbler.

Cobb salad A main-dish salad made famous at Hollywood's Brown Derby Restaurant. It consists of chopped chicken or turkey, tomatoes, avocado, bacon, hard-cooked eggs, scallions, Cheddar cheese, watercress, and lettuce dressed with a vinaigrette, and garnished with blue cheese.

cocktail A drink made of alcohol mixed with juice, soda, or other ingredients. Cocktails at typically served before a meal or at a party and might be called a "mixed" drink. The term "cocktail" also refers to an appetizer served before a meal.

cocktail sauce A spicy condiment often served with seafood. It's made of ketchup or chili sauce, horseradish, Worcestershire sauce, lemon juice, and hot sauce.

cocoa (KOH koh) A brown unsweetened powder made by removing most of the cocoa butter from pure chocolate. There are several types of cocoa powder: unsweetened, which is pure chocolate powder, and Dutch-process, which has a more mellow flavor because it has been treated with an alkali to neutralize the acids of the cacao bean. Other variations include presweetened cocoa, a drink mix made of cocoa, sugar, and flavorings; and instant cocoa mix, made of cocoa, milk powder, and sugar. **Storage:** Cocoa will keep for several years stored in a cool, dry spot in a tightly covered container. (*see also* **chocolate**)

Q **Can I substitute cocoa in recipes that call for other types of chocolate?**

A It's always best to use the type of chocolate called for in a recipe, but if you're in a pinch, make the following substitution:
• Use 3 tablespoons unsweetened cocoa plus 1 tablespoon shortening or cooking oil for 1 (1-ounce) square of unsweetened chocolate.
• Use 1/4 cup unsweetened cocoa plus 1/3 cup sugar plus 3 tablespoons shortening to substitute for 4 ounces sweet chocolate.

TEST KITCHEN SECRET

Use regular unsweetened cocoa in recipes that have a lot of ingredients, a large amount of sugar, or if the ingredients will be cooked. Use Dutch-process when you'll taste the cocoa straight up, without much added sugar; it's great for dusting cakes and candies and in coffee drinks or hot cocoa. JAN MOON

cocoa butter (KOH koh) The cream-colored fat removed from cocoa beans during the process of making cocoa powder. It's used to make bar chocolate, white chocolate, and is sometimes an ingredient in cosmetics. (*see also* **chocolate**)

coconut The large husk-covered fruit of the tropical palm tree; it's filled with a milky liquid and sweet white meat. The coconut has a hard outer shell that's hairy with three soft spots, sometimes referred to as eyes, on one end. Once the outer shell is broken open, the nut inside has a dark brown skin covering the white, firm-textured coconut meat. Fresh coconuts are at their peak from October through December; canned, frozen, or packaged coconut is sold shredded, flaked, and grated in sweetened or unsweetened forms. Coconut cream, coconut milk, and coconut oil are also available.

Storage: Store whole coconuts up to 1 month. Store fresh coconut meat in the refrigerator 4 or 5 days, or freeze it up to 6 months. Unopened canned coconut can be kept at room temperature up to 18 months; if packaged in plastic bags, it will keep up to 6 months. After canned or packaged coconut is opened, refrigerate in an airtight container up to a week.

Q How do you crack a coconut?

A Start by piercing the three eyes of the shell with a long nail, screwdriver, or ice pick, and draining the milky liquid; this can be used as a beverage, but should not be confused with coconut milk (*see* **coconut milk**). Next, place the shell on a hard surface, and gently, but firmly, tap it all around with a hammer until it cracks and splits. Break the shell apart with your hands, and carefully cut the white meat from the shell; peel the brown skin from the coconut meat. The meat can be grated or chopped using a grater, food processor, or knife.

TIMESAVING TIP
Use a vegetable peeler to quickly shave pretty garnishes of coconut curls from a piece of fresh coconut.

coconut cream A rich coconut-flavored liquid made by pouring one part boiling water or milk over four parts shredded fresh coconut. The mixture is simmered until foamy, cooled, and then strained. The rich liquid is often used in Asian cooking. Find canned coconut cream in the ethnic foods section of most markets. (*see also* **cream of coconut**)

coconut milk A coconut-flavored liquid made by combining equal parts water and shredded fresh coconut, and simmering until foamy. The mixture is cooled and then strained and used to make curries and Asian and Caribbean dishes. Coconut milk is similar to coconut cream but is more diluted. Look for canned coconut milk in the ethnic foods section of most markets. (*see also* **cream of coconut**)

coconut oil A dense, white buttery oil obtained from pressed coconut meat; often used in commercial frying and as an ingredient in commercially packaged candies, cookies, and margarine. Coconut oil is high in saturated fat, so some manufacturers now replace it with unsaturated fats to please more health-conscious consumers. (*see also* **fats and oils**)

cod A lean saltwater fish with a white, delicately flavored firm flesh. Cod can be baked, poached, braised, broiled, fried, or grilled. It's sold both fresh and frozen in steaks or fillets. Pollock and haddock are members of the cod family and make good substitutes. (*see also* **fish**)

Q **Is scrod the same thing as cod?**

A Sort of…you sometimes see the term scrod used on restaurant menus to describe a small cod or haddock.

coddle A very gentle cooking method that usually involves a water bath procedure, although it can also mean cooking food directly in hot to simmering water; boiling water is too hot. Coddled eggs are sometimes cooked in individual egg coddler dishes. The eggs are cracked into the dishes, covered with lids, and lowered into simmering water. Soft-cooked coddled eggs have long been a delicacy alone or in Caesar salads, but the USDA no longer recommends eating them unless they're cooked until both the yolks and whites are firm to prevent the possibility of salmonella. (*see also* **egg**)

coeur à la crème (KEWR ah la KREHM) This French term meaning "heart with cream" describes a classic cheese dessert made in a special cheesecloth-lined heart-shaped perforated mold. Cream cheese is mixed with sour cream or whipping cream and placed into the mold and then refrigerated overnight to allow the whey, or liquid, to drain out. The pretty white cheese is inverted and garnished with colorful berries or sliced fruit.

coffee A dark brown aromatic beverage made from brewing roasted, ground coffee beans. Coffee is usually served hot, but can be served iced; it's also used to flavor other foods such as desserts. Coffee is sold as whole beans or ground and is available in a variety of roasts. The darker the roast, the more bitter the flavor. The brewing method determines how coarsely coffee should be ground; the shorter the brewing method, the finer the grind. Instant coffee comes in powder and freeze-dried crystals. Both ground and instant coffees may be flavored. Most of these forms are available in regular and decaffeinated versions. There are many different types of coffees and blends. The flavor and body are determined by the type of bean used, where it was grown and harvested, and how it was roasted. Popular roasts are **American** (produces a moderate brew), **French** (produces a stronger coffee), **Italian** (used for espresso), **European** (a blend of two-thirds heavy-roast beans and one-third regular-roast beans), and **Viennese** (a blend of one-third heavy-roast beans and two-thirds regular-roast beans). **Storage:** Always remember that fresh is best, so buy in small quantities and store in an airtight container at room temperature up to a week. If you must store coffee longer, refrigerate it up to 2 weeks, or freeze up to 3 months. (*continued on the following page*)

Q **What is decaffeinated coffee?**

A Decaffeinated coffee is made from coffee beans that have been soaked or steamed to allow the caffeine to diffuse from the beans. The process removes about 97 percent of the caffeine.

Tips for Perfect Coffee:
• Start with fresh beans. Buy only what you can drink. If you have more than a week's worth of coffee on hand, you have too much.
• A good rule to remember when buying coffee beans: Tropical names like Sumatra, Jamaica, and Kenya refer to the source of the beans, while European names like French, Italian, and Viennese describe the roast.
• Store beans at room temperature in an airtight container, and grind them just before brewing. Do not freeze or refrigerate unless necessary.

TIMESAVING TIP
Keeping coffee warm in an electric coffeemaker or on the cooktop will result in a burnt flavor. Instead, pour freshly made coffee into an insulated container to keep it flavorful for hours.

RESCUE for leftover coffee:
Coffee does not reheat well, so use cold, leftover coffee to make iced coffee or a cold coffee drink.

READER TIP
"When I've brewed more coffee than we care to drink, I pour the remainder into ice-cube trays and freeze it. The cubes are perfect in iced coffee—when they melt, they don't dilute the drink."
L.C., Alexandria, VA

• Use good-tasting water.
• Make sure your coffeemaker has the correct brewing time of between 4 and 7 minutes.
• Use 1 to 2 tablespoons of ground coffee for every 8 ounces of water, depending on personal preference.
• Brew coffee at 200°.
• Keep coffee brewing equipment clean.

coffee cake A sweet, leavened breadlike cake that's usually eaten for breakfast or brunch. Coffee cakes can be flavored with nuts, fruit, and spices, and topped with frosting or glaze. They're usually best served warm and accompanied with a cup of coffee.

Cognac (KON yak) Named for the town of Cognac in France, this brandy is considered to be the finest of all brandies. To be a true Cognac, it must be aged in oak barrels for a minimum of three years; some are aged as long as 50 to 55 years. (*see also* **brandy**)

Cointreau (KWAHN troh) A clear, colorless orange French liqueur. (*see also* **liqueur**)

cola (KOH lah) A sweet carbonated soft drink flavored with a syrup made from an extract of cola leaves, nuts, and other flavorings. In recent years, diet, caffeine-free, and flavored colas have gained in popularity.

Southernism

The heat and humidity of the South drives Southerners to drink lots of cola. Several types—Coca-Cola, Pepsi, Dr Pepper, and RC Cola—rose to fame in the South and went on to become global stars. Today, the headquarters for Coca-Cola is located in Atlanta and features a museum on the history of this famous refresher.

colander A bowl-shaped cooking utensil made of metal or plastic with many perforations and, usually, short legs on the bottom. It's used to drain liquids from solids. Metal colanders can also be used as a steamer basket when placed in a large saucepan.

colby cheese (KOHL bee) A mild, firm Cheddar-style cow's milk cheese developed in Colby, Wisconsin, but now made all over the world. (*see also* **cheese**)

cold cuts Thin slices of various meats such as ham, roast beef, salami, and turkey that are served cold. Sometimes sliced cheese qualifies as a cold cut when making a sandwich or salad.

coleslaw A salad of Dutch origin that features shredded cabbage tossed with a mayonnaise or vinaigrette dressing. There are numerous recipes for coleslaw; some include shredded carrots, pickles, red or green bell peppers, and onion.

TIMESAVING TIP

For easy coleslaw, purchase a prepared package of coleslaw mix in the produce section of your market. To save even more time, look for bottled coleslaw dressing on the salad dressing aisle.

OUR FAVORITE COLESLAW

2 (10-ounce) packages finely shredded cabbage	½ cup mayonnaise
1 carrot, shredded	¼ cup milk
½ cup sugar	¼ cup buttermilk
½ teaspoon salt	2½ tablespoons lemon juice
⅛ teaspoon pepper	1½ tablespoons white vinegar

• Combine cabbage and carrot in a large bowl. Whisk together sugar and remaining 7 ingredients until blended; toss with vegetables. Cover and chill at least 2 hours. Yield: 8 to 10 servings.

READER TIP

"For crisp coleslaw, I soak the shredded cabbage in ice water for an hour, then drain and pat it dry before adding the dressing." C.P., Richmond, VA

collards (KAHL uhrds) A variety of cabbage that has large, dark green leaves with torn-looking edges. Collards grow on tall, tough stems, and are sometimes referred to as "collard greens." The cooked leaves taste sweeter than turnip greens; some say their flavor is reminiscent of cabbage and kale. Fresh collards are available year-round.

Selection: Young collards with small leaves are more tender and less bitter. Avoid collards with large leathery leaves that are withered or that have yellow spots.

Storage: Wash collards (see Secret below), and pat dry. Place in a plastic bag, and refrigerate up to 5 days. (*see also* **greens**)

Southernism

Collards are a staple food in the lower Southern states. Most cooks aren't too thrilled about cleaning and cooking collards, but they all adore the eating, especially with cornbread, black-eyed peas, and sweet potatoes. Collards are traditionally cooked in a seasoned broth with pork to tame any bitter flavors.

COLLARD GREENS SOUP

1 (8-ounce) ham hock	½ cup water
2 (32-ounce) containers chicken broth	2 (16-ounce) packages fresh collard greens, chopped
2 bacon slices, chopped	⅓ cup whipping cream
2 teaspoons olive oil	2 tablespoons cider vinegar
⅓ cup diced onion	1 tablespoon hot sauce
2 celery ribs, diced	1 teaspoon pepper
3 tablespoons all-purpose flour	

• Bring ham hock and broth to a boil in a Dutch oven; partially cover, reduce heat, and simmer 30 minutes.

• Cook bacon in hot oil in a skillet until crisp; remove bacon, and drain, reserving drippings in skillet.

• Sauté onion and celery in drippings 5 minutes or until tender; add bacon.

• Stir together flour and ½ cup water until smooth. Stir into bacon mixture. Stir bacon mixture and collard greens into broth mixture. Cover; simmer, stirring often, 1 hour or until tender.

• Remove ham hock; cool slightly. Remove meat; discard bone. Dice meat, and return to soup. Stir in cream and remaining ingredients. Yield: 15 cups.

TEST KITCHEN SECRET

"*Be prepared—cleaning collard greens can be a lot of trouble. One way is to pull the leaves from the stems by hand. Another is to hold each leaf over the sink and slash the leaf from the stem with a knife. You can also use kitchen shears to trim leaves from the stems. And be sure to wash the leaves by hand, once in warm water, and three times in cold water to get rid of all the grit. Like all greens, collards cook down considerably. A good rule of thumb is that 1 pound of raw greens yields 1½ cups cooked.*" VIE WARSHAW

collins A tall iced cocktail made of citrus juice, sugar syrup, and soda water, and garnished with a slice of lemon. If made with gin, it's called a Tom Collins; if vodka, a John Collins.

comfort food Foods that are considered to be nurturing, wholesome, and soul-satisfying. These foods tend to bring to mind thoughts and memories of special times and special people. Some typical examples include meat loaf, macaroni and cheese, and peach cobbler.

compote (KAHM poht) A dish of fresh or dried fruit slowly cooked in a light sugar syrup. The fruit may be flavored with cinnamon or lemon zest and served warm or cold, as a dessert, or as a light side dish for breakfast or brunch. This term also refers to a deep, stemmed glass or silver dish used to hold candy, nuts, or fruits.

compound butter Butter that has been creamed and flavored with herbs, garlic, wine, shallots, or other ingredients. Compound butters are used to enhance the flavor of other dishes and are often used as a garnish.

concassé (kawn ka SAY) Vegetables coarsely chopped into about ¼-inch pieces. (*see also* **chopping**)

concentrate A process of making a mixture less dilute, usually by boiling to remove excess liquid. Soups, sauces, and gravies are frequently concentrated to thicken their consistency and to maximize their flavor. Fruit juices are sometimes concentrated and frozen; water must be added to dilute them.

> **TIMESAVING TIP**
> For faster concentration when cooking a juice or other liquid, use a saucepan with a wide bottom to allow for quicker evaporation.

conch (KONGK) A mollusk that lives in the warm saltwaters of the Caribbean Sea and the Florida Keys. Its home is a beautiful spiral shell that's also prized. Conch has a delicate flavor and can be eaten raw in a salad, breaded and deep-fried, or chopped and used in chowders. Conch needs to be tenderized by pounding before it's cooked. **Storage:** Summer is the season for fresh conch; it can be stored in the refrigerator up to 2 days. Sometimes conch can be purchased canned or frozen. (*see also* **mollusk**)

Southernism

When you venture as far south as the Florida Keys, be sure to seek out conch fritters or a bowl of conch chowder. These delicacies, rarely found on menus north of the Keys, are worth the trip.

conchiglie (kon KEE lyay) Italian for "seashells," the term describes shell-shaped pasta that resembles little conch shells. Conchiglie is traditionally topped with a meat sauce. (*see also* **conch** *and* **pasta**)

condensed milk (*see* **sweetened condensed milk**)

condiment (KON duh muhnt) A food item used to add flavor to another food. A condiment might be a savory, spicy, or salty accompaniment such as a sauce, pickle, or relish, or it could be as simple as ketchup or salt.

Southernism

Southerners never hesitate to add condiments to vegetables, meats, fried fish, and even rice. In most home-style restaurants, you'll find a cluster of condiments such as Tabasco® sauce (a hot red pepper sauce), pepper sauce (small whole hot green peppers in vinegar), salt, pepper, and ketchup. You'll find the same in many homes, along with chutney, chowchow, and bread and butter pickles.

confection (kuhn FEHK shuhn) A term for any kind of candy or other sweet treats including gingerbread, ice cream, and even marmalade.

confectioners' sugar (*see* **powdered sugar** *and* **sugar**)

confit (kohn FEE) A French method of preserving meat, usually goose, duck, or pork. The meat is cooked in its own fat and refrigerated in a pot covered with that same fat, which acts as a seal and preservative. This improves the tenderness and flavor of the meat.

congeal The transition of a food from a liquid to a solid, usually by chilling until it becomes set.

congealed salad A chilled salad or side dish made of gelatin (often fruit flavored), and fruit or vegetables. The shimmery combinations can be molded into special shapes or cut into squares, and are often served on lettuce with a topping of mayonnaise.

Southernism

With the advent of refrigeration and powdered gelatin, Southerners began concocting all sorts of congealed salads. One of the oldest combinations is from Florida and combines lime-flavored gelatin with grapes and fresh melon or papaya. And almost every Southern kitchen has a cranberry congealed salad for the winter holidays.

CRANBERRY SALAD

1 (12-ounce) package fresh cranberries
1 cup sugar
1 (8-ounce) can crushed pineapple, undrained
1 (3-ounce) package raspberry gelatin
1 envelope unflavored gelatin

½ cup cold water
1 (15-ounce) can mandarin orange sections, undrained
2 large celery ribs, diced
1 medium apple, diced
½ cup finely chopped pecans
1 cup miniature marshmallows

• Process cranberries and sugar in a food processor until cranberries are coarsely chopped. Add pineapple, and pulse 3 times.
• Sprinkle raspberry gelatin and unflavored gelatin over ½ cup cold water in a large saucepan; stir and let stand 1 minute.

• Cook over low heat, stirring until gelatin dissolves (about 2 minutes). Stir in cranberry mixture, oranges, and next 3 ingredients. Cool to room temperature. Stir in marshmallows, and pour into a lightly greased 13- x 9-inch dish. Cover and chill 8 hours. Yield: 8 servings.

conserve (kuhn SURV) A jam or preserve that has nuts added to the mixture. Conserves are used as spreads for biscuits or other breads.

consommé (KON suh may) A concentrated, clarified meat or fish broth served hot or cold as a soup or used to form the base for a sauce.

continental breakfast A light breakfast of pastry or toast and coffee, tea, or juice, as opposed to the hearty English breakfast that can also include eggs, meat, and cereal. (*see also* **English Breakfast**)

convection oven An oven that uses internal fans to move hot air around. The rapidly moving hot air speeds cooking times by about 25 percent over a conventional oven and also browns foods more evenly. Convection ovens may be a separate appliance or built in tandem with a conventional oven or microwave.

converted rice Rice that has been parboiled, a process where the rice is pressure-steamed, dried, and milled. Converted rice requires more cooking liquid and a longer cooking time than regular rice, but cooks fluffier and drier; it's sold under brand names such as Uncle Ben's. (*see also* **rice**)

cookie Small, sweet baked pastries that vary in shape, thickness, and texture. Cookies can be plain or decorated and range from thin and crisp to thick and chewy.

Types of Cookies:

There are five basic types:

• *Bar cookies* are made from fairly stiff dough and can be chewy to cakelike. They're cut into squares or rectangles after they're baked.

• *Cutout cookies* are made from fairly soft dough that might require chilling before rolled out and cut into various shapes with a cookie cutter.

Q How do I tell when cookies are done?

A We give a range of baking times in our recipes. If you prefer soft and chewy, take them out of the oven at the lower end of time. Leave cookies in 1 or 2 minutes longer to make them crisper. We often include the phrase "until lightly browned" to help determine doneness. Also, unless the recipe states otherwise, remove cookies from baking sheets immediately after removal from oven. Transfer cookies to a wire rack to cool, being careful not to stack them or to let the sides touch as they cool. Cookies firm up as they cool.

• *Drop cookies* are made from soft dough dropped by the spoonful onto baking sheets. They can be crisp, chewy, or cakelike.

• *Shaped cookies* are made from firm dough that may require chilling before shaping. They are molded by hand or shaped with a cookie mold, stamp, or press, and are usually very crisp. Some shaped cookies are made from a thin batter and fried such as pizelles. (*continued on the following page*)

• *Refrigerator cookies* are made from soft dough shaped into rolls and chilled or frozen before being sliced and baked. Refrigerator cookies tend to be crisp.

Storage: Let cookies cool completely on a wire rack before storing. Store soft, chewy cookies in an airtight container to keep them from drying out. After 3 days, these cookies may harden, but can be softened by placing an apple wedge on wax paper in the container. Store crisp cookies in a container with a loose-fitting lid. Bar cookies can be stored in their baking pan; seal the top of the pan with aluminum foil. Unfrosted bar cookies can be stacked and stored in airtight containers with wax paper between the layers. Unfrosted cookies freeze well for 8 months if packed in heavy-duty zip-top plastic bags, metal tins, or plastic freezer containers. To serve, thaw in the container for about 15 minutes. Cookie dough can be frozen up to 6 months. Thaw the dough in the refrigerator or at room temperature until it's the right consistency for shaping into cookies as the recipe directs. Some refrigerator cookies can be sliced straight from the freezer without thawing.

> **TIMESAVING TIP**
>
> When making cookies, line baking sheets with parchment paper or special baking paper with a nonstick coating. The cookies won't stick, the liners minimize burning, and cleanup's a breeze.

Test Kitchen Cookie Secrets:

• Avoid using tub butter or margarine products labeled spread, reduced-calorie, liquid, or soft-style; they contain less fat than regular butter or margarine, and do not make satisfactory substitutions.

• Prevent stiff cookie dough from straining handheld portable mixers by stirring in the last additions of flour by hand.

• Keep the mixing of cookie dough to a minimum; stir just until the flour disappears. Overmixing toughens the dough.

• Lightly grease baking sheets only if the recipe specifies, and use only vegetable cooking spray or solid shortening. Butter or margarine encourages burning.

> **READER TIP**
>
> *"I used to skip the step in some cookie recipes that called for chilling the dough. But I found that chilling made the dough much easier to work with, and my cookies looked prettier. Now if I don't have time to chill the dough, I freeze it to hurry it along, but only until it's firm enough to shape."* B.M., Atlanta, GA

• Drop cookies 2 inches apart on shiny, heavy aluminum baking sheets. Dark sheets may absorb heat, causing cookies to brown too much on the bottom; nonstick baking sheets work well if not too dark. Insulated baking sheets will require a slightly longer baking time.

• Use 1 teaspoon (not a measuring spoon) to pick up drop cookie dough and another to push the dough onto the baking sheet.

• For brownies, line a lightly greased baking pan with foil before spreading batter in the pan to bake. After baking, lift foil with uncut baked brownies out of pan, peel back the foil, and the brownies will be easy to cut.

• Bake one batch at a time on the middle oven rack; if you have to bake more than one at the same time in the same oven, rotate the sheets from the top to the bottom rack halfway through baking time.

- Check cookies for doneness at the minimum baking time to promote even browning.
- Transfer baked cookies to a wire rack immediately after baking unless otherwise directed.
- Allow baking sheets to cool before reusing between baking; wipe surface with a paper towel or scrape off crumbs with a metal turner.
- If you're short on wire racks, place a sheet of wax paper on the counter, and sprinkle with sugar. Transfer cookies from baking sheet to sugared paper; cookies will cool without getting soggy. (*see also* **baking dishes and pans** *and* **brownie**)

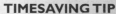

TIMESAVING TIP
When baking many batches of cookies, save time by spooning out the dough onto sheets of parchment paper, assembly-line fashion. Then slide each batch onto a baking sheet when ready to bake. Parchment eliminates the need to grease baking sheets.

cookie cutter A metal or plastic tool used to cut rolled cookie dough into various shapes. If the cookie cutter sticks to the dough when cutting cookies, dip the cutter into flour between every few cuts.

cookie mold A decorative mold used to create designs in some European cookie recipes. The dough is pressed into a floured mold, leveled off, and inverted onto a baking sheet.

cookie press Also called a "cookie gun," this tool consists of a hollow tube fitted at one end with a decorative template or nozzle and a plunger or trigger at the other end. The tube is filled with soft cookie dough that the plunger forces through the decorative tip.

cooking spray (*see* **vegetable cooking spray**)

cooking wine If labeled "cooking wine," it's an inexpensive, some say inferior, wine with added salt that would not be used for drinking purposes. Most cooks prefer to cook with a quality wine that they would be willing to drink and that complements the food being cooked.

cookware The kind and quality of pots and pans you own can greatly affect the outcome of a recipe. We suggest selecting a few pieces at a time and building your stock over time. Look for solid equipment that will last a lifetime, and won't warp, scorch, or dent. (*continued on the following page*)

RESCUE for dull pots and pans:
For copper cookware, mix a solution of 2 parts salt to 1 part vinegar and rub it lightly into the copper with a damp cloth; rinse and dry. *For stainless steel,* rub with dry baking soda and a moist cloth in the direction of the steel's grain; rinse and dry. Clean *aluminum cookware* with a paste of equal parts cream of tartar and water. Use the paste with a scrub brush. Always check with the manufacturer if you're unsure of what to do.

Cookware Materials: Different metals and alloys and different gauges or thicknesses work most effectively for different cooking tasks.

• *Aluminum cookware* heats rapidly, is durable, and is relatively inexpensive, but it does react with acid, which alters the taste and color of the food. It also tends to warp if not thick enough. Anodized aluminum has been treated to make it harder, denser, and resistant to corrosion.

• *Cast-iron* heats more slowly than other materials, but holds heat evenly, which makes it good for frying. It can react with acidic foods and impart a metallic taste. Enameled cast iron is prone to chipping and staining.

• *Copper cookware,* which is often lined with tin, is an excellent heat conductor, but is expensive and demands frequent polishing.

• *Stainless steel* and glass are poor conductors of heat but are non-reactive and easy to clean. However, clad stainless steel boasts rapid and uniform heat conduction, and aluminized steel also heats quickly and evenly, does not corrode, and is durable.

• *Enameled steel* is a good choice because it's heavy and durable and will not react with acidic foods.

• *Nonstick coated cookware* has been improved so that it does not affect the metal's ability to conduct heat. It's also durable and easy to clean. Nonstick cookware is helpful for making omelets, oatmeal, and rice, but it can hinder the browning of meats. Some nonstick cookware is also dishwasher safe.

Cookware Pieces You'll Need: Buy the best pots and pans you can afford. Consider buying individual pieces you know you'll use rather than a whole set. Look for pieces with thick bottoms, tight-fitting lids, and securely attached, heat-resistant handles.

• *Saucepans:* Select 1-, 2-, and 3-quart saucepans. Straight-sided saucepans with high sides are ideal for longer cooking, since the liquid will not boil away so quickly. Anodized aluminum or aluminized steel are good materials for saucepans.

• *Dutch oven:* A large round or oval pot with a lid and handles. The 8- to 9-quart size is the most useful size for a home kitchen. It can be made of enameled cast iron, regular cast iron, or other uncoated metals. A Dutch oven can be used for deep-frying, stewing, or simmering.

• *Stockpot:* This high, narrow pot is designed for minimal evaporation during long cooking. Most home cooks find the 10- to 12-quart stockpot to be the most useful. Stockpots are typically made of a heavy-gauge metal. It's often used for cooking pasta or soup, and has handles for easy lifting.

• *Double boiler:* It's a plus, but not absolutely necessary, to have a double boiler. This is basically a pair of stacking saucepans; a small amount of water is simmered in the lower pan, while ingredients to be heated gently, be kept warm, or to melt are placed in the top pan. Until you acquire a double boiler, you can improvise by placing a metal bowl over a saucepan of simmering water.

• *Sauté Pan:* A straight-sided skillet or frying pan that allows foods to be flipped and tossed with less spattering. The sides are typically 3 inches high; the pan itself may measure from 6 to 14 inches wide. They generally have a handle on one side and a lid.

• *Skillet:* A 12-inch heavy skillet with a lid will prove useful, as well as a 6-inch skillet for omelets, along with 8- and 10-inch skillets. These should be nonstick for healthy cooking. A well-seasoned cast-iron skillet is an inexpensive pan for making cornbread. Remember that a skillet or frying pan should have sides that flare outward, making it useful for cooking foods that must be stirred or turned out of the pan.

Q **How can I use my skillet in the oven if it's not ovenproof?**

A Wrap the handle in several layers of heavy-duty aluminum foil to protect it when finishing dishes, such as a frittata, in the oven.

• *A grill pan* is a griddle and grill in one. The ridged surface allows fat to drip away from food. Some are designed for use under the broiler and others for the cooktop. They're usually made of cast iron or anodized aluminum. (*see also* **baking dishes and pans, baking tools,** *and* **cast-iron cookware**)

cooling rack A grid of closely spaced metal wires resting on small feet that raise it above the level of the countertop. The raised surface allows air to circulate around baked goods while they cool and prevents them from getting soggy. You'll probably want to have two or three racks to handle multiple cake layers or sheets of cookies. Place the racks over a sheet of wax paper to catch the crumbs.

coquilles St. Jacques (koh KEEL san ZHAHK) A French dish of scallops cooked in a creamy wine sauce and topped with breadcrumbs or cheese. The mixture is traditionally spooned into a scallop shell and browned under the broiler before serving. Coquilles St. Jacques can be served as an entrée or as an elegant seated appetizer.

Q **What if I want to make coquilles St. Jacques, but don't have any scallop shells?**

A Scallop shells can usually be purchased at a kitchen supply store, but you can substitute individual au gratin dishes or tiny casserole dishes.

coral The roe or eggs of scallops or lobsters. They're typically eaten plain or added to a sauce or compound butter. When cooked, coral turns red.

cordial (*see* **liqueur**)

cordon bleu (kor dohn BLUH) A dish made of thin, boneless chicken breasts or veal scallops, topped with prosciutto or other ham, and Gruyère or Swiss cheese, then another thin piece of chicken or veal. The stacked meat and cheese is then breaded and sautéed until golden. Also a French term for "blue ribbon" that originally referred to an award given to outstanding women chefs; today it applies to any superior cook.

core To remove the central seed area from a fruit.

corer A utensil designed to remove the core from fruits or to hollow vegetables for stuffing. Corers are usually made of metal; an apple corer has a medium-length shaft with a circular cutting ring at the end; a pineapple corer has two concentric rings with serrated teeth—one ring removes the pineapple core and the other removes the outer pineapple shell.

coriander (KOR ee an der) A member of the parsley family, coriander is known for its seeds and dark green lacy leaves. The fresh leaves, considered an herb, are also known as cilantro and have a strong, pungent odor and flavor; they're used in Mexican, Asian, and Caribbean cuisines. The seeds, considered a spice, taste like a blend of lemon, sage, and caraway; they can be purchased ground or whole and are a major ingredient in curry powder and pickling spice. (*see also* **cilantro** *and* **herbs**)

corkscrew A tool used to remove a cork from a wine bottle.

corn We know corn as both a vegetable and a grain, which makes it one of our most important foods. The bright yellow or white kernels grow on a cob and are delicious boiled, steamed, baked, or creamed. The prized Southern variety of corn is "Silver Queen," a premium sweet white corn. If buying fresh corn, the peak season is May through September, but canned and frozen corn is plentiful anytime. Part of the value of corn is its versatility; it can be processed for oil, cornstarch, corn syrup, ground for cornmeal and flour, turned into popcorn, or fermented to make bourbon and beer.

RESCUE for corn past its peak:
To cook corn on the cob that's a day or so older than it should be, add a tablespoon of sugar, rather than salt, to the boiling water. Salt toughens corn kernels but sugar helps restore some of the natural sweetness. Bring the water to a boil, and add the corn; after the water returns to a boil, cook 3 more minutes.

Selection: The fresher the corn, the better it tastes. That's because as soon as it's picked, corn's sugar starts converting to starch, which lessens the natural sweetness. So, it's important to buy corn as soon as possible after it's picked. Look for ears with bright green, snug husks, golden brown silks, and plump, milky kernels. Fresh corn is best cooked and served the day it's purchased.

TIMESAVING TIP
For a quick addition to grilled meals, cook corn on the cob in the husks. Remove all but the innermost layer of husks, snip off the silk tassel with kitchen shears or scissors, and place the ears on the grill; cook, turning it often, until you can see the silhouette of the kernels through the husk, and the husk begins to pull away from the tip of the ear.

Storage: Refrigerate corn no more than 1 or 2 days. Remove the husks and silks just before cooking.

SOUTHERN-STYLE CREAMED CORN

8 ears fresh white corn
¼ cup butter or margarine
¼ cup water

½ cup half-and-half or milk
2 teaspoons cornstarch
½ teaspoon salt

• Cut off tips of corn kernels into a large bowl, scraping cobs well with a paring knife to remove all milk.

• Combine corn, butter, and water in a heavy saucepan; cover and cook over medium heat 10 minutes or until done, stirring occasionally.

READER TIP

When slicing corn from the cob, I set my tube pan or Bundt cakepan on the kitchen counter, and wedge the bottom of the cob in the hole of the pan. Then slice the kernels into the moat below. J.W., Winston-Salem, NC

• Combine half-and-half, cornstarch, and salt, whisking until cornstarch is blended; add to corn mixture, stirring well. Cover and cook 3 minutes or until thickened and bubbly, stirring often. Yield: 4 servings.

Q What's the trick to making creamed corn?

A First, be sure to get the freshest corn for this recipe because it will yield the most milk, which is what you'll need to make creamed corn. After slicing the kernels from the cob, reverse the knife and rub the dull side down the cob to extract the pulp and milk. Or, scrape the milk and pulp from the cob with a sturdy vegetable peeler.

TEST KITCHEN SECRET

"When I'm cleaning fresh corn on the cob, I wear a pair of rubber gloves to help remove stubborn silks. I just give the cob a quick twist while rubbing it down in my gloved hands, and in no time, the silks are off." VIE WARSHAW

cornbread A quick bread made of mostly cornmeal and usually a little flour that has a light, porous texture. Cornbread can be made in a square pan, but is most often made in a skillet. Corn muffins are made in a muffin pan, and corn sticks are made in a heavy cast-iron pan shaped like ears of corn. Corn pone is eggless cornbread made without flour and shaped into small ovals. Hush puppies are made from cornbread batter that's deep-fried.

Southernism

Cornbread carries a loyal following in the South. Its crispy crust and slightly gritty texture make it a popular staple— all by itself, crumbled over chili, or smothered in butter and honey. It's also a must for soaking up pot likker from greens and peas. And a well-seasoned cast-iron skillet for making cornbread is a must in Southern kitchens.

Cornbread can include flavorings such as cheese, onions, and bacon. True Southern cornbread has no sugar, but elsewhere it sometimes does. (*see also* **cornmeal, corn stick pan, hush puppy,** *and recipe on the following page*)

SKILLET CORNBREAD

2 teaspoons bacon drippings
1 large egg
2 cups buttermilk
1¾ cups white cornmeal

1 teaspoon baking powder
1 teaspoon baking soda
1 teaspoon salt

• Coat bottom and sides of a 10-inch cast-iron skillet with drippings. Heat in a 450° oven.

• Stir together egg and buttermilk. Add cornmeal, stirring well. Stir in baking powder, soda, and salt. Pour batter into hot skillet. Bake at 450° for 15 minutes or until browned. Yield: 6 servings.

Note: This recipe from our magazine was adapted from *Hoppin' John's Lowcountry Cooking* by John Martin Taylor (Bantam Doubleday Dell, 1992)

TEST KITCHEN SECRET

Cornbread batter should be fairly thin and pourable. If it seems too thick, add a little more liquid. Pouring the batter into a very hot skillet gives it a crispy exterior. MARGARET MONROE DICKEY

Q Should I use white or yellow cornmeal to make cornbread?

A It doesn't matter which type you use, though the white has a milder flavor.

READER TIP

"Sometimes I make cornbread croutons out of leftover cornbread. I let the leftover cornbread air dry, cut it into small cubes, place on a baking sheet, and bake at 350° for 30 minutes or until toasted. They're wonderful tossed into salads."

A.C., Fort Worth, TX

cornbread dressing A cornbread mixture that usually accompanies roast turkey. If placed inside the turkey, it's called stuffing; if baked separately in a pan, it's called dressing. Ingredients vary, but generally include crumbled cornbread, celery, onion, crumbled white bread, turkey or chicken broth, poultry seasoning, sage, and possibly eggs. Dressing can be crisp and crumbly or thick and moist, depending on personal preference, the amount of broth added, and length of cooking.

Southernism

All manner of dressings can be found in Southern cookbooks dating back to the early 1800s. Gradually, the dish came to be thought of as an essential part of holiday tables, often the most anticipated item on Thanksgiving and Christmas menus. Most agree that the dressing outranks the turkey, especially served with giblet gravy.

CORNBREAD DRESSING

2 cups cornmeal
½ cup all-purpose flour
2 teaspoons baking powder
1 teaspoon baking soda
1 teaspoon salt
1 teaspoon sugar (optional)
6 large eggs, divided
2 cups buttermilk

2 tablespoons bacon drippings or melted butter
½ cup butter or margarine
3 bunches green onions, chopped
4 celery ribs, chopped
1 (16-ounce) package herb-seasoned stuffing mix
5 (14-ounce) cans chicken broth

• Combine first 5 ingredients and, if desired, sugar in a large bowl. Stir together 2 eggs and buttermilk; add to dry ingredients, stirring just until moistened.

• Heat bacon drippings in a 10-inch cast-iron skillet or 9-inch round cakepan in oven at 425° for 5 minutes. Stir hot drippings into batter. Pour batter into hot skillet.

• Bake at 425° for 25 minutes or until cornbread is golden; cool and crumble. Freeze in large heavy-duty zip-top plastic bag up to 1 month, if desired. Thaw in refrigerator.

• Melt ½ cup butter in a large skillet over medium heat; add green onions and celery, and sauté until tender.

• Stir together remaining 4 eggs in a large bowl; stir in cornbread, onion mixture, stuffing mix, and chicken broth until blended.

• Spoon dressing into 1 lightly greased 13- x 9-inch baking dish and 1 lightly greased 9-inch square baking dish. Cover and freeze up to 3 months, if desired; thaw in refrigerator 8 hours.

• Place 13- x 9-inch dish (uncovered) and 9-inch square dish (uncovered) in oven at 350°. Bake 13- x 9-inch dish for 1 hour and 9-inch square dish for 50 minutes or until each is lightly browned. Yield: 12 servings.

TEST KITCHEN SECRET

You know you've added enough broth to the dressing mixture when you can shake it and it shimmies or jiggles. Adding any more will make it soupy. JAN MOON

corn dog A frankfurter dipped in a thick cornmeal batter and fried or baked. Corn dogs are usually served on a stick for easy eating.

Southernism

Corn dogs were created in 1942 by Texan Neil Fletcher for the Texas State Fair, and they're still popular fair food.

FAVORITE CORN DOGS

¾ cup self-rising flour
¼ cup self-rising cornmeal
2 tablespoons minced onion
1 tablespoon sugar
1 teaspoon dry mustard
6 tablespoons milk
1 large egg, beaten
1 (16-ounce) package frankfurters
Vegetable oil

• Combine flour, cornmeal, onion, sugar, and mustard; stir well. Combine milk and egg; add to dry ingredients, stirring well. Set aside.

• Wipe each frankfurter dry, and insert a 6- or 10-inch wooden stick into 1 end of each frankfurter, leaving a 2- to 3-inch handle. Dip each frankfurter into batter, coating completely.

• Pour oil to a depth of 3 to 4 inches into a deep skillet; heat to 375°. Fry frankfurters 2 to 3 minutes or until browned, turning once. Drain on paper towels. Repeat with remaining frankfurters. Serve with mustard and ketchup. Yield: 8 to 10 servings.

corned beef Beef cut from the brisket or round and cured or "corned" in a seasoned brine. Corned beef is grayish-pink to rosy-red in color and has a salty flavor. It's used to make corned beef hash and sandwiches. (*see also* **beef** *and* **corned beef hash**)

CORNED BEEF AND CABBAGE

1 (4-pound) corned beef brisket	¾ cup sour cream
3 tablespoons pickling spice	2 tablespoons prepared
2½ cups water	horseradish
1 cabbage, cut into wedges	

• Place brisket in a large Dutch oven; add pickling spice and water, and bring to a boil. Cover, reduce heat, and simmer 2 hours. Add cabbage; cover and cook 30 minutes.

• Combine sour cream and horseradish; serve with Corned Beef and Cabbage. Yield: 6 servings.

corned beef hash Finely chopped corned beef, potatoes, and seasonings fried until lightly browned. (*see also* **corned beef** *and* **hash**)

cornet (cor NAY) French for "horn" and cone-shaped. It might be a pastry filled with cream, a rolled piece of ham filled with cheese, or a paper cone filled with candy or nuts.

corn flour Finely ground yellow or white cornmeal used for breading or in combination with other flours for baking. It's similar to cornstarch; however cornstarch is made from the endosperm protein of the kernel and corn flour is made from the whole kernel. (*see also* **cornmeal** *and* **cornstarch**)

cornichon (KOR nih shohn) This French term describes a tiny pickled gherkin cucumber served as a condiment with pâté, smoked meats, and fish.

Cornish game hen One of the smallest members of the poultry family weighing from 1 to 2 pounds. One bird typically serves one, but larger or stuffed hens can be split to serve two. Cornish hens usually are sold frozen and must be thawed before cooking. (*see also* **poultry**)

TEST KITCHEN SECRET

Look for the smallest Cornish hens you can find; they'll be the most tender and have the best flavor. And be sure to split the hens if you grill them; this way they cook evenly throughout. VANESSA MCNEIL

Q How can a Cornish game hen be halved, especially when it's still frozen?

A Get the butcher to halve it while it's frozen, or once it's thawed, use kitchen shears to cut the hen in half.

cornmeal Dried, ground corn kernels; cornmeal can be yellow, white, or blue, depending on the type of corn used. When ground between two large rocks, the cornmeal is labeled water-ground or stone-ground. This type of meal retains some of the germ and hull of the corn, which shortens shelf life. When ground between steel cylinders or rollers, cornmeal is called roller ground.

Storage: Store cornmeal in an airtight container in a cool, dry place up to 6 months or in the refrigerator or freezer up to 1 year. (*see also* **cornbread, corn flour,** *and* **grain**)

Q **What's the difference between plain cornmeal, self-rising cornmeal, and cornmeal mix?**

A Plain cornmeal has no additives. Self-rising cornmeal has leavening agents and salt blended in the correct proportions to ensure that baked goods rise properly. Cornmeal mix is self-rising cornmeal plus flour added to lighten baked goods. Only liquid and sometimes egg are added to prepare cornbread batter from mixes.

corn oil An odorless, almost tasteless polyunsaturated oil made from the endosperm of corn kernels. It's good for frying because it has a high smoke point. Corn oil can also be used in baking, for making salad dressings, and to make margarine. (*see also* **fats and oils**)

corn pudding A baked custardlike Southern side dish that consists of corn kernels, eggs, milk, and sugar. (*see also* **corn**)

TEE'S CORN PUDDING

¼ cup sugar
3 tablespoons all-purpose flour
2 teaspoons baking powder
1½ teaspoons salt
6 large eggs

2 cups whipping cream
½ cup butter or margarine, melted
6 cups fresh sweet white corn kernels (about 12 ears)*

• Combine first 4 ingredients.
• Whisk together eggs, whipping cream, and butter. Gradually add sugar mixture, whisking until smooth; stir in corn. Pour mixture into a lightly greased 13- x 9-inch baking dish.
• Bake at 350° for 45 minutes or until golden brown and set. Let stand 5 minutes. Yield: 8 servings.
Note: For sweet white corn, we used "Silver Queen."

* 6 cups frozen whole kernel corn or canned shoepeg corn, drained, may be substituted for fresh corn.

corn relish A colorful and tangy combination of corn and other vegetables such as red and green bell peppers and onions. The vinegar-based mixture is usually tempered with sugar, making the relish sweet and sour. Corn relish is a popular Southern accompaniment with meats, poultry, sandwiches, or other main dishes. (*see also* **corn**)

SWEET WHITE CORN-AND-TOMATO RELISH

4 ears fresh sweet white corn	1 tablespoon olive oil
2 large tomatoes, peeled and chopped	½ teaspoon salt
	½ teaspoon pepper
3 green onions, sliced	¼ teaspoon garlic salt
2 tablespoons lemon juice	⅛ teaspoon hot sauce

• Cook corn in boiling water to cover 1 minute; drain and cool. Cut kernels from cobs.

• Stir together corn, tomato, and remaining ingredients; cover and chill 3 hours. Yield: 3 cups

Note: For sweet white corn, we used "Silver Queen."

corn salad A plant with narrow, dark green leaves that are tender and have a tangy, nutty flavor. The greens sometimes grow wild in cornfields, but otherwise has no relation to corn. It's considered a gourmet item and is expensive and hard to find. Corn salad is sometimes called field salad or mâche. (*see also* **greens** *and* **lettuce**)

cornstarch A white, powdery thickening agent made from the endosperm of corn kernels. Its thickening ability is activated when it's blended with a liquid and then cooked. Gravies, soups, puddings, and sauces thickened with cornstarch have a clearer, more translucent appearance than those thickened with flour. Cornstarch-thickened products break down if cooked too long or stirred too vigorously.

Storage: Cornstarch keeps up to 2 years in a cool, dry place. (*see also* **corn flour** *and* **thickening agent**)

TEST KITCHEN SECRET

"*Cornstarch has twice the thickening power of flour, so remember that 1 tablespoon of cornstarch supplies the same thickening as 2 tablespoons of flour. When substituting cornstarch for flour, use half as much cornstarch.*" JAMES SCHEND

Q When I cook with cornstarch, it always gets lumpy; how can I prevent this?

A Prevent lumps by first stirring cold water or other cold liquid into the cornstarch (about twice as much liquid as cornstarch) to make a paste. Then stir the cornstarch paste into the hot mixture you wish to thicken. Stirring constantly but gently, bring the mixture to a full boil over medium heat; continue to boil for 1 minute, stirring constantly.

corn stick pan A cast-iron baking pan with decorative depressions that resemble ears of corn. It's used for baking corn sticks. (*see also* **cast-iron cookware** *and* **cornbread**)

corn syrup A thick, sweet syrup made from cornstarch that can be either light or dark. Dark syrup has a stronger flavor than the light; light syrup has been clarified to remove color and cloudiness. Corn syrup is common in frostings, candy, and jellies because it minimizes formation of sugar crystals.

> **Q How do I know whether to use light or dark corn syrup?**
>
> **A** Dark syrup has a caramel flavor and color added; it's best for making pecan pie or dark-colored candies. Choose light corn syrup when you want to sweeten, not add color or caramel flavor to foods.

Côtes du Rhône (kot deuh ROHN) A generic name given to red, white, and rosé wines grown in France's Rhône Valley. (*see also* **wine**)

cottage cheese Soft, fresh, creamy cheese in curd form made from whole, low-fat or nonfat pasteurized cow's milk. It has a mild, slightly tart flavor, and is sold plain and flavored; because it's perishable, cartons are stamped with a "sell-by" date. Cottage cheese comes in three forms: small curd, medium curd, and large curd. Within these are creamed cottage cheese, containing 4 percent or more cream; low-fat cottage cheese, which has 1 to 2 percent cream; and dry-curd cottage cheese, which has less than 1 percent cream because it isn't mixed with milk or cream.
Storage: Use cottage cheese within a week of its sell-by date. (*see also* **cheese**)

cottage fries Sliced potatoes that are pan-fried, sometimes with onions and green bell peppers.

SOUTHERN-FRIED COTTAGE FRIES

3 large red potatoes, peeled and cut into 1½-inch chunks	1 small onion, chopped
½ cup vegetable oil	Salt and pepper to taste

• Fry potato chunks in hot oil in a 9- or 10-inch cast-iron skillet over medium-high heat 12 minutes, stirring often. Add onion, and cook 5 more minutes. Remove mixture to a serving bowl, using a slotted spoon. Sprinkle with salt and pepper to taste. Yield: 4 servings.

cottonseed oil A thick, colorless oil obtained from the seeds of the cotton plant. Cottonseed oil is usually blended with other oils to make vegetable oil products or margarine and salad dressings. (*see also* **fats and oils**)

coulis (koo LEE) A thick sauce made from a puree of vegetables or fruit, or a soup made from pureed shellfish.

country captain A spicy dish of chicken stew that includes onion, tomatoes, green bell pepper, celery, currants, parsley, curry powder, and seasonings slowly cooked in a covered skillet; it's sprinkled with toasted almonds and served with rice.

COUNTRY CAPTAIN

¾ cup all-purpose flour
½ teaspoon paprika
¼ teaspoon ground red pepper
12 chicken legs
¼ cup butter or margarine, divided
2 tablespoons vegetable oil
½ cup chopped fresh parsley
3 to 4 medium-size green bell peppers, chopped

2 to 3 medium onions, chopped
2 garlic cloves, minced
1½ tablespoons curry powder
1 teaspoon salt
½ to 1 teaspoon black pepper
½ teaspoon ground nutmeg
2 (14.5-ounce) cans diced tomatoes, undrained
½ cup raisins
6 cups hot cooked rice

• Combine first 3 ingredients in a large heavy-duty zip-top plastic bag.
• Place chicken, a few pieces at a time, in bag of flour mixture, shaking to coat. Melt 2 tablespoons butter in a large Dutch oven over medium heat. Add oil. Brown chicken on all sides in hot butter mixture. Remove pieces as they brown; set chicken aside, reserving pan drippings.
• Add remaining 2 tablespoons butter, parsley, and next 7 ingredients to drippings; sauté until onion is tender. Stir in tomatoes and raisins. Bring to a boil; reduce heat, and add chicken. Cover and simmer 30 minutes, stirring often, until chicken is done. Serve over rice. Yield: 6 servings.

country gravy Gravy made from meat or poultry pan drippings, flour, and milk or cream. Country gravy often accompanies chicken-fried steak. (*see also* **chicken-fried steak**)

COUNTRY GRAVY

¼ cup pan drippings
¼ cup all-purpose flour
2½ to 3 cups hot milk

½ teaspoon salt
⅛ to ¼ teaspoon pepper

• Pour off all except ¼ cup drippings from skillet in which steak or chicken was fried; place skillet over medium heat. Add flour; stir until browned. Gradually add hot milk; cook, stirring constantly, until thickened. Stir in salt and pepper. Serve hot over fried steak, chicken, or biscuits. Yield: 2¾ cups.

country ham Ham that has been preserved with a dry-rub cure and aged at least 6 months. The types are often named for the city in which they're processed. Smithfield ham, from Smithfield, Virginia, is one of the most popular types. Most country hams are very dry and salty and require soaking before cooking. Producers sell whole cooked country hams as well as the uncooked version. Most grocery stores also sell vacuum-packed slices ready for frying.

Uses: One of the greatest advantages of a whole country ham is that from the skin to the bone, every part serves a useful purpose. The skin, fat, and shank and butt ends of the ham are traditional seasoning for turnip and mustard greens, and the bone is used to make broth. Small bits and pieces left over after slicing are tasty stirred into scrambled eggs, omelets, potato salad, and deviled eggs.

Storage: Once a cured country ham is cooked, wrap it tightly in brown paper or aluminum foil, and refrigerate up to a month. Never wrap it in plastic because that holds in moisture and speeds spoilage. Country ham can be frozen up to 3 months. (*see also* **ham** *and* **redeye gravy**)

Southernism

By the end of the eighteenth century, cured ham was widely coveted as a Southern delicacy. In fact, the earliest manuscript of collected recipes from the Southern colonies contained instructions for salting, smoking, and aging hams. Today, traditional country hams are still being produced all over the South, though in more limited numbers. Virginia, North Carolina, Kentucky, and Tennessee reign as the places to go for the best country ham and biscuits.

COUNTRY HAM

1 (12- to 14-pound) uncooked country ham	1 tablespoon whole cloves
2 quarts cider vinegar	Hot biscuits

• Place ham in a large container. Add water to cover; soak 24 hours. Drain. Scrub ham 3 or 4 times in cold water with a stiff brush, and rinse well.

• Place ham, fat side up, in a large roasting pan.

• Pour vinegar over ham; sprinkle with cloves. Cover with lid or aluminum foil.

• Bake at 325° for 4 hours or until a meat thermometer registers 140°. Remove ham from oven, and cool slightly. Slice ham, and serve with hot biscuits. Yield: 35 to 40 servings.

Q **Can I do anything to keep country ham from tasting so salty?**

A You can remove some of the salt and add moisture back to the ham by soaking it in water for 24 hours. Or soak ham up to 3 days, changing the water daily.

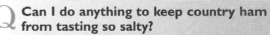
TEST KITCHEN SECRET

Many country hams are covered with mold when purchased. Just scrub or cut off the mold, and rinse the ham with a mixture of equal parts white vinegar and water. VANESSA MCNEIL

court-bouillon (kort boo YON) A broth made by simmering vegetables and herbs in water for about 30 minutes. Wine, lemon juice, or vinegar may be added. Court-bouillon is typically used for poaching fish, shellfish, or vegetables. (*see also* **broth**)

couscous (KOOS koos) A staple in North African cuisine, couscous is a tiny pasta made from coarsely ground semolina wheat. It can be cooked and eaten as porridge, sweetened and mixed with fruit, or served as a salad or side dish. It's quickly gaining popularity in today's fast-paced society because it cooks so quickly. Couscous is found in the rice section of your market. (*see also* **grain**)

> **TIMESAVING TIP**
> Couscous makes a great alternative to rice; the tiny pasta cooks almost instantly.

covered dish Prepared food taken to a social event where it's shared with other guests. Sometimes this event is known as a covered-dish dinner or a potluck supper. Especially in the South, this is a popular way to gather friends: The hostess isn't as frazzled because she doesn't have to prepare all the food, and the guests feel like an important part of the occasion because they bring a dish. It's fun to taste what everyone brings!

Southernism

In the South, family homecomings, wedding feasts, church dinners on the grounds, and other covered-dish dinners bring private cooking together with public eating. Such events not only provide good fellowship, they also allow us to swap recipes and taste the culinary creations of others. It's a chance to "peek" into another Southern kitchen. And no doubt, it's a chance to sample some awesome cakes and pies!

cowpea (*see* **black-eyed pea**)

crab A clawed crustacean prized for its delicately flavored, sweet white meat. The shellfish is often served with clarified butter for dipping. Along the Atlantic and Gulf coasts blue crabs are the catch; the waters of South Florida serve up stone crab; the Pacific coast yields Dungeness crab; the North Pacific brings us king crab and snow crab.
Selection: Purchase crab alive or already cooked. Don't cook a dead crab. If alive, look for the friskiest ones. If cooked, check for a fresh, sweet aroma. The best grades are lump or backfin, while flaked contains small pieces of meat.
Storage: Use live crabs on the day they're purchased or caught; refrigerate until just before cooking. Use cooked crabmeat within 2 days or freeze it up to 1 month. (*see also* **blue crab, Dungeness crab, king crab,** *and* **shellfish**)

> **RESCUE for canned crabmeat:**
> To make canned crabmeat taste fresher, soak it in ice water 10 minutes, then drain, and pat dry. This helps remove some of the metallic taste.

Crab Class

The source of the meat varies by the type of crab. Ounce for ounce, different varieties of cooked crabmeat substitute well in recipes.

Alaskan king crab: The sweet meat found in the long spindly legs are the prize of these extra-large crab that have little meat elsewhere. The legs are cooked, frozen, and then shipped.

Blue crab: These hard-shell crabs have blue claws and dark green to black shells that turn bright red when cooked. Blue crabs are the source for much of the cooked and canned crabmeat. Especially along the Maryland coast, however, they're frequently freshly steamed, coaxed from the shell, drenched in clarified butter, and heartily devoured with little more than the aid of a crab cracker, cocktail fork, and plastic bib to protect the connoisseur's clothing.

Dungeness crab: Weighing up to 4 pounds, this large crab is sold cooked and frozen outside its West Coast domain. *(continued on the following page)*

(continued on the following page)

TEST KITCHEN SECRET

Crab is expensive, and determining how much to buy can be confusing. We suggest 1 pound of blue crabs or ½ pound of crab legs per person. Dungeness crab varies, but half of a large crab or 1 whole small crab should be sufficient. If buying flaked or lump crabmeat, plan on 3 or 4 ounces per person. LYDA JONES

Q **How do I crack a cooked hard-shell crab and remove the meat?**

A

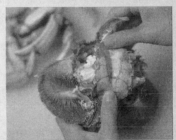

1. To get to cooked meat, first twist off crab legs and claws intact. Crack claws, and remove meat with a small cocktail fork.

2. Invert the crab, and pry off the apron (or tail flap), and discard it. Turn crab right side up again.

3. Insert thumb under shell by apron hinge; pry off the top shell, and discard it.

4. Pull away the inedible gray gills; discard them along with internal organs. Break the body; remove meat from pockets.

Snow crab: A spider-shaped crab noted for its leg portions and cocktail claws, both marketed cooked and frozen. The meat is also available prepicked by the pound in flake or lump pieces.

Soft-shell crab: Blue crabs that have shed their hard shells become a delicacy known as soft-shell crabs, which are in season from April to September. They are usually fried or sautéed and eaten whole, soft shell and all.

Stone Crabs: These crabs are a renewable resource because only the claw meat is consumed. During the stone crab's October to May season, fishermen remove one claw and return the crab back to the sea where it grows a new claw in a year or so. The sizeable, black-tipped claws are cooked immediately after harvest to prevent the meat from sticking to the inside of the shell. They're typically served cold with a spicy mustard or red cocktail sauce.

crab apple Small red apples with a very crisp, tart flesh that are available fresh only during fall months. Crab apples are too sour for eating out-of-hand, but are excellent for making jams and jellies. They can be purchased canned and spiced, and are often served alongside pork and poultry.

crab boil A prepackaged mixture of salt, herbs, and spices that's added to the water for cooking crab, shrimp, or lobster. The seasoning blend also comes in a convenient liquid form.

Southernism

A favorite outdoor get-together in the Chesapeake Bay area is called a "crab boil." The menu is simple and basically calls for about twice as many crabs as guests could be expected to eat, mallets for cracking the crabs, plenty of melted butter, and napkins.

crab cake Lump crabmeat, breadcrumbs, milk, eggs, green onions, and seasoning shaped into small patties and fried until crisp and golden.

FAIDLEY'S CRAB CAKES

This recipe is the specialty at Faidley's Seafood market in Baltimore. If you prefer a spicier crab cake, add finely chopped bell pepper, onion, and Old Bay seasoning to taste.

½ cup mayonnaise
1 large egg, lightly beaten
1 tablespoon Dijon mustard
1 tablespoon Worcestershire
   sauce
½ teaspoon hot sauce

1 pound fresh lump crabmeat,
   drained
1 cup crushed saltines (about 20
   crackers)
1 quart vegetable oil
Tartar sauce

• Stir together first 5 ingredients; fold in crabmeat and saltines. Let stand 3 minutes.

• Shape mixture into 8 patties. Place on a wax paper-lined baking sheet; cover and chill 1 hour.

• Fry crab cakes, in batches, in hot oil in a large skillet over medium-high

heat 3 to 4 minutes on each side or until golden. Drain on paper towels. Serve with tartar sauce, if desired. Yield: 8 servings.
Note: To sauté crab cakes, cook in 3 tablespoons butter or oil in a large nonstick skillet 3 to 4 minutes on each side or until golden.

crab imperial An American dish of crabmeat and flecks of onion and green bell pepper blended with mayonnaise or a sherry-flavored cream sauce. The mixture is spooned into scalloped baking shells, sprinkled with Parmesan cheese or breadcrumbs, and baked until golden.

crab Louis (LOO ee) This cold dish of premium crabmeat on a bed of shredded lettuce and topped with a spicy dressing is thought to have originated in San Francisco. Crab Louis is typically garnished with fresh tomato and hard-cooked egg wedges.

cracked wheat (see **grain** and **wheat**)

cracklings Crispy fried pieces of pork fatback that remain after fat is rendered. You can purchase this Southern phenomenon famous for baking into crackling cornbread in the meat department of some supermarkets.

Southernism

In the early South, when a hog was butchered, farmers let no part go to waste. The meat was preserved, hams were smoked, sausages were stuffed, and even the pig's feet were pickled. The leftovers were turned into lard and cracklings.

cranberry A small, tart, red berry of a plant that grows in parts of North America in bogs on low, trailing vines. It's harvested in the fall, available fresh during November and December, and frozen year-round. Canned cranberry sauce, cranberry relish, dried cranberries, and cranberry fruit drinks are available year-round.

Storage: Bags of fresh cranberries will keep in the refrigerator up to 4 weeks. They also can be frozen up to 9 months; it's not necessary to thaw frozen berries before using in baked goods. (see also **berry**)

READER TIP
"Frosted cranberries add a pretty, festive garnish to holiday plates. I brush the berries lightly with thawed egg substitute and then toss them with granulated sugar. After they dry, they can be arranged to garnish platters of turkey or meat." C.J., New Bern, NC

crappie (CRAW pee) Sometimes called "speckled perch," this freshwater sunfish has lean flesh and a mild, sweet flavor. Crappie is best suited to broiling, sautéing, or frying. (see also **fish**)

Southernism

There used to be signs in Cadiz, Kentucky, proclaiming it the "crappie capital of the world." Fishermen there know crappie spawn in the shallows of lakes in the spring. Thus the saying, "When the dogwoods are blooming, the crappie are spawning."

crawdads (*see* **crawfish**)

crawfish Also called "crawdads" or "mudbugs," and outside the South, "crayfish," these crustaceans resemble tiny lobsters. In fact, crawfish are prepared by most of the same methods as lobster, and like lobster, they turn bright red when cooked. Crawfish are sold live or boiled. Cooked, peeled tails are also available either fresh (from March to June) or frozen. Real crawfish fans know boiled crawfish are generally peeled and eaten with the juices and the sweet meat sucked from the heads.

Southernism

As the self-proclaimed "crawfish capital of the world," Louisiana harvests most of the nation's supply. It's no wonder that crawfish "boiling points" are so prevalent in modern day Louisiana. Out back of these eateries, you'll find giant boiling pots, perched atop propane-fired flames, bubbling with red crawfish. Inside, tables are covered with newspaper and set with rolls of paper towels, ready for the rush.

CRAWFISH BOIL

Soaking the crawfish in cooking liquid after removing them from the heat allows the seasonings to gently seep into the shells. The longer the soak, the more flavorful the crawfish.

1 onion, quartered	6 cups water
1 lemon, quartered	1 tablespoon salt
1 garlic clove, halved	2 teaspoons ground red pepper
1 bay leaf	2 pounds whole crawfish

• Tie first 4 ingredients in a cheesecloth bag. Place cheesecloth bag in a large Dutch oven, and add water, salt, and red pepper; bring to a boil, and boil 5 minutes. Add crawfish, and cook 5 minutes. Drain crawfish; peel and serve warm or chilled. Yield: 3 servings.

Q What's the correct way to eat crawfish?

A Remove the cooked meat from the shell by gently twisting the tail away from the body. Unwrap the first two or three sections of shell from the tail to expose more meat. Then pinch the end of the tail and, with the other hand, pull out the meat. Diehard fans suck the flavorful juices from the head of the crawfish.

crayfish (*see* **crawfish**)

cream A dairy product made from the fatty portion of unhomogenized milk that rises to the surface when milk is left to stand. Cream has a high fat content that gives it a rich butter flavor and velvety texture. Whipping cream is the richest cream you can buy, and there are two main types of cream that vary according to the amount of milk fat they contain. Heavy whipping cream is the richest. It has the highest percentage of milk fat—36% to 40%. Whipping cream contains 30% to 40% milk fat. Some recipes specifically call for heavy whipping cream for its ultimate rich attributes. Half-and-half, also called light cream, contains about half the amount of fat as whipping cream and is more like the consistency of milk than cream. It will not whip. Cream is also a term for beating or creaming a fat such as butter or shortening until light and fluffy. Creaming can be done by hand or with an electric mixer.

FAT AND CALORIES OF CREAM PER 1 TABLESPOON

TYPE CREAM	FAT GRAMS	CALORIES
Half-and-half	1.5	20
Whipping cream	4.5	45
Heavy whipping cream	5	50

TEST KITCHEN SECRET

Cream doubles when it's whipped, so if your recipe calls for 2 cups whipped cream, buy a half-pint (1 cup) of liquid cream. Use a metal bowl, and put the bowl, the beaters or the whisk, and the cream in the freezer for 15 minutes before whipping it. Beat it just until soft peaks form; if you overbeat, it'll turn into butter. MARY ALLEN PERRY

Q Can whipped cream be frozen?

A Just spoon whipped cream into mounds on a baking sheet lined with waxed paper, and freeze until firm. Transfer to a freezer container, and freeze 2 to 3 days. Let thaw 3 to 5 minutes before using.

RESCUE when you're short of cream: If you're making a cooked product and you need a little more cream, substitute 1 tablespoon melted butter plus enough whole milk to make 1 cup.

Storage: Refrigerate cream as soon as possible. It stays fresh for about a week. (*see also* **clotted cream**)

READER TIP
"When I'm making sweetened whipped cream, I add powdered sugar rather than granulated sugar because it dissolves better." B.R., Charleston, W. VA

cream cheese A white fresh cheese with a smooth, spreadable consistency and a mild, slightly tangy flavor. This rich cheese is made from a mixture of cow's cream and milk. Cream cheese blends deliciously with other ingredients such as herbs, chutney, jellies, chocolate, and fruit. It's a primary ingredient in cheesecake and many dips. And bagels are hardly bagels unless spread with cream cheese.

Several different types of cream cheese are available:

• *Regular* cream cheese comes in 3- and 8-ounce blocks.

• *Soft* or *whipped* cream cheese usually comes in tubs; there's no need to soften before using.

• *Flavored* cream cheese has added fruit or herbs that make the cheese sweet or savory.

• *Neufchâtel* cheese contains fewer calories, less fat, and more moisture than regular cream cheese.

• *Light* cream cheese contains fewer calories and less fat than regular or Neufchâtel cheese; it might also contain cottage cheese.

• *Nonfat* cream cheese contains no fat.

Storage: Cream cheese should be refrigerated. Once opened, use it within 2 weeks, and discard it if it becomes moldy. (*see also* **cheese** *and* **Neufchâtel cheese**)

> **TIMESAVING TIP**
>
> When guests show up unexpectedly and you need a quick appetizer, top a block of cream cheese with green or red pepper jelly, chopped dried tomatoes, chutney, or salsa. Serve with crackers.

cream filling A pie filling made of flavored pastry cream thickened with cornstarch or flour.

cream of coconut A commercial product consisting of sweetened coconut cream that's used in desserts and sweet mixed drinks. It's not a substitute for coconut cream, which does not have added sugar. (*see also* **coconut cream** *and* **coconut milk**)

cream of tartar A fine white powder that comes from the acid found on the inside of wine barrels after fermentation. Cream of tartar, sometimes called tartaric acid, gives volume and stability to beaten egg whites and prevents sugar crystallization when making candy or frosting. It's also used as the acid ingredient in some baking powders.

cream pie A single-crust pie with a sweet, rich, puddinglike filling that has a smooth, creamy texture. The crust can be made of pastry or cookie crumbs, and the pie is typically topped with meringue or whipped cream. Two popular types of cream pie are chocolate and coconut. (*see also* **meringue, pastry,** *and* **pie**)

Tips for better cream pie:

Southernism

People just can't resist cream pies. A Southern tradition, cream pies are the ethereal sweets of the dessert world. The phrase "a slice of heaven" must have been coined with silky cream pies in mind.

• If the cream filling is thickened with flour or cornstarch, never add it directly to a hot mixture—this would cause the mixture to lump. Typically, the thickening agent is blended with a cold liquid before the cooking process begins.

• Whether thickened with cornstarch or flour, cook the filling until it comes to a full boil; then boil 1 minute, stirring gently. If the filling contains eggs, you'll need to boil it longer to kill an enzyme present in eggs that could otherwise break down their thickening ability.

• Allow cream pies to cool completely before slicing and serving them. Otherwise, you run the risk of a runny pie.

• Always refrigerate cream pies.

COCONUT CREAM PIE

¾ cup sugar, divided
¼ cup cornstarch
2 cups half-and-half
4 egg yolks
3 tablespoons butter
1 cup flaked coconut

2 teaspoons vanilla extract, divided
1 baked (9-inch) pastry shell
1 cup whipping cream
Garnish: toasted coconut chips

• Combine ½ cup sugar and cornstarch in a heavy saucepan; gradually whisk in half-and-half and egg yolks. Bring to a boil over medium heat, whisking constantly; boil 1 minute. Remove from heat.

• Stir in butter, coconut, and 1 teaspoon vanilla. Cover tightly with plastic wrap, and cool to room temperature. Spoon custard mixture into pastry shell, and chill 30 minutes or until set.

• Beat whipping cream at high speed with an electric mixer until foamy; gradually add remaining ¼ cup sugar and remaining 1 teaspoon vanilla, beating until soft peaks form. Spread or pipe whipped cream over pie. Garnish, if desired. Store in refrigerator. Yield: 1 (9-inch) pie.

cream puff A crisp, hollow pastry puff made from choux pastry—flour, butter, water, and eggs—and filled with sweetened whipped cream, custard, or salad.

Storage: Store baked cream puff shells in an airtight container or plastic bag to prevent them from drying out; refrigerate and use within 24 hours. Cream puff shells can be frozen up to 2 months; thaw 5 to 10 minutes at room temperature before using. (*see also* **choux pastry**)

STRAWBERRY CREAM PUFFS

1 recipe Cream Puff Paste
1 cup whipping cream
⅓ cup sifted powdered sugar
3 cups fresh strawberries, sliced
Garnish: mint leaves

• Drop Cream Puff Paste into 10 equal mounds 3 inches apart on an ungreased baking sheet. Bake at 400° for 30 to 35 minutes or until golden and puffed. Cool away from drafts. Cut top off each cream puff; pull out and discard soft dough inside.

• Beat whipping cream at medium speed with an electric mixer until foamy; gradually add powdered sugar, beating until soft peaks form. Fold three-fourths of sliced strawberries into whipped cream; fill cream puffs with strawberry mixture. Arrange remaining sliced strawberries on top. Replace tops of cream puffs. Garnish, if desired. Yield: 10 servings.

CREAM PUFF PASTE

1 cup water
½ cup butter or margarine
1 cup all-purpose flour
⅛ teaspoon salt
4 large eggs

• Combine water and butter in a medium saucepan; bring to a boil. Add flour and salt, all at once, stirring vigorously over medium-high heat until mixture leaves sides of pan and forms a smooth ball. Remove from heat, and cool 4 to 5 minutes.

• Add eggs, 1 at a time, beating thoroughly with a wooden spoon after each addition; then beat until smooth. Shape and bake pastry immediately according to recipe directions. Yield: 10 (2-inch) cream puffs.

TEST KITCHEN SECRET

Before adding eggs to your cream puff dough, remove the saucepan from the heat and let the dough cool 5 minutes. If the dough is too hot, it will overcook the eggs and then the dough won't rise. I like to transfer the dough to the bowl of a stand mixer and add the eggs, one at a time, then beat with the dough hook or paddle attachment. Making a small slit with the paring knife in the side of a just baked puff allows the steam to escape and adds to the crispness. MARY ALLEN PERRY

cream sauce A classic béchamel or white sauce made with milk or cream. The thickness depends on the proportion of flour to liquid. Cream sauce is the base for many dishes, such as chicken à la king. (*see also* **béchamel sauce, mother sauces,** *and* **white sauce**)

RESCUE for a lumpy cream sauce:
Vigorously whisk the sauce until smooth, or whirl it in a food processor. Pour the sauce through a fine wire-mesh sieve. To thin an overly thick sauce, gradually add milk, 1 tablespoon at a time, as the sauce cooks.

CREAM SAUCE

3 tablespoons butter or
    margarine
3 tablespoons all-purpose flour

1¼ cups milk
¼ teaspoon salt
¼ teaspoon pepper

• Melt butter in a heavy saucepan over low heat; whisk in flour until smooth. Cook, whisking constantly, 1 minute. Gradually add milk; cook, whisking constantly, over medium heat until thickened. Whisk in salt and pepper. Yield: 1¼ cups.

cream sherry A sweet sherry with a deep golden color and full body. (*see also* **sherry**)

crème anglaise (krehm ahn GLEHZ) The French term for a rich vanilla custard sauce that can be served hot or cold over cake or fruit or spooned onto a dessert plate with a dessert on top. Southerners call the same sauce boiled custard. (*see also* **custard**)

crème brûlée (krehm broo LAY) French for "burnt cream," this rich custard served chilled is topped with a caramelized brown sugar crust formed by broiling. Small butane torches are also available for caramelizing the sugar atop the dessert. One hint: Use broiler-proof dishes when making this dessert; they'll need to withstand high broiler temperatures. (*see also* **brûlé, custard, salamander,** *and* **recipe on the following page**)

TEST KITCHEN SECRET

Get an even sprinkling of sugar on top of the custard by placing the sugar in a sieve. Hold the sieve over the custard, and push the sugar through with a spoon. MARY ALLEN PERRY

CRÈME BRÛLÉE

¾ cup sugar
3 cups whipping cream
7 egg yolks, lightly beaten

2 teaspoons vanilla extract
½ cup firmly packed brown
   sugar

• Combine ¾ cup sugar and whipping cream in a heavy saucepan; cook over medium heat, stirring constantly, until sugar melts and mixture comes to a simmer (do not boil). Remove from heat. Combine egg yolks and vanilla in a small bowl. Gradually stir about one-fourth of hot cream mixture into yolk mixture; add to remaining hot cream mixture, stirring constantly.
• Pour custard mixture evenly into 8 (4-ounce) ramekins. Place ramekins in a large roasting pan or 2 (9-inch) pans; add hot water to pan to a depth of 1 inch. Bake, uncovered, at 350° for 35 minutes. Remove ramekins from water; cool slightly on wire racks. Cover and chill until ready to serve.
• Place ramekins on a baking sheet. Sprinkle brown sugar evenly over custards. Broil 5½ inches from heat 3 minutes or until sugar melts. Cool on wire racks to allow sugar to harden. Yield: 8 servings.

crème caramel (krehm kair ah MEHL) A custard baked in a caramel-coated mold, chilled, served inverted on a dessert plate, and crowned with the caramel in the mold. In Italy, it's known as cream caramella, in Spain as flan, and in France as crème renversée. (*see also* **custard** *and* **flan**)

crème de cacao (krehm deuh kah KAH oh) Chocolate-flavored liqueur with a hint of vanilla; comes in clear and dark varieties. (*see also* **liqueur**)

crème de cassis (krehm deuh kah SEES) A reddish-purple currant-flavored liqueur and a key ingredient in kir. (*see also* **kir** *and* **liqueur**)

crème de menthe (krehm deuh MENTH) A syrupy mint-flavored clear or green liqueur used to flavor drinks and desserts. (*see also* **liqueur**)

crème fraîche A dairy product made from cultured cream with a slightly tangy, nutty flavor and velvety texture. Crème fraîche is ideal for adding to sauces and soups because it can be cooked without curdling; it's also delicious spooned over fruit or other desserts such as cobblers.

Q I can't find crème fraîche in the supermarket. Can I make it at home?

A Sometimes crème fraîche can be found only in gourmet markets and can be expensive. However, it's very easy to make an equally delicious version at home. Our recipe below simulates a true crème fraîche.

CRÈME FRAÎCHE SAUCE

⅓ cup sour cream
⅓ cup whipping cream

2 tablespoons powdered sugar

Combine all ingredients; cover and chill 8 hours. Yield: ⅔ cup.

Crenshaw melon An oval melon with a golden-green, lightly ribbed rind and salmon-orange flesh. The melon is available from July to October. A Crenshaw has a rich, sweet, spicy aroma and flavor. (*see also* **melon**)

Creole cooking (KREE ohl) In the eighteenth century, the Spaniards governing New Orleans described residents of European heritage as being Criollo; later, they became known as Creoles. The name represented residents with a refined cultural background and an elegant lifestyle. Even today, Creole cuisine is thought of as city cooking; it's more complex and sophisticated than Cajun cooking. Creole recipes place an emphasis on butter, cream, and tomatoes. It's similar to Cajun cooking in that it also uses an abundance of chopped green peppers, onions, celery, and filé powder. Grillades (small pieces of grilled meat) and grits is a traditional Creole dish. (*see also* **Cajun cooking, filé powder, grillade,** *and* **grits**)

Southernism

Creole cuisine was rooted in the soups and sauces and sweet confections of French cooking but over time was grafted with Spanish, American, Indian, and African influences. Ella Brennan, New Orleans native and "grande dame" of the Brennan family restaurants, says, "Creole is a more sophisticated cooking. Cajun is divine, but it's one-pot cooking. It's like if you're in France and you're eating in Paris or in the provinces." Several in New Orleans still reign as classic Creole restaurants: Galatoire's features a French Creole menu; Chez Helene offers up soul and Creole cooking; and Dooky Chase serves an authentic blend of Creole cuisine.

> **TIMESAVING TIP**
> To add a touch of Creole flavor to your favorite recipe, turn to the spice and seasoning section of your supermarket; prepared Creole seasoning mix jazzes up recipes.

Creole mustard (KREE ohl) A spicy, hot brown mustard flavored with horseradish and mustard seeds.

crêpe (KREHP) A delicate, unleavened pancake made from thin egg batter cooked in a hot sauté pan. Crêpes are paper-thin wrappers for sweet and savory fillings, and are rolled up or folded over. Dessert crêpes might be spread with fruit or jam and flamed with brandy or liqueur. Savory crêpes are filled with meat, cheese, or vegetables, and often topped with a cream sauce.
Storage: Crêpes can be cooked ahead and stacked with pieces of wax paper between the layers. Place the stack in an airtight container, and refrigerate up to 2 days or freeze up to 4 months. Thaw crêpes at room temperature about 1 hour before using. (*see recipe on following page*)

> **TIMESAVING TIP**
> You can purchase prepared crêpes in the supermarket; look for them in refrigerated cases or in the produce department.

CRÊPES

4 large eggs
2 cups all-purpose flour
¼ cup butter or margarine,
    melted

1 cup cold water
1 cup cold milk
½ teaspoon salt

• Process all ingredients in a blender or food processor until smooth, stopping to scrape down sides. Cover; chill 1 hour.
• Place a lightly greased 8-inch nonstick skillet over medium heat until hot.
• Pour 3 tablespoons batter into skillet; quickly tilt in all directions so that batter covers bottom of skillet.
• Cook 1 minute or until crêpe can be shaken loose from skillet. Turn crêpe, and cook about 30 seconds. Repeat procedure with remaining batter. Stack crêpes between sheets of wax paper. Yield: 2 dozen.

crêpes Suzette (KREHPS soo ZEHT) Dessert crêpes that have been sautéed in orange butter, then flamed with an orange liqueur.

crimp To pinch or press pastry or dough together using the fingers, a fork, or another utensil. (*see also* **pastry** *and* **pie**)

Fork Edge: Press firmly around pastry edge with tines of fork. To prevent sticking, dip fork in flour.

Pinch Edge: Place index finger on outside of pastry rim and thumb and other index finger on inside. Pinch pastry into V shape along the edge.

Rope Edge: Place side of thumb on pastry rim at an angle. Pinch pastry by pressing knuckle of index finger into pastry toward thumb.

crisp To refresh limp vegetables by soaking them in ice water, or baked goods, such as crackers, by heating in the oven. Vegetables that are crisp will be firm and fresh, not soft or wilted; baked goods should be hard and brittle, not soft.

RESCUE for limp salad greens:
Restore crispness to limp salad greens by placing them in ice water and refrigerating up to 1 hour. Drain well, wrap greens in paper towels, and refrigerate in plastic bags at least 4 hours.

crisp-tender A term that describes vegetables cooked until they are just tender, but still somewhat crunchy. This preserves nutrients and increases flavor. (*see also* **vegetables**)

Q **How do I know when vegetables have cooked to the crisp-tender stage?**

A When you can pierce the vegetable with a fork with only slight pressure, it's crisp-tender.

Crock-Pot™ The brand name of an electrical appliance known as a slow cooker that simmers food slowly for several hours. (*see also* **slow cooker**)

croissant (kwah SAHN) A French term for rich, flaky crescent-shaped yeast rolls. Croissants get their flaky texture from layers of dough that have been rolled, spread with butter, and folded. The layers separate slightly as the rolls bake and produce a puffy texture. Croissants are generally thought of as a breakfast pastry but also can be used for sandwiches. Fresh and frozen croissants are sold in most supermarkets.
Storage: Croissant dough can be frozen up to 1 month if wrapped tightly in aluminum foil or placed in freezer bags. Baked croissants can also be frozen in an airtight container up to 2 months; to serve, heat in foil at 400° for 6 to 7 minutes.

croquembouche (kroh kuhm BOOSH) French for "crisp in the mouth," croquembouche is an elaborate pyramid-shaped dessert made of bite-sized custard-filled cream puffs held together with a sugar glaze and covered with caramel. The outside of the creation is decorated with delicate spun sugar. Croquembouche is traditionally served at weddings, baptisms, or christenings. (*see also* **choux pastry, cream puff,** *and* **profiterole**)

croquette (kroh KEHT) A mixture of ground or chopped meat, fish, poultry, or vegetables held together by a thick white sauce and shaped into ovals or rounds. The croquettes are dipped into beaten egg, coated with breadcrumbs, and deep-fried until crisp and golden. (*see also* **white sauce**)

crostini (kroh STEE nee) An Italian term for thin slices of toasted bread with a savory topping. Crostini is usually served as an appetizer.

croustade (kroo STΛHD) An edible container used to hold creamed meat or vegetables. A croustade can be made from pastry, a hollowed-out bread loaf, or pureed potatoes. Before it's filled, the croustade is typically deep-fried or toasted until golden and crisp.

croûte, en (ahn KROOT) French for "crust." Meat, poultry, fish, or pâté encased in pastry and baked. (*see also* **pâté**)

crouton (KROO tawn) A small cube or piece of bread made crisp by toasting, sautéing, baking, or frying. Croutons are used to garnish and add flavor. Commercial croutons are available plain or seasoned with herbs.

HOMEMADE CROUTONS

3 to 4 tablespoons olive oil
1 garlic clove, minced
½ teaspoon salt
½ teaspoon pepper
6 (1-inch) slices French bread, cubed

• Combine all ingredients in a large zip-top plastic bag; seal and shake well. Spread cubes on a 15- x 10-inch jellyroll pan; bake at 425° for 10 minutes, stirring after 5 minutes. Yield: 4 cups.

crown roast A special-occasion pork or lamb roast made from the loin of the rib section. The ribs are trimmed and the meat side is turned inward into a circle to form a stately crown shape. The center is filled with vegetables, rice, or stuffing. After cooking, the tips of the rib bones are often decorated with paper frills. (*see also* **lamb** *and* **pork**)

CROWN PORK ROAST WITH CRANBERRY-SAUSAGE STUFFING

½ teaspoon salt
½ teaspoon pepper
1 (16-rib) crown pork roast, trimmed
½ pound ground pork sausage
1 (8-ounce) package herb-seasoned stuffing mix
1 (16-ounce) can whole-berry cranberry sauce
1½ cups chopped cooking apple
¼ cup butter or margarine, melted

• Rub salt and pepper over all sides of roast; place roast, bone ends up, on rack in a roasting pan.
• Cook sausage in a skillet, stirring until crumbled and no longer pink; drain. Combine sausage, stuffing mix, and remaining 3 ingredients, stirring well. Spoon into center of roast. Cover stuffing and ends of ribs with aluminum foil.
• Bake at 325° for 2½ hours or until a meat thermometer registers 160°. Remove foil; let roast stand 15 minutes before slicing. Serve with pan drippings if desired. Yield: 8 to 12 servings.

crudités (kroo dee TAY) French term for raw vegetables served as an appetizer and accompanied with dipping sauce.

cruet (KREW et) A small container with a pouring spout used for storing and pouring vinaigrette dressing, oil, or vinegar at the table.

cruller (KRUHL uhr) A Dutch doughnut-style pastry that's shaped into a twist, then fried and sprinkled with sugar or brushed with a glaze. (*see also* **doughnut**)

crumble To break food into small pieces. For example, crumbled bacon is often added to omelets, salads, or vegetable dishes.

crumpet (KRUHM piht) A small round, yeast-raised British batter bread cooked on a griddle. The unsweetened crumpet has a smooth, brown bottom and a top filled with tiny holes. Similar to an English muffin, crumpets can be toasted and spread with butter or jam.

crush To reduce food to crumbs, paste, or powder, often by using a mortar and pestle or rolling pin. Sometimes herbs and spices are crushed to release their flavors.

> **TIMESAVING TIP**
> To quickly crush cracker crumbs, place crackers in a zip-top plastic bag and alternately pound and roll with a rolling pin.

crust The crisp, usually browned outer layer of baked, fried, or roasted foods such as on bread or fried chicken. The term also refers to a thin layer of pastry serving as a pie shell or covering for pâté. (*see also* **pastry** and **pie**)

> **TEST KITCHEN SECRET**
> *Years ago, our staff never used commercial pastry crust. But the quality has improved and the time we have to cook has decreased, so we now use them often. Our favorite is refrigerated pastry crust found in the refrigerated section of your store. Just spread it out on your counter and pat smooth.* MARGARET MONROE DICKEY

crustacean (kruh STAY shuhn) Shellfish with elongated bodies and jointed soft shells, such as crabs, lobsters, and shrimp. (*see also* **shellfish**)

crystallized flowers Flowers soaked in a thick sugar syrup, then drained and dried; after drying, they're sometimes sprinkled with superfine sugar. The flowers most often crystallized are violets, miniature rosebuds, and rose petals; they're generally used for decorating desserts. It's easy to make crystallized flowers, but they can also be purchased at gourmet markets and specialty shops.

CRYSTALLIZED FLOWERS

• To crystallize rosebuds, rose petals, violas, and mint leaves, rinse them gently and let dry on paper towels.
• Beat 2 cups powdered sugar, 1 tablespoon meringue powder, and ⅓ cup water at low speed with an electric mixer until blended; beat at high speed 4 to 5 minutes or until fluffy.
• Brush powdered sugar mixture on all sides of flower petals and mint leaves; sprinkle petals and leaves with 1 cup superfine sugar. Let stand on wire racks 24 hours to dry. Do not refrigerate.

Cuban bread Hard, crusty white bread made with flour, water, yeast, salt, and sugar. Cuban bread resembles French bread, but the sugar makes it slightly sweeter. (*see also* **French bread**)

cube To cut food into pieces ½ inch or larger on each side. If food is cut into cubes, it's generally larger than diced, which means the pieces are ⅛ to ¼ inch on each side. (*see also* **chopping** *and* **dice**)

TIMESAVING TIP

To cube an onion quickly, halve it from top to root end. Place the onion halves, flat side down, and make a couple of parallel vertical slices, then make a couple of cuts across the slices.

cubed steak A thin cut of beef taken from the top or bottom round and tenderized by pounding or scoring the surface or by running it through a butcher's tenderizing machine. Without tenderizing, cube steak would be too tough to eat. Cube steak is generally fried and smothered in gravy and simmered for extra tenderness. (*see also* **beef** *and* **score**)

cucumber A long, slender vegetable with dark green skin and edible seeds surrounded by a mild and crisp white flesh. Cucumbers are usually eaten raw in salads or used for making pickles. Cucumbers are available year-round; however, the small ones used for pickling are plentiful only during summer months. There are several types of cucumbers:

TIMESAVING TIP

It's not necessary to remove the seeds from a cucumber, but if you prefer them seedless, cut the cucumber in half lengthwise, and scrape out the seeds with a spoon or melon baller.

- *Regular cucumbers* are large and thick and have green slick skin.
- *English cucumbers* are longer and thinner than regular cucumbers and are more expensive because they're seedless; they're sometimes called "burpless" cucumbers.
- *Pickling cucumbers,* also called salad cucumbers, are small and easily identified by their bumpy skins.

Q **Do cucumbers need to be peeled?**

A There's no reason to peel cucumbers even if they're waxed, and those sold in supermarkets often have a waxy finish to help prolong their freshness. Just wash the cucumbers thoroughly to remove the waxy coating if you don't peel them.

Storage: Refrigerate cucumbers up to 2 weeks. However, use pickling cucumbers as soon after picking as possible. (*see also* **English cucumber**)

TEST KITCHEN SECRET

Add a decorative touch to cucumber slices by pulling the tines of a fork down the length of an unpeeled cucumber; then slice crosswise into thin slices. LYDA JONES

cuisine (kwih ZEEN) A French term that pertains to a specific style or manner of cooking, or to a particular country's food habits or the food prepared by a restaurant. Nowhere, except perhaps in France where the term originated, is the gastronomical perspective of history more important than in the South. Southern cuisine is gradually being influenced by modern demands, but many Southerners are fiercely loyal and intent upon protecting the integrity of Southern recipes.

Southernism

True Southern cuisine is the richest and most completely developed of all American regional cuisines. From the start, Spanish and English explorers introduced and discovered good things to eat when they came ashore in the South, and that process of exchange has continued with the arrival of other Europeans, Africans, and Asians. Through it all, there has evolved an abundance of elaborate rituals, generations-old stories, and guarded secrets revolving around food.

cumin (KUH mihn) Small crescent-shaped seeds that are the dried fruit of a plant in the parsley family. The seeds have a nutty flavor and aroma and are available either whole or ground. Cumin is often an ingredient in Indian, Middle Eastern, and Asian cuisines, but its most popular use is in chili and curry powders. (*see also* **chili powder, curry powder,** *and* **spice**)

cup A unit of measurement in the United States equal to 8 fluid ounces. Cup measures are available for dry and liquid ingredients. (*see also* **measuring**)

curaçao (KYEUR uh soh) Orange liqueur made from bitter oranges harvested on the Caribbean island of Curaçao. (*see also* **liqueur**)

curd When milk coagulates, it separates into liquid (whey) and semisolids (curds), which are used for making cheese. (*see also* **cheese** *and* **lemon curd**)

curdle The breaking down of milk or egg mixtures into liquid and solid components, usually as a result of excessive heat, overcooking, or the addition of an acid, such as lemon juice or wine.

TEST KITCHEN SECRET

When making cream soups or sauces, be sure to thicken them with flour or cornstarch before adding any acid ingredients. Also, once you add sour cream or yogurt to a hot mixture, it will curdle if it continues to boil. VIE WARSHAW

cure To preserve food by drying, salting, pickling, or smoking. Common cured foods include smoked ham or salmon, pickled herring, dried fruit, and salted fish.

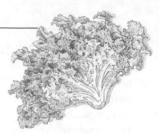

curly endive Grows in loose heads of lacy, green-rimmed outer leaves that curl at the tips. The leaves have a prickly texture and slightly bitter taste. Curly endive is used in salads, but can be eaten as a vegetable or in soups. (*see also* **chickory** *and* **endive**)

currant (KUR uhnt) Two fruits are classified as currants: tiny dried grapes that are used mainly in baked goods and tiny fresh berries that are related to the gooseberry and named by color—black, red, or white currants. Fresh berry currants are delicious in jams, jellies, sauces, or served with sugar and cream. The season for fresh currants is June through August. Tiny dried grape currants taste like raisins. (*see also* **gooseberry** *and* **grape**)

curry Any number of hot, spicy, gravy-based stews of East Indian origin that include curry powder. Curry recipes are usually served with rice and a variety of condiments.

> ### TEST KITCHEN SECRET
>
> *Typical condiments to serve alongside your favorite curry dish are coconut, chopped peanuts, raisins, chopped green onion, and crumbled bacon. It looks nice when you surround the curry with the various condiments.* JAMES SCHEND

curry powder Widely used in Indian cooking, curry powder is a blend of several ground spices, herbs, and seeds, including cardamom, cumin, coriander, red pepper, fennel seeds, saffron, and turmeric. (*see also* **spice**)

> ### TEST KITCHEN SECRET
>
> *To keep curry powder from tasting too strong and bitter, cook it in a little oil before adding it to the recipe.* MARGARET MONROE DICKEY

cushaw (koo SHAH) A large ivory-colored crookneck squash with yellow-orange flesh and a mild flavor. (*see also* **squash**)

custard A sweet puddinglike dessert made of milk and eggs that can either be baked or stirred on the cooktop; both methods require slow, gentle cooking in order to prevent curdling. For this reason, stirred custards are usually made in a heavy saucepan or double boiler and baked custards in a water bath. Custards can be flavored with chocolate, vanilla, or fruit; stirred custard often serves as the base for ice cream or as a dessert sauce. Stirred custards are a vital part of popular recipes such as crème

Q **How can I tell if custard is done?**

A The most reliable way is to remove custard from the heat when it reaches 170° to 175° on a candy thermometer. The more traditional way to tell is to dip a clean metal spoon into the custard; the custard should coat the spoon and hold its shape. Baked custard can be tested for doneness by inserting a knife near the center; the knife should come out clean if it's done.

anglaise and pastry cream. Baked custard classics include crème brûlée and flan.
Storage: Always store custard in the refrigerator. Made with eggs, it's susceptible to harmful bacteria, so never leave it at room temperature over 2 hours. (*see also* **crème anglaise, créme brûlée, crème caramel,** *and* **flan**)

<u>STIRRED CUSTARD</u>

¼ cup cornstarch
1 cup sugar
⅛ teaspoon salt
2 cups milk

1 cup whipping cream
3 large eggs
3 tablespoons butter
2 teaspoons vanilla extract

• Stir together first 3 ingredients in a heavy saucepan. Gradually whisk in milk and cream. Add eggs, and whisk until foamy. Cook over medium heat, whisking constantly, 10 minutes or until thickened. (Do not boil.) Remove from heat; stir in butter and vanilla.

• Pour into a 1½-quart bowl. Cover and chill. Yield: 6 servings.

TEST KITCHEN SECRET

To prevent custard from forming a skin on top, press a sheet of greased wax paper or plastic wrap directly onto the surface of the custard before refrigerating. REBECCA KRACKE GORDON

cut in To work a solid fat, such as butter or shortening, into dry ingredients, such as flour, until the mixture resembles coarse meal. Southern biscuits get their flakiness from this important step.

Q **How do you cut in shortening?**

A The simplest way is to press the fat into the flour using a tool called a pastry blender; a food processor can also be used, but be careful not to overwork the dough. You can also use 2 table knives; draw the knives across each other to cut through the mixture.

cutlet Thin boneless slices of meat, typically pork, veal, or lamb, taken from the leg or rib section and cooked quickly by sautéing or grilling. This term also describes chopped and processed meat, fish, or poultry that's formed into the shape of a cutlet, then breaded and fried. (*see also* **veal Oscar**)

cutting board A flat surface of either wood or plastic polyethylene on which food is sliced or chopped. Some cutting boards have a carved edge to catch meat drippings. Always wash plastic boards in hot, soapy water, or run dishwasher-safe ones through the dishwasher to disinfect. Clean wooden boards with a mixture of 1 part bleach to 8 parts water, then rinse. We suggest using two boards: one just for meats and one for everything else. Or, if you have only one board, mark a side of the board exclusively for meat.

TEST KITCHEN SECRET

Place your cutting board on a damp kitchen towel before you use it. The cloth provides a skidproof surface, which keeps the board from moving.

VANESSA MCNEIL

daikon (DI kuhn) A large Asian radish with a sweet, fresh flavor. The flesh of the daikon is crisp, juicy, and white, and the skin can be either creamy white or black. Daikon is used raw as a garnish and in salads or cooked in stir-fried dishes.
Storage: Refrigerate daikons in a plastic bag up to 1 week.

daiquiri (DAK uh ree) A cocktail made of rum, lime juice, and sugar. A frozen daiquiri contains additional ice and is processed in the blender until smooth. Sometimes pureed fruit is blended into the drink mixture. (*see also* **cocktail**)

STRAWBERRY DAIQUIRIS

1 (6-ounce) can frozen lemonade concentrate, undiluted
1½ cups light rum
½ cup sifted powdered sugar
4 cups sliced fresh strawberries
Ice cubes

• Process first 4 ingredients in a blender until smooth, stopping to scrape down sides. Pour half of strawberry mixture into a bowl, and set aside.
• Add ice to remaining mixture in blender to 4-cup level; process until smooth. Repeat with remaining strawberry mixture and ice. Yield: 2 quarts.

dandelion greens (DAN dl i uhn) Dark green, thick, jagged-edged leaves of a weed that grows wild and cultivated. The leaves can be cooked like spinach; the roots can be eaten as vegetables or roasted and ground to make a coffeelike beverage. The tenderest dandelion greens are found in early spring.
Storage: Refrigerate dandelion greens in a plastic bag up to 5 days. Wash the leaves thoroughly before using. (*see also* **greens**)

Southernism

In the Appalachian and Ozark mountain regions, the spring ritual of harvesting wild dandelion greens dates back to Native Americans. But more treasured than the greens were the pert dandelion blossoms because these were turned into dandelion wine.

Danish pastry A flaky, rich, buttery breakfast pastry made from yeast dough. Danish pastries can be filled with a variety of fruit, nuts, or cheese, and are sometimes topped with a sugar glaze.

dash A measurement that refers to a small amount of a seasoning added to a dish. A dash is ⅛ teaspoon or less. (*see also* **measuring**)

dasheen (*see* **taro root**)

dashi (DA shee) A Japanese soup made with dried bonito tuna flakes, dried kelp, and water.

date The fruit of a palm tree native to the Middle East. Most dates are small, oblong, have a single pit, and a golden brown to deep amber color. Dates are plump and have extremely sweet flesh, chewy texture, and are eaten fresh or dried. Dates can be purchased whole, with or without pits, and chopped.
Storage: Refrigerate in an airtight container up to several months or freeze up to 1 year.

Q Is there a way to soften dried-out dates?

A Heat a cup of water or fruit juice to boiling and pour it over the dates; let stand 5 to 10 minutes, and drain well. If the dates aren't really dried out, but just stuck together, microwave them on MEDIUM (50% power) for 30 to 45 seconds.

TEST KITCHEN SECRET

It's easier to chop dates if you dip your knife in water as you go. The water helps keep the dates from sticking to the knife. But the easiest way to cut dates is with kitchen shears; just dip the shears in water between cuts. JAN MOON

daube (DOHB) A French stew made with beef, red wine, vegetables, and seasonings and slowly braised for several hours.

dauphine (doh FEEN) French for pureed potatoes mixed with puff pastry dough, shaped into balls, and fried. Term also refers to fried sole fillets garnished with mushrooms, crayfish, truffles, and quenelles. (*see also* **sole**)

debone To remove bones from meat, fish, or poultry. Tweezers work well for removing fine fish bones.

decant To gently pour a wine from its original bottle into a carafe or other container. The goal of decanting is to separate the wine from the sediment in the bottom of the original bottle. In addition, the process allows the wine to "breathe" before being served, improving its flavor. Decanting is not recommended for older wines, as their bouquet fades quickly after pouring.

decanter A narrow-necked glass container used to hold wine or liqueur.

decorator's icing A soft, smooth icing made with powdered sugar, shortening, water, and vanilla or other flavoring that's typically tinted with food coloring. Cakes and cupcakes are frosted and trimmed with the icing using special cake-decorating tips. Decorator's frosting, while not the tastiest frosting, because it contains shortening rather than butter, is the best frosting for beginners to use when piping icing from decorator tips. That's because the shortening will not soften or melt from the heat of the hand. Experienced pipers use buttercream icing or royal icing for decorations; royal icing hardens when dry, which makes it a good choice for making durable decorations. (*see also* **buttercream** *and* **royal icing**)

D **deep-fry** A technique that cooks food in hot fat or oil deep enough to cover the item being fried. Shortening or peanut or canola oil are best for deep-frying because each can be heated to a high temperature before it starts smoking. (*see also* **fats and oils**)

Southernism

It's not surprising that many Southern foods were traditionally fried, given the golden brown and crispy texture that lard—the original Southern frying medium—gave to fritters cooked in a cast-iron skillet. In addition, frying was a simple technique, easily taught to new cooks.

deer (*see* **venison** *and* **wild game**)

deglaze (dee GLAYZ) To add a liquid such as wine or cream to a pan after food is braised, roasted, or fried to loosen the browned, caramelized bits of food left on the bottom. The deglazed mixture often becomes the base for a sauce to accompany the food cooked in the pan.

degrease (dee GREES) Removing the fat from the top of a liquid. For example, a spoon can be used to skim fat from the surface of a hot soup or gravy. Another method is to chill the mixture until the fat solidifies in a layer on top and can be lifted off the surface. (*see also* **skim**)

dehydrate (dee HY drayt) A process of removing the natural moisture from food by slowly drying it. Dehydrating slows the growth of bacteria and minimizes spoilage so food can be stored longer. Fruits, vegetables, herbs, spices, soups, meats, and milk can all be dehydrated. Some foods can be dehydrated naturally by being left in the open air and sun. Another way is to use an electric dehydrator.

Delmonico potatoes (dehl MAHN ih coh) The owner of Delmonico's, a nineteenth-century New York restaurant bearing his name, is credited with creating this dish. It consists of cooked, mashed potatoes topped with grated cheese and buttered breadcrumbs, then baked until golden.

Delmonico steak (dehl MAHN ih coh) Made famous at Delmonico's restaurant in New York City, this tender, flavorful steak is a boneless cut of beef from the short loin. In some areas, it's also referred to as a New York steak or a Kansas City strip steak; it can be broiled, grilled, or fried. (*see also* **beef**)

demi-glace (DEHM ee glahs) A French term used to describe a rich brown sauce made from a mixture of a rich brown sauce and beef stock that has slowly cooked until it's reduced to a thick glaze. Demi-glace is used as a base for many other sauces. (*see also* **brown sauce** *and* **mother sauces**)

demi-sec (DEHM ee sehk) A French term that describes sparkling wines or champagnes as being "half dry" or relatively sweet. (*see also* **champagne, dry, sec,** *and* **wine**)

demitasse (DEHM ee tahs) French for "half cup"; term also describes a tiny cup of strong black coffee usually served after dinner.

Derbyshire cheese (DAHR bee sheer) A pressed English cheese that is similar to Cheddar cheese. It has a pale golden-orange interior that flakes when broken. The British have long flavored this cheese with sage and given it as gifts at Christmas.

Derby-Pie® (DER bee) A trademark referring to a rich chocolate-chip and pecan pie concoction flavored with bourbon. It was developed at the Melrose Inn in Prospect, Kentucky, as its signature dish. The name, "Derby pie," was drawn from a hat as members of the family who owned Melrose Inn all contributed ideas for naming the luscious pie.

dessert (dess AHRT) A sweet food served as the last course of a meal or as a refreshment. Desserts include all types of sweets; they can be quite elaborate or as simple as a piece of fruit.

dessert wine A variety of sweet wines that can be served with dessert or after a meal. Some popular dessert wines include Madeira, port, Sauternes, or sherry. (*see also* **wine**)

Q **How should a dessert wine be served?**

A The average serving is 2 to 2½ ounces. Formal dessert wine glasses are available; however, it can be served in a 6-ounce stemmed glass. Most dessert wines are served chilled, although several styles of port and sherry are served at room temperature.

devein (dee VAYN) A process of removing the gray-black intestinal vein from the back of a shrimp. (*see also* **shrimp**)

Q **Is it necessary to devein shrimp?**

A For small and medium shrimp, it's a personal preference. In these sizes, removing the dark vein is done mostly for looks. Once cooked, veins are harmless. However, the intestinal vein of large or jumbo shrimp is not only more noticeable, it sometimes contains grit and is frequently removed.

TIMESAVING TIP
Deveining can be done with the tip of a sharp knife. But it can be done faster with a special tool called a deveiner. It slides underneath the shell and along the back of the shrimp and lifts out the vein. Another quick way is to use kitchen shears to snip down the back of the shrimp; rinse out the dark vein, and then remove the shell.

deviled (DEV eld) A term that refers to highly seasoned food such as deviled eggs or deviled crab. The hot, spicy flavor might come from red pepper, mustard, hot sauce, chili powder, black pepper, or horseradish.

DEVILED EGGS

The potato flakes make a full-bodied filling, perfect for piping. One basic recipe makes two variations to chill overnight.

1 dozen hard-cooked eggs, peeled	¼ teaspoon salt
¾ cup light mayonnaise	¼ teaspoon pepper
1 tablespoon Dijon mustard	½ cup instant potato flakes
	Garnish: fresh dill sprigs

• Cut eggs in half lengthwise. Remove yolks. Process egg yolks, mayonnaise, and next 4 ingredients in a food processor until smooth, stopping to scrape down sides.
• Spoon or pipe filling into egg whites. Cover and chill up to 8 hours. Garnish, if desired. Yield: 2 dozen.

Bacon-Stuffed Eggs: Stir ⅔ cup (8 slices) crumbled cooked bacon, 3 tablespoons pickle relish, and ¼ cup chopped fresh chives into yolk mixture. Proceed as directed.

Shrimp-Stuffed Eggs: Stir ¾ pound shrimp, cooked, peeled, and chopped; 2 tablespoons prepared horseradish; and 6 green onions, minced, into yolk mixture. Proceed as directed.

devil's food cake A rich, moist, dark chocolate cake leavened with baking soda. Typically, extra chocolate or cocoa distinguish a devil's food cake from an ordinary chocolate cake, theoretically making it more "sinful."

DEVIL'S FOOD CAKE

Slather this all-purpose rich chocolate cake in Rich Chocolate Buttercream or a whipped cream frosting.

4 (1-ounce) squares unsweetened chocolate	1 teaspoon baking soda
½ cup shortening	¾ teaspoon salt
2 cups sugar	¾ cup buttermilk
2 large eggs	¾ cup water
2 cups sifted cake flour	1 teaspoon vanilla extract
½ teaspoon baking powder	Rich Chocolate Buttercream (optional)

• Place chocolate in top of a double boiler; bring water to a boil. Reduce heat to low; cook until chocolate melts.

• Beat shortening at medium speed with an electric mixer until creamy; gradually add sugar, beating well. Add eggs, 1 at a time, beating after each addition. Add chocolate, mixing well.

• Combine flour and next 3 ingredients; add to chocolate mixture alternately with buttermilk, beginning and ending with flour mixture. Mix at low speed after each addition until blended. Add water, mixing well. Stir in vanilla. Pour batter into 2 greased and floured 9-inch round cakepans.

• Bake at 350° for 30 to 35 minutes or until a wooden pick inserted in center comes out clean. Cool in pans on wire racks 10 minutes; remove from pans, and cool completely on wire racks. Frost as desired. Yield: 12 servings.

RICH CHOCOLATE BUTTERCREAM

2 (1-ounce) squares unsweetened chocolate	4 cups sifted powdered sugar
2 (1-ounce) squares semisweet chocolate	¼ cup cocoa
1 cup butter, softened	¼ cup milk
	2 teaspoons vanilla extract

• Place chocolate in top of a double boiler; bring water to a boil. Reduce heat to low; cook until chocolate melts, stirring often. Remove from heat.

• Beat butter at medium speed with an electric mixer until creamy. Add chocolate, powdered sugar, and remaining ingredients; beat until spreading consistency. Yield: 3¾ cups.

Devonshire cheese (DEHV uhn sheer) A soft, creamy, rich cheese made by draining all the whey from Devonshire cream. (*see also* **cheese**)

Devonshire cream (DEHV uhn sheer) (*see* **clotted cream**)

dewberry (DOO beh ree) A variety of blackberry grown on trailing vines; the berry is smaller than an ordinary blackberry. (*see also* **blackberry**)

dice To cut food with a knife into small ⅛- to ¼-inch cubes. (*see also* **cube**)

Dijon mustard (dee ZHOHN) Created in the Dijon region of France, this pale yellow, creamy mustard is made from brown mustard seeds, white wine, unfermented grape juice, and seasonings. Dijon mustard has a clean, sharp, medium-hot flavor that makes it ideal for dishes in which the flavor of the food shouldn't be covered up. (*see also* **mustard**)

HONEY-DIJON VEGETABLES

1 cup water	2 tablespoons all-purpose flour
3 carrots, diagonally sliced	1 cup milk
1½ cups cauliflower florets	2 tablespoons Dijon mustard
1 (10-ounce) package frozen brussels sprouts, thawed	1 tablespoon honey
2 tablespoons butter	½ teaspoon chicken bouillon granules
2 tablespoons diced onion	¼ teaspoon hot sauce

• Bring 1 cup water to a boil in a saucepan. Add carrot and cauliflower; cover and simmer 8 minutes. Add brussels sprouts, and cook 8 minutes or until tender; drain and keep warm.
• Melt butter in a skillet; add onion, and sauté until tender. Whisk in flour until smooth; cook, whisking constantly, 1 minute. Gradually add milk; cook over medium heat, whisking constantly until thickened. Stir in mustard and remaining 3 ingredients; toss with vegetables. Yield: 8 servings.

dill An annual herb that has feathery green leaves and a delicate, refreshing flavor. Dillweed can be used fresh or dried to flavor dishes such as salads, vegetables, meats, seafood, and sauces. The dried fruit of dillweed is the tan, flat dill seed. The seeds have a sharper, stronger flavor than dillweed. Dill seed is commonly used to flavor the brine of dill pickles. (*see also* **herbs**)

dill pickle Preserved cucumbers prepared in a brine flavored with dill seed. Kosher dill pickles are similar to regular dill pickles, but have garlic added to the pickling solution.

Southernism

Playing off Southerners' love for fried foods, fried dill pickles originated somewhere deep in Mississippi—so deep, in fact, that local restaurants debate which establishment deserves credit.

Storage: Pickles, especially those you make yourself, reach their best flavor if stored after processing for 4 or 5 weeks before opened. However, always watch for signs of spoilage, such as a leaking or a bulging lid. When opened, check for mold, foul odor, color change, spurting liquid, or unusual softness. If there is any indication of spoilage, immediately discard. (*see also* **pickle**)

dilute (dih LOOT) A process where the flavor or strength of a mixture is reduced by adding additional liquid, usually water.

dim sum (DIHM SUHM) A variety of small snacks such as steamed or fried dumplings, shrimp balls, spring rolls, or Chinese pastries. Dim sum is regularly served in Chinese teahouses.

dip A thick creamy sauce or condiment that can be served hot or cold and is generally made from a base of mayonnaise, sour cream, or cream cheese. Dips are typically accompanied with raw vegetables, crackers, or various types of chips to use for dunking.

dirty rice A Cajun dish of rice cooked with ground chicken livers or gizzards and onions, and flavored with broth, bacon drippings, green bell pepper, and garlic. The dish gets its name from the dirty look the giblets give the rice, but the flavor is delicious. (*see also* **Cajun cooking**)

DIRTY RICE

2 cups long-grain rice, uncooked
1 quart water
5 chicken wings (about ¾ pound)
5 chicken gizzards (¼ pound)
5 chicken hearts (about 1 ounce)
5 chicken livers (about ¼ pound)
2 pounds ground hot pork sausage
¼ cup butter or margarine
1 large onion, chopped
¾ cup chopped green pepper
2 celery ribs, chopped
½ cup sliced green onions
½ cup chopped cooked ham
1 tablespoon dried parsley flakes

• Cook rice according to package directions; set aside.
• Combine water and next 3 ingredients in a Dutch oven; bring to a boil. Cover, reduce heat, and simmer 20 minutes; add chicken livers, and cook 10 minutes or until tender. Drain, reserving 1 cup liquid. Remove meat from wings; coarsely chop wing meat, gizzards, hearts, and livers. Set chopped meat aside.
• Brown sausage in Dutch oven, stirring until it crumbles. Drain sausage, and set aside.
• Melt butter in Dutch oven; add onion, pepper, and celery. Sauté 5 minutes or until tender, stirring often. Add green onions, and cook 2 minutes. Add ham, sausage, chopped meat, and reserved liquid. Bring to a boil; cover, reduce heat, and simmer 15 minutes. Stir in cooked rice and parsley. Yield: 10 servings.

Southernism
This side dish takes advantage of what some might consider the "throw-away" pieces of poultry and transforms them into a prized side dish. In South Carolina, the dish is called "hash." It uses pork livers and is a staple at barbecues.

disjoint To separate meat at the joint such as a chicken leg cut from the thigh. (*see also* **chicken**)

dissolve To stir a dry ingredient such as sugar, salt, yeast, or gelatin into a liquid so that none of the solid remains.

ditali (dee TAH lee) An Italian term used to describe small, short tubes of pasta. Ditalini (diht ah LEE nee) are even smaller than ditali; ditali is often used in minestrone. (*see also* **minestrone** *and* **pasta**)

divan (dih VAN) A term that refers to a dish that contains broccoli and a cream sauce. Chicken divan made with chicken, broccoli, and a creamy cheese sauce is a classic.

CHICKEN DIVAN

4 skinned chicken breast halves	½ cup mayonnaise
1 fresh rosemary sprig	½ teaspoon grated lemon rind
½ teaspoon salt	2 tablespoons lemon juice
¼ teaspoon pepper	½ teaspoon salt
2 tablespoons butter or margarine	¼ to ½ teaspoon curry powder
¼ cup all-purpose flour	2 (10-ounce) packages frozen broccoli spears, thawed and drained
1 cup milk	
1 egg yolk, beaten	⅓ cup grated Parmesan cheese
1 (8-ounce) container sour cream	Paprika

• Place first 4 ingredients in a large saucepan; add water to cover. Bring to a boil. Cover, reduce heat, and simmer 15 to 20 minutes or until chicken is tender. Drain, reserving ½ cup broth. Discard rosemary.
• Cool chicken slightly. Bone and chop chicken; set aside.
• Melt butter in a heavy saucepan over low heat; add flour, stirring until smooth. Cook 1 minute, stirring constantly. Gradually add milk and reserved broth; cook over medium heat, stirring constantly, until thickened and bubbly.
• Stir one-fourth of hot mixture into egg yolk; add to remaining hot mixture, and cook, stirring constantly, 1 minute. Remove from heat; stir in sour cream and next 5 ingredients.
• Layer half each of broccoli, chicken, and sauce in a greased 2-quart casserole. Repeat layers. Sprinkle with Parmesan cheese.
• Bake, uncovered, at 350° for 30 to 35 minutes. Sprinkle with paprika. Yield: 4 to 6 servings.

divinity (dih VIHN ih tee) A delicate, soft, white candy made by slowly beating hot sugar syrup into stiffly beaten egg whites. Chopped nuts, candied fruit, food coloring, and flavoring can be added.

MRS. FLOYD'S DIVINITY

Mrs. Louise Floyd, of Selma, Alabama, is the mother of John Floyd, the editor-in-chief of Southern Living. *She shares our definitive recipe for this pearly confection.*

2½ cups sugar
½ cup water
½ cup light corn syrup
¼ teaspoon salt

2 egg whites
1 teaspoon vanilla extract
1 cup chopped pecans, toasted
Garnish: toasted pecan halves

• Cook first 4 ingredients in a heavy 2-quart saucepan over low heat until sugar dissolves and a candy thermometer registers 248° (about 15 minutes). Remove from heat.
• Beat egg whites at high speed with an electric mixer until stiff peaks form. Pour half of hot syrup in a thin stream over egg whites, beating constantly at high speed, about 5 minutes.
• Cook remaining half of syrup over medium heat, stirring occasionally, until a candy thermometer registers 272° (about 4 to 5 minutes). Slowly pour hot syrup and vanilla over egg white mixture, beating constantly at high speed until mixture holds its shape (about 6 to 8 minutes). Stir in chopped pecans.
• Drop mixture quickly by rounded teaspoonfuls onto lightly greased wax paper. Garnish, if desired. Cool. Yield: 4 dozen (1¾ pounds).

TEST KITCHEN SECRET

When you're making divinity, set egg whites out at room temperature 20 minutes before heating so they'll whip to their fullest. Also, use a sturdy, freestanding electric mixer; it's easier on your arm, plus a portable doesn't have the power to beat divinity. MARY ALLEN PERRY

dollop (DOLL uhp) A small amount of a soft food, such as whipped cream or sour cream spooned or added atop a dessert or soup.

dolma (DOHL mah) A term that refers to various fruits, vegetables, or leaves stuffed with a savory filling. Among the most popular dolmas are grape leaves stuffed with ground lamb, rice, onion, currants, pine nuts, and seasoning. Others used as casings for stuffings include squash, eggplant, bell pepper, cabbage leaves, and apples. Dolmas are typically braised or baked, but they can be eaten hot or cold as an appetizer or entrée.

dolphin (DAHL fihn) (*see* **mahi mahi**)

Dom Perignon (DOM peh ree nyonh) The finest and most expensive sparkling wine produced by Moët and Chandon wineries in France; it's named after a 17th-century cellar master who is popularly credited with developing the art of blending wines to create champagnes with superior flavor. (*see also* **champagne**)

dot To place small pieces of an ingredient, usually butter, over the surface of a food. For example, putting bits of butter over the top of a fruit pie or a casserole before baking it.

double boiler An arrangement where two pots fit together snugly with one sitting on top and partway inside the other. The lower pot is used to hold simmering water, which gently heats the contents of the top pot. Double boilers are used to cook heat-sensitive foods such as custards, mousses, and cream sauces, and to melt chocolate. Sometimes a double boiler might be referred to as a double saucepan. (*see also* **cookware**)

> **RESCUE when you don't have a double boiler:**
> You can easily create your own double boiler by placing a heat-resistant mixing bowl or slightly smaller saucepan over a larger one, although it may not be as steady or fit as tight. Remember, a tight fit between the pans ensures that no water or steam mixes with the ingredients, which can cause melting chocolate to stiffen or "seize." In some cases, a heavy saucepan will work.

dough (DOH) A mixture of flour, liquid, and other ingredients used in baking that's dry enough and pliable enough to roll or knead, but stiff enough to cut into shapes. Dough generally has a low moisture content and contains less fat, sugar, and liquid than a batter.

doughnut A small, round or ring-shaped pastry of sweet dough leavened with baking powder or yeast, and deep-fried or baked until golden. Doughnuts are often coated with a glaze, confectioner's sugar or frosting, or filled with jelly or pudding.

READER TIP
"My husband and I have found that when making doughnuts, it's important to use a deep pan with high sides to prevent splattering. Also, we cook only 2 or 3 doughnuts at a time; too many will lower the temperature of the oil, and you want the oil to stay hot." A.G., Macon, GA

GLAZED DOUGHNUTS

Cook doughnuts, a few at a time. Turn them once, and dip in glaze while warm.

1 (¼-ounce) envelope active dry yeast	½ teaspoon salt
2 tablespoons warm water (100° to 110°)	½ teaspoon ground nutmeg
	⅛ teaspoon ground cinnamon
¾ cup warm milk (100° to 110°)	1 large egg
¼ cup sugar	2½ cups bread flour
3 tablespoons shortening	Vegetable oil
	Glaze

- Combine yeast and warm water in a 1-cup liquid measuring cup; let stand 5 minutes.
- Combine yeast mixture, milk, next 6 ingredients, and 1 cup flour in a large mixing bowl; beat at medium speed with an electric mixer about 2 minutes or until blended. Stir in remaining 1½ cups flour. Cover and let rise in a warm place (85°), free from drafts, 1 hour or until doubled in bulk.
- Punch dough down; turn dough out onto a well-floured surface, and knead several times. Roll dough to ½-inch thickness, and cut with a 2½-inch doughnut cutter. Place doughnuts on a lightly floured surface. Cover and let rise in a warm place, free from drafts, 30 minutes or until doubled in bulk.
- Pour oil to a depth of 2 to 3 inches in a Dutch oven; heat to 375°. Cook doughnuts 4 or 5 at a time in hot oil about 1 minute or until golden on 1 side; turn and cook other side about 1 minute. Drain well on paper towels. Dip each doughnut while warm in glaze, letting excess drip off. Cool on wire racks. Yield: 1½ dozen.

GLAZE

2 cups sifted powdered sugar   **¼ cup milk**
- Combine ingredients, and stir until smooth. Yield: ⅔ cup.

draft beer Unpasteurized beer served from a keg through a tap or spigot.

dragée (dra ZHAY) Tiny silver or gold ball decorations made of sugar and used for decorating cakes, cookies, and other baked goods. Dragées are for decoration only and are no longer considered edible in the United States because they contain traces of metal, although they're sold as edible in some other countries. Dragées can be purchased in the cake decorating section of your supermarket or at cake decorating stores. The term also refers to candied almonds with a hard sugar coating.

drain To put food in a colander, strainer, or sieve, and pour off the liquid or fat from a solid food before it's served or before other ingredients are added.

TEST KITCHEN SECRET

It's easy to reduce the fat content in recipes calling for ground meat; just drain the cooked meat in a strainer or colander, and discard the excess fat. VIE WARSHAW

Drambuie (dram BOO ee) A Scottish amber-colored liqueur made with malt whiskey, heather honey, and herbs. (*see also* **liqueur**)

draw To remove the entrails from game, poultry, or fish. The term also refers to clarifying a mixture, as in drawn butter. (*see also* **clarify** *and* **eviscerate**)

drawn butter (*see* **clarified butter**)

dredge (DREGH) To coat a food with flour, finely ground bread-crumbs, or cornmeal. Food is usually dredged before it's sautéed, fried, or baked. For example, chicken might be dipped in egg and milk and dredged in flour before it's fried. (*see also* **breading** *and* **coat**)

TIMESAVING TIP

Dredging can be messy, but several options make it neater. Use tongs to dip food into liquid and to transfer the food to a pieplate filled with flour or other coating. If using your hands, remember this tip: Use 1 hand to dip in the liquid and the other to dredge. The easiest way is to use 1 hand to dip in the liquid, and then place the food in a plastic bag and shake with the coating.

dressing A sauce usually served cold and used to dress salads or cold vegetables. This term also refers to a bread mixture used to stuff chicken or turkey; it can be cooked separately in a pan or inside the bird. (*see also* **cornbread dressing**)

dried beef Wafer thin slices of smoked, salted, and dried beef. Dried beef usually is sold in small jars and was once a popular ingredient in a Depression-era recipe known as creamed beef on toast. Sometime dried beef is referred to as "chipped" beef.

dried fruit Fruit with most of its moisture removed by exposure to the sun or through a mechanical dehydration process that concentrates the sweetness and flavor. Dried fruit usually has four or five times the calories by weight of fresh fruit. Eat it as a snack, use in baked goods, or reconstitute it in water.

Storage: Most dried fruit can be stored at room temperature in a plastic bag up to a year.

Q How can I plump up dried fruit?

A Cover it with water or other flavored liquid, such as broth or wine, and bring to a boil. Remove the fruit from the heat; cover and let stand 5 minutes.

TEST KITCHEN SECRET

To keep dried fruit from sticking to your knife when you're chopping it, use a sharp knife, and dip it often in hot water. Or, try using kitchen shears dipped in hot water. MARGARET MONROE DICKEY

dried tomato A tomato that has been dehydrated by drying and has a red color, chewy texture, and intense flavor. Dried tomatoes are available packed in oil or dry-packed. They can be used to add rich, tangy flavor to appetizers, sauces, soups, pizza, and many other dishes. **Storage:** Refrigerate open jars of oil-packed dried tomatoes up to 2 weeks. Dry-packed tomatoes will keep indefinitely if kept in a moisture-proof container in a cool, dry place. (*see also* **dehydrate** *and* **tomato**)

Q How are dried tomatoes rehydrated?

A Rehydrate dry-pack dried tomatoes by allowing them to stand in hot water for 10 to 15 minutes. Or, cover the tomatoes in oil and let stand overnight.

drippings The melted fat and juices that are released in the pan in which meat or other food has been cooked. The drippings might be used as the base for a sauce or gravy. Drippings from salt-cured smoked bacon provided a splendid flavoring ingredient for beans, greens, and other veggies in old-time Southern cooking. We still crave the combinations today, although we don't indulge in the high-fat seasoning as often for health concerns.

drizzle To slowly pour a fine stream of liquid over a food or plate. For example, a glaze might be drizzled over a cake as decoration, or butter might be drizzled over a casserole before baking for flavor and browning.

drop cookie A cookie made by dropping spoonfuls of soft dough onto a baking sheet. (*see also* **cookie**)

CHOCOLATE CHIP-PEANUT BUTTER COOKIES

½ cup chunky peanut butter	½ teaspoon vanilla extract
¾ cup shortening	1¼ cups all-purpose flour
½ cup firmly packed light brown sugar	½ teaspoon baking soda
½ cup sugar	¼ teaspoon salt
1 large egg	1 cup (6 ounces) semisweet chocolate morsels

• Beat first 6 ingredients at medium speed with an electric mixer until creamy.
• Stir together flour, soda, and salt. Gradually add to peanut butter mixture, beating at low speed until blended; stir in semisweet chocolate morsels. Drop batter by rounded tablespoonfuls onto ungreased baking sheets.
• Bake cookies at 350° for 10 to 15 minutes. Let stand 2 minutes. Remove cookies to wire racks, and cool completely. Yield: 3 dozen.

drum A large and diverse family of fish named for the drumming or croaking noise they make during mating season. Drum, or croaker, is a firm, low-fat fish found in the temperate waters of the Atlantic and Pacific oceans. Some varieties include the Atlantic croaker, black drum, kingfish, redfish, spotted bass and white sea bass. (*see also* **fish**)

dry A tasting term that describes wine that isn't sweet because it retains very little sugar. Sometimes the French word "sec" is used instead. (*see also* **champagne, demi-sec, sec** *and* **wine**)

dry ice A form of crystallized and solidified carbon dioxide that's used as a coolant or long-term refrigerant such as during a power outage. Dry ice doesn't turn into water when it melts; it passes directly from a solid to a gas. Touching dry ice with bare hands can result in burns.

TEST KITCHEN SECRET

"When there's a power outage, keep in mind that 25 pounds of dry ice will keep a full 10-cubic-foot freezer cold for 3 to 4 days, or a half-full freezer cold for 2 to 3 days. Place heavy cardboard on top of frozen packages, and put the dry ice on the cardboard. Ask the ice company to wrap each piece of ice in newspaper so you won't have to touch it." LYDA JONES

dry milk This pantry staple is sometimes called "powdered" milk; it can serve as a stand-in for regular milk, especially for low-fat baking. (*see also* **milk**)

dry rub A mixture of ground spices and herbs that's rubbed or pressed onto the surface of meat or poultry before it's baked or grilled. Many recipes suggest the food be refrigerated several hours to absorb the flavor of the rub.

MASTER CLASS BARBECUE RUB

1 cup granulated brown sugar	2 tablespoons ground black pepper
¼ cup garlic salt	
¼ cup celery salt	1 tablespoon lemon pepper
¼ cup onion salt	2 teaspoons ground sage
¼ cup seasoned salt	1 teaspoon dry mustard
½ cup paprika	½ teaspoon ground thyme
3 tablespoons chili powder	½ teaspoon ground red pepper

• Combine all ingredients. Chill in an airtight container up to 3 weeks, or freeze up to 6 months. Rub on beef, lamb, pork, chicken, or fish, and cook over indirect heat. Yield: 2⅔ cups.

Dubonnet (doo boh NAY) A French aperitif made from red wine and flavored with quinine and herbs. Dubonnet blanc, a drier version made from white wine, is also available.

duchess potatoes (DUH shees) A fluffy puree of potatoes, egg yolks, butter, and seasoning. The mixture can be piped through a pastry tube into individual rosettes and baked, or it can be a decorative garnish or border for meats, poultry, fish, or casseroles.

duck, duckling A wild or domestic bird with rich, succulent dark meat. The flavor of the duck is affected by the diet of the bird as well as its age and size. Generally, older, heavier birds have a stronger flavor and are less tender.
Domestic ducks are commercially raised and fed a special diet to produce sweet, tender meat; wild ducks include mallards, wigeon, and teal. (*see also* **wild game**)

Q Is there a way to prepare duck so it won't be fatty or greasy?

A This is mainly a problem with domestic ducks, because they have a thick layer of fat under their skin. So, when roasting a domestic duck, prick the skin to allow the fat to escape. Also, trim any excess skin from the duck, especially around the neck. Dry the bird inside and out to reduce spattering; season it with salt and pepper, and place breast side down, uncovered, in the refrigerator overnight. These steps allow the skin to dry out even more.

duck sauce A thick, sweet-and-sour Chinese condiment made from plums, apricots, sugar, and seasonings. Duck sauce, sometimes called "plum sauce," is served with duck, pork, spareribs, egg rolls, and spring rolls.

du jour (doo ZHOOR) A French term that means "of the day." The term is used most often in restaurants to introduce a special menu item such as the soup of the day.

dulce (DOOL say) A very sweet Spanish confection made with sugar and cream.

dump cake Cake made by combining and mixing all the ingredients in the same pan in which the batter is baked. Dump cakes often are made with oil instead of butter or margarine.

TIMESAVING TIP
This is the cake of choice for harried cooks. There's no mixer to wrestle and no extra pans to wash.

dumpling A Southerner has a repertoire of dumplings, each tailored in texture and composition to the dish for which they're prepared. Chicken and dumplings is probably the most beloved dish, with a flour-based ball of dough cooked in chicken broth. For lovers of turnip greens, a ball of cornmeal and water is often plopped into the pot likker (the juice from cooking greens in water and bacon or pork fat) and cooked. Dessert found its niche in the dumpling family with recipes for apple dumplings, featuring a dough of flour, water or milk, cooked in a sweetened mixture of apple juice, butter, and/or water. Dumpling recipes vary as keenly as the cooks who make them; some are lightened with baking powder or soda, some are made from commercial baking mixes, and others use shortening, lard, or butter.

TEST KITCHEN SECRET

"When adding dumplings to a liquid, make sure the liquid is hot and bubbling; otherwise the dumplings will become soggy. After the dumplings are added, cover with the lid; this will keep the dumplings from deflating." JAN MOON

CHICKEN AND DUMPLINGS

1 (2½-pound) whole chicken, cut up	1 teaspoon chicken bouillon granules
2½ teaspoons salt, divided	3 cups self-rising flour
¾ teaspoon pepper, divided	½ teaspoon poultry seasoning
½ teaspoon garlic powder	⅓ cup shortening
½ teaspoon dried thyme	2 teaspoons bacon drippings
¼ teaspoon ground red pepper	1 cup milk

• Cover chicken with water, and bring to a boil in a large Dutch oven. Add 1½ teaspoons salt, ½ teaspoon pepper, and next 3 ingredients; cover, reduce heat, and simmer 1 hour. Remove chicken, reserving broth in Dutch oven; cool chicken. Skim fat from broth; bring to a simmer.

• Skin, bone, and coarsely chop chicken. Add chicken, bouillon, and remaining salt and pepper to broth. Return to simmer.

• Combine flour and poultry seasoning in a bowl. Cut in shortening and bacon drippings with a pastry blender until mixture is crumbly. Add milk, stirring until dry ingredients are moistened.

• Turn dough out onto a lightly floured surface. Roll out to ⅛-inch thickness; cut into 1-inch pieces.

• Bring broth to a boil. Drop dumplings, a few at a time, into boiling broth, stirring gently. Reduce heat, cover, and simmer, stirring often, 25 minutes. Yield: 8 servings.

Dungeness crab (DUHN juh nehs) The most important commercially harvested crab in the Pacific. This large reddish-brown or purplish crab has succulent pink flesh with a sweet flavor. (*see also* **crab**)

durum wheat (DOOR uhm) (*see* **wheat**)

dust Lightly coating a food or utensil with a powdery ingredient such as flour, powdered sugar, or cocoa. Laying strips of wax paper over a cake to be dusted with powdered sugar, such as in the illustration, creates decorative strips across the cake once wax paper is removed.

Dutch oven A large pot or kettle with a tight-fitting lid and sturdy handles that's used for slow cooking on the cooktop or in the oven. Dutch ovens can be made of enameled cast iron, regular cast iron, or other metals, and they range in size from 4 to 12 quarts. Dutch ovens are said to be of Pennsylvania Dutch heritage.

duxelles (dook SEHL) A French term for a mixture of finely chopped mushrooms, shallots, and herbs slowly cooked in butter until it forms a thick paste. Duxelles are used to flavor sauces and soups, or they can serve as a garnish or as a stuffing mixture. (*see also* **mushroom**)

Earl Grey A popular black tea named for Charles Grey, British prime minister to King William IV. The tea is a mixture of Indian and Sri Lankan teas, flavored with oil of bergamot, which comes from small, acidic oranges. (*see also* **tea**)

earthenware Bakeware made of glazed clay. Earthenware tends not to conduct heat well, but once hot, will retain heat, which makes it useful for dishes requiring lengthy cooking such as baked beans and stews.

Q How do I clean earthenware dishes?

A Take care to cool earthenware dishes slowly and completely before washing in order to prevent the glaze from cracking. Once the glaze cracks, the exposed surface can affect the flavor of foods cooked in the container. If the glaze cracks and a lead painted surface is underneath, don't use the container for cooking or serving food anymore.

F

éclair (ay KLAIR) A finger-shaped cream puff or choux pastry shell filled with pudding, pastry cream, or whipped cream and served as a dessert. Éclairs are usually topped with a sweet icing or glaze. (*see also* **choux pastry**)

VANILLA CREAM-FILLED ÉCLAIRS

1⅓ cups water
1 (11-ounce) package
    piecrust mix
3 large eggs

2 egg whites
Vanilla Pastry Cream
Chocolate Glaze

• Bring 1⅓ cups water to a boil in a 3-quart saucepan over medium-high heat. Stir in piecrust mix, beating vigorously with a wooden spoon 1 minute or until mixture leaves sides of pan.
• Place dough in bowl of a heavy-duty electric stand mixer; cool 5 minutes. Beat dough at medium speed with electric mixer, using paddle attachment. Add eggs and egg whites, 1 at a time, beating until blended after each addition. (If desired, eggs and egg whites may be added 1 at a time and beaten vigorously with a wooden spoon instead of using the mixer.)
• Spoon dough into a large heavy-duty zip-top plastic bag. (A large pastry bag may also be used.) Cut a 1½-inch opening across 1 corner of the bag. Pipe 4-inch-long strips of dough 2 inches apart onto ungreased baking sheets.
• Bake at 425° for 20 to 25 minutes or until puffed and golden. (Do not underbake.) Remove from oven, and cut a small slit in side of each éclair to allow steam to escape. Cool on wire racks.
• Split éclairs, using a serrated knife, starting at 1 long side without cutting through opposite side. Discard soft dough inside. Carefully spoon about ¼ cup Vanilla Pastry Cream into each éclair; close top of each éclair. Top with Chocolate Glaze. Chill 2 hours or freeze up to 1 month. Yield: 1 dozen.

VANILLA PASTRY CREAM

2 large eggs
2 egg yolks
½ cup sugar
⅓ cup cornstarch

2 cups half-and-half
2 tablespoons butter, softened
2 teaspoons vanilla extract

• Whisk together first 4 ingredients in a 3-quart saucepan. Gradually whisk in half-and-half. Cook over medium heat, whisking constantly, until mixture comes to a boil. Cook 1 minute or until mixture thickens. Remove from heat; whisk in butter and vanilla. Cover and chill 4 hours. Yield: 3 cups.

CHOCOLATE GLAZE

1 cup semisweet chocolate morsels
¼ cup whipping cream

2 tablespoons butter, softened

• Microwave morsels and whipping cream at HIGH in a 2-cup glass measuring cup 30 seconds to 1 minute or until melted, stirring twice. Whisk in butter until blended, and spoon immediately over éclairs. Yield: 1⅓ cups.

Edam cheese (EE duhm) This mellow, nutty, sometimes salty cheese from Holland has a pale yellow interior with a red or yellow paraffin coating. A great all-purpose cheese, it's made from part-skimmed milk and comes in spheres that weigh from 1 to 4 pounds. (*see also* **cheese**)

egg The oval, hard-shelled reproductive body produced by birds. There are many different types of eggs—duck, goose, and quail—but hen eggs are the most common ones used in cooking. Domestic hen eggs have white or brown shells, though the color does not affect the flavor or nutritional value of the egg. Eggs have many purposes in the kitchen; they serve as leaveners, as a base for dressings such as mayonnaise, and as a thickener in sauces and custards. The USDA recommends that all dishes containing raw eggs be avoided because of salmonella risk. All eggs should be cooked to an internal temperature of at least 160°.

Q **How can I prevent that unattractive greenish ring around the yolk of a hard-cooked egg?**

A The secret lies in never cooking them longer than necessary. The best way is to place the eggs in a single layer in a saucepan and add enough water to come 1 inch above the eggs. Bring them to a boil, and immediately cover and remove from the heat. Let the eggs sit, covered, for 15 minutes. Pour off the water and immediately place the eggs under cold, running water.

TEST KITCHEN SECRET

"*When testing recipes, we use only Grade A large eggs.*"

REBECCA KRACKE GORDON

Egg grades and sizes:
Eggs are sold by both grade and size.
• The grade measures the egg's interior and exterior appearance. Most eggs are sold as Grade AA or A; AA eggs spread less and have a slightly higher, firmer yolk and white than the A eggs. Grade B eggs spread more; the white is weak and watery, and the yolk is large and flat. Most eggs sold in supermarkets today are Grade AA or A; most grade B eggs are sold for use by food manufacturers.

RESCUE for an older recipe that calls for using raw eggs:
For Caesar Salad, just omit the egg and adjust the recipe, if needed. If an ice cream recipe calls for raw eggs, cook the mixture like a custard to 160°. For uncooked soufflés, cook the egg whites and sugar in the top of a double boiler to 160°, then remove from heat and beat until soft peaks form. In some cases, such as casseroles and custards, you can replace raw eggs with a refrigerated or frozen egg product or imitation eggs. Use ¼ cup egg substitute for each egg that you replace.

• The sizes of eggs include jumbo, extra large, large, medium, small, and peewee. Prices are based primarily on egg size, with the larger sizes costing more per dozen than the smaller sizes. (*continued on the following page*)

E

An egg is composed of many parts, including the shell, yolk, chalazae, and albumen. Most eggs are sold in the shell by the dozen, but eggs are also available frozen and powdered. Commercially frozen egg products are generally pasteurized and may contain a stabilizing ingredient. Imitation eggs or egg substitutes also are available; these usually contain a blend of egg whites, food starch, corn oil, and skim milk powder; they contain no cholesterol, but they do contain quite a bit of sodium. Dried eggs are sold in camping stores; frozen omelets and frozen scrambled eggs also can be purchased.

TEST KITCHEN SECRET

"Separating eggs can be tricky. You can use a special egg separator or you can do it by hand. Tap the egg on a hard surface and hold it over a bowl. Pull the halves apart, holding one-half like a cup to cradle the yolk, and let the white part flow into the bowl underneath. Then rock the yolk back and forth between the two shells until all the white has dripped into the bowl." VANESSA MCNEIL

Storage: Refrigerate eggs preferably in the carton with their large ends up on an inside shelf. The egg-sized spaces on some refrigerator doors subject the eggs to frequent changes in temperature because the door is opened and closed. Fresh, uncooked eggs in the shell can be kept refrigerated in their carton up to 5 weeks. Cool, hard-cooked eggs should be refrigerated and used within a week. Keep unbroken raw yolks covered with water in a tightly covered container and use within a day or two. Refrigerate leftover raw whites in a tightly covered container for no more than 4 days.

Freezing Eggs: If you find yourself with more eggs than you'll use in a few weeks, lightly beat them, add ⅛ teaspoon salt per egg, and pour into freezer containers; if freezing several at once, make a note of the number of eggs on the freezer container. Whole, beaten eggs can be frozen up to 6 months. Thaw eggs in the refrigerator overnight and use immediately. Be sure to thoroughly cook eggs that have been frozen. (*see also* **egg substitute**)

READER TIP

"My husband and I are on a low-cholesterol diet, so I replace whole eggs with egg whites. I substitute 2 eggs whites for 1 whole egg. For scrambled eggs, I use 1 whole egg plus 2 whites for each serving." M.T., Columbia, SC

egg foo yong (foo YUHNG) A Chinese-American dish of eggs mixed with various ingredients such as bean sprouts, scallions, water chestnuts, pork, chicken, and shrimp. Egg foo yong is typically pan-fried into small pancake-size portions, which are sometimes topped with a thin sauce of chicken broth and soy sauce. While *Southern Living* has specialized in offering readers our unique regional cuisine, we've also shared reader favorites from other cuisines, such as the recipe that follows.

EGG FOO YONG

½ cup soy sauce
½ cup water
2 tablespoons sugar
2 tablespoons white vinegar
2 garlic cloves, minced
1 tablespoon all-purpose flour
2 tablespoons water
1 (16-ounce) can bean sprouts, drained

1 (5-ounce) package frozen cooked shrimp or
1 (6-ounce) can crabmeat, drained
1 (7-ounce) can sliced mushrooms, drained
1 small onion, chopped
4 green onions, chopped
4 large eggs, beaten

• Combine first 5 ingredients in a small saucepan. Bring to a boil; reduce heat, and simmer, uncovered, 2 minutes.

• Combine flour and 2 tablespoons water in a small bowl, stirring with a wire whisk until smooth. Stir flour mixture into soy sauce mixture; cook, stirring constantly, until mixture is thickened and bubbly. Set aside, and keep warm.

• Combine bean sprouts and next 4 ingredients in a large bowl; stir beaten eggs into bean sprout mixture.

• Preheat griddle to 350° or place a large skillet over medium heat. Lightly grease griddle or skillet. For each patty, pour about ¼ cup batter onto hot griddle. Cook patties 30 seconds to 1 minute or until edges are set and golden; turn and cook other side. Serve immediately with reserved sauce. Yield: 4 servings.

LITE BITE
Use reduced-sodium soy sauce in this recipe if you're watching your sodium intake.

eggnog A rich, chilled Christmas beverage made of eggs, cream or milk, sugar, nutmeg, flavoring, and sometimes liquor. The recipe name comes from the word "noggin," a small mug or cup in which eggnog was served in earlier days. Refrigerated eggnog and canned eggnog are available in supermarkets during the holiday season. (*see recipe on the following page*)

Southernism

With Kentucky the hotbed of whiskey distilleries in the 1800s (and even today), it's not surprising that one of our favorite holiday drinks is eggnog spiked with bourbon.

TEST KITCHEN SECRET

Some older recipes for eggnog call for using raw eggs. Instead, cook the eggs, sugar, and about half of the milk over low heat, like custard, until it reaches 160°. Then stir in the remaining milk and flavoring. Remember to keep eggnog cool when it's served, because even after cooking, eggs and milk remain perishable. LYDA JONES

AUNT KAT'S CREAMY EGGNOG

Jan Moon from our Test Kitchen shares this recipe that's been in her family for many years.

1 quart milk
12 eggs
¼ teaspoon salt
1½ cups sugar
¾ cup to 1½ cups bourbon*
1 tablespoon vanilla extract
½ teaspoon ground nutmeg, divided
1 quart whipping cream

• Heat milk in a large saucepan over medium heat. (Do not boil.)
• Beat eggs and salt at medium speed with an electric mixer until thick and pale; gradually add sugar, beating well. Gradually stir about one-fourth of hot milk into egg mixture; add to remaining hot milk, stirring constantly.
• Cook over medium-low heat, stirring constantly, 25 to 30 minutes or until mixture thickens and reaches 160°.
• Stir in bourbon, vanilla, and ¼ teaspoon nutmeg. Remove from heat; cool. Cover and chill up to 2 days.
• Beat whipping cream at medium speed with an electric mixer until soft peaks form. Fold whipped cream into egg mixture. Sprinkle with remaining ¼ teaspoon nutmeg before serving. Yield: 3 quarts.

*Substitute 1½ to 2 cups milk for bourbon.

eggplant A member of the nightshade family that's actually a fruit though used as a vegetable. There are many varieties of eggplant, ranging from rich purple to white, from 2 to 12 inches in length, and from oblong to round. The most common eggplant is the large, pear-shaped variety with a smooth, glossy, dark purple skin. Eggplant flesh is creamy white with tiny edible seeds, and its mild flavor combines well with many other ingredients. Eggplants can be prepared in a variety of ways including baking, broiling, frying, and grilling. **Storage:** Refrigerate fresh, uncut eggplants up to 2 days. (*see also* **vegetables**)

pear-shaped eggplant

white eggplant

Japanese eggplant

Q **Is there a way to prevent eggplant from discoloring?**

A Since eggplant flesh discolors rapidly, cut it just before using. The cut flesh can be brushed with lemon juice or dipped in a mixture of lemon juice and water to prevent browning.

TEST KITCHEN SECRET

Sometimes eggplant tastes a little bitter; this can be remedied by salting and letting it sit for about 20 minutes. Eggplant also has a tendency to soak up oil, so coat with a batter or crumb mixture before it's fried. JAMES SCHEND

egg roll A deep-fried Chinese appetizer made from a thin flour and water dough wrapper that's folded and rolled around a savory filling of chopped vegetables that sometimes includes meat.

eggs Benedict A dish consisting of an English muffin topped with ham or Canadian bacon, a poached egg, and hollandaise sauce. It's believed the dish originated in Manhattan's famous Delmonico's Restaurant when regular patrons, Mr. and Mrs. LeGrand Benedict, asked to have a new dish created for the lunch menu. (*see also* **English muffin** *and* **hollandaise sauce**)

EGGS BENEDICT

4 (½-ounce) Canadian bacon slices	4 eggs, poached
2 English muffins, split and toasted	Hollandaise Sauce
	Coarsely ground pepper

• Cook bacon in a skillet coated with cooking spray over medium heat until thoroughly heated, turning once. Drain on paper towels.
• Place 1 bacon slice on each muffin half. Top each with a poached egg, and drizzle evenly with Hollandaise Sauce. Sprinkle with pepper, and serve immediately. Yield: 2 servings.

HOLLANDAISE SAUCE

4 egg yolks	¾ cup butter or margarine, melted
2½ tablespoons fresh lemon juice	¼ teaspoon salt

• Whisk egg yolks in top of a double boiler; gradually whisk in lemon juice. Cook over hot water, stirring constantly with a wire whisk, until mixture thickens.
• Add butter, ¼ cup at a time, whisking until smooth. Whisk in salt; cook, whisking constantly, until smooth and thickened. Serve immediately. Yield: about 1 cup.

egg slicer A utensil with a hinged upper portion of taut, stainless steel wires and a base with an oval depression in slats that correspond to the wires. When the upper portion is brought down onto a hardcooked egg sitting in the depression, it cuts the egg into even slices.

> **TIMESAVING TIP**
> An egg slicer is great for slicing mushrooms. Just trim a piece from the stem end of each mushroom, then cut the trimmed mushrooms, one at a time, in the slicer. The slices will be even and thin.

eggs Sardou (sahr DOO) A dish of poached eggs topped with creamed spinach, artichoke hearts, ham, anchovies, truffles, and hollandaise sauce that originated at Antoine's in New Orleans. It's named for Victorien Sardou, a famous French dramatist. (*see also* **hollandaise sauce**)

egg substitute Found in both the refrigerated and frozen food sections of the supermarket, egg substitutes are typically made of egg whites and may also contain food starch, corn oil, skim milk powder, artificial coloring, and other additives that make the product taste and perform like whole eggs. Most substitutes contain no cholesterol, very little fat, and can be used sparingly in baking and cooking. This product does not perform well in cases where eggs act as leaveners, such as popovers and delicate pastries, but they're a good substitute for eggs for those on low-cholesterol diets.

LITE BITE
Substitute ¼ cup egg substitute for 1 whole egg when trying to reduce your cholesterol. Be sure to cook egg substitutes slowly over low heat; they can be tough and dry if cooked over high heat.

egg timer A tiny hourglass tool that holds just enough sand to run from top to bottom in 3 minutes. This is the time it takes to soft-cook an egg, which was the original intent of the device. The USDA, however, no longer recommends eating soft cooked eggs because they may contain salmonella.

egg wash A mixture of beaten egg yolk or egg white and water or milk. An egg wash can be brushed over baked goods before baking to add sheen and color to the finished product. Our recipes generally give the ingredient proportions to use, but if not, 1 egg white or yolk to 1 tablespoon water or milk is standard.

Q Will baked goods look different if an egg yolk wash is used rather than an egg white wash?

A If a yolk wash is used, it will add a golden-yellow finish, and an egg white wash will add a clear sheen.

elbow macaroni Small, semicircular tubes of pasta. Elbow macaroni comes in several sizes and is the pasta traditionally found in macaroni and cheese. (*see also* **pasta**)

Q How do I know how much elbow macaroni to add to soups and stews?

A One cup of uncooked elbow macaroni will make 2½ cups of cooked, so add it accordingly. If you add too much dry macaroni to a soup, it will consume all the liquid by the time the macaroni cooks.

elderberry The purple-black, tart fruit of the elder tree. The berries are used for preserves, pies, and wine.

elephant ears A thin, crisp French pastry baked or fried until golden, and then sprinkled with granulated sugar. Because the pastry is folded and rolled into large, thin ovals, it takes on the appearance of an elephant's ear.

elephant garlic A member of the leek family, the cloves from this large head have a white outer layer with a pinkish-white interior. Compared to other varieties of garlic, this one's timid in flavor. Elephant garlic is about the size of a small grapefruit. It's grown mainly in California. (*see also* **garlic**)

Q **Where is elephant garlic sold, and how is it used?**

A Elephant garlic abounds in most gourmet markets. While it looks like a large bulb of garlic, it's actually a member of the leek family. Its mild aroma and flavor make it perfect for baking whole, by itself or with meats, or for sautéing as you would regular garlic.

empanadas (em pah NAH dahs) Mexican and Spanish deep-fried turnovers with pastry crusts and fillings of meat, vegetables, or fruit.

emulsion (ih MUHL shuhn) A smooth mixture of two liquids that normally don't mix, such as oil and water. Emulsifying is done by slowly adding one ingredient to another, while rapidly whisking or mixing. Mayonnaise and vinaigrette are two examples of emulsified mixtures. (*see also* **mayonnaise** *and* **vinaigrette**)

enchilada (en chuh LAH dah) A Mexican dish consisting of a soft corn tortilla wrapped around a meat or cheese filling. Enchiladas are typically served hot and topped with red sauce, cheese, guacamole, or sour cream.

CHICKEN ENCHILADAS

3 cups chopped cooked chicken
2 cups (8 ounces) shredded Monterey Jack cheese with peppers
½ cup sour cream
1 (4.5-ounce) can chopped green chiles, drained
⅓ cup chopped fresh cilantro
8 (8-inch) corn tortillas
1 (8-ounce) container sour cream
1 (8-ounce) bottle green taco sauce
Toppings: diced tomato, chopped avocado, chopped green onions, sliced ripe olives, chopped fresh cilantro

• Stir together first 5 ingredients. Spoon chicken mixture evenly over tortillas, and roll up.
• Arrange in a lightly greased 13- x 9-inch baking dish. Coat tortillas with cooking spray.
• Bake at 350° for 35 to 40 minutes or until golden brown.
• Stir together sour cream and taco sauce in a bowl.
• Spoon sour cream mixture over hot enchiladas; sprinkle with desired toppings. Yield: 4 servings.

en croûte (ahn KROOT) (*see* **croûte, en**)

endive (EN dyv) Any of several varieties of salad greens that grow in bunchy heads. Endive, sometimes called "chickory," has slender, whitish green leaves or frilly green or red leaves, and a mild, bitter taste, depending on the variety. The most familiar types of endive include Belgian endive, curly endive, escarole, and radicchio.

Belgian endive

escarole

Storage: Refrigerate endive in plastic bags in the refrigerator up to 3 days. (*see also* **Belgian endive, chicory, curly endive, escarole,** *and* **radicchio**)

English breakfast A hearty breakfast than can include eggs, ham or other meat, fish, broiled tomatoes, mushrooms, baked pastries, fruit, jam, juice, and tea or coffee. Contrast it to continental breakfast, both of which hail from England. (*see also* **continental breakfast**)

English breakfast tea A robust, full-flavored, and richly colored blend of several different black teas. (*see also* **tea**)

English cucumber A long, seedless cucumber with dark green skin and a mild flavor. These cucumbers also are known as "hothouse" or "burpless" cucumbers. (*see also* **cucumber**)

English muffin A round, flat, unsweetened yeast bread that's baked on a griddle. Coarse-textured English muffins are usually split with a fork and toasted and served with butter or jam.

English pea (*see* **sweet green peas**)

English walnut A nut with a hard, wrinkled, tan-colored shell enclosing two distinct halves of nutmeat. The English walnut is the most common type of walnut and has a sweet flavor that makes it good for eating out-of-hand and for using in sweet and savory dishes. It's also used to produce walnut oil. California is the world's leading producer of English walnuts. (*see also* **nuts** *and* **walnut**)

enoki mushrooms (en OH kee) A crisp, delicate, Japanese mushroom that grows in clumps. The mushrooms have long, thin stems, with tiny white or pale orange caps and a mild, almost fruity flavor. Enoki mushrooms can be eaten raw in salads or used to garnish soups or other hot dishes. If part of a cooked dish, they should be added at the last minute, as heat tends to make them tough. Enoki mushrooms can be purchased fresh or canned in Asian markets and some supermarkets. (*see also* **mushroom**)

en papillote (pah pee YOHT) A cooking technique where delicate food, usually seafood or chicken with vegetables, is enclosed in a wrapper of greased parchment paper and then baked. As the food bakes and lets off steam, the parchment puffs up; for serving, the paper is slit and peeled back so the diner can enjoy the escaping aroma. (*see also* **parchment paper**)

Q How is parchment paper prepared for cooking en papillote?

A Cut a piece of parchment paper that's twice as long as it is wide; coat with cooking spray or brush with melted butter. Place the food and seasonings on one-half of the paper, and fold the wrapper over to cover the food. With a series of small double folds, seal all the way around the outer edge of the paper, then place on a baking sheet, and bake as usual.

enrich When a product is thickened or enhanced at the last minute by the addition of another product, such as butter, egg yolks, or cream, to enhance a sauce, or vitamins to enhance the nutrition of flour.

entrée (AHN tray) In the United States, this term refers to the main course of a meal; in Europe, it refers to the first course.

epicure (EHP ih kyoor) This term describes someone with discriminating taste and appreciation of fine foods and wines.

escalope (eh SKAL ohp) A French term for a thin, usually flattened, slice of meat or fish. Because it's so thin the escalope only requires a few seconds of sautéing on both sides. Sometimes this cut is referred to as a "scallop" of meat or fish.

escargot (ehs kahr GOH) The French term for "snail." Escargot is typically an appetizer dish of snails cooked in butter flavored with herbs and served hot in their shells or in ceramic cups. (*see also* **mollusk**)

escarole (EHS kuh rohl) A variety of endive with broad green leaves with slightly curled edges. It has a firm, chewy texture, mildly bitter flavor, and can be eaten raw or cooked. (*see also* **endive**)

espresso (ehs PREHS oh) Dark, strong beverage made by forcing steam or hot water through finely ground and packed Italian-roast coffee. When espresso is made, a thin layer of beige froth appears on the surface; if topped with foam made from steamed milk, espresso becomes cappuccino. (*see also* **cappuccino** *and* **coffee**)

TEST KITCHEN SECRET

If you don't have an espresso maker, make a close substitute in a regular coffee maker using 3 to 4 tablespoons ground espresso roast coffee beans to ¾ cup water. Serve espresso in demitasse cups with cream, lemon peel, raw sugar, or brandy, as you prefer. Lyda Jones

essence A concentrated, usually oily extract made from an herb, spice, or flower and used in small amounts to flavor various dishes. It can be found in specialty food stores and catalogs.

étouffée (eh too FAY) A French term that means "smothered," but Southerners know it as a Cajun dish of either shrimp or crayfish cooked with onions and peppers in a roux base. (*see also* **Cajun cooking, crayfish,** *and* **roux**)

CRAWFISH ÉTOUFFÉE

½ cup butter or margarine	¼ teaspoon ground white pepper
1 large onion, chopped	½ teaspoon hot sauce
¼ cup finely chopped celery	1½ tablespoons all-purpose flour
¼ cup chopped green pepper	¾ cup water
2 garlic cloves, minced	½ cup finely chopped green
1 pound peeled crawfish tails	onions
1 teaspoon salt	¼ cup finely chopped fresh
½ teaspoon ground black pepper	parsley
½ teaspoon onion powder	Hot cooked rice

• Melt butter in a large skillet over medium heat. Add onion and next 3 ingredients; cook, stirring constantly, 5 minutes.
• Stir in crawfish and next 5 ingredients; cook 5 minutes. Stir in flour; cook, stirring constantly, 2 minutes.
• Stir in water gradually; cook over low heat 20 minutes, stirring mixture occasionally.
• Stir in green onions and parsley; cook 3 minutes. Serve over rice. Yield: 3 to 4 servings.

Southernism

Acadian (Cajun) folklore testifies that when making an étouffée, the first thing to do is to marinate the chef. So, in the spirit of Cajun country, be sure to douse yourself with the cup that cheers before you get started!

evaporated milk Concentrated milk made by removing 60 percent of the water from milk. This process gives evaporated milk a slight caramel flavor. The milk is sealed in cans so no refrigeration is necessary until the can is opened. Evaporated fat-free milk and low-fat milk also are available.

Storage: Store unopened cans of evaporated milk at room temperature up to a year. Once opened, cover and refrigerate milk no more than a week. (*see also* **milk**)

Q **Is there a difference between evaporated milk and sweetened condensed milk?**

A Yes; both canned milk products have had 60% of the water removed, but sweetened condensed milk has a significant amount of sugar added. (*see also* **sweetened condensed milk**)

eviscerate (eh VIHS uh rayt) (*see* **draw**)

extracts Concentrated flavorings made from plants such as vanilla beans or almonds. Extracts are created by evaporating or distilling plant's essential oils and then suspending the oils in alcohol. If the extract is labeled "pure," it must contain only essential oils distilled from natural plants.

Q When would an extract be used?

A All types of baked goods, frostings, pies, ice creams, beverages, and dessert recipes benefit from extracts. A favorite Southern example is vanilla extract in pound cake.

Imitation flavoring, such as imitation vanilla extract, replicates the flavor of pure vanilla extract by using synthetic compounds. Artificial flavorings mimic foods that do not exist naturally, such as root beer or butterscotch. Extracts add a burst of flavor to foods without adding extra volume, calories, or changing the consistency. Extracts will keep indefinitely if they are tightly covered and stored in a cool, dark place. (*see also* **essence** *and* **flavoring**)

eye of round A cut of beef from the round that's flavorful, but somewhat tough because it has little fat and marbling. Moist-heat methods of cooking make the cut more tender. Sometimes it's combined with the bottom round for a roast. (*see also* **beef**)

fagioli (fa ZOHO lee) The Italian word for "beans." In most cases, fagioli refers to white kidney beans. Cannellini beans and great Northern beans are substitutes.

Fahrenheit (FAIR uhn hyt) A temperature scale with 32° as the freezing point of water and 212° as its boiling point. (*see also* **Celsius, metric measure,** *and* **thermometer**)

fajitas (fah HEE tuhs) A Mexican-American dish traditionally made from skirt or flank steak that has been marinated in a mixture of oil, lime juice, pepper, and garlic before being grilled. The grilled meat is cut into thin strips and wrapped in a flour tortilla, and accompanied with a variety of garnishes including grilled onions and bell peppers, guacamole, salsa, refried beans, and sour cream. Many restaurants give diners the choice of beef, chicken, or vegetable fajitas. (*see also* **flank steak, skirt steak,** *and recipe on following page*)

READER TIP
"It's easy to plan a party around fajitas. I marinate the meat the night before, and when guests arrive, all I have to do is grill and slice the meat. It's very colorful when the meat and all the toppings are arranged on the buffet. Another plus is guests get to select what they want on their fajitas, so everyone's happy." J.E., San Antonio, TX

CHICKEN FAJITAS

1 cup vegetable oil	1 avocado, peeled and sliced
½ cup lime juice	2 cups (8 ounces) shredded
½ cup chopped fresh cilantro	Monterey Jack cheese
4 garlic cloves, pressed	1 red bell pepper, cut into strips
2 teaspoons salt	1 yellow bell pepper, cut into
1½ tablespoons pepper	strips
12 skinned and boned chicken	12 romaine lettuce leaves
breast halves	Sour cream
12 (6-inch) flour tortillas	Salsa

• Whisk together first 6 ingredients in a shallow dish or large heavy-duty zip-top plastic bag; add chicken. Cover or seal, and chill 1 to 2 hours, turning occasionally.
• Remove chicken from marinade, discarding marinade.
• Grill, covered with grill lid, over medium-high heat (350° to 400°) 20 to 25 minutes or until done. Cut chicken breast halves into thin strips.
• Top tortillas evenly with chicken, avocado, and next 4 ingredients; roll up, and serve with sour cream and salsa. Yield: 6 servings.

falafel (feh LAH fehl) A Middle Eastern dish of deep-fried balls of spiced, ground chickpeas. They're usually served inside pita bread with a yogurt or tahini sauce. (*see also* **chickpea, pita,** *and* **tahini**)

farfalle (fahr FAH lay) An Italian term for "butterfly" used to describe bow tie pasta.

farina (fuh REE nuh) Made from cereal grains, farina is a bland-tasting flour or meal. Sometimes farina is an ingredient in breakfast cereals, baby foods, and pasta. Farina is available in instant, malt, or cocoa-flavored forms. When cooked in boiling water, farina makes a hot breakfast cereal.

farmer cheese (*see* **cheese**)

fatback The layer of fat that runs along a hog's back. It's used to make lard and cracklings and sometimes for cooking, especially in Southern recipes. Fatback is not to be confused with salt pork from the sides and belly of the hog. (*see also* **cracklings**)

Southernism

Pigs were cheap and quick to raise, and provided culinary substance for early Southerners. One such delicacy was fatback. It yielded an inexpensive and conventional seasoning for leafy greens and veggies of all varieties. Many of today's Southerners remain true to their palates and still simmer fatback in a pot of down-home greens. Because of fatback's high-fat content, many Southerners sample it selectively.

fats and oils Cooking fats and oils include a wide array of edible, greasy, solid, or liquid substances that are by-products of animals or plants. They're used primarily in cooking to deliver richness and flavor, to tenderize baked goods, and for frying. All forms of fat are made up of a combination of fatty acids that are either saturated, monounsaturated, or polyunsaturated. Saturated fats are found primarily in animal products and tropical oils, and are usually solid enough to hold their shape at room temperature. They are the least desirable fats to include in a healthy diet. Unsaturated fats (monounsaturated and polyunsaturated) come mainly from vegetables, nuts, and grains, and are usually liquid oils at room temperature. They are more desirable in a healthy diet. Hydrogenated or partially hydrogenated fats are those that have gone through a process where unsaturated oils have been turned into semisolids or saturated fat such as margarine in tub or in stick form.

Selecting: When deciding which fat or oil to use, consider what you're going to make. Some recipes require solid fat and some call for liquid oil. Another factor to consider is whether the particular flavor of an oil or fat is desired. Also important is the temperature you can heat a fat or oil before it starts to smoke and taste unpleasant.

LITE BITE

In general, the softer and more pourable the fat, the less harmful it is to your heart. Exceptions are palm, coconut, and palm kernel oils, which are high in saturated fat. By choosing fats wisely and using them sparingly, you can eat well and enjoy a heart-healthy diet.

• *Almond oil:* Has the delicate flavor and aroma of toasted almonds, but has a low smoke point. Can be used to make salad dressings.
• *Butter:* Has a rich, creamy flavor, but is high in saturated fat. Used for brief, lower heat sautéing because it tends to burn; also used to enrich sauces or baked goods.
• *Canola oil:* Has a bland flavor, light yellow color, fairly high smoke point, and is high in monounsaturated fat. Is good for salad dressings, sautéing, frying, and baking.
• *Coconut oil:* Is popular for deep-frying because it imparts rich flavor, but is high in saturated fat and not widely used in the United States.
• *Corn oil:* Deep gold and mild flavored, all-purpose oil used for general cooking and deep-frying. Is high in polyunsaturated fat.
• *Grapeseed oil:* Has mild flavor and high smoke point so it's suitable for sautéing and frying. Also popular in salad dressings and marinades.

TEST KITCHEN SECRET

When oil becomes fragrant and begins to shimmer, it's hot enough to begin cooking. Once it begins to smoke, it's too hot. LYDA JONES

• *Hazelnut oil:* Fragrant hazelnut flavor, generally combined with lighter oils. It can be used in salad dressings, sauces, main dishes, and baked goods.
(continued on the following page)

• *Lard:* Pure pork fat, rich in flavor. Used by bakers to give flaky texture and rich taste to pastry. Has a high smoke point so it's suitable for deep-frying. Is high in saturated fat.

• *Margarine:* Butter substitute made from hydrogenated vegetable oil. With exception of reduced-fat margarine, it can be used for baking or frying.

• *Olive oil:* Oil produced from the fruit of the olive tree. Extra virgin is a term applied to oil pressed without use of heat or chemicals; it's considered the finest olive oil and is low in acidity. Olive oils labeled superfine, fine, and pure will have less fragrance and color than extra virgin and are better suited to sautéing. Generally, the deeper the color of the olive oil, the more intense the flavor. Olive oil is high in monounsaturated fat and has a fairly low smoke point, which means it can be used for low- or medium-heat sautéing, salad dressings, as a seasoning, and for marinades.

Q Is cholesterol related to cooking fats and oils?

A Cholesterol is a substance present in foods and fats of animal origin; the human liver also produces it. Although cholesterol is necessary for the body to function properly, it's only needed in moderate amounts, and the body usually manufactures an adequate supply. It's carried in the blood in units called lipoproteins, of which there are 2 types: low-density lipoproteins (LDL), which is often called bad cholesterol because it tends to clog arteries and may lead to heart disease and stroke; and high-density lipoproteins (HDL), containing what is sometimes called good cholesterol because it appears to clear fat and excess cholesterol from the blood. Eating foods high in saturated fat may increase total cholesterol and LDL levels. For this reason, a diet low in cholesterol and saturated fat is the first line of defense against high cholesterol. Recent research shows that monounsaturated fats such as those found in avocados, nuts, and peanut, canola, and olive oils may help lower total cholesterol and increase the ratio of good cholesterol to bad cholesterol.

• *Palm oil:* Reddish-orange oil from the fruit of the African palm. It's high in saturated fat. It's used in West African and Brazilian cooking.

• *Palm kernel oil:* Extracted from the nut or kernel of palms. It has a yellowish-white color and mild flavor, but is also high in saturated fat. It's used in some margarines and commercial baked products.

• *Peanut oil:* Clear oil pressed from peanuts, which gives it a hint of nutty flavor. Has a high smoke point so it's prized for stir-frying and frying. It's high in monounsaturated fat and polyunsaturated fat.

• *Safflower oil:* Flavorless, colorless oil from safflower seeds. Has a high smoke point so it's good for sautéing and deep-frying, and is also popular for salad dressings. It's high in polyunsaturated fat.

• *Sesame oil:* Extracted from sesame seeds; can be deep or light amber colored. The darker oil has a stronger flavor and fragrance than the light and is used to flavor Asian dishes. The lighter is excellent for salad dressings or sautéing.

• *Shortening:* A type of hydrogenated solid vegetable fat mostly used for baking or deep-frying.

- *Soybean oil:* Extracted from soybeans and has a light yellow color. Is high in polyunsaturated fat and monounsaturated fat. Used to make margarine and shortening. It has a high smoke point so it's good for sautéing and frying.
- *Sunflower seed oil:* Pale yellow, flavorless oil high in polyunsaturated fat and monounsaturated fat. Has a fairly low smoke point, but can be used for sautéing and salad dressings.
- *Vegetable oil:* All-purpose oil made up of a mixture of other oils such as corn, safflower, and canola. It has a pale color, neutral flavor, and a high smoke point that makes it good for frying.
- *Walnut oil:* Distinctively nutty flavor and fragrance. Used in salad dressings, sauces, and baked goods. It has a low smoke point.

Storage: Fats and oils are sensitive to light, water, and heat. Exposure to these will promote rancidity. Store all fats and oils in airtight containers, especially butter and margarine, which absorb odors easily. Refrigerate butter, margarine, and lard up to 1 month. Store oil and shortening at room temperature—oil up to 9 months and shortening up to 1 year. Olive oil can be stored at room temperature up to 6 months or in the refrigerator up to a year. Flavored nut oils go rancid quicker than other cooking oils and should be bought in small quantities and kept refrigerated. (*see also* **smoke point**)

LITE BITE

To lower the risk of heart attack and some forms of cancer, watch the amount of total fat, especially saturated fat and cholesterol in your diet. The total fat should be no more than 30 percent of your calorie intake. One way to do this is to pay attention to nutrition facts on food labels. Another way is to calculate how many calories and grams of fat are in the food you eat; to do this, you need to know that 1 gram of fat contains 9 calories. Plug those numbers into these 2 equations:

1. Total fat in grams x 9 = total calories from fat

2. $\dfrac{\text{Total fat calories}}{\text{total calories x 100}}$ = % calories from fat

fava bean (FAH vuh) Large, flat, kidney-shaped bean that can be purchased dried, canned, and fresh. Fava beans have a very tough skin, which should be removed by blanching before cooking. Sometimes known as a "broad" bean, favas are often used in Mediterranean and Middle Eastern dishes. They can be cooked in a variety of ways and are often used in soups. (*see also* **beans, dried;** *and* **beans, fresh**)

feijoa (fay YOH ah) A small, egg-shaped fruit that's native to South America and grown in New Zealand and California. Also referred to as a pineapple guava, the feijoa has thin, bright green skin surrounding a fragrant, cream-colored flesh and soft center. Enjoy the feijoa in fruit salads, desserts, or as a garnish.

fennel (FEHN uhl) Florence fennel is a vegetable with a bulbous base, celery-like ribs, and a feathery, bright green top. When raw, this fennel is licorice flavored and has a crisp texture; when cooked, the flavor becomes more delicate and the texture softens. The feathery green tops also have a delicate licorice flavor and are used for seasoning salads and soups. Common fennel is the variety of fennel that produces oval, brown fennel seeds. Fennel seeds are available whole and ground and are used in sweet and savory food as well as to flavor some liqueurs. Fennel is available from fall through spring.
Storage: Store fresh fennel in a plastic bag in the refrigerator up to 5 days. Fennel seeds should be stored in a cool, dark place up to 6 months. (*see also* **spice**)

fennel seeds (*see* **fennel** *and* **spice**)

fermented black beans Small black soybeans preserved in salt. They have a very salty, pungent flavor and are used in Asian cooking for flavoring meat and fish dishes.

feta cheese (FEHT uh) (*see* **cheese**)

fettuccine (feht tuh CHEE nee) Flat, narrow, egg noodles that are cooked in boiling water, drained, and usually served with a sauce. (*see also* **pasta**)

fettuccine Alfredo (feht tuh CHEE nee al FRAY doh) A popular dish of fettuccine coated with a rich cream sauce, Parmesan cheese, and freshly ground pepper. Serve it as a meatless main dish or side dish. (*see also* **Alfredo sauce**)

FETTUCCINE ALFREDO

8 ounces fettuccine, uncooked	**¼ teaspoon ground white pepper**
½ cup butter	**2 tablespoons chopped fresh**
½ cup whipping cream	**parsley**
¾ cup grated Parmesan cheese	**Garnish: fresh parsley**

• Cook fettuccine according to package directions, omitting salt. Drain well, and place in a large bowl; keep warm.
• Combine butter and whipping cream in a small saucepan; cook over low heat until butter melts. Stir in cheese, pepper, and parsley.
• Pour mixture over fettuccine; toss until fettuccine is coated. Garnish, if desired. Yield: 4 servings.

fiber The indigestible or partially digestible parts of plants. High-fiber foods are essential because they provide roughage to aid in digestion and excretion of waste. Some experts also suggest that a diet high in fiber may reduce the risk of heart disease and certain forms of cancer. There are two types of fiber:

• **Insoluble:** Fiber that cannot be dissolved in water. The sources for insoluble fiber include dried beans, vegetables, fruit skins, and bran from grains such as wheat. Insoluble fiber helps keep the digestive system working and may help reduce the risk of colon cancer. Fiber increases the speed at which food passes through the gastro-intestinal tract, thus reducing exposure time of potential cancer-causing substances.

> **Q How can I increase the level of fiber in my diet?**
>
> **A** A: One way is to start eating more fruits such as oranges or peaches, or whole foods such as apples or potatoes with the skin on. Select high-fiber vegetables such as corn, peas, or beans more often. Eating whole grain bread and high-fiber cereals also will help.

• **Soluble:** Fiber that dissolves in water to form a gel-like mixture to slow down absorption of nutrients into the bloodstream. Sources are fruits, vegetables, dried beans, brown rice, barley, and oats. Soluble fiber may help lower blood cholesterol levels.

fiddlehead fern Young, edible fern that resembles the spiral end of a violin or fiddle; the tightly coiled, deep green fronds have a flavor similar to asparagus or green beans. The fern fronds are generally available in specialty produce markets from April through July. Steam, simmer, or sauté them like a vegetable, or serve raw in salads.
Storage: Refrigerate, unwashed, in a plastic bag up to 2 days.

fideos (fih DAY ohs) Thin, vermicelli-type noodles used often in Spanish cooking.

field pea A type of yellow or green pea grown for drying. Once dried, the peas usually are split along a natural seam and are then called "split peas." Dried field peas do not usually require presoaking before cooking. (*see also* **pea**)

field salad (*see* **corn salad**)

fig A soft, teardrop-shaped fruit with edible seeds. There are hundreds of varieties of figs; they range in color from purplish and reddish brown, to green or greenish yellow, and from round to oval. Fig meat ranges from pale pink to purple and tastes delicate and sweet. Fresh figs are available from June through October, and are delicious eaten out-of-hand or in baked goods or preserves. Figs also can be purchased candied, dried, or canned in syrup.

Storage: Fresh figs are very perishable; handle them gently. Place them in a single layer in a paper towel-lined container and refrigerate only 2 or 3 days. Dried figs can be stored in an airtight container and refrigerated up to 6 months or in the freezer up to a year.

Southernism

Southerners have never grown figs commercially since Spaniards first introduced the sweet fruit to this country more than 400 years ago. Enough backyard fig trees dot our region, however, to provide fresh figs for making homemade jams and preserves to share year-round with family and friends.

figaro sauce (FIHG uh roh) A French compound sauce made from hollandaise sauce flavored with tomato puree and minced parsley. Figaro sauce is typically served with fish or poultry. (*see also* **hollandaise sauce**)

filbert (*see* **hazelnut**)

filé powder (fih LAY) Ground young sassafras leaves considered by many to be an essential contribution to gumbo and other Creole dishes. It lends an earthy flavor and thickening properties to soups and sauces. Find filé with spices or gourmet foods in your supermarket, and store it in a cool, dark place up to 6 months.

TEST KITCHEN SECRET

If filé is added after gumbo is removed from the heat, it mixes in obediently. But if it's added while the gumbo is cooking, it turns tough and stringy. Sometimes we serve filé as a condiment that can be sprinkled over an individual serving of gumbo. MARGARET MONROE DICKEY

Southernism

Choctaw Indians from the marshlands of southern Louisiana introduced filé powder to the Creole cooks of the region in the late 1800s. Filé quickly became a thickening alternative to okra in the famous gumbos simmering throughout Louisiana, and is a staple seasoning in kitchens throughout the bayou.

filet mignon (fih LAY mihn YON) An expensive, boneless cut of beef that comes from the tenderloin. A filet can be up to several inches thick and two to three inches in diameter. Cook filet mignon by broiling, grilling, or sautéing. (*see also* **beef**)

fillet (fih LAY) A piece of meat or fish that has been carefully removed from the bone. This term can also refer to removing the bone from a piece of meat or fish.

filo (*see* **phyllo**)

fines herbes (FEEN erb) A French term that describes a mixture of very finely chopped herbs, including chervil, chives, parsley, and tarragon, though others might also be part of the blend. Dried fines herbes, available in the spice section, are typically added to a cooked mixture near the end of cooking. (*see also* **herbs**)

fino (FEE noh) Pale gold, very dry Spanish sherry that's often served chilled as an apéritif.

firm ball stage (*see* **candy**)

fish Fish have fins, backbones, and gills, and provide some of the most versatile forms of animal protein available.

Fish come from saltwater (such as flounder and grouper) and freshwater (such as catfish and trout), and may be both wild and farmed. Fish are further divided into two categories: fat or oily and lean.

Fat fish have an oil content of more than 5 percent and tend to be higher in calories and stronger in flavor than lean fish. The color of oily fish is usually darker due to oil distributed throughout the flesh. Fat fish are suited to grilling, broiling, and smoking. Lean fish contain less than 5 percent oil. Lean fish are therefore milder in favor and whiter in appearance than fat fish. They are better suited to moist-heat cooking such as poaching and baking; they can be grilled if basted often. Use the chart at right to determine if the fish you're cooking is classified as fat or lean, and then cook accordingly.

Selecting fish: When shopping for fish, deal with a store that has quick turnover, regularly

FISH CLASSIFICATION

FAT FISH	LEAN FISH	
Amberjack	Cod	Scamp
Freshwater Catfish	Flounder	Scrod
Herring	Grouper	Sea Bass
Lake Trout or Rainbow Trout	Haddock	Snapper
	Halibut	Sole
Mackerel	Mahi mahi	Swordfish
Mullet	Ocean Perch	Tilapia
Pompano	Orange Roughy	Tilefish
Salmon	Pike	Triggerfish
Sardines	Pollock	Turbot
Tuna	Redfish	Walleye
Whitefish	Rockfish	Whiting

replenishes its stock, and uses refrigerated cases for storage. The eyes of a fresh fish should be clear, clean, and full, almost bulging. The gills should be pinkish-red and not slippery. The flesh should be firm and elastic, and the skin should have no faded markings, and be shiny with scales firmly attached. But most important is the odor; fish should have a clean, mild aroma and not an offensive fishy or ammonia smell.

FISH FORMS

You can purchase fresh fish in a variety of forms.

- A **whole fish** makes a dramatic presentation when cooked. Purchase 1 pound per serving.

- A **drawn fish** is a whole fish that has been eviscerated and scaled. Purchase 1 pound per serving.

- A **dressed fish** has been eviscerated, scaled, and has head and fins, and sometimes the tail removed. Pan-dressed fish is simply smaller fish that has been dressed. Purchase ½ pound per serving.

- **Fish steaks** are crosscut slices of large dressed fish. They're usually cut about 1 inch thick. The only bone is a cross section of the backbone and ribs. Purchase about ⅓ to ½ pound per serving.

- **Fillets** are the sides of fish cut lengthwise away from the backbone. They're often skinned and are usually, though not always, boneless. Purchase ⅓ to ½ pound per serving.

TIMETABLE FOR COOKING FISH

COOKING METHOD	FORM	WEIGHT OR THICKNESS	COOKING TEMPERATURE	TOTAL COOKING MINUTES
Baking	Dressed	3 to 4 pounds	350°	40 to 60
	Pan-dressed	½ to 1 pound	350°	25 to 30
	Steaks	½ to 1 inch	350°	25 to 30
	Fillets	1 inch	350°	10 per inch
Broiling	Pan-dressed	½ to 1 pound	Broil	10 to 15
	Steaks	½ to 1 inch	Broil	10 to 15
	Fillets	1 inch	Broil	10 per inch
Frying	Pan-dressed	½ to 1 pound	375°	2 to 4
	Steaks	½ to 1 inch	375°	2 to 4
	Fillets	1 inch	375°	1 to 5
Grilling	Fillets	1 inch	medium high (350° to 400°)	10 per inch
Poaching	Pan-dressed	½ to 1 pound	Simmer	10
	Steaks	½ to 1 inch	Simmer	10
	Fillets	1 inch	Simmer	9 per inch

Cooking Fish: Fresh fish can be baked, broiled, fried, grilled, steamed, or microwaved. When selecting your cooking method, keep in mind if the fish is fat or lean (see chart on page 197). Overcooking or cooking at too high a temperature will cause fish to become dry and tough. Be sure to check for doneness occasionally while cooking. Test for doneness by inserting a fork into the thickest part of the fish, and twist slightly; if done, the fish will flake easily and come away from the bones. The flesh becomes opaque and the juices should be milky white.

When Grilling: Choose a fish fillet or steak that's at least 1 inch thick for grilling. Our Test Kitchens staff recommends spraying the food rack with cooking spray before placing it over a hot fire. Use a fish basket if you'd like; be sure to grease the basket before adding the fish.

When Poaching: It's easy to poach fish in a fish poacher—a long, narrow piece of cookware with a removable tray.

TEST KITCHEN SECRET

If you have to scale a fish, use a knife or a utensil called a fish scaler. We prefer to scale fish outside on newspaper; if inside, insert the fish in a large plastic bag. The scales will fly off, but be trapped in the bag. Vie Warshaw

Or, cut fish in half crosswise and use a large skillet. Fill the pan with liquid deep enough to cover the fish; bring to a boil, reduce heat, and simmer liquid. Add fish to liquid, and simmer 9 to 10 minutes per inch of thickness, turning halfway through cooking time. (*continued on the following page*)

When Microwaving: It's best to microwave fish, covered, at HIGH power for 3 to 5 minutes per pound to quickly seal in juices and flavor. Arrange thicker portions to the outside of the dish so they'll get done without overcooking the thinner areas. When fish turns opaque, it's done.

Storage: Fresh fish is perishable, so it's best to cook it the same day you buy it or catch it. If that's not possible, store fish wrapped in plastic in the coldest part of the refrigerator up to 2 days, or refrigerate, covered with ice, in a colander over a drip pan. Freeze fish in an airtight wrap up to 3 months.

> **LITE BITE**
>
> Swordfish, halibut, rainbow trout, canned solid white tuna, and sockeye salmon are good sources of omega-3 oil, an essential type of fat that may help protect your heart and also may be beneficial for rheumatoid arthritis, psoriasis, and hypertension (high blood pressure).

fish and chips A British dish of deep-fried fish fillets (usually cod or haddock) and French fries, usually served with malt vinegar.

five-spice powder A mixture of five ground spices used in Chinese cooking. The combination usually consists of cinnamon, cloves, fennel seeds, star anise, and Szechuan peppercorns.

fizz Gin fizz is the most popular of this type cocktail drink made with liquor, lemon juice, sugar, and soda served over ice.

flagolet (fla zhoh LAY) A small, tender kidney-shaped bean cultivated in France with a pale green to creamy white color. Flagolet beans are rarely available fresh in the United States, but they can be purchased dried or canned. They're often served as an accompaniment with lamb.

flake To break food into small pieces. For example, using a fork to break off small pieces of fish or canned tuna.

flambé (flahm BAY) A French term that describes a dramatic method of preparing or serving food with flaming brandy or liqueur. This presentation is particularly appealing for dessert, where fruits or fruit-flavored desserts are flamed and served over ice cream, such as Cherries Jubilee or Bananas Foster.

BANANAS FOSTER

¼ cup butter or margarine
⅓ cup firmly packed dark brown sugar
½ teaspoon ground cinnamon
4 bananas, quartered

⅓ cup banana liqueur
⅓ cup dark rum
1 pint vanilla ice cream

• Melt butter in a large skillet over medium-high heat; add brown sugar and next 3 ingredients. Cook, stirring constantly, 2 minutes or until bananas are tender. Pour rum into a small long-handled saucepan; heat just until warm. Remove from heat. Ignite with a long match, and pour over bananas. Baste bananas with sauce until flames die down. Serve immediately over ice cream. Yield: 4 servings.

TEST KITCHEN SECRET

“To flame brandy or a liqueur, use a long match to ignite the warmed liqueur. Then pour it carefully over the food in a flameproof dish. Never use 150-proof alcohol; it's too volatile and might explode when ignited.” Mary Allen Perry

flan (FLAHN) The Spanish term for a caramel custard baked in a mold, then chilled and served inverted onto a dessert plate, and drizzled with the caramel from the mold. Also refers to a round tart with either a sweet or savory filling. It's usually baked in a bottomless metal ring called a flan ring that's placed on a baking sheet before adding the pastry. (*see also* **crème caramel** *and* **custard**)

FLAN

⅔ cup sugar
4 large eggs, lightly beaten
1 (14-ounce) can sweetened condensed milk

1¾ cups milk
2 teaspoons vanilla extract

• Sprinkle ⅔ cup sugar in a large heavy skillet. Cook over medium heat, stirring constantly with a wooden spoon, until sugar melts and turns light brown. Quickly pour hot caramel into an oiled 9-inch round cakepan, tilting to coat bottom evenly; set aside. (Caramel syrup will harden and crack.)
• Combine eggs and remaining 3 ingredients; beat with a wire whisk. Pour custard mixture over syrup in cakepan. Cover cakepan, and place in a large shallow pan. Add hot water to pan to a depth of 1 inch. Bake at 325° for 50 minutes or until a knife inserted near center comes out clean.
• Remove pan from water bath, and uncover; cool completely on a wire rack. Cover and chill at least 8 hours. Loosen edges of flan with a spatula, and invert onto a rimmed serving plate, letting melted caramel drizzle over the top. Yield: 8 servings.

F

flank steak A long, thin, fibrous cut of beef that comes from the lower hindquarter. It can be tenderized by marinating, and then broiled or grilled whole and cut into thin, across-the-grain slices. (*see also* **beef** *and* **fajitas**)

FLANK STEAK IN MEXICAN MARINADE

1 (6-ounce) can pineapple juice	1 tablespoon ground cumin
½ cup reduced-sodium soy sauce	1 teaspoon garlic salt
¼ cup fresh lime juice	1 (1¾-pound) flank steak

• Combine first 5 ingredients, stirring well; reserve ¼ cup pineapple mixture, and chill.
• Place steak in a large shallow dish or zip-top plastic bag; pour remaining pineapple mixture over steak. Cover or seal, and chill 3 to 4 hours, turning steak occasionally.
• Remove steak from marinade, discarding marinade.
• Grill, covered with grill lid, over medium-high heat (350° to 400°) 15 minutes or until a meat thermometer inserted into thickest portion registers 145° (medium rare), turning occasionally and basting with reserved ¼ cup pineapple mixture.
• Slice steak; serve with tortillas, tomato, lettuce, guacamole, shredded cheese, and sour cream. Yield: 6 servings.

flapjack (*see* **pancake**)

flatbread A Scandinavian crisp, crackerlike bread made with rye, wheat, or barley flour. Flatbread is a nice accompaniment for soup, salad, or cheese.

flauta (FLAUW tah) A Mexican corn tortilla rolled around a savory meat or poultry filling and fried until crisp.

flavor A complex combination of aroma, taste, and texture. To enjoy the fullest flavor of food, all three of these sensations work in harmony. Scientists believe there are four basic flavors that our taste buds recognize: sweet, sour, salty, and bitter. Most foods that we enjoy are a combination of several or all of these basic flavors.

flavoring An imitation extract made of chemical compounds that doesn't contain any of the original food it resembles. Common imitation flavorings include banana, cherry, coconut, strawberry, and vanilla. (*see also* **extracts**)

float A scoop of ice cream added to a carbonated beverage. For example, vanilla ice cream added to root beer for a root beer float.

floating islands A French dessert of poached meringues floating in a thin vanilla custard sauce and drizzled with caramel. Floating islands are sometimes referred to as "snow eggs."

florentine (FLOHR uhn teen) A thin, crisp Italian cookie made of butter, sugar, cream, honey, and candied fruit. After baking, the cookies are often coated with chocolate on one side.

Florentine, à la A phrase meaning in the style of Florence, Italy, and traditionally refers to dishes that are served on a bed of spinach. Florentine dishes are typically topped with Mornay sauce and sometimes sprinkled with cheese and browned in the oven. The term can also refer to any dish containing spinach. (*see also* **Mornay sauce**)

flounder A type of flat fish native to Southern coastal waters as well as the Pacific Ocean. They have a brownish-gray skin, and the meat is lean, firm, white, and mild-flavored. Flounder can be baked, broiled, poached, steamed, sautéed, or deep-fried. (*see also* **fish**)

CRAB-STUFFED FLOUNDER

1 celery rib, chopped	1 large egg, lightly beaten
3 green onions, chopped	2 tablespoons fresh lemon juice
2 garlic cloves, minced	1 tablespoon chopped fresh
¼ cup olive oil	parsley
½ pound fresh lump crabmeat, drained	¼ teaspoon salt
	¼ teaspoon pepper
1 cup soft breadcrumbs (homemade)	6 (4-ounce) flounder fillets
	½ cup butter or margarine,
½ cup grated Parmesan cheese	melted
1 plum tomato, chopped	Garnish: lemon wedges

• Cook celery, green onions, and garlic in hot oil in a large skillet over medium-high heat, stirring constantly, until tender. Remove from heat; add crabmeat and next 8 ingredients, stirring well.

• Brush fillets evenly with melted butter. Spoon 1 heaping tablespoon crabmeat mixture on top of each fillet. Roll up fillets, and secure each with a wooden pick. Place fillets in a lightly greased 13- x 9-inch baking dish. Spoon remaining crabmeat mixture over each stuffed fillet, and drizzle with any remaining butter.

• Cover and bake at 375° for 20 minutes. Uncover and bake 10 more minutes or until fish flakes with a fork. Garnish, if desired. Yield: 6 servings.

F

flour The very finely ground meal of an edible grain. Flour is milled from all kinds of grains: wheat, corn, rye, oats, and barley, and each grain produces one or more kinds of flour. Differences in flour are due to the particular grain used and how it's processed.

Southernism

Staunch, native Southern cooks believe that soft wheat flour such as White Lily and Martha White make the softest, tenderest biscuits. Believe it or not, wheat grown in the South is softer than wheat grown in the North, so these brands are Southern-bred.

Types of Flour:

Wheat flours are classified by the amount of protein they contain. Soft wheat flours are relatively low in protein and generally are best for making cakes, cookies, and pastries. Wheat flours made from hard wheat are high in protein and are generally used for breads. Durum wheat, the hardest wheat of all, produces flour very high in protein that's used for making pasta. By using different types of wheat in the milling process, a variety of flours are produced. It's important to note that the following different types of flours are not generally interchangeable in our recipes:

LITE BITE

To add more fiber to your diet, replace part of the all-purpose flour in a recipe with whole wheat flour. Replace no more than half of the all-purpose with whole wheat. Gradually add liquid because you may need less than when using only all-purpose flour. Keep in mind that the end product may have less volume and a denser texture.

• *Bread flour* is a blend of hard wheat flour and a bit of malted barley flour, and is produced especially for bread making. Its high-protein content produces sturdy yeast breads.

• *All-purpose flour* is a combination of hard wheat and soft wheat flours and can be used for all types of baking. There are some all-purpose flours produced in the South such as White Lily and Martha White that have a higher content of soft wheat, and these are good for baking biscuits, cakes, quick breads, and sweet rolls. National brands, such as Pillsbury and Gold Medal, are considered hard wheat flours and may be used in a variety of baked goods.

• *Unbleached flour* is all-purpose flour that has no bleaching agents added during processing and can be used interchangeably with all-purpose flour.

• *Self-rising flour* is all-purpose flour that has leavening and salt added. It's best not to substitute self-rising flour for all-purpose; however, you can substitute all-purpose for self rising with these adjustments: For 1 cup self-rising, use 1 cup all-purpose plus 1 teaspoon baking powder and ¼ teaspoon salt.

• *Cake flour* is soft wheat flour with a lower protein content than all-purpose; it produces a tender, delicate crumb in cakes. Substitute all-purpose flour for cake flour by using 2 tablespoons less all-purpose flour per cup.

• *Instant flour*, sometimes called instant-blending flour or shake-and-blend flour, is made by a special process that produces quick-mixing flour for use in thickening gravies and sauces. This flour dissolves best in cold water, but novice cooks like it because it's more forgiving than regular flour when added directly to hot sauces. If you whisk constantly while adding this flour, it blends in smoothly.

• *Pastry flour* is a soft wheat blended flour with less starch than cake flour, and is used only for making pastry.

• *Whole wheat flour* is coarse-textured and ground from the entire wheat kernel, which makes it higher in fiber, nutrients, and fat content. Also called graham flour, whole wheat flour is good in breads and some cookies, but is not the best choice for pastry or other delicate baked goods.

Q **Is it necessary to sift flour before using?**

A Since flour is sifted during milling, there's no need to sift before measuring. When measuring flour, stir the flour lightly, and spoon it lightly into a standard dry measuring cup. Then level with the straight edge of a spatula. The only flour we sift before measuring is cake flour.

Storage: Store all-purpose flour in an airtight container in a cool, dry place for 10 to 15 months. Whole grain flours can be stored up to 5 months. For longer storage, refrigerate or freeze the flour in an airtight container. Be sure to bring refrigerated or frozen flour to room temperature before using.

flowers, edible
Flower blossoms that are used as an ingredient in a recipe or as a garnish. Before using flowers in recipes, make sure they haven't been sprayed with chemicals or pesticides. Also, make sure the flower itself isn't poisonous. Rinse edible flowers with water and gently pat dry before use.

Q **How do I find out if a flower is safe to eat?**

A Contact the poison control center or your local botanical society or county Extension service. The flowers in the chart are generally considered safe.

Storage: Refrigerate edible flowers in an airtight container up to 1 day.

EDIBLE FLOWER BLOSSOMS AND HOW TO USE

FLOWER	FLAVOR	USE
Borage	Mild cucumber	Salad
Calendula	Tangy	Salads, soups, dips
Chive blossoms	Mild sweet onion	Salads, soups
Daisy	Mild	Salads
Dandelion	Mild	Soups
Daylily	Sweet to tart	Salads
Lavender	Sweet	Fruit salads, desserts
Marigold	Citrus	Salads, soups
Nasturtium	Peppery	Salads
Pansy	Spicy grapes	Salads
Rose	Perfumy, slightly sweet	Beverages, desserts
Squash blossoms	Slightly sweet, squashlike	Salads
Violets	Sweet, tangy, or spicy	Fruit salads, desserts

flute (*see* **crimp**)

focaccia (foh CAH chee ah) Italian flat, round bread leavened with yeast and flavored with olive oil and herbs. Focaccia can be eaten as a snack or served as an accompaniment with soups or salads.

> ⏱ **TIMESAVING TIP**
> Ready-to-eat focaccia is available at the supermarket and can be used as a quick pizza crust. Just add your favorite toppings and bake.

foie gras (FWAH GRAH) A French term that refers to the liver of a goose or duck that has been force-fed for fattening. The rich livers are typically used to make pâté, an appetizer, which is served chilled with thin, sliced toast. The livers also are delicious quickly sautéed. (*see also* **pâté**)

fold A technique where a light and airy ingredient, such as beaten egg whites, is gently mixed with a heavier ingredient, such as custard. To fold, place the lighter mixture on top of the heavier one in a large bowl; use a rubber spatula or wire whip to cut down through the mixtures, move across the bottom of the bowl, and come back up, folding some of the mixture from the bottom over close to the surface. Turn the bowl often so the ingredients are evenly distributed.

> **TEST KITCHEN SECRET**
> *Folding is the way to "stir" delicate dishes, such as soufflés, that would collapse with too much regular stirring. These dishes lose their fluffiness if folded incorrectly. So for best results, use a firm, but light hand, and don't overdo it. Stop folding once the mixtures are just blended.* JAN MOON

fondant (FAHN duhnt) A sweet, thick opaque paste of sugar, water, and cream of tartar. Once a fondant mixture is cooked and cooled, it can be beaten and kneaded until extremely pliable. Fondant is used for making candy, but heating makes it soft enough to use for decorating cakes.

fondue (fahn DOO) A French word referring to food cooked at the table in a ceramic or metal pot with its own heat source. There are three types of fondue. Cheese fondue is a melted cheese mixture into which chunks of French bread can be dipped. Meat fondue is small pieces of beef cooked in the fondue pot and then dipped into sauces. Dessert fondue is a heated dessert sauce, often chocolate, into which fruit or cake can be dipped.

PUB FONDUE

1 (10¾-ounce) can Cheddar
   cheese soup, undiluted
¾ cup beer
2 teaspoons prepared mustard

1 teaspoon Worcestershire sauce
2 cups (8 ounces) shredded
   mild Cheddar cheese

• Combine first 4 ingredients in a heavy saucepan; bring to a boil over
medium heat, stirring constantly. Gradually add shredded cheese, stirring
constantly, until cheese melts. Spoon into a fondue pot. Serve with cubes of
French bread for dipping Yield: 2½ cups.

fontina cheese (fahn TEE nah) (*see* **cheese**)

food coloring Liquid or paste edible dyes that are used to tint foods
different colors. A tiny
amount of food coloring
goes a long way, so add it
gradually with caution.
Liquid coloring comes in
little bottles that can be
purchased at most super-
markets. Paste coloring
comes in a wider variety of colors and is sold in cake decorating shops.

Q What's the difference between liquid and
paste food coloring?

A Paste coloring is good to use when tinting a mixture
that doesn't combine easily with liquid, such as
white chocolate. Paste works especially well to create
darker colors, such as black and red. Liquid coloring
is handy for creating lighter colors in foods.

food groups To help consumers make nutritious food choices, the
USDA developed the Food Guide Pyramid. The pyramid stresses that good
nutrition begins
with three food
groups: grains, veg-
etables, and fruits.
Foods from the
dairy and meat
groups follow next
and are among the
richest sources of
protein and calcium.
Foods from the fats,
oil, and sweets group
should be eaten only
occasionally and in
moderation.

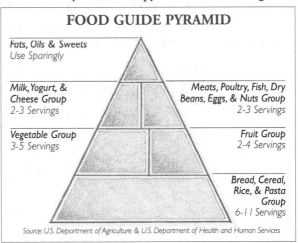

FOOD GUIDE PYRAMID

Fats, Oils & Sweets
Use Sparingly

Milk, Yogurt, &
Cheese Group
2-3 Servings

Meats, Poultry, Fish, Dry
Beans, Eggs, & Nuts Group
2-3 Servings

Vegetable Group
3-5 Servings

Fruit Group
2-4 Servings

Bread, Cereal,
Rice, & Pasta
Group
6-11 Servings

Source: U.S. Department of Agriculture & U.S. Department of Health and Human Services

food mill A kitchen utensil used to strain and puree foods. A food mill usually has a hand-turned paddle that forces food through a strainer plate at the bottom, removing skins, seeds, and pulp. Southerners savvy in making jellies often use food mills to help clarify the pulp.

food processor An appliance brought to the United States from France in the 1970s. It's used to puree, chop, grate, slice, and shred foods. A food processor consists of a plastic work bowl that sits on a motorized driveshaft. The cover has a feed tube through which foods can be added. Food processors are sold in different sizes to accommodate different amounts of food; many come with a set of blades for different tasks.

TEST KITCHEN SECRET

"When chopping, shredding, or slicing multiple foods, the food processor can save lots of time. It makes quicker work of Southern specialties such as Brunswick stew than our forefathers could ever imagine. Food processors are so powerful that they can overwork foods if you aren't careful. Don't use them for mashing potatoes, beating egg whites, or whipping cream." MARGARET MONROE DICKEY

food safety Protecting food from the growth of organisms that can cause illness or death. Food safety is such an important issue that the USDA maintains regulations governing the food industry and offers advice for consumers. Basic rules of food safety include:

FOOD-BORNE ILLNESS ISSUES

These bacteria can cause mild to severe intestinal flulike symptoms, and even death. Careful attention to food safety can prevent potential ingestion.

BACTERIA	FOOD CULPRITS	PREVENTION
Salmonella	Meat, poultry, fish, eggs, milk, custards, cream-filled desserts	Thoroughly cook all meat, eggs, poultry, and fish. Keep raw food separate from cooked food. Do not drink unpasteurized or raw milk
Staphylococcus aureus	Meat, poultry, cheese, eggs, starchy salads, meat and poultry salads, custards, cream-filled desserts	Wash hands and utensils before preparation. Do not leave at room temperature more than 2 hours.
Clostridium perfringens	Large portions of foods that cool slowly, chafing-dish foods not kept hot, poultry, gravies, stews, meat casseroles	Keep hot food hot, over 140°, and keep cold food cold, under 40°. Divide foods cooked in bulk into shallow containers to cool.
Clostridium botulinum	Home-canned foods and commercial canned foods	Use only reliable recipes. Don't use canned goods with cloudy liquids, loose lids, spurting liquid, or goods in cracked jars; avoid swollen or dented cans and lids

- **Shop smart.** Buy perishable items last and avoid buying items that you won't use before the expiration date.
- **Keep cold foods cold.** Keep cold foods at 40° or below. Set your refrigerator to no higher than 40° and your freezer to 0°. As soon as you return home from shopping, refrigerate or freeze perishables. Defrost and marinate foods in the refrigerator rather than at room temperature. At picnics, keep perishables in a closed ice chest in the shade. Set out small amounts of food at a time and, when possible, surround it with ice.
- **Keep hot foods hot.** Keep hot foods over 140°. To be certain that food is cooked to a safe temperature, use an instant-read thermometer (cook pork to at least 160°, beef to at least 145°, chicken breasts to 170°, and whole chickens to 180°). When reheating leftovers, make sure they reach at least 165°.
- **Keep things clean.** Wash your hands with hot, soapy water before and after handling food. Use hot, soapy water on all dishes, utensils, and work surfaces. Soak cutting boards in a mild bleach solution and replace them if they get deep cuts. Wash kitchen towels in the hot water cycle of your washing machine, and wash sponges daily in hot water or in the dishwasher.
- **Avoid cross-contamination.** Keep raw meat, poultry, seafood, and eggs away from ready-to-eat foods. When preparing foods, cut vegetables and salad ingredients first, then raw meats and poultry. Be careful to avoid placing cooked food on a plate that previously held raw meat, poultry, eggs, or seafood unless it has been thoroughly washed. Discard all unused marinades, or, if used, bring to a boil first to kill bacteria. (*see also* **cutting board**)

> ### TEST KITCHEN SECRET
>
> *We stay abreast of current recommendations of the USDA regarding food safety. Visit the Web site at **www.foodsafety.gov** for up-to-date information.*
>
> JAN MOON

fool A British dessert made by folding pureed fruit into whipped cream. The British traditionally used gooseberries to make this dessert.

fortified wine Wine that has been enhanced with brandy. Such wines include port, sherry, and many dessert wines. (*see also* **wine**)

Frangelico (fran JELL ih koh) A sweet hazelnut liqueur often used for flavoring desserts and coffees. (*see also* **liqueur**)

frankfurter A smoked, seasoned, precooked sausage made from beef, pork, chicken, or turkey, and known by several other names including hot dog, wiener, coney, and frank. Frankfurters can contain up to 30 percent fat and 10 percent water. They range in size from the tiny "cocktail frank" to the famous footlongs. Although precooked, frankfurters taste better if heated, and can be grilled, fried, steamed, braised, or microwaved. (*see also* **hot dog**)

frappé (fra PAY) A French term for a drink that consists of a liqueur poured over shaved or crushed ice.

freeze-drying Preserving food by freezing it in a vacuum chamber and removing moisture. Although brittle and crumbly, freeze-dried foods maintain their color and shape better than other dried foods. Freeze-dried foods are light, compact, easily transported, and can be stored at room temperature. A variety of freeze-dried foods are available for camping or backpacking and can be purchased at outdoor stores.

freezing A method of preserving foods by storing them at 0° or below. Meats, fish, poultry, fruits, vegetables, bread, and many other dishes freeze well. The key to good results is to select good quality, fresh food, and freeze it as quickly as possible. The longer it takes to freeze, the larger the ice crystals are that form, and larger ice crystals eventually cause the food to deteriorate. Protect foods from the dry, cold air of the freezer, or they will get freezer burn, which is extreme drying that ruins texture and flavor. Protect foods by wrapping them carefully in airtight packages.

> ### TEST KITCHEN SECRET
>
> *Tray freezing is ideal for berries, shrimp, or other small foods. Spread foods in a single layer on a baking sheet or tray, and freeze until the pieces are firm. Then transfer to a plastic bag or rigid plastic container for continued storage.* MARGARET MONROE DICKEY

Best freezer containers and wrappings:
- *Freezer paper:* Must be labeled and sealed completely with freezer tape. Is often used over cardboard, plastic, or foil for additional protection.
- *Heavy-duty zip-top bags made for freezing:* Fill and eliminate excess air before sealing and labeling. Plastic wrap is even better because it seals out more air than bags and doesn't waste space; however at least two layers are needed for best protection.
- *Rigid, plastic containers with lids:* (less than 2 quarts) are ideal, but must leave at least ½-inch headspace for dry foods and at least 1 inch for liquids to allow for expansion during freezing. Vacuum-sealed plastic requires a machine to suck out the air before sealing in the heavy-duty plastic wrap.

SHELF LIFE OF FROZEN FOODS

Here's how long to expect common foods to last in the freezer. Use this chart to write an expiration date on foods before freezing.

FOOD	STORAGE TIME
Breads, rolls, biscuits	3 months
Cakes, cupcakes	6 months
Casseroles	1 to 3 months
Cookies (unbaked)	6 months
Cookies (baked)	8 to 12 months
Fruits (except citrus)	8 to 12 months
Leftovers	1 to 3 months
Pies	2 months
Soups and Stews	1 to 3 months
Vegetables (blanched)	8 to 12 months

Storage: Always label packages with the contents, quantity, date frozen, and any special instructions, such as suggested expiration date. When adding food to the freezer, add only about 2 pounds of food per cubic foot of freezer space at one time. Adding too much at one time delays the freezing and affects the quality of the food. If possible, place foods so air can circulate around them.

Some foods don't freeze well—cream sauces, custards, cooked rice, meringues, cooked egg whites, or icings made from egg whites, cheese, cooked potatoes (except for French fries), salad greens, celery, cabbage, and cucumbers.

RESCUE when the power goes out:
Foods stay frozen longer if the freezer door is kept shut. Usually the food in a full freezer will stay frozen 2 to 4 days, but a half-full freezer will last only about 24 hours. Generally foods that have been partially thawed, but still have visible ice crystals, can be refrozen safely, though their overall quality won't be as good. (*see also* **dry ice**)

Q **Is it OK to eat foods that have freezer burn?**

A The food is safe to eat, but probably won't taste good. Prevent freezer burn by making sure the food is packaged in an airtight wrap or container.

FREEZING PROBLEMS AND SOLUTIONS

PROBLEM	CAUSE	PREVENTION
Freezer burn	Torn or unsealed packages	Be sure all packages are sealed tightly so no air can seep in.
	Packaging not moisture- and vapor-resistant	Use only packaging appropriate for freezing
	Too much air in package	Press out all air in wrapped foods. With containers, use just the right size for the amount of food that will leave the proper headspace.
Gummy liquid in fruits	Fruits frozen too slowly	Freeze foods at 0° or below immediately after packaging. Don't overload your freezer.
	Freezer temperature too warm	Always keep the temperature set at 0° or below.
	Fluctuating temperature	Maintain a constant temperature of 0° or below. Open door as infrequently as possible.
Grassy flavors in vegetables	Not blanching vegetables before freezing	Blanch all vegetables 2 to 4 minutes before freezing.
Green vegetables turn olive-brown	Not blanching vegetables before freezing	Blanch all vegetables 2 to 4 minutes before freezing.
Mushy food	Large ice crystals form on food, damaging the cell structure	Freeze foods at 0° or below immediately after packaging and maintain that temperature throughout storage.

freezer burn When the surface of frozen food dries and discolors as a result of moisture loss at below-freezing temperatures. (*see also* **freezing**)

French bread Long, slender loaf of light, crust, yeast bread that contains no fat and is made with water instead of milk. French bread is usually shaped into the classic long loaf or long, thin baguette. (*see also* **baguette**)

FRENCH BREAD

2 (¼-ounce) envelopes	1 tablespoon butter, softened
rapid-rise yeast	6½ to 7 cups all-purpose flour,
2 tablespoons sugar	divided
2½ cups warm water	Cornmeal
(100° to 110°)	1 egg white
1 tablespoon salt	1 tablespoon cold water

• Combine first 3 ingredients in a 1-quart liquid measuring cup; let stand 5 minutes.
• Stir together yeast mixture, salt, and butter in a large bowl. Gradually stir in enough flour to make a soft dough. Place in a well-greased bowl, turning to grease top.
• Cover and let rise in a warm place (85°), free from drafts, 40 minutes or until doubled in bulk.
• Punch dough down; turn out onto a lightly floured surface. Knead lightly 5 times. Divide dough in half. Roll 1 portion into a 15- x 10-inch rectangle. Roll up dough, starting at long side, pressing firmly to eliminate air pockets. Pinch ends to seal; turn under.
• Place dough, seam side down, on a greased baking sheet lightly sprinkled with cornmeal. Repeat procedure with remaining dough.
• Cover and let rise in a warm place, free from drafts, 20 minutes or until doubled in bulk. Make 4 or 5 (¼-inch-deep) cuts on top of each loaf with a sharp knife.
• Combine egg white and water; brush over loaves. Bake at 400° for 25 minutes or until golden. Yield: 2 loaves.

Q **Is there a difference between Italian bread and French bread?**

A The differences are that French bread loaves are usually a bit longer, narrower, and have a crisper crust than Italian bread loaves.

French Colombard A French white grape that's widely grown in California. These pale grapes have a tart flavor. French Colombard is often blended with Chenin Blanc to make California Chablis. (*see also* **wine**)

French dressing Classic French salad dressing, or vinaigrette, is made with oil and vinegar and seasoned with salt, pepper, and herbs. In the United States, we think of French dressing as being a commercially prepared, creamy, tart but sweet, reddish-orange salad dressing.

french To cut meat or vegetables into long, slender strips. This term also refers to removing the meat from the end of a chop or rib of a roast and exposing the bone prior to cooking.

French fries Potatoes cut into lengthwise strips and deep-fried until crisp and golden.

French green bean A green bean cut lengthwise into very narrow strips.

French toast A breakfast dish of bread dipped in an egg and milk mixture, and fried or sautéed in butter until golden on both sides. Sometimes, French toast is served with syrup or sprinkled with powdered sugar. The French call this dish *pain perdu*, which means lost bread because it's a way to revive slightly stale French bread.

fricassee (FRIHK uh see) A thick, chunky French stew in which meat or poultry is slowly stewed in stock and served in a cream sauce.

fried rice An Asian dish of cooked rice that's fried with other ingredients, such as bits of meat, shrimp, chicken, and vegetables, and seasoned with soy sauce. A scrambled egg is also often tossed into the mixture.

CASHEW FRIED RICE

2 large eggs, lightly beaten	5 cups cooked rice
2 tablespoons vegetable oil, divided	1/8 teaspoon turmeric
1 small onion, chopped	1/4 cup lite soy sauce
1 garlic clove, minced	1 teaspoon sugar
1/2 teaspoon grated fresh ginger	1/4 teaspoon dried crushed red pepper
1 (10-ounce) package frozen sweet green peas, thawed	1/2 cup chopped roasted cashews
	1/4 cup chopped green onions

• Stir-fry eggs in 1 tablespoon hot oil in a skillet 3 minutes. Remove eggs from skillet. Heat remaining oil; add onion and next 5 ingredients; stir-fry 3 minutes.
• Whisk soy sauce, sugar, and red pepper. Add to skillet; stir-fry 5 minutes. Stir in eggs and cashews; top with green onions. Yield: 4 servings.

F

frijoles (free HOH lehs) The Mexican term for beans. Frijoles can refer to kidney or pinto beans.

frill A fluted paper decoration slipped over protruding meat bones to garnish crown pork roasts or lamb chops before serving. (*see also* **crown roast**)

frittata (frih TAH tuh) An Italian omelet that resembles a crustless quiche. It's a mixture of eggs, cheese, and other ingredients such as vegetables cooked slowly in a skillet until firm. A frittata is different from an omelet because it can be finished under a broiler, is cut into wedges for serving, and is not folded during the cooking process.

fritter Small portions of batter or dough that are deep-fried. Fritters can be sweet or savory; chopped fruit or vegetables can be stirred into the batter before it's fried. Popular fritters include those made with apples, corn, or crab.

CORN-AND-CRAB FRITTERS

We're sure you'll enjoy this recipe from Criolla's restaurant in Grayton Beach, Florida, as much as we did.

3 tablespoons butter or margarine	1 teaspoon salt
1½ cups frozen whole kernel corn	1 teaspoon pepper
⅓ cup chopped red bell pepper	2 large eggs, lightly beaten
3 green onions, chopped	1 cup ricotta cheese
1 cup yellow cornmeal	½ cup buttermilk
½ cup all-purpose flour	1 tablespoon lime juice
1 teaspoon baking powder	1 pound fresh lump crabmeat
1 teaspoon baking soda	Vegetable oil
	Criolla Rémoulade

• Melt butter in a large skillet; add vegetables, and sauté 5 minutes.
• Combine cornmeal and next 5 ingredients in a large bowl.
• Combine eggs and next 3 ingredients; stir into cornmeal mixture. Stir in vegetables. Drain and fold in crab.
• Shape ¼ cup mixture into a patty. Repeat with remaining mixture.
• Pour oil into a heavy skillet to a depth of ¼ inch; place over medium-high heat until hot.
• Cook half of patties 2 to 3 minutes on each side; drain. Repeat with remaining patties. Serve with Criolla Rémoulade. Yield: 20 fritters.

CRIOLLA RÉMOULADE

1 cup mayonnaise	2 teaspoons Worcestershire sauce
¼ cup Creole mustard	2 teaspoons prepared horseradish
¼ cup chopped sweet pickle	2 teaspoons anchovy paste
2 tablespoons capers	1 teaspoon paprika
2 teaspoons seafood seasoning	1 teaspoon minced fresh parsley

• Combine all ingredients; cover and chill at least 1 hour. Yield: 1¾ cups.

frog legs The long, hind legs of large, edible frogs. Frog legs have a delicate flavor similar to white chicken meat. Most frog legs found in supermarkets or gourmet markets have been farm-raised. Because their flavor is so subtle, frog legs should be lightly seasoned with flour and sautéed in butter or olive oil.

fromage (froh MAHZH) A French term for cheese. For example, fromage blanc is an extremely soft, fresh cream cheese that has the consistency of sour cream and is usually eaten with fruit as a dessert.

frost To cover or spread a cake with frosting or icing. This term might also refer to chilling a glass or mug in the freezer until it's frosted with a thin coating of ice crystals.

frosting Sometimes called "icing," this sweet, sugar-based mixture is used to top cakes, cupcakes, and cookies. Besides sugar, frosting can also contain butter, milk, water, eggs, and flavoring. It can be cooked, as in boiled frosting, or uncooked, as in buttercream frosting, and can range from thick (for spreading) to thin (for pouring). Frostings need to be thick enough to adhere to the item being coated, but be soft enough to spread easily; they can be made from a recipe or be purchased ready-to-use. (*see also* **cake decorating**)

Secrets for Perfect Frostings:
• Before frosting a cake, make sure the layers are completely cool.
• Brush off excess crumbs from top and sides of cake layers before you begin frosting.
• To keep frosting off the serving plate, tuck strips of wax paper under all sides of bottom cake layer before you begin frosting.
• Stack cake layers with the first layer (or first 2 layers for a 3-layer cake), bottom sides up on the serving plate; then place top cake layer right side up. This makes a straighter, taller cake. Spread about one-fifth to one-fourth of frosting between each cake layer.
• Spread a thin layer of frosting on sides to set any remaining crumbs (this is called a "crumb" coat); then spread a generous amount of frosting over the thin layer.
• Always keep the frosting just ahead of the spatula; don't backstroke until the entire area is frosted or the spatula may drag up cake crumbs.
• Spread remaining frosting on top of cake, joining the frosting at the top and sides, making decorative swirls.
• Gently pull strips of wax paper from under the frosted cake.

Favorite Frostings:
• *Butter or cream cheese:* These frostings do not require cooking. The ingredients are simply beaten together and thinned or thickened by adding more liquid or powdered sugar. (*continued on the following page*)

• *Fudge:* A cooked frosting that's made like fudge candy, except it's beaten only until it reaches spreading consistency.

• *Boiled:* A cooked frosting in which hot sugar syrup is beaten into stiffly beaten egg whites.

• *Glaze:* A thin, uncooked frosting poured or drizzled over cakes.

• *Seven-minute:* A light, fluffy cooked frosting named for the amount of time the mixture of egg whites and sugar syrup is beaten while heated in a double boiler.

frothy A cooking term that describes a foamy mixture.

fructose (FRUHK tohs) An extremely sweet substance that occurs naturally in fruits and honey. It's more water soluble than glucose and sweeter than table sugar (sucrose). Fructose comes in granulated and syrup forms, but it shouldn't be substituted for regular sugar unless specified in a recipe. (*see also* **glucose** *and* **sucrose**)

fruitcake A rich, dense holiday cake full of candied or dried fruit, spices, nuts, and just enough batter to hold the ingredients together. Dark fruitcakes are generally made with molasses or brown sugar, while light fruitcakes are made with granulated sugar or light corn syrup. Most fruitcakes are baked slowly, cooled, and covered in cheesecloth moistened with liquor or brandy and tightly wrapped in foil; the flavor of the cake improves when stored in this manner for several weeks.

Southernism

Say "fruitcake" in the South, and the immediate word association is "Claxton." In 1910, Savino Tos, an Italian pastry maker, tired of the hectic pace he'd found when he immigrated to New York, traveled to the South and instantly fell in love with its quieter lifestyle. He was charmed by the friendliness of the people of Claxton, Georgia, and especially liked that there was no bakery. He made Claxton his home and his new bakery became an instant success. To share the spirit of the coming holiday season, he spent the fall baking fruitcakes. Thirty years later, Tos retired and sold his bakery to long-time employee Albert Parker. By then, the fruitcakes were so popular that Parker halted production of all other bakery items to concentrate on fruitcakes, and the old-fashioned horse and buggy label became a Southern institution.

Q How do I prevent fruitcake from drying out?

A Wrap the cake in a linen towel or cheesecloth dampened with brandy, bourbon, or your favorite spirits. Place the wrapped cake in a cake tin or carefully wrap it in heavy-duty aluminum foil; then store at room temperature, or if your recipe specifies, refrigerate it.

SHERRY-NUT FRUITCAKE

2 cups golden raisins	¾ cup firmly packed brown sugar
¾ cup dry sherry	6 large eggs
2 cups chopped candied pineapple (about 1 pound)	¼ teaspoon salt
1½ cups chopped red candied cherries (about ¾ pound)	1 teaspoon ground allspice
1½ cups chopped green candied cherries (about ¾ pound)	1 teaspoon ground cinnamon
4 cups chopped pecans	¾ teaspoon ground mace (optional)
3 cups all-purpose flour, divided	¾ cup whipping cream
¾ cup butter or margarine, softened	1 (10-ounce) jar strawberry preserves
¾ cup sugar	¾ teaspoon almond extract
	¾ teaspoon orange extract
	¾ teaspoon vanilla extract

• Soak raisins in sherry 8 hours; drain and set aside.

• Combine pineapple, candied cherries, pecans, and 1 cup flour, tossing to coat. Set aside.

• Beat butter at medium speed with an electric mixer until fluffy; gradually add sugars, beating mixture well. Add eggs, 1 at a time, beating well after each addition.

• Combine remaining 2 cups flour, salt, allspice, cinnamon, and, if desired, mace. Add to butter mixture alternately with whipping cream, beginning and ending with flour mixture. Beat at low speed just until blended after each addition. Add preserves and flavorings, beating well. Stir in reserved raisins and fruit mixture. Spoon mixture into a greased and floured 10-inch tube pan.

• Bake at 275° for 3 hours or until a long wooden pick inserted in center comes out clean. Cool in pan on a wire rack 20 minutes; remove from pan, and cool completely on wire rack. If desired, soak cheesecloth in ⅔ cup dry sherry, wrap around cake, and place in an airtight container; refrigerate 7 to 10 days. Yield: 1 (10-inch) cake.

READER TIP

"When making fruitcake, instead of chopping candied fruit with a knife, I simply put the measured amount of sugar in my food processor, toss in the fruit, and pulse several times. It saves me from the tedious job of chopping the sticky fruits." J.C., Lightfoot, VA

fruit cocktail A mixture of chopped fruits, such as pineapple, peaches, pears, grapes, and cherries. The fruit is usually served chilled as an appetizer or dessert. Canned fruit cocktail is also available.

fruit leather Pureed fruit, sometimes sweetened with sugar or honey, spread into a thin layer and dried. After drying, the fruit leather is often cut into strips or rolled up and eaten as a snack. It's sold in most supermarkets, where it might be referred to as a fruit roll-up.

F

fry To cook food in hot fat or oil, giving it a crisp, golden crust. Frying methods vary depending on the amount of fat or oil used. Here are some common methods:

• **Pan-frying** is cooking food in a skillet in a small amount of hot fat or oil. Pan-fried foods usually have a light breading or coating.

• **Shallow frying** is cooking food in about 1 inch of hot fat or oil.

Most shallow-fried foods are breaded or coated with batter.

• **Deep-fat frying** is food fried in enough hot fat or oil to cover it. The cooking time varies with the food, and the cooking temperature usually ranges from 365° to 375°, depending on the food. It's important to maintain the oil's temperature during the entire deep-frying process. Deep-fat-fried foods generally have a thicker coating. A deep-fat fryer, Dutch oven, or outdoor fryer can be used.

Q **How can I prevent hot oil from spattering and popping when foods are added for frying?**

A Always pat food dry with a paper towel before frying. If adding frozen food to hot oil, ice crystals may cause some spattering. You might want to use a spatter guard or spatter screen that can be placed over the frying pan to catch the spatters. Or use a long-handled skimmer to gently submerge and remove food.

Southernism

Long before the discovery of cholesterol, Southerners developed a love affair with fried foods: fried chicken, fried okra, fried green tomatoes, fried catfish, country-fried steak, and fried peach pies. Sounds like a line from Forrest Gump, minus the shrimp! And like Bubba's hankering for shrimp, so is a Southerner's affinity for things fried.

RESCUE for fat that catches on fire:

If hot fat or oil catches on fire when frying, don't douse it with water. First, turn off the burners and the range fan. Then, extinguish the fire by carefully sliding a lid over the pan to smother the flames. Or, pour baking soda on the fire until it's out. If baking soda doesn't work, go for the fire extinguisher. If the fire gets out of control, leave the house and call 911.

• **Stir-frying** is an Asian method of quickly cooking small pieces of food in a small amount of hot oil in a wok or skillet while stirring constantly. High heat is used in stir-frying.

• **Oven-frying** really isn't frying but the end result resembles fried products; the food is breaded or coated, rolled or drizzled with melted butter or oil, or coated with vegetable cooking spray, and placed on a baking sheet and baked in a hot oven.

• **Sautéing** is a dry-heat method of cooking food quickly over a high temperature in a nonstick skillet and with very little fat or oil. (*see also* **breading, coat,** *and* **fats and oils**)

fry bread A specialty bread of Native Americans, particularly the Navajo and Hopi. The bread is made of flour, water or milk, and salt, and formed into thin rounds, which are deep-fried and served hot with a sweet or savory topping.

frying pan A round pan with a long handle and low, sloping sides. Also called a skillet, this pan is used for frying foods over high heat so it should conduct heat evenly and be thick enough not to warp. Frying pans usually are available in 8-, 10-, and 12-inch sizes. Electric frying pans are square or oblong, and heat is controlled by an adjustable thermostat attached to the skillet. (*see also* **cookware**)

Southernism

The frying pan of the old South was a black iron skillet. It holds heat at an even temperature and browns foods evenly.

fudge A semisoft candy usually made with sugar, butter or cream, corn syrup, flavoring, and usually chocolate. Fudge can be plain and creamy smooth, or it can contain nuts, dried fruit, or marshmallows. (*see also* **candy**)

Foolproof Fudge
Our Test Kitchens staffers turn out countless pounds of fudge each year. Here's their advice for making perfect fudge:
• If it's a humid day, the candy may have a more sugary texture. Make it on a dry day for best results.
• Have all your ingredients chopped, measured, and ready before you begin cooking.
• Use a heavy saucepan with thick sides and bottom. It will conduct heat evenly.
• Butter the inside of the saucepan before you begin. This keeps sugar from clinging to sides of pan and helps prevent fudge from becoming grainy.
• An important early step in making creamy fudge is to be sure sugar dissolves completely before boiling the candy mixture. Otherwise, fudge

Q Why do candy stores make fudge in foil-lined pans?

A They do this because lining the pan with buttered foil allows the completed fudge to be lifted out of the pan in one piece. Cutting the candy outside the pan produces firm, straight cuts for even pieces of candy. Buttering the foil keeps the candy from sticking to the foil and cuts down on pan washing. Note that the pans are always lined before making the fudge because there's no time to do this once the fudge is in the saucepan.

may be grainy and crumbly. To test this, dip a metal spoon into sugar syrup mixture and press spoon against sides of pan. If sugar's dissolved, you shouldn't feel any grains of sugar on the back of the spoon.
• Use a clip-on candy thermometer. Always read thermometer at eye level. Test it for accuracy by placing thermometer in boiling water 2 minutes; it

should register 212°. If not, adjust temperature given in recipe by the amount that your reading deviates from 212°. For example, if your thermometer registers 210° in boiling water, it's 2 degrees low. And you should remove candy from heat when thermometer registers 2 degrees below what the recipe specifies. (*see also* **thermometer**)

• Adjust heat as candy cooks, if necessary, to maintain a gentle rolling boil. The candy mixture should be boiling at least halfway up sides of pan.

• Don't scrape sides of pan clean when pouring out fudge. This could lead to grainy fudge.

• Let fudge cool without any stirring before you beat it.

CHOCOLATE-PEANUT BUTTER FUDGE

2½ cups sugar	½ cup butter or margarine,
¼ cup cocoa	divided
1 cup milk	1 cup chopped peanuts
1 tablespoon light corn	½ cup creamy peanut butter
syrup	2 teaspoons vanilla extract

• Butter sides of a heavy 3-quart saucepan. Combine sugar and cocoa in saucepan, stirring well. Stir in milk and corn syrup. Cook over medium heat, stirring constantly, until sugar dissolves. Add 2 tablespoons butter; stir until butter melts. Bring to a boil; cover and boil 2 to 3 minutes. Uncover and continue to cook, without stirring, until mixture reaches soft ball stage or candy thermometer registers 234°.

• Remove from heat, and without stirring, add remaining ¼ cup plus 2 tablespoons butter, peanuts, peanut butter, and vanilla. Cool 10 minutes.

• Beat mixture with a wooden spoon just until well blended (about 3 minutes); pour immediately into a buttered 8-inch square pan. Cool; cut fudge into squares. Yield: 3 dozen squares (2 pounds).

TEST KITCHEN SECRET

If your fudge recipe calls for beating, do it with a wooden spoon just until it begins to thicken, then stir in nuts or other ingredients, and continue beating until it becomes thick and just starts to lose its gloss. At this point, pour the fudge into the prepared pan. If you beat it too long, you won't be able to pour the fudge; you'll have to scrape it out, knead it with your fingers, and shape it into logs or roll it into balls. LYDA JONES

Note: If you don't have peanuts on hand or time to chop them, substitute chunky peanut butter for creamy peanut butter.

Fumé Blanc (FYOO may BLAN) A crisp, dry California white wine made from the Sauvignon Blanc grape. This term distinguishes this wine from other semisweet wine traditionally made from Sauvignon Blanc grapes. (*see also* **wine**)

funnel cake A deep-fried, spiral-shaped Pennsylvania Dutch pastry that gets its name because the batter is poured through a funnel into hot fat for frying. Funnel cakes are served hot and sprinkled with powdered sugar.

CARNIVAL FUNNEL CAKES

2½ cups all-purpose flour
2½ teaspoons baking powder
1¼ teaspoons salt
¼ cup sugar
1½ cups milk
⅓ cup half-and-half

2 eggs, lightly beaten
Vegetable oil
½ cup sifted powdered sugar
1 teaspoon ground cinnamon
⅛ teaspoon ground nutmeg

• Combine flour, baking powder, and salt in a medium mixing bowl, stirring well. Add ¼ cup sugar; stir well to combine. Add milk, half-and-half, and eggs; beat at medium speed with an electric mixer until smooth.
• Pour vegetable oil to a depth of ¼ inch in a large skillet; heat to 375°. Cover bottom opening of funnel with finger. (A funnel with a ⅜-inch opening works best.) Fill funnel with batter. Hold funnel over skillet. Remove finger from funnel end to release batter into hot oil; move funnel in a slow, circular motion to form a spiral.
• Fry each funnel cake 1 minute or until edges turn golden brown; turn and fry until golden brown. Drain well on paper towels. Repeat procedure with remaining batter.
• Combine ½ cup powdered sugar, cinnamon, and nutmeg; stir well. Sprinkle cakes with powdered sugar mixture. Serve warm. Yield: 12 (5-inch) cakes.

fusilli (fyoo SEE lay) Italian for "twists." The term describes spiral-shaped pasta usually served with a thick sauce.

fusion cuisine A modern style of cooking that draws from other cuisines, particularly the European and Asian cuisines. This term usually refers to Asian cooking techniques that are incorporated and used with European or American ingredients.

Fuzzy Navel A cocktail made of peach schnapps and orange juice. (*see also* **schnapps**)

galette (gah LEHT) A round, thin French cake made of flaky pastry with a savory or sweet filling. The best-known example is the "Galette des Rois," the traditional cake that originated in sixteenth century France to commemorate King's Day, which falls 12 days after Christmas. The cake often contains a tiny plastic baby or other token, which is guaranteed to bring the recipient good luck. The New Orleans King cake tradition celebrating the feast of the three magi that preceeds Mardi Gras is rooted in this French cake. (*see also* **King cake**)

G

Galliano (gal LYAH noh) Sweet, anise-flavored golden Italian liqueur. (*see also* **Harvey Wallbanger** *and* **liqueur**)

game (*see* **wild game**)

ganache (gahn AHSH) A rich blend of chocolate and whipping cream heated and then cooled until lukewarm and poured like a glaze over cakes or tortes. Sometimes, cooled ganache is whipped and used as a filling for pastries.

CHOCOLATE-ALMOND PETITS FOURS

¾ cup butter, softened	1½ cups all-purpose flour
2 (8-ounce) cans almond paste	1 (12-ounce) can apricot filling
1½ cups sugar	Chocolate Ganache
8 large eggs	6 ounces white chocolate, melted

• Grease bottom and sides of 2 (15- x 10-inch) jellyroll pans, and line with wax paper; grease and flour wax paper. Set aside.
• Beat butter and almond paste at medium speed with a heavy duty electric mixer until creamy. Gradually add sugar, beating well. Add eggs, 1 at a time, beating after each addition. Stir in flour. Spread batter evenly into prepared pans. Bake at 400° for 8 to 10 minutes. Cool in pans on wire racks.
• Turn out 1 cake onto a flat surface; remove wax paper, and spread with apricot filling. Top with remaining cake; cut with a 1½-inch round cutter.
• Place small cakes on a wire rack in a large, shallow pan. Using a squeeze bottle, coat top and sides with warm Chocolate Ganache. (Spoon up excess frosting that drips through rack; reheat and refill bottle, and use to continue frosting cakes.) Chill cakes at least 30 minutes. Pipe dots on frosted cakes with white chocolate. Freeze up to 3 months. Yield: 3½ dozen.

CHOCOLATE GANACHE

1 cup whipping cream	2 cups (12-ounces) semisweet chocolate morsels

• Heat whipping cream in a heavy saucepan over low heat. Add chocolate, stirring until smooth. (Mixture thickens as it cools; reheat over low heat if necessary.) Yield: 2 cups.

garam masala (gah RAHM mah SAH lah) A flavorful and aromatic blend of roasted and ground spices used in Indian cuisines. The blend of spices varies, but typically contains peppercorns, cardamom, cinnamon, cloves, coriander, nutmeg, turmeric, and fennel seeds. Garam masala is usually added to a dish toward the end of cooking or sprinkled over the finished dish.

garbanzo beans (*see* **chickpea**)

garlic A powerfully flavored member of the onion family and an indispensable ingredient in many cuisines and dishes. Garlic is grown in bulbs, which are made up of sections called cloves. Each garlic clove is encased in its own parchmentlike skin. Heating garlic mellows its flavor, while chopping intensifies the taste. Besides fresh garlic, there's dried minced garlic, garlic juice, garlic powder, garlic salt, and bottled minced garlic.

There are three major types of garlic available: the white skinned, strongly flavored American garlic; the purple colored, milder flavored Mexican and Italian garlic; and the giant white skinned, very mild-flavored elephant garlic. Cloves of American, Mexican, and Italian garlic range from ½ to 1½ inches in length, while elephant garlic has bulbs the size of a large orange, and cloves that weigh about an ounce each.

TIMESAVING TIP

The fastest way to mash garlic is by crushing it under the weight of your hand with a chef's knife. When you do this, the skins slip right off.

Storage: Store firm, plump fresh garlic in a cool, dry, dark place. Leave bulbs whole because individual cloves dry out quickly. Don't store garlic in the refrigerator because it will dry out quickly. (*see also* **elephant garlic**)

garlic bread Slices of Italian or French bread spread with garlic butter and toasted in the oven. Garlic bread can also be broiled or grilled. (*see also* **garlic**)

garlic butter Softened butter mixed with minced or crushed garlic. Garlic butter can be used to flavor other foods or spread on bread for toasting. (*see also* **garlic**)

garlic press A gadget used to press garlic cloves through a perforated grid to extract the pulp and juice. (*see also* **garlic**)

garlic salt A mixture of garlic powder blended with salt and a moisture-absorbing agent. It's a real time-saver for the busy cook to be able to use 2 common seasonings in one quick measuring step. (*see also* **garlic**)

To make homemade garlic salt, just combine ⅛ teaspoon garlic powder with ⅞ teaspoon of salt. It's also handy to know that 1 fresh clove of garlic equals ⅛ teaspoon garlic powder. VIE WARSHAW

garni (gahr NEE) A French term for garnished that's used to describe a food not served alone but accompanied with side dishes or garnishes. For example, steak garni usually means the meat is accompanied with vegetables and potatoes. (*see also* **garnish**)

garnish A decorative, edible accompaniment with completed food dishes that gives them a finished look. Garnishes should be simple and echo or compliment the flavor of the dish, and appeal to the eye.

If you're trying to decide how to garnish a dish, look at the ingredients in it. For example, if a chicken dish is seasoned with basil, then tuck in a sprig of fresh basil. Add garnishes just before serving; if they sit too long, they begin to wither. JAN MOON

gastronomy (gas TRON uh mee) The art and science of fine dining.

gâteau (ga TOH) A French term for cake that can refer to any plain or fancy cake-type dessert.

gazpacho (gahz PAH choh) A cold, uncooked Spanish soup made of fresh tomatoes, bell peppers, onions, and cucumbers, and flavored with garlic, olive oil, hot sauce, and vinegar. Some Spanish argue vehemently that authentic gazpacho contains bread as well. Gazpacho is often garnished with croutons.

READER TIP
"I make a batch of gazpacho in the summer when there are so many fresh tomatoes. If I make it in the winter, I use Roma or plum tomatoes; they have a meaty flesh that's good in soup." J.S., Lexington, KY

SOUTHWESTERN GRILLED GAZPACHO

1 garlic bulb	⅓ cup chopped fresh cilantro
12 plum tomatoes	3 tablespoons lime juice
4 medium-size sweet onions, quartered	1 teaspoon salt
	1 teaspoon sugar
2 zucchini, cut in half lengthwise	1 teaspoon dried chervil
1 red bell pepper, cut in half and seeded	1 teaspoon ground cumin
	½ teaspoon pepper
1 jalapeño pepper	1 cucumber, seeded and diced
1 (32-ounce) can vegetable juice	Garnishes: chopped avocado,
2 (10-ounce) cans diced tomatoes and green chiles	sour cream

• Cut off pointed end of garlic bulb. Arrange garlic, plum tomatoes, and onion in a lightly greased grill basket. Place zucchini, bell pepper, and jalapeño pepper on lightly greased grill rack.
• Grill, covered with grill lid, over medium-high heat (350° to 400°), 15 to 20 minutes or until lightly charred, turning occasionally.
• Place bell pepper in a heavy-duty zip-top plastic bag; seal and let stand 10 minutes to loosen skin. Peel peppers.
• Cut jalapeño pepper in half lengthwise; discard stem and seeds.
• Pulse grilled vegetables and jalapeño, in batches, in a food processor until coarsely chopped, stopping to scrape down sides.
• Combine vegetables, vegetable juice, and next 8 ingredients in a bowl. Stir in cucumber. Cover and chill 8 hours. Garnish, if desired. Yield: 4 quarts.
Note: Vegetable mixture may be frozen up to 12 months, omitting cucumber. Thaw mixture, and stir in cucumber before serving.

gefilte fish (geh FIHL teh) A popular Jewish dish consisting of ground fish mixed with eggs, matzo meal, and seasonings. The mixture is shaped into balls or patties and simmered in vegetable or fish stock. After chilling, the fish is served in its own stock.

gelatin (JEHL uh tihn) An unflavored, colorless, odorless thickening agent made from natural animal protein. When gelatin is dissolved in hot water and then cooled, it forms a jellylike substance. Gelatin is used primarily for making molded desserts and salads. Generally, an envelope of gelatin will jell 2 cups of liquid. (*see also* **congealed salad**)

TIMESAVING TIP

To set gelatin quickly, use ice water rather than tap water. Also, try spreading the gelatin in a shallow layer in a metal baking pan. Or, set the gelatin bowl or mold in a bowl of ice water. You could also speed up chilling by placing gelatin in the freezer, but transfer it to the refrigerator after 20 minutes; any longer and it will begin to freeze and get chewy.

(*continued on the following page*)

Q **What is the correct way to soften gelatin?**

A The key to working with gelatin is to soften it in cold liquid for 3 to 5 minutes before completely dissolving it over heat. This step allows the gelatin granules to soften and swell so they will dissolve smoothly when heated.

TEST KITCHEN SECRET

There are a few fresh foods that shouldn't be used in gelatin mixtures because they contain an enzyme that prevents gelatin from firming. These include pineapple, kiwifruit, figs, guava, papaya, and gingerroot, which need to be cooked or canned before they're combined with gelatin. JAMES SCHEND

gelato (jel LAH toh) An Italian-style ice cream made with milk, egg yolks, and sweetener. Gelato has a more velvety texture than American ice cream because it doesn't contain as much air and is usually not as sweet.

génoise (zhehn WAHZ) A rich, light French sponge cake made with flour, sugar, eggs, butter, and vanilla. Génoise serves as the base for many elegant desserts, such as petits fours, cake rolls, and baked Alaska.

German chocolate cake A rich layer cake made with sweet chocolate and filled and frosted with cooked coconut and pecan frosting.

German potato salad A salad made of potatoes, bacon, onions, celery, and green pepper, and flavored with a dressing made from bacon drippings, vinegar, and sometimes sugar. The salad can be served warm or cold.

GERMAN POTATO SALAD

5 red potatoes, unpeeled	¼ cup cider vinegar
4 bacon slices, chopped	1 teaspoon salt
1 bunch green onions, chopped	1 teaspoon pepper
1 tablespoon all-purpose flour	1 (2-ounce) jar diced pimiento,
⅔ cup water	drained

• Cook potatoes in boiling water to cover 25 to 30 minutes or until tender; drain and cool. Cut into thin wedges.

• Sauté bacon in a large skillet over medium-high heat 2 minutes. Add green onions, and sauté 2 minutes.

• Stir in flour; cook, stirring constantly, 1 minute. Gradually stir in ⅔ cup water and vinegar; cook, stirring constantly, until thickened. Stir in salt and pepper. Toss with potatoes and pimiento. Serve warm. Yield: 4 servings.

ghee (GEE) Originally from India, ghee is clarified butter that's been cooked until it begins to brown, giving a nutty, caramel-like flavor. Ghee is good for sautéing and frying; make it at home or purchase in gourmet markets.

gherkin (GER kihn) A small, dark green cucumber used for making pickles. Cornichons are the French version of pickled gherkins.

giblet gravy (JIHB liht) A gravy made from giblets and pan drippings of roasted turkey or chicken. The giblets are simmered in water with onion, celery, and seasonings until tender, and the resulting broth is combined with the pan drippings and thickened for gravy. If desired, the cooked giblets and a hard-cooked egg can be chopped and added to the gravy before serving.

ROAST TURKEY AND GIBLET GRAVY

1 (12-pound) turkey	1 teaspoon salt
¼ teaspoon salt	2 tablespoons butter, melted
1 medium onion, chopped	⅓ cup cornstarch
1 celery rib, sliced	½ cup water
1 carrot, sliced	¾ teaspoon salt
2 quarts water	½ teaspoon pepper

• Combine giblets and neck from turkey, ¼ teaspoon salt, and next 3 ingredients in a medium saucepan; add 2 quarts water. Bring to a boil over medium heat; cover, reduce heat, and simmer 1 hour or until giblets and neck are tender. Drain mixture, reserving broth; cover and refrigerate. Coarsely chop neck meat and giblets; refrigerate.

• Rinse turkey with cold water; drain and pat dry. Sprinkle cavity with 1 teaspoon salt. Tie ends of legs together with string. Lift wing tips up and over back, and tuck under bird. Place turkey, breast side up, on a rack in a shallow, lightly greased roasting pan; brush entire bird with melted butter.

• Bake at 325° until a meat thermometer inserted into meaty part of thigh registers 180° (about 2½ hours). If turkey starts to brown too much, cover loosely with aluminum foil. Remove turkey and rack from roasting pan, reserving drippings in pan; let the turkey stand 15 minutes before carving.

• Remove and discard fat from drippings; return drippings to roasting pan. Add reserved broth and enough water, if necessary, to equal 5 cups. Stir to loosen browned particles.

• Stir together cornstarch and ½ cup water in a saucepan. Add broth mixture; cook over medium heat, stirring constantly, 10 minutes or until thickened. Stir in neck meat and giblets, ¾ teaspoon salt, and pepper. Serve with turkey. Yield: 12 servings.

READER TIP

"When I make giblet gravy, I always add a chopped egg, but since I've been watching my cholesterol, I just add the chopped white." J.A., Valdosta, GA

giblets (JIHB liht) The edible internal organs of a bird. Generally, this term refers to the heart, liver, gizzard, and sometimes the neck.

Gibson (GIHB suhn) A martini cocktail garnished with a tiny white onion and named for the famous American "Gibson Girl" illustrator, Charles Dana Gibson.

gimlet (GIHM liht) A cocktail made with vodka or gin, lime juice, and sugar syrup.

gin (JIHN) A clear liquor made from grains such as barley, corn, or rye and flavored with juniper berries. (*see also* **liquor**)

ginger; gingerroot A tropical plant grown for its gnarled, bumpy root. Gingerroot has tan skin and pale greenish-ivory flesh; its flavor is peppery and slightly sweet, and it has a pungent, spicy aroma. Gingerroot is especially popular in Asian cooking, but most Americans are more familiar with the dried, ground form of ginger. The flavor of dried ground ginger is very different from fresh gingerroot and is not an appropriate substitute for dishes specifying the fresh. Dried ground ginger is often used in curries, fruit compotes, gingerbread, and gingersnaps. Gingerroot and ground ginger can be purchased in most supermarkets. Gingerroot is also available candied, crystallized, or pickled in vinegar.

Storage: Store fresh, unpeeled gingerroot at room temperature for a week, or wrap it in paper towels and refrigerate 2 to 3 weeks; it can be frozen up to 2 months. Store ground and candied ginger in a cool, dark, dry place. (*see also* **spice**)

Q Should fresh gingerroot be peeled before it's used?

A If gingerroot is to be eaten, it should be peeled, but if used just to flavor a dish, such as a marinade or tea, it's not necessary to peel it. Gingerroot can be peeled with a vegetable peeler or paring knife, or you can scrape off the skin with the side of a spoon. Like garlic, ginger has a more intense flavor when crushed or grated. It can be crushed with the flat side of a knife blade or pressed in a garlic press.

TEST KITCHEN SECRET

The next time you see fresh ginger, buy several large pieces. Grate all of it, and seal in a plastic zip-top freezer bag. Your can store it in the freezer for several months, and when a recipe calls for freshly grated ginger, it's in the bag. Measure what you need, then reseal the rest. MARGARET MONROE DICKEY

ginger ale A sweetened carbonated beverage flavored with ginger extract.

gingerbread A dense, ginger-spiced cookie flavored with molasses or honey and cut into decorative shapes, or a dark, moist cake flavored with molasses, ginger, and other spices. Gingerbread cake is usually baked in a square pan and often topped with lemon sauce, ice cream, or whipped cream. (*see also* **ginger**)

GINGERBREAD MEN

1 cup butter or margarine, softened	½ teaspoon baking soda
	⅛ teaspoon salt
1½ cups firmly packed dark brown sugar	2½ teaspoons ground ginger
	2 teaspoons ground cinnamon
2 large eggs	½ teaspoon ground cloves
⅔ cup molasses	¼ teaspoon ground nutmeg
⅓ cup fresh lemon juice	½ cup raisins
6½ to 7 cups all-purpose flour	¼ cup red cinnamon candies
2 tablespoons baking powder	White Frosting

• Beat butter at medium speed with an electric mixer until creamy; gradually add brown sugar, beating well. Add eggs, molasses, and lemon juice; beat mixture well.

• Combine 2 cups flour, baking powder, and next 6 ingredients; stir well. Add to butter mixture, beating at low speed until blended. Gradually add enough remaining flour to make a stiff dough, mixing well. Shape dough into 2 balls. Cover and chill at least 1 hour.

• Roll 1 portion of dough to ¼-inch thickness on a large greased baking sheet. (Place a damp towel under cookie sheet, if necessary, to prevent baking sheet from moving.) Cut gingerbread men with a 5½-inch cookie cutter. Remove excess dough, using the tip of a knife. Add excess dough to remaining half of dough; wrap in wax paper, and chill until needed.

• Press raisins and cinnamon candies in each gingerbread man for eyes, nose, mouth, and buttons.

• Bake at 350° for 10 to 14 minutes or until golden. Cool 1 minute on baking sheet. Remove to wire racks to cool completely. Repeat procedure with remaining dough. Decorate Gingerbread Men with White Frosting. Yield: 2½ dozen.

WHITE FROSTING

1 (16-ounce) package powdered sugar, sifted	⅓ cup half-and-half
	1 teaspoon vanilla extract
½ cup shortening	

• Combine all ingredients in a large bowl; beat at medium speed with an electric mixer until mixture is spreading consistency. Use frosting to outline gingerbread and to make cuffs, collars, belts, and shoes. Yield: 2 cups.
Note: If desired, use different size cookie cutters. For an 8½-inch cookie cutter, bake 12 to 14 minutes (Yield: 11 cookies). For a 3-inch cookie cutter, bake 8 minutes; use currants instead of raisins (Yield: 8 dozen).

G

gingersnap A crisp round cookie flavored with ginger and molasses. Gingersnaps often are crushed and used to make crusts for cheesecakes or pies.

ginkgo nut (GING koh) The fruit of the ginkgo tree. This buff-colored, sweet nut is sold dried or canned and is used in Asian cooking. Ginkgo nuts must be shelled and blanched before they're used.

ginseng (JIHN sing) A plant native to China revered more as a medicine than as a food. Throughout history, ginseng has been credited with all manner of healthful and aphrodisiac qualities. For culinary purposes, ginseng leaves are brewed in tea and sipped as a pick-me-up. Ginseng or ginseng tea can be purchased in Asian markets, health-food stores, pharmacies, and some supermarkets.

gizzard An internal stomach organ from poultry. It's used in giblet gravy, but it's tough and needs to be simmered until tender. Before using, the gizzard should be split open and cleaned under cold, running water. (*see also* **giblet gravy**)

glacé (glah SAY) A French term that describes food with a glossy coating, such as fruit that has been dipped in a syrup that hardens when cold, or a cake coated with shiny, sweet icing.

glögg (GLUHG) A Swedish beverage of spiced wine punch flavored with brandy. Glögg is often served hot in cups and garnished with cinnamon sticks, almonds, and raisins.

glucose (GLOO kohs) A simple sugar found in the blood. It's made either by digesting food or from other carbohydrate and protein sources in the body. (*see also* **fructose** *and* **sucrose**)

gluten (GLOO tihn) An elastic protein found in flour, especially wheat flour, that when moistened and kneaded, helps hold in the gas bubbles formed by the leavening agent. Gluten provides most of the structure for baked products. The amount and strength of gluten varies with different flours. Bread flour is high in gluten and provides good framework for yeast breads. Cake flour has less gluten and yields tender cakes. Martha White and White Lily make a soft wheat flour (less gluten) that many Southerners prefer for tender biscuits.

gnocchi (NYOH kee) An Italian dumpling made from potatoes and flour. The dumplings are made into squares, strips, or balls and are simmered in liquid, baked, or fried. Gnocchi also can include eggs, cheese, or finely chopped spinach, and can be served as a side dish, appetizer, or main dish, with or without butter, Parmesan cheese, or a savory sauce.

goat cheese (*see* **cheese** *and* **chèvre**)

golden nugget squash A small, pumpkin-shaped winter squash with a dull orange skin, orange flesh, and a sweet flavor. Often used in fall and winter table decorations, golden nugget squash can be stored at room temperature up to a month. It's typically baked or steamed. (*see also* **squash**)

goober A Southern name for peanuts. Sometimes, goobers are referred to as goober peas. Peanuts were brought to North America in the 1700s by West African slaves who spoke the Bantu language. The Bantu word for peanuts is "nguba" (GOO bah). Southerners misheard the slaves calling peanuts "goober peas" and adopted the term. (*see also* **peanut**)

goose A wild or domestic waterfowl. Much larger than a duck, a goose weighs from 6 to 15 pounds. The meat, which is mostly dark, tastes moist and rich. Because geese are so fatty, they're not as popular in the United States as they are in France. Most geese are sold frozen and can be purchased throughout the year. Fresh geese can be found in some specialty markets and are available from early summer through December. Geese are best roasted; however, a larger, older goose might be tough, so you would want to use a moist-heat cooking method such as braising. (*see also* **wild game**)

gooseberry A tart berry grown on bushes, mostly in northern Europe and New Zealand that comes in many varieties, including green, white, yellow, and red. Fresh gooseberries are difficult to find, but they're available canned. They're used to make jam, jelly, pies, and desserts. (*see also* **berry**)

goose liver (*see* **foie gras**)

gordita (gohr DEE tah) A corn tortilla that's fried and filled with ground pork or chorizo and topped with cheese and lettuce. (*see also* **chorizo**)

Gorgonzola (gohr guhn ZOH lah) (*see* **cheese**)

gorp A snack mixture of nuts, raisins, seeds, dried fruit, and toasted oats. Gorp is often used by athletes as an energy booster. (*see also* **granola**)

FANCY GORP

1 (16-ounce) package candy-coated chocolate pieces
1 (12-ounce) jar unsalted roasted peanuts
1 (6-ounce) can salted natural almonds
1 cup (6 ounces) semisweet chocolate morsels
1 cup butterscotch morsels
1 cup raisins

• Combine all ingredients; store in an airtight container. Yield: 2 quarts.

Gouda cheese (GOO dah) (*see* **cheese**)

goulash (GOO lahsh) A Hungarian stew made with beef or veal and vegetables, and flavored with paprika. Goulash is sometimes garnished with dollops of sour cream and served over noodles. (*see also* **paprika**)

gourd (GOHRD) The nonedible fruit of various plants of the gourd family. Gourds have extremely hard, tough shells that can be dried and used as decorative containers.

gourmand (goor MAHND) A connoisseur of fine food and drink, often to excess. (*see also* **epicure** *and* **gourmet**)

gourmet (goor MAY) One who appreciates fine food and drink. Gourmet foods are those that are considered the highest quality, perfectly prepared, and beautifully presented. A gourmet restaurant is considered to serve food of the highest quality that has been prepared with care.

graham cracker A flat, rectangular-shaped cracker made with whole wheat flour and sweetened with honey. Sometimes graham crackers are crushed and combined with sugar and butter and used as a crust for pie. We use the original honey graham cracker the most, but cinnamon, chocolate, and low-fat variations also are available.

GRAHAM CRACKER CRUST

1 (5⅓-ounce) packet graham
    crackers, crushed
    (about 1⅔ cups)

¼ cup sugar
6 tablespoons butter or
    margarine, melted

• Combine all ingredients, mixing well. Firmly press crumb mixture evenly in bottom and up sides of a 9-inch pieplate.

• For frozen pies, crust may be used without baking. For other pies, bake at 350° for 7 to 9 minutes. Yield: 1 (9-inch) crust.

TEST KITCHEN SECRET

To easily press graham cracker crumbs into a pieplate, slip your hand inside a plastic sandwich bag; this allows you to keep the crumbs in the pieplate and protects your hand from becoming a buttery mess. LYDA JONES

graham flour Coarsely milled whole wheat flour that lends extra texture to some breads and cookies. (*see also* **flour**)

grain The edible seeds of any plants from the grass family. Common cereal grains include barley, bulghur, couscous, grits, kasha, millet, oats, quinoa, rice, rye, and wheat. Grains can be used in casseroles, salads, and stuffings. Grits, the small flakes of hulled, dried corn, are popular in the South as a side dish with fried fish or with eggs and bacon for breakfast. Oatmeal is also a breakfast dish, while bulghur and barley are eaten as side dishes.

Storage: Whole grains have a short shelf life and are prone to turning rancid because they contain an oil-rich germ. It's best to buy whole grains in small quantities and keep them in airtight containers, if possible, in the refrigerator. Polished grains, such as white rice, have been hulled and the germ removed, so they generally keep well in an airtight container at cool room temperature up to a year. (*see also* **barley, bulghur, couscous, grits, kasha, millet, oat, quinoa, rice, rye,** *and* **wheat**)

READER TIP

"It may seem natural to use a wooden spoon for stirring grits, but try using a stainless steel wire whisk instead. Pour the grits into the boiling water, bit by bit, whisking constantly, and lumps will disappear." C.G., Smyrna, GA

GRAINS COOKING GUIDE

This chart provides basic cooking instructions for 1 cup of grain; salt can be added, if desired.

GRAIN	WATER	DIRECTIONS	YIELD
Barley, pearl	4 cups	Add to boiling water; simmer 45 minutes, then drain.	3 to 3½ cups
Bulghur	2 cups	Add to cold water; bring to boil, then cover and simmer 10 to 12 minutes.	2½ to 3 cups
Couscous	1½ cups	Remove boiling water from heat; stir in couscous. Cover and let stand 5 minutes.	2½ cups
Grits, regular	6 cups	Add to boiling water; cover and simmer 15 to 20 minutes until thickened, stirring often with a wire whisk.	6 cups
Kasha	1½ cups	Add to cold water; bring to a boil; cover and simmer 10 to 12 minutes.	2 cups
Millet	2 cups	Add to boiling water; simmer, uncovered, 15 minutes. Remove from heat, cover, and let stand 10 minutes.	3 cups
Quick-cooking oats	2 cups	Add to boiling water; cover and simmer 1 minute. Remove from heat, and let stand, covered, 3 minutes.	2 cups
Rolled oats	2 cups	Add to boiling water; simmer, uncovered, 5 minutes.	1¾ cups
Quinoa	2 cups	Rinse thoroughly; add to boiling water. Cover and simmer 12 to 15 minutes.	3 cups
Cracked wheat	2 cups	Add to cold water. Bring to a boil; cover and simmer 30 to 45 minutes or until tender.	3 cups

---

Grand Marnier (GRAN mahr NYAY) Orange-flavored, brandy-based French liqueur that's dark golden in color. (*see also* **liqueur**)

G

granita (grah nee TAH) An Italian frozen ice made from water, sugar, and a fruit or wine flavoring. Granitas are stirred frequently during freezing so they have a grainy, slushy texture. (*see also* **ice**)

GINGER TEA GRANITA

2 quarts water	4 family-size tea bags
¼ to ⅓ cup grated fresh ginger	1½ cups sugar
⅓ cup lemon juice	Garnish: fresh mint sprigs
¼ cup honey	

• Bring first 4 ingredients to a boil in a large saucepan. Reduce heat, and simmer, stirring occasionally, 5 minutes. Remove from heat.
• Add tea bags; cover and steep 5 minutes. Remove tea bags, squeezing gently; add sugar, stirring until dissolved. Cool.
• Pour tea through a wire-mesh strainer into a 13- x 9-inch baking dish.
• Freeze 8 hours. Remove mixture from freezer 20 minutes before serving. Process mixture, one-fourth at a time, in a food processor or blender until smooth. Serve immediately, and garnish, if desired. Yield:10 cups.

granola (gruh NOH luh) A mixture of oats, nuts, and dried fruits similar to gorp, but is coated with oil and honey, and toasted. Granola is typically eaten for breakfast or as a snack.
Storage: Store in an airtight container in a cool, dry place up to 1 month or in the refrigerator up to 3 months. (*see also* **gorp**)

GRANOLA

4 cups uncooked regular oats	½ cup honey
1 cup sunflower seeds	⅓ cup vegetable oil
½ cup whole almonds	2 tablespoons water
½ cup sesame seeds	1 cup dried apricots, coarsely
¾ cup wheat germ	chopped
1 (3.5-ounce) can flaked coconut	1 cup raisins

• Combine first 6 ingredients in a large bowl. Stir together honey, oil, and 2 tablespoons water; pour over oat mixture, tossing well. Spread mixture into a lightly greased 15- x 10-inch jellyroll pan.
• Bake at 225° for 1 hour and 45 minutes, stirring every 15 minutes.
• Stir in apricot and raisins. Cool completely. Store in an airtight container. Yield: 10 cups.

granulated sugar (*see* **sugar**)

grape Small, juicy, edible berries that grow in clusters on vines. There are thousands of varieties of grapes; some are grown for snacking, others for making wine. There also are special varieties of grapes for making raisins, grape juice, and jelly.

READER TIP
"For a fun snack on a hot day, my kids love little clusters of frozen grapes." J.W., Pensacola, FL

Storage: Store grapes, unwashed, in plastic bags, in the refrigerator, up to a week. Always wash grapes thoroughly before eating. (*see also* **currant**)

Varieties of Grapes

Green and red seedless grapes are the most common edible grapes, but there are many other flavorful varieties:

- *Black Corinth,* also called champagne grapes; these tiny purple grapes grow in small, tight clusters. When dried, their sweet richness is intensified and they become known as currants.
- *Concord grapes* are blue-black with a silvery bloom; most are used for making grape juice and jelly, or they can be eaten as a snack.
- *Emperor grapes* are large, oval, red to purplish grapes with a mild flavor and small seeds.
- *Flame seedless grapes* are round purplish-red grapes. Their texture is also a bit crunchy, and their mild flavor is sweet, but tart.
- *Muscadine grapes,* sometimes called scuppernongs, are found in the Southern states; they have thick skins, are greenish-purple, and have a strong, musky flavor. They can be eaten as a snack or used to make wine.
- *Muscat grapes* can be white or black; they're sweet with a musky flavor, and are grown mostly for making raisins, but can also be used to make muscatel wine.
- *Scuppernong grapes,* sometimes called muscadines, are found in Southern states; they have thick skins, are a bronze color, and have a strong, musky flavor. Enjoy them as a snack or in jams, jellies, or homemade wine.
- *Thompson seedless grapes* are medium-sized grapes with thin, pale green skins. These grapes have a sweet flavor and are widely available.

Southernism

Scuppernongs can still be found growing wild in parts of the South. These grapes are most often used to make jam or jelly. The recipe for scuppernong pie originated in the Appalachian Mountains area. Thomas Jefferson compared wines made from North Carolina scuppernongs to fine wines from Europe.

grapefruit A round, tropical citrus fruit commonly grown in Florida, Texas, Arizona, and California. Grapefruits have yellow to pink skins and sweet-tart juicy meat that grows in sections like an orange. Grapefruit can be seedless or seeded; they also can have white, pink, or ruby-red meat. The heavier the grapefruit is, the juicer it will be. Grapefruit often is cut in half and eaten for breakfast or sectioned for salads. (*see also* **citrus fruit**)

GRAPEFRUIT COMPOTE IN ROSEMARY SYRUP

1 cup sugar	6 large grapefruit
½ cup water	½ cup maraschino cherries with
3 tablespoons honey	stems
3 sprigs fresh rosemary	Garnish: fresh rosemary sprigs

- Combine first 4 ingredients in a saucepan. Bring to a boil over medium heat. Boil 5 minutes. Remove from heat; let cool. Discard rosemary.
- Peel and section grapefruit over a serving bowl to catch juice. Add grapefruit to bowl. Pour rosemary syrup over fruit in bowl. Add cherries. Cover and chill until ready to serve. Garnish, if desired. Yield: 10 servings.

grapefruit knife A small knife with a curved double-edged blade that is serrated on both sides. The knife can be used to section any kind of citrus fruit, but is especially useful for cutting grapefruit meat from the rind and membrane. Grapefruit spoons also are useful; they also have serrated edges to free the juicy sections from the membrane.

grape leaves Large, green leaves from grapevines that often are used by Greek and Middle Eastern cooks to wrap foods for cooking. Grape leaves are rarely available fresh, but can be purchased canned, packed in salty brine. Rinse the leaves before using to remove some of the saltiness; simmer in water for about 10 minutes to make pliable for wrapping.

grasshopper pie Airy, creamy, chilled pie made of marshmallow cream and whipped cream flavored with crème de menthe. Grasshopper pies typically have a chocolate cookie-crumb crust. (*see also* **crème de menthe**)

GRASSHOPPER PIE

1¼ cups chocolate wafer crumbs (about 32 wafers)
⅓ cup butter, melted
1 (6-ounce) package chocolate-covered mint wafer candies
4 cups miniature marshmallows
¼ cup sugar
2 tablespoons butter
⅓ cup green crème de menthe
1½ cups whipping cream, whipped

• Combine chocolate crumbs and melted butter; press into bottom and up sides of a greased 9-inch pieplate. Bake at 350° for 6 to 8 minutes. Cool completely.
• Cut 3 mint candies in half; set aside. Reserve 10 whole candies for garnish. Chop remaining candies; set aside.
• Combine marshmallows, sugar, and 2 tablespoons butter in top of a double boiler. Bring water to a boil. Reduce heat to low; cook until marshmallows melt, stirring frequently. Remove from heat. Stir in crème de menthe. Cool to room temperature. Fold in chopped candies and whipped cream.
• Spread mixture evenly into prepared crust. Arrange reserved candy halves in a circle in center of pie; freeze until firm.
• Pull a vegetable peeler down sides of reserved whole candies to make tiny shavings. Garnish pie with candy shavings. Yield: 1 (9-inch) pie.

grate To scrape a piece of food against a coarse, serrated surface until it's reduced to small particles or thin shreds. Grating is similar to shredding, however grating produces smaller pieces. (*see also* **grater** *and* **shred**)

TEST KITCHEN SECRET

"*For all but very hard cheese, grating is easiest if the cheese is well chilled. In fact, some soft cheeses need to be briefly frozen before grating. For example, processed cheese is too soft for grating unless it's been frozen first.*" MARY ALLEN PERRY

grater A kitchen tool that comes in several shapes and sizes and is used to scrape hard foods into small pieces. Graters are made of metal or plastic, and can be flat, round, or box shaped, but all have perforated, sharp-edged holes or slits for grating. Rotary or hand-turned graters force food through a chute and into contact with a rotating grating surface. Most food processors are equipped with grating dishes. Specialty rotating graters and ginger graters also are available. (*see also* **Mouli grater**)

> **TIMESAVING TIP**
> For easy cleanup, spray graters with cooking spray before grating cheese or citrus rind.

gratin dish (GRAW ten) Shallow oval ovenproof dishes made of metal or ceramic with small handles on both ends. Many gratin dishes are sized small for individual servings and are used when preparing recipes that are topped with cheese or breadcrumbs and cooked in a hot oven. (*see also* **au gratin**)

gratinée (grah teen NAY) A French term that describes a dish topped with cheese, breadcrumbs or sauce, and browned in the oven or under the broiler.

gravy A sauce made from the drippings or juices left in the pan after cooking meat or chicken. The juices are usually combined with liquid, such as broth, wine, water, or milk, and thickened with flour, instant flour, cornstarch or other thickening agent. Gravy often is served over meat, poultry, mashed potatoes, rice, or split biscuits. (*see also* **drippings** *and* **flour**)

PAN GRAVY

Pan Drippings (fat and juice)	¼ teaspoon salt
2 tablespoons all-purpose flour	⅛ teaspoon pepper
1 cup meat juices, broth, or water	

• Pour off all but 2 tablespoons pan drippings from pan. Add flour, stirring until smooth. Cook 1 minute, stirring constantly.

• Gradually add meat juice; cook over medium heat, stirring constantly, until thickened and bubbly. Stir in salt and pepper. Yield: 1 cup.

> **TEST KITCHEN SECRET**
>
> *If you want smooth gravy, stir the flour or cornstarch until dissolved in a small amount of cold liquid before adding it to the gravy. Then, cook and stir constantly with a wire whisk until the gravy thickens. Another trick is to use instant flour that's guaranteed not to lump.* Vie Warshaw

gravy boat A short, squatty, elongated pitcher, also called a sauce boat, which is used for serving gravy. The pitcher often is permanently attached to a matching saucer underneath that catches drips.

grease To rub fat or shortening over the surface of a pan to help prevent food from sticking. Some baking recipes suggest greasing pans and then dusting them lightly with flour.

great Northern beans Large white beans with a mild flavor; popular in baked bean recipes. (*see also* **beans, dried**)

grecque, à la (ah lah GREHK) A French term for "Greek style." When prepared à la grecque, a dish usually contains vegetables and herbs that have been cooked in olive oil and lemon juice; it's served cold, sometimes as an appetizer.

green bean The entire long, slender green bean pod is edible; it's often called a "string" bean or "snap" bean. When steamed, sautéed, or simmered, this vegetable makes a popular side dish. The wax bean is a pale yellow variety of the green bean; it can be purchased fresh and stored in the refrigerator in a plastic bag 3 to 4 days. Green beans also are available canned or frozen. (*see also* **beans, dried;** *and* **beans, fresh**)

Southernism

Green beans may have undergone more of a cooking transformation that any other popular Southern vegetable in the last couple of generations. Our grandmothers simmered them for hours, usually flavored with a ham hock, proclaiming them done only after they showed no resistance to the fork whatsoever. Today's cooks forgo the ham bone in favor of lower fat flavor alternatives such as broth, and get them in and out of the pot as quickly as possible to maximize color, texture, and nutrients.

green goddess Made from mayonnaise, tarragon vinegar, and anchovies, this salad dressing can also be used as a sauce for fish or shellfish.

GREEN GODDESS DRESSING

⅓ cup coarsely chopped fresh parsley
1 cup mayonnaise
⅓ cup chopped chives
3 tablespoons tarragon vinegar
1 tablespoon anchovy paste
⅛ teaspoon salt
1 garlic clove, crushed

• Process parsley in a blender 1 minute. Add mayonnaise and remaining ingredients; process until smooth. Cover and chill. Yield: 1¼ cups.

green onions (*see* **onion**)

green pea (*see* **pea** *and* **sweet green peas**)

green pepper (*see* **bell pepper** *and* **peppers**)

greens The green leafy parts of various plants that are eaten raw or cooked. In general, those greens with dark, hearty leaves require cooking, while those that have lighter leaves can be eaten raw in salads.
Selection: Purchase fresh, crisp leaves free of blemishes or tiny insect holes. Small, young leaves will have a milder flavor; most are at their peak from late winter to early spring, though turnip greens peak in late fall, spinach in the spring and fall, beet greens during the summer and early fall, and Swiss chard in early spring through the fall. Most of these greens are best cooked, though a few of the following can be eaten raw:

• *Beet greens* have smooth, thin leaves and an earthy flavor. Prepare them similar to spinach.
• *Chard* is made of large, crinkled leaves on fleshy, ribbed stems that can be red or white. It has a flavor similar to spinach and can be cooked like spinach.
• *Collard greens* are large, thick dark green leaves with a mild flavor but tough texture. Be sure to simmer until tender.
• *Dandelion greens* are pale green with jagged-edged leaves that are slightly bitter and tangy. Cook them like spinach.
• *Escarole* has broad, curly-edged, green, outer leaves that are tangy and slightly bitter; chop and enjoy them raw or cooked.
• *Kale* has firm, frilly leaves on long stems with mild cabbage flavor that are best cooked.
• *Mustard greens* are light green with yellow overtones and have a peppery, pungent flavor. Cook them like collard greens.
• *Sorrel* has triangular or spear-shaped leaves that have a tart, sour flavor and can be eaten raw or cooked.
• *Spinach* has dark green, smooth, spear-shaped leaves that have a slightly bitter flavor; it can be eaten raw or cooked.
• *Turnip greens* have crinkly green leaves with a bold, sweet, peppery flavor that tastes best cooked.
Storage: Wrap greens, unwashed, in a clean, damp kitchen towel or damp paper towel, and place inside a loose plastic bag; refrigerate 3 to 5 days. Because most dark greens grow close to the ground and have sturdy, curly leaves, they collect large amounts of dirt and sand, so wash thoroughly before using. In fact, we suggest washing most dark greens repeatedly in several changes of water. (*see also* **beet, chard, collards, lettuce, spinach,** *and* **turnip**)

green tea Popular among Asian cultures, green tea has steamed, dried, unfermented leaves. Green tea has a slightly bitter flavor and a greenish-yellow color. Some believe drinking it provides health benefits. (*see also* **tea**)

gremolata (greh moh LAH tah) A mixture of minced parsley, lemon peel, and garlic that's often served with osso buco and other hearty meat dishes. (*see also* **osso buco**)

grenadine (grehn uh DEEN) A thick, sweet, red syrup made from pomegranates that's used to color and flavor cocktails and nonalcoholic drinks. Sometimes it contains alcohol; check the label if this is a concern.

griddle A large flat pan or cooking surface designed for cooking foods, such as pancakes, with a minimal amount of oil or fat. Some griddles are made of thick, heavy metals, and some have a nonstick coating.

griddle cake (*see* **pancake**)

grillade (gruh LAHD) A Creole dish of pounded round steak, veal, or pork cooked in a rich, seasoned sauce with tomatoes and other vegetables and served with grits. (*see also* **Creole cooking** *and* **grits**)

GRILLADES AND GRITS

1½ **pounds top round steak**	1 **small onion, chopped**
3 **tablespoons all-purpose flour**	½ **cup chopped celery**
1½ **teaspoons salt**	1 **green bell pepper, chopped**
¾ **teaspoon black pepper**	4 **garlic cloves, minced**
½ **teaspoon dried thyme**	1 **(14.5-ounce) can diced**
⅛ **teaspoon ground red pepper**	**tomatoes, undrained**
3 **tablespoons butter or margarine,**	1 **cup water**
melted and divided	4 **cups hot cooked grits**

• Pound steak to ¼-inch thickness with a meat mallet or rolling pin. Cut steak into 2-inch squares; set aside.
• Combine flour and next 4 ingredients in a large heavy-duty zip-top plastic bag. Add steak; seal bag, and shake to coat.
• Brown half of steak in 1 tablespoon butter in a Dutch oven over medium-high heat about 2 minutes on each side. Remove from Dutch oven; keep warm. Repeat procedure with 1 tablespoon butter and remaining steak.
• Remove from Dutch oven. Add remaining 1 tablespoon butter, onion, and next 3 ingredients to Dutch oven. Cook over medium heat, stirring constantly, 5 minutes or until vegetables are tender. Add tomatoes and

water; return steak to Dutch oven. Cover, reduce heat, and simmer 45 minutes, stirring once. Spoon grillades over grits, and serve hot. Yield: 4 servings.

grilling Cooking food on a grill over direct or indirect heat; this usually requires cooking over hot coals or lighting a gas grill. **Direct grilling** provides intense heat that's ideal for small foods such as burgers, steaks, chops, and poultry pieces; the lid is typically left off a charcoal grill, but is closed with a gas grill. However, **indirect grilling,** which cooks with the heat source to the side of the food, is always done with the lid on. It allows for roasting large or fatty cuts of meat without burning; it's the choice for whole birds, ribs, brisket, large roasts, and whole fish. For indirect grilling, usually a drip pan is placed between divided coals, and the grill must be covered.

> **RESCUE for grill flare-ups:**
> Flare-ups happen when fat and meat juices drip on hot coals. If there's a flare-up, raise the grill rack, cover the grill, or spread the coals farther apart. If needed, remove the food from the grill and mist the coals with water from a spray bottle, then return food to the grill.

When grilling, you need to be able to determine how hot the fire is. Many cooks determine coal temperature by how long they can hold their hands above the coals at cooking level, but a grill thermometer offers a more accurate measurement; the only problem with a thermometer is it gives an accurate reading only when the grill is covered. For a "hands-on" technique, follow this guide: A hot fire allows a 2-second hand count and is between 400° and 500°, with coals that are barely covered with ash. A medium fire allows a 4-second hand count, is between 300° and 350°, and has coals that are glowing through the gray ash. A low fire allows a 5-second hand count

> **LITE BITE**
> Recent studies point to charred portions of grilled foods as carcinogens or cancer-causing compounds. Charred areas are created when meat drippings fall onto hot coals and create carcinogens that are transferred to the food through smoke. To minimize the risk, trim meats of visible fat before grilling and limit the amount of oil or butter in marinades. Also keep a spray bottle handy to keep flare-ups at bay.

> **TEST KITCHEN SECRET**
> *"To add even more flavor to grilled foods, soak a handful of hardwood chips in water at least 1 hour and toss them on the fire. Fruit woods such as apple and cherry add subtle aromas, while stronger woods such as mesquite or hickory add bolder aroma and flavor."* Vanessa McNeil

and is under 300°; the coals are covered with a thick layer of ash. (*see also* **barbecue** *and chart on the following page*)

GROUND RULES FOR GRILLING

Use this chart as a guide when cooking beef, fish, lamb, pork, or poultry on the grill.

MEAT	COOKING TIME	METHOD	INSTRUCTIONS
BEEF			
Ground beef patties	8 to 12 minutes	Direct	Cook, without grill lid, until no longer pink.
Steaks (1 to 1½ inches thick)	8 to 12 minutes	Direct	Cook, without grill lid, to at least 145°.
Steaks (2 inches thick)	8 to 10 minutes	Direct	Cook, covered with grill lid, to at least 145°.
Tenderloin	30 to 45 minutes	Indirect	Cook, covered with grill lid, to at least 145°.
Brisket (6 pounds)	3 to 4 hours	Indirect	Cook, covered with grill lid, to at least 145°.
FISH			
Whole fish (per inch of thickness)	10 to 12 minutes	Direct	Cook, covered with grill lid.
Fish fillets (per inch of thickness)	10 minutes	Direct	Cook, without grill lid.
LAMB			
Chops or steaks (1 inch thick)	10 to 12 minutes	Direct	Cook, without grill lid, to at least 145°.
Leg of lamb (boneless or butterflied)	40 to 50 minutes	Indirect	Cook, covered with grill lid, to at least 145°.
PORK			
Pork chops (½ inch thick)	7 to 11 minutes	Direct	Cook, covered with grill lid, to 160°.
Pork chops (¾ inch thick)	10 to 12 minutes	Direct	Cook, covered with grill lid, to 160°.
Pork chops (1½ inches thick)	16 to 22 minutes	Direct	Cook, covered with grill lid, to 160°.
Kabobs (1-inch cubes)	9 to 13 minutes	Direct	Cook, covered with grill lid, to 160°.
Pork tenderloin (½ to 1½ pounds)	16 to 21 minutes	Indirect	Cook, covered with grill lid, to 160°.
Ribs	1½ to 2 hours	Indirect	Cook, covered with grill lid, to 160°.
POULTRY			
Chicken (whole, halves, quarters, and thighs)	50 to 60 minutes	Indirect	Cook, covered with grill lid, to 180°.
Chicken (bone-in breast)	30 minutes	Indirect	Cook, covered with grill lid, to 170°.
Chicken (boneless breast)	10 to 12 minutes	Direct	Cook, without grill lid.
Turkey (bone-in breast, cut lengthwise in half	45 minutes	Indirect	Cook, covered with grill lid, to 170°.

grind To reduce food to small particles, usually by pounding, crushing, or milling. For example, coffee beans can be ground in a coffee grinder, or can be finely ground in a food processor.

grissini (gruh SEE nee) Thin, crisp Italian breadsticks that can be purchased in supermarkets. They're great with soups and salads.

grits Also known as hominy grits, this ground grain is made from white or yellow corn; cooked until thick, they're a favorite breakfast dish throughout the South. Grits are available in four forms: instant grits, which have been precooked and dehydrated and just boiling water; quick grits, which are finely ground and cook in 5 minutes; regular grits, which are more coarsely ground and cook in 10 minutes; and whole-ground or stone-ground grits, which usually are sold at gristmills or specialty food stores and cook in 15 to 20 minutes. **Storage:** Store uncooked grits in an airtight container in a cool, dry place up to 6 months. (*see also* **grain** *and* **hominy**)

Southernism

Through the years, grits have been the workhorse of the Southern table. Enlisted to fill plates when more expensive ingredients were scarce, grits also acted as a foundation for flavorful items such a gravy or over-easy eggs. However, in the past decade or so, grits have experienced a renaissance, appearing on menus in upscale restaurants with ingredients such as peppers, cheese, and shrimp.

CREAMY GRITS

2 cups half-and-half or
   whipping cream
¼ teaspoon salt
⅛ teaspoon garlic powder
⅛ teaspoon pepper
½ cup uncooked quick-cooking
   grits

2 ounces cream cheese, cubed
¾ cup (3 ounces) shredded sharp
   Cheddar cheese
¼ teaspoon hot sauce

• Bring first 4 ingredients to a boil in a Dutch oven; gradually stir in grits. Return to a boil; cover, reduce heat, and simmer, stirring occasionally, 5 to 7 minutes or until thickened.
• Add cheeses and hot sauce, stirring until cheeses melt. Serve immediately. Yield: 4 servings.

RESCUE for leftover grits:
It's easy to turn leftover grits into a delicacy that resembles polenta (a mush made from cornmeal), which can be served with a flavorful topping. Spoon the grits into a plastic wrap-lined loafpan, smoothing the top with a spatula; cover and chill until firm. Remove from pan, peel off the plastic wrap, and cut into ½-inch-thick slices. Slices can be pan-fried or baked and topped with a variety of flavorful meat or vegetable sauces.

groats The crushed, hulled kernel of a grain, such as buckwheat (also known as kasha), barley, or oats. Groats come in varying degrees of grindings, from coarse to fine, and are widely used in cereals, as a side dish with vegetables, or in soups. (*see also* **grain**)

grog A hot, spiced drink made from boiling water, sugar or honey, and rum. Grog often is served in a mug and garnished with a slice of lemon.

ground beef Beef that has been put through a meat grinder. It's mostly used for hamburgers. Ground beef must be at least 70% lean according to federal regulations. Ground chuck must be at least 80% lean, while ground round must be 85% lean. Generally, the more fat the ground beef contains, the paler the meat will be and the less expensive it will be.

We prefer the flavor and texture of burgers and meat loaves made from ground chuck. Ground beef works well for spaghetti sauce; just be sure to drain it well.

Storage: Ground beef is more perishable than roasts or steaks, which means it has a shorter shelf life. Immediately freeze any ground beef you don't plan to use within a few days. And refrigerate leftovers containing ground beef within 2 hours after cooking. Frozen ground beef will keep up to 2 weeks in its original packaging, but for longer storage, rewrap in moisture-proof airtight material, and freeze up to 6 months. Shape into individual patties or loaves before freezing, if desired.

Checking doneness: Cook round meat patties and meat loaves to 170° or until no pink remains. Check for doneness with a meat thermometer or instant-read thermometer. (*see also* **beef**)

grouper (GROO puhr) A lean, white, firm-fleshed saltwater fish. Grouper can be baked, broiled, fried, poached, or steamed; it's sold as whole fish, fillets, and sometimes steaks. (*see also* **fish**)

HEAVENLY BROILED GROUPER

2 pounds grouper fillets	3 tablespoons chopped green
½ cup grated Parmesan cheese	onions
1 tablespoon butter or	1 garlic clove, pressed
margarine, softened	¼ teaspoon salt
3 tablespoons reduced-fat	Dash of hot sauce
mayonnaise	

• Place fillets in a single layer in a lightly greased 13-x 9-inch pan. Stir together Parmesan cheese and remaining 6 ingredients; spread over fillets.
• Broil 6 inches from heat 10 minutes or until lightly browned and fish flakes with a fork. Yield: 6 to 8 servings.
Note: Do not broil closer to heat than 6 inches or topping may burn before fish is done.

gruel (GROO uhl) A thin cereal or porridge typically made with oatmeal and cooked with water or milk. (*see also* **porridge**)

grunt A fish found in Florida's coastal waters so named because of the grunting noise it makes; it's best broiled or sautéed. "Grunt" or "slump" is also an old-fashioned spicy, sweet dessert made from fresh fruit cooked with a biscuit-dough topping.

Gruyère cheese (groo YAIR) (*see* **cheese**)

guacamole (gwah kah MOH lee) An avocado dish that's a popular Mexican dip, sauce, side dish, or salad. Guacamole is made from mashed avocado mixed with lemon or lime juice, and variations often include chopped tomato, green onions, chile peppers, and cilantro. Guacamole turns brown when exposed to air for very long, so it's best served within an hour of making. Store guacamole in the refrigerator with plastic wrap pressed directly on the surface to help prevent browning. If, despite your efforts, browning does occur, don't panic; just scrape off the browned part before serving. (*see also* **avocado**)

GUACAMOLE

8 ripe avocados, peeled
1 medium-size ripe tomato, diced
1 small onion, minced
½ teaspoon salt
⅛ teaspoon pepper
1 to 1½ tablespoons lemon juice
3 tablespoons minced fresh cilantro
1 tablespoon hot sauce (optional)

• Mash avocados with a fork until smooth; stir in tomato, next 5 ingredients, and, if desired, hot sauce. Serve immediately, or cover and chill up to 2 hours. Serve with tortilla chips. Yield: about 5 cups.

guava (GWAH vah) A sweet, tropical fruit grown mostly in South America and Hawaii. The small, oval-shaped fruit has yellowish-green to purple-black skin, and meat that ranges from off white to red. The flavor of a guava is similar to that of a lemony pineapple. Fresh guavas are usually only available in the area where they're grown, but guava jelly and juice are available in many supermarkets. This fruit is popular in South Florida with the Latin American community.
Storage: Guavas should be very ripe before they're eaten. Ripen them at room temperature, and then refrigerate up to 4 days.

guinea fowl (GIHN ee) A small bird weighing ¾ pound to 4 pounds that is all dark meat. The guinea is a relative of the chicken and partridge, has very little fat, a tender texture, and strong gamey flavor. Because guinea meat is lean, it can easily dry out, so it's best prepared by moist cooking methods. Guinea is sold frozen and fresh. (*see also* **poultry**)

G

gumbo (GHUM boh) A Cajun stew almost always containing a dark roux and is sometimes thickened with okra or filé powder. Gumbo usually contains a variety of vegetables, meats, seafood, or shellfish, and is served over rice. Most Cajuns agree that the secret to a good gumbo is the roux, a mixture of flour and oil and the foundation of gumbo.

Some insist that the roux must be cooked in an iron pot to develop proper flavor, however, the iron will darken the okra in the recipe, so many use pots made of other materials. Whichever you use, cook the roux over low heat, and stir it constantly until it's the color of a copper penny.

Ask five Cajuns which kind of meat or fish makes the best gumbo, and you'll hear as many different answers. They most often opt for different combinations of shrimp, crabmeat, oysters, and fish, while others have found that ham, sausage, or chicken also can enhance the flavor. Just which seasonings to add stirs up equal controversy.

Gumbo is thickened with either okra or filé powder, which is ground sassafras leaves. Okra gives the gumbo a rich, earthy flavor and thickens the stew as it simmers. Filé imparts a delicate taste similar to thyme. Add filé only after the gumbo has finished cooking because the filé becomes stringy if it's allowed to boil. A small amount can thicken a whole pot of gumbo, so add it sparingly. Or pass the filé at the table so each person can thicken the gumbo to his own preference. (*see also* **filé powder** *and* **roux**).

SPICY SEAFOOD GUMBO

1 cup vegetable oil
1 cup all-purpose flour
4 medium onions, chopped
8 celery ribs, chopped
3 garlic cloves, minced
4 (14½-ounce) cans chicken broth
2 (28-ounce) cans whole tomatoes, undrained and chopped
2 (10-ounce) packages frozen sliced okra, thawed
1 pound crab claws
¼ cup Worcestershire sauce
1 tablespoon hot sauce
5 bay leaves
½ cup minced fresh parsley
2 teaspoons dried thyme
2 teaspoons dried basil
2 teaspoons dried oregano
2 teaspoons rubbed sage
1 teaspoon pepper
2 pounds unpeeled medium-size fresh shrimp
2 (12-ounce) containers Standard oysters, undrained
1 pound fresh crabmeat, drained and flaked
1 pound firm white fish fillets, cut into 1-inch cubes
Hot cooked rice
Gumbo filé (optional)

- Combine oil and flour in a cast-iron skillet; cook over medium heat, stirring constantly, until roux is chocolate colored (about 20 minutes).
- Stir in onion, celery, and garlic; cook 10 minutes, stirring often. Transfer mixture to a Dutch oven.
- Add chicken broth and next 12 ingredients. Bring to a boil; reduce heat, and simmer, uncovered, 2 hours, stirring occasionally.
- Peel shrimp, and devein, if desired. Add shrimp, oysters, crabmeat, and fish to Dutch oven. Bring to a boil; reduce heat, and simmer, uncovered, 10 minutes or until seafood is done. Discard bay leaves.
- Serve gumbo over rice; sprinkle with filé, if desired. Yield: 7 quarts.

Southernism

It's lucky for Southerners that the French who settled in south Louisiana lacked some of the ingredients to make their favorite fish stew, bouillabaisse. It was the Cajuns who learned to substitute available seafood, local herbs, and new vegetables such as okra for the traditional ingredients of bouillabaisse. The result was gumbo—a dish that made the Cajuns famous.

gunpowder tea A green Chinese tea whose leaves are rolled into tiny balls, which gives the tea a granular appearance. Considered the finest of the green teas, it has a pale color and a mild, slightly bitter flavor. (*see also* **green tea**)

gyro (JEER oh) A Greek sandwich based on minced lamb that has been molded around a spit and roasted. The meat is sliced, wrapped in pita bread, along with grilled onions and bell peppers, and capped with a cucumber-yogurt sauce.

habanero chile pepper (ah bah NEH roh) This small, squatty, very hot chili pepper has green to bright orange skin and is generally used for making spicy sauces. The habanero is the hottest pepper on the Scoville scale, a scale that measures the pungency of peppers. We recommend that you wear disposable gloves when you handle habaneros. (*see also* **peppers**)

haddock (HAD uhk) A low-fat, firm-textured, mild-flavored white saltwater fish related to the cod, but smaller. Haddock are found in the north Atlantic Ocean from Cape Cod to Newfoundland. They can be baked, poached, sautéed, or grilled, and are sold as whole fish, fillets, or steaks. Frozen and smoked haddock also are available. (*see also* **cod** *and* **fish**)

hake (HAYK) A low-fat, delicately flavored, white saltwater fish that's related to the cod. Hake are found in the Atlantic Ocean from southern Canada to North Carolina and in the Pacific Ocean along the West Coast. They can be baked, poached, braised, broiled, and fried. Hake is sold as whole fish, fillets, or steaks. Frozen, smoked, and salted hake are also available. (*see also* **cod** *and* **fish**)

half-and-half (*see* **cream**)

halibut (HAL uh buht) A very large, low-fat, firm-textured, mild-flavored, white saltwater fish that's a member of the flatfish family. Halibut are abundant in northern Pacific and Atlantic waters. They can be baked, grilled, poached, and broiled. Fresh and frozen halibut are sold as fillets and steaks. (*see also* **fish**)

ham The hind leg of pork that's cured and smoked. The label on the ham will identify the type of processing and whether the ham has been cooked. If labeled "fully cooked," the ham does not require further heating and can be eaten cold, but is actually more flavorful if heated to 140°. Ham marked "fresh ham" and/or "cook before eating" actually hasn't been cured or smoked and must be cooked to 160° before serving. Always assume, unless the wrapper indicates otherwise, that a ham needs cooking.

You'll find ham available for purchase as bone-in or boneless. Bone-in hams are sold whole, as halves, in butt or shank portions, or as center-cut slices. The butt half generally has a higher proportion of meat to bone, and is more expensive than the shank. Boneless hams are easy to slice and have very little waste. They're commonly sold as halves, quarters, or steaks. Canned hams are always boneless and fully cooked; those labeled "water added" have been injected with a seasoned water solution before smoking.

Storage: Refrigerate cured hams up to 1 week, cooked or uncooked. Refrigerate canned hams before and after opening unless they're otherwise marked; unopened, they'll typically keep up to a year. (*see also* **country ham, cure, Parma ham, pork,** *and* **Smithfield ham**)

TIME SAVING TIP
To cook ham faster, cut it into steaks, which heat quicker than a whole ham. Heat the steaks in a skillet, or broil, bake, or grill them.

Southernism

The popularity of ham in the early South is easy to explain: Virtually every part of the pig was edible; the hind leg was particularly flavorful when salted and smoked to preserve it. The goal of the early South for curing ham was to keep food on the table in tough times; today we cure hams for that distinctive salty flavor we crave.

HAM DICTIONARY:

Bone-in ham: This ham has the entire bone intact. It's available whole, butt end, or shank end only.

Boneless ham: This ham has the entire bone removed, and the ham is rolled or packed in a casing.

Country ham: Ham prepared with a dry rub cure. Most country hams are very dry and salty and require soaking before cooking. They're often named for the city in which they're processed. Smithfield ham, from Smithfield, Virginia, is one of the most popular types of country-cured ham.

Dry-cured ham: The ham's surface is rubbed with a mixture of salt, sugar, nitrites, and seasonings, and then air-dried.

Fresh ham: Uncured, uncooked pork hind leg.

Prosciutto ham: Prosciutto is a broadly used term to describe ham that has been seasoned, salt-cured, and air-dried. Italy's Parma ham is a true prosciutto. It's usually sold very thinly sliced and eaten as an appetizer.

Smoked ham: Ham that's been hung in a smokehouse after the curing process in order to take on the smoky flavor of the wood used.

Q **Why do some recipes call for a smoked, fully cooked ham half, and then instruct you to cook the ham again to 140°?**

A Fully cooked ham heated to 140° is the optimum temperature for serving a cooked ham to bring out the most flavor.

READER TIP

"I save leftover ham bones to make soup. If I can't make it right away, I just wrap the bone in aluminum foil and freeze. Ham bones make great split pea or bean soup."

J.S., Cullman, AL

BAKED HAM WITH BOURBON GLAZE

1 cup honey	¼ cup orange juice
½ cup molasses	2 tablespoons Dijon mustard
½ cup bourbon	1 (7-pound) smoked ham half

• Microwave honey and molasses in a 1-quart microwave-safe dish at HIGH 1 minute; whisk to a blend. Whisk in bourbon, juice, and mustard. Set glaze aside.

• Remove skin and excess fat from ham; place ham in a roasting pan. Bake at 325° on lower oven rack for 1½ hours or until a meat thermometer inserted into thickest portion registers 140°, basting occasionally with glaze. Bring drippings and remaining glaze to a boil in a saucepan. Remove from heat; serve with ham. Yield: 12 to 14 servings.

hamburger Ground beef that has been shaped into a patty cooked and served between a split hamburger bun. Some sources trace the first record of the hamburger to a menu from Delmonico's Restaurant in New York in 1834, despite its name relation to the city of Hamburg, Germany. The popularity of the hamburger soared in the 1920s with the advent of White Castle roadside restaurants, which led the growth of the fast food burger chain industry. Today a family favorite, hamburger patties are often cooked outdoors on the grill and served with a variety of condiments, including lettuce, tomatoes, onions, ketchup, mayonnaise, mustard, and pickles. If a slice of cheese is added to the warm patty, it becomes a cheeseburger. (*see also* **beef** *and* **ground beef**)

hamburger press A kitchen gadget used to form perfectly round, flat hamburger patties. The press can be made of plastic or metal.

ham hock The lower portion of a hog's hind leg that has been cut into 2- to 3-inch pieces. Hocks are comprised of meat, fat, bone, and connective tissue, which contribute a lot of flavor to dishes such as soups and beans. (*see also* **ham** *and* **pork**)

hard ball stage (*see* **candy**)

hard crack stage (*see* **candy**)

hard sauce Sometimes called "brandy butter," this sweet dessert sauce traditionally accompanies plum pudding. Hard sauce is made from creamed butter and sugar, which is flavored with vanilla, brandy, rum, or whiskey. The sauce may be spread into a decorative mold and refrigerated until "hard" or the consistency of butter, and unmolded just before serving. (*see also* **plum pudding**)

SHERRIED HARD SAUCE

Leave the sherry out and enjoy basic hard sauce, if you wish.
  ½ **cup butter, softened**   2 **tablespoons sherry**
  1 **cup sifted powdered sugar**
• Beat butter at medium speed with an electric mixer until creamy. Gradually add sugar and sherry, beating until fluffy. Cover and chill. Serve sauce over warm plum pudding (page 400). Yield: 1 cup.

haricot vert (ah ree koh VAIR) A French term that describes young, tiny, slender green beans prized for their thinness. They're generally cooked whole. (*see also* **green bean**)

harissa sauce (hah REE suh) A hot, spicy sauce from North Africa made from hot chile peppers, garlic, cumin, coriander, and caraway. Harissa sauce is traditionally served with couscous, soups, or stews, and can be made fresh or purchased canned in Middle Eastern markets.

harusame (hah roo SAH mee) A translucent vermicelli-like Japanese noodle made from mung bean starch, cornstarch, or sweet potato flour. Harusame is commonly chopped and used instead of a batter as a coating for tempura. The noodles sometimes are called cellophane noodles. (*see also* **Asian noodle**)

Harvard beets Sliced beets cooked in a thickened mixture of vinegar, sugar, water, butter, and cornstarch. They're generally served hot.

Harvey Wallbanger A sweet cocktail beverage made of vodka, orange juice, and Galliano. (*see also* **Galliano**)

hash Finely chopped meat, potatoes, and seasonings that are fried together until lightly browned. Traditionally, hash was made with corned beef, but it might also be made with other meats. (*see also* **corned beef**)

hash browns A breakfast dish or side dish of finely chopped or grated potatoes that are fried until browned. The potatoes are usually pressed down into a flat cake as they're cooked until golden brown on both sides. Hash browns can be made fresh or purchased frozen.

HASH BROWN POTATOES

2 **pounds round red potatoes,** halved	2 **tablespoons minced fresh** parsley
2 **tablespoons bacon drippings**	½ **teaspoon dried oregano**
2 **tablespoons butter or** margarine	2 **garlic cloves, minced**
1 **small onion, chopped**	¼ **teaspoon salt**
	⅛ **teaspoon pepper**

• Place potatoes in a Dutch oven with water to cover; bring to a boil. Cook, uncovered, 8 minutes; drain and chill at least 20 minutes. Dice potatoes, and set aside.

• Melt bacon drippings and butter in a 9-inch cast-iron skillet over medium-high heat. Add diced potato, stirring until coated. Cook potato 10 minutes, turning occasionally. Add onion and remaining ingredients, stirring gently; cook 10 minutes or until potato is browned on all sides. Yield: 4 servings.

Q **What's the best type of potato to use when making hash browns?**

A The red or white potato, also known as a boiling or an all-purpose potato, has a waxy flesh that keeps its shape, making it perfect for hash browns.

hasty pudding A cornmeal mush, also known as "Indian pudding," made with water or milk and sweetened with molasses, maple syrup, or honey. Our colonial ancestors enjoyed hasty pudding served for breakfast or as a dessert. (*see also* **Indian pudding**)

haute cuisine (OHT kwih ZEEN) A French term for fine food elegantly prepared and served.

Havarti cheese (hah VAHR tee) (*see* **cheese**)

hazelnut A nut grown on the bushy hazel shrub. Also known as "filberts," sweet, rich hazelnuts have a hard, smooth, helmet-shaped shell with a light cap. The shelled nuts are covered in a brown skin that can be removed by heating the nuts at 350° for 10 to 15 minutes. The small, round, pale gold nuts can be used to flavor salads, sweets, and main dishes, and can be purchased whole or chopped. (*see also* **nuts**)

head cheese A type of sausage made of the meat from the head of a hog. The meat is cooked and chopped, seasoned, and spiced, then combined with its own jelled meat broth and formed into a loaf or mold. Head cheese is usually served cold as a luncheon meat. (*see also* **sausage**)

heaping A term that describes when a dry measure is filled slightly more than full, such as a heaping teaspoon. (*see also* **measuring**)

hearts of palm The cream-colored, tender, edible core of a young cabbage palm tree, which grows in tropical climates. The cabbage palm or "swamp cabbage" is Florida's state tree, and is protected from indiscriminate cutting. So most of the hearts of palm that we consume are imported from Brazil, where they are grown for eating. Hearts of palm have a delicate flavor similar to artichokes; they're expensive and rarely available fresh. Canned hearts of palm are sold in gourmet markets and large supermarkets. This delicacy is used most often in salads or main dishes.

HEARTS OF PALM SALAD
WITH BASIL-AND-GARLIC DRESSING

This recipe has long been a favorite at luncheons served in our test kitchens.

2 (14-ounce) cans hearts of
    palm, drained and cut into
    ½-inch slices
2 red or yellow bell peppers,
    cut into thin strips

1 pint cherry tomatoes
1 purple onion, sliced and
    separated into rings
3 to 4 heads Bibb lettuce
Basil-and-Garlic Dressing

• Combine first 4 ingredients; toss gently, and set aside.
• Arrange lettuce in a salad bowl or on individual plates; top with vegetable mixture, and drizzle with Basil-and-Garlic Dressing. Yield: 12 servings.

BASIL-AND-GARLIC DRESSING

½ cup white wine vinegar
¼ cup lemon juice
8 fresh basil leaves
3 garlic cloves

¼ teaspoon salt
¼ teaspoon pepper
¾ cup olive oil

• Combine first 6 ingredients in a blender. With blender on high, gradually add olive oil in a slow, steady stream. Process 2 minutes. Cover and refrigerate at least 8 hours, if desired; process again before serving or let stand at room temperature 30 minutes, and whisk vigorously to blend. Yield: 1½ cups.

hen (*see* **chicken**)

herbs The fragrant leaves of various plants and shrubs whose leaves, non-woody stems, or flowers are used to season most any type of entrée, side dish, or salad. Herbs can be grown at home or they can be purchased. If purchased, they come in three forms: fresh, dried, or ground. If a recipe doesn't specify when to add herbs, it's best to add them near the end of cooking to release their full flavor. Bay leaves are the exception; they typically simmer at length in soups, and are then removed and discarded before serving.

READER TIP

"I grow lots of herbs, so I had to learn how to preserve my harvest. To air-dry, I invert bundled herbs in brown paper bags, and hang them in a cool, dry place; after a few weeks, when they're dry, I store them in an airtight container. I also dry herbs in the microwave. I spread them on a paper plate and microwave at HIGH for 1 or 2 minutes or until they look dry; when cool, I store them in airtight containers." A.C., Franklin, KY

Storage: Treat fresh herbs like a bouquet of flowers. Douse the leaves with cool water, wrap stems in a damp paper towel. Place the towel-wrapped herbs in a zip-top plastic bag, remove as much air as possible from bag, and refrigerate up to a week. (*See herb dictionary on the following page.*)

TIMESAVING TIP
To chop fresh herbs, stuff the leaves into a glass measuring cup and insert kitchen shears or scissors; snip in cup, rotating shears with each snip.

HERB DICTIONARY:

Basil: One of the easiest herbs to grow, basil has a heady fragrance and a faint licorice flavor. Use it in salads, pestos, pasta dishes, pizza, and meat and poultry dishes. Purple ruffles basil has ruffled purple-black leaves and a mild fragrance and flavor. Cinnamon basil, Thai basil, and lemon basil are very flavorful, fragrant basils for cooking.

Bay leaves: Use fresh or dried bay leaves in soups, stews, vegetables, and bouquet garnis. Discard bay leaves before serving food.

Borage: The nodding purple flowers of borage are popular edible garnishes in green salads, on fancy cakes, or floating in a glass of wine or tea. You can use the young leaves, too. They wilt quickly, so chop and add to salads or cucumber tea sandwiches just before serving.

Chervil: A fragile herb, chervil is commonly known as French parsley. It has a subtle anise flavor and is best fresh or cooked only briefly. Add chervil to egg dishes, soups, and salads, or use it as a substitute for parsley.

Q Which herbs have the strongest flavor?

A The strong herbs are rosemary, cilantro, tarragon, thyme, oregano, and sage, so use these sparingly. Medium-flavored herbs are basil, dill, mint, and fennel. Delicate herbs like parsley and chives can be used more generously.

Chives: Chives are attractive, rugged herbs that are easy to grow. Snip the leaves and they'll provide a mild onion or garlic flavor to soups, salads, and vegetable dishes. In spring, chives boast globelike lavender-colored blooms that make ideal edible garnishes for salads. The wild (nodding) onion is a type of chive in bloom.

Cilantro: Also known as Chinese parsley, cilantro is grown for its spicy-flavored foliage and for its seeds called coriander. Cilantro is the leaf; coriander is the seed or powder; the two are not interchangeable in recipes. Slightly bruise a cilantro leaf and it will give off an unmistakable pungent peppery fragrance. Use the leaves in southwestern, Mexican, and Asian dishes. Cumin and mint are seasonings often paired with cilantro. Coriander seeds are used in Indian dishes as well as in pickles and relishes.

Dill: Finely chop feathery fresh dill foliage for fish and shrimp dishes, eggs, soups, sandwiches, potato salad, and sauces. Dill is a good salt substitute. You can harvest and dry dill seeds and use them in pickles, breads, and salad dressings.

Geranium, scented: The foliage and flowers of scented geranium are edible. Use scented leaves for flavoring pound cakes, cookies, herb butters, jellies, and iced tea. Some scented varieties are apple, lemon, orange, peppermint, rose, and strawberry.

Lavender: This edible ornamental herb has purple flowers that spike in early summer. Harvest the flowers just before they're fully opened, and use them in ice cream or other desserts, marinades, and sauces. Spanish lavender is a gray-leafed plant with needlelike leaves that look like rosemary.

Lemon balm: This hardy, bushy member of the mint family has a mild lemony flavor. Chop the aromatic leaves to use in tea bread, scones, and salads, or use leaves whole in tea or other cold beverages.

Lemon Verbena: The strongest scented lemon herb, lemon verbena has a healthy lemony essence. Use it as you would lemon balm leaves. Pulse a handful of leaves with a cup of sugar in a food processor to make lemon sugar. Store it in a jar. Use the sugar in sweets and teas.

Mint: Add this popular herb to lamb, poultry, salads, sauces, teas, and punches. Try cooking with flavorful types of mint such as peppermint, orange mint, apple mint, or chocolate mint.

Nasturtiums: These bright red and orange edible flowers have a peppery taste. Use them in salads, sandwich spreads, or as a versatile garnish.

Oregano: These small green leaves produce strong flavor. Greek oregano is the most popular oregano for cooking because of its strong flavor and aromatic leaves. Add oregano to Italian dishes, meat, fish, eggs, fresh and cooked tomatoes, vegetables, beans, and marinades.

Rosemary: Unlike other herbs, rosemary has a stronger flavor when fresh than when dried. It's a hardy herb with a piney scent and flavor. To harvest rosemary, strip leaves from the stem. Use the strong-flavored leaves sparingly. Rosemary adds a wonderful accent to soups, meats, stews, breads, and vegetables.

> ### TEST KITCHEN SECRET
>
> *If you want to substitute fresh herbs for dried herbs, which have more concentrated flavor, use 3 times the amount of fresh as dried. (Example: 1½ teaspoons fresh equals ½ teaspoon dried.) The only exception to this rule is rosemary. Use equal amounts of fresh versus dried for rosemary.* LYDA JONES

Sage: This fuzzy gray-green hardy herb is best known for use in holiday dressings. Sage flavors sausage, too. Sage leaves are soft and pliable, which makes them easy to tuck under the skin of poultry before roasting.

Tarragon: This leafy herb plays a classic role in béarnaise sauce. It also adds flavor to soups, poultry, seafood, vegetables, and egg dishes. It's used often to make herb butter or vinegar. French tarragon's leaves have a bittersweet, peppery scent with a hint of anise.

Thyme: Strip the tiny leaves from stems just before using. Use fresh thyme in marinades for basting seafood, chicken, or pork. Add thyme to mayonnaise for sandwiches or to beans, meat stews, vegetables, or rice. There are many varieties of thyme.

herbs de Provence (AIRB duh proh VAWNS) A mixture of dried
herbs that represents the most often used herbs in southern France. The mixture usually contains basil, fennel seeds, lavender, marjoram, rosemary, sage, summer savory, and thyme. Herbs de Provence can be used to season meat, poultry, and vegetable dishes.

herb vinegar Flavored vinegar made by steeping fresh herbs, such as dill and tarragon, in wine vinegar. They add a lot of flavor when added to simple salad dressings and sauces. (*see also* **vinegar**)

ROSEMARY-RED WINE VINEGAR

7 (6-inch) fresh rosemary sprigs   4 cups red wine vinegar

• Place rosemary in a hot, sterilized 1-quart jar. Bring vinegar to a boil in a saucepan; then pour hot vinegar into jar. Cover and let stand at room temperature 2 days.

• Strain vinegar into hot, sterilized jars, discarding rosemary; store vinegar in refrigerator up to 6 months. Yield: 3¾ cups.

Making Vinegars

• Use 4 large fresh herb sprigs or 10 spice berries or hot peppers for each pint of vinegar.

• If you harvest herbs from your garden, pick the leaves before the plant blooms, and clip the healthiest herbs early in the morning. Wash leaves, and pat dry.

• Put herb leaves, berries, or peppers into sterilized glass bottles. Find bottles at kitchen and home stores or recycle your own bottles. Always wash and sterilize the bottles in boiling water 10 minutes before filling.

• Bring vinegar just to a boil; pour into bottles, making sure leaves and peppers are completely covered.

• Cover bottles tightly with nonmetallic caps; contact with metal spoils the vinegar.

• Flavored vinegar tastes best when allowed to age a couple of days at room temperature. At this point, strain vinegar, and pour into sterilized, airtight bottles with nonmetallic lids. Store vinegar in refrigerator up to 6 months.

hermit A spicy, chewy cookie filled with chopped fruits and nuts and sweetened with molasses or brown sugar. It's believed these cookies were named by colonial New Englanders, who claimed the cookies were better after they had been hidden away like a hermit for several days.

hero sandwich A huge sandwich also known as a "submarine," "grinder," "hoagie," "poor boy," or "po' boy." It basically consists of a small loaf of Italian or French bread that has been split and filled with layers of thinly sliced meats, cheese, tomatoes, pickles, lettuce, and peppers.

herring A large family of saltwater fish found in the waters of the northern Atlantic and Pacific. Fresh herring has a soft texture and flavorful dark meat that's high in fat and suited for baking, sautéing, and grilling. Small, young herring are sold as sardines; the largest member of the herring family is the shad, which is prized for its eggs, known as shad roe. The alewife, or spring herring, is sold pickled or smoked. (*see also* **fish** *and* **sardine**)

hibachi (hih BAH chee) A small, inexpensive, uncovered square-cornered grill usually made of cast iron. Hibachis are easy to transport, but they cook only a small amount of food at a time.

hickory nut A nut that grows on hickory trees and has a very hard shell and a rich, buttery flavor. Hickory nuts are generally available only in certain parts of the country and are sold unshelled. There are a number of varieties of hickory trees, and all of them bear nuts. The most prized is the pecan. Pecans make a great substitute for hickory nuts, and vice versa, in sweet and savory recipes. (*see also* **nuts**)

high altitude Altitudes of more than 3,000 feet above sea level have lower atmospheric pressure or thinner, drier air, which makes foods react differently when cooked. For example, water boils at a lower temperature, so foods cooked in water take longer to cook. Foods also dry out more quickly. These differences require that some adjustments be made to recipes. (*see also* **boil**)

APPROXIMATE BOILING POINTS OF WATER AT HIGHER ALTITUDES

Sea level	212°
2,000 feet	208°
5,000 feet	203°
7,500 feet	198°
10,000 feet	194°

RECOMMENDED ADJUSTMENTS FOR BAKING AT HIGH ALTITUDES

Finding what works best in your location is largely a process of trial and error, but these suggestions give you an idea of how recipes might be adjusted.

INGREDIENT	3,000 FEET ALTITUDE	5,000 FEET ALTITUDE	7,000 FEET ALTITUDE
Baking powder	Reduce ⅛ teaspoon	Reduce ⅛ to ¼ teaspoon	Reduce ¼ teaspoon
Sugar	Reduce up to 1 tablespoon	Reduce up to 2 tablespoons	Reduce up to 3 tablespoons
Liquid	Increase 1 to 2 tablespoons for each cup	Increase 2 to 4 tablespoons for each cup	Increase 3 to 4 tablespoons for each cup

highball A tall cocktail served over ice. Most highballs are simple mixtures, such as whiskey and water or soda water.

high tea A British tradition of a late-afternoon or early evening meal. Food for high tea is usually substantial, and might include a meat or fish dish, crumpets, biscuits and jam, cakes and pastries, and a pot of hot tea. (*see also* **crumpet, tea,** *and* **tea time**)

hoagie (*see* **hero sandwich**)

hoecake (*see* **johnnycake**)

hog jowl A vital seasoning for true Southern cooking, the hog jowl comes from the cheek of the hog that has been cut into sections and cured and smoked. Southerners use the jowls to season and flavor vegetables and beans. Hog jowls can be refrigerated up to a week or frozen for longer storage.

Southernism

There are a few culinary subjects which Southerners feel free to discuss only among themselves. Hog jowl is one, without which we'd be hard put to cook our dried beans and peas. Another is pot likker, the "nectar" obtained in no other way than seasoning a mess of greens with jowl. Southerners today don't season with jowl as much as in the past, but they enjoy their veggies cooked that way when the opportunity presents itself.

hoisin sauce (HOY sihn) A sweet, spicy, thick, reddish-brown sauce that's widely used as a flavoring in Chinese cooking. Hoisin sauce is made from a mixture of soybeans, garlic, and chili peppers, and is most often used in meat, poultry, and shellfish dishes. Hoisin sauce is sold in Asian markets and most large supermarkets. If kept in a glass jar with a tight lid, the sauce will keep indefinitely in the refrigerator.

hollandaise sauce (HOL uhn dayz) A rich, lemony, yellow sauce made with butter, egg yolks, and lemon juice. Hollandaise usually is served warm over vegetables, poultry, fish, or egg dishes, such as Eggs Benedict. Since this sauce contains egg yolks, it should be cooked to 160°, usually in a double boiler. (*see also* **eggs Benedict** *and* **mother sauces**)

RESCUE for curdled hollandaise:
As soon as the sauce starts to curdle, quickly whisk 1 or 2 more tablespoons butter into the sauce and beat vigorously with a wire whisk until smooth.

HOLLANDAISE SAUCE

3 egg yolks	2 tablespoons lemon juice
⅛ teaspoon salt	½ cup butter or margarine, cut
⅛ teaspoon ground red pepper	into pieces

• Whisk first 3 ingredients in top of a double boiler; gradually add lemon juice, stirring constantly. Cook over hot water, stirring constantly with a wire whisk, until mixture thickens.

• Add about one-third of butter to egg mixture; cook over hot water, stirring constantly with a wire whisk until butter melts. Add another third of butter, stirring constantly. As butter melts, stir in remaining butter. Cook, whisking constantly, until smooth and thickened. Serve immediately. Yield: about ¾ cup.

home fries (*see* **cottage fries**)

hominy Dried white or yellow corn kernels with the hull and germ removed. Hominy resembles soft, white, puffed kernels of corn and has a slightly sweet, cornlike flavor. Most hominy is sold canned; dried hominy is also available, but must be reconstituted before using. Hominy is served with butter or cream as a side dish. When ground, hominy becomes grits. **Storage:** Store dried hominy in airtight containers and canned hominy in a cool, dry place up to a year. (*see also* **grits**)

homogenize (huh MAHJ uh nyz) A process by which the fat globules in milk are broken up and dispersed evenly throughout the milk instead of rising to the top. This term applies mainly to milk, but some commercial salad dressings also are homogenized. (*see also* **milk**)

honey A sweet, sticky substance produced by bees from the nectar of flowers. Honey is deposited by the bees in a waxy network of cells known as a honeycomb. The flavor of honey depends on the flowers from which it's made, the location, and the climate. There are hundreds of different types of honey, but in general, the darker the color, the stronger the flavor. Much honey is made from clover, which has a mild flavor; other popular honeys are produced from orange blossoms and sage. Honey is sold in supermarkets and fruit stand markets. **Storage:** Store honey at room temperature in a dry

Q **Can honey be used in recipes instead of granulated sugar?**

A It's best to use what the recipe specifies, but it's possible to substitute honey for sugar in some recipes, although some experimenting may be required. Try replacing 1 cup of granulated sugar with one-half to two-thirds cup of honey. Since honey contains a large amount of water, you'll need to reduce the liquid; for every cup of sugar replaced by honey, the total liquid should be reduced by one-fourth cup. Also, reduce the baking temperature by 25 degrees.

place up to 1 year; if refrigerated, it will crystallize and become grainy. Store comb or chunk honey at room temperature up to 6 months.

Forms of honey
Honey is available in several different forms:
- *Liquid or regular honey* has been removed from the comb and often is pasteurized to remove yeasts and debris, and to help prevent crystallization.
- *Comb honey* still contains the chewy, edible beeswax honeycomb.
- *Chunk honey* has pieces of the honeycomb included in the jar, but is mostly liquid honey.
- *Honey butters* and *honey spreads* are processed and spreadable at room temperature.

RESCUE for crystallized honey:
Grainy honey can be made smooth again; microwave the opened jar on HIGH about 30 seconds. Or, place the jar in a container of hot water, and stir the honey until the crystals dissolve.

TEST KITCHEN SECRET

There are so many different flavors of honey available. For example, there's alfalfa, buckwheat, dandelion, heather, linden, raspberry, spearmint, and thyme. And some of these have strong flavors. When cooking, it's important to be aware of the flavor intensity of the honey you're using because a bold honey could overwhelm a delicate-flavored recipe. REBECCA KRACKE GORDON

honeydew melon (*see* **melon**)

hoppin' John
A dish of black-eyed peas (sometimes called cowpeas) cooked with salt pork and other seasonings and served with rice. Served on New Year's Day, it's a popular dish in the South to bring good luck the rest of the year. This dish is typically made with dried black-eyed peas, but if you're in a rush, substitute canned peas; just rinse with water before using. (*see also* **black-eyed pea**)

Southernism
Several stories exist about how hoppin' John got its name, so pick your favorite. One theory is that children loved the dish so that they hopped around the table in eager anticipation. Another story surmises that hoppin' John was a busy waiter who served the dish. Another theory credits a man named John who loved the dish so much he would hurry, or hop, to the table when it was on the menu.

HOPPIN' JOHN

2 cups dried black-eyed peas	½ teaspoon pepper
¾ pound ham, chopped	½ teaspoon hot sauce
1 quart water	2 cups hot cooked rice
1 cup chopped onion	½ cup chopped green onions
1 teaspoon salt	

• Sort and wash peas; place in a Dutch oven. Cover with water 2 inches above peas.
• Bring to a boil; cook 2 minutes. Remove from heat; cover and let stand 1 hour. Drain.
• Bring ham and 1 quart water to a boil in Dutch oven; boil 15 minutes. Add peas; cover, reduce heat, and simmer, stirring occasionally, 45 minutes.
• Add onion and next 3 ingredients, and return to a boil. Cover, reduce heat, and simmer 15 minutes or until peas are tender. Stir in rice and green onions. Yield: 6 to 8 servings.

hops A plant whose conelike flowers are a major ingredient in making beer. The dried hops flower imparts a pleasantly bitter flavor to beers and ales. (*see also* **ale** *and* **beer**)

hors d'oeuvre (or DERV) Small, bite-size portions of hot or cold foods served before a meal with cocktails or beverages. (*see also* **appetizer,** **canapé,** *and* **crudités**)

horseradish A thick, gnarled root of a plant of the mustard family that has a hot, pungent flavor. Fresh horseradish is usually grated and used to season salads, soups, sauces, and spreads. Prepared, bottled horseradish also is available; it's usually ground and blended with white vinegar and used as a condiment. Dried horseradish, called "wasabi," also can be purchased and is frequently used in Japanese cooking.
Storage: Store fresh horseradish root in the refrigerator in a plastic bag up to 3 weeks or freeze it in a plastic freezer bag up to 6 months. Prepared horseradish begins to lose its hotness once it has been opened; replace it after 4 months. (*see also* **wasabi**)

hot cross buns Small, round, tender, sweet yeast rolls that have the shape of a cross snipped into or frosted on the top of the bun. Traditionally served at Easter, hot cross buns sometimes contain currants, raisins, or candied fruits.

hot dog A warmed frankfurter eaten in an oblong roll and topped with mustard, ketchup, relish, chili, slaw, or other condiments. Traditionally the franks were pork, but now are beef, turkey, or even vegetable-based for today's health-conscious consumer. They're a popular street vendor food in large cities. (*see also* **frankfurter**)

hot fudge A luscious, rich sauce made from chocolate, butter, sugar, and cream, and served warm over ice cream or other desserts.

HEAVENLY HOT FUDGE SAUCE

4 (1-ounce) unsweetened chocolate squares	3 cups sugar
	1 (12-ounce) can evaporated milk
½ cup butter	½ teaspoon salt

• Melt chocolate and butter in a large heavy saucepan over low heat, stirring constantly. Add sugar, 1 cup at a time, alternately with evaporated milk, beginning and ending with sugar; stir constantly over medium heat 5 minutes or until smooth. Stir in salt. Serve warm, or spoon sauce into hot sterilized jars, and seal. Store in refrigerator up to 1 month. Yield: about 4 cups.

hot sauce A fiery sauce made from chile peppers and vinegar. Hot sauce is strong, and only a drop or two is needed to season and flavor cocktails, sauces, greens, and other dishes. It's a condiment on many Southern tables. (*see also* **cayenne pepper, chile pepper, red pepper,** *and* **vinegar**)

Q **Is vinegar pepper sauce the same thing as Tabasco® sauce?**

A Tabasco® is a trade name for hot sauce produced by the McIlhenny family on Avery Island in Louisiana. It's made from a very hot, small red pepper that originally came from Mexico, but now grows in Louisiana and is used exclusively for making Tabasco® sauce. Vinegar pepper sauce is vinegar bottled with whole small, green chile peppers that flavor the vinegar.

hubbard squash A large, irregularly shaped squash with a greenish-gray to bright orange shell and orange flesh. Hubbard is available from September to March, and is best cut into pieces and boiled or baked. Mash or puree the cooked flesh and mix it with butter and seasonings.(*see also* **squash**)

huckleberry A wild berry that's similar to a blueberry, but has 10 small, hard seeds. The skin of the huckleberry also is thicker than a blueberry, and its flavor is more acidic. Huckleberries are difficult to find unless you pick them yourself. They're in season from June through August and can be prepared in pies or muffins. (*see also* **berry**)

huevos rancheros (WEH vohs rahn CHER ohs) A Mexican dish of eggs baked atop a casserole of tortillas, tomato, and chile salsa.

hull To remove the protective outer covering of nuts, seeds, or grains, or in the case of strawberries, to remove the leaves from the tops of the berries.

hummingbird cake A popular, moist layer cake flavored with pineapple and bananas and frosted with rich cream cheese frosting.

HUMMINGBIRD CAKE

3 cups all-purpose flour	1½ teaspoons vanilla extract
1 teaspoon baking soda	1 (8-ounce) can crushed
1 teaspoon salt	pineapple, undrained
2 cups sugar	1 cup chopped pecans
1 teaspoon ground cinnamon	2 cups chopped bananas
3 large eggs, beaten	Cream Cheese Frosting
1 cup vegetable oil	½ cup chopped pecans

• Combine first 5 ingredients in a large bowl; add eggs and oil, stirring until dry ingredients are moistened. (Do not beat.) Stir in vanilla, pineapple, 1 cup pecans, and bananas.
• Pour batter into 3 greased and floured 9-inch round cakepans. Bake at 350° for 25 to 30 minutes or until a wooden pick inserted in center comes out clean. Cool in pans on wire racks 10 minutes; remove from pans, and cool completely on wire racks.
• Spread Cream Cheese Frosting between layers and on top and sides of cake; sprinkle ½ cup chopped pecans on top. Store in refrigerator. Yield: 16 servings.

Southernism

We don't know how this cake got its name, but it certainly caught our readers' attention when it ran in our February, 1978, issue of Southern Living *magazine. It quickly became our all-time most requested recipe, and requests still come in today. According to letters sent from readers, it's won numerous blue ribbons at county fairs across the South since its debut. Thanks to Mrs. L.H. Wiggins from Greensboro, NC, for sharing it with us.*

CREAM CHEESE FROSTING

1 (8-ounce) package cream cheese, softened	1 (16-ounce) package powdered sugar, sifted
½ cup butter softened	1 teaspoon vanilla extract

• Beat cream cheese and butter at medium speed with an electric mixer until smooth. Gradually add powdered sugar, beating at low speed until light and fluffy. Stir in vanilla. Yield: 3 cups.

hummus (HU mes) A Mediterranean puree of cooked garbanzo beans, also known as chickpeas, that are mashed and mixed with tahini (sesame seed paste), lemon juice, and garlic. Hummus is typically served as an appetizer dip, along with pieces of pita bread to be used as dippers or as a sandwich spread. (*see also* **chickpea, pita, sesame seed,** *and* **tahini**)

HUMMUS

1 (15-ounce) can chickpeas, drained
¼ cup tahini
2 tablespoons chopped fresh parsley
1 large garlic clove
⅓ cup lemon juice
1½ teaspoons ground cumin
¼ teaspoon ground red pepper
2 tablespoons chopped onion
1 tablespoon reduced-sodium soy sauce

• Process all ingredients in a food processor until smooth. Yield: 1⅔ cups.

Hungarian goulash (*see* goulash)

hurricane A cocktail beverage made of dark rum, passion fruit, and other citrus juices, and served in a hurricane glass, which is a large, lantern-shaped glass.

Southernism

The world-famous Hurricane originated at Pat O'Brien's Restaurant in New Orleans where there's a Mardi Gras celebration 365 days a year. It's served in signature souvenir glasses that hold a full 26 ounces of the potent brew.

hush puppy A deep-fried cornbread fritter or dumpling popular in the South and often served with fried fish. Hush puppies are flavored with chopped onion, and sometimes cooked corn or beer is added.

TIMESAVING TIP
Whenever you fry up hush puppies and there are extras left over, just pop them into a zip-top plastic freezer bag, and store in the freezer up to 1 month. That way they're ready to enjoy anytime after a brief stint in a 400° oven to crisp them.

Southernism

The theory that the term started as a mixture of hash and batter called "hash puppy" has a few believers. Others say some fishermen were sitting by their campfire while eating fried fish when their "huntin' dawgs" started to bark. The men fried some cornbread batter in the skillet they had used for frying the fish and tossed it to the dogs. "Hush, puppies," they said.

BUTTERMILK HUSH PUPPIES

2 cups self-rising flour
2 cups self-rising white
    cornmeal
1 teaspoon sugar
½ teaspoon salt
½ teaspoon pepper

1 large onion, grated
1 jalapeño pepper, seeded and
    minced (optional)
2 cups buttermilk
1 large egg
Vegetable oil

• Combine first 5 ingredients; stir in onion and, if desired, jalapeño.

• Whisk together buttermilk and egg; add to flour mixture.

• Pour oil to a depth of 3 inches in a Dutch oven; heat to 375°. Drop batter by level tablespoonfuls into oil; fry in batches 5 to 7 minutes or until golden. Drain on paper towels. Yield: 5 dozen.

TEST KITCHEN SECRET

The oil for frying hush puppies should be 2 to 3 inches deep and heated until very hot, about 375°. Fry only a few at a time so the oil doesn't cool down; you want them to be crisp and golden. VANESSA MCNEIL

husk (*see* **hull**)

hydrogenation (*see* **fats and oils**)

hydroponics A method of growing plants, such as tomatoes, in a liquid nutrient solution, rather than in soil. Since there's no soil to attract weeds or pests, the produce is pesticide-free. The climate and season of production are irrelevant since things are grown under controlled conditions. So, in theory, the "perfect" tomato can be grown anywhere and anytime of year. Some may question that theory, but others pay a steep price to buy the prized produce.

hyssop (HIHS up) A member of the mint family with pungent, slightly bitter leaves. Hyssop can be added to salads, fruit dishes, soups, and stews, but is grown more for its oil, which is extracted and used to flavor liqueurs. (*see also* **herbs** *and* **liqueur**)

ice A sorbetlike mixture of sugar syrup, and fruit juice, wine, liqueur, or coffee often stirred during freezing to form a slightly granular texture; it's called granité in France and granita in Italy. Before serving, most ices are scraped with the tines of a fork to fluff up the crystals. You won't get a firm scoop when serving an ice, so just mound it in glasses and serve immediately. This term also refers to frozen water used to chill foods or beverages. The process of icing could mean chilling a glass or serving dish until coated with frost, or it could refer to spreading a frosting on a cake or cookie. (*see also* **granita**)

TEST KITCHEN SECRET

To give your ice the smooth icy consistency of sorbet, process the mixture in a food processor just until fluffy after it's almost frozen. Freeze again until firm. REBECCA KRACKE GORDON

LEMON ICE

1 (12-ounce) can frozen lemonade concentrate, thawed	1 cup water
3 cups ice cubes	⅓ cup sugar

• Process all ingredients in a food processor or blender until smooth. Pour mixture into a 13- x 9-inch pan, and freeze 45 minutes.
• Process mixture in food processor or blender until smooth. Return to pan, and freeze 8 hours. Yield: 4 cups.

iceberg lettuce (*see* **greens** *and* **lettuce**)

icebox cookie Cookie dough that has been shaped, usually into a log, and refrigerated until chilled; it later can be sliced into rounds for baking. (*see also* **cookie** *and* **refrigerator cookie**)

ice cream A creamy, frozen blend of milk products, a sweetener, various flavorings, and sometimes eggs. Ice cream can be churned at home in an ice cream freezer or it can be purchased in pints, quarts, half gallons, and gallons from supermarkets or ice cream establishments. Most commercial ice creams have additional air incorporated in them as well as stabilizers to improve their texture and body and to make them slow to melt. Fat from cream

TEST KITCHEN SECRET

For the best flavor and texture, most homemade ice creams need to stand an hour or so before serving. To do this, remove the freezer dasher and cover the ice cream with foil before replacing the lid. Pack the freezer bucket with ice and salt, using a high ratio of salt to ice, and wrap the top with a towel or newspaper. After it ripens, be careful not to let any salty brine get into the ice cream. VANESSA MCNEIL

and milk imparts richness, smoothness, and flavor to ice cream. Generally, the higher the fat content, the smoother and creamier the ice cream.

Storage: If storing commercially prepared ice cream longer than a few days, place in an airtight plastic bag or container to protect against drying out. Homemade ice cream can be frozen up to 2 months in a freezer container that has a tight-fitting lid. (*see also* **gelato, ice cream freezer, ice milk,** *and* **sherbet**)

Q **If my ice cream recipe contains eggs, do they have to be cooked, even though they're going to be frozen in the ice cream?**

A In keeping with today's food safety standards, eggs must be cooked, and then chilled, for ice cream custards, or you can substitute pasteurized eggs. But there are also many easy ice cream recipes that don't contain eggs.

VANILLA CUSTARD ICE CREAM

2 cups milk
1 vanilla bean, split
8 egg yolks
¾ cup sugar

½ teaspoon salt
¼ cup (2 ounces) vanilla extract
2 cups whipping cream
Topping: crumbled pralines

• Cook milk in heavy saucepan over medium heat, stirring often, just until bubbles appear; remove from heat. Add vanilla bean; cover and let stand 20 minutes. Discard vanilla bean.
• Whisk together yolks and next 3 ingredients in a large bowl until thick and pale. Gradually whisk warm milk mixture into yolk mixture; return to saucepan.
• Cook over very low heat, stirring constantly, 5 minutes or until mixture thickens and coats a spoon. Remove from heat; pour through a wire-mesh strainer into a bowl. Cool, stirring occasionally.

TIMESAVING TIP

When entertaining, ice cream can be scooped ahead and placed on a chilled baking sheet; cover tightly with plastic wrap, and return to freezer up to 24 hours before serving.

Southernism

Southern Living *has a sweet spot for ice cream, and it shows in the recipes. In the last 20 years, we've shared 9 recipes for strawberry ice cream, 10 for vanilla, 11 ways to make peach, and 12 variations of chocolate. For variety, we've made fennel, piña colada, fig, and even scuppernong ice cream.*

• Stir in cream; cover and chill 1 hour.
• Pour mixture into freezer container of a 1-gallon hand-turned or electric freezer. Freeze according to manufacturer's instructions.
• Pack freezer with additional ice and rock salt; let stand 1 hour before serving. Top with pralines. Yield: 2 quarts.

ice cream freezer An appliance used to make homemade ice cream. Most freezers have a canister with a central paddle or dasher; the canister is placed inside a container that holds either ice and salt, a chemical coolant, or an electric refrigeration unit.

A manual freezer consists of a wooden bucket with a metal inner canister; it requires ice, rock salt, and energetic volunteers to turn the crank that rotates the dasher. It usually takes 30 to 40 minutes of churning to make 4 to 5 quarts of ice cream in a manual freezer. An updated version of the manual freezer consists of a pre-frozen canister that sits inside a plastic container; the canister is placed in the freezer overnight to freeze the coolant, and the ice cream mixture is added to the frozen canister, and hand-cranked intermittently for 15 to 30 minutes.

Q Can I use table salt when preparing the freezer container with ice and salt?

A Rock salt is preferred over table salt because rock salt is slower to dissolve.

Electric freezers also are available; they're equipped with motors that rotate the canister or the dasher. Some electric freezers are just like manual wooden bucket-type freezers except you don't have to crank them. There is also a self-contained electric countertop model that uses refrigerator ice and table salt. Another version is a small electric freezer unit model that can be placed directly in the freezer of your refrigerator. You might also consider a countertop electric freezer that has a built-in refrigeration unit. Always read the instructions provided by the manufacturer; manual and electric freezers can be made of different materials, which can make a difference in the recommended ice-salt ratio. (*see also* **ice cream**)

TEST KITCHEN SECRET

When freezing ice cream, don't skimp on the ice and salt. If you use too little salt, the brine won't get cold enough. With too much salt, large ice crystals may form. When adding ice and salt, make four fairly thick layers of ice and four thin layers of salt, beginning with ice and ending with salt. Add more ice and salt as the ice melts during the freezing process and afterwards, if you let it stand before serving. MARGARET MONROE DICKEY

ice cream soda A drink made from ice cream, flavored syrup, and soda water served in a tall glass. Most ice cream sodas are topped with whipped cream and served with both a long-handled spoon and straws.

iced tea Freshly brewed tea that's diluted with water and served over ice. It can be sweetened or unsweetened, and is sometimes flavored with fresh mint, berries, or fruits. (*see also* **tea**)

RESCUE for cloudy tea:
Avoid this problem by allowing tea to cool to room temperature before chilling. Adding a bit of boiling water to cloudy tea will help clear up the cloudiness.

SOUTHERN SWEETENED TEA

6 cups water	**1 to 1¾ cups sugar**
4 family-size tea bags	

• Bring 6 cups water to a boil in a saucepan; add tea bags. Boil 1 minute; remove from heat. Cover and steep 10 minutes. Remove tea bags, squeezing gently.
• Add sugar, stirring until dissolved. Pour into a 1-gallon pitcher, and add enough water to fill pitcher. Serve over ice. Yield: 1 gallon.

Southernism

According to Martha McCulloch-Williams in her cookbook, Dishes and Beverages of the Old South, *written just after the turn of the twentieth century, "My teamaking is unorthodox, but people like to drink the brew. Bring fresh water to a bubbling boil in a clean, wide kettle, throw in the tea—a tablespoonful to the gallon of water, let boil just one minute, then strain from the leaves into a pot that has stood five minutes full of freshly boiled water, and that is instantly wrapped about with a thick napkin, so it shall not cool. Serve in tall glasses with rum and lemon or with a sherry syrup, flavored with lemon; add a maraschino cherry or so, or a tiny bit of ginger-flavored citron." Her attention to detail is a testament to how Southerners cherish their sweet brew. It's as true today as it was then.*

ice milk A frozen dessert similar to ice cream, but made with less milk fat and milk solids. Ice milk contains fewer calories than ice cream, is lighter in texture, and not as creamy. (*see also* **ice cream**)

icing A sweet frosting or filling used for covering cakes and decorating pastries. Icing is sometimes thought of as being slightly thinner and shinier than frosting, but the two terms are often used interchangeably. (*see also* **frosting**)

immersion blender A narrow, oblong handheld kitchen appliance with a rotary blade on one end. This portable stem-type blender can be immersed directly into a pot, bowl, or glass of liquid. It's particularly useful for making sauces, dips, shakes, smoothies, and for pureeing soups.

Indian nut (*see* **pine nut**)

Indian pudding A hearty baked puddinglike dessert, similar to hasty pudding. Indian pudding is made from cornmeal, milk, molasses, and spices; the flavor is similar to pumpkin pie. This dish originated in the Northeast; it was based on supawn, a Native American dish made from cornmeal. Early settlers added the molasses, and later, the spices. Sometimes the pudding is flavored with apples and served with whipped cream, hard sauce, or ice cream. (*see also* **hard sauce** *and* **hasty pudding**)

infusion (ihn FYOO zhuhn) Extracting flavor from tea leaves, herbs, or fruit while they steep in hot liquid. For example, an oil or vinegar might be infused with various herbs and later used to flavor other dishes. (*see also* **steep** *and recipes on the following page*)

MAKING INFUSED OILS

Herb Oil: Place 1 cup chopped fresh basil, chives, dill, mint, oregano, or thyme in a heavy saucepan; add 1 cup canola oil. Warm over low heat 20 minutes, stirring occasionally; cool at least 8 hours. Pour through a wire-mesh strainer, discarding solids. Cover and chill up to 2 weeks.

Roasted Garlic Oil: Place 8 heads garlic on a sheet of aluminum foil. Drizzle garlic with ¼ cup canola oil; seal foil over garlic. Bake at 400° for 45 minutes; cool. Squeeze pulp from each clove into a heat-proof container. Heat 1 cup canola oil; pour over garlic. Then pour through a wire-mesh strainer, discarding garlic. Cover and chill up to 2 weeks.

insalata (ihn sah LAH tah) An Italian term for salad, with insalata mista being a mixed salad and insalata verde referring to a salad of tossed greens.

instant flour (*see* flour)

Irish coffee
A cold-weather drink made of Irish whiskey, hot black coffee, and sugar. It's typically served in a glass mug and topped with a generous dollop of whipped cream. For authentic Irish coffee, don't stir the cream in. Irish tradition calls for sipping the hot coffee through the cream.

Irish soda bread
A traditional Irish quick bread leavened by baking soda and buttermilk. The round, free-form bread contains currants, raisins, and/or caraway seeds, and may have a cross or an "X" slashed in the top of the loaf.

IRISH SODA BREAD

6 cups all-purpose flour	4 teaspoons sugar
1 tablespoon baking powder	2½ cups buttermilk
1½ teaspoons baking soda	2 tablespoons butter, melted
2 teaspoons salt	1½ cups raisins

• Combine first 5 ingredients in a large bowl; set aside. Combine buttermilk, butter, and raisins; add to flour mixture, stirring until moistened.
• Turn dough out onto a well-floured surface, and knead until smooth and elastic (about 5 minutes). Press dough into a 1½-inch-thick circle on a greased baking sheet.
• Bake at 325° for 1 hour or until bread sounds hollow when tapped. Remove to a wire rack; cool 5 minutes. Yield: 8 to 12 servings.

Irish stew
A simple, hearty stew made from lamb or mutton, potatoes, and onions that simmers for several hours in stock or water until thickened. Irish stew is sometimes served with pickled red cabbage.

Irish whiskey
A light, dry whiskey from Ireland. It's similar to Scotch whiskey, except the barley for Irish whiskey isn't smoked. (*see also* whiskey)

irradiation A preservation process in which certain fruits, vegetables, dried spices and herbs, teas, pork, and grains are subjected to low doses of radiation in order to extend shelf life. Radiation slows the ripening process and eliminates microorganisms and insects, but it doesn't seem to affect the food's texture, flavor, or appearance. Although irradiation is FDA-approved, there is still some concern about the long-term side effects of eating treated food products. On the other hand, proponents suggest that irradiation is safer and better than preserving foods with chemicals and other preservatives.

Italian bread A long, cylindrical loaf of chewy, crusty bread. Italian bread is shorter and usually plumper than French bread or French baguettes. (*see also* **baguette** *and* **French bread**)

Italian meringue A glossy meringue made by slowly beating hot sugar syrup into whipped egg whites. Since the egg whites are cooked by hot sugar syrup, they can be served with no further cooking. Similar to a boiled icing, Italian meringue can be used to frost cakes, top pies, or be served over fruit. It may also be incorporated into dessert soufflé or pudding mixtures. (*see also* **boiled icing, frosting,** *and* **meringue**)

Italian parsley Also known as flat-leaf parsley, Italian parsley is darker in color and stronger in flavor than curly parsley. (*see also* **parsley**)

Italian sausage Pork sausage flavored with garlic and fennel seeds, first used in the South as a pizza topping and in spaghetti sauce. Today it's included in pastas, casseroles, sandwiches, and a variety of dishes. It's typically sold in links, but usually removed from the casings and crumbled for cooking; buy it sweet or hot. (*see also* **sausage**)

Italian seasoning This dry seasoning blend includes varying combinations of oregano, basil, rosemary, marjoram, thyme, and garlic powder.

jaggery (JAG uh ree) Dark brown sugar made from the sap of palm trees or sugarcane and used mostly in India and Southeast Asia. Jaggery can be purchased in East Indian markets as a soft or solid cake; the flavor resembles molasses or maple sugar. (*see also* **sugar**)

jalapeño (hah lah PEH nyoh) A smooth-skinned chile pepper with a hot to very hot, green vegetable flavor and dark green color. This short, tapering chile is usually about 2 inches long and ¾ to 1 inch in diameter. When seeding a jalapeño, it's best to wear rubber gloves because the seeds and veins are also hot and can burn your hands. Jalapeños can be purchased fresh or canned, and are a popular ingredient in a variety of Mexican and Southwestern dishes. (*see also* **chile pepper** *and* **peppers**)

jam A mixture of fruit and sugar that's cooked to a thick consistency and used as a spread for bread, toast, and biscuits, or as a filling for pastries and cookies. Jam is generally less firm than jelly and is made with crushed or finely chopped fruit rather than juice. Sometimes commercial pectin is added to homemade jams to create the desired consistency. (*see also* **boiling water bath, canning, jelly,** *and* **preserves**)

Q **What's the difference between jelly, jam, and preserves?**

A Jelly is made from fruit juice and is translucent. Jams and preserves are similar except preserves contain larger pieces of fruit than jams. Preserves are sometimes made from whole fruits, such as strawberries and other berries; hence the term "preserves," because the shape of the whole fruit is "preserved."

BLUEBERRY JAM

1½ quarts stemmed blueberries, crushed
¼ cup lemon juice
1 (1-inch) cinnamon stick
7 cups sugar
2 (3-ounce) packages liquid pectin

• Combine first 4 ingredients in a Dutch oven; bring to a boil until sugar dissolves, stirring often. Boil 2 minutes, stirring often; remove from heat. Discard cinnamon stick. Add pectin, and stir 5 minutes. Skim off foam with a metal spoon.

TEST KITCHEN SECRET

Select good quality fruit that's fully ripe for making jams and jellies. Contrary to popular belief, less-than-perfect fruit is not good for preserving because the quality of the canned product depends on the quality you begin with. JAN MOON

• Pour hot jam quickly into hot, sterilized jars, filling ¼ inch from top. Remove air bubbles; wipe jar rims. Cover at once with metal lids, and screw on bands. Process in boiling water bath 10 minutes. Yield: 5 half-pints.

jambalaya (juhm buh LI yah) A highly seasoned Creole rice dish flavored with tomatoes, onions, and green pepper, and often any combination of beef, pork, chicken, sausage, ham, or seafood. (*see also* **Creole cooking**)

SMOKY CAJUN JAMBALAYA

1 pound andouille or Cajun-style sausage
4 skinned and boned chicken breast halves
2 tablespoons peanut oil
1 cup chopped cooked ham
2 teaspoons Cajun seasoning
1 large onion, finely chopped
1 green bell pepper, chopped
½ cup chopped celery
3 garlic cloves, minced
1 (14½-ounce) can Cajun-style stewed tomatoes, undrained
½ cup chicken broth
1 tablespoon Worcestershire sauce
½ teaspoon hot sauce
3 cups hot cooked rice
1 cup chopped green onions

- Cut sausage into ½-inch slices; cut chicken into ½-inch pieces.
- Cook sausage in oil in a Dutch oven over medium-high heat 3 minutes or until no longer pink. Add chicken; cook, stirring often, until browned.
- Stir in ham, and cook until heated. Remove meat mixture, reserving 1 tablespoon drippings in Dutch oven. Return mixture to Dutch oven; stir in Cajun seasoning and next 5 ingredients. Cook, stirring constantly, 5 minutes.
- Stir in chicken broth and remaining ingredients; cook, stirring constantly, 2 minutes or until thoroughly heated. Yield: 6 servings.

Southernism

Louisiana chefs are notorious for tossing just about everything but the kitchen sink into a pot of jambalaya! Best associated with the brief period of Spanish domination in New Orleans, jambalaya is deemed by many as the trademark of Cajun cuisine. It's particularly revered in Gonzales, Louisiana, the self-professed Jambalaya Capital of the World. The city is heralded for its Jambalaya Festival hosted each year in honor of the first Cajun settlers.

jardinière, à la (jahr duh NIHR) A French term that refers to dishes garnished with vegetables.

Jarlsberg (*see* **cheese**)

jasmine rice Young, tender rice with a strong floral aroma and delicate flavor. Jasmine rice is often used in Thai and Vietnamese cuisines and in American cuisine as an aromatic alternative to long-grain rice. (*see also* **rice**)

java (JAH va) A type of coffee bean grown on the island of Indonesia; the beans produce full-bodied coffee with a strong, peppery flavor. Java is also a slang term that refers to coffee. (*see also* **coffee**)

jell (*see* **congeal**)

jelly Translucent gelatin-like spreads that are the result of cooking sugar and fruit juice. Pectin is often added to jelly mixtures to achieve the desired consistency, but some recipes rely on the natural pectin in the fruit and don't require additional pectin. In Britain, the term jelly refers to gelatin desserts. (*see also* **boiling water bath, jam,** *and* **preserves** *and recipes on following page*)

Q **I'm cutting back calories, so is it okay to reduce the sugar in my grandmother's jelly recipe?**

A Don't skimp on sugar in canning recipes. The proper amount of sugar is important for achieving a good gel. Sugar also contributes to the taste of the product and acts as a preservative, preventing the growth of microorganisms. You can substitute honey or light corn syrup for some of the sugar, but adjustments are sometimes necessary in other ingredient amounts. If you choose to use another sweetener, be sure to consult with a local county Cooperative Extension System or check the Web site for the Ball and Kerr companies at **homecanning.com** for advice.

HERB JELLY

1½ cups white grape juice
½ cup water
3½ cups sugar

Prepared herbs (variations follow)
Liquid food coloring (optional)
1 (3-ounce) package liquid pectin

• Combine first 4 ingredients and, if desired, food coloring in a Dutch oven. Bring to a rolling boil; cook 1 minute, stirring constantly. Add pectin, and bring to a rolling boil. Boil 1 minute, stirring often. Remove from heat; skim off foam with a metal spoon.

• Pour hot jelly through a sieve into hot, sterilized jars, filling to ¼ inch from top; wipe jar rims. Cover at once with metal lids, and screw on bands. Process in boiling water bath 5 minutes. Yield: 4 half-pints.

> ### TEST KITCHEN SECRET
>
> *When making jelly without added pectin, it's tricky to tell when the hot fruit mixture has reached the proper consistency since it thickens as it cools. To test for doneness, we always dip a cool metal spoon into the boiling jelly and lift it out of steam so the syrup runs off the side of the spoon. When two drops of the syrup come together and fall as a single drop or "sheet" off the spoon (usually at 220° to 222°), the jellying point has been reached.* JAMES SCHEND

Rosemary Jelly: Add 3 tablespoons chopped fresh rosemary before boiling.
Thyme Jelly: Add 3 tablespoons crushed fresh thyme leaves before boiling.
Basil Jelly: Add 3 tablespoons chopped fresh basil and, if desired, 4 drops yellow liquid food coloring before boiling.
Mint Jelly: Add ¾ cup crushed fresh mint leaves and, if desired, 2 drops green liquid food coloring before boiling.

jelly bag A tightly woven cloth bag used for draining and straining crushed fruit when making jelly. Jelly bags are made so they can be hung over a bowl that collects the strained juice; they are often left to drain for several hours or overnight.

jellyroll A thin layer of sponge cake baked in a jellyroll pan that measures 15 x 10 inches. After baking, the cake is spread with jam, jelly, whipped cream, or frosting, and rolled up into a log shape. Jellyrolls can be sprinkled with powdered sugar or frosted. (see also **baking dishes and pans** and **cake**)

> ### TEST KITCHEN SECRET
>
> *Jellyrolls are very easy to make. The secret is to turn the cake out onto a cloth towel that's heavily sprinkled with powdered sugar as soon as it comes out of the oven. Then, immediately roll up the towel and cake together, and let it cool. The towel keeps the cake from sticking together as it cools, and makes it easy to reroll after it's filled.* JAN MOON

jerk A Jamaican cooking term used when pork or chicken is rubbed with a sweet-hot paste made from spices, herbs, and chile peppers, and cooked slowly over a fire of green pimiento wood. Commercial jerk seasoning blends, sauces, and pastes are available in most large supermarkets.

jerky Thin strips of meat (usually beef or venison), that have been salted and dried in the sun or oven. Jerky has a very tough, chewy texture, salty flavor, and is high in protein; it's also lightweight and keeps indefinitely, which makes it popular with hikers and backpackers.

Jerusalem artichoke A brown-skinned, iron-rich tuber of the sunflower family that looks like gingerroot and is sometimes referred to as a sunchoke. This vegetable has white flesh, a nutty, sweet flavor, and crunchy texture, making it perfect for eating raw in salads or for boiling or steaming as a side dish or soup. Fresh Jerusalem artichokes are at their best fall through winter; select those that are firm and avoid any tinged with green.
Storage: Refrigerate in a plastic bag up to a week. (*see also* **vegetables**)

jewfish A type of giant sea bass found in waters off the coast of Florida and the Gulf of Mexico. Jewfish is characterized by firm, white meat, and is usually sold in steaks and fillets. (*see also* **fish**)

jícama (HEE kah mah) A round, tropical root vegetable, also known as the Mexican potato. Jícama has a thin, sandy brown skin that should be peeled before it's used; the white, crisp flesh has a sweet, nutty flavor. It's most often eaten raw with dips or in salads.
Storage: Fresh jícamas can be stored, unwrapped, in the vegetable bin of your refrigerator up to 3 weeks.

READER TIP
"Jícama is great teamed with citrus fruits and chile peppers for a spicy salad or side dish. I also like it cut into thin slices and tossed with olive oil and lime juice." M.M., Tampa, FL

jigger A standard shot glass used by bartenders to measure liquor for mixed drinks. In some cases, the size of the jigger can vary, but it's typically from 1 to 2 ounces. (*see also* **beverage**)

jimmies Tiny chocolate or sugar candies used to decorate desserts, ice cream, or cookies. Find them at the supermarket on the cake decorating supplies aisle with colored sugars.

Johannisberg Riesling (yoh HAH nihs boerg REEZ ling) A type of light, white wine grape grown in Germany and California from which fine, fruity white wines are produced. (*see also* **wine**)

J

johnnycake A thin, flat simple bread made of cornmeal, salt, and boiling water or cold milk. Johnnycake, sometimes called "hoe cake," is typically baked on a griddle like a pancake and served with vegetables.

Jordan almond A large, plump almond imported from Spain and typically sold plain or coated with a hard pastel candy coating. (*see also* **almond**)

juicer An electric or manual kitchen device that simplifies the extraction of juice from fruits. The simplest type features a shallow bowl with a rigid, fluted cone in the center onto which a cut fruit is placed and pressure is applied; there's also a spout on the side of the bowl for pouring juice. Fancier versions look like tall presses with levers that are pulled to press juice into a cup below. There's also a hand version made of wood known as a reamer. (*see also* **reamer**)

> **TIMESAVING TIP**
> Juicing goes faster if the fruit is at room temperature. Also, before juicing, roll lemons, limes, and oranges on a hard surface, pressing firmly with the palm of your hand; this breaks membranes inside the fruit and allows it to be juiced more easily. Another trick is to microwave fruit for 10 to 20 seconds on HIGH before juicing.

jujube (JOO joo bee) A fruit-flavored candy with a firm, chewy, gelatinous texture. Sometime jujubes are referred to as gummi candy.

julep A cool, syrupy-sweet alcoholic drink flavored by the leaves or extract of an aromatic plant, such as mint. The most famous is the Southern mint julep. (*see also* **mint julep**)

julienne (joo lee EHN) To cut food into thin matchstick-size strips (⅛ x ⅛ x 1½-inches) which, once cut, are called "julienne" strips. Julienned vegetables are sometimes used in stir-fry recipes, or they might be added as a garnish to salads or meat dishes. (*see also* **chop**)

> **TIMESAVING TIP**
> A fast way to cut julienne strips is to cut the vegetable into pieces the desired length and about ⅛ inch thick. Then stack the slices and cut lengthwise into thinner strips. Another fast way to julienne carrots or celery is to slice them on the bias into thin ovals about ¼ inch thick and 2 inches long. Then fan several ovals out and cut into ⅛-inch strips.

juniper berry Dried, aromatic, blue-black berries used most often to flavor gin, but also to flavor meats, wild game, and other savory dishes. The berries are too bitter to eat raw. (*see also* **gin**)

junket (JUHNG kith) A British dessert made with milk, sugar, flavoring, and rennet, which coagulates and gives the mixture a soft, puddinglike texture. Junket is usually served chilled with fresh fruit. (*see also* **rennet**)

jus (ZHEW) (*see* **au jus**)

kabob A grilled or broiled skewer of meat, poultry, shellfish, fish, or vegetables. The food for kabobs is usually cut into chunks and marinated before being threaded onto skewers. Sometimes kabobs are brushed with sauce or oil during cooking for flavor and to prevent drying. (*see also* **brochette, shish kabob,** *and* **skewer**)

BEEF TENDERLOIN KABOBS

½ cup dry sherry or beef broth
¼ cup olive oil
2 tablespoons soy sauce
1 garlic clove, minced
¼ teaspoon pepper
1 pound beef tenderloin steaks
    or boneless top sirloin steaks,
    cut into 1-inch cubes
8 large mushrooms
1 red bell pepper, cut into 1-inch
    pieces
8 cherry tomatoes
2 small onions, quartered
1 green bell pepper, cut into
    1-inch pieces

• Combine first 5 ingredients in a shallow dish or a large heavy-duty zip top plastic bag; add steak and remaining ingredients. Cover or seal, and chill for 2 hours, turning steak occasionally.
• Remove steak and vegetables from marinade, discarding marinade. Thread onto 4 (12-inch) skewers.
• Grill kabobs, covered with grill lid, over medium-high heat (350° to 400°) 5 to 7 minutes on each side or until desired doneness. Yield: 4 servings.

kabocha (kah BOH chah) A medium to large winter squash that has a dark green rind with lighter green streaks; the orange-colored flesh is smooth, tender, and sweet. Kabocha squash can be baked much like acorn squash after it has been cut in half and the seeds removed. (*see also* **squash**)

Kahlúa (kah LOO ah) This dark brown, coffee-flavored Mexican liqueur is often used in making white or black Russian cocktails. (*see also* **liqueur** *and* **white Russian**)

kaiser roll A large, round yeast roll with a crisp crust that can be used for making sandwiches. (*see also* **yeast**)

kalamata olive (kahl uh MAH tuh) A large, purple-black Greek olive that's often slit before packing to allow better absorption of the olive oil or vinegar in which it's packed. (*see also* **olive**)

kale A member of the cabbage family with attractive dark green, frilly leaves arranged in a loose bunch. Kale has a mild, cabbagelike flavor, and can be cooked similar to spinach. Ornamental, colorful varieties are also available.

Storage: Wash fresh kale in cold water and pat dry. Place leaves in a plastic bag lined with a slightly damp paper towel; store in the coldest section of the refrigerator up to 3 days. If stored too long, kale becomes bitter. (*see also* **greens**)

HOMESTYLE KALE

2 bunches fresh kale
  (about 1 pound)
6 bacon slices, chopped

1 small onion, chopped
1 to 2 tablespoons cider vinegar

• Remove stems and discolored spots from kale; rinse with cold water, and drain. Tear kale into bite-size pieces.
• Place in a steamer basket over boiling water. Cover and steam 5 minutes.
• Cook bacon in a skillet until crisp; remove and drain on paper towels, reserving 2 tablespoons drippings in skillet.
• Sauté onion in hot drippings until tender. Stir in kale and bacon. Drizzle with vinegar. Yield: 4 to 6 servings.

TEST KITCHEN SECRET

Don't relegate the curly leaves of kale to the side of the plate as just a garnish. More and more, we find we're adding the earthy flavor of kale to salads, soups and stews, or cooking it as a side dish. VANESSA MCNEIL

kamut (kah MOOT) Egyptian for wheat, kamut is a natural variety of large kernel, high-protein wheat grown mostly in Montana. It has a nutty flavor and is used to make pastas, puffed cereal, and crackers. Kamut and kamut products are generally available in health food stores. (*see also* **wheat**)

kasha (KAH shuh) A Russian term that refers to buckwheat kernels that have been hulled, roasted, and cracked. Kasha is a reddish-brown color, has a strong, nutty flavor, and chewy texture. In Russia, kasha is typically prepared as a sweetened porridgelike dish or cooked in salted water as a risotto and served with butter. (*see also* **grain** *and* **risotto**)

kelp Long, dark brown to grayish-black algae that's dried, folded into sheets, and used in Japanese and other Asian cuisines to flavor dashi and sushi. Also known as "kombu," kelp is sometimes pickled and served as a condiment. Find kelp in Japanese markets; it keeps indefinitely until opened, and then it can be refrigerated up to 6 months. (*see also* **dashi** *and* **sushi**)

ketchup (KEHCH uhp) Also called catsup, this time-honored condiment is extremely popular in the South. More ketchup is sold in the South than in any other part of the country. It's on the menu where French fries or hamburgers are served. Ketchup is tomato-based and includes the tang of vinegar, but is sweetened with sugar and spices. Some gourmet ketchups include other ingredients, such as walnuts, mangoes, or mushrooms.

Key lime (see **Key lime pie** and **lime**)

Key lime pie A tart pie created by pioneer settlers of the Florida Keys; it's made with egg yolks, sweetened condensed milk, and lime juice from yellowish-green Key limes. The tart filling is spooned into a pastry or graham cracker crust, spread with meringue, and baked until golden. The filling of authentic Key lime pie never includes green food coloring. This pie is best served chilled. (see also **lime**)

TEST KITCHEN SECRET

Real Key limes are sometimes hard to find, but the bottled juice is available in most grocery stores. If you're in a pinch, substitute lemon juice, but the flavor won't be as tart. MARY ALLEN PERRY

KEY LIME PIE

1¼ cups graham cracker crumbs
¼ cup firmly packed light
 brown sugar
⅓ cup butter or margarine, melted
2 (14-ounce) cans sweetened
 condensed milk

1 cup fresh Key lime juice
2 egg whites
¼ teaspoon cream of tartar
2 tablespoons sugar

• Combine first 3 ingredients. Press into a 9-inch pieplate. Bake at 350° for 10 minutes; cool. Stir together milk and lime juice. Pour into crust.
• Beat egg whites and cream of tartar at high speed with an electric mixer just until foamy. Add sugar, 1 tablespoon at a time, beating until soft peaks form and sugar dissolves (2 to 4 minutes). Spread meringue over filling.
• Bake at 325° for 25 to 28 minutes. Chill 8 hours. Yield: 1 (9-inch) pie.

kibbe (KIH bee) A Middle Eastern dish, also known as kibbeh, that contains ground lamb, bulghur wheat, and onions. (see also **bulghur**)

kidney Considered a variety or organ meat, kidneys are small and reddish-brown, have a tender texture, and strong flavor. The kidneys used most often come from beef, veal, lamb, and pork; they may be simmered, broiled, or cooked in casseroles, stews, or in famous steak and kidney pie.

kidney bean A dark red, medium-size, kidney-shaped bean. Kidney beans can be eaten alone or stirred into soups; they're often added to chili con carne. Dried and canned kidney beans are plentiful and can be purchased at most supermarkets. (see also **beans, dried;** and **chili con carne**)

kielbasa (kihl BAH sah) Also referred to as Polish sausage, kielbasa is made from ground pork, beef, or turkey, and is flavored with garlic. Kielbasa is sold smoked, precooked, and in large links. Even though it's precooked, kielbasa tastes better if heated before serving. (*see also* **sausage**)

kimchi (KIHM chee) A very spicy-hot Korean condiment of pickled cabbage or turnips; it's seasoned with garlic, chiles, green onions, and ginger. Kimchi can be purchased in Korean markets and will keep indefinitely in the refrigerator.

King cake A round, briochelike dessert decorated with bands of purple, green, and yellow icing that's a traditional part of Mardi Gras celebrations in Louisiana as well as in Mobile, Alabama, and in other Gulf Coast cities. The cake is traditionally decorated in royal colors—yellow, purple, and green—honoring the three kings who visited the Christ child on the Epiphany (also known as the Twelfth Night or King's Day). (*see also* **galette**)

KING CAKE

¼ cup butter or margarine	2 large eggs
1 (16-ounce) container sour cream	6 to 6½ cups all-purpose flour
⅓ cup sugar	½ cup sugar
1 teaspoon salt	1½ teaspoons ground cinnamon
2 (¼-ounce) envelopes active dry yeast	⅓ cup butter or margarine, softened
1 tablespoon sugar	Colored Frostings
½ cup warm water (100° to 110°)	Colored Sugars

• Cook first 4 ingredients in a saucepan over low heat, stirring often, until butter melts. Cool mixture to 100° to 110°.

• Dissolve yeast and 1 tablespoon sugar in ½ cup warm water in a large bowl; let stand 5 minutes. Add butter mixture, eggs, and 2 cups flour; beat at medium speed with an electric mixer 2 minutes or until smooth. Gradually stir in enough remaining flour to make a soft dough.

• Turn dough onto a floured surface; knead until smooth and elastic, about 10 minutes. Place in a well-greased bowl, turning to grease top. Cover dough, and let rise in a warm place (85°), free from drafts, 1 hour or until doubled in bulk.

• Stir together ½ cup sugar and cinnamon; set aside.

• Punch dough down; divide in half. Turn 1 portion out onto a lightly floured surface; roll to a 28- x 10-inch rectangle. Spread half each of cinnamon mixture and softened butter on dough. Roll up dough, jellyroll fashion, starting at long side. Place dough roll, seam side down, on a lightly greased baking sheet. Bring ends together to form an oval ring, moistening and pinching edges together to seal. Repeat with remaining dough, cinnamon mixture, and butter. Cover and let rise in a warm place, free from drafts, 20 minutes or until doubled in bulk.

• Bake at 375° for 15 minutes or until golden. Decorate with bands of Colored Frostings, and sprinkle with Colored Sugars. Yield: 2 cakes.
Note: Once the cake cools, randomly insert a plastic baby doll, if desired, before frosting. (Read the "Southernism" about the doll's significance.)

COLORED FROSTINGS

3 cups powdered sugar
3 tablespoons butter, melted
3 to 6 tablespoons milk
¼ teaspoon vanilla extract

1 or 2 drops each of green, yellow, red, and blue liquid food coloring

• Stir together powdered sugar and melted butter. Add milk to reach desired consistency for drizzling; stir in vanilla. Divide frosting into 3 batches, tinting 1 green, 1 yellow, and combining red and blue food coloring for purple frosting. Yield: about 1½ cups.

COLORED SUGARS

1½ cups sugar

1 or 2 drops each of green, yellow, red, and blue liquid food coloring

• Place ½ cup sugar and drop of green food coloring in a jar or zip top plastic bag; seal. Shake vigorously to evenly mix color with sugar. Repeat procedure with ½ cup sugar and yellow food coloring. For purple, combine 1 drop red and 1 drop blue food coloring before adding to remaining ½ cup sugar. Yield: ½ cup of each colored sugar.

Southernism

The King Cake tradition is thought to have been brought to New Orleans from France in 1870. The Creoles placed a bean or pea inside the cake before serving it, and the favor's finder was named king or queen for a day. Today, a tiny plastic doll is the common prize meant to bring good luck, and the honored recipient is bound by custom to host the next party and provide the next cake.

king crab A giant crab weighing as much as 10 to 15 pounds found off the coast of Alaska and Japan. King crab has white flesh with red edges and a delicate, sweet flavor. (*see also* **crab**)

king mackerel A type of mackerel also known as a kingfish; found in the Atlantic Ocean from Florida to Massachusetts. (*see also* **fish** *and* **mackerel**)

king orange A large orange grown in Florida that has a flattened shape with loose, rough, orange-colored skin. The flesh of the king orange is pale orange and juicy with a sweet-tart flavor. (*see also* **orange**)

kir (KEER) An apéritif made of white wine and crème de cassis, a black currant liqueur. Kir Royale is an apéritif made of crème de cassis and Champagne or other sparkling wine. (*see also* **apéritif** *and* **crème de cassis**)

kirsch (KEERSH) A clear cherry brandy that has been double-distilled from small, semisweet cherries. Kirsch is often used as an ingredient in cherries jubilee. (*see also* **brandy** *and* **cherries jubilee**)

kishke (KIHSH keh) A Jewish sausage made with matzo meal, fat, onions, and ground beef or other meat. The kishke mixture is stuffed into a beef casing, steamed, and roasted. (*see also* **matzo meal** *and* **sausage**)

kitchen shears A pair of scissors used to cut parchment paper, kitchen string, cheesecloth, fresh herbs, fruits, and other food-related items. Basic kitchen shears should have stainless-steel blades and one serrated edge. They're similar to poultry shears, but not as long or as heavy. (*see also* **poultry shears**)

> **TIMESAVING TIP**
> One of our favorite tools, kitchen shears, makes quick work of cutting up a whole chicken. Or to "chop" herbs, place a handful of herbs in a cup and "snip" with the shears. You can also use them to trim the fat from large cuts of meat.

kiwifruit (KEE wee) A fuzzy, brown-skinned, egg-shaped fruit native to New Zealand. The beautiful bright green flesh of kiwifruit has a sunburst pattern of tiny edible black seeds; its sweet-tart flavor is similar to that of pineapple and strawberries. Kiwifruit can be halved and scooped out with a tablespoon, peeled and sliced for salads and desserts, or used as a garnish.

> **TEST KITCHEN SECRET**
> "*Kiwifruit contains the same enzyme as fresh pineapple, so don't add it to gelatin salads or desserts; it will prevent the mixture from setting up. However, the same enzyme makes kiwifruit good for tenderizing meats; just rub or marinate meats with kiwifruit before they're cooked.*" MARGARET MONROE DICKEY

> **TIMESAVING TIP**
> To hasten ripening, place kiwifruit in a brown paper bag with an apple or a banana. Seal tightly, and let stand at room temperature overnight.

Q **Is it necessary to peel kiwifruit?**

A The skin of the kiwi is similar to that of a peach, so it isn't necessary to peel it. You might want to gently wash the skin to remove any excess fuzz.

Storage: Kiwifruit can be kept at room temperature until ripe. Then they should be stored in the refrigerator, where they'll keep several weeks.

knackwurst (NAK wurst) Plump German sausage links of precooked, garlic-seasoned beef and/or pork. Knackwurst, also known as knockwurst, is usually boiled or grilled before it's served with sauerkraut. The name of this sausage originated from the German word knack, which means "crack" and wurst, which means "sausage." (see also **sauerkraut** and **sausage**)

knead A process of working dough by hand, in a heavy-duty mixer, or in a food processor to distribute ingredients and develop gluten. Kneading is an important step in making dough because it creates a network of stretchy gluten strands that captures gases given off by the leavening agent, and allows dough to stretch and rise. (see also **breads, yeast**)

Q What's the correct way to knead dough?

A If kneaded by hand, the dough is worked using a folding-back-and-pressing-forward motion. The dough is then folded in half, given a quarter turn, and the process is repeated, adding a small amount of flour, if needed, to prevent sticking. The kneading-by-hand process can take 10 minutes or longer to form a smooth, elastic dough. Kneading in a heavy-duty mixer requires about 4 to 7 minutes; a food processor requires just 30 to 50 seconds with the steel knife blade or 2 minutes with the plastic dough blade.

TEST KITCHEN SECRET

A good test to see if you've kneaded a dough long enough is to push your fingertips into the dough. If the indentation springs back, the dough has been kneaded sufficiently. If it's extra soft, try using a scraper to gather and turn the dough. JAN MOON

knife An important tool used for cutting, peeling, and slicing. Select knives made of high-quality material that won't rust or corrode; carbon-stainless steel is an ideal choice for the knife blade. For good balance, look for knives with full tangs, where the metal of the blade visibly extends the entire length of the handle and is anchored by several rivets. The handle can be made of wood, resin-impregnated wood, plastic, rubber, or metal. Although knives come in sets, many professionals recommend buying knives individually so that the cutlery fits an individual's hand. After determining quality and comfort, follow the maker's recommended way of sharpening, and keep your knife consistently sharp. (continued on the following page)

Q What's the best way to store knives?

A When knives are stored loose in a drawer, users risk getting cut—and picking up a dull knife that's bumped against other items and lost its edge. Store knives in a slotted knife block or special drawer insert containing slots for blades or on a magnetic bar attached to the wall.

TEST KITCHEN SECRET

Remember to wash your knives immediately after using them, and dry them thoroughly. Washing knives by hand rather than in the dishwasher is critical to keeping their edges sharp. VIE WARSHAW

Knives are available in several different sizes and shapes:

- A **chef's knife** has a broad, stiff, slightly curved blade averaging about 8 inches long, and is used for chopping as well as for slicing, dicing, julienning, or mincing. The broad side can be used to crush garlic and gingerroot. Smaller, less broad chef's knives are also available.
- **Paring knives** look like a small chef's knife with a tapered blade usually 3 to 4 inches long and are used for peeling and slicing fruits and vegetables or for chopping small quantities.
- A **bread knife** has a straight, serrated blade at least 8 inches long and is used to cut through soft or crusty breads, cakes, and baked goods.
- **Slicing or carving knives** have long, slender blades and are used to slice or carve meats and large vegetables.
- A **utility knife** is like a larger paring knife with a slightly curved blade, and can be used for carving small cuts of meat.
- A **boning knife** has a narrow, slightly flexible curved blade 5 to 7 inches long and is excellent for separating cooked or uncooked meat from the bone, carving a roast, or peeling fruits and vegetables.

RESCUE for dull knives:

There are several options for sharpening knives. Sharpening steels are included in many knife sets; while they won't actually sharpen a knife, they will keep the edge in proper alignment. According to Neil Crumley, president of Wüsthof-Trident knife company, "The key to using a steel is holding the knife blade at a consistent 20-degree angle as you simulate the motion of the blade 'shaving' off the surface of the steel itself. To use the steel, hold it tip down on a sturdy surface. Holding the knife blade at a 20-degree angle, with the wide end of the blade at the top of the steel, draw the blade down along the steel, curving slightly so that the entire edge touches the steel; repeat the procedure for the other side of the blade using the opposite side of the steel. Do this five or 10 times, alternating the right and left side of the blade.

"You can also use a sharpening stone or whetstone to restore the cutting edge of a blade. First, moisten the stone with water or mineral oil to help prevent friction. Then place the stone on a damp towel near the edge of a sturdy surface. If using the fine-grain side of the stone, position the wide end of the knife blade against the upper corner of the stone and tilt the blade up at a 20-degree angle; use a 25- to 35-degree angle for the coarse-grain side. Move the blade toward you in a slight arc over the stone, beginning with the wide end and ending with the tip. Repeat several times, then do the other side of the knife."

Because sharpening stones can be difficult and confusing to use, Crumley advises home cooks to regularly use a sharpening steel, and if really needed, have knives sharpened by a professional. Electric knife sharpeners are also available; just be careful not to overuse them as they can damage the blades.

knish (kuh NISH) A baked or deep-fried Jewish pastry stuffed with mashed potatoes, cheese, ground meat, and buckwheat. (*see also* **buckwheat**)

knockwurst (*see* **knackwurst**)

Kobe beef (KOH bee) An exclusive grade of beef from cattle raised in Kobe, Japan. The cattle receive special treatment that consists of massages with sake and a diet high in beer. The end result is beef that's exceptionally tender, full flavored, and expensive. (*see also* **beef**)

kohlrabi (kohl RAH bee) A member of the cabbage and turnip family with a pale green or pale purple bulb-like stem that grows above the ground and is topped with dark green leaves. The kohlrabi bulb has a mild, nutty-sweet, turniplike flavor and is cooked the same way turnips or other root vegetables are cooked; it's available from mid-spring to mid-fall. **Storage:** Refrigerate kohlrabi in a plastic bag up to a week. (*see also* **vegetables**)

> ### TEST KITCHEN SECRET
>
> *If possible, don't peel the kohlrabi bulb until after it's cooked because this will give it a better flavor. After cooking, the bulb can be peeled and sliced or diced.* MARY ALLEN PERRY

kolache; kolacky; kolachke (koh LAH chee) A sweet Eastern European pastry made with yeast dough. Kolache is typically made into small rounds; each round has an indentation in the middle, which is filled with poppy seeds, jam, nuts, or crushed fruit.

Kona A type of coffee bean grown in the Kona region of the island of Hawaii. The beans produce superior aromatic coffee with a smooth, mellow flavor. (*see also* **coffee**)

kosher (KOH sher) A term indicating that food has been prepared or processed in accordance with Jewish dietary laws. Kosher laws not only indicate which types of foods can be eaten, but how they can be combined at mealtime. Most of the guidelines concern meat, fish, and dairy products. For example, beef, veal, lamb, and goat are considered kosher, but pork and wild game are not. It's also necessary for these animals to be slaughtered quickly and painlessly by a specially trained butcher using a sharp knife to kill the animal in a single stroke, and all meat must be drained of blood by salting. In addition, meat and poultry should not be combined with dairy products, and only seafood with fins and scales are allowed. In order for commercially prepared foods to be considered kosher, their preparation must be supervised by a rabbi. Kosher food products are specially labeled as being kosher and can be purchased in most supermarkets.

kosher salt Purified coarse rock salt that has been approved for use on kosher meats. It's used in the preparation of meat by Jews who observe kosher standards as well as by gourmet cooks who prefer its texture and flavor. (*see also* **salt**)

kraut (*see* **sauerkraut**)

kreplach (KREHP luhkh) Small Jewish noodle dumplings, similar to ravioli, that are stuffed with chopped meat or cottage cheese and simmered in chicken stock. (*see also* **ravioli**)

küchen (KOO khehn) A yeast-leavened German coffee cake filled with fruit or cheese and topped with nuts or crumbs. Küchen often appears at breakfast, but it can also be served as a dessert. (*see also* **coffee cake**)

kudzu (KUD zoo) A vine native to Japan that grows rampant in the South. The plant has mild-flavored roots that can be boiled and eaten or processed into a starch similar to arrowroot and used as a thickener. The starch can also be used as a coating for foods before frying. Kudzu is available in some Japanese and health food markets. (*see also* **arrowroot**)

kugel (KOO guhl) A creamy Jewish baked noodle or potato pudding that can be served as a side dish or sweetened and served as a dessert.

NU AWLINS KUGEL

The traditional Jewish noodle pudding takes on South Louisiana flavor with the addition of pralines.

3 large eggs, lightly beaten
1 (8-ounce) package cream cheese, softened
1 (8-ounce) container sour cream
½ cup butter, melted
¼ cup sugar
1 teaspoon vanilla extract
1 teaspoon salt
8 ounces ½-inch-wide noodles, cooked without salt or fat
4 pecan pralines, finely crumbled

• Combine first 7 ingredients in a large bowl, and stir in cooked noodles. Pour mixture into a buttered 8-inch square baking dish. Bake, uncovered, at 350° for 35 minutes.
• Sprinkle with praline crumbs, and bake 12 more minutes. Let stand about 10 minutes; cut into squares. Serve warm. Yield: 6 to 8 servings.
Note: You can substitute ¼ cup firmly packed brown sugar and 2 tablespoons chopped pecans for the pralines, if desired.

kugelhopf (KOO guhl hopf) A sweet, yeast-leavened, breadlike cake filled with raisins, candied fruits, and nuts, and baked in a special fluted tube pan known as a kugelhopf mold. Popular in Central Europe, kugelhoph is typically served for breakfast or afternoon tea.

kulich (koo LIHCH) A tall, cylindrical, yeast-leavened cake filled with candied fruit, raisins, and saffron. The top of the cake is usually drizzled with powdered sugar icing and sprinkled with chopped candied fruit and almonds. Kulich is traditionally prepared for Russian Easter celebrations.

kumquat (KUHM kwaht) A small oval citrus fruit that looks like a miniature orange. The edible rind is tangy-sweet, while the inside flesh is very tart. Kumquats can be sliced and served in salads or used as a garnish, but they're more likely to be candied or pickled whole or cooked into preserves and marmalades. Fresh kumquats are available from November to March.
Storage: Kumquats can be kept at room temperature up to a week or refrigerate in a plastic bag for 3 or 4 weeks. (*see also* **citrus fruit**)

kung pao (GONG bao) A spicy-hot Chinese stir-fry dish made with chicken or shrimp, and vegetables. Kung pao is flavored with garlic, ginger, dried chiles, and fried peanuts.

lactic acid (LAK tihk) An acid formed when milk sugar is fermented with certain bacteria. Lactic acid is found in sour milk and is responsible for the tart taste of yogurt, cheese, sauerkraut, pickles, and olives.

lactose (LAK tohs) A sugar that occurs naturally in milk. It's the least sweet of all natural sugars and is often used in baby formulas. However, as people age, they sometimes develop intolerance to lactose in varying degrees.

ladle A kitchen utensil with a cuplike bowl on one end of a long, hooked handle. Ladles come in different sizes and capacities, but are generally used to serve sauces, soups, and other liquids or to transfer them to a container.

Lady Baltimore cake A multilayered white cake filled with a rich mixture of raisins, nuts, and other fruit, and typically covered with fluffy white boiled frosting. (*see also* **Lord Baltimore cake** *and recipe on the following page*)

Southernism

In her 1930 cookbook, Two Hundred Years of Charleston Cooking, *Alicia Rhett Mayberry officially took credit for creating the original Lady Baltimore cake. Years before, novelist Owen Wister had immortalized Mrs. Mayberry's cake when he described it in his romantic novel entitled* Lady Baltimore, *writes food historian John Egerton in* Southern Food.

BOURBON-LACED LADY BALTIMORE CAKE

1 cup butter or margarine,
  softened
2 cups sugar
3½ cups sifted cake flour
1 tablespoon plus ½ teaspoon
  baking powder
¾ teaspoon salt
1 cup milk
1 teaspoon vanilla extract
8 egg whites
Coconut-Bourbon Filling
Boiled Frosting

• Grease 4 (9-inch) round cakepans; line with wax paper. Grease and flour wax paper.
• Beat butter at medium speed with an electric mixer until creamy; gradually add sugar, beating well. Combine flour, baking powder, and salt; add to butter mixture alternately with milk, beginning and ending with flour mixture. Mix at low speed after each addition until blended. Stir in vanilla.
• Beat egg whites at high speed until stiff peaks form. Gently fold into flour mixture. Pour batter into prepared pans.
• Bake at 375° for 20 minutes or until a wooden pick inserted in center comes out clean. Cool in pans on wire racks 10 minutes; remove from pans, and peel off wax paper. Cool layers completely on wire racks.
• Spread Coconut-Bourbon Filling between layers and on top of cake. Spread Boiled Frosting on sides of cake. Yield: 20 servings.

COCONUT-BOURBON FILLING

1½ cups raisins
1½ cups red candied cherries,
  halved
1½ cups coarsely chopped pecans
1½ cups flaked coconut
12 egg yolks, lightly beaten
1¾ cups sugar
¾ cup butter
½ teaspoon salt
½ cup bourbon

• Place raisins in a small saucepan, and cover with water. Bring to a boil; cover, remove from heat, and let stand 5 minutes. Drain and pat dry.
• Combine raisins, cherries, pecans, and coconut in a large bowl; set aside.
• Combine egg yolks and next 3 ingredients in top of a double boiler; bring water to a boil. Reduce heat to medium; cook, stirring constantly, 20 minutes or until mixture is thick. Add bourbon; stir well. Pour over fruit and nut mixture, stirring well; cool completely. Yield: 6 cups.

BOILED FROSTING

1½ cups sugar
½ cup water
½ teaspoon cream of tartar
⅛ teaspoon salt
4 egg whites
½ teaspoon almond extract

• Combine first 4 ingredients in a heavy saucepan. Cook over medium heat, stirring constantly, until clear. Cook, without stirring, until mixture reaches soft ball stage or candy thermometer registers 240°.
• While syrup cooks, beat egg whites at high speed with an electric mixer until soft peaks form; continue to beat, adding hot syrup in a heavy stream. Add almond extract. Beat until stiff peaks form. Yield: 7 cups.

ladyfinger A small oblong-shaped sponge cake about 3 inches long sometimes served alongside ice cream and pudding or used to line spring-form pans or molds for other desserts, such as charlottes, trifles, and tiramisu. Ladyfingers can be purchased from bakeries or supermarkets, or they can be made from scratch. (*see also* **charlotte, tiramisù,** *and* **trifle**)

lager (LAH guhr) A type of beer that's stored until it becomes light, bub-bly, and clear of sediment. Served cold, lager is one of the most popular types of beer in America. (*see also* **beer**)

lahvosh (LAH vohsh) Crispy Armenian cracker bread leavened with yeast and baked in round, thin, flat sheets. It's usually eaten as a mild-flavored cracker, but can also be softened with water to be used to make a sandwich. Find lahvosh in Middle Eastern markets and most supermarkets.

lait (LAY) A French term for milk. (*see also* **café au lait**)

lamb The meat from sheep slaughtered when less than a year old. Yearling and mutton, from older sheep, has a stronger flavor, is less tender, and is popular in England. Lamb has gained a widespread following in America on restaurant menus and with home cooks.

The USDA has a grading system that indicates the quality and tenderness of lamb based on the proportion of fat to lean. These grades are, beginning with the best: Prime, Choice, Good, Utility, and Cull. A certification pro-gram used in the United States identifies superior lamb products; the amount of fat and the age of the animal are considered. For exam-ple, meat from a sheep less than a year old must have ¼ inch or less fat trim and is cer-tified as the highest quality lamb available. Yearling is certified as meat from sheep between one and two years old, and mutton from sheep two years old or older.

Most lamb raised in the United States is sold fresh; imported frozen lamb from New Zealand and Australia is also available. Domestically raised lamb tends to be larger, meatier, and milder in flavor than most

> **Q** Should I get the butcher to remove the silvery skin that surrounds large cuts of lamb?
>
> **A** This skin is called "fell" and is sometimes left on whole roasts to hold in natural juices while the lamb cooks. However, trim the fell from small cuts before cooking or the meat may curl.

TEST KITCHEN SECRET

Most lamb is best cooked at 325° because higher temperatures cause the fat to burn. You'll know it's done when the internal temperature registers 145° for medium rare or 160° for medium. Also, we've found it's best to allow cooked meats, including lamb, to stand 10 to 15 minutes after they're removed from the oven before carving. MARY ALLEN PERRY

imported lamb. This is because domestic lamb is usually grain-fed rather than grass-fed.

Selecting: Purchase lamb with a bright pink color, pink bones, and white fat. If the meat and bones are dark red, it usually means the meat is older.

Storage: Ground lamb can be refrigerated 1 day or frozen up to 4 months, while all other lamb cuts can be refrigerated 2 days or frozen up to 9 months. Cooked lamb can be refrigerated 4 days; freezing is not recommended.

LAMB CHOPS WITH MINT AIOLI

6 garlic cloves, minced	16 (2-inch-thick) lamb chops
2 teaspoons dried summer savory	1 tablespoon olive oil
1 teaspoon salt	Mint Aioli
1 teaspoon pepper	Garnish: fresh mint sprigs

• Combine first 4 ingredients, and rub evenly into both sides of lamb chops. Brown chops in hot oil in a nonstick skillet over medium-high heat 2 to 3 minutes on each side. Arrange on a lightly greased rack in a broiler pan.
• Bake chops at 350° for 35 to 40 minutes or until a meat thermometer inserted into thickest portion registers 145° (medium rare). Serve with aioli. Garnish, if desired. Yield: 6 to 8 servings.

MINT AIOLI

1 cup mayonnaise	1 teaspoon grated lemon rind
¼ cup coarsely chopped fresh mint	2 tablespoons fresh lemon juice
4 garlic cloves, minced	½ teaspoon salt
	½ teaspoon pepper

• Process all ingredients in a blender or food processor until smooth, stopping to scrape down sides. Yield: 1¼ cups.

TIMETABLE FOR ROASTING LAMB

CUT	APPROXIMATE WEIGHT IN POUNDS	INTERNAL TEMPERATURE	APPROXIMATE TOTAL COOKING TIMES IN HOURS AT 325°
Leg			
Whole (bone-in)	6 to 7	160° (medium)	2½ to 3½
Half (bone-in)	3 to 4	160° (medium)	2 to 2¾
Shoulder (boneless)	4 to 6	160° (medium)	2½ to 3¾
Rib roast	1½ to 2½	160° (medium)	1 to 1⅔*
Crown roast (unstuffed)	2 to 3	160° (medium)	1 to 1½*
Sirloin tip	3	145° (medium rare)	1½
		160° (medium)	2
		170° (well done)	2¼

*Oven set at 375° and not preheated

LAMB CUTS

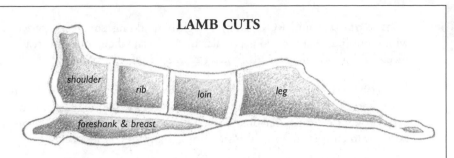

Lamb sent to market is divided into large wholesale cuts that butchers later divide into smaller cuts. It's important to have an idea where each cut comes from because this will tell you how tender it will probably be. Keep in mind that all lamb tends to be tender because it comes from such a young animal. However, the tenderest cuts come from the lightly used muscles along the upper back (rib and loin sections), and the less tender cuts come from the more heavily used muscles (shoulder, leg, foreshank, and breast). Except for the shank cuts, you can use dry-heat cooking methods. Roast, grill, broil, or panbroil the rack, loin, shoulder, and leg cuts. Braising or cooking in liquid, which are moist-heat methods, are better when preparing the less-tender shank cuts.

- **Shoulder:** A large cut that yields firm but flavorful meat, including blade and arm chops that can be grilled or broiled, and shoulder roasts for roasting or braising.

square cut shoulder roast

- **Rib:** This cut also yields tender meat, including rib chops for sautéing, broiling, or grilling, as well as the crown roast.

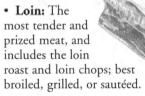

rib roast

rib chop

- **Loin:** The most tender and prized meat, and includes the loin roast and loin chops; best broiled, grilled, or sautéed.

loin roast

- **Leg:** The firm, but flavorful meat from this cut is roasted whole or cut into cubes for kabobs or stew. A small leg of lamb can be boned, butterflied, marinated, or grilled.

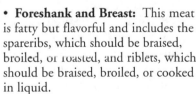

shank portion roast

- **Foreshank and Breast:** This meat is fatty but flavorful and includes the spareribs, which should be braised, broiled, or roasted, and riblets, which should be braised, broiled, or cooked in liquid.

lambrusco (lam BROO skoh) A lightly sparkling, somewhat sweet red wine from Italy. Lambrusco is popular in America; when chilled, it teams nicely with moderately spiced foods. (*see also* **wine**)

lamprey (LAM pree) A fish that resembles an eel; found in fresh and salt waters of North America and Europe. The black-skinned lamprey has a very fatty but delicately flavored flesh. The most common method of preparation is to cut the lamprey into small pieces and stew it in wine.

Lancashire cheese (LANG kuh sheer) A moist, firm cow's milk cheese made in Lancashire, England; it has an ivory-white color and a mild flavor that sharpens as it ages. Because it melts so easily, Lancashire cheese is a great choice for making Welsh rarebit. (*see also* **cheese** *and* **Welsh rarebit**)

Lane cake A white or yellow cake made in several layers and filled with a rich mixture of coconut, raisins, pecans, and bourbon or brandy. The top and sides of the original Lane cake were also spread with fruit filling, though later cooks opted to cover their creations with fluffy white frosting.

Southernism

Food writer and historian John Egerton expresses deep affection for Lane cake in his book, Southern Food, *when he says, "When I made a Lane cake for the first time, using a recipe similar to Mrs. Lane's original, my three hours of painstaking labor were richly rewarded with a beautiful and delicious confection that left me with a warm feeling for Emma Lane and all the patient bakers of the South who once performed these labors for the benefit and pleasure of others."*

LANE CAKE

1 cup butter, softened	1 cup milk
2 cups sugar	1 teaspoon vanilla extract
3¼ cups all-purpose flour	8 egg whites
1 tablespoon baking powder	Lane Cake Filling
¾ teaspoon salt	

• Beat butter at medium speed with an electric mixer until creamy; gradually add sugar, beating well. Combine flour, baking powder, and salt; add to butter mixture alternately with milk, beginning and ending with flour mixture. Beat at low speed after each addition until blended. Stir in vanilla.
• Beat egg whites at high speed until stiff. Stir one-third of egg whites into batter; gently fold in remaining egg whites. Spoon into 3 greased and floured 9-inch round cakepans. Bake at 325° for 25 minutes or until a wooden pick inserted in center comes out clean. Cool in pans on wire racks 10 minutes; remove from pans, and cool completely on wire racks.
• Spread Lane Cake Filling between layers and on top and sides of cake. Yield: 1 (3-layer) cake.

LANE CAKE FILLING

12 egg yolks	½ cup bourbon
1½ cups sugar	1½ cups finely chopped pecans
¾ cup butter	1½ cups finely chopped raisins
1½ teaspoons vanilla extract	1½ cups flaked coconut

• Combine egg yolks, sugar, and butter in a heavy saucepan. Cook over medium heat, stirring constantly, until thickened (about 20 minutes).
• Remove from heat; stir in vanilla and remaining ingredients. Cool completely. Yield: 5 cups.

lard Rich, processed pork fat, often used by early Southerners for frying or for making flaky biscuits and pastries. It's not used as often today for health reasons, but you'll still find it in many Southern grocery stores. Store it at room temperature or in the refrigerator. (*see also* **fats and oils**)

larding A process where long, thin strips of fat are inserted into and over a dry cut of meat to make it more juicy and flavorful.

lasagna, lasagne (luh ZAHN yuh) A wide, flat Italian noodle with ruffled or smooth edges used to make lasagna. Lasagna is an Italian dish made with lasagna noodles that have been boiled and layered with various cheeses (cottage cheese or ricotta cheese, Parmesan cheese, and mozzarella cheese), and a tomato and meat sauce or béchamel sauce. After baking until bubbly, let lasagna stand for at least 10 minutes to set before serving.

> **TIMESAVING TIP**
>
> For faster lasagna, use "no-boil" lasagna noodles. These special noodles go straight into the casserole and must be covered generously with sauce or cheese so that they can absorb enough moisture to become tender. Follow the package directions to make sure the noodles rehydrate properly.

GOURMET WHITE LASAGNA

8 uncooked lasagna noodles	1 (3-ounce) package cream cheese, softened
1 pound ground beef	½ cup dry white wine
½ pound ground pork sausage	2 cups (8 ounces) shredded Cheddar cheese
1 cup chopped onion	1½ cups (6 ounces) shredded Gouda cheese
½ cup chopped celery	1 (12-ounce) container small-curd cottage cheese
1 garlic clove, minced	1 large egg, lightly beaten
2 teaspoons dried basil	2 cups (8 ounces) shredded mozzarella cheese
1 teaspoon dried oregano	
½ teaspoon dried Italian seasoning	
½ teaspoon salt	
1 cup half-and-half	

(*recipe continued on the following page*)

• Cook noodles according to package directions; drain and set aside.
• Cook ground beef, ground pork sausage, and next 3 ingredients in a large skillet, stirring until meats crumble and are no longer pink; drain. Stir in basil and next 5 ingredients. Stir in wine and Cheddar and Gouda cheeses; cook, stirring constantly, until cheese melts. Set aside.
• Combine cottage cheese and egg; set aside. Arrange half of noodles in a lightly greased 13- x 9-inch baking dish; top noodles with half each of meat mixture, cheese mixture, and mozzarella cheese. Repeat layers with remaining ingredients.
• Bake, uncovered, at 350° for 40 minutes; let stand 10 minutes before serving. Yield: 6 to 8 servings.

latke (LAHT kuh) A Jewish potato pancake made from grated potatoes, eggs, onions, matzo meal or flour, and seasoning. The potato mixture is fried and served hot as a side dish, often with applesauce. Latkes are traditionally served at Hanukkah. (*see also* **matzo meal**)

POTATO LATKES

4 medium baking potatoes, peeled	4 large eggs, lightly beaten
1 small onion	1 teaspoon salt
¼ cup all-purpose flour	½ teaspoon freshly ground pepper
	¾ cup vegetable oil

• Shred potatoes and onion in a food processor; squeeze potatoes and onion between papers towels to remove excess moisture. Transfer to a bowl. Stir in flour and next 3 ingredients until blended.
• Drop mixture by 2 tablespoonfuls into hot oil in a large skillet; fry over medium-high heat, turning once, until browned. Drain on paper towels. Yield: 12 servings.

lattice Strips of pastry crisscrossed on top of a pie or tart. (*see also* **pie**)

laurel leaf (*see* **bay leaf**)

lavender (*see* **herbs**)

layer cake A cake with two or more layers stacked with icing, filling, or frosting in between. Cake layers are typically baked separately, but they can be baked in one thick layer that's split or sliced horizontally into thinner layers after baking. (*see also* **cake**)

leaf lettuce (*see* **greens** *and* **lettuce**)

leaven To raise or infuse (as in bread or cake) with a substance such as yeast or baking powder to incorporate air, and ultimately, to make it rise.

leavening agent An ingredient that causes a food product to rise or to become light and airy. Common leavening agents used in cooking include:
• **Chemical substances** such as baking powder and baking soda react with liquids and heat to create carbon dioxide.
• **Yeast**, a biological substance, gives off carbon dioxide, a natural by-product, created as microorganisms digest sugar and starch.
• **Eggs**, whether whole, just yolks, or whites alone, are natural leaveners and can be beaten to create a foamy network of tiny protein air bubbles that when heated, coagulate and help maintain structure.
• **Hot air and steam** are also natural leavening agents. They come into play when heat changes some of the water or liquid in a food or recipe into steam, such as in popovers and cream puffs.

The gases created or trapped by leavening agents cause foods to rise. By the time the gases dissipate, the food's structure, formed by the starches and proteins from other ingredients, such as flour and sugar, will have become stable enough to hold its shape. (*see also* **baking powder, baking soda,** *and* **yeast**)

lebkuchen (LAYB koo kuhn) A German cookie made with spices, honey, ground nuts, and citron. The cookie dough is often pressed into decorative molds or cut into fanciful shapes or designs. Lebkuchens are best made ahead; they're sometimes decorated with a powdered-sugar glaze. (*see also* **citron** *and* **cookie**)

leche (LEH cheh) A Spanish term for milk.

lecithin (LEHS uh thihn) A fatty substance that occurs naturally in animal and plant tissue and is used as an ingredient in some vegetable cooking sprays. (*see also* **vegetable cooking spray**)

leckerle (LEH kehr lee) There are two versions of this festive Swiss cookie; one is made with honey and the other with ground almonds. Leckerle dough is traditionally pressed into decorative wooden molds that leave an imprinted design on the surface of the cookies.

Lee cake A white layer sponge cake with citrus juice and rind in the filling and frosting. The cake is named after General Robert E. Lee. (*see recipe on the following page*)

Southernism

As commander of the Army of Northern Virginia during the Civil War, General Robert E. Lee earned the reputation for two things: an excellence in the art of war and an unyielding hunger for a spectacular sponge layer cake with a citrus filling and frosting. The Confederate commander so dearly loved the confection that it has been dubbed Robert E. Lee Cake ever since.

GENERAL ROBERT E. LEE ORANGE-LEMON CAKE

2 cups sifted cake flour
1½ teaspoons baking powder
½ teaspoon cream of tartar
9 eggs, separated
2 cups sugar

½ cup vegetable oil
4 teaspoons grated lemon rind
2 tablespoons lemon juice
Pinch of salt
Orange-Lemon Frosting

• Combine first 3 ingredients, and sift 6 times; set aside.
• Combine egg yolks and sugar in a large mixing bowl; beat at high speed with an electric mixer until mixture is thick and lemon colored. Reduce speed to medium, and gradually add vegetable oil. Add flour mixture; mix until well blended. Stir in lemon rind and juice.
• Beat egg whites and salt until stiff peaks form. Fold whites into batter. Pour batter into 4 wax paper-lined and greased 8-inch round cakepans.
• Bake at 325° for 20 to 25 minutes or until cake springs back when lightly touched. Cool in pans 10 minutes; loosen cake from sides of pan, using a small metal spatula. Remove cake from pan, and peel off wax paper. Cool layers completely on wire racks.
• Spread Orange-Lemon Frosting between layers and on top and sides of cake. Store cake in refrigerator until serving time. Yield: one 4-layer cake.

ORANGE-LEMON FROSTING

½ cup butter, softened
2 tablespoons sour cream
2 (16-ounce) packages powdered
  sugar, sifted

¼ cup grated orange rind
2 tablespoons grated lemon rind
2 tablespoons lemon juice
4 to 5 tablespoons orange juice

• Beat butter; add sour cream, and beat well. Add powdered sugar and grated rind alternately with juices, beating well. Yield: 4 cups.

leek A member of the onion family that looks like a giant green onion with a bright white stalk with a bulbous end and long, overlapping green leaves. Leeks have a mild, subtle onion-garlic flavor, and can be cooked whole as a vegetable or chopped and sliced and used in salads, soups, or to flavor other dishes. Leeks are available year-round.

Q **How can I best remove all the dirt and grit from leeks?**

A Because they grow partly underground, leeks are often very dirty. To clean, trim off the roots and the tough tops of the green leaves. Then cut the leek stalk in half and rinse well under cold running water, gently separating the layers and rubbing the leaves to remove trapped dirt. If the recipe calls for chopped or sliced leeks, try rinsing the leeks and then slice; place the slices in a deep bowl of water. Swish the leeks around and then let them stand about 15 minutes; dirt will sink to the bottom. Remove the clean leeks with a slotted spoon.

Storage: Refrigerate leeks in a plastic bag up to 5 days. (*see also* **vegetables**)

leg of lamb Is available boned or bone-in; if purchasing bone-in, look for a French-style or three-quarter leg of lamb with its upper pelvic bones removed, allowing for easier carving. (*see also* **lamb**)

legume (lehg YOOM) A group of plants that have double-seamed seed pods. Depending on the plant variety, the seeds, the pod and the seeds, or just the dried seeds can be eaten. Commonly eaten legumes include beans, lentils, peanuts, peas, and soybeans. They're a good source of protein and are used in soups, stews, and casseroles. Note that many legumes require soaking and long cooking. (*see also* **beans, dried; black-eyed pea; lentil; peanut;** *and* **yard-long bean**)

lemon An oval citrus fruit with a bright yellow skin, juicy yellow flesh, and tart, acidic juice. Lemons are available year-round; their juice and zest can be used in sweet and savory recipes. Lemon juice is available bottled or frozen in most supermarkets. **Storage:** Lemons can be stored at room temperature for about a week. For longer storage, place in plastic bags and refrigerate up to 3 weeks. (*see also* **citrus fruit** *and* **lime**)

TEST KITCHEN SECRET

One large lemon usually yields 2 to 3 tablespoons juice and 2 teaspoons zest. Get double-duty from lemons by removing the zest before squeezing the juice. To remove the zest, use a special zester or fine grater (we like the Microplane Food Grater, which peels several strips at a time). Or, you can peel the lemon, being careful to remove as little of the white pith as possible, and combine it with a little sugar in a food processor and pulse to make a fine zest. Once the zest or peel is removed, the remaining fruit can be refrigerated up to a week. LYDA JONES

LEMON BARS

2½ cups all-purpose flour, divided
½ cup sifted powdered sugar
¾ cup butter or margarine
½ teaspoon baking powder
4 large eggs, lightly beaten
2 cups sugar
½ teaspoon grated lemon rind (optional)
⅓ cup fresh lemon juice
Powdered sugar

• Combine 2 cups flour and ½ cup powdered sugar; cut in butter with a pastry blender until crumbly. Spoon mixture into a greased 13- x 9-inch pan; press firmly and evenly into pan, using fingertips. Bake at 350° for 20 to 25 minutes or until crust is lightly browned.
• Combine remaining ½ cup flour and baking powder. Combine eggs, 2 cups sugar, lemon rind, if desired, and lemon juice; stir in flour mixture. Pour over prepared crust.
• Bake at 350° for 25 minutes or until lightly browned and set. Cool on a wire rack. Dust lightly with powdered sugar; cut into bars. Yield: 2 dozen.

lemonade A slightly tart beverage made of sugar, water, and lemon juice. Lemonade is usually served chilled in a tall glass, sometimes over ice.

FRESH-SQUEEZED LEMONADE

1½ cups sugar
½ cup boiling water
1 tablespoon grated lemon rind

1½ cups fresh lemon juice
(8 large lemons)
5 cups water

• Stir together sugar and ½ cup boiling water until sugar dissolves.
• Stir in rind, juice, and 5 cups water. Chill. Serve over ice. Yield: 8 cups.

lemon balm (*see* **herbs**)

lemon curd A thick, creamy spread made from lemon juice, sugar, butter, and egg yolks. The mixture is cooked in the top of a double boiler until it thickens and coats a spoon. It's used to fill tarts and cakes, spread on breads, gingerbread, or scones, or layered with pound cake and whipped cream for a quick trifle. (*see also* **curd**)

TIMESAVING TIP
Commercially prepared lemon curd is available in most supermarkets and makes a fine substitute in a pinch.

LEMON CURD

2 cups sugar
1 cup butter or margarine
3 tablespoons grated lemon rind

⅔ cup fresh lemon juice
2 teaspoons cornstarch
4 large eggs, lightly beaten

• Combine first 5 ingredients in top of a double boiler; bring water to a boil. Reduce heat to low; cook until butter melts. Gradually, stir about one-fourth of hot mixture into eggs; add to remaining hot mixture, stirring constantly.
• Cook, stirring constantly, over simmering water until mixture thickens and coats a spoon (about 15 minutes). Remove from heat; cool.
• Cover and refrigerate up to 2 weeks. Serve with pound cake, angel food cake, or gingerbread. Yield: 3¼ cups.

lemon grass An aromatic herb with long, greenish, grassy stalks and a scallionlike base. Lemon grass imparts a strong lemon flavor to many Southeast Asian dishes; it can be purchased fresh or dried in Asian markets and in the gourmet produce section of many supermarkets.

Q What's a substitution for lemon grass?

A Try lemon zest or lemon verbena. If a recipe calls for 1 tablespoon chopped lemon grass, use ½ teaspoon lemon zest or 1 teaspoon verbena.

lemon meringue pie A flaky pie pastry filled with lemon custard and topped with a layer of soft meringue. (*see also* **lemon** *and* **meringue**)

BEST-EVER LEMON MERINGUE PIE

1½ cups sugar
 ½ cup cornstarch
 ¼ teaspoon salt
 4 egg yolks
1¾ cups water
 ⅔ cup lemon juice
 3 tablespoons butter or margarine

1 teaspoon grated lemon rind
1 baked 9-inch pastry shell
3 egg whites
¼ teaspoon cream of tartar
⅓ cup sugar
½ teaspoon vanilla extract

• Combine first 3 ingredients in a large heavy saucepan; set mixture aside.
• Combine egg yolks and water; stir into sugar mixture. Cook over medium heat, stirring constantly, until mixture thickens and boils. Boil 1 minute, stirring constantly. Remove from heat. Stir in juice, butter, and lemon rind. Spoon into pastry shell.
• Beat egg whites and cream of tartar in a grease-free bowl at medium speed with an electric mixer until soft peaks form. Gradually add ⅓ cup sugar, 1 tablespoon at a time, beating at high speed until stiff peaks form and sugar dissolves (2 to 4 minutes). Add vanilla, beating just until blended. Spread meringue over hot filling, sealing to edge of pastry. Bake at 325° for 25 to 28 minutes. Yield: 1 (9-inch) pie.

TEST KITCHEN SECRET

The key to perfect lemon custard is to thicken the cornstarch and sugar mixture before adding lemon juice. If the lemon juice is added too early, you'll reduce the thickening ability of the cornstarch. Also, be careful to temper the beaten egg yolks into the hot mixture to prevent curdling. JAMES SCHEND

lemon verbena (ver BEE nuh) (*see* **herbs**)

lentil Small dried seeds of various legumes that supply high protein and are often eaten as a meat substitute. There are two main types. Egyptian lentils are small and round, don't have a seed coat, and are reddish-orange in color. French lentils are slightly larger, have a seed covering, and are grayish-brown; both types have a beanlike texture when cooked, and a mild, nutty flavor. Lentils cook in minutes, are economical, and can be used in salads, soups, stews, and other vegetable dishes.

Storage: Store in an airtight container in a cool, dry place up to a year. (*see recipe on the following page*)

TEST KITCHEN SECRET

Unlike dried beans, lentils don't require long soaking and cooking, but they need to be sorted and washed before they're used. Spread them out on a baking sheet, and pick out any pebbles. Then, dump into a bowl of water and swish them around, discarding any trash that floats. Transfer to a colander and rinse under running water. Cooking time can vary considerably, depending on lentils' point of origin. MARGARET MONROE DICKEY

VEGGIE BURGERS

1 cup dried lentils, sorted and
 washed
2½ cups water
¼ cup ketchup
¼ teaspoon garlic powder
1 small onion, finely chopped
½ cup shredded carrot
1 cup uncooked quick-cooking
 oats
1 large egg

1 teaspoon salt
¼ teaspoon pepper
1 tablespoon whole wheat flour
2 tablespoons vegetable oil
8 hamburger buns
8 slices tomato
8 lettuce leaves
16 dill pickle slices
Mayonnaise or Thousand Island
 Dressing

• Combine lentils and water in a saucepan; bring to a boil over medium high heat. Cover, reduce heat, and simmer 25 minutes. Cook, uncovered, 10 minutes or until water is absorbed and lentils are tender.
• Stir ketchup and next 7 ingredients into lentils. Shape into 8 patties; sprinkle with flour. Cover and chill 1 hour.
• Pour 1 tablespoon oil into a large skillet. Fry 4 patties over medium-high heat 1 to 2 minutes on each side or until golden. Repeat procedure with remaining 1 tablespoon oil and 4 patties.
• Place a patty on bottom half of each bun; top with tomato, lettuce, and pickles; add top half of bun. Serve with mayonnaise or Thousand Island Dressing. Yield: 8 servings.

lettuce A term that describes a huge variety of leafy greens that serve as the basis for green salads. Most are available year-round, but during the cool months of spring and fall, there is an increased variety. The leaves range in texture from crisp to soft, and in flavor from sweet and mild to bitter and peppery:

Arugula

• **Arugula**, also called rocket, has dark green spiky leaves with a strong, spicy flavor.
• **Belgian endive** has crisp, slightly bitter, tightly closed leaves in a small, oblong-shaped head. (*see also* **Belgian endive** *and* **endive**)
• The **butterheads** include **Boston** and **Bibb** lettuces. Boston lettuce has a green, smooth, loose head. Its close relative, Bibb lettuce, is smaller, darker, and more delicate. Their tender, buttery flavor makes them good for salads, but they must be treated gently because they bruise easily.

TIMESAVING TIP
For the prettiest salads, tear lettuce leaves by hand. However, you can quickly shred large amounts of lettuce by first removing the ribs and stacking three or four leaves together. Starting on the long side, roll the leaves into a tight cylinder like a cigar. Then slice the cigar crosswise. The slices will unravel into fine shreds. (*see also* **chiffonade**)

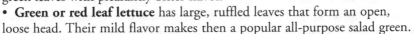

- **Curly endive** is a bushy head of narrow, frilly leaves with bitter flavor. (*see also* **curly endive**)
- **Frisée** is a young, curly endive with yellowish-green leaves with pleasantly bitter flavor.

Frisée

- **Green or red leaf lettuce** has large, ruffled leaves that form an open, loose head. Their mild flavor makes then a popular all-purpose salad green.
- **Iceberg** has a tightly closed head, crisp texture, bland flavor, and has less nutritional value than other lettuces. However, it's by far the most popular and widely available lettuce in North America.
- **Mâche**, also called corn salad, has tangy, nutty-flavored, oval leaves that grow in small, loose bunches. (*see also* **corn salad**)
- **Mesclun** is a mix of baby greens; it usually includes a range of colors and textures and offers a variety of pleasant flavors.

Mâche

- **Oakleaf** lettuce has mild-flavored, tender leaves shaped like those of an oak tree; sometimes they're tinged in red.
- **Radicchio** has tender but firm leaves with a slightly bitter flavor; they're usually in shades of burgundy with white ribs. (*see also* **radicchio**)
- **Romaine** lettuce, also called cos lettuce, has a large, cylindrical head and a slightly tough leaf that's juicy and sweet. Romaine is best used for salads when it's still small and relatively tender; it adds interesting crunch to salads and is an irreplaceable ingredient in Caesar salad. (*see also* **Caesar salad**)
- **Watercress** has small, round, dark green leaves on short, delicate stems; it has a pungent, peppery flavor.

Watercress

TIMESAVING TIP

A centrifugal salad spinner makes quick work of drying lettuce. Just place the cleaned leaves in the plastic spinner basket inside the spinner container, cover with the top, and whirl the leaves dry. Dressings cling better to dry leaves. (*see also* **salad spinner**)

Since leaves can be dirty as well as delicate, wash them gently in cool water, and then dry thoroughly. A salad spinner (*see Timesaving Tip*) can be used to dry greens, or you can shake them free of excess moisture and blot dry with paper towels. If time permits, return the washed greens to the refrigerator to stay crispy. When purchasing, look for lettuce that's unbruised, unwilted, and has robust color. Avoid leaves that are browning along the tips.

Storage: Refrigerate clean lettuce in a plastic bag or an airtight container up to 5 days. (*see also* **endive** *and* **escarole**)

TEST KITCHEN SECRET

Don't add salad dressing until just before serving. However, you can put the dressing in the bottom of the bowl and pile the greens on top and toss just before serving. Rebecca Kracke Gordon

lichee (LEE chee) (*see* **litchi**)

licorice (LIHK uh rihs) A feathery-leafed plant grown in Europe. The root of the licorice plant, as well as the extract taken from the root, has a distinctive, sweet flavor similar to anise or fennel, and can be used to flavor sweets, baked goods, and beverages. This term also refers to a red- or black-colored candy flavored with licorice extract. (*see also* **anise** *and* **fennel**)

lima bean (LY muh) Named for Lima, Peru, this flat, kidney-shaped bean has a pale green color, and plump body. There are two main varieties of lima beans—Fordhook and baby lima. The Fordhook is larger, plumper, and has a stronger flavor. Fresh limas, available from June to September, are usually sold in their pods and must be shelled before eaten. Frozen, canned, and dried limas are also available year-round. Limas can be cooked alone as a side dish, in soups, and are sometimes cooked and cooled for salads. (*see also* **beans, dried;** *and* **beans, fresh**)

Southernism

One of the best reasons to eat lima beans in the South is succotash, a dish handed down from Native Americans. Corn and limas are cooked together and, sometimes, other garden-fresh produce is added, depending on the season.

Limburger cheese (LIHM buhr guhr) A semisoft cheese made from cow's milk and well known for its pungent aroma. Limburger has a yellow to reddish-brown rind and a beige interior. When limburger is young it's very firm, crumbly, and salty, but at 2 to 3 months, it's soft and spreadable. The cheese has a kind of sweet flavor; older than 3 months, the smell and flavor are intense. Limburger is best served with other full-flavored foods such as onions, dark breads, and dark beer. Though it originated in Belgium and is made in the United States on a small scale, most limburger cheese comes from Germany. (*see also* **cheese**)

lime An oval, green or greenish-yellow citrus fruit with pale green pulp that yields juice ranging from tart to sour. Most of the limes we see are called Persian limes; they are bright green, large, and have few seeds. The Mexican or Key lime is smaller and has a thinner skin. Lime enthusiasts claim it has a better, more tart flavor and would never use anything else to make Key lime pie. Like lemons, limes are dual purpose; both their juicy pulp and rind can be used to provide bold, tart flavor.

Storage: Limes can be stored at room temperature for about a week. For longer storage, place in plastic bags and refrigerate 2 or 3 weeks. (*see also* **citrus fruit, Key lime pie, lemon,** *and* **limón**)

TEST KITCHEN SECRET

"Grated lime zest and fresh-squeezed juice can be frozen up to 6 months. Pour the juice into ice cube trays and freeze. When the cubes are solid, transfer them to zip-lock freezer bags." JAN MOON

limeade A slightly tart beverage made of sugar, water, and lime juice. Limeade is usually served chilled in a tall glass, sometimes over ice.

limón (lee MON) A Mexican lime also known as a Key lime and traditionally served with tequila drinks. (*see also* **Key lime, lime,** *and* **tequila**)

limpa bread (LIHM puh) A moist, fragrant Swedish rye bread leavened with yeast and flavored with fennel or anise and orange peel.

line A process where a pan is covered with parchment paper, wax paper, or aluminum foil to prevent the mixture in it from sticking to the pan. A pan can also be lined to give structure to a soft mixture, such as a soufflé. Sometimes the lining is an edible material, such as ladyfingers or thin slices of cake used to line a bowl for a trifle or charlotte. Another example would be when slices of bacon are used to line a mold for pâté. Even coating a pan or pieplate with breadcrumbs or cookie crumbs qualifies as a lining.

lingonberry (LING on bear ree) A member of the cranberry family that has red skin, a tart flavor, and grows wild. They're hard to find fresh, but can be purchased as sweet sauces or preserves. (*see also* **berry**)

linguine (lihn GWEE nee) Long, narrow, flat strands of pasta. Linguine's first introduction for most Southerners was in linguine with clam sauce. Today, however, the pasta is paired with everything from fresh vegetables to cream sauce and ethnic cuisines. (*see also* **pasta**)

CREAMY LINGUINE WITH GREENS

1 (16-ounce) package fresh turnip or collard greens, chopped
6 to 8 bacon slices, diced
1 large onion, diced
2 garlic cloves, minced
1 (7-ounce) jar roasted sweet red peppers, drained and diced
½ teaspoon salt
¼ teaspoon ground black pepper
¼ teaspoon dried crushed red pepper
2 cups whipping cream
1 (5-ounce) package shredded Parmesan cheese, divided
12 ounces linguine, cooked

• Cook greens in boiling water to cover in a Dutch oven 10 minutes. Drain and set aside. Cook bacon in Dutch oven until crisp; remove and drain on paper towels, reserving 2 tablespoons drippings in skillet.
• Sauté onion and garlic in hot drippings until tender. Add greens, roasted red peppers, and next 3 ingredients; cook over medium heat, stirring occasionally, 5 minutes or until thoroughly heated.
• Heat cream in a small saucepan over medium heat 5 minutes or until thoroughly heated (do not boil). Set aside 2 tablespoons Parmesan cheese. Stir in remaining cheese. Toss together cream mixture and pasta; top with greens and sprinkle with bacon and reserved cheese. Yield: 4 servings.

linzertorte (LIHN zuhr tort) An Austrian tart made with buttery pastry, which incorporates ground almonds, grated lemon rind, and spices. The bottom crust is usually spread with raspberry jam before being topped with a lattice crust and baked. (*see also* **lattice**)

liqueur (lih KUHR) A sweet, strong alcoholic beverage made from a base of distilled spirits, such as brandy, rum, or whiskey, and flavored with a variety of ingredients. These flavoring ingredients typically include extracts, oils, fruit syrups, and sugar syrup made from fruits, herbs, flowers, nuts, chocolate, coffee, or spices. Some liqueurs are described as being crème liqueurs; these are especially sweet and syrupy. Liqueurs are high in alcohol and usually range from 50 to 100 proof. Also called cordials, liqueurs are intended to be sipped in small quantities as an after-dinner drink, or used to flavor desserts and sauces, or for making cocktail beverages.

LIQUEUR FLAVORS

FLAVOR	LIQUEUR
Almond	Amaretto, crème d'almond
Anise	anisette, Galliano, ojen, ouzo, Pastis, Pernod, Ricard, Sambuca Romana
Apricot	Abricotine, Apry, crème d'abricots
Banana	crème de banane
Caramel	caramello
Caraway	kummel
Cherry	Cherristock, crème de cerise, crème de kirsch, maraschino, Peter Heering, wishniak
Chocolate	Chocolat Suisse, crème de cacao, Sabra, Vandermint
Coffee	Brazilia, Café Brizard, crème de café, crème de moka, Kahlúa, Pasha, Sabroso, Tia Maria
Currant	crème de cassis
Hazelnut	crème de noisette, Frangelico
Herbs and Spices	Bénédictine, cascarilla, Chartreuse, Fior d'Alpe, Strega
Mint	crème de menthe, peppermint schnapps
Orange	Cointreau, curaçao, Grand Marnier, Halb and Halb, Triple Sec
Pineapple	crème d'ananas
Plum	prunelle
Raspberry	crème de framboises, himbeer
Strawberry	crème de fraises
Tea	O-Cha, Tea Breeze
Vanilla	crème de vanille
Walnut	crème de noix

TEST KITCHEN SECRET

When cooking with liqueurs, use a cautious hand; their concentrated flavor can easily overpower a dish. You should always remove a pan from the heat before stirring in a liqueur, and avoid letting the mixture sit too long before serving, since the liqueur flavor dissipates quickly when exposed to heat and air. MARY ALLEN PERRY

liquid smoke A commercial product made by diffusing smoke in liquid. It's used as a basting or flavoring ingredient to add hickory-smoke flavor to foods; add it to marinades or brush it on meats, poultry, or fish.

liquor (LIH kuhr) A general term that refers to any distilled alcoholic beverage, the most popular being whiskey, gin, vodka, and rum. This term can also refer to the juices of a shellfish, as in oyster liquor. It can also refer to the liquid resulting from cooking meats or vegetables, as in pot liquor or "pot likker." (*see also* **alcohol, bourbon, gin, pot liquor, rum, vodka,** *and* **whiskey**)

Southernism

What's the difference between whiskey and bourbon? In the 1790s, Scotch or Scotch-Irish immigrants fled Pennsylvania to escape taxes on their home brews and settled in Kentucky. By 1820, "Kentucky whiskey" was an established name and product. Dr. James C. Crow, a doctor and chemist, came up with a new sour-mash distilling process and standardized the method for making whiskey. The new process caught on with Kentucky distillers, and the libation was called bourbon.

litchi (LEE chee) A small tropical fruit native to China and Southeast Asia. The litchi has a rough, red shell and flesh that looks like a soft, white grape and tastes similar to a sweet Muscat grape. Litchis are rarely available fresh, but they can be purchased canned in Asian grocery stores or in the international or canned fruit sections of some supermarkets; they add flavor to salads, or they can be eaten as a snack.

liter A metric measure of liquid volume. One liter is equal to 33.8 fluid ounces or 1.06 quarts. (*see also* **beverage** *and* **metric measure**)

liver A nutritious organ meat that tastes best when it comes from a young animal. Calf's liver has a pinkish-brown color, is tenderer, and has a better flavor than beef liver. Goose livers receive high praise when transformed into foie gras and pâté, while mild chicken livers make popular appetizers wrapped in bacon for rumaki. Most livers are available fresh, though beef and chicken livers are also usually offered frozen. Look for liver that has a bright reddish-brown color and a fresh aroma.

TEST KITCHEN SECRET

Nobody likes tough, fried liver, but if it's sliced thin and skillfully cooked, it's surprisingly good. The key is to avoid overcooking; sautéing is the most popular way to cook liver. For example, thinly sliced calf's liver should be sautéed over medium-high heat just until it's no longer pink in the center, about 2 or 3 minutes per side. Vie Warshaw

Storage: Refrigerate liver in the package it which it was purchased for no more than a day. (*see also* **foie gras, pâté, rumaki, variety meats,** *and recipe on the following page*)

FRIED CHICKEN LIVERS

1 pound chicken livers	1 teaspoon pepper
2 cups all-purpose flour	1 cup buttermilk
1½ teaspoons seasoned salt	Vegetable oil

- Pierce chicken livers several times with a fork.
- Combine flour, salt, and pepper in a shallow dish; dredge livers in flour mixture. Dip livers into buttermilk, and dredge in flour mixture again.
- Pour oil to depth of 2 inches into a Dutch oven; heat to 365°. Cook in batches, 4 minutes or until golden. Serve immediately. Yield: 4 to 5 servings.

liverwurst (LIHV uhr wurst) Ready-to-eat liver sausage made of pork liver and seasonings. It's sold smoked or plain and comes in links, loaves, and slices. It's usually eaten as a snack or on sandwiches. (*see also* **sausage**)

lobster Perhaps the most prestigious of all shellfish; although found in most oceans of the world, the two most important species are the Maine or American lobster, and the spiny lobster. The difference between these two is that Maine lobster has five pairs of legs, the first of which are two large, heavy claws. The spiny lobster has five pairs of legs with no claws. Therefore, most of the meat on spiny lobsters is in the tail, whereas Maine lobsters also contain claw meat. Sometimes spiny lobsters are sold as frozen "rock lobster" tails. When buying a live lobster, make sure it's lively; pick it up and see if it wiggles its legs and curls its tail. Live lobsters usually have a mottled greenish-brown color, but their shells turn red once cooked. If boiled or steamed, the lobster can be cleaned after cooking, but if broiled, clean and split them first.

PREPARING LIVE LOBSTER

1. Grasp live lobster just behind the eyes with long tongs. Plunge lobster, headfirst, into boiling water.

2. Place lobster on its back. Using kitchen shears, cut the body shell and the tail shell apart.

3. Scoop out the green tomalley (liver) and the coral roe (in female lobster only).

4. Using kitchen shears, cut down center of tail underside. Pull meat from shell in one piece.

5. Cut ¼ inch deep along outer tail to expose vein. Discard vein.

6. Crack claws with a seafood cracker or nutcracker, and extract meat.

Storage: It's best to purchase lobsters on the day they're to be cooked. If you must keep them a few hours, store on a bed of ice in the refrigerator. All fresh lobsters must be cooked while still alive or killed just prior to cooking.

RESCUE for a lobster that's overly active:
To subdue an active lobster, place it in the freezer for 5 to 10 minutes before cooking.

CRAB-STUFFED LOBSTER TAILS

2 quarts water	2 tablespoons fine, dry bread-
1 tablespoon salt	crumbs (store-bought)
2 (1½- to 1¾-pound) live lobsters	¼ teaspoon Old Bay seasoning
½ pound fresh lump crabmeat	¼ teaspoon pepper
1 garlic clove, minced	2 tablespoons butter, melted
1 tablespoon chopped fresh parsley	1 teaspoon lemon juice
2 tablespoons freshly grated	Garlic-Butter Sauce
Parmesan cheese	

• Combine water and salt in a large Dutch oven; bring to a boil. Plunge lobsters headfirst into boiling water; return to a boil. Cover, reduce heat, and simmer 10 minutes; drain and cool.

• Break off large claws and legs. Crack claw and leg shells, using a seafood or nutcracker; remove meat, and set aside. Break off tail. Cut top side of tail shell lengthwise, using kitchen shears. Cut through center of meat, and remove vein. Leave meat in shell, or for easier serving, loosen and lift meat out of shell. Return to shell intact. Rinse and set aside.

• Drain crabmeat, removing any bits of shell. Combine crabmeat, garlic, and next 7 ingredients; toss gently. Spoon into lobster tails. Place on a baking sheet. Bake at 400° for 12 minutes or until thoroughly heated. Serve with Garlic-Butter Sauce and claw and leg meat. Yield: 2 servings.

TEST KITCHEN SECRET

"Lobsters are traditionally boiled, but they can be steamed over a few inches of water. Be careful not to overcook them because that makes the meat stringy and chewy. When broiling, you know it's done as soon as the meat turns opaque. If boiling, cook 10 minutes for 2 (1-pound) lobsters." LYDA JONES

Q When purchasing lobster, do I buy one per person?

A Plan on purchasing a 1- to 1½-pound whole lobster or 1 (8-ounce) lobster tail for each person.

GARLIC-BUTTER SAUCE

½ cup butter	1 garlic clove, minced
2 tablespoons whipping cream	2 tablespoons lemon juice

• Melt butter in a small saucepan over low heat; add whipping cream and garlic, and cook 1 minute, stirring constantly with a wire whisk.
• Stir in lemon juice. Remove from heat. Yield: ⅔ cup.

lobster Newburg A dish of cooked, chopped lobster meat heated in a sauce of cream, egg yolks, and sherry or Madeira wine. Lobster Newburg is typically served over buttered toast points or, more elegantly, in delicate puff pastry shells.

lobster Thermidor (THUHR mih dohr) An elaborate dish made from cooked, chopped lobster tail meat and a creamy béchamel sauce flavored with wine, shallots, tarragon, and mustard. After cooking, the lobster mixture is spooned back into the lobster tail shell, sprinkled with cheese, and broiled until golden. It's believed that Napoleon named the dish after he first tasted it. (*see also* **béchamel sauce**)

loganberry A cross between a raspberry and blackberry, and named after its developer, Judge James H. Logan. The loganberry, grown mostly in Oregon and Washington states, looks like a large raspberry, is juicy with a tart flavor, and turns purple-red when ripe. Like most other berries, rinse loganberries just before you're ready to use them; store in a plastic bag in the refrigerator for 2 to 3 days. Most loganberries are eaten fresh or made into preserves or canned. (*see also* **berry**)

loin The upper midsection of pork, extending from the shoulder to the leg, or from the rib to the leg in beef, lamb, and veal. Beef loin is usually divided into the short loin and sirloin. The loin is generally a very tender cut from which steaks, chops, and the tenderloin are taken. (*see also* **beef, lamb, pork,** *and* **veal**)

lo mein A term that refers to fresh Chinese egg noodles. Lo mein also describes a Chinese-American dish of chicken, shrimp, or beef that has been cooked with vegetables, such as bean sprouts, mushrooms, water chestnuts, bamboo shoots, and green onions, and is served over soft noodles.

London broil Actually the name of a recipe, but when sold in the market, it's usually sold as a cut of beef from the flank area. Because this is a tougher cut, err on the side of caution when cooking; it's easily overcooked. For best results, London broil is tenderized by marinating, then grilled or broiled, and thinly sliced across the grain. London broil takes its name from London, England, where it was first served. (*see also* **beef**)

LONDON BROIL

1 (1½-pound) flank steak*	2 green onions, minced
½ cup dry red wine or red wine vinegar	1 teaspoon dry mustard
½ cup vegetable oil	2 teaspoons coarsely ground pepper
¼ cup chopped fresh parsley	¼ teaspoon salt
2 large garlic cloves, minced	

- Score steak by making shallow diagonal cuts at 1-inch intervals in a diamond pattern on both sides of meat. Place steak in a large heavy-duty zip-top plastic bag or large shallow dish.
- Combine wine and next 7 ingredients; pour over steak. Seal or cover; marinate in refrigerator 8 hours, turning occasionally.
- Drain meat, discarding marinade. Place steak on a rack in broiler pan. Broil 3 to 5 inches from heat 5 minutes; turn steak. Broil 6 to 8 more minutes or to desired doneness. Slice steak diagonally across the grain into thin slices. Yield: 4 servings.

*For this recipe, if your steak is 1 inch thick or less, broil it on the top rack. If it's more than 1 inch thick, broil on the second rack.

longhorn cheese Cheddar-style cheese made in Wisconsin and named after the longhorn cow. Longhorn cheese has a mild flavor, an orange color, and is available in various shapes. (*see also* **cheese**)

Long Island tea A potent cocktail made of gin and vodka and sometimes, tequila. The drink is mixed with cola-flavored soda and lemon, and served in a tall glass over ice.

loquat (LOH kwaht) Also known as a Japanese plum, the loquat is a small to medium, slightly pear-shaped fruit that has a slightly downy, yellowish-orange skin, juicy, crisp flesh, and a large seed. The delicate, sweetly tart flavor of the loquat brings to mind a pleasant combination of apples and apricots.
Because loquats bruise easily and quickly deteriorate after picking, they're rarely available in areas other than where they're grown. However, they can be purchased dried or canned in Asian markets.

Lord Baltimore cake A multilayered yellow cake filled with a mixture of chopped pecans or almonds, maraschino cherries, and macaroon crumbs. The cake is typically covered with fluffy white boiled frosting. (*see also* **Lady Baltimore cake** *and recipe on the following page*)

Southernism

Where did the cake get its name? Supposedly Charles Calvert, the third Lord Baltimore, was sent from England in 1661 to govern the territory that was to become Maryland. By all accounts, his rule was so unpopular that his subjects hated him, and he eventually was forced to return to England. So, it's more likely the cake was named after the regal city of Baltimore than the lordship himself.

LORD BALTIMORE CAKE

¾ cup shortening
2¼ cups sugar
  8 egg yolks
3¾ cups sifted cake flour
1½ tablespoons baking powder
  ½ teaspoon salt
1¾ cups milk
  ½ teaspoon almond extract
  ½ teaspoon vanilla extract

Boiled Frosting
1 cup chopped mixed candied
  fruit
1 cup chopped pecans or walnuts
½ cup macaroon crumbs (about
  3 cookies)
1 teaspoon vanilla extract
½ teaspoon almond extract

• Beat shortening at medium speed with an electric mixer until fluffy; gradually add sugar, beating at medium speed 5 to 7 minutes. Add egg yolks, 1 at a time, beating after each addition.
• Combine flour, baking powder, and salt; add to shortening mixture alternately with milk, beginning and ending with flour mixture. Mix at low speed after each addition until blended. Stir in ½ teaspoon almond extract and ½ teaspoon vanilla. Pour into 3 greased and floured 9-inch round cakepans.
• Bake at 350° for 22 to 25 minutes or until a wooden pick inserted in center comes out clean. Cool in pans on wire racks 10 minutes; remove from pans, and cool completely on wire racks.
• Combine 2 cups Boiled Frosting, candied fruit, and remaining ingredients; spread between layers. Spread remaining Boiled Frosting on top and sides of cake. Yield: 16 servings.

BOILED FROSTING

1½ cups sugar
  ½ cup water
  ½ teaspoon cream of tartar

⅛ teaspoon salt
4 egg whites
½ teaspoon almond extract

• Combine first 4 ingredients in a heavy saucepan. Cook over medium heat, stirring constantly, until mixture is clear. Cook, without stirring, until mixture reaches soft ball stage or candy thermometer registers 240°.
• While syrup cooks, beat egg whites at high speed with an electric mixer until soft peaks form; continue to beat egg whites, adding the hot syrup mixture in a heavy stream.
• Add almond extract. Beat until stiff peaks form and frosting is thick enough to spread. Yield: 7 cups.

lotus A water lily whose various parts are frequently used in Asian cooking. For example, the large leaves can be dried and used as wrappers for sweet and savory mixtures for steaming. The ivory-colored root has a crisp texture and sweet flavor; thin slices can be stir-fried or fried for tempura, while thicker slices are good braised with vegetables. Lotus seeds can be candied and added to desserts and pastry fillings. The leaves, root, and seeds can be found in Asian markets; the leaves come fresh and dried, while the root comes fresh, canned, dried, and candied.

lovage (LUHV hij) A large, stalky herb that looks like celery. Lovage stalks have a strong celery-like flavor and can be cooked as a vegetable. Fresh lovage leaves and seeds can also be used to flavor salads, stews, and meat dishes. Dried leaves and chopped or powdered stalks can be purchased at health food stores and gourmet markets; the dried seeds are commonly referred to as celery seed, which can be purchased in most supermarkets. (*see also* **celery** *and* **herbs**)

low calorie A food-labeling term defined at publishing date by the Food and Drug Administration (FDA) that describes a food or food product with 40 or fewer calories per serving.

low cholesterol A food-labeling term defined at publishing date by the FDA that describes a food with 20 milligrams or less of cholesterol and 2 grams or less of saturated fat per serving. (*see also* **cholesterol**)

low fat A food-labeling term defined at publishing date by the FDA that describes a food with 3 grams or less of fat per serving.

low-fat milk A food-labeling term defined at publishing date by the FDA that describes milk with 3 grams or less of fat per 8-ounce serving. Milk with 99% of the milk fat removed (1% milk) is considered low fat. (*see also* **milk**)

low sodium A food-labeling term defined at publishing date by the FDA that describes a food with 140 milligrams or less of salt per serving.

lox Salmon that has been cured in brine and then cold-smoked. Because lox is brine-cured, it's slightly saltier than other smoked salmon. However, some lox does have a bit of sugar added to the brine, which reduces the salty taste. A favorite in American-Jewish cuisine, lox is often teamed with bagels and cream cheese. (*see also* **brine** *and* **smoked salmon**)

luau (LOO ow) A traditional event in Hawaii that centers around a feast highlighted by the serving of a roasted pig. This festive occasion is also marked by hula dancers and Hawaiian music.

luncheon meat A term that describes ready-to-eat, thinly sliced meat that's often used to make sandwiches, salads, and cold meat platters. Luncheon meat might also be referred to as "cold cuts" and comes packaged or sliced to order from the deli case.

lychee (LEE chee) (*see* **litchi**)

lyonnaise, á la (ly uh NAYZ) A term used by the French to indicate cuisine associated with Lyon, France, a city in central France that's recognized for its outstanding food. Typically, the term refers to dishes prepared or garnished with onions.

lyonnaise sauce (ly uh NAYZ) A French sauce that starts with demi-glace or thick brown base sauce, and is seasoned with white wine and sautéed onions. Lyonnaise sauce is usually strained before it's served over sliced meat or poultry. (*see also* **demi-glace**)

macadamia nut (mak uh DAY mee uh) A highly prized nut with a rich, buttery flavor and crisp texture that's native to Australia but now plentiful in Hawaii, and to some degree, in California. Because it's very difficult to crack, the macadamia is usually sold shelled.
Storage: Macadamias have a high fat content, and they can quickly become rancid. For best results, store in an airtight container in the refrigerator or freezer, and use within a month. (*see also* **nuts**)

macaroni (mak uh ROH nee) A well-known type of Italian pasta made with semolina flour and water, but no eggs. While macaroni is generally a tube-shaped pasta, as in elbow, ditalini, penne, rigatoni, and ziti, it's also available as shells, twists, and ribbons. (*see also* **ditali, elbow macaroni, pasta, rigatoni, semolina,** *and* **ziti**)

macaroni and cheese A casserole dish of cooked macaroni layered with grated American or Cheddar cheese, and baked until the cheese is melted and the top is golden brown. Passionate macaroni eaters argue that a true mac and cheese is made with a sauce of flour, milk, and cheese. Others prefer the addition of eggs. Quick and easy macaroni casseroles sometimes rely on condensed soups for thickening.

Southernism

There are rigorous standards for the perfect macaroni and cheese—just ask our Foods staff. The custard-versus-creamy debate raged at the tasting table for days with advocates on both sides advancing their causes.

CREAMY MACARONI AND CHEESE

½ cup butter or margarine
½ cup all-purpose flour
½ teaspoon salt
½ teaspoon ground black pepper
¼ teaspoon ground red pepper
¼ teaspoon garlic powder
2 cups half-and-half
2 cups milk

2 (10-ounce)blocks sharp
    Cheddar cheese, shredded
    and divided
1 (10-ounce) block extra-sharp
    Cheddar cheese, shredded
1 (16-ounce) package elbow
    macaroni, cooked

- Melt butter in a large skillet over medium-high heat. Gradually whisk in flour until smooth; cook, whisking constantly, 2 minutes. Stir in salt and next 3 ingredients. Gradually whisk in half and half and milk; cook, whisking constantly, 8 to 10 minutes or until thickened.
- Stir in half of sharp Cheddar cheese. Stir in extra-sharp Cheddar cheese until smooth. Remove from heat.
- Combine pasta and cheese mixture, and pour into a lightly greased 13-x 9-inch baking dish. Sprinkle with remaining sharp Cheddar cheese.
- Bake at 350° for 20 minutes (bake 15 minutes longer for a crusty top). Yield: 6 to 8 servings.

Note: For testing purposes only, we used Kraft Cracker Barrel cheeses.

macaroon (mak uh ROON) An elegant drop cookie made with egg whites, sugar, almond paste or ground almonds, and flavoring. Some macaroons are light and crisp, while others are dense and chewy. For example, coconut macaroons tend to be a bit chewy, while Italian amaretti macaroons are crisp and crunchy. (*see also* **amaretti**)

mace (MAYS) A fragrant, yellow-orange ground spice made from the lacy outer covering of the nutmeg seed. The flavor of mace is more intense and pungent and not as sweet as nutmeg. Mace is particularly suited for flavoring pickles and relishes, whipped cream, seafood sauces, various desserts, and savory root vegetable casseroles. (*see also* **nutmeg** *and* **spice**)

macerate (MAS uh rayt) A process of soaking, steeping, or marinating food in liquid to infuse it with the flavor of the liquid. This process is most often applied to fruit soaked in brandy, rum, or liqueur. (*see also* **infusion**)

mâche (MAHSH) (*see* **corn salad** *and* **lettuce**)

mackerel (MAK uhr uhl) A family of saltwater fish that has a firm, high-fat flesh and a strong, but pleasant flavor; common types include Spanish, Atlantic, Pacific, and king mackerel. This fish can be purchased fresh, frozen, smoked, canned, and salted.

Storage: Because of its high-fat content, fresh mackerel doesn't keep well; try to cook it the same day it's purchased. (*see also* **fish**)

Madeira (muh DEER uh) A sweet fortified white wine named for the Portuguese island on which it was originally produced. Madeira is an excellent cooking wine because it leaves a rich taste after the alcohol has cooked off and blends nicely with meats without being excessively sweet. However, Madeira is sweet enough to be served as an apéritif or after-dinner beverage. (*see also* **apéritif** *and* **fortified wine**)

madeleine (MAD l ihn) A small, light French sponge cake eaten as a cookie. Madeleine batter is poured into a pan that has shell-shaped indentations; the baked teacakes look like scallop shells and are particularly popular served with tea, lemonade, or coffee.

MADELEINES

2 large eggs
⅛ teaspoon salt
⅓ cup sugar
½ cup all-purpose flour

1 teaspoon grated lemon rind
½ cup butter, melted and cooled
Powdered sugar

• Beat eggs and salt at high speed with an electric mixer until foamy. Gradually add sugar; beat at high speed 15 minutes or until thick and pale. Combine flour and lemon rind; fold in 2 tablespoons at a time. Fold in butter, 1 tablespoon at a time. Spoon 1 tablespoon batter into greased and floured madeleine molds.
• Bake at 400° for 8 to 10 minutes or until lightly browned. Cool in molds about 3 minutes. Remove from molds, and cool on a wire rack, flat side down. Sprinkle with powdered sugar. Yield: 2 dozen.

magnum (*see* **wine bottles**)

mahi mahi (MAH hee MAH hee) The Hawaiian name for a type of fish called dolphin fish or dorado. Mahi mahi is lean, firm-textured, and has a mild to moderate flavor; it can be baked, broiled, grilled, or poached. (*see also* **fish**)

MAHI MAHI WITH LEMON MAYONNAISE

4 mahi mahi fillets (1½ pounds)
1 tablespoon vegetable oil
¼ teaspoon salt

¼ teaspoon pepper
Lemon Mayonnaise

• Brush fillets with oil; sprinkle with salt and pepper. Place in a lightly greased grill basket.
• Grill, covered with grill lid, over medium heat (300° to 350°) 4 minutes on each side or until fish flakes with a fork. Serve with Lemon Mayonnaise. Yield: 4 servings.

LEMON MAYONNAISE

½ cup mayonnaise
1½ teaspoons grated lemon rind
1 tablespoon fresh lemon juice

¼ teaspoon salt
⅛ teaspoon ground red pepper

• Stir together all ingredients; cover and chill. Yield: ½ cup.

mai tai (MY ty) A cocktail made of light and dark rum, lime juice, curaçao, orgeat syrup, and grenadine. This popular party drink is served over finely crushed ice and is sometimes garnished with pineapple sticks or paper umbrellas. (*see also* **curaçao, grenadine,** *and* **orgeat**)

maître d' (may truh DEE) A French term for head waiter. The maître d'hotel is in charge of the dining room and is often responsible for dishes finished at dining tables, such as bananas Foster or steak au poivre. (*see also* **bananas Foster** *and* **steak au poivre**)

malt (MAWLT) The name given to barley after it has germinated and the germ has been eliminated from the grain, dried, and ground into a powder. Powdered malt is used for brewing beer, distilling liquor, making vinegar, and as a nutritious drink when mixed with hot water. Malt can be purchased in most health food stores.

malted milk When malt powder is mixed with dried milk and sugar; if combined with regular milk, ice cream, and flavoring, it becomes a malted milk shake. (*see also* **milk shake**)

malt vinegar A mild-flavored vinegar made from malted barley. It's typically pale or caramel-colored and popular in pickle recipes.

mamey (ma MAY) A fruit native to the West Indies that's the size of a large orange. The mamey has a tough, pale russet-colored, bitter rind and firm, golden pulp, which tastes a little like an apricot.

mandarin orange (MAN duh rihn) An aromatic, thin-skinned citrus fruit that resembles a small orange. There are several varieties including tangerines, clementines, Dancy oranges, Japanese satsumas, and tangelos; all are easy to peel, and their segments are easy to separate. In addition, mandarins can be sweet or tart; some have seeds while others don't. Most canned mandarin oranges are made from satsumas and are delicious in salads, sauces, desserts, and salsas. (*see also* **citrus fruit, orange,** *and* **tangelo**)

mandoline (MAHN duh lihn) A hand-operated slicing tool equipped with an assortment of adjustable blades for cutting uniform pieces of fruits or vegetables. Mandolines can be made from wood, plastic, or metal; some must be steadied by hand or placed over a bowl, while others have folding legs that permit slicing on a 45° angle.

TIMESAVING TIP

A mandoline makes quick work of thinly slicing a large number of vegetables, but if it's just one vegetable or a small piece that must be cut, it's probably best to use a knife because of the time it takes to assemble and clean the mandoline's blades.

M

mango (MANG goh) Called the "apple" of the tropics, this oval or kidney-shaped fruit tastes like a blend of peach, apricot, and pineapple. Most mangoes have a green-to-yellow peel tinged with red and deep golden-yellow flesh surrounding a huge, flat seed. For the sweetest flavor, choose a ripe mango; those that are unripe taste bitter. Mangoes are in season from May to September, and are delicious simply peeled and eaten plain, sliced into fruit salads, or made into chutney or salsa.

Q What's the best way to slice around the huge mango seed?

A With the peel still on, stand the mango up so that the stem end points toward you. With a sharp knife, cut straight down about an inch to one side of the stem, just grazing the side of the pit. Repeat on other side of the fruit, and trim off the flesh left around the pit. Then, carefully score the cut side of the mango halves in a crisscross pattern through the flesh, just down to the peel (see illustration above). Bend the peel back and turn the halves inside out; cubes of fruit will pop out. Cut across the bottom, next to the peel, to remove the cubes.

Storage: To ripen mangoes, place them in a paper bag at room temperature. Once ripe, they can be placed in a plastic bag and refrigerated for several days.

FRESH MANGO SALSA

2 ripe mangoes, peeled and finely chopped
½ red bell pepper, finely chopped
½ purple onion, finely chopped
2½ tablespoons chopped fresh cilantro
2 to 3 tablespoons chopped fresh mint

1 jalapeño pepper, seeded and minced
2 tablespoons fresh lime juice
½ teaspoon salt
¼ teaspoon pepper

• Stir together all ingredients. Cover and chill 3 hours. Yield: 2 cups.

Manhattan

A cocktail beverage consisting of bourbon or blended whiskey, sweet vermouth, and bitters served over ice and garnished with a maraschino cherry. To make a perfect Manhattan, use equal parts sweet and dry vermouth; a dry Manhattan contains only dry vermouth.

manicotti

(man uh KOT tee) Long, wide pasta tubes that are usually boiled, then stuffed with a meat or cheese mixture. The stuffed manicotti is typically covered with a tomato sauce and baked.

> **TIMESAVING TIP**
> Use a small, long-handled baby spoon or iced-tea spoon to stuff manicotti shells. Or, pipe the filling with a pastry bag or plastic bag; cut off one corner of bag and squeeze mixture into shells. For thicker fillings, slice the shell lengthwise, fill it, then reshape, placing cut side down in the baking dish.

MEATY STUFFED MANICOTTI

8 ounces uncooked manicotti shells
½ pound hot Italian sausage
½ pound ground round
1 large egg
⅓ cup milk
2 white bread slices, cubed
2 cups (8 ounces) shredded mozzarella cheese
1 (16-ounce) container small-curd cottage cheese
1 tablespoon dried Italian seasoning
½ teaspoon salt
½ teaspoon garlic powder
½ teaspoon pepper
2 (16-ounce) jars spaghetti sauce with mushrooms, divided
¼ cup shredded Parmesan cheese

• Cook pasta according to package directions; rinse with cold water. Drain.
• Remove casings from sausage, and discard. Cook sausage and beef in a large skillet, stirring until meat crumbles and is no longer pink. Drain.
• Combine sausage mixture, egg, and next 8 ingredients. Spoon into manicotti shells; arrange stuffed shells in a lightly greased 13- x 9-inch baking dish. Pour 1½ jars spaghetti sauce over shells.
• Bake, covered, at 350° for 30 minutes. Uncover and pour remaining ½ jar spaghetti sauce over shells; sprinkle with Parmesan. Bake, uncovered, 10 more minutes. Yield: 6 to 8 servings.

Note: Casserole may be assembled and frozen up to 1 month. Thaw in refrigerator overnight; bake, covered, at 350° for 40 minutes or until heated.

maple syrup Pure maple syrup is made from maple sap that has been boiled down until it's thick and syrupy; it can be used in baking, frostings, and glazes, but is most popularly used as a topping for pancakes or waffles. Maple-flavored syrup is a blend of pure maple syrup and corn syrup and is usually less expensive than pure syrup.

Storage: Small amounts of maple syrup that can be used within 2 months can be kept in an airtight container in a cool, dry place. Larger amounts can be kept up to a year in the refrigerator or can be frozen indefinitely.

Q Why is maple syrup graded, and what does it mean?

A Maple syrup is graded according to its color and flavor; the darker the color, the stronger the flavor. The lightest syrup is Grade A; it has the most delicate flavor and is the most expensive. Grades B and C are darker, have a stronger flavor, and are less expensive. When buying maple syrup, always look for the word "pure" on the label.

RESCUE for crystallized maple syrup:
If crystals have started to form in a bottle of maple syrup, simply heat the bottle in a pan of hot water over very low heat until the crystals dissolve. If the container is plastic, pour the syrup into a saucepan and melt the crystals over low heat. You can also heat the container (if it's microwave-safe) in the microwave oven on MEDIUM power 10 to 15 seconds.

maraschino cherry (mar uh SHEE noh) A type of cherry known as the Royal Ann that has been pitted and marinated in a flavored sugar syrup or maraschino liqueur and dyed red or green. Red maraschino cherries are usually flavored with almond, while the green are flavored with mint. The cherries are used for garnishing cocktails, desserts, baked goods, and fruit salads. Candied cherries, often used in fruitcakes, have been boiled or dipped in sugar syrup and dried. (*see also* **cherry**)

marbling Flecks or streaks of whitish fat that appear throughout meat and make it more flavorful, tender, and juicy. Marbling is typically found in only the best cuts of meat, especially beef.

margarine (MAHR juh rihn) A butter substitute made from vegetable oil that has been hydrogenated to transform it into a solid fat; sometimes flavoring and coloring are added. There are many different margarine products:
• **Regular margarine,** also known as oleo, must contain 80 percent fat; it's available salted and unsalted, and it often comes in a stick form.
• **Diet spreads** contain only 40 percent fat and half the calories of regular margarine; they can't be substituted for regular margarine in baked goods. Fat-free margarine is also available; it's often available in tubs.
• **Liquid margarine** is soft enough to be squeezed, and is available in plastic squeeze-type bottles. Fat-free liquid or spray margarine is also available.
• **Soft margarine** is made with vegetable oils and processed to make it spread easily.
• **Whipped margarine** has air incorporated to make it spread easily; it can't be substituted for regular margarine in baked goods.
• **Butter-margarine blends,** such as Land O' Lakes Country Morning Blend, combine butter and margarine into a single product.
• **Vegetable oil spreads** contain more fat than diet margarine, but less than regular margarine.
• **Some brands** of margarine, such as Benecol, are trans-free margarines, and do not contribute to atherosclerosis (hardening of the arteries). In fact, they reduce LDL cholesterol levels.

TEST KITCHEN SECRET

In many cases, margarine can be used as a substitute for butter, except in special recipes where butter is more desirable, like in shortbread, pound cake, or puff pastry dough. In general, tub-style or reduced-fat margarines are not suitable for baking or frying because of their high water content. If you use stick margarine, you're almost always safe when baking. MARY ALLEN PERRY

Storage: Margarine can be stored tightly wrapped in the refrigerator up to 2 months or in the freezer up to 18 months. (*see also* **butter** *and* **fats and oils**)

margarita (mahr gah REE tah) A cocktail made of tequila, lime juice, and an orange-flavored liqueur such as Triple Sec or Cointreau. Margaritas are typically served in a stemmed glass with a large bowl, and the rim might be dipped in lime juice and coated with salt. To make slushy, frozen margaritas, blend the cocktail mixture with crushed ice. (*see also* **liqueur**)

ORANGE-LIME MARGARITAS

2 (6-ounce) cans frozen limeade concentrate, thawed, undiluted, and divided	3 tablespoons powdered sugar, divided
1¼ cups tequila, divided	Ice cubes
1 cup orange juice, divided	Coarse salt
½ cup orange liqueur, divided	Lime wedges
	Garnish: lime slices

• Process half of each of first 5 ingredients in a blender 30 seconds or until smooth. Add ice cubes to bring to 3½-cup level; process until slushy. Pour into a large heavy-duty zip-top plastic bag. Repeat procedure with remaining half of first 5 ingredients and ice cubes; add to bag. Seal and freeze 8 hours.
• Place salt in a saucer. Rub rims of glasses with lime wedges; dip rims in salt. Let margaritas stand at room temperature 20 minutes or until slushy; pour into glasses, and garnish, if desired. Yield: 6 cups.

marinade (MAIR ih nayd) A tenderizing and flavoring liquid in which meats, seafood, or vegetables are soaked before cooking. Most marinades contain an acid such as lemon juice, vinegar, or wine and an oil to lubricate or add moisture; herbs or spices, minced garlic, and sugar or sweeteners might be included for additional flavor. If cooks coat their grill racks

TEST KITCHEN SECRET

Never use the marinade from meat or poultry for basting or as a sauce for serving without first bringing it to a boil for 1 minute. These marinades contain raw juices and are unsafe until they have been thoroughly cooked. JAMES SCHEND

with vegetable cooking spray prior to firing up the grill, the oil can be eliminated in most marinades, especially if the marinade isn't too sugary.

marinara sauce (mah ree NAHR uh) A red Italian pasta sauce made from tomatoes and flavored with garlic, onions, and oregano.

MARINARA SAUCE

1 medium onion, thinly sliced	3 tablespoons chopped fresh parsley
3 garlic cloves, minced	1½ teaspoons dried oregano
3 tablespoons olive oil	1½ teaspoons dried basil
2 (16-ounce) cans tomato sauce	1 teaspoon salt
1 (16-ounce) can crushed tomatoes	½ teaspoon pepper

• Sauté onion and garlic in hot olive oil in a large skillet 5 minutes; add tomato sauce and remaining ingredients. Reduce heat, and simmer, uncovered, 15 minutes. Yield: 2 cups.

marinate (MAIR ih nayt) The process of soaking food in a marinade to absorb additional flavors or for tenderizing. (*see also* **marinade**)

Q **How long do foods need to marinate?**

A It depends on what you're marinating. To simply add flavor, marinate most foods 30 minutes to 2 hours. To tenderize meat, marinating 8 hours or overnight is ideal, but large cuts of meat such as a rump roast or chuck eye roast can go up to 24 hours. Delicate fish and seafood only need 30 to 45 minutes of marinating, but chicken breasts can go 1 to 2 hours. Beef and lamb can spend several hours in a marinade without becoming mushy; tougher cuts such as round or flank steak can easily marinate 24 hours. Many of our recipes say to marinate 8 hours; these can usually go overnight in the refrigerator.

Marinating Tips

• Use containers made of glass, ceramic, or plastic because marinades usually contain acids, which can react with aluminum and create undesirable flavor.
• Plastic zip-top bags can be used for marinating; you'll need less marinade, and you can turn the bag occasionally to evenly distribute the marinade over the food. For extra protection against spills, place the plastic bag inside a bowl to hold the food being marinated.
• Always marinate meat, poultry, and seafood in the refrigerator.
• Take care when marinating delicate, tender foods such as fish and shellfish; if left in the marinade too long, they will develop a soft, mushy texture.

TIMESAVING TIP
Bottled vinegar-based salad dressings can be used as a convenient marinade. Italian salad dressing is a favorite for almost any meat. Red wine vinegar or balsamic vinaigrette also work well with red meat.

marjoram (MAHR juhr uhm) Sometimes called sweet marjoram, this member of the mint family has oval green leaves and a mild, sweet oregano-like flavor. Marjoram is available fresh in some markets, but is available more often in the dried and ground forms; it's used to flavor meats and vegetables. (*see also* **herbs**)

marmalade (MAHR muh layd) A citrus preserve that contains pieces of fruit and fruit rind. Marmalade is often made from oranges, but lime and ginger varieties are sometimes available. This spread typically has a tangy sweet flavor and can be used on toast, biscuits, or scones.

TEST KITCHEN SECRET

When making marmalade, be sure to omit the white, fleshy pith in between the rind and the citrus fruit. It gives the marmalade a bitter taste. VIE WARSHAW

SUNNY ORANGE MARMALADE

| 12 oranges (about 6 pounds) | 4 cups water |
| 2 lemons | 9 cups sugar |

• Peel oranges, and cut rind into thin strips. Chop pulp, discarding seeds. Cut lemons into thin slices, discarding seeds.
• Combine orange rind, chopped pulp, lemon slices, and 4 cups water in a large Dutch oven; bring to a boil. Reduce heat, and simmer 15 minutes. Remove from heat; cover and chill 8 hours or overnight.
• Combine fruit mixture and sugar in a Dutch oven; bring to a boil. Reduce heat, and simmer, stirring occasionally, 1½ hours or until a candy thermometer registers 215°.
• Pack hot marmalade into hot, sterilized jars, filling to ¼ inch from top. Remove air bubbles; wipe jar rims. Cover at once with metal lids, and screw on bands. Process in boiling water bath 5 minutes. Yield: 5 pints.

marrow The soft, fatty tissue found in the central cavity of a bone. Marrow has an ivory color after it's cooked, and is considered a flavorful delicacy by many Europeans.

Marsala (mahr SAH lah) An Italian fortified wine with a rich, smoky flavor that ranges from dry to sweet. Sweet Marsala is used as a dessert wine or as a flavoring in dessert recipes such as zabaglione. Dry Marsala serves as an apéritif or cooking wine. (*see also* **apéritif, fortified wine,** *and* **zabaglione**)

marshmallow (MAHRSH mehl oh) A light, spongy, pillow-shaped candy made from sugar, corn syrup, gelatin, and egg whites. Commercially made marshmallows are available large and miniature, white, and colored. Enjoy marshmallows by toasting them over a campfire; they can also be used to fill or frost cakes, or to top dishes such as sweet potato casserole. Marshmallow creme is a thick, creamy commercial product that looks like melted marshmallows and is sometimes used in making candies and ice cream toppings. It can also serve as a filling for cakes and cookies.

> **Q How many large marshmallows equal a cup of miniature?**
>
> **A** One cup of miniature marshmallows equals about 10 large marshmallows. Also, a 7-ounce jar of marshmallow creme equals a 16-ounce package of marshmallows, melted, plus 3½ tablespoons of light corn syrup.

Storage: Marshmallows can be frozen in a zip-top plastic bag.

martini (mahr TEE nee) A cocktail made of gin and dry vermouth. Martinis are typically served straight up (no ice) or on the rocks (with ice), and are garnished with a green olive or a twist of lemon. If made with vodka, it becomes a vodka martini. A Gibson is a martini garnished with a tiny cocktail onion. In addition, flavored martinis are becoming so popular that martini bars are appearing in some locales. (*see also* **Gibson, on the rocks,** *and* **straight up**)

marzipan (MAHR zih pan) A sweet paste of ground almonds, sugar, and egg whites. Marzipan is often colored and shaped into decorative designs and figures, but it can also be used as a filling for candy or as an icing that covers fancy cakes. Marzipan is available in most supermarkets.

masa; masa harina (MAH sah ah REE nah) A Spanish term that refers to a traditional dough made of dried corn kernels that have been soaked and cooked in limewater and then ground. Masa is vital to Mexican cooking because it's the key ingredient in corn tortillas.

mascarpone cheese (mas cahr POHN ay) (*see* **cheese**)

mash To press or beat a food in order to remove lumps and to create a smooth texture. Vegetables, such as potatoes and squash, can be boiled, baked, roasted, and then mashed. This term can also refer to a grain or malt mixture used in brewing beer or in the fermentation of whiskey; if some of the previous batch of already fermented mash is added as a starter, the result is known as sour mash.

TEST KITCHEN SECRET

Tensions fly high at our tastings as to whether a masher, ricer, or mixer should be used for mashing potatoes. If your mother or grandmother used an electric mixer for her mashed potatoes, you likely prefer them that way. If she mashed them with the back of a spoon, you probably like that version best. The real key is not to overbeat; the potatoes take on a gummy texture if they are overbeaten. Lyda Jones

matsutake mushroom (maht soo TAH kay) (*see* **mushroom**)

matzo (MAHT suh) A flat, brittle bread made only with water and flour and baked without any leavening. Matzo is traditionally eaten during Passover. (*see also* **matzo meal**)

matzo ball A Jewish dumpling made from matzo meal, sometimes flavored with chicken fat and usually served in chicken soup. A matzo ball might also be referred to as a knaidel. (*see also* **matzo meal**)

matzo meal A meal ground from matzo bread; it can be used like breadcrumbs to bind, thicken, or coat other foods. Matzo meal is also the base for matzo balls, and sometimes replaces flour in baked goods. The meal can be purchased in Jewish markets and most supermarkets.

Maui onion A large golden yellow onion with moist white flesh and a mild, sweet flavor. Maui onions are similar in taste to Vidalia, Texas Supersweet, and Walla Walla onions, but are grown in Maui, Hawaii. (*see also* **onion, Vidalia onion,** *and* **Walla Walla**)

mayonnaise (MAY uh nayz) A cold, thick, creamy dressing, spread, or sauce made from an emulsion of oil, egg yolks, and vinegar or lemon juice. If egg yolks aren't used, the product is called salad dressing, which is sweeter than mayonnaise. Commercial mayonnaise should contain at least 65 percent oil; reduced-calorie mayonnaise contains less oil and fewer calories. It's easy to make homemade mayonnaise with a food processor or blender, but we don't recommend using uncooked eggs. Instead, use egg substitute, or you can heat the yolk mixture in the top of a double boiler to 160°.

TEST KITCHEN SECRET

Many people think mayonnaise is often the culprit in cases of food poisoning. Think again. Mayonnaise, with its high acid content—from the lemons—often protects against foodborne illness. JAN MOON

Storage: Refrigerate mayonnaise once it's opened. Store the commercial product up to 6 months. Use homemade mayonnaise within 3 or 4 days.

HOMEMADE MAYONNAISE

2½ tablespoons white wine vinegar	½ to ¾ teaspoon salt
¼ cup egg substitute	½ teaspoon pepper
1½ tablespoons coarse-grained mustard	⅔ cup vegetable oil

• Process first 5 ingredients in a blender until smooth, stopping to scrape down sides. With blender running, add oil in a slow, steady stream, blending until thickened. Yield: 1 cup.

mead A drink made from a fermented mixture of honey, water, and yeast or hops, and flavored with herbs, spices, or flowers. Also known as honey wine, mead was popular in early England and is still consumed today.

meal Coarsely ground seeds of edible grains, such as oats or corn. Meal can also be made from other dried substances, such as bone meal or dried fish meal.

mealy When a food or mixture has a dry, grainy, crumbly texture similar to meal. Sometimes this term is used to describe the texture of a baked potato or an apple that's slightly dry and almost crumbly.

M

measuring A process of determining the amount or size of a food, an ingredient, or a utensil. It's important to use the right utensil to correctly measure; use a ruler to determine dimensions, liquid measuring cups to measure liquids, dry measuring cups to measure dry ingredients, and measuring spoons to measure small amounts of dry or liquid ingredients.

Measuring liquid ingredients:
Measure liquids on a level surface in a glass or clear plastic measuring cup with a pouring lip. Read liquid measurements at eye level.

Measuring dry ingredients:
Measure dry ingredients in stainless steel or plastic dry measuring cups. For flour, lightly spoon it into measuring cup, letting it mound slightly.

Leveling dry ingredients: Level the top using the straight edge of a spatula or knife.

• **Liquid measuring cups** look like little pitchers with ounce and cup amounts printed on the sides; they typically range in size from 1 to 4 cups. When measuring a liquid, place the cup on a flat surface, pour in the liquid, and then read it at eye level.

• **Dry measuring cups** are graduated cups in a standard set ranging from one-fourth cup to 1 cup. When measuring a dry ingredient, spoon it into the cup, and then level it off with the straight edge of a knife. However, brown sugar and shortening should be packed tightly into the cups before being leveled.

TEST KITCHEN SECRET

It's easy to lose track of what and how much you've measured. The best remedy for this is to measure all of your ingredients before you begin a recipe. Place unmeasured ingredients to the left of your workspace and move to the right as they are measured. Some people find it helpful to measure out loud, and to set aside measured ingredients on paper plates or paper towels. VANESSA MCNEIL

Q **What's the best way to measure sticky solid ingredients such as peanut butter or vegetable shortening?**

A These ingredients can be easily measured by first spraying the inside of dry measuring cups with vegetable cooking spray.

• **Measuring spoons** come in a sets and always include a one-fourth teaspoon, one-half teaspoon, 1 teaspoon, and 1 tablespoon; some also include a one-half tablespoon or one-eighth teaspoon. After filling, level off dry ingredients with a flat edge. (*see also* **baking tools, cup, metric measure,** *and* **volume**)

Measuring brown sugar: To measure accurately, use the measuring cup that holds the exact amount called for in a recipe. Pack brown sugar firmly into a dry measuring cup; then level it off. The sugar will hold its shape when turned out of the cup.

EQUIVALENT MEASURES

3 teaspoons	1 tablespoon
4 tablespoons	¼ cup
5⅓ tablespoons	⅓ cup
8 tablespoons	½ cup
16 tablespoons	1 cup
2 tablespoons (liquid)	1 ounce
1 cup	8 fluid ounces
2 cups	1 pint (16 fluid ounces)
4 cups	1 quart
4 quarts	1 gallon
⅛ cup	2 tablespoons
⅓ cup	5 tablespoons plus 1 teaspoon
⅔ cup	10 tablespoons plus 2 teaspoons
¾ cup	12 tablespoons

Measuring syrupy ingredients: When measuring honey, molasses, corn syrup, or other sticky ingredients, first coat the measuring spoon or cup with vegetable cooking spray. Then the ingredient will slip out easily, and clean up will be simple.

meat (*see* **beef, lamb, pork,** *and* **veal**)

meatballs Minced or ground meat rolled into small rounds and often augmented with onions, herbs, spices, breadcrumbs or egg, and spiced according to preference. Meatballs are usually pan-fried or baked and can be served with or without a sauce. They can be cooked in soup, served over pasta, or eaten alone as the main dish.

TIMESAVING TIP

Plan ahead by placing uncooked meatballs on a baking sheet and freezing, uncovered; transfer to a zip-top plastic bag to store. When ready to cook, defrost only the number of meatballs that you need. Cooked meatballs can also be frozen. Just cool after cooking, then freeze and store.

TEST KITCHEN SECRET

When making meatballs, I start by wetting my hands with cold water to keep the meat from sticking as I shape the meat mixture into a long, narrow log the same diameter of what I want my meatballs to be. Then I cut the log crosswise into equal pieces and roll each piece into a ball. Margaret Monroe Dickey

M

meat loaf A ground meat mixture shaped into a loaf and baked. Meat loaves can be made from beef, veal, lamb, or pork and usually include onions, breadcrumbs, eggs, and seasoning. Slice leftover meat loaf and make into sandwiches.

MEAT LOAF WITH TOMATO GRAVY

2 pounds ground chuck
1 (1¼-ounce) envelope taco seasoning
½ cup Italian-seasoned breadcrumbs
1 small sweet onion, diced
2 large eggs, lightly beaten
⅓ cup ketchup
1 (10-ounce) can diced tomato and green chiles
½ cup (2 ounces) shredded Monterey Jack cheese
Tomato Gravy

• Stir together first 6 ingredient until blended. Shape into a 10- x 6-inch loaf; place in a lightly greased 13- x 9-inch pan. Cover; chill 8 hours, if desired. Top with tomatoes and green chilies.

TIMESAVING TIP

For faster cooking, shape a long, narrow, free-form meat loaf in an aluminum foil-lined baking pan.

• Bake at 425° for 45 to 50 minutes or until meat is not longer pink. Pour off juices. Sprinkle meat loaf with cheese; let stand 15 minutes. Serve with Tomato Gravy. Yield: 6 to 8 servings.

TOMATO GRAVY

3 tablespoons butter
3 tablespoons all-purpose flour
2 (10-ounce) cans diced tomato and green chiles
1 (16-ounce) can tomato sauce
3 tablespoons chopped fresh cilantro
1 teaspoon sugar

• Melt butter in a large saucepan over medium-high heat; whisk in flour until smooth. Cook, whisking constantly, 1 minute.
• Whisk in tomatoes and green chilies and remaining ingredients. Cook 5 minutes or until thoroughly heated. Serve warm or chilled. Yield: 4½ cups.

meat tenderizer There are four main methods for tenderizing meat. The first is by adding a commercial powder containing an enzyme, such as papain, to break down the tissues of tough meat. Another is to marinate the meat in an acid-based marinade. Long, slow cooking will also help tenderize meat. And last, meat can be pounded with a meat mallet, a metal or wooden hammerlike tool with a toothlike surface. (*see also* **papain**)

meat thermometer (*see* **thermometer**)

medaillon (meh DAL yuhn) Beef, veal, or pork that has been cut into small rounds or ovals. Medaillons are usually taken from a tender cut of meat such as the tenderloin.

medium rare A degree of doneness for meat. The meat should have a bright red center and be slightly springy when pressed. For most meat, medium-rare doneness is 145° to 150°. (*see also* **beef**)

medium well A degree of doneness for meat. The meat should have very little pink in the center, be almost brown, and feel firm and springy when pressed. For most meat, medium well is 160°. (*see also* **beef**)

mein A Chinese term for thin noodles made from wheat flour. The term is usually preceded by another descriptive word indicating the type of noodle or noodle dish such as chow mein. (*see also* **Chinese noodle**)

Melba sauce A dessert sauce made from pureed and strained raspberries, red currant jelly, sugar, and cornstarch. Melba sauce was created by French chef Auguste Escoffier, who made it for Australian opera singer Dame Nellie Melba. The sauce usually tops peach Melba, but it can also adorn ice cream or pound cake. (*see also* **Melba toast** *and* **peach Melba**)

Melba toast Very thin slices of white bread that have been baked until golden brown and very crisp. Melba toast was created by French chef Auguste Escoffier for Australian opera singer Dame Nellie Melba. Melba toast is sold in most supermarkets and is usually served with soups or salads.

melon A member of the gourd family that grows on a vine. These sweet fruits generally have thick, hard rinds, many seeds, and a sweet, juicy flesh. There are two basic types: the muskmelon and the watermelon. Muskmelons are those with netted skins such as the cantaloupe, and smooth skins, such as casaba, Crenshaw, and honeydew. The watermelon family is smaller, but does include different sizes, different colored flesh, and seedless varieties. Melons are most plentiful in the summer, but are generally available year-round in supermarkets. They're delicious eaten plain, in cold soups, or in fruit salads.
Storage: Ripe muskmelons will keep up to 5 days in the refrigerator or in a cool, dark place. Seal in plastic wrap or an airtight container, because they readily absorb the odors and flavors of other foods, plus give off strong aromas. Watermelon is best eaten as soon as possible, but a whole watermelon can stay in the refrigerator up to a week; if too big for the refrigerator, store in a cool, dark place for no more than 3 days. Cut watermelon should be wrapped with plastic wrap or placed in an airtight container. (*see also* **cantaloupe, casaba, Crenshaw melon,** *and* **watermelon**)

melon baller A tool used to scoop round balls from melons, cucumbers, or other foods. Most of these tools are designed with a single middle handle and a different sized scoop at either end.

melt A process where heat is used to transform a food such as butter or chocolate from a solid to a liquid or a semi liquid. Melting is generally done in a microwave oven, in the top of a double boiler, or in a heavy saucepan over low heat.

meringue (muh RANG) A white, fluffy mixture produced by gradually beating sugar into stiffly beaten egg whites. Meringues can be classified as soft or hard. Soft meringues are glossy, smooth, and tender; they're often used to top pies, puddings, and baked Alaska. Soft meringues can also be folded into cake batters to lighten them, used to frost cakes, or poached to make floating "islands." Hard meringues are generally sweeter than soft meringues and are baked to form crisp, dry meringue shells or cookies. Italian meringue is slightly different because it's made by gradually pouring hot sugar syrup over stiffly beaten egg whites and beating until the mixture is smooth and shiny; it can also be soft or hard. (see also **baked Alaska, cream pie, floating islands, Italian meringue,** *and* **lemon meringue pie**)

Q How can I make sure that hard meringues are crisp and dry?

A Hard meringue dessert shells or cookies should be baked at a very low temperature, usually between 200° and 225°. Bake the meringues until they're firm and almost dry; then turn off the oven, and leave them in the oven to cool several hours or overnight. Hard meringues can be stored in an airtight container at room temperature up to 2 days. For longer storage, they can be frozen up to a month in an airtight freezer container.

TEST KITCHEN SECRET

Always let meringue pie cool completely before serving; if sliced in haste, the filling will most likely be runny. In fact, it's best to make meringue pie several hours before serving. Using a hot, wet knife will also make it easier to neatly slice the meringue. MARY ALLEN PERRY

RESCUE for improperly beaten egg white: Make sure you are working with beaters and bowls that are grease-free and very clean. Even the smallest bit of oil or grease in a bowl can keep whites from reaching their full volume. Also, adding a small amount of cream of tartar to the whites will increase their stability.

MERINGUE

4 to 6 egg whites
½ to ¾ teaspoon cream of tartar

½ cup sugar
½ teaspoon vanilla extract

• Beat egg whites and cream of tartar at high speed with an electric mixer just until foamy.

• Gradually add sugar, 1 tablespoon at a time, beating until stiff peaks form and sugar dissolves (2 to 4 minutes). Add vanilla, beating well. Spoon onto pie and bake according to recipe (usually at 325° for 25 to 28 minutes or until golden). Yield: enough for 1 (9-inch) pie.

Q **What causes meringue on a pie to weep?**

A When soft meringue on a pie weeps, it's usually because the meringue was not spread on the pie while the filling was hot, and therefore did not get thoroughly cooked on the bottom. Meringue should be quickly spread onto hot filling; anchor it to the edge of the pasty to seal and keep it from shrinking. Bake the pie immediately, and afterwards, cool it away from drafts. Also, avoid making meringue on humid days; sugar will absorb moisture, making it impossible to create a stable meringue.

Making a Perfect Meringue

• For a meringue with great volume, let the egg whites stand at room temperature for a full 30 minutes before beating.

• Be sure to use the size bowl called for in your recipe. Copper, stainless-steel, or glass bowls work best. Be sure your electric mixer beaters are clean.

• Begin to add the sugar gradually as soon as soft peaks form (tips will curl).

• After adding all the sugar, continue beating until stiff peaks form and the sugar is completely dissolved. Rub a little of the meringue between your fingers; it should feel completely smooth.

meringue powder A fine, white powder made with dried egg whites. Meringue powder is used to replace fresh egg whites in recipes where icings and meringues are uncooked. The powder can be found in most cake decorating stores or in the cake decorating department of some large retail stores. (*see also* **powdered eggs**)

Merlot (mer LOH) A red wine grape that produces a wine by the same name. Merlot has a dark, rich color and earthy, fruity flavor. (*see also* **wine**)

mesclun (MEHS kluhn) (*see* **lettuce**)

mesquite (meh SKEET) A hardwood tree found mostly in the southwestern United States and Mexico. Mesquite is popularly used when grilling and smoking foods to impart a distinctive aroma and slightly sweet flavor to whatever is being cooked.

metric measure A system of weights and measures used in other parts of the world, but used in the United States only for scientific work. The basic units for measuring are gram for weight, meter for length, and liter for volume. (*see Metric Equivalents chart, page 572*)

Mettwurst (MEHT wurst) A soft, fatty German sausage made from pork and seasoned with coriander and white pepper. Bright red Mettwurst is cured, smoked, and ready to eat. Mettwurst is typically eaten as a spread on bread or crackers. (*see also* **sausage**)

meunière (muhn YAIR) A style of cooking in which food is seasoned, dusted with flour, and sautéed in butter.

Mexican chocolate A grainy chocolate flavored with almonds, cinnamon, and vanilla. Mexican chocolate is often used in preparing Mexican hot chocolate drink and for flavoring mole-type dishes. The chocolate can be purchased in Mexican markets and some supermarkets.

Mexican wedding cookies Small, round, buttery cookies made from ground almonds, pecans, or hazelnuts, and rolled in powdered sugar after baking. Sometimes these cookies are called Mexican wedding cakes or Russian teacakes.

MEXICAN WEDDING COOKIES

½ cup butter, softened
1 cup all-purpose flour
¼ cup sugar
1 teaspoon vanilla extract
1 cup finely chopped pecans
1 cup powdered sugar

• Beat butter at medium speed with an electric mixer until creamy.
• Add flour, ¼ cup sugar, and vanilla, beating until blended. Stir in pecans. (Dough will be stiff.)
• Shape into 1-inch balls, and place on ungreased baking sheets.
• Bake at 400° for 10 minutes. Remove to wire racks, and cool slightly.
• Roll warm cookies in powdered sugar; cool cookies completely on wire racks. Yield: 4 dozen.

mezzaluna (mehz zuh LOO nuh) A crescent-bladed, two-handled knife useful for chopping or mincing vegetables or nuts; it's also known as a mincing knife.

microwave cooking A heating method that uses high-frequency radio waves to penetrate food, causing friction among vibrating molecules, which results in heat; this heat then spreads throughout the food by conduction. A microwave oven is a handy oven alternative, noted for cooking vegetables and bacon and for heating and reheating foods efficiently. Microwave ovens vary in wattage, ranging from 600 watts to 1,200 watts. Some microwave ovens have revolving trays inside to turn the food so it can cook more evenly. All foods cooked in the microwave oven are cooked on either HIGH (100% power), MEDIUM-HIGH (70% power), MEDIUM (50% power), MEDIUM-LOW (30% power), or LOW (10% power); varying the power level enables you to essentially control the "heat" the oven is producing. Periodically stir foods being microwaved to allow the hotter portion on the outside to be mixed into the cooler center. If the food can't be stirred, then rearrange or turn the food halfway through cooking time.

Q **Do I need to use special cookware in the microwave?**

A You should use cookware that's labeled microwave safe. This should include heat-resistant glass, oven-tempered glass, glass-ceramic cookware, ceramic dishes, plastic containers, and paper products. If uncertain, test the dish by placing a 1-cup glass measure filled with water in the microwave along with the container you are testing. Microwave at HIGH for 1 minute. If the dish remains cool, it's safe to use; if hot, avoid using.

TEST KITCHEN SECRET

It's safe to use heavy-duty storage and freezer bags in the microwave, but be sure to vent the bags to allow steam to escape. Use them only on the defrost or reheat setting, but not on HIGH. Do not use the bags for steaming vegetables in the microwave. LYDA JONES

Midori liqueur (mih DOOR ee) A green-colored Japanese liqueur with the taste of honeydew melon. (*see also* **liqueur**)

milanaise (mee lah NEHZ) A French term associated with the cuisine of Milan, Italy; it describes pasta that has been tossed with butter and grated cheese and topped with a tomato sauce that includes shredded ham, pickled tongue, mushrooms, and truffles.

milk A white or ivory liquid produced by adult female mammals. Milk is composed of water, milk fat, and milk solids. In the United States, milk from cows is the most popular kind of milk used, but outside the United States, goats, sheep, and camels are popular sources of milk. Most milk is very nutritious because it contains protein, calcium, phosphorus, vitamins A and D, lactose, and riboflavin; in fact, milk and its by-products compose one of the fundamental food groups in the United States Food Guide Pyramid.
Shopping: A wide range of cow's milk products are available; they come in cartons, cans, bottles, and boxes; some appear on the regular shelf and others in the refrigerated case. They include:
Whole milk: Fresh cow's milk that contains about 3½% fat. (*continued on the following page*)

Low-fat milk: May contain either 1 or 2% fat and fewer calories than whole milk.

Fat-free milk: Nonfat contains less than ½% fat.

Buttermilk: Was traditionally the liquid drained from churned butter, but today is made by adding special bacteria to nonfat milk or low-fat milk; it has a tangy flavor and a creamy texture.

Q **What do the terms pasteurized and homogenized mean on my milk label?**

A Pasteurized milk has been heated briefly and then quickly cooled to destroy most of the harmful bacteria in raw milk; this process also extends its shelf life. Homogenized milk has been processed so that particles of butterfat are broken down until they are evenly suspended throughout the milk. Homogenization prevents cream from separating and rising to the top of the milk. Most milk sold in the United States has been pasteurized and homogenized.

Acidophilus milk: Low-fat or nonfat milk with special bacteria added to help maintain a balance of beneficial microorganisms in the digestive tract.

Lactose-reduced milk: Special low-fat milk that has the lactose, a common source of food allergies, reduced to only 30%.

Chocolate milk: Whole or low-fat milk that has chocolate or cocoa and sugar added.

Soy milk: Made from soybeans and is higher in protein than cow's milk and is cholesterol-free; it's available plain, sweetened, or flavored.

Several types of powdered milk and canned milk are also available.

Storage: Milk should be refrigerated. Never pour milk that has been left at room temperature back into a carton of chilled milk. Check sell-by dates on milk cartons at the time of purchase; if properly stored, it should be fine to drink for several days even after the date has expired. Evaporated milk will keep at room temperature up to a year, but it must also be refrigerated and used within 2 to 3 days after opening. Dry milk keeps up to a year in a cool, dry place; once reconstituted, it must be refrigerated and used within 3 days. (*see also* **butter, cheese, cream, evaporated milk, food groups, powdered milk, sour cream, soy milk, sweetened condensed milk,** *and* **yogurt**)

milk chocolate (*see* chocolate)

milk punch
A beverage made of liquor, sugar, milk, and sometimes flavored with vanilla extract. The mixture is stirred until smooth and served over ice.

milk shake
Originally a soda fountain specialty of milk, a flavored syrup or fruit, and ice cream blended in a blender until thick and smooth. (*see also* **malted milk**)

DOUBLE-BERRY MILK SHAKE

1 pint fresh strawberry halves, frozen
¾ cup milk
¼ cup powdered sugar
½ teaspoon vanilla extract
1 pint strawberry ice cream
Garnishes: sweetened whipped cream, fresh strawberries

- Process first 4 ingredients in a blender until smooth.
- Add ice cream; process until blended. Garnish, if desired. Yield: 4 cups.

milk toast Buttered toast, sometimes sprinkled with sugar and cinnamon, and topped with hot milk. Milk toast was traditionally served as a comfort food for the sick.

millet (MIHL leht) A cereal grain used mostly in the United States as birdseed and animal feed. However, in disadvantaged regions of Asia and Africa, millet is ground into flour or boiled like rice to make hot cereal. Millet can be found in Asian markets and health food stores.
Storage: Store millet in a cool, dry place in an airtight container up to 2 years. (*see also* **cereal grains** *and* **grain**)

mimosa (mih MOH suh) A cocktail made of equal parts of orange juice and sparkling wine. Mimosas are served cold, but not over ice; they're often served at brunch.

MIMOSAS

1 (12-ounce) can frozen orange juice concentrate, thawed and undiluted
⅓ cup orange liqueur
1 (750-milliliter) bottle champagne, chilled

- Prepare orange juice according to can directions; stir in liqueur. Cover and chill thoroughly. Stir in champagne just before serving. Yield: 10 cups.

Parson's Mimosas: You can substitute 1 (750-milliliter) bottle sparkling white grape juice for the champagne, and omit the liqueur. Yield: 9⅔ cups.

mince (MIHNS) To finely cut food into pieces usually less than ⅛ inch. Something that has been minced is cut into smaller pieces than something that has been chopped. (*see also* **chopping**)

mincemeat A finely chopped mixture of dried fruit, apples or pears, citrus peel, nuts, beef suet, spices, and brandy or rum. Mincemeat traditionally included minced, cooked beef, which contemporary versions don't use. Today, mincemeat can be purchased commercially in jars or cans; it also can be made from scratch. It's popular during the holiday season as a filling for pies, tarts, and cookies. (*see also* **suet**)

mineral water Carbonated or noncarbonated water with a high mineral content taken from wells or natural springs. The carbonated version is sometimes referred to as sparkling mineral water. (*see also* **water**)

minestrone (mee ness TROH nay) An Italian vegetable soup made with pasta and dried beans; it's thick enough to usually be considered a one-course meal. Sometimes minestrone includes beef for flavoring; if so, the meat might be left in the soup. The hearty mixture is often topped with a sprinkling of Parmesan cheese.

MEATBALL MINESTRONE

3 garlic cloves, minced
1 tablespoon olive oil
3 (15-ounce) cans cannellini
   beans, undrained and
   divided
1 (32-ounce) container chicken
   broth
1 (1.4-ounce) envelope vegetable
   soup mix
60 to 64 frozen cooked meatballs

1 (14½-ounce) can diced
   tomatoes with basil, garlic,
   and oregano
½ teaspoon dried crushed red
   pepper
8 ounces uncooked rotini pasta
1 (10-ounce) package fresh
   spinach, torn
Garnishes: shredded Parmesan
   cheese, chopped fresh parsley

• Sauté garlic in hot oil in a stockpot over medium-high heat 1 minute. Stir in 2 cans beans and chicken broth, and bring to a boil.
• Stir in vegetable soup mix until dissolved. Add meatballs, tomatoes, and red pepper; return to a boil.
• Add rotini, and cook, stirring often, 15 minutes.
• Stir in remaining can beans and spinach; cook 5 more minutes. Garnish, if desired. Serve with breadsticks. Yield: 4 quarts.
Note: For testing purposes only, we used Knorr Vegetable Soup Mix.

mint (*see* **herbs**)

mint julep A cocktail made of bourbon, fresh mint, and sugar, and served over finely crushed ice. Juleps have been around since the 1700s, but no state claims the mint julep like Kentucky. Mint juleps became the official drink of the Kentucky Derby in 1875. Run on the first Saturday in May, the Derby marks the ordering of an average of 80,000 mint juleps at the racetrack during Derby Week. (*see also* **muddle**)

Southernism

The Southern nuances of serving a mint julep vary. Some people stress the precise time for harvesting the mint. Others prefer shaved ice to crushed. Others argue over whether to serve it in an engraved sterling silver cup, a crystal goblet, or a plastic container. But all agree that the vessel should be cold.

MINT JULEP

¼ cup bourbon
1 tablespoon Mint Syrup

Garnish: fresh mint sprigs

• Combine ¼ cup bourbon and 1 tablespoon Mint Syrup; serve mixture over crushed ice. Garnish, if desired. Yield: 1 serving.

MINT SYRUP

1½ cups coarsely chopped
  fresh mint

2 cups sugar
2 cups water

• Tie mint in a cheesecloth bag, and place in a saucepan. Add sugar and water; bring to a boil. Cook, stirring constantly, until sugar dissolves.
• Remove from heat; cover and cool. Remove and discard cheesecloth bag. Yield: 2¾ cups.

minute steak A small, thin, boneless cut of beef that has been cubed or scored for tenderness. Because it's so thin, it needs to be cooked only about 1 minute per side over high heat.

mirepoix (mihr PWAH) A mixture of two parts chopped onions, one part chopped carrots, and one part celery cut into ½-inch cubes. The mixture is sautéed in butter and used as a flavor enhancer for a variety of sauces, stocks, stews, and other foods.

mirin (MIHR ihn) A low-alcohol, sweet, syrupy, thin, golden-colored Japanese rice wine. Mirin is often used to add a touch of sweetness and flavor to glazes, sauces, and other dishes; it's available in Asian markets and some supermarkets. Some refer to mirin as "rice wine." (*see also* **rice wine**)

mirliton (MIHR lih ton) (*see* **chayote**)

miso (MEE soh) A fermented soybean paste that also contains rice or barley and is used as a basic flavoring in many Japanese dishes. Miso comes in different strengths and flavors; generally, the darker the color, the stronger the taste. Miso can be purchased in Asian markets and some health food stores. (*see also* **soybean**)

mix To stir, blend, or beat ingredients so they are evenly dispersed throughout a mixture.

mixer An appliance equipped with beaters, and sometimes dough hooks and other attachments, that's used for mixing, kneading, whipping, or creaming foods. The two basic types of motorized electric mixers are the stationary or stand mixer and the portable or handheld mixer.

Stationary or stand mixers are good for mixing large amounts and heavy batters; heavy-duty versions of stand mixers, such as that shown, usually come with wire whisks for beating egg whites or whipping cream, a paddle for creaming butter and sugar, and dough hooks for kneading bread. Brands such as KitchenAid, which is a heavy-duty mixer, mix more quickly and forcefully than regular stand mixers or portable handheld mixers. Purchasers of new KitchenAid mixers will need to back off standard mixing times given in our recipes. For instance, if a dough is to be kneaded for 10 minutes, KitchenAid instructs consumers to knead for 3 to 4 minutes. Owners of regular stand mixers or handheld mixers might not be able to knead dough with these less powerful mixers.

Portable or handheld mixers have a smaller motor and don't have as many attachments, but are usually adequate for mixing most batters. These lightweight mixers offer great control and are preferred by some home cooks.

We've used all of these mixers successfully in our kitchens. The trick is knowing how long to mix for desired results. Here's one example: When creaming 1 stick butter, the KitchenAid mixer knocked it out in 1 minute on medium speed; a Hamilton Beach stand mixer took 7 to 8 minutes on high speed, stopping several times to scrape down the sides of the bowl; a Hamilton Beach high-powered handheld mixer creamed butter in 3 minutes on medium speed. With a handheld mixer, you won't have to stop and scrape down the sides of the bowl.

mocha (MOH kah) The flavor combination of coffee and chocolate.

CHOCOLATE MOCHA CRUNCH PIE

Mocha Pastry Shell
1 (1-ounce) square unsweetened
   chocolate, chopped
⅓ cup butter or margarine
¾ cup firmly packed brown sugar
¼ cup all-purpose flour
2 teaspoons instant coffee
   granules

1½ cups milk
2 egg yolks, lightly beaten
2 cups whipping cream
½ cup sifted powdered sugar
1½ tablespoons instant coffee
   granules
½ (1-ounce) square semisweet
   chocolate, grated (optional)

• Prepare Mocha Pastry Shell; set aside. Place 1 square chopped chocolate and butter in top of a double boiler; bring water to a boil. Reduce heat to low; stir in brown sugar, flour, and 2 teaspoons coffee granules. Gradually stir in milk, and cook 10 minutes or until mixture thickens.

• Gradually add one-fourth of hot mixture to egg yolks. Add to remaining hot mixture, stirring constantly. Cook, stirring constantly, 20 to 25 minutes or until mixture is very thick. Remove from heat. Pour filling into cooled pastry shell. Cover and chill at least 6 hours.

• About 2 hours before serving, beat cream, powdered sugar, and 1½ tablespoons coffee granules in a large mixing bowl at medium speed with an electric mixer until soft peaks form (do not overbeat). Spoon over chilled filling. Sprinkle with grated chocolate, if desired. Chill. Yield: 8 servings.

MOCHA PASTRY SHELL

1 piecrust stick, crumbled, or ½ (11-ounce) package piecrust mix
1 (1-ounce) square unsweetened chocolate, grated
¾ cup finely chopped walnuts
¼ cup firmly packed brown sugar
1 tablespoon water
1 teaspoon vanilla extract

• Use a fork to combine crumbled piecrust stick and chocolate in a medium bowl. Stir in walnuts and brown sugar. Combine water and vanilla; sprinkle over pastry mixture. Mix with fork until mixture forms a ball.

• Line a 9-inch pieplate with aluminum foil. Press pastry mixture evenly into pieplate. Bake at 375° for 15 minutes; cool completely. Invert crust onto another pieplate; remove foil. Return to 9-inch pieplate. Yield: 1 (9-inch) pastry shell.

moist-heat cooking A process of simmering, poaching, boiling, or steaming. Moist-heat cooking methods are used to emphasize the natural flavors of foods. When slow, moist-heat cooking is applied to tougher cuts of meat, they generally become much more tender and flavorful.

molasses (muh LAS ihz) A thick, sweet, brownish-black liquid made from the juices pressed from sugarcane during refining. Molasses has a rich, heavy, sweet flavor that's concentrated by boiling; during the first boiling, light molasses is produced. Light molasses has a mild flavor and can be used as syrup for pancakes or waffles. During the second boiling, dark molasses is made; it isn't as sweet as light molasses but has a robust flavor that makes it better for gingersnaps, gingerbread, baked beans, and Indian pudding. The third boiling yields blackstrap molasses, which is very thick, dark, and bitter, and mostly used in feed for cattle; it should not be substituted for light or dark molasses in recipes.

Storage: Molasses can be kept in a cool, dark place up to a year. (*see also* **gingerbread, gingersnap,** *and* **Indian pudding**)

Q Is it better to cook with light molasses or dark molasses?

A The two are generally interchangeable. The main differences are that dark molasses isn't quite as sweet as light molasses, and foods prepared with the dark take on a darker color.

TIMESAVING TIP
Coat measuring cups or spoons with vegetable cooking spray before measuring molasses; this way the molasses will pour right out.

M

mold To shape food either by hand or by pouring it into a decorative container. For example, bread dough or meat loaf can be molded and formed by hand into a desired shape and baked. An ice cream bombe or congealed salad can be molded in a decorative container and be refrigerated or frozen until firm.

mole (MOH lay) A dark, reddish-brown sauce usually served with poultry. This Mexican specialty typically consists of onions, garlic, chiles, ground pumpkin or sesame seeds, and a small amount of Mexican chocolate. In mole, chocolate is the most unique ingredient; it adds richness to the sauce without being overly sweet.

mollusk (MOL uhsk) A class of soft-bodied shellfish having no internal skeleton. However, mollusks do generally have a shell of some sort. Snails, clams, oysters, octopus, and squid are categorized as mollusks. (*see also* **crustaceans** *and* **shellfish**)

Mongolian grill A small grill that's popular in Chinese cooking; it typically sits in the center of the dining table so each diner can cook his own food. The food usually consists of small amounts of meat dipped in a sauce, threaded on skewers, and grilled.

Mongolian hot pot A type of Chinese fondue in which each diner dips food into a pot of simmering stock placed in the center of the table. After the food is cooked, it's often dipped into a sauce or condiment. (*see also* **condiment** *and* **fondue**)

monkey bread A sweet or savory yeast bread made by piling small balls of dough in a tube pan. The balls of dough can be dipped in melted butter and flavored with any combination of raisins, nuts, sugar, herbs, or spices. The dough is allowed to rise, and after baking, can be pulled apart for serving. Monkey bread recipes can be made from convenient frozen bread dough from the supermarket or homemade yeast dough.

CHEESE-FILLED MONKEY BREAD

1 (8-ounce) package sharp Cheddar or Monterey Jack cheese, cut into 24 (¾-inch) cubes	1 (25-ounce) package frozen roll dough, thawed 2 tablespoons butter or margarine, melted

• Place 1 cheese cube in center of each roll, shaping dough into a ball around cheese cube. Pinch dough to seal. Dip in butter.
• Layer dough balls, seam side up, in a greased 12-cup Bundt pan. Cover and let rise in a warm place (85°), free from drafts, 40 minutes or until doubled in bulk. Bake at 350° for 30 to 35 minutes or until golden. Invert onto a platter, and serve warm. Yield: 2 dozen.

monkfish A fish found in the waters of the Atlantic Ocean and Mediterranean Sea, and known as "poor man's lobster" because it has a mild, sweet flavor similar to that of lobster. The only edible portion of this fish is the tail, which is usually cut into fillets. Monkfish is a lean fish with a very firm texture. (*see also* **fish**)

monosodium glutamate (mon uh SOH dee uhm GLOO tuh mayt) Referred to as MSG, this white, powdery flavor enhancer is made from an amino acid found in seaweed and vegetables. MSG is often used in Chinese and Japanese cooking; some people have an adverse reaction to too much of it and complain of dizziness, headaches, flushing, and burning sensations. MSG can be purchased in the spice section of most supermarkets; it's also an ingredient in many seasoning mixes and processed foods, so check package ingredient lists if you're sensitive to it.

Monte Cristo sandwich (MON tee KRIHS toh) A sandwich made of cooked, sliced chicken or turkey, cheese, and sometimes baked ham. The sandwich is dipped into beaten egg and fried in butter until golden.

MONTE CRISTO SANDWICH

3 tablespoons mayonnaise	6 Swiss cheese slices
1½ teaspoons prepared mustard	2 large eggs, lightly beaten
12 sandwich bread slices, trimmed	1 cup milk
6 cooked turkey slices	1½ cups pancake mix
6 cooked ham slices	Butter or margarine

• Stir together mayonnaise and mustard; spread mixture on 1 side of each bread slice.
• Place 1 slice each of turkey, ham, and cheese on each of 6 bread slices. Top with remaining bread slices. Cut each sandwich in half diagonally; secure with wooden picks.
• Stir together eggs, milk, and pancake mix in a shallow dish until blended. Dip each sandwich into batter, letting excess batter dip into bowl.
• Melt butter in a large heavy skillet. Cook 3 sandwiches at a time, 3 to 4 minutes on each side or until lightly browned and cheese begins to melt. Serve immediately. Yield: 6 sandwiches.

Monterey Jack cheese (*see* **cheese**)

Montrachet cheese (mohn truh SHAY) A soft cheese made in France from goat's milk. Montrachet has a creamy texture and mild, tangy flavor; it's sold in logs covered in a gray, salted ash. (*see also* **cheese**)

M

MoonPie® A confection consisting of two large graham cracker rounds holding a marshmallow filling; the cookie-pie usually has a chocolate, vanilla, or banana-flavored waxy-like coating.

Southernism

The MoonPie® was developed in the early 1900s by Earl Mitchell at the Chattanooga Bakery in Tennessee. One story says Mitchell talked to a coal miner about what kind of snack he would like. The miner noticed the rising moon and raised his hands to the sky, saying, "About that big!" Inspired, Mitchell headed back to the bakery and watched employees dipping graham crackers into marshmallows. Soon, the chocolate-coated MoonPie was born to rave reviews. The pairing of "RC Cola and a MoonPie" soon became synonymous with Southern snacking.

moo shu (MOO shoo) A Chinese stir-fried dish containing shredded pork, chicken, or beef, scallions, tiger lily buds, mushrooms, and scrambled eggs; the mixture is rolled in a small, thin pancake, which is sometimes spread with hoisin sauce. (*see also* **hoisin sauce** *and* **tiger lily buds**)

Moravian cookies Very thin, spicy ginger cookies traditionally served at Christmas in the Czech province of Moravia by a church group called Moravians. The Moravians living in North Carolina still make and sell these popular cookies.

Southernism

If you're looking for a gingery, thin, crisp, wafer-of-a-cookie, look to the many bakeries in and around Winston-Salem, North Carolina, the landing spot for many Moravians after their migration from Germany and then to Bethlehem, PA. While the cookies can be purchased year-round, they are a "must" on the Christmas list for many individuals from the region. The cookies are often sold in signature red cannisters and tins. Many of the bakeries now offer flavors in addition to the classic ginger.

Mornay sauce (mohr NAY) A French sauce created by adding grated Parmesan, Gruyère, or Swiss cheese to a basic white sauce or béchamel sauce. Mornay sauce is served with fish, shellfish, eggs, vegetables, and chicken. (*see also* **béchamel sauce**)

mortar and pestle A bowl and pestle used to pound ingredients, such as herbs, spices, and nuts, into a powder or paste. The bowl-shaped mortar holds the ingredients, while the club-shaped pestle crushes and grinds them.

TEST KITCHEN SECRET

Use a mortar and pestle to bruise fresh or dried herbs and spices to release their flavors. If you don't have a mortar and pestle, you can use a coffee grinder or food processor or rub dried herbs in your hands. JAN MOON

mostaccioli (mos tah chee OH lee) Italian term meaning "little mustaches" that describes 2-inch-long pasta tubes with ends cut on the diagonal.

mother sauces The five leading French sauces are béchamel (basic white sauce), velouté (light stock sauce), demi-glace (brown stock sauce), hollandaise and mayonnaise (emulsified sauces), and tomato sauce. These sauces are referred to as "mother sauces" because they're the basis for many other sauces. (*see also* **béchamel sauce, brown sauce, demi-glace, hollandaise sauce, mayonnaise, tomato sauce, velouté sauce,** *and* **white sauce**).

Mouli grater (MOO lee) A handheld rotary grater used for grating small amounts of food, such as cheese. It's easy to operate; the food is placed in a hopper above a grating cylinder, which is rotated by a turn handle.

moussaka (MOO sah kah) A Greek casserole consisting of layers of sliced eggplant and ground lamb or beef covered with a rich white sauce or cheese.

MOUSSAKA

1 pound ground beef or lamb	1 large egg, lightly beaten
2 large onions, chopped (3 cups)	6 tablespoons butter
¼ cup tomato paste	6 tablespoons all-purpose flour
1 tablespoon dried parsley flakes	3 cups milk
¼ teaspoon salt	½ teaspoon salt
¼ teaspoon pepper	¼ teaspoon pepper
1 cup water	⅛ teaspoon ground nutmeg
2 medium eggplants (2 pounds)	2 large eggs, lightly beaten
2 teaspoons salt	1 cup freshly grated Parmesan
6 tablespoons olive oil	cheese
½ cup cracker crumbs, divided	

• Cook ground beef and onion in a large skillet until beef is browned and no longer pink, stirring until it crumbles; drain well. Stir in tomato paste and next 4 ingredients. Cover and simmer 30 minutes.

• Peel eggplants, if desired, and cut into ¼-inch-thick slices. To extract bitterness, sprinkle 1 teaspoon salt on each side of slices; let stand 30 minutes. Rinse and pat dry with a paper towel. Brush eggplant slices with olive oil; place on a lightly greased rack of a broiler pan. Broil 5½ inches from heat 3 minutes. Turn, brush with olive oil, and broil 3 more minutes or until tender.

• Layer half of eggplant slices in a lightly greased 13- x 9-inch baking dish. Sprinkle ¼ cup cracker crumbs over eggplant. Add 1 egg and remaining ¼ cup cracker crumbs to meat sauce. Spoon half of meat sauce over eggplant. Repeat layers with remaining eggplant and meat sauce. Set aside.

• Melt butter in a large heavy saucepan over low heat; add flour, stirring until smooth. Cook 1 minute, stirring constantly. Gradually add milk; cook over medium heat, stirring constantly, until thickened and bubbly. Stir in ½ teaspoon salt, ¼ teaspoon pepper, and nutmeg.

• Gradually stir about 1 cup white sauce into 2 eggs; add to remaining white sauce, stirring well. Pour over meat. Bake, uncovered, at 350° for 40 minutes. Sprinkle with cheese; bake 6 more minutes. Yield: 8 servings.

M

mousse (MOOS) A French term meaning "froth" or "foam" that describes a rich, airy creamy dessert or main dish. A dessert mousse is typically flavored with fruit puree, chocolate, or coffee and made light by folding beaten egg whites or whipped cream into a custard or gelatin mixture; most are served chilled or frozen. A main-dish mousse can be made with meat, fish, shellfish, or vegetables and can be molded and served hot or cold; those served hot are usually made light by the addition of beaten egg whites and might require baking in a bain-marie or water bath to achieve the proper texture. (*see also* **bain-marie, mold,** *and* **water bath**)

CHOCOLATE TRUFFLE MOUSSE

8 (1-ounce) squares semisweet chocolate	2 tablespoons powdered sugar
¼ cup light corn syrup	½ teaspoon vanilla extract
¼ cup butter or margarine	½ cup fresh raspberries
2 egg yolks, lightly beaten	½ cup whipping cream, whipped
1 cup whipping cream, divided	Garnish: chocolate curls

• Combine first 3 ingredients in a heavy saucepan; cook over low heat, stirring constantly, until chocolate melts.

• Combine egg yolks and ¼ cup whipping cream. Gradually stir about ½ cup chocolate mixture into yolk mixture; add to remaining chocolate mixture, stirring constantly. Cook over medium-low heat 1 minute or until mixture reaches 160°. Remove from heat; cool to room temperature.

• Beat ¾ cup whipping cream at medium speed with an electric mixer until foamy; gradually add powdered sugar, beating until soft peaks form. Stir in vanilla.

• Stir ½ cup whipped cream mixture into chocolate mixture (to lighten it); then fold in remaining cream mixture. Spoon into 4 stemmed glasses. Cover and chill at least 8 hours. Top each serving with fresh raspberries and a dollop of whipped cream. Garnish, if desired. Yield: 4 servings.

mousseline (moos LEEN) A sauce that has whipped cream or beaten egg whites incorporated to give it a light, airy texture. A mousseline might also lighten dishes of fish, shellfish, poultry, or foie gras. (*see also* **foie gras**)

mozzarella cheese (maht suh REHL lah) An Italian cheese originally made from water buffalo's milk, though today most is made from cow's milk. Fresh mozzarella comes in a creamy white ball, has a mild, delicate flavor, and can be sliced for salads or spread on bread for an appetizer. Fresh mozzarella can be purchased in Italian markets, cheese shops, at deli counters, and some supermarkets. Factory-produced mozzarella is drier and stringier than fresh and is often thought of as pizza cheese because it melts smoothly and has an elastic texture; it can be purchased in chunks or shredded in packages of various sizes in supermarkets. (*see also* **cheese**)

MSG (*see* **monosodium glutamate**)

muddle A process of crushing or mixing ingredients in the bottom of a bowl or glass. This technique is used mostly when preparing drinks; in the case of mint juleps, mint leaves and sugar are muddled with a spoon in order to release the flavor of the mint before bourbon and ice are added. (*see also* **mint julep**)

Muenster cheese (MUHN stuhr) A creamy semisoft cow's milk cheese of French origin, but also made in the United States. The French version has red or orange rind, a smooth, yellow interior with small holes, and a flavor that ranges from mild to quite robust. The American version also has an orange rind, a lighter yellow interior, and a fairly bland flavor. (*see also* **cheese**)

muesli (MYOOS lee) A mixture of raw or toasted cereals, dried fruits, nuts, bran, wheat germ, sugar, and dried milk solids. The combination is typically eaten with milk, yogurt, or fruit juice for breakfast. Muesli can be purchased on the cereal aisle in most supermarkets and is sometimes labeled as granola. (*see also* **granola**)

muffin A tender, cakelike bread baked in small, cup-shaped pans, and often contains fruit and nuts. Most muffins are categorized as quick breads and are leavened with baking powder or baking soda; they are identified by slightly rounded, pebbly-type tops. Muffins can be sweet or savory, made in sizes that range from giant to miniature, and can be served at breakfast, tea, lunch, or dinner. English muffins are a totally different product; they are leavened with yeast and precooked on a griddle.
Storage: Store in a plastic bag at room temperature up to 3 days. To freeze, wrap in heavy-duty aluminum foil or place in a zip-top plastic freezer bag and freeze up to 3 months. (*see also* **English muffin** *and* **quick bread** *and recipes on the following page*)

> **TEST KITCHEN SECRET**
>
> *Be careful not to overmix muffins. If you stir the batter until all the lumps are smooth, the muffins will be tough and have pointed tops. For tender muffins stir the batter just enough to moisten the dry ingredients, and no more.* MARY ALLEN PERRY

BLUEBERRY STREUSEL MUFFINS

1¾ cups all-purpose flour
2¾ teaspoons baking powder
¾ teaspoon salt
½ cup sugar
2 teaspoons grated lemon
   rind
1 large egg, lightly beaten
¾ cup milk
⅓ cup vegetable oil

1 cup fresh or frozen blueberries,
   thawed and drained*
1 tablespoon all-purpose flour
1 tablespoon sugar
¼ cup sugar
2½ tablespoons all-purpose flour
½ teaspoon ground cinnamon
1½ tablespoons butter or
   margarine

- Combine first 5 ingredients in a large bowl; make a well in center of mixture. Combine egg, milk, and oil; stir well. Add to dry ingredients, stirring just until moistened.
- Combine blueberries, 1 tablespoon flour, and 1 tablespoon sugar, tossing gently to coat. Fold blueberry mixture into batter. Spoon batter into greased muffin pans, filling two-thirds full.
- Combine ¼ cup sugar, 2½ tablespoons flour, and cinnamon; cut in butter with a pastry blender until mixture is crumbly. Sprinkle over batter. Bake at 400° for 18 minutes or until golden. Remove from pans immediately. Yield: 1 dozen.

TIMESAVING TIP
To save on cleanup time, line muffin pans with paper muffin liners. You won't have to grease the pan, and it'll be a cinch to clean.

Q How can I make muffins with evenly rounded tops?

A For standard-size muffins, fill muffin cups no more than two-thirds full. For larger muffin cups, fill each three-quarters full.

*If using frozen blueberries, thaw and drain them, and pat dry with paper towels. This will prevent discoloration of batter.

Jumbo Blueberry Streusel Muffins: Spoon batter into 6 (3½- x 1¾-inch) greased muffin pans, filling two-thirds full. Sprinkle with streusel mixture. Bake at 400° for 20 minutes or until golden. Yield: ½ dozen.

muffin pan (*see* **baking dishes and pans**)

muffuletta (muhf fuh LEHT tuh) An Italian hero-style sandwich made famous in New Orleans. A muffuletta is made from a large, round sesame seed Italian loaf that has been split and filled with layers of ham, salami, provolone and mozzarella cheese, and a dressing called olive salad made from olives, lettuce, tomato, and garlic.

Southernism

This Italian sandwich, which originated at the turn of the twentieth century in New Orleans, has the usual meats and cheeses, and the bread is always round. But the key ingredient—"olive salad"—makes the big difference. Central Grocery in New Orleans often gets the credit for creating this Crescent City classic, but you can find wonderful variations at other eateries, too.

NAPOLEON HOUSE MUFFULETTA

Napoleon House, an historic French Quarter eatery, shares this recipe for making one muffuletta at a time. Invite friends for a muffuletta-thon and just multiply the sandwich ingredients to feed the extra folks. There may even be enough olive salad left over to send home in small jars as party favors.

2 slices ham (about 2 ounces)
3 slices Genoa salami (about 2½ ounces)
2 slices pastrami (about 2 ounces)
¼ cup Italian Olive Salad

1 slice provolone cheese
1 slice Swiss cheese
1 (5-inch) sandwich bun with sesame seeds

• Layer first 6 ingredients on bottom half of bun; top with remaining bun half, and wrap in aluminum foil.
• Bake at 350° for 20 minutes or until sandwich is thoroughly heated.
Yield: 1 serving.

ITALIAN OLIVE SALAD

4 cups pimiento-stuffed olives, drained and coarsely chopped
1 cup canned mixed vegetables, drained
1 (14-ounce) can artichoke hearts, drained and coarsely chopped
1 (16-ounce) can chickpeas, drained and coarsely chopped
1 (8-ounce) jar cocktail onions, drained and coarsely chopped

¼ cup capers, drained
⅔ cup pickled vegetables, drained and coarsely chopped
1 large green pepper, chopped
3 celery ribs, chopped
2 garlic cloves, minced
1 cup olive oil
½ cup red wine vinegar
1½ tablespoons dried oregano
½ teaspoon pepper

• Combine all ingredients; cover and chill 8 hours.
• Store salad in refrigerator up to 1 week. Use in sandwiches or serve with bagel chips Yield: 11½ cups.

mulberry A berry that's similar in size and shape to a blackberry and has a rather bland, sweet taste. There are three varieties of the mulberry: red, black, and white; the red is the only one found in the United States. Mulberries can be eaten raw or used to make jams, jellies, preserves, baked goods, or mulberry wine. (*see also* **berry**)

mull To infuse or flavor a beverage such as wine, cider, fruit juice, or beer by heating it with herbs, citrus fruit, and sugar or spices such as cinnamon, cloves, allspice, or nutmeg. Mulled beverages are especially popular in the wintertime. (*see also* **infusion** *and recipe on the following page*)

MULLED WINE PUNCH

2 cups cranberry juice cocktail
½ cup firmly packed brown sugar
3 whole cloves
3 whole allspice
1½ cups dry red wine
Garnish: cinnamon sticks

• Combine first 4 ingredients in a saucepan; bring to a boil over medium heat, stirring until sugar dissolves.

• Reduce heat, and simmer, uncovered, 5 minutes. Remove from heat. Discard whole spices. Stir in wine. Garnish, if desired. Serve warm. Yield: 3½ cups.

mullet (MUHL iht) A silvery-gray, moderate to high-fat fish with a firm, white flesh and mild, nutty flavor. Mullet can be found in the waters of the southern Atlantic Ocean and in the Gulf of Mexico; they can be fried, baked, broiled, or poached. They are most popular on the Gulf Coast and especially in the Florida Panhandle, where they are fried or smoked. (*see also* **fish**)

Southernism

"On the Gulf Coast, mullet is also called Biloxi bacon, or lisa, the latter apparently intended to give a more romantic image to a good fish that suffers low esteem because of its unmelodic common name. Smoked mullet is an excellent specialty that deserves a wider reputation." — John Egerton, Southern Food: At Home, on the Road, in History

mulligan stew (MUHL ee gahn) A catchall stew of meat, potatoes, and vegetables reputed to have originated in hobo camps during the early 1900s. However, the name indicates that the stew might have originated in Ireland; it's also very similar to another stew concoction called burgoo. (*see also* **burgoo**)

mulligatawny soup (muhl ih guh TAW nee) A spicy soup from southern India consisting of meat or vegetable broth flavored with curry and containing chicken or other meats, rice, eggs, coconut, and cream.

mung bean (*see* **bean sprouts**)

muscadine grape (MUHS kuh dihn) (*see* **grape**)

muscat grape (MUHS kat) (*see* **grape**)

mush A type of porridge or cereal made by cooking cornmeal with water or milk. This old Southern dish can be served for breakfast with milk and topped with maple syrup; it can also be poured into a pan, cooled, and cut into squares and sautéed until golden brown. Like polenta, fried mush can be served hot topped with a gravy or sauce. (*see also* **polenta**)

mushroom A member of the fungus family that's available in many different varieties, but usually consists of a stem and a cap. Mushrooms have a rich, earthy flavor and basically fall into two categories: cultivated and wild. Cultivated mushrooms are commonly found in most supermarkets, but many modern cooks consider the flavors of wild mushrooms to be more exotic and exciting. However, it's vitally important to know which species are edible and which are poison-

ous. Some wild mushrooms are fatally toxic and closely resemble edible varieties. Never pick or eat wild mushrooms unless a trained expert collector has identified them. Many supermarkets now carry wild mushrooms that have been professionally farmed and are not poisonous. Most cultivated mushrooms are available fresh, but many varieties are canned or dried. Common button or white mushrooms are used often for canned mushrooms; these are available whole, sliced, chopped, and in stems and pieces.

Here's a guide to the types of mushrooms now available:

Mushroom Dictionary

Chanterelle: A trumpet-shaped wild mushroom with a delicate flavor and chewy texture; it ranges in color from golden to yellow-orange. It can be cooked separately or added to other dishes.

chanterelle

Crimini: The cultivated brown variety of the button mushroom; it's usually a little larger and firmer, but can be used in place of white mushrooms.

Cloud or wood ear: A ruffled, brown-black Chinese mushroom with almost no flavor. It's crunchy and used to add texture to soups and stir-fries. It's sometimes available fresh, but it's usually sold dried.

cloud or wood ear

Enoki: An Asian cultivated mushroom that grows in clumps. It has long, slender stems and tiny caps. Cut away and discard the mass at the base of the clump before using. This mushroom is good eaten raw in salads.

enoki

Matsutake: A delicate wild Japanese mushroom with a slightly pointed, thick, dark brown cap and meaty stem. To prepare, sauté or wrap in foil and place on the grill. The matsutake is available fresh or canned.

Morel: A wild mushroom with an elongated honeycomb cap and a rich, smoky flavor that pairs well with chicken, veal, cream sauces, and eggs. It's available fresh, dried, and canned.

Oyster: A wild or cultivated gray mushroom with a short stem

morel

and a ruffled cap that resembles an oyster shell. It's best grilled, roasted, stir-fried, or sautéed in butter. It's available fresh, dried, and canned.

Porcini: Also known as wild cèpe mushrooms, porcini are available fresh, but are more commonly sold dried. They are brown with a strong woodsy, nutty flavor and can be used in soups, sauces, and risotto.

Portobello: A cultivated mushroom that's actually a large, mature cremini. It's prized for its huge cap that has a meaty flavor and texture; the underneath gills and stems aren't always used. The gills tend to turn foods a gray color, so grill or roast portobellos separately and then add to pasta sauces or polenta. If using portobellos in a light sauce, remove the dark gills to avoid darkening the sauce.

portobello

Shiitake: A cultivated Asian mushroom that's fresh or dried. It has a floppy, flat cap and rich, meaty flavor. Typically, only the cap is eaten.

Straw: Grown on straw left in rice paddies, these small, globe-shaped mushrooms have an earthy flavor and beige or brown color. The mushrooms are available only canned outside Asia and can be used in soups and stir-fries.

straw

White button: A cultivated all-purpose mushroom that's fairly bland, but absorbs flavor when added to savory dishes. It comes in several sizes; the small are good for sautéing in butter; the larger are good for stuffing or broiling. They come fresh, dried, or canned.

Storage: Refrigerate fresh mushrooms, unwashed, for no more than 3 days; they're best kept in a paper or cloth bag that allows them to breathe. Spread delicate varieties in a single layer on a tray and cover with a damp cloth. Do not store mushrooms in plastic because this causes them to deteriorate more quickly. (*see also* **duxelles** *and* **vegetables**)

Q **What is the best way to reconstitute dried mushrooms?**

A Cover them in hot water, wine, broth, or vinegar, and soak for about 30 minutes. Then squeeze them with your fingers to drain thoroughly. The soaking liquid is also very flavorful; if possible, strain the liquid and add it to your recipe.

muskmelon (*see* melon)

mussel (MUHS uhl) A bivalve mollusk found in fresh and saltwater, but only the ones in the shallow waters of the Atlantic Ocean and Pacific Ocean and the Mediterranean Sea are eaten. Mussels generally have a thin, oblong shell that can range in color from blue to green; they hold creamy-tan meat that's tough, but tastes slightly sweet, and turns red when cooked. In the United States, most mussels are cultivated and tend to be plumper and milder than those grown wild. Mussels are sold live, fresh shucked, frozen, canned, and smoked. Fresh mussels can be steamed, fried, baked, or used in bouillabaisse or paella. (*see also* **bouillabaisse, mollusk,** *and* **paella**)

Storage: Live mussels should be covered with a damp cloth and refrigerated for no more than a day or two before cooking; discard any that aren't alive.

Once shucked, mussels can be kept in their liquor in the refrigerator for several days, or they can be frozen in the liquor up to 3 months.

MUSSELS STEAMED IN WINE

6 dozen raw mussels in shells
½ cup butter, divided
1 large onion, chopped
2 shallots, chopped
2 garlic cloves, minced
2½ cups finely chopped fresh parsley
½ teaspoon freshly ground pepper
1½ cups dry white wine
½ cup fresh lemon juice

- Scrub mussels with a brush, and remove beards. Discard opened, cracked, or heavy mussels (they're filled with sand).
- Melt ¼ cup butter in a large Dutch oven over medium-high heat. Add mussels, onion, and next 5 ingredients. Cover and cook 4 minutes or until mussels open, shaking pan several times.
- Transfer mussels to a serving dish with a slotted spoon, discarding any unopened mussels. Cover and keep warm.
- Pour remaining liquid in pan through a strainer into a large skillet, discarding parsley mixture. Bring to a boil. Cook 20 minutes or until thickened. Remove from heat; whisk in remaining butter. Stir in lemon juice; pour over mussels. Yield: 6 servings.

mustard The leafy greens of the mustard plant are cooked and eaten like turnip greens. When the plant blooms, its flowers produce mustard seeds, which can be used whole as a pickling spice, ground into a powder to make dry mustard for seasoning, or processed with liquid and other seasonings to make prepared mustard. Several types of mustard seeds—white or yellow, brown, and sometimes, black—are used in making mustard products. The white and yellow seeds are larger, but not as pungent as the brown or black. The white seeds are usually the main ingredient in American-style mustard, which is made yellow by the addition of turmeric. While brown, black, and yellow seeds are blended to make hot English mustard, only the brown seeds are used for pickling and seasoning, and for making hot, yellow Chinese mustards. The French are known for tangy, smooth Dijon mustard made from brown seeds and white wine. German mustards range from very hot to sweet and mild and have a coarse or smooth texture; they are usually made from brown seeds. The seeds, powder, and a great variety of prepared mustards are readily available in supermarkets. Once opened, prepared mustard should be refrigerated. (*see also* **condiment, Dijon mustard,** *and* **turmeric**)

mustard greens (*see* **mustard** *and* **greens**)

mustard seed (*see* **mustard** *and* **spice**)

mutton (*see* **lamb**)

nacho (NAH choh) A crisp tortilla or tortilla chips topped with melted cheese and chile peppers. Nachos might also be topped with salsa, sour cream, or refried beans; they're usually served as an appetizer. (*see also* **tortilla**)

napa cabbage (*see* **Chinese cabbage**)

Napa Valley A grape-growing and wine-producing region near San Francisco, California. Several varieties of grapes are grown in this area, but the principal ones are Cabernet Sauvignon and Chardonnay. (*see also* **Cabernet Sauvignon, Chardonnay,** *and* **wine**)

napoleon (nuh POH lee uhn) A French pastry made into small rectangular shapes with crisp layers of puff pastry and rich pastry cream. Napoleons are glazed with icing or dusted with powdered sugar. In addition, some restaurant menus feature sweet and savory napoleons that have alternating stacked ingredients. For example, tomato napoleons are made from sliced tomatoes, sliced mozzarella, and fresh basil. (*see also* **puff pastry**)

navel orange A large orange with a thick, bright orange rind and sweet, flavorful meaty flesh with no seeds. This orange gets its name because the blossom end resembles a human navel. (*see also* **orange**)

navy bean A type of kidney bean named for the fact that the United States Navy has long served it as a staple on their menus. Navy beans are also widely used for making commercially canned pork and beans. Today, white beans such as cannellini and navy beans are used in soups, pastas, and salads. (*see also* **beans, dried;** *and* **cannellini beans**)

Neapolitan ice cream (nee uh PAHL uh tuhn) A commercially prepared ice cream made of three layers: chocolate, vanilla, and strawberry. The ice cream is usually sliced so that each serving displays the three flavors.

nectar A sweet, thick juice extracted from fruits such as apricots, peaches, and pears. Nectar is much thicker than other types of fruit juices; according to Greek and Roman mythology, it was the drink of the gods. Canned nectar can be found in the canned fruit section of most supermarkets.

nectarine (nehk tah REEN) A medium-sized fruit with smooth, yellow and red skin, and flesh that's sweet, but firmer than that of a peach. Like peaches, nectarines also have pitlike seeds. Nectarines do not have to be peeled, and they can be eaten out of hand or used in a variety of salads and desserts.
Storage: If nectarines are on the firm side, speed their ripening by placing them in a paper bag for several days at room temperature. Once ripened, store nectarines in the refrigerator and use within 2 or 3 days.

WARM BLUEBERRY-NECTARINE SHORTCAKE

2 pounds ripe nectarines, cut into wedges	¾ cup butter or margarine, cut into pieces
½ cup sugar	2 large eggs, lightly beaten
¼ teaspoon ground nutmeg	1 cup sour cream
¼ teaspoon almond extract	1 teaspoon vanilla extract
2 cups whipping cream	1 tablespoon sugar
3 tablespoons sugar	¼ cup butter or margarine, softened
2¾ cups all-purpose flour	
¼ cup sugar	1 cup fresh blueberries
4 teaspoons baking powder	Garnish: nectarine wedges

• Stir together first 4 ingredients in a medium saucepan; cook over medium heat, stirring often, 3 to 4 minutes or until sugar dissolves. Remove pan from heat.
• Beat whipping cream at medium speed with an electric mixer until foamy; gradually beat in 3 tablespoons sugar at high speed until stiff peaks form. Cover and chill.
• Combine flour, ¼ cup sugar, and baking powder in a large bowl; cut in ¾ cup butter with a pastry blender until crumbly.
• Stir together eggs, sour cream, and vanilla until blended; add to flour mixture, stirring just until dry ingredients are moistened.
• Turn dough out onto a lightly floured surface, and knead 10 times. Pat dough into a 9-inch square; cut into 9 (3-inch) squares, and place on a lightly greased baking sheet. Sprinkle with 1 tablespoon sugar.
• Bake at 450° for 12 minutes or until golden; remove from oven. Split squares in half horizontally; spread bottom halves with ¼ cup butter.
• Stir blueberries into nectarine mixture. Spoon fruit mixture evenly onto warm shortcake bottoms; cover with shortcake tops. Serve with sweetened whipped cream, and garnish, if desired. Yield: 9 servings.

Nesselrode pudding (NEHS uhl rohd) Count Nesselrode, a nineteenth-century Russian diplomat, had a number of dishes named after him, including Nesselrode pudding. This mixture consists of rich custard mixed with chestnut puree, candied fruits, currants, raisins, and maraschino liqueur. The pudding was often frozen or made into a pie. (*see also* **chestnut, custard, liqueur,** *and* **maraschino cherry**)

Neufchâtel cheese (noo shuh TELL) A soft, creamy, white unripened cow's milk cheese with a mild, delicate flavor. Named after the town in Normandy, Neufchâtel has a taste and appearance similar to cream cheese, but contains less milk fat and more moisture. If a recipe calls for light cream cheese, this is what you use. (*see also* **cheese** *and* **cream cheese**)

Newburg A dish of lobster, crabmeat, or shrimp served in a rich sauce made from cream, egg yolks, and sherry. Newburg is traditionally served over buttered toast points, but other bread bases are sometimes substituted.

New England boiled dinner An East Coast American specialty usually consisting of corned beef, but sometimes ham, salt pork, or chicken, and a mixture of cabbage, potatoes, parsnips, onions, and carrots. This hearty one-pot meal is slowly simmered and then served with horseradish and mustard.

new potato (*see* **potato, red potato,** *and* **vegetables**)

niçoise, à la (nee SWAHZ) A term that refers to a method of cooking associated with the cuisine of Nice, France. This cooking style is characterized by the use of tomatoes, garlic, black olives, and anchovies.

noisette (nwah ZEHT) A French term for hazelnut; it can also be used in reference to small, tender, round slices of meat taken from the rib or loin of beef, veal, or lamb. In addition, beurre noisette refers to butter that has been cooked until it's a light hazelnut color. (*see also* **hazelnut**)

nondairy creamer A product used to lighten and dilute coffee or tea. Though described as a creamer, this product doesn't contain cream; instead, it contains hydrogenated oil or saturated fats such as coconut or palm oil, sweeteners, preservatives, and emulsifiers. Nondairy creamer is available in powdered, liquid, or frozen form. (*see also* **fats and oils**)

nonpareil (non puh REHL) Tiny, colored sugar candies used to decorate cakes and other confections. This term also describes small disks of chocolate candy that are coated with colored candies. In France, small pickled capers might also be referred to as nonpareils. (*see also* **caper**)

noodle A type of pasta made from flour, water, and eggs. Noodles can be homemade or produced commercially in flat, thick, or thin strips of various lengths. A wide variety of noodles are available in most supermarkets; they can also be purchased in Asian markets. Noodles made from mung bean starch, rice flour, or buckwheat play an important role in Asian cuisines. (*see also* **Asian noodle, buckwheat, Chinese noodle, mung bean,** *and* **pasta**)

CHICKEN NOODLE SOUP

6 bone-in chicken breast halves	1 small onion, chopped
3 quarts water	1 tablespoon dried parsley flakes
1¼ teaspoons salt	2 (3-ounce) packages chicken-
¼ teaspoon pepper	flavored ramen soup mix
1 (16-ounce) package frozen mixed vegetables	

• Bring first 4 ingredients to a boil in a large Dutch oven. Cover, reduce heat, and simmer 30 to 40 minutes or until chicken is tender. Remove chicken, reserving broth in Dutch oven. Skin, bone, and shred chicken.
• Add frozen vegetables, onion, and parsley to reserved broth. Cover and cook over medium heat 20 minutes.
• Add ramen noodles with seasoning packet; cook, stirring occasionally, 5 minutes. Stir in chicken; cook 10 minutes. Yield: about 3 quarts.

nopales (noh PAH lays) (*see* **cactus**)

nougat (NOO guht) A candy made of roasted nuts and sugar syrup or honey. White nougat, which includes beaten egg white and sometimes chopped candied fruit, is soft and chewy. Brown nougat, made with caramelized sugar, has a firmer texture.

nouvelle cuisine (noo vehl kwee ZEEN) A French term used to describe a new style of cooking that rose to popularity in France in the 1970s and later in America in the 1980s. Nouvelle cuisine emphasizes lighter foods served in smaller quantities, reliance on natural flavors, shorter cooking times, and creative combinations of ingredients; it marked a departure from the traditional, rich cooking methods so characteristic of classic French cooking.

nutmeg The hard seed of a fruit from a tropical evergreen tree native to the East Indies. When first picked, nutmeg is surrounded by a lacy membrane, which later becomes the spice, mace. The hard, oval-shaped nutmeg seed is grayish-brown and about 1-inch long; it has a strong, sweet, spicy aroma and flavor. Nutmeg is sold ground or whole, and is used to flavor baked goods, eggnog, custard, fruit dishes, and some vegetables. (*see also* **mace** *and* **spice**)

nutmeg grater A small, handheld grater with a curved surface used to turn whole nutmeg into powder. Nutmeg grinders that operate similar to a pepper mill can also be used. (*see also* **nutmeg**)

N

nuts An edible seed or fruit or in the case of peanuts, a legume, surrounded by a shell that's thin and brittle or woody and tough. Nuts are sold shelled or unshelled; once shelled, they can be roasted or dry-roasted, salted or unsalted, sugared or spiced. Nuts are also available ground or whole, in halves, slices, slivers, chopped, blanched, and in pieces. Among the more popular nuts are almonds, Brazil nuts, cashews, chestnuts, hazelnuts, macadamias, peanuts, pecans, pine nuts, pistachios, and walnuts. **Storage:** Because they contain high amounts of oil, nuts can go rancid and develop a stale taste fairly quickly. Unshelled nuts will keep well for 6 months to a year if stored in a cool, dark, dry place. If shelled, nuts should be kept in an airtight container; they will stay fresh at room temperature up to a month, and if refrigerated, for 3 to 6 months. Nuts can also be frozen in zip-top freezer bags up to a year. Vacuum-packed nuts can be stored at room temperature. (*see also individual nuts and* **legume**)

Q Why do so many recipes call for toasting nuts?

A Toasting helps the nuts stay crisp when combined with moist ingredients. Toasting also brings out the full flavor of nuts. You can toast small amounts of nuts in a dry skillet over medium heat for just a few minutes, stirring often. Use your sense of smell to judge when they're toasted, and watch them closely; the smaller the pieces, the quicker they cook, so don't turn your back!

TEST KITCHEN SECRET

"For the best results, chop nuts by hand with a large, sharp knife. But for large quantities, the easiest way is to use the food processor. However, be alert, and don't overwork them; try pulsing the machine rather than running it continuously. If the nuts are to be used in baked goods, try adding a little flour or sugar from the list of ingredients to absorb any oil that's produced during processing. This will keep the nuts dry, and they can spread more evenly throughout the batter or dough." LYDA JONES

READER TIP

"The easiest way to remove skins from shelled nuts is to pour boiling water over them and let them stand 1 minute. Then drain the nuts and transfer to a clean towel. Wrap the towel around the nuts and gently rub; the skins will slip right off. Take your towel outside and shake it out to discard the skins." B.T., Raleigh, NC

oat An edible cereal produced from oat grass. Whole oats are used mostly as animal feed; after cleaning, toasting, hulling, and another cleaning, they become oat groats and are pronounced ready for human consumption. There are several different ways oat groats can be further processed:

• **Rolled oats** are oat groats that have been steamed and flattened by steel rollers into flakes; they are also called old-fashioned oats.

• **Quick-cooking oats** are oat groats that have been cut into several pieces before rolling flat; this shortens the cooking time.

• **Instant oatmeal** is made from oat groats that are cut into very small pieces and processed so they need no cooking, just the addition of boiling water. Some types of instant oatmeal are flavored with various spices and fruits.
• **Steel cut oat groats,** also known as Scottish or Irish oatmeal, have been sliced by steel blades; they take longer to cook and have a chewier texture.
• **Oat flour** is made from groats that have been ground into powder; it doesn't contain gluten, so when used for baking, it must be combined with regular flour.
• **Oat bran** is the outer casing of the oat and is high in soluble fiber; it's used in baked goods and as a hot cooked breakfast cereal.
Storage: Store oats in an airtight container in a cool, dry place up to 6 months. Or, oat products can be frozen in a moisture-proof container up to a year. (*see also* **bran, cereal grain,** *and* **grain**)

RAISIN-OATMEAL COOKIES

1 cup butter or margarine, softened	2 cups self-rising flour
1 cup sugar	2 teaspoons ground cinnamon
1 cup firmly packed brown sugar	3 cups uncooked regular oats
2 large eggs	1 cup raisins
	1 cup chopped pecans

• Beat first 3 ingredients at medium speed with an electric mixer until fluffy.
• Add eggs, beating until blended. Gradually add flour and cinnamon, beating at low speed until blended. Stir in oats, raisins, and pecans. Cover and chill 8 hours.
• Divide dough into 2 equal portions. Roll each portion into a 12-inch log.
• Cut each log into 1-inch-thick slices. Place slices on ungreased baking sheets. Bake at 400° for 12 minutes or until golden brown; remove to wire racks to cool. Yield: 2 dozen.

O'Brien potatoes A hearty dish, probably named by the Irish, that consists of diced potatoes fried with onions and red or green bell peppers.

octopus (OH tuh puhs) A saltwater mollusk with 8 tentacles or arms that have richly flavored white meat. Octopus is popular in Japanese and Mediterranean cuisines. It's available fresh and frozen in many supermarkets and fish markets; it can also be purchased smoked and canned. Octopus is quite tough and rubbery if not prepared correctly; it's best cooked quickly over high heat or very slowly over low heat. It can be eaten raw, boiled, pickled, sautéed, or deep-fried. (*see also* **mollusk** *and* **shellfish**)

oenology (ee NOL uh jee) The science of wine production including the growing of grapes, harvesting, vinification, and bottling.

oeuf (OUF) A French term for egg.

oils (*see* **fats and oils**)

okra (OH kruh) Slender, green, fuzzy, fingerlike pods containing numerous small, edible seeds. Brought to the South by African slaves, okra is still popular in Southern cuisine; it's an ingredient in many dishes, such as gumbo, but it can also be fried, steamed, or grilled as a vegetable. Okra has a mild flavor, but when cooked in liquid, it gives off a viscous substance that thickens the liquid. Okra is at its peak during summer months, but it's also available canned and frozen.

Storage: Store okra in a plastic bag in the refrigerator up to 3 days. (*see also* **gumbo** *and* **vegetables**)

FRIED OKRA

Okra connoisseurs have their favorite recipe. If bacon drippings aren't used, try adding them. We did in this recipe, and it made a great recipe even better.

1 **pound fresh okra**	1 **teaspoon salt**
2 **cups buttermilk**	¼ **teaspoon ground red pepper**
1 **cup self-rising cornmeal**	**Vegetable oil**
1 **cup self-rising flour**	¼ **cup bacon drippings**

• Cut off and discard tip and stem ends from okra; cut okra into ½-inch-thick slices. Stir into buttermilk; cover and chill 45 minutes. Combine cornmeal and next 3 ingredients. Remove okra from buttermilk with a slotted spoon; discard buttermilk. Dredge okra, in batches, in cornmeal mixture.

• Pour oil to a depth of 2 inches into a Dutch oven or cast-iron skillet; add bacon drippings. Heat to 375°. Fry okra, in batches, 4 minutes or until golden; drain on paper towels. Yield: 4 servings.

Southernism

"We use only fresh okra. It's cut, dipped in buttermilk and egg, salted and peppered, dredged in cornmeal, and then deep-fried. Fried okra and okra cooked in soup are the only ways I like it. No boiled or steamed okra for me."

—Louis Van Dyke of Blue Willow Inn in Social Circle, GA

Old Bay seasoning The name of a commercially prepared spice blend basically consisting of celery salt, dry mustard, and paprika. The seasoning is often used in preparing shellfish, and it originated in the Chesapeake Bay area.

old-fashioned A cocktail made of bourbon, a little water, a dash of bitters, and a sugar cube or sugar syrup. The mixture is served over ice in a glass called an old-fashioned glass and is typically garnished with an orange slice and maraschino cherry.

oleo (*see* **margarine**)

Olestra (oh LESS trah) A molecularly restructured fat made of sucrose polyester that passes through the human body without being absorbed. Olestra adds no calories or cholesterol to the foods in which it's used.

olive The small, oval fruit of the olive tree. Fresh olives are too bitter to eat; after harvest, they are either pressed to make olive oil or cured into table olives. Their color varies according to when they're picked. For example, green olives are harvested before they ripen, while black olives are left on the tree until completely ripe. There are many different varieties of olives; some are named according to their area or origin, while others are named according to the way they are cured.

Some of the most familiar olives include:
• **Spanish olives,** picked young, soaked in lye, and fermented in brine for 6 to 12 months; they are sold pitted, unpitted, or stuffed with pimientos, almonds, or anchovies.
• **Kalamata olives** from Greece are often referred to as Greek olives; they are almond-shaped, purplish-black in color, are brine-cured, and packed in oil or vinegar.
• The tiny, dark brown **niçoise olive** (nee SWAHZ) from Provence, France, is brine-cured, then packed in olive oil with lemon and herbs.
• **Sicilian olives,** sometimes flavored with red pepper or fennel, are large, green, and tart.
• Various other types include the nutty-flavored **gaeta olive** from Italy, the large, salty-tart **Moroccan olive,** and the medium-sized, salty **picholine** from France.

Many of the olives grown in America are bathed in lye and oxidized to develop a black color; they are referred to as California or Mission olives and are the soft, mild-flavored olives available in cans and often used in Mexican cooking. Olives packed in brine will stay plump and relatively firm, but some olives are packed in salt; they become dry, wrinkled, and bitter.
Storage: Olives should be covered completely with water, brine, or oil; they keep for up to a year in the refrigerator. Refrigerate salt-packed olives in an airtight, plastic container up to 6 months. (*see also* **kalamata olive**)

olive oil (*see* **fats and oils**)

omelet (AHM leht) A popular egg dish in which a mixture of beaten eggs, seasonings, and sometimes water or milk are cooked in butter until firm. The omelet is usually folded over a savory filling such

> **RESCUE for omelets that fall apart:**
> If it's just a tear, add an attractive garnish to cover it up, but if the omelet falls apart, then chop it up and serve it as scrambled eggs or make an egg sandwich.

as cheese, ham, mushrooms, onions, peppers, sausage, and herbs. Some omelets can be sweet; these are filled with jelly or fruit and sprinkled with powdered sugar or flamed with liqueur. For puffy or soufflé omelets, the whites and yolks are beaten separately and then folded together; these omelets are usually finished in the oven. There are also flat omelets, which resemble frittatas. Omelets can be made with whole eggs or just egg whites; they can be made in any skillet, but a nonstick, shallow omelet pan with rounded sides makes it easier to fold the omelet and to slide it out of the pan. (*see also* **egg, frittata, omelet pan,** *and* **soufflé**)

PUFFY DESSERT OMELET

1 pint fresh strawberries, sliced	1 teaspoon vanilla extract
2 tablespoons sugar	2 tablespoons butter or
6 large eggs, separated	margarine
¼ teaspoon salt	Sweetened whipped cream
¼ cup sugar	Powdered sugar
2 tablespoons all-purpose flour	Garnishes: strawberries, lemon
2 teaspoons grated lemon rind	twist

• Toss sliced strawberries with 2 tablespoons sugar; set aside.
• Beat egg whites and salt at high speed with an electric mixer until stiff peaks form. Beat egg yolks, ¼ cup sugar, and next 3 ingredients at medium speed until blended. Fold in beaten egg whites.
• Melt butter in a 10-inch ovenproof skillet over low heat.
• Add egg mixture to skillet. Cook, without stirring, 6 minutes or until bottom of omelet is golden. Remove skillet from heat.
• Broil 5½ inches from heat 1 minute or until golden.
• Invert omelet onto a serving plate.
• Top with sliced sweetened strawberries, whipped cream, and powdered sugar. Garnish, if desired. Yield: 4 servings.

omelet pan A shallow pan with gently curved sides, a flat bottom, and a long handle. The pan is designed to make it easy to fold and to remove an omelet; an omelet pan has a nonstick finish and is 6 to 10 inches in diameter.

onion An aromatic and flavorful underground bulb that's a member of the lily family. Onions are practically indispensable in food preparation; they're crisp and pungent when raw and soft and sweet when cooked. There are two main classifications of onions: green onions, also called scallions, and dry onions, which are mature onions with juicy flesh covered with dry, papery skins.

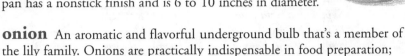

TEST KITCHEN SECRET

If chopping a large quantity of onions, start by coarsely chopping, and then finish the chopping in the food processor. For individual onions, use a sharp knife to cut through the stem end and peel back the papery skin. Place the peeled onion on the cut end, and cut it down the middle lengthwise. Place each half, cut side down, on a cutting board, and make several parallel horizontal cuts almost to the root end. Then make several parallel vertical cuts through the onion layers, but again, not cutting through the root end. Finally, cut across the grain to make chopped pieces. REBECCA KRACKE GORDON

scallions

Green onions include:

Scallions: Also known as green onions or spring onions, are the immature shoots of the bulb onion with a narrow white base and long, flat green leaves. They have a mild flavor and can be eaten raw or cooked.

Leeks: similar in appearance to scallions, but much larger. They have straight, thick white shanks instead of bulbs, flat, solid-green leaves, and ropelike roots. Their flavor is sweeter, milder, and more delicate than that of other onions. (*see also* **leek**)

Chives: Also considered an herb, are made up of pencil-thin, long, green leaves, and have a delicate flavor. (*see also* **chive**)

RESCUE for hands that smell of onion: Rub your hands with a little lemon juice, or try rubbing fingertips on the bowl of a stainless steel spoon under warm, running water or rub hands over the stainless kitchen faucet.

Dry onions include:

All-purpose onions: Also called yellow globe; they are usually 2 to 2½ inches in diameter and have a strong flavor. Globe onions can also have white skins.

Jumbo Spanish onions: Are round, yellow-skinned, mild in flavor, and slightly sweet.

Bermuda onions: Also known as Granex onions; they are medium to large, round or semiflat, white or yellow skinned, and mild and sweet. (*continued on the following page*)

Jumbo Spanish

Grano onions: Are mild-flavored, yellow-skinned onions shaped like tops.
Red, purple, or Italian onions: Are mild and slightly sweet with a purplish-red color. Sweet elongated varieties are called red torpedo onions.

Vidalia

Vidalia, Walla Walla, Texas SuperSweet, and Maui onions: Are mild, sweet and juicy and named for their place of origin, since, due to soil and climate, they lose their characteristic sweetness if grown elsewhere. Because they are so sweet, they have a shorter storage life than other dry onions.

Southernism

Texas and Georgia will never agree on who grows the sweetest onion. Both states are known for their sweet onion harvests. In fact, only 20 counties in the state of Georgia are licensed to use the name "Vidalia" on their onions.

TIMESAVING TIP

Frozen chopped onions are especially good time-savers for casseroles or one-dish-type recipes. Simply substitute the frozen onions for the same amount of fresh in your recipe.

RESCUE for tears:

Start with a sharp knife because a dull blade will bruise the onion and cause even more juices to fly. Then, try to avoid cutting off the root end before chopping the onion. Also, chilling the onion for 20 to 30 minutes before chopping should help.

Pearl and boiling onions: Pearl onions are small onions about the size of a marble and are traditionally white; boiling onions are slightly larger, about 1 inch in diameter, and white. Both have a mild flavor similar to that of green onions.

Shallots: Look like large cloves of garlic covered with papery bronze skin; their flavor is delicate and subtle yet tangy.

Dried or freeze-dried onion products: These include onion powder, onion salt, and onion flakes.

Onions can also be purchased canned, pickled, and frozen.

Storage: Green onions should be wrapped in plastic and refrigerated up to 3 weeks, depending on the variety. Dry onions can be stored in a cool, dry, well-ventilated place 2 to 3 months. To extend the life of Vidalia, Walla Walla, Texas Supersweet, and Maui onions, store so that they aren't touching each other; some cooks hang them in old panty hose with knots tied in between each onion. For longer storage, freeze sliced or chopped onions in zip-top freezer bags up to a year. (*see also* **vegetables**)

READER TIP

"When a recipe calls for only a tablespoon or two of grated or minced onion, I put a small chunk of onion through my garlic press. It's fast and it saves on cleanup." C.B., Greensburg, KY

TIMESAVING TIP

When chopping onions, save the excess and freeze in a zip-top freezer bag. Also, when sautéing onions or onion and garlic mixtures, sauté more than you need and freeze the leftovers; this will save time when preparing soups, sauces, and stews.

onion soup A soup that uses onions as the main flavoring ingredient; it can be clear or creamy. French onion soup, the most popular, is clear soup with a beef-broth base and is topped with croutons or a slice of toasted French bread, and cheese. Commercially prepared onion soups can be purchased canned or as a dried mix. (*see also* **crouton** *and* **French bread**)

CARAMELIZED FRENCH ONION SOUP

1 recipe Caramelized Onions	½ teaspoon dried thyme
1 (10½-ounce) can beef consommé, undiluted	¼ cup dry white wine
	6 cups large croutons
1 (10½-ounce) can beef broth, undiluted	1 cup (4 ounces) shredded Swiss cheese
2 cups water	

• Combine first 5 ingredients in a 3½-quart slow cooker.
• Cook, covered, at HIGH 2½ hours or until thoroughly heated. Stir in wine.
• Ladle soup into 6 ovenproof bowls, and top evenly with croutons and cheese. Place bowls in a jellyroll pan.
• Broil 3 inches from heat 5 minutes or until cheese is melted. Serve immediately. Yield: 6 servings.

CARAMELIZED ONIONS

2 extralarge sweet onions (about 3 pounds)	1 (10½-ounce) can chicken or beef broth, undiluted
¼ cup butter or margarine	

• Cut onions in half; cut each half into ½-inch-thick slices.
• Combine all ingredients in a 3½-quart slow cooker. Cook, covered, at HIGH 8 hours or until golden brown and very soft. Store in an airtight container; chill up to 2 weeks, or freeze up to 2 months. Yield: 2 cups.

on the half shell A phrase that describes when raw or cooked oysters are served in their bottom shell. If served raw, they are presented on a bed of crushed ice, but if cooked, as in oysters Rockefeller, they will be on a bed of rock salt. Oysters on the half shell are usually accompanied with lemon juice, cocktail sauce, hot sauce, and crackers. (*see also* **hot sauce, oysters Rockefeller,** *and* **salt**)

on the rocks When a beverage, usually alcoholic, is served over ice without water or a mixer. A beverage served on the rocks might also be referred to as a lowball.

open-faced A term that's used in reference to a sandwich made from one slice of bread topped with various meats, cheeses, etc. Open-faced sandwiches can be served hot or cold; when served hot, they are often topped with gravy or sauce.

orange A round to oval-shaped citrus fruit with juicy, orange-colored segmented flesh, surrounded by a peel or rind. Depending on the variety, the peel can be thin to moderately thick, and the flavor of the flesh can range from bitter to tart to sweet. Most oranges are eaten fresh or squeezed for juice, but they can also be cooked in sweet or savory dishes.

There are three basic types of orange: sweet, loose-skinned, and bitter.

• **Sweet oranges** include the Hamlin, navel, Valencia, and blood orange. The Hamlin is a thin-skinned, medium-sized, juicy orange. The navel is sweet, easy to peel, and

almost always seedless. The Valencia is often used for juicing because of its thin skin. The blood orange has a distinctive red flesh and juice.

Southernism

How do you tell the difference between a Florida and a California orange? California oranges tend to have a golden orange-yellow color and a thick, even skin. Florida oranges range in color from orange to yellow-orange to greenish-yellow and tend to have a thinner skin. You'll often see tiny brown lines on the outer skin that mark where the leaves of the orange tree gently rubbed against the orange as it grew.

Q **What's the easiest way to section an orange?**

A Slice off the top and bottom of the orange; then stand it upright. Following the contour of the fruit, slice off the peel, pith, and membrane in thick strips. Holding the fruit over a bowl, cut along each side of the membrane between the sections, letting each segment drop into the bowl as it's sliced.

• **Loose-skinned oranges** have rinds that easily slip off the fruit and segments that divide with ease. Mandarin, tangelo, and temple oranges fall into this category.

• **Bitter oranges** include the Seville and bergamot. These often have a thick rind, dry pulp, and are too sour to eat raw; they're usually used in marmalades, candies, and liqueurs.

Storage: Oranges can be left at room temperature for a week, sometimes longer if kept in a cool, dry place. They can also be refrigerated up to 3 weeks. (*see also* **blood orange, citrus fruit, mandarin orange,** *and* **navel orange**)

orange blossom honey Clear, pale reddish-gold honey with delicate flavor. Orange blossom honey is produced primarily in Florida and California. (*see also* **honey**)

orange roughy (RUHF ee) A low-fat fish found in the coastal waters of New Zealand and Australia; it has a firm, white flesh and a mild flavor, which lends itself to poaching, baking, broiling, or sautéing. Flounder or other lean white fish make good substitutes for orange roughy. (*see also* **fish**)

oregano (*see* **herbs**)

organic A term describing foods produced by farmers who use renewable resources and conserve water and soil to conserve the environment. Organic meats, poultry, eggs, and dairy products come from animals given no antibiotics or growth hormones. Organic food is produced without common pesticides and fertilizers, irradiation, sewage sludge, or genetic engineering. Organic foods generally do not contain any artificial coloring, flavoring, or additives; most are produced and sold in local markets and are usually fresher. The USDA has just established national standards that foods labeled Aorganic® must meet to certify that they follow proper standards.

orgeat (OHR zhat) Sweet syrup made from almonds, sugar, and rose water or orange flower water. Orgeat is used as a flavoring for cocktail beverages such as the mai tai. (*see also* **mai tai**)

orzo (OHR zoh) An Italian term for barley; but orzo is actually tiny, rice-shaped pasta. Orzo can be cooked in soups, tossed in pasta salads, or served as a substitute for rice. (*see also* **pasta**)

Oscar (OS kuhr) A dish, such as veal Oscar, where the main ingredient is sautéed and topped with crabmeat or crawfish meat, béarnaise sauce, and asparagus. (*see also* **béarnaise sauce** *and* **veal Oscar**)

osso buco (AW soh BOO koh) A flavorful Italian dish made of veal shanks braised in olive oil, white wine, and stock with onions, tomatoes, garlic, carrots, celery, and lemon peel. The finished dish is traditionally garnished with gremolata, a mixture of chopped fresh lemon rind, parsley, and garlic, and served with risotto. (*see also* **gremolata, risotto, veal,** *and recipe on the following page*)

OSSO BUCO

8 (2-inch-thick) veal shanks	1 bay leaf
½ teaspoon salt	4 cups hot water
1 teaspoon pepper	4 teaspoons beef bouillon
¼ cup olive oil, divided	granules
2 large onions, chopped	1 tablespoon all-purpose flour
3 large carrots, chopped	1 tablespoon butter, softened
3 celery ribs, chopped	3 tablespoons chopped fresh
2 cups dry white wine	parsley
3 fresh parsley sprigs	1 teaspoon grated lemon rind
1 fresh thyme sprig	1 clove garlic, minced

• Rub veal with salt and pepper. Brown veal, in 2 batches, in 3 tablespoons hot oil in a large skillet over medium-high heat 5 minutes, turning often. Remove to a roasting pan; keep warm.

• Sauté onion, carrot, and celery in remaining 1 tablespoon hot oil in skillet until tender. Add wine; bring to a boil, and boil, stirring occasionally, until reduced by two-thirds (about 15 minutes).

• Tie herbs with string. Add herbs, 4 cups hot water, and bouillon granules to skillet; cover. Bring to a boil. Pour over veal. Cover; bake at 375° for 1 hour and 45 minutes or until veal is tender. Remove veal; keep warm.

• Pour drippings through a wire-mesh strainer into a skillet, discarding solids. Bring to a boil; boil until reduced by half (about 40 minutes). Whisk flour and butter until smooth; whisk into drippings. Cook, whisking constantly, 1 minute. Set gravy aside.

• Combine 3 tablespoons parsley, lemon rind, and garlic. Serve veal in wide-rimmed pasta bowls; top with gravy and sprinkle with parsley mixture. Yield: 8 servings.

ostrich A large bird whose flesh is lean and purple and sometimes substituted for beef. You'll find ostrich on some restaurant menus. Ostrich eggs can also be eaten, though one egg can weigh up to three pounds.

oven A large appliance used for baking, roasting, and broiling. Three basic types of ovens are available for home use: thermal or conventional ovens, convection ovens, and microwave ovens. Thermal ovens use radiant heat from gas flames or electric elements to cook food with dry heat; most electric ovens cook food more quickly and evenly than gas ovens. Convection ovens have a fan that blows heated air throughout; the food cooks quickly and evenly in the moving air. Microwave ovens use heat generated by the food itself, produced when molecules are agitated by short, high-frequency microwaves. One of the latest developments in oven technology is the halogen oven, which uses powerful halogen lights to cook the outside of food, much like conventional radiant heat, but also penetrates the surface so the inside is cooked at the same time. In addition, other types of ovens beginning to be marketed employ superfast technologies such as thermal pulsing (a combination of infrared and halogen cooking) or shooting jets of ultrahot air. (*see also* **convection oven** *and* **microwave cooking**)

oven-fry A method of cooking where food is dipped in melted butter or margarine, dredged in flour or crumbs, and placed in a hot oven to bake. Oven-frying achieves a final product similar to frying, but with less fat.

OVEN-FRIED CHICKEN

1¼ cups Italian-seasoned breadcrumbs	½ teaspoon poultry seasoning
¼ cup grated Parmesan cheese	¼ teaspoon ground red pepper
½ cup fat-free mayonnaise	8 skinned and boned chicken breast halves
½ teaspoon salt	

• Stir together breadcrumbs and Parmesan cheese in a shallow dish.
• Stir together mayonnaise and next 3 ingredients.
• Brush both sides of chicken with mayonnaise mixture, and dredge in breadcrumb mixture. Place in an aluminum foil-lined 15- x 10-inch jellyroll pan coated with vegetable cooking spray.
• Bake at 425° for 20 minutes or until done. Yield: 8 servings.

oven thermometer (*see* **thermometer**)

oxtail A term that generally refers to beef or veal tail. Oxtails are flavorful, but contain many bones, and are best cooked in soups or stews.

oyster A bivalve mollusk found in saltwater regions throughout the world. Oysters usually have a rough, gray shell that contains gray, soft, slippery-textured flesh that can be eaten raw or cooked. There are three main species of oysters sold in the United States: Pacific or Japanese, Eastern or Atlantic, and Olympia. Pacific oysters are found along the Pacific seaboard and can reach up to a foot long. Atlantic oysters come in various sizes, have a briny flavor, and are known for their place of origin, such as Apalachicola or Chesapeake Bay. Olympia oysters are usually very small and are harvested from Washington's Puget Sound. Fresh oysters are available year-round; however, they are at their peak during fall and winter months. Oysters in the shell can be served raw, baked, steamed, or in special recipes such as oysters Rockefeller.

Q Is it still safe to eat fresh, raw oysters?

A Since oysters are susceptible to water contaminants and harmful organisms, it's recommended that pregnant women and other high-risk individuals with serious medical conditions cook oysters thoroughly before eating. If you plan to eat raw oysters, buy them from reputable markets and make sure the oysters were harvested in waters that were certified as safe.

(*continued on the following page*)

Shucked oysters can be fried, sautéed, used in soups or stews, in dressings or stuffings, or made into appetizers such as angels on horseback. The flavorful, clear liquor that fresh, shucked oysters are packed in can also be used in soups and stews. Oysters are also available canned and smoked.

Storage: Live oysters are best eaten as fresh as possible; reject those that do not have tightly closed shells or that don't snap shut when tapped. Live oysters can be covered with a damp towel and refrigerated up to 3 days; however, the sooner they're used, the better they'll taste. Refrigerate shucked oysters, covered in their liquor, up to 2 days, or freeze up to 3 months. Canned oysters can be kept in a cool, dry place up to 2 years. (*see also* **mollusk** *and* **oysters Rockefeller**)

oyster cracker A small, round cracker that's traditionally served with oyster stew.

oyster knife A hand tool used to pry open oysters during the shucking process. The knife has a fat, pointed, arrow-shaped blade and a flange to protect the hand.

oyster mushroom (*see* **mushroom**)

oyster sauce A thick, dark brown sauce made from oyster extracts and soy sauce. Oyster sauce is popular in Asian cooking, where its smoky-sweet flavor imparts interest to stir-fries, noodle dishes, and meat, vegetable, and seafood dishes. It can be purchased in many supermarkets and Asian markets.

oysters Rockefeller A dish of oysters served hot on the half shell with a topping of spinach, breadcrumbs, and seasonings. The oyster shells are usually presented on a bed of rock salt to keep them from moving around and from toppling over. (*see also* **on the half shell, oysters,** *and* **salt**)

Southernism

The expression "too rich for my blood" is the gist of the on-the-half-shell dish, Oysters Rockefeller. In the1890s, Jules Alcaitore, son of Antoine (founder of Antoine's restaurant in New Orleans) created the signature concoction so rich and elegant that he named it for prominent business tycoon, John D. Rockefeller. There are many adaptations of the dish, but the original recipe remains a secret. On his deathbed, Jules requested that the exact ingredients never be disclosed—a feat that has been achieved despite many attempts at replication.

OYSTERS ROCKEFELLER

1 (10-ounce) package frozen
  chopped spinach, thawed and
  well drained
1 cup Italian-seasoned
  breadcrumbs
¼ cup grated Parmesan cheese
2 large eggs, lightly beaten
1 garlic clove, minced

¼ teaspoon salt
¼ teaspoon pepper
¼ teaspoon hot sauce
Rock salt
2 dozen oysters on the half shell,
  drained
6 bacon slices, each cut crosswise
  into 4 pieces

• Combine first 8 ingredients. Sprinkle a thin layer of rock salt in a large shallow pan. Arrange oysters, in shells, over rock salt. Spoon spinach mixture onto oysters; top with bacon. Bake at 350° for 15 minutes. Broil 5 inches from heat 3 minutes. Yield: 6 servings.

Ozark pudding A baked pudding made with chopped apples and pecans from orchards in the Ozark Mountains of Arkansas. Ozark pudding is sometimes served with rum-flavored whipped cream.

pad thai A Thai stir-fry dish made of cooked rice noodles, tofu, shrimp, crushed peanuts, nam pla (a salty condiment made of fermented fish), bean sprouts, eggs, garlic, and chiles.

paella (py AY yuh) A Spanish dish consisting of a mixture of rice, peas, onions, sausage, chicken, fish, and shellfish. Paella is often flavored with saffron, which turns the rice an attractive yellow color. Paella is named after the wide, shallow, two-handled pan in which it's traditionally cooked and served.

READER TIP

"We cook paella on the grill in a large paella pan. It's great for entertaining because guests can serve themselves directly from the pan. If you don't have a paella pan, use a very large skillet with a cover." G.M., Savannah, GA

SHORTCUT PAELLA

1½ pounds unpeeled, medium-size
  fresh shrimp
1 (16-ounce) package chorizo
  or smoked sausage, sliced
1 (¾-pound) package chicken
  tenders
2 (10-ounce) cans diced tomatoes
  with lime juice and cilantro

2 (14-ounce) cans low-sodium
  fat-free chicken broth
½ teaspoon ground cumin
1 (10-ounce) package saffron rice
1 (9-ounce) package frozen sweet
  green peas

• Peel shrimp, and devein, if desired; set shrimp aside.
• Sauté sausage and chicken tenders in a large, deep skillet over medium-high heat 10 minutes. Add tomatoes, chicken broth, and cumin. Bring to a boil. Stir in rice, and cook, uncovered, over medium heat 45 minutes or until liquid is almost absorbed, stirring occasionally. Stir in shrimp and peas, and cook 4 minutes or until shrimp turn pink. Yield: 6 servings.

pain perdu (pahn pehr DOO) (*see* **French toast**)

palacsinta (pah lah SHIHN tuh) Thin Hungarian pancakes or crêpes spread with a savory filling of minced ham and mushrooms or a sweet filling of jam; they are usually stacked and cut into wedges for serving. (*see also* **crêpe** *and* **pancake**)

palmier (pahlm YAY) (*see* **elephant ears**)

palm oil (*see* **fats and oils**)

pan (*see* **baking dishes and pans**)

pan-broil A dry-heat cooking method used to quickly cook meat or fish in a skillet without any fat.

pancake A flat, round, tender quick bread made from batter poured onto a hot griddle or skillet. Pancakes vary in thickness from the very thin French crêpe to the much thicker breakfast pancake; they're traditionally served with butter and sweet syrup at breakfast, although they can also be eaten at lunch or dinner as appetizers, entrées and desserts. Through the years, Americans have referred to pancakes by other names including hot cakes, griddle cakes, and flapjacks. Other countries and religious groups have their own special versions of the pancake, such as the Hungarian palacsinta and the Jewish blintz. Convenient pancake mixes are available in supermarkets. (*see also* **blintz, crêpe,** *and* **palacsinta**)

> **TEST KITCHEN SECRET**
>
> *For nice, evenly shaped pancakes, mix the batter in a large (pint or quart) liquid measuring cup. Pour the same amount of batter onto the griddle for each pancake. If you have children and want to make shaped pancakes, use a bulb baster; it allows you be creative, but also control the amount of batter that's released.* MARGARET MONROE DICKEY

Q How do I determine when to flip pancakes, and how do I know when they're done?

A Start by making sure the griddle is preheated over medium-high heat; sprinkle a few drops of water on the hot surface. If the water bounces off the griddle, it's too hot; if it doesn't bounce at all, it isn't hot enough. Then make a test pancake. Lightly oil the hot griddle, and pour the batter in the center; let it cook until bubbles appear and then burst. When the edges look dry, turn the pancake over with a pancake turner, and cook an additional minute. Lift the edge of the pancake and peek underneath; it should be golden brown.

BANANA PANCAKES WITH
PEANUT BUTTER AND JELLY SYRUPS

2 cups biscuit mix	3 tablespoons butter or margarine
1 cup buttermilk	¾ cup maple syrup
1 cup mashed banana	¼ cup reduced-fat creamy peanut
2 large eggs	butter spread
½ teaspoon ground cinnamon	Strawberry syrup

• Whisk together first 5 ingredients in a large bowl just until dry ingredients are moistened.
• Melt 1 tablespoon butter on a hot griddle. Pour about ¼ cup batter for each pancake onto griddle. Cook pancakes until tops are covered with bubbles and edges look cooked; turn and cook other side.
• Repeat procedure with remaining butter and batter. Whisk together maple syrup and peanut butter until smooth.
• Serve pancakes with peanut butter mixture and strawberry syrup.
Yield: 12 (4-inch) pancakes.
Note: For smaller pancakes, pour 1 tablespoon batter onto hot griddle. Proceed as directed.

TIMESAVING TIP
Combine dry ingredients in one bowl and wet ingredients in another bowl the night before so they are ready to stir together the next morning. Or, mix the batter in a heavy-duty zip-top plastic bag and refrigerate until ready to cook; then snip off a bottom corner and dispense the batter. Another trick is to make pancakes ahead and freeze in an airtight container; reheat in a 350° oven until warmed.

pancetta (pan CHEH tuh) Italian bacon cured with salt, pepper, and other spices rather than with smoke. Pancetta comes in a roll and can be sliced or chopped. It adds subtle flavor to soups, sauces, meats, and vegetables.

pandowdy A simple, deep-dish dessert made with apples, brown sugar or molasses, spices, and butter. Pandowdy is typically topped with a biscuit-like batter and baked until crisp and golden; it's best served hot with a scoop of ice cream.

panettone (pan uh TOH nee) A sweet Italian yeast bread flavored with anise and filled with raisins, candied citrus peel, and pine nuts. Panettone is traditionally baked in a tall, cylindrical mold and served as a breakfast bread or dessert on festive occasions such as Christmas, weddings, or christenings. (*see also* **anise** *and* **pine nut**)

pan-fry (*see* **fry**)

panini (pah NEE nee) A sandwich served on hard rolls or other European-style bread such as French baguettes or Italian hard rolls. Panini can be eaten cold or wrapped in aluminum foil and heated. (*see also* **baguette**)

panzanella (pahn tsah NAYL lah) An Italian bread salad made from bread cubes mixed with capers, anchovies, tomatoes, and cucumbers. Panzanella is typically dressed or tossed with olive oil. Cornbread salad would be the Southern equivalent.

papain (puh PAY ihn) Derived from papaya, this enzyme is used as a meat tenderizer since it has the ability to break down the protein in meat. (*see also* **meat tenderizer**)

papaya (puh PY yuh) A large pear-shaped tropical fruit with orange to yellow skin and juicy orange flesh; it has an exotic astringent flavor that resembles a cross between peaches and melons. The seed cavity of the papaya contains a mass of slick, black seeds. Native to Central America, the papaya, sometimes called "paw paw," is now also grown in Hawaii and Florida. In Latin America and Southeast Asia, the unripe fruit is often shredded and tossed in salads and harvested for papain, an enzyme that breaks down proteins and is used as a meat tenderizer. To eat fresh papaya, cut in half lengthwise, remove the seeds, and cut the flesh like a melon. Papayas are most plentiful in the spring and fall; papaya juice or nectar and dried papaya are also available.
Storage: Slightly green papayas will ripen quickly at room temperature, especially if placed in a paper bag. Refrigerate the ripe fruit and use as soon as possible. Peel, cut, and store the fruit in an airtight container in the refrigerator for several days. (*see also* **papain**)

papillote (pah pee YOHT) (*see* **en papillote** *and* **parchment paper**)

paprika (pa PREE kuh) A blended powder made from dried red peppers; the flavor ranges from slightly sweet and mild to pungent and moderately hot. The color of paprika can also vary from bright orange-red to deep brownish-red. Most commercial paprika comes from Spain, South America, California, and Hungary, with the Hungarian variety considered by many to be superior. Hungarian cuisine has long used paprika as a mainstay flavoring rather than simply as a garnish, but it's used more often as a garnish in American cooking. All supermarkets carry mild paprika, while ethnic markets sell the more pungent varieties. It can be stored in a cool, dark place for up to 6 months before the flavor begins to deteriorate. (*see also* **spice**)

paraffin A wax that can be applied to the rinds of some cheeses and vegetables such as rutabagas and cucumbers for protection during transport and to increase shelf life. Until recently, homemade jelly was often sealed with paraffin; however, it doesn't form an airtight seal. So the USDA recommends that for long-term storage, all jam, jellies, and preserves be processed in a boiling water bath for 5 to 10 minutes. (*see also* **boiling water bath**)

parboil Partially cooking a food in a boiling or simmering liquid. Sometimes a food is parboiled before it's combined with other ingredients that don't cook as long. For instance, when preparing a stir-fried dish, some vegetables require a longer cooking time, so they might be parboiled before they're added to the wok. The parboiling process is actually similar to the blanching process, but requires a longer cooking time, usually until the food is half-done. (*see also* **blanch**)

parboiled rice (*see* rice)

parchment paper Heavy grease-resistant paper used to line cakepans or baking sheets, to wrap foods for baking en papillote, or for making disposable pastry or piping bags. Parchment paper can be purchased in most large supermarkets. (*see also* **en papillote** *and* **pastry bag**)

pare Removing the thin skin or peel from fruits and vegetables. This process is usually done with a paring knife or vegetable peeler. (*see also* **knife**)

parfait (pahr FAY) A chilled or frozen dessert served in a tall, narrow, footed parfait glass. Parfait fillings can vary, but might include ice cream, whipped cream, flavored syrups, chopped fruit or fruit puree, and nuts; they're often layered in parfait glasses. French parfaits usually consist of a frozen custard or ice flavored with fruit puree.

paring knife (*see* knife)

parisienne sauce (puh ree zee EHN) A rich, creamy sauce made by blending cream cheese with olive oil, lemon juice, chervil, and sometimes paprika. Parisienne sauce is often used as a topping for cold asparagus.

Parker House rolls A yeast roll made famous in the late 19th century at the Parker House, a Boston hotel. Parker House rolls are shaped by folding each individual round of dough in half along an off-center crease before baking. (*see recipe on the following page*)

PARKER HOUSE REFRIGERATOR ROLLS

2 (¼-ounce) envelopes active dry yeast	⅔ cup shortening
1 cup warm water (100° to 110°)	1 cup water
½ cup sugar	2 large eggs, beaten
1½ teaspoons salt	6 cups all-purpose flour
	Melted butter or margarine

• Dissolve yeast in 1 cup warm water, and set aside.
• Combine sugar, salt, shortening, and 1 cup water in a small saucepan; heat, stirring often, until shortening melts. Cool mixture to 100° to 110°.
• Combine yeast mixture, shortening mixture, and eggs in a large bowl. Gradually stir in flour. Turn dough out onto a floured surface, and knead 5 to 8 minutes or until smooth and elastic. Place in a well-greased bowl, turning to grease top; cover and refrigerate 1½ hours.
• Punch dough down; turn out onto a floured surface. Roll out to ¼-inch thickness. Cut into 2½-inch circles, and brush with melted butter. Make a crease across each circle, and fold one half over. Gently press edges to seal. Place on greased baking sheets, and let rise in a warm place (85°), free from drafts, 30 minutes or until doubled in bulk. Bake at 375° for 9 minutes or until lightly browned. Brush rolls with melted butter. Yield: about 4 dozen.

Parma ham (PAHR muh) Produced in Parma, Italy, this ham is seasoned, salt-cured, and air-dried, but not smoked; it has a rosy-brown color and firm, dense texture. Parma ham is usually known as prosciutto; it's served thinly sliced with honeydew melon as an appetizer, or used to flavor soups or other dishes. (*see also* **ham**)

Parmesan cheese (*see* **cheese**)

parmigiana, à la (pahr muh ZHAH nuh) A term that refers to a dish prepared with Parmesan cheese. For example, Parmesan cheese is an important flavoring ingredient in veal parmigiana and eggplant parmigiana as well as in many au gratin dishes. (*see also* **au gratin**)

parsley A popular herb for seasoning and garnishing. Parsley has long, very slender stems; small, green leaves; and a slightly peppery, tangy-fresh flavor. Varieties include Italian or flat-leaf parsley and curly-leaf parsley. Fresh and dried parsley is widely available; fresh is sold in bunches in the produce department. It's often next to cilantro, a more pungent herb, so be sure you pick up the bunch you desire! **Storage:** Like most herbs, wash parsley and shake off excess moisture. Wrap in damp paper towels; chill in a plastic bag up to a week. (*see also* **Italian parsley**)

TEST KITCHEN SECRET

If fresh parsley (or any herb) wilts, just snip the lower stems and place the bunch in a glass of cold water; loosely cover leaves with a plastic bag, and chill. It will perk up in no time. LYDA JONES

parsnip A root vegetable with bright green, feathery leaves. The long tapering vegetable is shaped like a carrot and has beige-white skin with a sweet, nutty flavor. Parsnips can be refrigerated in a plastic bag up to a month; they are suitable for baking, boiling, sautéing, roasting, or steaming and are often boiled and mashed like potatoes or served in combination with potatoes. They are also wonderful roasted; it brings out their sweetness. (*see also* **vegetables**)

partridge (*see* **wild game**)

passion fruit An egg-shaped, purple-skinned tropical fruit named by South American Jesuit missionaries who thought the plant's flowers resembled the crucifix. Passion fruit is native to Brazil, but is now grown in California, Florida, and Hawaii. The soft golden flesh of the passion fruit is sweet, but tart, and filled with tiny, edible black seeds. Passion fruit can be sliced open and eaten, or it can be added to fruit salads, sauces, dressings, desserts, and beverages. Purchase fresh passion fruit during the summer months in some supermarkets; the canned nectar is also available.
Storage: Ripen passion fruit at room temperature until wrinkled, then refrigerate and use within 3 to 5 days.

pasta (PAH stuh) An unleavened dough formed from a liquid (eggs and/or water), mixed with a flour (usually semolina made from durum wheat), and cut into shapes. Pasta can be purchased dried or refrigerated fresh; dried is inexpensive and has a long shelf life. Look for fresh pasta in the refrigerated section at the supermarket or make your own. Uncooked dried pasta of similar shapes can be interchanged in recipes if it's measured by weight, not volume. Cooked pasta, however, can be substituted cup for cup. When cooked, noodles swell slightly; spaghetti and macaroni double in size. Pasta is done when it's "al dente," or chewy, not soft or overdone. Allow 2 ounces of uncooked dried pasta, 3 ounces of uncooked refrigerated fresh pasta, or 1 to 1½ cups cooked pasta per person. (*continued on the following page*)

TEST KITCHEN SECRET

Pasta needs plenty of room to boil; use 3 quarts rapidly boiling water for every 8 ounces of dried pasta, and stir during the first couple of minutes, because this is when the starch is released and causes the noodles to stick together. If desired, add a small amount of vegetable oil to the water to help prevent sticking. When the pasta is cooked, toss it with a sauce as soon as possible after draining because pasta begins to stick as it cools. Sometimes, a recipe calls for rinsing pasta, as in pasta salads, which benefit from having less starch and less "stickiness" once chilled. MARY ALLEN PERRY

TIMESAVING TIP
Fresh pasta cooks in 1 to 3 minutes, while dried pasta requires 6 to 15 minutes.

Storage: Store uncooked dry pasta in an airtight container in a cool, dry place free from dust and moisture up to a year. Store uncooked egg noodles up to 6 months. Plain, cooked pasta can be kept in the refrigerator up to 4 days or in the freezer for 1 month. Refrigerate prepared pasta dishes 1 to 2 days, or freeze as long as 6 months. (*see also* **al dente, lasagna, manicotti, noodle, orzo,** *and* **pasta machine**)

Pasta and Sauce Pairings

• Serve thin sauces such as marinara or pesto with thin pastas.

• Serve thick, chunky meat and vegetable sauces with tubular and shell pastas that are designed to "trap" the sauce. Thick pastas such as rigatoni, ziti, and fettuccine also pair well with thick sauces.

• Rich, thick, smooth sauces blend best with flat pastas that won't trap too much sauce.

> **RESCUE for overdone pasta:**
> Don't toss with sauce; instead, just spoon the sauce over the pasta. If the pasta is very soft, use in another dish such as an omelet or frittata.

Pasta and Rice ID

Long Shapes: Spaghetti, fettuccine, linguine, vermicelli, and angel hair are the most popular and versatile. Team thick strands with hearty sauces and thin strands with light, delicate sauces.

Medium Shapes: Penne, rigatoni, and mostaccioli have holes and ridges and pair well with chunky, hearty sauces. Farfalle (bow ties), elbow macaroni, radiatore (little radiators), wagon wheels, and medium shells are popular in salads, casseroles, and stews.

Small Shapes: Ditalini (thimbles) and orzo (rice-shaped pasta) are suited for soups, salads, and sauces with chopped vegetables.

Egg Noodles: Available in fine, medium, and wide, these are commonly used in casseroles and soups. As the name implies, egg noodles contain egg; most other dried pastas do not.

Specialty Shapes: Lasagna, manicotti, and jumbo shells are always used in baked dishes. Ravioli and tortellini are filled with meat, cheese, or other ingredients.

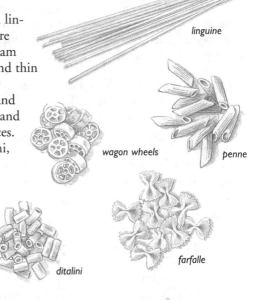

linguine

wagon wheels

penne

ditalini

farfalle

lasagna

manicotti

MAKING FRESH PASTA

1. Place flour on surface; make a well in center, using a measuring cup.

2. Add egg mixture to well; whisk with a fork, stirring in flour from bottom.

3. Knock in a little flour from the sides, and blend it into the eggs.

4. Knead dough, continually dusting with flour, until dough feels smooth and resilient.

5. Use a pastry brush to brush dough sheets with flour on both sides after first pass in pasta machine.

6. Pass each dough sheet through the cutting rollers of pasta machine. Two pairs of hands are helpful here.

HOMEMADE PASTA

3 to 4 cups all-purpose flour	4 to 6 tablespoons water
3 large eggs, lightly beaten	3 quarts water
1 tablespoon olive oil	1 teaspoon salt
1 teaspoon salt	

• Place flour on work surface; make a well in center (photo 1). Combine eggs, oil, and 1 teaspoon salt; place in center of flour well. Whisk eggs with a fork, gradually stirring in flour from bottom of well (photo 2). Push some flour from sides of well into the center as mixture thickens (photo 3). Continue whisking until mixture becomes very stiff.

• Begin kneading dough by hand; gradually work in more flour and 4 to 6 tablespoons water (1 tablespoon at a time). Scrape up remaining flour and sift out any dried bits. Continue kneading and dusting with flour (photo 4) until dough is no longer sticky and springs back when pressed in center. Reserve any remaining flour. Cover dough with plastic wrap; let rest 1 hour.

• Divide dough in half, keeping reserved dough covered to prevent drying. Working with 1 portion at a time, pass dough through smooth rollers of pasta machine on widest setting. Brush dough with flour, using a pastry brush (photo 5); fold in half, and brush both sides with flour. Repeat procedure 8 times for each portion of dough until smooth and pliable.

• Cut each portion of dough into 3 pieces. Pass each piece once through rollers 2 through 6, brushing with flour if dough becomes sticky. Pass each piece through cutting rollers of pasta machine (photo 6). Hang pasta to dry on a wooden rack no longer than 30 minutes. Repeat with remaining dough.

• Combine 3 quarts water and 1 teaspoon salt in a Dutch oven, and bring to a boil. Add pasta, and cook 2 to 3 minutes or until al dente. Serve with desired sauce. Yield: 8 cups.

pasta machine There are two types of pasta machines: the roller type and the extruder type. Roller-type machines can be hand-cranked or electric with smooth rollers that roll and flatten the dough; another notched roller is attached, which cuts the dough into ribbonlike noodles. Extruder machines are electrical appliances that mix dough and force it through plates of various sizes and shapes, producing solid or hollow-shaped pastas.

pasteurize (PAS chuh rys) To heat milk or other liquids to a high temperature to kill bacteria and destroy enzymes that cause spoilage. All grade A milk must be pasteurized prior to retail sale. (*see also* **homogenize** *and* **milk**)

pastitsio (pah STEE tshis oh) A Greek casserole consisting of pasta, ground beef or lamb, grated cheese, tomatoes, and a béchamel sauce flavored with cinnamon. (*see also* **béchamel sauce**)

pastrami (puh STRAH mee) A cut of beef from the plate, brisket, or round that has been rubbed with salt and a seasoning paste of garlic, peppercorns, red pepper, cinnamon, cloves, and coriander, then dry-cured, smoked, and cooked. Pastrami is typically served hot or cold in sandwiches.

pastry This term generally describes unleavened dough made with flour and shortening that's used for pie or tart shells. Pastry is also sometimes used to wrap meats, poultry, game, or seafood for baking and special presentation. But several other types of pastry are also popular: Puff pastry is made from extra rich pastry dough and has butter layered or worked into it; choux pas-

STEPS TO PERFECT PASTRY

1. Cut fat into flour mixture, using a pastry blender, until mixture is crumbly.

2. Sprinkle ice water evenly over surface. Stir just until the dry ingredients are moistened.

3. Gather dough into a ball or flat disc. Cover and chill at least 30 minutes.

4. Roll dough with a rolling pin to ⅛-inch thickness; carefully roll dough onto pin, and then unroll into pieplate.

5. Another way to transfer dough is to fold it in half and then in half again; place point in center of pieplate. Unfold.

6. When baking pastry without a filling, prick bottom and sides with a fork. Do not prick pastry if it is to be filled before baking.

try is made with butter, milk, flour, and eggs; and paper-thin phyllo pastry is made with flour and water and usually layered with butter or vegetable cooking spray. Sometimes the term "pastry" is used broadly and imprecisely to describe all fancy sweet baked goods including cakes, sweet rolls, and cookies. (*see also* **choux pastry; crimp; croûte, en; crust; phyllo; pie;** *and* **puff pastry**)

RESCUE for solving pastry problems:

Tough pastry: Too little fat, too much water, overmixing, too much flour added, kneading the dough

Crumbly crust: Too little water, too much fat, self-rising flour used, insufficient mixing

Soggy bottom crust: Filling too moist, oven temperature too low, too much liquid in pastry

Crust shrinks: Pastry stretched to fit in the pan, dough uneven in thickness, rolling dough back and forth with rolling pin

TIMESAVING TIP

If you're in a pinch for time, use a 15-ounce package of refrigerated piecrusts instead of homemade pastry. Note that two piecrusts come in each package, so be sure to refrigerate or freeze the one that's leftover. For testing, we use the Pillsbury Ready Crust brand.

BASIC PASTRY FOR A SINGLE 9-INCH PIE

1¼ cups all-purpose flour
½ teaspoon salt

⅓ cup plus 1 tablespoon shortening
3 to 4 tablespoons ice water

• Combine flour and salt; cut in shortening with a pastry blender until mixture is crumbly (photo 1). Sprinkle ice water, 1 tablespoon at a time, evenly over surface; stir with a fork until dry ingredients are moistened (photo 2). Shape into a ball; cover and chill until ready to use (photo 3).

• Roll pastry to ⅛-inch thickness on a lightly floured surface. Place in 9-inch pieplate (photos 4 and 5); trim off excess pastry along edges. Fold edges under, and crimp. Chill.

• For baked pastry shell, prick bottom and sides of pastry shell

TEST KITCHEN SECRET

The key to making flaky pastry begins with measuring ingredients accurately and mixing them properly. If proportions of fat to flour to liquid are off even slightly or if you overwork the dough, your pastry can turn out tough or crumbly. Jan Moon

with a fork (photo 6). Chill pastry until ready to bake. Bake at 450° for 10 to 12 minutes or until golden. Yield: 8 servings.

DOUBLE-CRUST PASTRY

2 cups all-purpose flour
1 teaspoon salt

⅔ cup plus 2 tablespoons shortening
4 to 5 tablespoons ice water

• Combine flour and salt; cut in shortening with a pastry blender until mixture is crumbly. Sprinkle ice water, 1 tablespoon at a time, evenly over surface; stir with a fork until dry ingredients are moistened. Shape into a ball; chill until ready to use. Roll and fit pastry into pieplate as recipe directs. Follow desired pie recipe for baking. Yield: 8 servings.

pastry bag A cone-shaped bag with two open ends, the smaller of which can be fitted with a plastic or metal decorative tip. The large end of the bag is filled with icing, whipped cream, custard filling, or dough or batter, which is squeezed through the tip to form decorative patterns or designs; the bags are an efficient tool for decorating cakes and shaping batters for cookies and pastries. Pastry bags, also known as piping bags, come in various sizes and are made of nylon and plastic-lined cotton or canvas; they can be purchased in gourmet shops, cake decorating shops, and some supermarkets. (*see also* **cake decorating** *and* **parchment paper**)

> **TIMESAVING TIP**
> To quickly improvise a pastry bag, fill a heavy-duty zip-top plastic bag and snip off the tip of one corner with scissors. Parchment paper can also be used to fashion a pastry bag.

pastry blender (*see* **baking tools**)

pastry brush (*see* **baking tools**)

pastry wheel A sharp wheel on a wooden or metal handle used for cutting or scoring pastry; it's preferable to a knife since it cuts evenly and doesn't disturb the dough. Most pastry wheels have straight edges, but some have fluted edges. Pastry wheels are popularly used to cut pizza into slices.

pâte (PAHT) French term for pastry, paste, batter, or dough.

pâté (pah TAY) An elegant mixture of ground meat that resembles meat loaf. Pâté, made from seasoned, ground pork, veal, liver, ham, fish, poultry, or game can have a smooth or coarse texture; cream, cognac, eggs, vegetables, nuts, and spices might also be included. Some pâtés are cooked in a pastry crust, in which case they are referred to as pâté en croûte; others are cooked in a terrine or mold. Pâté may be served hot or cold as a first course or appetizer; it can be prepared at home or purchased in the deli section of gourmet markets or supermarkets.

> **LITE BITE**
> Modern variations of pâtés are popping up that are meatless. They may be made of mushrooms or vegetables for example.

Storage: Wrap pâté in plastic wrap and keep in the refrigerator up to a week. Often the flavor actually improves if the pâté is left to rest in the refrigerator for several days. (*see also* **croûte, en;** *and* **terrine**)

pattypan squash Small, round, flat, white summer squash with scalloped edges. Pattypan squash are prepared in the same manner as other summer squash. (*see also* **squash**)

patty shell A small, baked cup-shaped shell, usually made of puff pastry, used to hold individual servings of creamed meat, chicken, or shellfish. Freshly baked patty shells can be purchased in some bakeries, but frozen, unbaked shells are available in most supermarkets. (*see also* **puff pastry**)

paw paw (PAW paw) (*see* **papaya**)

pea All of the many varieties of peas are members of the legume family. Some varieties, such as the sweet green pea, are eaten fresh, removed from their pods; others, such as yellow and green split peas, are used dried. There are also varieties that are eaten pod and all, such as the sugar snap pea or snow pea.
Storage: The sugar in fresh peas quickly converts to starch, so it's important that they be prepared and eaten as soon as possible after picking, usually within 2 to 3 days; they should be stored in a plastic bag in the refrigerator. Store dried peas in an airtight container at room temperature in a cool, dry place up to a year. (*see also* **black-eyed pea, chickpea, field pea, snow pea, sugar snap pea, sweet green pea,** *and* **vegetables**)

pea bean Also known as a French kidney bean, this is the smallest of the dried white beans. Pea beans are typically used in baked beans and soups; they require long, slow cooking. (*see also* **beans, dried**)

peach A golden yellow, fuzzy round fruit with yellow or white meat surrounding a brownish-red pit. Peaches are sweet, juicy, and fragrant; they are often classified as clingstone or freestone, depending on how difficult or easy it is to separate the pit from the flesh. Peaches make excellent jams, pies, and sauces; they can also be used in salads, desserts, pies, cakes, and ice cream.
Selection: A deep gold or yellow skin is the sign of a ripe peach, not the rosy blush, which distinguishes certain varieties. A strong, perfumy aroma is also a sign of ripeness. Don't buy peaches with wrinkles or brown spots.
Storage: Peaches bruise easily, so handle them with care. Use the softest fruit first. Serve ripe peaches immediately, or store in refrigerator. For the fullest flavor, serve ripe peaches at room temperature. Store unripe peaches in a loosely covered paper bag or bowl. Check them daily; peaches are ripe when they yield slightly to gentle pressure.
Peach poundage: 1 pound of peaches (2 large or 3 medium) yields:
- 2 cups sliced peaches, or
- 1⅔ cups chopped peaches, or
- 1½ cups pureed peaches

TEST KITCHEN SECRET

To prevent sliced peaches from browning, sprinkle lemon juice or orange juice over them and toss gently. LYDA JONES

TIMESAVING TIP
To speed ripening, place peaches in a loosely closed paper bag at room temperature for 1 to 3 days. Check them daily because ripening can occur very rapidly.

peach Melba A dessert made with poached peach halves, vanilla ice cream, and raspberry sauce. Peach Melba was created in the late 1800s by French chef Auguste Escoffier for Dame Nellie Melba, a popular Australian opera singer. (*see also* **Melba sauce**)

PEACH MELBA

1 (10- or 12-ounce) package frozen raspberries (not in syrup)	1 tablespoon orange liqueur
½ cup red currant jelly	1 tablespoon cornstarch
1 tablespoon water	6 canned peach halves
	Vanilla ice cream

• Place raspberries in a 1½-quart glass bowl; microwave at MEDIUM (50% power) for 3 to 4½ minutes or until thawed. Press raspberries through a food mill or sieve; discard seeds. Add jelly to raspberry puree; microwave at MEDIUM for 2 to 4 minutes or until jelly melts. Stir well.

• Combine water and liqueur; stir in cornstarch. Add cornstarch mixture to raspberry mixture, stirring well; microwave at HIGH for 1½ to 3 minutes or until mixture thickens. Stir well. Chill.

• Place each peach half cut side up in an individual dessert dish; top each peach with a scoop of vanilla ice cream. Pour raspberry sauce over top of ice cream. Yield: 6 servings.

peanut Though we use them as a nut, peanuts are actually legumes from a plant that bears seeds in pods grown underground. Peanuts have a papery brown skin and are contained in a thin, netted, tan-colored shell or pod. Each year, much of the peanut crop is used to make peanut butter and peanut oil. Peanuts can also be used in making candy, soups, breads, cookies, and cakes; they can also be added to Asian stir-fries and noodle dishes. Purchase peanuts unshelled and shelled, with or without their papery skins, raw or roasted, salted or unsalted, and mixed with other nuts in bags or vacuum-sealed jars and cans.

Southernism

Jimmy Carter, the favorite son of Plains, Georgia, made the humble peanut famous in 1976, when he became the first and only peanut farmer to be elected President of the United States. Suddenly the world was cooking peanuts…they roasted and fried them. The boiled peanut stepped into the spotlight, as well. The recipe was simple: wash a gallon of fresh, unshelled green peanuts and place in a large pot. Cover with water, add salt, and boil until tender. Then let stand in the water until cool. Eat one and you'll eat a dozen, so grab something to catch the hulls!

TEST KITCHEN SECRET

Raw peanuts can be roasted in the shell by spreading them out in a shallow baking pan. Bake at 350° for 25 to 30 minutes, stirring occasionally. Roast shelled peanuts the same way for 15 minutes or until golden. JAN MOON

Storage: Raw peanuts in the shell keep about 9 months in the refrigerator or indefinitely, if frozen. Raw, shelled peanuts keep 3 to 6 months in the refrigerator and indefinitely if frozen. Roasted peanuts will keep at room temperature for about a month; for longer storage, keep in an airtight container in the refrigerator up to 6 months. Vacuum-packed peanuts will keep up to a year, but once opened, should be refrigerated in an airtight container. (*see also* **fats and oils** *and* **peanut butter**)

Q **Is there any real difference between cocktail peanuts, dry-roasted peanuts, boiled peanuts, and raw peanuts?**

A Cocktail peanuts have usually been roasted in oil, and sometimes still wear their red skins. Dry-roasted peanuts are roasted by dry heat so they aren't quite as moist. Boiled peanuts have been boiled and are wet and mushy. Raw peanuts have an uncooked taste and are typically used in recipes, such as peanut brittle, where they will be cooked; they can also be fried and eaten as a snack. Sometimes raw peanuts can be difficult to find; look for them at produce stands or in the produce section of your supermarket.

peanut butter A spreadable blend of ground peanuts, vegetable oil, and salt sold in two forms: smooth or chunky. Most peanut butter is used as a sandwich spread, but it can also be used in recipes for pies, cakes, and cookies. While commercially made peanut butter is by far the most popular, it can be made at home in a blender or food processor.

Storage: An unopened jar of regular peanut butter will stay fresh in a cool, dry place up to 2 years; once opened, the flavor will deteriorate after 3 months. If refrigerated, it will keep up to 6 months. (*see also* **peanut**)

PEANUT BUTTER-BANANA PIE

40 vanilla wafers
⅓ cup honey-roasted peanuts
½ cup butter or margarine, melted
1⅓ cups firmly packed dark brown sugar, divided
1 (8-ounce) package cream cheese, softened

¾ cup creamy peanut butter
1 cup whipping cream, divided
1 teaspoon vanilla extract
2 bananas
Chopped honey-roasted peanuts (optional)

• Process first 3 ingredients and ⅓ cup brown sugar in a food processor until crumbly. Press mixture into bottom and up sides of a 10-inch deep-dish pieplate. Bake at 350° for 5 minutes. Set piecrust aside.
• Beat remaining 1 cup brown sugar, cream cheese, peanut butter, and 1 tablespoon whipping cream at medium speed with an electric mixer until mixture is light and fluffy. Set aside.
• Beat remaining whipping cream and vanilla until stiff peaks form. Fold one-third of whipped cream into peanut butter mixture; fold peanut butter mixture into remaining whipped cream.
• Slice bananas, and place on crust. Spread peanut butter mixture evenly over bananas. Sprinkle with chopped peanuts, if desired. Chill 2 hours. Yield: 1 (10-inch) pie.

P

peanut oil (*see* **fats and oils**)

pear A sweet, fragrant tree fruit that has a soft, juicy flesh. There are hundreds of varieties; some of the more commonly available ones include:
• **Anjou:** Egg-shaped with greenish-yellow or red skin. They're good for slicing into salads, cooking in desserts, or baking whole, and are available from October to May.
• **Asian:** Round, firm, applelike with golden brown to green skin. They're juicy and sweet, have a crunchy texture, and are good for eating or cooking.
• **Bartlett:** Bell-shaped with yellow or red skin. They're good for eating, canning, and cooking, and are available from August to November.

TEST KITCHEN SECRET

If you need to speed the ripening process, wrap pears separately in newspaper, and put in a cardboard box or paper bag. Let stand at room temperature until they yield to gentle pressure at the stem end. VANESSA MCNEIL

• **Bosc:** Has a long, tapered neck and green skin with a distinct brown-russet-colored skin. They're good for eating fresh or for baking, poaching, and broiling, and are in season from September to May.
• **Comice:** Chubby and round and has green or greenish-yellow skin that sometimes has a red blush on one side and a thick, short stem. They're good for eating fresh, but aren't recommended for cooking.
• **Nelis:** Egg-shaped with russet-colored skin. They're a good choice for eating fresh, for baking, or poaching, and are available from November to May.
• **Seckel:** Small, egg-shaped with dark green to red or totally reddish skin. They're good for eating fresh, for pickling, canning, and preserves, and are available from August to January.

Q **What is the best way to core a pear?**
A Cut pears in half lengthwise and scoop out the core with a melon baller or grapefruit spoon. Toss cut pears with a little citrus or pineapple juice to prevent discoloring.

Pears don't ripen well on trees; they're picked when mature, but not ripe. You'll know when a pear is ripe by applying gentle pressure at the base of the stem. If it yields slightly to pressure, it's ripe. Remember that color is not always a good indicator of ripeness. Pears are also available dried as well as canned.
Storage: Once ripened, fresh pears will keep for several days in the refrigerator. Don't store in plastic bags.

pearl barley (*see* **barley** *and* **grain**)

pearl onion (*see* **onion**)

pecan A native American nut from the pecan tree. A member of the hickory family, pecan trees are widely grown in Georgia, Oklahoma, and

Texas. Pecans have a smooth, oval, tan and brown shell that contains two deeply crinkled lobes of golden brown nutmeat. The flavor of pecan is sweet and delicate, but rich and buttery. Shelled pecans can be purchased chopped or in halves in supermarkets; unshelled pecans are at their peak during autumn months.

While pecans are good for eating, they are most prized for the contribution they make to cakes, pies, and cookies as well as to many meat and vegetable dishes.

Storage: Pecans in the shell will stay fresh in a cool, dry place up to 6 months. Shelled nuts can be kept in an airtight container in the refrigerator up to a year or in the freezer for 2 years or longer. (*see also* **hickory nut** *and* **nuts**)

Southernism

Whether it's pronounced pih-KAHN pie, pih-KAN pie, or even PEE-kan pie may still be up for debate, but the verdict is in on the palatability. It's 100% delicious and 100% Southern. Of the many varieties of nut pies that appear on Southern tables, the pecan pie is probably the most popular. This golden, gooey pie is beloved for its sweet contribution to the Southern holiday sideboard.

PECAN PIE

½ (15-ounce) package
   refrigerated piecrusts
4 large eggs
¾ cup sugar
1 cup light corn syrup
½ cup butter or margarine,
   melted

¼ cup firmly packed light brown
   sugar
1 teaspoon vanilla extract
¼ teaspoon salt
1 cup pecans, coarsely chopped

• Unfold 1 piecrust, and roll to press out fold lines. Fit into a 9-inch pieplate according to package directions; fold edges under, and crimp.
• Whisk together eggs and next 6 ingredients in a saucepan over low heat until well blended. Pour into piecrust, and sprinkle with pecans.
• Bake at 350° on lower rack 30 minutes or until pie is set. Yield: 1 (9-inch) pie.

pectin (PEHK tihn) A natural, water-soluble substance used to help thicken jams, jellies, and preserves. Pectin occurs naturally in some fruits. How much pectin a fruit contains depends upon the fruit and its stage of ripeness; it's usually concentrated in the seeds and skin of tart, underripe fruits, and diminishes as the fruit ripens. If the fruit doesn't have enough natural pectin, then commercial pectin must be added to make the jam or jelly "jell." Commercial pectin is available in liquid and powdered forms. Keep in mind that pectin will work correctly only when the proper balance of sugar and acid is present. (*see also* **jam, jelly,** *and* **preserves**)

peel The skin, rind, or outer covering of a fruit or vegetable. This term also refers to the process of removing the skin or rind from a fruit or vegetable.

Peking duck (PEE king) A Mandarin Chinese dish consisting of a duck whose skin is separated from the meat by pumped air. The duck is then coated with a honey mixture and hung until the skin is dry; afterwards, the duck is roasted. When served, the duck has a shining golden exterior, crisp skin, and is moist and succulent inside. The most common way to eat Peking duck is to cut it into thin slices, and roll it up with pieces of cucumber in fine pancakes brushed with bean paste. (*see also* **duck** *and* **duckling**)

pekoe tea (PEE koh) The medium-size grade of slightly coarse, black tea leaves. Orange pekoe is the grade for the smallest leaves. (*see also* **tea**)

penuche (puh NOO chee) A fudgelike Mexican candy made with brown sugar, butter, milk or cream, and vanilla; sometimes nuts are added. Penuche has a golden brown color and caramel flavor. (*see also* **candy** *and* **fudge**)

pepitas (puh PEE tahs) Roasted pumpkin seeds that are eaten as a snack or used in Mexican cooking. The hulled seeds have a pale green color and delicate flavor. Pepitas can be purchased in health-food stores, Mexican markets, and some supermarkets, or you can make your own from leftover pumpkin seeds.

TEST KITCHEN SECRET

"To toast pumpkin seeds, sauté them in a little canola oil until lightly browned. Then transfer them to a baking sheet and sprinkle with salt. Bake the seeds at 350° for 10 minutes or until crisp; drain on paper towels and cool. Store the seeds in an airtight container in the refrigerator up to a month." REBECCA KRACKE GORDON

pepper, black (*see* **peppercorn** *and* **spice**)

peppercorn The tiny berries of the pepper plant, which is a climbing vine native to India and Indonesia. The berries have a brown color when fully ripened, but are available in

Q **Does ground red pepper come from peppercorns? Where do pink peppercorns come from?**

A Ground red pepper comes from dried red cayenne peppers, not peppercorns. Pink peppercorns aren't really peppercorns at all, but the berry of a South American rose plant; they have a bitter, pinelike flavor, and are available dried or pickled.

three varieties that are harvested at different stages of maturity:
• *Black peppercorns* are picked immature and sun-dried until they turned dark and wrinkled. Inside, is a lighter colored core; that's why ground black pepper has a mixture of dark and light powder. It has a warm, pungent aroma and flavor, and comes whole, cracked, and ground.
• *Green peppercorns* are tender, immature berries that can be freeze-dried or

packed in brine, water, or vinegar. They have a milder flavor, a softer texture, and are easier to crush than other varieties.

• *White peppercorns* are mature berries that have been hulled, exposing a white inner core. They have a pungent flavor, but are milder than a black peppercorn and come whole or ground.

Storage: Store ground pepper and peppercorns in a cool, dry, dark place. Whole peppercorns will keep almost indefinitely, but ground pepper needs to be replaced every 3 months. (*see also* **spice**)

pepperoni (pehp puh ROH nee) A hard, spicy, air-dried Italian sausage made of beef and pork and seasoned with red and black pepper. Pepperoni comes ready to eat and is often sliced thin and served as an appetizer; it's a popular topping for pizza. (*see also* **sausage**)

peppers Though classified as a fruit and a member of the capsicum family, peppers are enjoyed as a vegetable and a seasoning. They vary in size and shape, but most peppers are hollow pods with internal white ribs to which tiny seeds are attached. Peppers come in a variety of colors and range in flavor from delicately sweet to fiery hot.

The sweet varieties include red, green, yellow, orange, brown, or purple bell peppers; the green version is usually a bit sharper in flavor and less expensive. These mild-flavored peppers can be used raw in salads, cooked in sauces, simmered in soups or stews, and in relishes and baked dishes. In addition, large bell peppers can be stuffed and roasted or grilled. Red bell peppers are often roasted and peeled, and sometimes flavored with

olive oil or preserved in brine and turned into pimiento. Bell peppers can be stored in a plastic bag in the refrigerator up to a week.

The hot varieties, often called chiles or chile peppers, can pack a fiery punch. Many types of chiles, including fresh and dried, are widely available. Among the most popular are:

• **Anaheim (AN uh hym):** A mild, fresh green chile about 6 to 10 inches long used for making chiles rellenos; they are also available chopped and canned.

Anaheim

ancho

• **Ancho (AHN cho):** A dried poblano pepper; it has a dark reddish-brown color and is used for making chili powder. (*continued on the following page*)

- **Banana:** Long, yellow fresh chile with a mild flavor; it turns red when mature. It's used in salads, stuffed, or pickled.
- **Cascabel (KAHS sah behl):** Small, round dried chile with a dark red color; it has a medium-hot, slightly acidic, toasted flavor that's good in sauces and soups.
- **Cayenne (KI yen):** Tiny, narrow red pepper about 3 inches long with a hot, smoky flavor. It's often ground into red pepper.

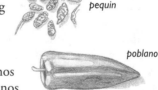
cayenne

- **Chipotle (chih POHT lay):** A smoked and dried jalapeño pepper about 3 inches long with wrinkled skin and a dull reddish color. It can be purchased dried or canned, and is sometimes used to made adobo sauce, a seasoning paste.
- **Fresno:** A mild to very hot fresh chile about 3 inches long; it can be red, yellow, or green. It's used mostly for seasoning, sauces, and pickling.
- **Guajillo (gwah HEE yoh):** A narrow, dark red dried chile about 5 or 6 inches long with a hot, bold flavor. If fresh, it's called a mirasol pepper and is popular for stews and sauces.

guajillo

- **Habanero (ah bah NEH roh):** A small fresh or dried chile about 1 to 2 inches long and considered one of the hottest chiles. If fresh, they are most often green; the dried are dark red.
- **Jalapeño:** A fresh green chile with a mildly hot to fiery hot flavor. It's also sold canned, whole or sliced, and pickled.

jalapeño

- **Mulato (moo LAH toh):** A sweet mild-to-hot dried chile about 5 inches long and almost black.
- **Pasilla (pah SEE yah):** A long, slender dried chile with a brownish black color and hot flavor.
- **Pequin (pay KEEN):** A tiny, oval, very hot fresh or dried chile about ½-inch long and orange-red in color.

pequin

- **Poblano (poh BLAH noh):** A large, fairly mild dark green, fresh chile about 5 inches long. Often stuffed for chiles rellenos or roasted and peeled. When dried, poblanos become ancho chiles.

poblano

- **Serrano (seh RAH noh):** Small, slender fresh green to red chiles with hot flavor. It's often made into salsa.
- **Tabasco:** Red or yellow pods used almost exclusively for making Tabasco® hot sauce.
- **Thai:** Also known as bird chiles, these are small, thin, green or red chiles about 1 inch long with a very hot flavor.

Storage: Fresh chiles should be kept at room temperature and used within 2 days. If refrigerated, they will keep up to a week. Dried chiles can be hung

in a corner of your kitchen or pantry, but they last longer if stored in an air-tight container away from light and moisture.
(*see also* **Anaheim chile pepper, ancho chile pepper, banana pepper, bell pepper, cayenne pepper, chile pepper, chiles rellenos, chipotle chile pepper, habanero chile pepper, jalapeño, pimiento, poblano chile, serrano chile, Tabasco pepper,** *and* **vegetables**)

pepper steak A Chinese stir-fry dish made from thin strips of beef, green pepper, and onions cooked in a soy sauce mixture. In France, pepper steak is made from a beef steak that has been coated with coarsely ground black peppercorns, sautéed in butter, and served with a sauce made from pan drippings, wine, and cream; sometimes it's flamed with brandy or Cognac and called steak au poivre. (*see also* **brandy, Cognac,** *and* **steak au poivre**)

SIMPLE AND SUMPTUOUS PEPPER STEAK

¼ cup cornstarch, divided	1 pound boneless top sirloin
½ teaspoon ground ginger	steak, cut into thin slices
1 (10½-ounce) can beef broth	1 tablespoon vegetable oil
2 tablespoons soy sauce	2 teaspoons sesame oil
½ teaspoon dried crushed red	1 garlic clove, pressed
pepper (optional)	1 green bell pepper, sliced
½ teaspoon salt	1 medium onion, sliced
½ teaspoon pepper	Hot cooked rice

• Whisk together 2 tablespoons cornstarch, ginger, beef broth, soy sauce, and, if desired, red pepper; set aside.
• Combine remaining 2 tablespoons cornstarch, salt, and pepper; dredge steak in mixture.
• Heat vegetable oil and sesame oil in a large skillet over high heat 3 minutes; add steak slices and garlic, and sauté 4 minutes or until browned.
• Add bell pepper and onion; sauté 8 minutes or until tender. Stir in broth mixture; reduce heat, and simmer 3 to 5 minutes or until thickened. Serve over rice. Yield: 6 servings.

perch Various freshwater fish with spiny fins found in North America and Europe. The most familiar variety in the United States is the yellow perch with an olive-green back, dark vertical bands, and red-orange fins. They have firm flesh with a delicate, mild flavor, and are best pan-fried, broiled, sautéed, baked, or used in soups and stews. There are also several saltwater fish that are incorrectly identified as perch including the white perch (a member of the bass family), and ocean perch (a member of the rockfish family).

Pernod (pair NOH) Anise- or licorice-flavored liqueur that's popular in France. Pernod cocktails are mixed with water, sugar, and angostura bitters. (*see also* **bitters** *and* **liqueur**)

persimmon (puhr SIHM uhn) A soft-
textured winter fruit with red-orange skin and flesh.
Sometimes called "the apple of the Orient," persimmons come in two varieties: the Hachiya or Japanese persimmon and the Fuyu persimmon. The Hachiya is larger, acorn-shaped,
softer, and is bitter unless ripe; the Fuyu tends to be smaller, tomato-shaped,
firmer, and sweeter. Persimmons can be eaten out-of-hand or added to quick
breads, custard, ice cream, or pie.
Storage: Always allow persimmons to ripen at room temperature; the
Hachiya will be soft to the touch when ripe, but the Fuyu will be firm.
Once ripened, refrigerate persimmons, and use as soon as possible, or place
in an airtight container whole and freeze up to 3 months.

pesto (PEH stoh) An Italian sauce made from basil, garlic, olive oil, pine
nuts, and Parmesan cheese. Pesto can be made by crushing the ingredients
with a mortar and pestle
or by using a food processor; it's used as an ingredient in appetizers or as a
topping for pasta. (*see also*
basil, food processor,
and **mortar and pestle**)

> **TIMESAVING TIP**
> When you're in a hurry for pesto or don't
> have enough fresh basil, try commercially made
> pesto; you can find it in jars near the Parmesan
> cheese or pasta section of your supermarket or
> in tubs in the refrigerated section.

PESTO

2 cups fresh basil leaves (1 large bunch)	2 garlic cloves
¼ cup chopped walnuts or pine nuts	1 teaspoon salt
¼ cup olive oil	¼ cup freshly grated Parmesan cheese
2 teaspoons lemon juice	2 tablespoons freshly grated Romano cheese

• Process first 6 ingredients in a food processor or blender 2 minutes or
until smooth, stopping twice to scrape down sides. Stir in cheeses.

TEST KITCHEN SECRET

"*A batch of pesto can usually be used for more than
one recipe, so make sure the leftovers are properly
stored. Press a sheet of plastic wrap directly onto the
surface of the leftover pesto, and refrigerate for several days. Or, spoon the leftover pesto into ice cube
trays and freeze; pop the frozen cubes out, and store
in a freezer bag up to a month.*" MARY ALLEN PERRY

• Toss desired
amount of pesto with
hot cooked pasta, or
spoon 2 tablespoons
pesto into 6 sections
of an ice cube tray;
cover and freeze up to
3 months. Thaw and
reheat slowly before
serving. Yield: ⅔ cup.

petit four (PEH tee fohr) Bite-size sponge or layer cake cut into squares, diamonds, or circles and glazed with a ganache or other icing. Petit fours are sometimes elaborately decorated with icings of contrasting colors, melted chocolate, or piped flowers and leaves. They're usually served on special occasions such as bridal or baby showers or for tea. (*see also* **ganache**)

pfeffernüesse (FEHF fuhr noos) Hard, round German Christmas cookies flavored with spices and black pepper.

pheasant (*see* **wild game**)

phyllo (FEE loh) Greek pastry dough that comes in tissue-thin layers made of flour and water. Multiple sheets of phyllo are typically layered with melted butter or vegetable cooking spray and used in making sweet and savory dishes such as baklava and spanakopita. Phyllo can be made at home, but it can also be purchased frozen in many supermarkets; some Greek markets sell fresh phyllo pastry. (*see also* **baklava, pastry,** *and* **spanakopita**)

> ### TEST KITCHEN SECRET
>
> *Thaw phyllo in its package as the label directs, typically overnight, and work with only one sheet of pastry at a time, keeping the remaining sheets covered with a damp towel; if left uncovered, it will become brittle. Also, brush each sheet generously with melted butter; this makes the layers crisp when baked.* VANESSA MCNEIL

> ### LITE BITE
> We've had equally good luck coating phyllo with vegetable cooking spray instead of butter, saving calories and fat.

picadillo (pee kah DEE yoh) A Spanish hash made from ground pork and beef or veal, and tomatoes, garlic, and onions. In Mexico picadillo is used as a stuffing; in Cuba it's served as a sauce over black beans and rice.

piccalilli (PIHK uh lih lee) A zesty pickled English relish made from a mixture of pickled tomatoes, sweet peppers, onions, zucchini, cucumber, cauliflower, and cabbage. Piccalilli is flavored with brown sugar, allspice, and vinegar, and is typically served as an accompaniment with other vegetable or meat dishes.

piccata (pih CAH tuh) An Italian dish of thinly sliced meat or poultry that has been lightly floured, sautéed in butter, and sprinkled with lemon juice. (*see recipe on the following page*)

VEAL PICCATA

1 pound veal cutlets	3 tablespoons lemon juice
1 teaspoon salt	2 garlic cloves, minced
½ teaspoon pepper	3 tablespoons dry white wine
½ cup all-purpose flour	1 tablespoon chopped fresh
3 tablespoons butter	parsley
2 tablespoons olive oil	

• Place veal between 2 sheets of plastic wrap or wax paper, and flatten to ¼-inch thickness, using a meat mallet or rolling pin. Cut veal into 6 serving-size pieces. Pat veal dry. Rub salt and pepper on veal, and dredge in flour.
• Heat butter and oil in a large skillet over medium-high heat. Add veal in 2 batches, and cook 1 to 2 minutes on each side. Remove veal to a warm platter; cover and keep warm. Drain drippings.
• Add lemon juice, garlic, and white wine to skillet, stirring to loosen particles from bottom of skillet; cook over medium heat 1 to 2 minutes. To serve, spoon juices over veal; sprinkle with parsley. Yield: 4 servings.

pickle Food that has been preserved in seasoned brine or vinegar. Some foods frequently pickled include beets, cucumbers, okra, onions, cauliflower, baby corn, watermelon rind, pig's feet, herring, and peeled, hard-cooked eggs. Pickles are often served as condiments and sometimes as appetizers or snacks. Pickles can be made at home or bought in jars at the supermarket.

When making pickles at home, start with fresh, firm ingredients; for extra crispness, refrigerate vegetables prior to pickling. Make sure your vinegar is at least 5% acidity; distilled white vinegar, white wine vinegar, and cider vinegar can be used. Season pickles with granulated uniodized pickling or canning salt. Also, use white, granulated sugar and whole spices; ground spices will make the brine cloudy.

RESCUE for pickle problems:
Soft or slippery pickles:
• Blossom ends not removed
• Vinegar of too low acidity used
• Not enough salt in brine
• Cucumbers not submerged in brine
• Improper processing

Hollow pickles:
• Cucumbers too large
• Too much time between picking and brining
• Improper brining process

Shriveled pickles:
• Brine or vinegar too strong
• Syrup too heavy
• Overcooking or overprocessing
• Too much time between picking and brining
• Dry weather during vegetable growth

Dark or discolored pickles:
• Hard water used
• Spices left in pickles
• Iodized salt used
• Ground spices used

Spoilage:
• Processing time too short
• Canning jars and/or new lids not used
• Ingredients not measured accurately
• Vinegar that has lost strength used

For best results, invest in a water-bath canner with a rack, standard canning jars, new metal lids, metal bands, jar filler or funnel, jar lifter, nonmetal spatula, kitchen timer, and a slotted spoon. Always use sterilized jars and lids. When the pickles are ready, place them firmly in the hot, sterilized jars, and cover with boiling syrup or brine, leaving ¼-inch headspace. Run a non-metal spatula around the inside edge of jars to remove air bubbles, and wipe jar rims clean before putting the metal lids in place. Then screw on metal bands.

> **TIMESAVING TIP**
> Refrigerator pickles, made in small batches, stored in the refrigerator, and eaten within 1 to 2 weeks, do not need to be packed in sterilized jars or processed.

To process pickles in a water bath, put the jars on a rack in the canner filled with simmering water covering the jar tops by 2 to 3 inches. Start to count processing time when the water reaches a boil. The USDA recommends processing at least 10 minutes for pint-size jars and 20 minutes for quart-size jars. After processing, let the jars cool and then store 4 to 5 weeks before opening. For more information about canning, visit **homecanning.com** or contact your local county Extension Cooperative System. (*see also* **boiling water bath, brine, pickled eggs, pickling spice, salt,** *and* **vinegar**)

pickled eggs Shelled hard-cooked eggs that have been immersed in a brine or vinegar. Pickled eggs are sometimes available for purchase at casual bars, where their salty, vinegar flavor compliments cold beer.

pickling spice A pungent blend of herbs, spices, and seeds used to flavor the brine or vinegar solution used in making pickles, relishes, and preserved meats. The spice blend varies, but often includes whole or broken allspice, bay leaves, cardamom, coriander, cinnamon, cloves, ginger, mustard seeds, and peppercorns. Packaged pickling spice mix is sold in most supermarkets.

picnic ham A cut of pork taken from the arm shoulder or the foreleg. True ham comes from the pig's back leg, so this cut is actually a picnic shoulder or pork shoulder, even though it looks and tastes similar to ham. Picnic ham is often deboned and smoked, which gives it hamlike flavor; it's a less-expensive substitute for regular ham. (*see also* **ham**)

pico de gallo (PEE koh day GI yoh) A zesty relish made of chopped jícama, onions, bell pepper, oranges, jalapeño, and cucumbers; it's popular throughout Mexico and South America.

pie A sweet or savory dish consisting of a filling in a pastry shell which lines a slope-sided pan or dish. Pies can have just a bottom crust, a top crust, a lattice top crust, or both a bottom and top crust. Sweet pies are usually served for dessert, and savory pies as the main course or appetizer. Savory pies include a range of pot pies and quiches, but there are many different types of sweet pies. They include:

• **Fruit pies:** Double or single-crust pies made with fresh, canned, frozen, or dried fruit filling. Double-crust fruit pies can have a solid or lattice top crust. Single-crust fruit pies can have either a pastry or crumb crust.

• **Chiffon:** Single-crust pie with light, fluffy filling made with gelatin, egg whites, and sometimes whipped cream. They are made with either a pastry or crumb crust and usually require refrigeration.

• **Cream:** Single-crust pie with sweet, creamy, pudding-like filling. They have either a pastry crust or a crumb crust and are topped with meringue, whipped cream, or fruit.

• **Custard:** Single-crust pie with rich, smooth, but firmer filling made from eggs and milk. They usually have a pastry crust and are sometimes topped with whipped cream.

• **Frozen:** Single-crust pie filled with ice cream or a chiffon-type filling. They can have a pastry or crumb crust and are often topped with whipped cream.

Q **Can I freeze my homemade pies?**

A Ice cream pies and some baked pies, particularly fruit pies, freeze well. The texture of the pastry, however, may lose crispness in the freezing and defrosting. The texture of the fruit may soften slightly, too. To freeze baked pies, freeze them unwrapped first, then wrap them so that they're airtight; label and return them to the freezer. Use frozen pies within two months. Thaw baked pies at room temperature for 30 minutes; then reheat at 350° until warm. It's not a good idea to freeze custard, cream, or chiffon pies that contain meringue toppings. The meringue will deteriorate in the freezing and thawing stages. Pies with a primarily egg base in the filling won't freeze well either.

• **Meringue:** Single-crust pie filled with a custard or cream filling and topped with mounds of swirling white meringue. They have a pastry or crumb crust and are always baked after the meringue is spread over a hot filling.

• **Nut and vegetable pies:** Single-crust pies filled with sweet potatoes, pumpkin, pecans, or other nuts. They have a pastry crust and are sometimes served with a dollop of whipped cream on each serving.

Storage: Refrigerate pies containing eggs or dairy products; this includes chiffon, cream, custard, meringue, nut, and vegetable pies. You can store fruit pies at room temperature for a day, but then refrigerate them. Freeze frozen ice cream pies in freezer bags up to 2 weeks. (*see also* **lattice, meringue, pastry, pot pie, quiche,** *and* **tart**)

RESCUE for ailing pies:
- **If the crust shrinks,** the pastry was stretched too tightly. Loosely drape and press pastry into the pieplate or pan to avoid shrinkage; chill it briefly before baking, and add pie weights if prebaking.
- **If the crust browns too fast,** your oven may be too hot or isn't heating evenly. Shield the crust edges with strips of aluminum foil after it turns golden.
- **If the filling bubbles over,** the pie may be too full, the pieplate may not be deep enough, or the filling could contain too much liquid and need to be thickened with additional starch. Place a sheet of aluminum foil on the rack below the pie to catch drips.
- **If the top crust of a double-crust pie sags,** the pie may not have enough filling or the dish could be too deep. Top slices with ice cream before serving.
- **If the pie looks cooked, but is underdone inside,** then loosely wrap it in foil and return it to the oven to cook through.
- **If the top crust of a double-crust pie puffs up too high,** cut slits in the crust before baking to allow steam to escape.
- **If the top crust of a double-crust pie looks dull,** then brush it with milk or water or sprinkle with sugar before baking.
- **If it's hard to cut a neat slice of frozen, cream, or chiffon pie,** then wipe the knife and dip it into hot water between each cut.
- **To avoid messy spills when carrying custard pie to the oven,** place the unfilled pie shell on the oven shelf and then pour in the custard filling.
- **To prevent a skin from forming on a custard pie filling during chilling,** apply plastic wrap directly to the surface of the filling; remove plastic wrap before adding a topping.
- **If custard filling is too firm or tough,** it probably cooked too long. Remove it from the oven when it slightly jiggles 2 inches from the center when you gently pull the oven rack.

---

piecrust (*see* **pastry** *and* **pie**)

pierogi (peer OH gee) Polish in origin, pierogi are small crescent-shaped dumplings filled with seasoned, minced mixtures such as pork, onions, and cottage cheese. They're dropped in boiling water, sautéed in butter, topped with toasted breadcrumbs, and served as a first course or side dish.

pie weights Small metal or ceramic pellets used to keep an unfilled pie pastry shell from puffing up and bursting during baking. (*see also* **pastry**)

pigeon A domesticated type of poultry with dark meat and an earthy, wild flavor. Pigeons are slaughtered when more than 4 weeks old; if less than 4 weeks old, it's referred to as squab. (*see also* **poultry**)

pignoli (*see* **pine nut**)

pig's feet The feet and ankles of pigs; they contain many small bones and connective tissues and require long, slow cooking. Pig's feet can also be served pickled or smoked. They make a flavorful addition to soups and stews. (*see also* **pork** *and* **variety meats**)

pigs in a blanket Sausages wrapped in pastry dough, biscuit dough, or a pancake. The most common example is a cocktail sausage wrapped in pastry dough; it's baked and served as an appetizer.

pike (PYK) A family of freshwater fish that includes the muskellunge and pickerel. They are sometimes referred to as the "shark" of fresh water because of their long body, large mouth, and fierce-looking teeth. The pike has lean, firm, low-fat flesh with a mild flavor, but does contain many small bones. Pike is the traditional fish used in quenelles and gefilte fish. (*see also* **fish, gefilte fish,** *and* **quenelles**)

pilaf (PEE lahf) A grain dish made by sautéing rice or bulghur in butter or oil and cooking in stock. The mixture is simmered without stirring until the liquid is absorbed. Pilaf can be flavored with curry, cooked vegetables, meats, seafood, or poultry, and is served as a side dish or main dish. (*see also* **bulghur** *and* **rice**)

LEMON RICE PILAF

2 tablespoons butter or margarine	3 cups hot cooked rice
4 celery ribs, sliced	2 tablespoons grated lemon rind
6 green onions, chopped	½ teaspoon salt
	¼ teaspoon pepper

• Melt butter in a skillet over medium-high heat; add celery and onions. Sauté until celery is tender. Stir in rice and remaining ingredients; cook over low heat until heated. Yield: 6 servings.

Pilsner (PIHLZ nuhr) A fine, light lager beer in the style of beer originally brewed in Pilsen, a city in the Czech Republic. A pilsner glass is a tall, slender V-shaped, footed glass typically used for serving beer. (*see also* **beer**)

pimiento (pih MYEHN toh) A large, heart-shaped sweet red pepper. Pimiento adds color and flavor to casseroles, sauces, and other dishes; also used to stuff olives. (*see also* **olive** *and* **peppers**)

PIMIENTO CHEESE

1½ cups mayonnaise
1 (4-ounce) jar diced pimiento, drained
1 teaspoon Worcestershire sauce
1 teaspoon finely grated onion

¼ teaspoon ground red pepper
1 (10-ounce) block extra-sharp Cheddar cheese, finely shredded
1 (10-ounce) block sharp Cheddar cheese, shredded

• Stir together first 5 ingredients in a large bowl; stir in cheeses. Store in refrigerator up to 1 week. Yield: 4 cups.

Pimm's cup A gin-based British drink with a refreshing, slightly herbal flavor. Pimm's cup can be mixed with lemonade, soda water, or ginger ale, and is garnished with orange, lemon, or cucumber slices.

piña colada (PEEN yuh koh LAH duh) A cocktail made of rum, pineapple juice, and cream of coconut. This popular tropical drink is served over ice and is sometimes garnished with a wedge of pineapple. To make frozen piña coladas, blend the mixture with crushed ice or ice cream.

THICK 'N' RICH PIÑA COLADAS

1 (8½-ounce) can cream of coconut
1 (8-ounce) can crushed pineapple, drained
⅓ cup flaked coconut

½ cup light rum
½ teaspoon banana extract
2 cups vanilla ice cream, slightly softened

• Process all ingredients in a blender until smooth. Serve immediately. Yield: 4 cups.

Mock Coladas: Omit rum, and add 1 teaspoon rum extract. Yield: 3½ cups.

pinch A measuring term that refers to a tiny amount that can be picked up by pinching together the thumb and forefinger. A pinch is approximately 1/16 of a teaspoon. (*see also* **measuring**)

pineapple A tropical fruit named for its resemblance to the pine cone. The pineapple has a spiny, diamond-patterned greenish-brown skin, sword-like leaves sprouting from its crown, and a fragrant, sweet, juicy flesh. Grown in warm, tropical areas from Hawaii to Malaysia, pineapple is one

Q **How do you peel a pineapple?**

A Slice off the bottom stem end and the green top. Stand the pineapple on one cut end and slice off the skin, cutting just below the surface, in wide vertical strips, leaving the small brown eyes. The eyes can be removed by cutting diagonally around the fruit, following the pattern of the eyes and making shallow, narrow furrows, cutting away as little of the flesh as possible. Finally, slice the pineapple into rings, and use a small, round cookie cutter or knife to remove the center core.

P

of the world's most popular fruits and a symbol of hospitality. Pineapple is available canned, crushed, in chunks, slices, or tidbits. It can also be found frozen and candied. Pineapple is used in a variety of dishes including fruit desserts, salads, cakes, and as a garnish for meats. **Storage:** Pineapple will not become any sweeter once picked, but it will soften if left at room temperature for a few days. Once ready, it should be refrigerated and used as soon as possible. Cut pineapple will last a few more days if placed in a tightly covered container and refrigerated, or frozen in a freezer container.

TEST KITCHEN SECRET

Fresh pineapple contains an enzyme called bromelain that prevents gelatin from congealing. Since heat destroys the enzyme, you can use cooked or canned pineapple in congealed salads. Bromelain also helps tenderize meat, so add fresh pineapple juice to marinades for tough cuts of beef. However, it's too potent for marinating poultry or seafood, and will make them mushy. JAMES SCHEND

FRESH PINEAPPLE UPSIDE-DOWN CAKE

¼ cup butter or margarine
1 cup firmly packed light brown
   sugar
4 (½-inch-thick) fresh pineapple
   slices*
½ cup dried cherries
½ cup macadamia nuts, chopped
3 large eggs, separated
1 cup sugar
1 cup all-purpose flour
¼ teaspoon baking soda
1 teaspoon salt
⅓ cup milk

• Melt butter in a 10-inch cast-iron skillet over medium heat, and sprinkle with brown sugar.
• Arrange pineapple slices, cherries, and nuts over brown sugar; cook until sugar bubbles. Remove from heat.
• Beat egg yolks until thick and pale; gradually add 1 cup sugar, beating well. Combine flour, soda, and salt. Add to yolk mixture, beating just until blended. Stir in milk. Beat egg whites until stiff but not dry; fold into batter. Spoon batter evenly over fruit in skillet.
• Bake at 350° for 30 minutes or until a wooden pick inserted in center comes out clean. Run a knife around edge of cake to loosen; cool in pan on a wire rack 10 minutes. Invert onto a serving plate. Yield: 1 (10-inch) cake.

*You can substitute 4 canned pineapple slices instead of the fresh, if desired.

pine nut A small nut that comes from several varieties of pine trees. Also known as the Indian nut, piñon (in Spanish), pignoli (in Italian), or pignon (in French), the creamy-white pine nut has a rich, but delicate pine flavor, and a high fat content. Pine nuts can be purchased in most supermarkets.

They're used in pasta sauces, pesto, and rice dishes. Because of their high fat content, they turn rancid quickly, so refrigerate them in an airtight container for 2 to 3 months, or freeze for 6 to 9 months. (*see also* **nuts**)

pink peppercorn (*see* **peppercorn**)

piñon (PIHN yuhn) (*see* **pine nut**)

Pinot Blanc (PEE noh BLAHN) White grapes used to produce crisp, dry white wine. Most Pinot Blanc wines are less intense and more delicate in flavor than Chardonnay. Pinot Blanc pairs well with chicken and seafood. (*see also* **wine**)

Pinot Noir (PEE noh NWAHR) Red wine grapes that produce spicy, rich, red Burgundy. Pinot Noir grapes are also used to make rosé wine and sparkling wines. Pinot Noirs pair well with roasted poultry, pork, and veal. (*see also* **wine**)

pinto bean A medium-size pale pink bean with reddish-brown streaks. Also referred to as "red Mexican beans," pinto beans are mixed with rice or used in soups and stews. In addition, refried beans and chili con carne are two popular dishes based on pinto beans. Pinto beans are available dried and canned. (*see also* **beans, dried; chili con carne;** *and* **refried beans**)

piquante sauce (pee KAHNT) A brown French sauce made from shallots, wine, vinegar, and flavored with gherkins, parsley, and herbs. Piquante sauce is usually served with sliced meats. (*see also* **gherkin**)

piroshki (pih ROSH kee) Russian or Polish turnovers made of flaky pastry filled with meat, fish, cheese, or mushrooms. Piroshki are usually baked or deep-fried and served as an appetizer or as a soup accompaniment.

pirouettes (pir oh ET) Dainty, thin, rolled-up wafer cookies whose ends are sometimes dipped in melted chocolate. Pirouettes are often served with ice cream.

pistachio nut (pih STASH ee oh) A pale green nut with a hard, tan shell sometimes dyed red or blanched until white. According to the California Pistachio Commission, pistachio shells were originally dyed red to disguise blemishes and now consumers expect them to be red; the dye makes them easy to identify. Pistachios have a delicate, subtle flavor and are good for adding to sweet and savory dishes. (*see also* **nuts**)

pit A stone or seed found in fruits such as cherries, peaches, or plums. This term can also refer to the process of removing such stones from fruit.

pita (PEE tah) A round, hollow Middle Eastern flatbread, sometimes called "pocket bread," made of white or whole-wheat flour, and leavened with yeast. Pita rounds can be split open, cut crosswise to form pockets for stuffing, cut into wedges and used as dippers for hummus, or simply enjoyed as a bread or snack. Pita bread can be purchased in Middle Eastern markets and most supermarkets. (*see also* **hummus** *and* **pita chip**)

pita chip Toasted wedges of pita bread used as a snack or dipper. Pita chips are often sprinkled with herbs and spices for added flavor.

pith Bitter, white membrane found on citrus fruits between the outer rind or peel and the inner pulp or flesh. (*see also* **section** *and* **zest**)

pizza (PEE zuh) An Italian dish made of flattened baked, yeast dough topped with tomato sauce, mozzarella cheese, and any of a variety of other ingredients such as peppers, onions, Italian sausage, mushrooms, anchovies, and pepperoni. Updated versions include deep-dish pizza, thick or thin crust, and a range of creative toppings such as dried tomatoes, duck, basil, salmon, goat cheese, or wild mushrooms. In commercial pizza parlors, thin-crust pizza is known as Neapolitan pizza, while thick-crust pizza is referred to as Sicilian pizza. Frozen pizzas are sold in most supermarkets; they can also be made at home with frozen or refrigerated fresh pizza dough and your choice of toppings.

> **TIMESAVING TIP**
> For quick pizzas or snacks, try these as crust ideas: focaccia or flatbread, Boboli bread, flour tortillas, whole wheat pitas, halved English muffins, and halved bagels.

ROASTED POTATO PIZZAS

2 bacon slices	6 small red potatoes, thinly sliced
1 garlic clove, minced	1 small onion, sliced
½ (8-ounce) package fresh mushrooms, chopped	1 tablespoon olive oil
1 (15-ounce) can tomato sauce	1 teaspoon chopped fresh or dried rosemary
1 teaspoon dried Italian seasoning	1 (8-ounce) can refrigerated crescent rolls
6 dried tomatoes, chopped	1 (3-ounce) package shredded Parmesan cheese
1 teaspoon salt, divided	
1 teaspoon freshly ground pepper, divided	

• Cook bacon in a large skillet until crisp; remove bacon, reserving 2 tablespoons drippings. Crumble bacon, and set aside.

• Sauté garlic and mushrooms in 1 tablespoon reserved drippings in skillet. Stir in tomato sauce, Italian seasoning, dried tomatoes, ¼ teaspoon salt, and ¼ teaspoon pepper. Cook over medium heat, stirring occasionally, 30 minutes. Set aside.

• Combine sliced potatoes, onion, remaining 1 tablespoon drippings, oil, remaining ¾ teaspoon salt, remaining ¾ teaspoon pepper, and rosemary in a roasting pan, tossing gently.
• Bake at 450° for 18 to 20 minutes, stirring once. Set aside.
• Unroll crescent rolls, and separate into 8 triangles; shape each triangle into a 4-inch circle, and place on ungreased baking sheets.
• Bake at 375° for 6 minutes. Top each with tomato sauce mixture, potato mixture, bacon, and Parmesan cheese. Bake 5 to 6 more minutes. Yield: 8 servings.

plantain (PLAN tihn) (*see* **banana**)

Planter's punch Rum punch made of lime juice, sugar syrup, and water; it's served in a tall glass over cracked ice.

plastic wrap Thin sheets of clear polyethylene or polyvinyl chloride formed on rolls for conveniently wrapping and storing foods. Plastic wrap also provides excellent moisture retention, which is useful in microwave cooking. Plastic wrap can form an airtight seal, which increases the shelf life of many foods.

plum A small, round fruit that grows in clusters on trees. There are hundreds of plum varieties; they're smooth-skinned, have juicy, sweet flesh surrounding a center pit, and can be yellow, green, red, purple, or indigo blue. Plums can be used for fruit compotes, desserts, jams, jellies, sauces, snacks, and tarts; some are dried. Among the most common varieties are:
• **Red ace:** A medium-size plum with reddish-purple skin and reddish flesh; it has sweet flavor and is good in fruit compotes and as snacks.
• **Damson:** A small, oval-shaped plum with indigo blue skin and yellow-green flesh; its tart taste makes good pies and jams.
• **Friar:** A large plum with deep black skin and amber flesh; it has a very sweet flavor that works in preserves, sauces, and tarts.
• **Italian:** A small oval plum with dark blue to purple skin and firm golden flesh; it's used to make prunes.
• **Queen Ann:** A large plum with dark reddish-purple skin and golden flesh; it's a good eating plum.
• **Red beauty:** A small- to medium-size plum with bright red skin and yellowish flesh; it can be used in desserts or for eating.
• **Santa Rosa:** A small- to medium-size plum with purple-crimson skin and yellow flesh that's dark red around the pit; it has tart flavor and is great for canning, freezing, or for making jams and jellies.
Storage: Firm plums can be stored at room temperature until they become slightly soft. Refrigerate ripe plums in a plastic bag up to 4 to 5 days. (*see also* **compote** *and* **prune**)

plum pudding A steamed breadlike British Christmas dessert, originally made with plums, but now made with suet, dried currants, raisins, almonds, and spices. The pudding is usually steamed or boiled in a special pudding mold and served warm, and flamed with rum or brandy; sometimes it's accompanied with hard sauce. (*see also* **currant, hard sauce,** *and* **suet**)

PLUM PUDDING WITH SHERRIED HARD SAUCE

3 cups all-purpose flour
1 teaspoon baking soda
½ teaspoon salt
2 teaspoons ground cinnamon
½ teaspoon ground allspice
½ teaspoon ground cloves
2 cups raisins

1 medium Granny Smith apple, peeled and chopped (1 cup)
1 cup currants
1 cup light molasses
1 cup cold water
2 cups finely chopped suet*
Sherried Hard Sauce (page 250)

• Combine first 6 ingredients in a large bowl; mix well. Stir in raisins, apple, and currants.
• Combine molasses, water, and suet; add to dry ingredients, mixing well. Spoon mixture into a well-greased 2½-quart metal steamed pudding mold; cover tightly with lid or aluminum foil.
• Place mold on rack in a large deep kettle with enough boiling water to come halfway up mold. Cover kettle; steam pudding 3 hours in boiling water, replacing water as needed. Uncover and let pudding stand 5 minutes before unmolding. Cut into slices, and serve with Sherried Hard Sauce. Yield: 12 servings.

*Suet is solid white fat rendered from beef. If it's not packaged in your supermarket meat case, ask the butcher to cut some. It lends richness to puddings such as this one. Shortening does not substitute well.

plum sauce (*see* **duck sauce**)

plum tomato (*see* **tomato**)

poach A moist-heat cooking method where food is partially or completely submerged in water, stock, court-bouillon, or sugar syrup and gently simmered until it's done. (*see also* **court-bouillon** *and* **egg**)

TEST KITCHEN SECRET

Consider poaching not only for cooking eggs, but also in preparing other fragile foods such as fruit and fish. Delicate foods should be poached in liquid that's simmering rather than boiling. MARGARET MONROE DICKEY

poblano chile (poh BLAH noh) A large, dark green fresh chile pepper with a rich, mild-to-hot flavor. Poblanos are often stuffed with cheese for chiles rellenos. They're available fresh, canned, or dried; when dried, poblanos become known as ancho chile peppers. (*see also* **chiles rellenos** *and* **peppers**)

po' boy (*see* **hero sandwich**)

poire (PWAHR) A French term for pear.

pokeweed A tall, leafy green plant that tastes similar to spinach; the leaves and stems are edible, but the berries and roots are poisonous. Poke-weed, sometimes called poke sallet, is gathered wild along roadsides; the leaves can be cooked as spinach, and the stems can be prepared like asparagus. Only experienced people should gather it because similar-looking plants can be poisonous.

polenta (poh LEHN tah) An Italian dish made by cooking cornmeal with liquid until it forms a soft mush. Polenta can be eaten hot with butter or cooled until firm and cut into squares and grilled or fried. For added flavor, polenta is sometimes served or mixed with cheese or topped with tomato sauce. Polenta can be enjoyed as a first course, side dish, or eaten for breakfast.

Polish sausage (*see* **kielbasa** *and* **sausage**)

polonaise, à la (poh loh NEHZ) A French term that describes cooked vegetables, usually cauliflower and asparagus, that are topped with chopped hard-cooked eggs, breadcrumbs, parsley, and melted butter.

pomegranate (POM uh gran uht) A deep red fruit with thick, leathery skin. Inside are hundreds of crunchy red seeds packed in compartments separated by tough white membranes. Pomegranates have a fruity, sweet flavor and a deep red juice often used in Middle Eastern stews, sauces, marinades, glazes, salads, and drinks; they can also be used to flavor sorbet and ice cream, and the seeds can be sprinkled in salads, tarts, and fruit desserts. Because of their attractive color and long shelf life, pomegranates are often part of holiday table decorations. Fresh pomegranates are available in Middle Eastern markets and large supermarkets in the fall and early winter; canned pomegranate juice is also available.

Q&A: How do you seed a pomegranate?

Working over a bowl, cut off a thin slice of rind from the blossom end of the fruit, being careful not to pierce any seeds. Lightly score the skin of the fruit from stem to blossom end in four to six places, without cutting through to the seeds. Gently break the fruit apart along the scored lines, and bend back the rind of each piece to reveal the seeds. Remove the seeds with your fingertips.

TEST KITCHEN SECRET

Always work over a bowl and wear an apron when seeding pomegranates. Their bright red juice leaves stubborn stains on whatever they touch. LYDA JONES

Storage: Pomegranates can be kept at room temperature up to a week, or refrigerated in a plastic bag up to 3 weeks. The seeds can be frozen for a year.

pomelo (pom EH loh) A giant citrus fruit with a thick, coarse yellow to pink rind and yellow to pink segmented, tart-flavored flesh. Pomelos can range from cantaloupe-size to as large as a watermelon and are used in the same way as a grapefruit.

pomme (POM) A French term for apple.

pommes frites (pom FREET) (*see* **French fries**)

pompano (PAHM puh noh) A saltwater fish found in the waters off the coast of Florida; it has a firm, white, mild-flavored flesh with a moderate amount of fat. Pompano is sold whole and in fillets, both fresh and frozen. Though this versatile fish can be prepared by most any cooking method, it is often served en papillote. (*see also* **en papillote** *and* **fish**)

pone A Native American term that means "baked." The first pones were made from a batter of coarsely ground cornmeal, water, salt, and bear grease, and baked on flat rocks or metal surfaces. This term includes all manner of easy-to-make corn patties or corn cakes. (*see also* **cornbread**)

popcorn A type of corn that explodes into white or yellow puffs when exposed to heat. Popcorn is enjoyed as a snack and is often seasoned with butter and salt. Popcorn kernels are available in all supermarkets; special microwave popcorn is also available as well as already popped and flavored popcorn.
Storage: Moisture in the kernels is what makes popcorn pop. As it ages, popcorn dries out; to ensure that yours pops, buy it where turnover is fast and then store it in an airtight container at room temperature or the freezer.

CARAMEL-NUT POPCORN CLUSTERS

1 (14-ounce) package caramels	12 cups popped corn
2 tablespoons whipping cream	1 cup dry-roasted peanuts

• Combine caramels and whipping cream in a glass bowl. Microwave at HIGH 3 minutes or until melted, stirring mixture once.
• Place popcorn and peanuts in a large bowl. Drizzle with caramel sauce, tossing gently to coat.
• Place popcorn mixture on a lightly greased 15- x 10-inch jellyroll pan.
• Bake at 250° for 1 hour. Cool. Yield: about 13 cups.

popover A puffy, muffinlike bread leavened with eggs and steam. Popovers have crisp, brown, crusty exteriors and moist, airy interiors; they can be plain or flavored with cheese, spices,

RESCUE for soggy popovers:
Pierce the popovers with a knife at the end of baking to allow steam to escape; return them to the oven for 5 more minutes to become crisp.

or herbs. Serve popovers for breakfast, as a side dish, or with roast beef; they can also be split and filled with scrambled eggs, seafood, salad, pudding, ice cream, or custard. (*see also* **baking dishes and pans** *and* **quick bread**)

PARMESAN POPOVERS

2 tablespoons grated Parmesan cheese
1 cup all-purpose flour
1 cup milk
2 large eggs
2 egg whites
1 tablespoon butter, melted
2 teaspoons Worcestershire sauce
½ teaspoon salt
¼ teaspoon garlic powder

• Sprinkle bottom and sides of well-greased popover pans or 8-ounce custard cups with Parmesan cheese.

• Whisk together flour and remaining ingredients until blended. Spoon into pans, filling three-fourths full.

• Bake on lowest oven rack at 450° for 15 minutes. Reduce temperature to 350°, and bake 30 minutes or until golden brown. Serve immediately. Yield: 6 servings.

Q Do I need a special pan to make popovers?

A Custard cups, small ovenproof bowls, ramekins, or 2½-inch muffin pans will work. Remember to grease the cups or pans completely and fill them three-fourths full of batter. If the recipe calls for preheating the pans and you are using custard cups or ramekins, don't preheat the cups. Special popover pans are convenient to use because they have deep cups that are attached to one another.

poppy seed Tiny, round, blue-gray seeds of the poppy plant. They have a crunchy texture, nutty flavor, and can be used in breads, cakes, muffins, and salad dressing. They're also used in a variety of cooked dishes, and are especially popular in Middle Eastern and Indian cuisines. Poppy seeds can be purchased whole or ground in most supermarkets. (*see also* **spice**)

POPPY SEED DRESSING

⅔ cup light sour cream
½ cup apricot or pear nectar
2 tablespoons white wine vinegar
1 tablespoon vegetable oil
1 tablespoon honey
1 teaspoon poppy seeds

• Whisk together all ingredients in a bowl. Chill, if desired. Serve with fresh fruit. Yield: 1¼ cups.

porcini (*see* **mushroom**)

pork The meat from hogs raised for food. Pork is light pink in color, full-flavored, and has a finely grained texture. Most pork in the marketplace today is cured or smoked, such as bacon, sausage, and ham, or sold fresh. Some slaughterhouses have their pork graded by the USDA on a system based on the proportion of fat to lean. The grades are 1, 2, 3, 4, and utility, with grade 1 being the best. All pork is subjected to state and federal inspection for wholesomeness to insure the slaughter and processing took place under sanitary conditions.

TEST KITCHEN SECRET

" *Almost all cuts of pork are tender and can be cooked by dry heat. But keep in mind that pork is lean and cooks quickly; overcooking can make it dry and tough. We test thicker cuts of pork for perfect doneness with a meat thermometer. For thin chops, a quick sear on each side will usually be all you need.* " VIE WARSHAW

TIMETABLE FOR ROASTING FRESH PORK

CUT	APPROXIMATE WEIGHT IN POUNDS	INTERNAL TEMPERATURE	APPROXIMATE TOTAL COOKING TIMES AT 325° IN MINUTES PER POUND
Loin			
Center	3 to 5	160°	20 to 25
Half	5 to 7	160°	30 to 35
End	3 to 4	160°	35 to 40
Roll	3 to 5	160°	30 to 35
Boneless top	2 to 4	160°	20 to 30
Crown	4 to 6	160°	20 to 25
Picnic shoulder			
Bone in	5 to 8	170°	40 to 45
Rolled	3 to 5	170°	40 to 45
Boston shoulder	4 to 6	170°	40 to 45
Leg (fresh ham)			
Whole (bone-in)	12 to 16	160°	18 to 20
Whole (boneless)	10 to 14	160°	20 to 25
Half (bone-in)	5 to 8	160°	22 to 25
Tenderloin	½ to 1	160°	20 to 30 minutes (Roast at 375°)
Back ribs		165° to 170° (well done)	1½ to 2 hours total
Country-style ribs		165° to 170° (well done)	1½ to 2½ hours total
Spareribs		165° to 170° (well done)	1½ to 2½ hours total
Pork loaf	1½ to 2	165° to 170° (well done)	1 to 1½ hours total

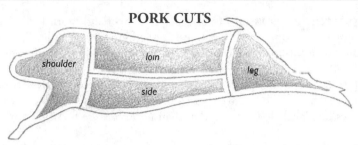

PORK CUTS

A butchered pig is divided into wholesale cuts from which smaller pieces of meat are carved for sale in supermarkets. The two wholesale cuts most often sold fresh are the loin and the blade shoulder. The other wholesale cuts—the leg or ham, the side, and the arm shoulder—are often cured but are sometimes sold fresh.

• **Shoulder:** Meat from the blade shoulder is marbled with fat, juicy, and flavorful. It produces the blade roasts and steak. Meat from the arm shoulder is usually smoked for picnic ham, hocks, and pig's feet.

smoked picnic

blade roast

smoked hocks

• **Loin:** The loin is the tenderest part of the pig. From this cut come loin chops, the tenderloin, loin roasts, and back rib and country-style rib sections.

loin

• **Leg:** The leg is usually either roasted as a fresh leg of pork or smoked to make ham.

smoked ham

• **Side:** The side produces spareribs that are usually barbecued and side meat that's smoked and turned into bacon.

Selecting: Look for pork that has pink flesh, a clean smell, and white fat. Cured pork should be rosy pink. Pork takes on a gray color when it's been in the meat case too long. Vacuum-sealed pork will be slightly darker because the meat isn't exposed to air.

Storage: Store pork in the package in which it was purchased, in the refrigerator 2 to 3 days; ground pork should be stored in the refrigerator no longer than 2 days. To freeze, wrap and seal tightly in freezer wrap or heavy-duty aluminum foil; ground pork can be frozen up to 3 months, and other fresh pork 6 to 9 months.

Cooking: Though pork is virtually free of any trichnae, it's still recommended that you cook all pork to 160°. Pork that's smoked or grilled sometimes remains pink even when it's well done; this is desirable. Rely on a meat thermometer for accurate doneness.
(*see also* **bacon, ham, sausage,** *and* **trichinella**)

RESCUE for pork questions:
Get the answers by calling the USDA's Meat and Poultry Hot Line at 800-535-4555.

porridge (POR ihj) Once a staple of Scotland, porridge is a thick pudding made from cereal or oatmeal cooked in water or milk. Porridge is usually eaten hot for breakfast and is served with cold milk or cream and sugar.

port Sweet fortified red wine traditionally served with dessert or after a meal. The highest quality port comes from the Portuguese city of Oporto; these are labeled "Porto," rather than port. (*see also* **fortified wine**)

porterhouse steak A steak cut from the large end of the beef short loin; this tender cut contains portions from the tenderloin and the top loin. It's considered one of the most flavorful and prized steaks. (*see also* **beef**)

portobello (*see* **mushroom**)

posole (poh SOH leh) A Mexican soup of pork and broth, hominy, onions, chile peppers, and cilantro. Posole is often garnished with lettuce, radishes, onions, and cheese, according to individual taste. This hearty soup is typically eaten as a main course and served during the Christmas season.

potato A tuberous vegetable with a fairly smooth skin that can be brown, yellow, red, or purple. Potato flesh also varies; it can be yellow or white, and have a waxy or dry texture. Some potatoes have buds or eyes that need to be removed before cooking. In addition to fresh, there are a wide variety of canned, frozen, refrigerated, and dehydrated potato products; potato chips are also popular. Potato flour is also available. There are several basic categories of fresh potatoes in America:
• The *russet* or *Idaho* potato is long, slightly rounded, and has brown, rough skin and numerous eyes. Its dry mealy texture makes it good for baking and frying.
• *Long white* potatoes have pale gray-brown skins with few eyes. Because they're firm and waxy, they're an all-purpose potato and can be baked, boiled or roasted.

MICRO-BAKED POTATOES

Rinse potatoes and pat dry; prick several times with a fork. Arrange potatoes in microwave oven, leaving 1 inch between each. (If microwaving more than 2 potatoes, arrange them in a circle.)

Microwave at HIGH according to the times in chart, turning and rearranging potatoes once. Let potatoes stand 5 minutes before serving. (If potatoes are not done after standing, microwave briefly and let stand 2 minutes.)

NUMBER OF POTATOES	MINUTES AT HIGH POWER
1	3 to 4
2	5 to 7
3	8 to 10
4	11 to 13
6	14 to 16

Times are for medium potatoes (6 to 7 ounces). If larger, allow more time.

- *Round white* and *round red* potatoes have a waxy flesh that's good for boiling, frying, and roasting.
- *New potatoes* are young red potatoes that haven't had time to become starchy and therefore have a waxy texture that's good for boiling and making potato salad or for pan roasting. They are usually available from spring to early summer.
- *Yukon gold* are medium-size round potatoes with a thin yellowish skin and a pale yellow flesh which gives the illusion that they're buttered.

Storage: Store potatoes in a cool, dry, dark, well-ventilated place up to 2 weeks. New potatoes should be used within 2 or 3 days of purchase. (*see also* **potato chips, potato flour, potato salad, red potato, vegetables,** *and* **Yukon gold**)

ROASTED GARLIC-PARMESAN MASHED POTATOES

2 garlic bulbs	¼ cup shredded Parmesan cheese
Olive oil (optional)	3 tablespoons butter or
3 pounds potatoes, peeled and	margarine, softened
quartered	⅓ cup chopped fresh parsley
2 teaspoons salt, divided	½ teaspoon pepper
¼ cup whipping cream	Garnish: fresh thyme sprigs

- Cut off pointed ends of garlic bulbs; place garlic on a piece of aluminum foil, and drizzle with oil, if desired. Fold foil to seal.
- Bake at 425° for 30 minutes; cool. Squeeze pulp from garlic cloves; set aside.
- Bring potato, 1 teaspoon salt, and water to cover to a boil in a Dutch oven; boil 20 to 25 minutes or until potato is tender. Drain.
- Mash potato, or

Q How do you make mashed potatoes that aren't lumpy or pasty?

A There are some who believe the best way is to use a ricer or food mill; many on our staff recommend mashing with a potato masher, as seen in these photos:

1. Cook potatoes in boiling water until tender; drain well. Return potatoes to warm pan.

2. Add butter and mash. Then add milk and seasonings, and mash until desired texture.

press through a ricer. Stir in garlic pulp, remaining 1 teaspoon salt, whipping cream, and next 4 ingredients. Garnish, if desired. Yield: 6 servings.

potato chips Thinly sliced, deep-fried potatoes, invented by the chef of a Saratoga Springs, New York, hotel for a mid-nineteenth century guest. Classic chips are soaked in cold water, then deep-fried, and salted. This popular snack is now available in a variety of sizes, cuts,

thicknesses, and flavors. Potato chips should be stored in an airtight container in a cool, dark place; some packages are stamped with a freshness date.

potato flour Cooked, dried potato that has been milled into starchy, gluten-free flour. Potato flour is used as a thickener and for baking.

potato salad Cooked, sliced, or diced potatoes bound with mayonnaise or sour cream dressing and flavored with ingredients such as chopped onion, green peppers, celery, and hard-cooked eggs. Most potato salad is served cold, although German potato salad is sometimes served hot and is bound with a dressing of vinegar and bacon drippings. (*see also* **German potato salad**)

CLASSIC POTATO SALAD

2½ pounds red potatoes or yellow Finn potatoes	2 green onions, chopped
1 celery rib, diced	1 cup mayonnaise
⅓ cup sweet pickle relish or	2 tablespoons lemon juice
½ cup chopped sweet pickles	1 teaspoon salt
2 large hard-cooked eggs, sliced	¼ teaspoon pepper
	½ teaspoon dry mustard (optional)

• Cook potatoes in boiling water to cover 25 minutes or just until potatoes are tender.
• Drain well, and cool slightly. Peel and cube potatoes. Combine potato, celery, and next 3 ingredients in a large bowl; toss gently.
• Combine mayonnaise, next 3 ingredients, and, if desired, dry mustard in a small bowl. Pour mayonnaise mixture over potato mixture, tossing gently to combine. Serve warm or chilled. Yield: 7 servings.

pot liquor The liquid remaining after cooking greens or other vegetables. Flavorful pot liquor, or "pot likker," as it's called in the South, can be served hot as soup or soaked up with dry pieces of cornbread; it's also wonderful for cooking cornmeal dumplings.

Southernism
Pot liquor from greens is a delicacy enjoyed by most greens lovers, and even by some who don't care for the vegetables themselves. Some Southerners spoon it like soup or soak it up with dry pieces of cornbread.

DOWN-HOME TURNIP GREENS

1 bunch fresh turnip greens (about 4½ pounds)	3 quarts water
	¼ teaspoon freshly ground pepper
1 pound salt pork (streak of lean) or smoked pork shoulder	2 teaspoons sugar (optional)

- Remove and discard stems and discolored spots from greens. Wash greens thoroughly; drain and tear greens into pieces. Set aside.
- Slice salt pork at ¼-inch intervals, cutting to, but not through, the skin.
- Combine salt pork, 3 quarts water, pepper, and, if desired, sugar in a Dutch oven; bring mixture to a boil. Cover, reduce heat, and simmer 1 hour. Add greens, and cook, uncovered, 30 to 35 minutes or until tender. Serve greens with a slotted spoon, and dip cornbread into the pot liquor. Yield: 4 to 6 servings.

pot pie A savory main dish of meat or poultry and vegetables in a rich, creamy sauce. Most pot pies have either a single or double-crust pastry, but sometimes they're topped with a biscuitlike crust. Pot pie can be made at home, but commercially prepared frozen pot pies are also available at the supermarket.

CHICKEN-AND-EGG POT PIE

2 cups chopped cooked chicken	1 cup (4 ounces) shredded Cheddar cheese
2 hard-cooked eggs, chopped	
1 (15¼-ounce) can whole kernel corn, rinsed and drained	1 (2-ounce) jar diced pimiento, drained
1 (15¼-ounce) can sweet green peas, rinsed and drained	¼ teaspoon pepper
1 (10¾-ounce) can cream of chicken soup, undiluted	2 (8-ounce) cans refrigerated crescent rolls, divided

- Stir together first 8 ingredients in a large bowl until mixture is blended.
- Unroll 1 can crescent roll dough, and press dough into a lightly greased 9-inch square baking dish.
- Bake at 350° for 15 minutes. Remove from oven.
- Spoon chicken mixture over crescent roll dough in dish.
- Unroll remaining can crescent roll dough; roll into a 9-inch square.
- Place dough over chicken mixture, pressing edges of top and bottom crusts to dish to seal.
- Bake 18 to 20 more minutes or until golden. Yield: 4 to 6 servings.

pot roast A large piece of meat from the beef chuck or round that's usually tough, but when cooked slowly by moist heat becomes tender and flavorful. The roast is typically browned in hot fat, then covered and cooked in a small amount of liquid either on top of the range or in the oven. (*see also* **beef**)

pots de crème (poh duh KREHM) A French dessert of creamy pudding, often served in special little porcelain cups or tiny pots with lids. Pots de crème can be chocolate, vanilla, caramel, or lemon flavors.

CHOCOLATE POTS DE CRÈME

2 cups half-and-half	3 tablespoons amaretto
2 egg yolks, lightly beaten	2 teaspoons vanilla extract
2 tablespoons sugar	Pinch of salt
3⅓ cups (20 ounces) semisweet chocolate morsels	1 cup sweetened whipped cream
	Garnish: chocolate shavings

• Combine first 3 ingredients in a heavy saucepan; cook over medium heat 12 minutes or until mixture reaches 160°, stirring constantly. Add chocolate morsels and next 3 ingredients, stirring until smooth.
• Spoon into 8 (4-ounce) ramekins or chocolate pots; cover and chill at least 4 hours. Top with whipped cream. Garnish, if desired. Yield: 8 servings.

pot stickers Small Chinese dumplings made of won ton skins filled with ground meat, fish, shellfish, chopped water chestnuts, and scallions; they're typically fried or browned, then cooked in broth or steamed, and served as an appetizer along with a dipping sauce. (*see also* **won ton**)

Pouilly Fumé (POOY yee fu may) Dry white wine from Sauvignon Blanc grapes that's produced in Pouilly-sur-Loire, France. (*see also* **wine**)

Pouilly Fuissé (POOY yee fwee say) Light, dry, fruity white wine made from Chardonnay grapes that's produced in Burgundy, France. (*see also* **wine**)

poulet (poo LAY) French for a young spring chicken. (*see also* **chicken**)

poultry Any domestic bird raised for food. The USDA recognizes six kinds of poultry including chicken, turkey, duck, goose, pigeon or squab, and guinea fowl. However, other domesticated birds are also found at the meat counter of most supermarkets including Cornish hens, capons, and free-range or free-roaming chickens and pheasant.

RESCUE for poultry questions: Get the answers by calling the USDA's Meat and Poultry Hot Line at 800-535-4555.

Storage: Fresh poultry is highly perishable. When shopping, check the "sell by" date and choose the freshest available. As soon as possible, store poultry, wrapped in plastic wrap, in the coldest part of your refrigerator; it will keep up to 2 days. Most cooked poultry can be refrigerated up to 4 days. You can freeze properly packaged poultry parts up to 9 months and a whole bird up to a year; wrap in heavy-duty plastic wrap or freezer paper before freezing. Cooked poultry dishes can be frozen 4 to 6 months. (*see also* **chicken, Cornish game hen, duck, duckling, goose, guinea fowl, pigeon, squab,** *and* **wild game**)

HERB-ROASTED CHICKEN

½ cup butter, softened	1 (3- to 3½-pound) whole
2 shallots, diced	chicken
3 garlic cloves, minced	6 to 8 fresh parsley sprigs
2 tablespoons fresh rosemary,	½ teaspoon salt
crushed	¼ teaspoon pepper

• Stir together first 4 ingredients. Loosen skin from chicken breast without detaching it; carefully rub butter mixture over chicken, and insert parsley under skin. Rub butter mixture inside cavity.

• Sprinkle chicken with salt and pepper. Place chicken, breast side up, in a roasting pan. Bake at 425° for 20 minutes. Reduce oven temperature to 325°, and bake 40 more minutes or until done. Yield: 4 servings.

TIMETABLE FOR ROASTING POULTRY

	READY TO COOK WEIGHT IN POUNDS	OVEN TEMPERATURE	INTERNAL TEMPERATURE (IN THIGH)	APPROXIMATE TOTAL ROASTING TIME IN HOURS
Chicken (unstuffed)*	2 to 2½	375°	180°	¾ to 1
	2½ to 3	375°	180°	1 to 1¼
	3 to 4	375°	180°	1¼ to 1¾
	4 to 5	375°	180°	1¾ to 2
Capon (unstuffed)	4 to 7	325°	180°	1¾ to 2½
Cornish hen (stuffed)	1 to 1½	375°	180°	1 to 1¼
Duckling (unstuffed)	3½ to 5½	325°	180°	2 to 2¾
Goose (unstuffed)	7 to 9	350°	180°	2 to 2½
	9 to 11	350°	180°	2½ to 3
	11 to 13	350°	180°	3 to 3½
Turkey (unstuffed)**	8 to 12	325°	180°	2¾ to 3
	12 to 14	325°	180°	3 to 3¾
	14 to 18	325°	180°	3¾ to 4¼
	18 to 20	325°	180°	4¼ to 4½

*Stuffed chickens and turkeys require about 5 additional minutes per pound.

poultry seasoning A blend of thyme, sage, pepper, marjoram, rosemary, and other herbs and spices used to season poultry and stuffings.

poultry shears Strong scissors with slightly curved blades, one of which has a notched edge. Poultry shears are used to cut through poultry flesh and bones; they can also be used for trimming firm vegetables.

pound To beat food with a mallet to crush it or to break down meat texture and make it more tender. This term also refers to a basic measurement of weight in the U.S. system in which 16 ounces equals a pound. (*see also* **measuring** *and* **meat tenderizer**)

pound cake A dense, rich cake originally made with 1 pound each of flour, butter, sugar, and eggs. Today, pound cake recipes might include a variety of other ingredients such as baking powder, sour cream, coconut, nuts, fruits, and flavorings. To ensure that your pound cake has the best texture, always measure ingredients precisely and mix batter properly. A critical step is beating the butter or shortening and sugar until light and fluffy. This procedure takes about 5 minutes using an electric mixer and ingredients that have been at room temperature for 20 minutes (but no longer for food safety reasons). When adding eggs, flour, and liquid, mix just until blended. Overbeating can cause the cake to be tough.

Southernism

Thought to be of British origin, discrepancy remains today, particularly among Virginians, as to the genesis of the pound cake. Despite the queries over development, the cake nonetheless receives its name from the original ingredient measurements: A pound of sugar, a pound of flour, a pound of butter, and a pound of eggs. While the amounts of ingredients have changed over time, the sturdy, classic cake remains a favorite. Some Southerners even confess to toasting it for breakfast.

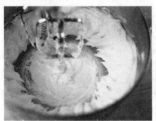

1. Beat butter at medium speed with an electric mixer until creamy.

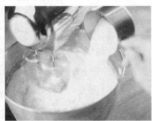

2. Gradually add sugar, beating well.

3. Add eggs, one at a time, beating just until yellow disappears.

4. Add milk to butter mixture alternately with flour mixture.

5. Spoon thick batter into greased and floured tube pan, and bake.

READER TIP
"I try to keep a pound cake in my freezer to have on hand for emergency desserts. When needed, I slice it, and toast the slices; sometimes I top it with sliced fresh fruit, whipped cream, or ice cream." J.J., Lexington, VA

MILLION DOLLAR POUND CAKE

1 pound butter, softened	¾ cup milk
3 cups sugar	1 teaspoon almond extract
6 large eggs	1 teaspoon vanilla extract
4 cups all-purpose flour	

- Beat butter; gradually add sugar, beating at medium speed with an electric mixer until light and fluffy. Add eggs, 1 at a time, beating after each addition. Add flour to butter mixture alternately with milk, beginning and ending with flour mixture. Mix after each addition. Stir in flavorings.

- Spoon batter into a greased and floured 10-inch tube pan. Bake at 300° for 1 hour and 40 minutes or until a wooden pick inserted in center comes out clean. Cool in pan 10 to 15 minutes; remove to wire rack. Cool. Yield: 1 (10-inch) cake.

powdered eggs Dehydrated whole eggs are often used in commercial food production. Only a few dried egg products are available to consumers, but lightweight single- or double-serving foil pouches of freeze-dried eggs are found in camping and outdoor stores. Dried meringue powder is also available in some gourmet cooking shops; it can be used to replace raw egg whites in some recipes. (*see also* **egg, egg substitute,** *and* **meringue powder**)

powdered milk Milk that has all the moisture removed; it's less expensive and easier to store than fresh milk, but never tastes quite like the real thing. Powdered whole milk must be refrigerated before and after it's reconstituted. Nonfat dry milk has most of the butterfat removed; it's available in regular and instant form. Powdered buttermilk is also available, but generally used for baking or making pancakes. Powdered milk is also great to take along on camping trips. (*see also* **milk**)

powdered sugar Refined sugar ground into a fine, white, easily dissolved powder, also known as confectioners' sugar or 10X sugar. Powdered sugar is often used to make icings and candy; it can also be used decoratively as a fine dusting on desserts. It's handy to know that a 1-pound box of powdered sugar contains about 4½ cups, sifted. (*see also* **sugar**)

Q **Does powdered sugar need to be sifted before measuring?**

A Powdered sugar measures differently depending on whether it's sifted or not. Our recipes specify "sifted powdered sugar" (meaning we sifted before measuring it), if we sifted it. If it's not critical to the recipe, we do not sift. If sifting is important for achieving a smooth icing, for instance, we tell you to sift. Powdered sugar is very light and has a tendency to pack down during shipping. Sugar packed in an airtight plastic bag tends to stay lighter and usually doesn't need sifting. Powdered sugar exposed to air, such as in boxes, tends to pack down more. If it's lumpy, you may want to sift it before using.

TIMESAVING TIP
Save preparation steps when you open a new box of powdered sugar by sifting the entire contents into an airtight plastic container. Next time you need this ingredient, it will be ready to use.

praline (PRAH leen or PRAY leen) A rich, patty-shaped caramel-flavored candy made with sugar, cream, butter, and pecans. After cooking, the praline mixture is beaten with a wooden spoon just until the mixture begins to thicken; then it's quickly dropped in mounds onto wax paper. (*see also* **candy**)

Southernism

This delectable Louisiana brittle candy dates back to 1750. Originally the patty-shaped, fudge-like delicacy was made with almonds—the preferred nut of the French—and was considered an aid to digestion at the end of a meal. However, the Creoles quickly found a better alternative in the abundant pecan and replaced the white sugar with brown. Today it's considered one of the paramount sweets in the South, particularly in Texas and Louisiana.

PRALINES

3 cups firmly packed light brown sugar	¼ teaspoon salt
1 cup whipping cream	¼ cup butter or margarine
2 tablespoons light corn syrup	2 cups chopped pecans
	1 teaspoon vanilla extract

• Bring first 4 ingredients to a boil in a 3-quart saucepan over medium heat, stirring constantly. Cook, stirring occasionally, 6 to 8 minutes, or until a candy thermometer registers 236° (soft ball stage).

RESCUE for a praline mixture that's too stiff to spoon into mounds:
Stir a few drops of hot water into the mixture, and then work quickly. You can also try returning the mixture to the cooktop and heating gently, stirring just until the mixture is no longer dry.

• Remove mixture from heat, and add butter. (Do not stir.) Let stand until candy thermometer reaches 150°. Stir in pecans and vanilla, using a wooden spoon; stir constantly until candy begins to thicken. Drop by heaping teaspoonfuls, working rapidly, onto wax paper. Let stand until firm. Yield: 2½ dozen.

prawn Giant and jumbo shrimp are often called prawns in the United States, although true prawns are actually either a type of freshwater shrimp or certain miniature members of the lobster family. Prepare prawns as you would shrimp. (*see also* **shellfish** *and* **shrimp**)

preheat To turn on and bring an oven, broiler, or pan to the desired temperature before adding the food to cook. Preheating ensures that food cooks evenly and in the time specified in your recipe.

Q **Is it necessary to preheat the oven?**

A Preheating is important for foods such as breads, cakes, and cookies, but not so important when just baking or reheating a casserole. It takes about 10 minutes for an oven to preheat.

preserves A fruit mixture cooked with sugar and usually pectin that contains medium to large chunks of fruit. Preserves are cooked to a jamlike consistency and used as a spread on bread or toast. (*see also* **jam, jelly,** *and* **pectin**)

FIG PRESERVES

2 quarts fresh figs (about 4 pounds)   **8 cups sugar**

- Layer figs and sugar in a Dutch oven. Cover and let stand 8 hours.
- Cook over medium heat 2 hours, stirring occasionally, until syrup thickens and figs are clear.
- Pack hot figs into hot jars, filling to ½ inch from top. Cover fruit with boiling syrup, filling to ½ inch from top. Remove air bubbles; wipe jar rims. Cover jars at once with metal lids, and screw on bands. Process in boiling-water bath 15 minutes. Cool completely; chill, if desired. Yield: 4 quarts.

pressure cooker An appliance made of heavy-gauge stainless steel and aluminum that's designed for cooking food quickly with compressed steam. Most such cookers have a locking, airtight lid and a valve to regulate pressure; they range in size from 4 to 10 quarts. Generally, the more pounds of pressure used, the higher the temperature and the quicker the food cooks. The cookers drastically cut the cooking time for foods, such as soups, stews, and tough cuts of meat, that would normally require lengthy simmering. They can also be used for canning; special pressure canners are made just for this purpose.

ROAST WITH ONION-AND-MUSHROOM GRAVY

1 (2- to 3-pound) boneless chuck roast, trimmed
½ teaspoon pepper
1 (10¾-ounce) can cream of mushroom soup, undiluted
1 (1-ounce) envelope dry onion soup mix
2 beef bouillon cubes
2 cups water
2 tablespoons cornstarch
2 tablespoons water

- Sprinkle roast evenly with pepper; place in a 6-quart pressure cooker. Add mushroom soup and next 3 ingredients. Cover cooker with lid, and seal securely; place pressure control over vent and tube.
- Cook over medium-high heat 20 minutes or until pressure control rocks quickly back and forth. Reduce heat to medium-low; cook 20 more minutes.
- Remove from heat; run cold water over cooker to reduce pressure. Carefully remove lid so that steam escapes away from you.
- Remove roast, and keep warm. Stir together cornstarch and 2 tablespoons water; add to liquid in pressure cooker. Bring to a boil; cook 1 minute. Serve gravy with roast. Yield: 4 to 6 servings.

> ### TEST KITCHEN SECRET
>
> *It's important to thoroughly clean your pressure cooker after each use to ensure the steam vent isn't clogged. Store the cooker with the cover turned upside down over the pot rather than attaching it; this allows all moisture to escape.* JAMES SCHEND

pretzel (PREHT zuhl) A hard and crispy or soft and chewy snack food made from a slender rope of leavened dough coated with salt and baked into a knot or stick shape.

prick To make small holes in the surface of a food to allow steam to escape. When baking an unfilled pie pastry, the bottom and sides are pricked with a fork to prevent blistering and puffing. (*see also* **pastry** *and* **pie**)

prickly pear The pear-shaped, edible fruit of various cactus plants. The skin can range in color from green to purplish-red, and the soft, porous flesh, studded with black seeds, is light yellow-green to deep golden. The fruit has a melonlike aroma and a sweet but rather bland flavor that lends itself to being peeled, seeded, and served cold or cut up and cooked as a vegetable. The juice can be served plain or in a mixed drink with vodka or rum. Prickly pears are available in Mexican markets and some produce markets from fall through spring.
Storage: Ripen prickly pears at room temperature until slightly softened; then refrigerate and use within a few days. (*see also* **cactus**)

primavera (pree muh VAIR uh) An Italian term that means "first green" and refers to using tender, young, raw or blanched fresh vegetables of spring as a garnish or ingredient in various dishes.

prime rib A term used in reference to rib roast. The "prime" designation actually refers to the highest USDA grade of beef. However, when shopping for prime rib, be aware that the best grade of beef generally sold in supermarkets is USDA choice, so even though a rib roast might be packaged as prime rib, it's really choice. (*see also* **beef**)

prix fixe (PREE FIHKS) A French phrase that indicates a complete meal served by a restaurant or hotel for a predetermined price.

processed cheese (*see* **American cheese**)

profiterole (pro FIHT uh rohl) A small mound of cream puff pastry filled with a sweet or savory mixture. Sweet profiteroles might be filled with custard or ice cream, and topped with chocolate sauce. Savory profiteroles are usually served as appetizers and are filled with meat or chicken mixtures. The elaborate French dessert known as croquembouche consists of profiteroles mounded into a pyramid shape and coated with caramel sauce. Baked, unfilled profiteroles can be frozen in a heavy-duty zip-top freezer bag up to 1 month. (*see also* **choux pastry, cream puff,** *and* **croquembouche**)

proof A term that indicates the alcohol content of liquor. In the United States, the proof level is twice the percentage of alcohol, so if liquor is labeled 80 proof, then it contains 40 percent alcohol. This term also refers to the process of dissolving yeast in warm liquid; it's allowed to rest in a warm place for 5 to 10 minutes or until it swells and becomes bubbly. This test indicates whether the yeast is alive and active and able to work as a leavening agent. (*see also* **alcohol, liquor,** *and* **yeast**)

prosciutto (proh SHOO toh) (*see* **ham** *and* **Parma ham**)

proteins A class of nutrients that occurs naturally in animals and plants and are essential to build, maintain, and repair body cells. Proteins also produce antibodies that ward off disease and contribute to the production of enzymes and hormones that regulate the body. Proteins are abundant in foods such as meats, poultry, fish, dairy products, nuts, dried peas, and dried beans.

provençal (proh vahn SAHL) A French term that describes a style of cooking popular in the Provence region of France where garlic, tomatoes, and olive oil are commonly used. Onions, olives, mushrooms, anchovies, and eggplant are frequently a part of provençal dishes.

provolone cheese (*see* **cheese**)

prune The original name given to a dried or dehydrated plum. Today, most companies label them dried plums. The Italian plum is the best-known type of plum for drying, but other varieties are sometimes used. Store in an airtight container in a cool, dry place up to 6 months. They can be eaten out-of-hand or used in a variety of sweet and savory dishes. (*see also* **plum**)

pudding Several different types of desserts are classified as puddings. One is a soft, creamy boiled pudding made with eggs, milk, sugar, and flavoring. Boiled pudding is thickened with flour, cornstarch, or tapioca, and is usually flavored with chocolate, vanilla, butterscotch, banana, or coconut. Rice puddings are thickened custard style with egg or the starch from the rice. Bread puddings start with firm bread soaked in milk and eggs, and sweetened with sugar; most are baked. Other starchy, cakelike pudding may also be baked, such as Indian pudding or steamed pudding. (*see also* **bread pudding, hasty pudding, Indian pudding, steamed pudding, Yorkshire pudding,** *and recipe on the following page*)

> ### TEST KITCHEN SECRET
>
> *For cornstarch puddings, use a heavy-bottomed saucepan to prevent sticking and scorching, and stir constantly with a wooden spoon.* Margaret Monroe Dickey

VANILLA PUDDING

⅓ cup sugar
1½ tablespoons cornstarch
⅛ teaspoon salt
2 cups milk

2 egg yolks
1 tablespoon butter or margarine
1 teaspoon vanilla extract

• Combine first 3 ingredients in a large saucepan; gradually stir in milk. Cook over medium heat, stirring constantly, 6 minutes or until mixture comes to a boil. Cook 1 more minute, stirring constantly. Remove mixture from heat.

• Beat egg yolks 2 minutes or until thick and pale. Gradually stir about one-fourth of hot mixture into yolks; add to remaining hot mixture, stirring constantly. Bring mixture to a boil over medium heat, and cook 3 minutes, stirring constantly.

•Remove from heat; stir in butter and vanilla. Pour mixture into custard cups. Cover and chill, if desired. Yield: 4 servings.

Q **How can "skin" be prevented from forming on cooked puddings?**

A Covering the surface of the pudding with wax paper or plastic wrap after removing from the heat will prevent the skinlike film from forming.

Puerto Rican rum A dry, brandylike rum that comes in a light or dark color. The light is clear with a delicate flavor, while the dark is amber or golden and has a stronger flavor.

puff pastry Delicate, crisp, multilayered pastry made by placing pats of chilled butter between layers of pastry dough, then rolling it out, folding it in thirds, and chilling, then repeating the rolling, folding, and chilling process 6 to 8 times. When baked, the moisture in the butter creates steam, causing the dough to puff and separate into hundreds of fine, flaky layers. Puff pastry is used to make croissants, napoleons, and patty shells. Commercial puff pastry is sold frozen in sheets and as patty shells.(*see also* **croissant, napoleon, pastry,** *and* **patty shell**)

pullet A young hen less than a year old. Because of its age, a pullet is generally tender. (*see also* **chicken**)

pulp The flesh of a fruit.

pulverize A process of reducing a food to a fine texture, usually a powder or dust; it's done by processing, grinding, pounding, or crushing. This process is sometimes used to give fresh herbs and spices a finer texture. (*see also* **mortar and pestle**)

pumpernickel (PUHM puhr nihk uhl) Dense, dark German bread made of rye flour augmented with wheat flour. Pumpernickel bread has a slightly sour flavor; sometimes molasses and caraway seeds are added.

pumpkin A large, orange, hard-shelled member of the gourd family. Pumpkins are round to oblong, have a distinctive ridged shell, and range in color from pale ivory to deep red-tinged orange. Pumpkin's orange flesh has a mild, sweet flavor, and the seeds, also known as pepitas, can be husked and roasted. For cooking, look for small, sweet varieties of pumpkin with a thick flesh and a fairly small seed cavity. Most large pumpkins have fibrous flesh that's not good for cooking; they are best used for Halloween jack-o'-lanterns. Fresh pumpkins are available in the fall and winter. Convenient canned pumpkin puree is also available; some purées are plain and others, labeled as pie filling, include sugar and spices.
Storage: Most pumpkins will keep for a month or longer if stored in a cool, dry place. Once cut, pumpkins should be wrapped tightly in plastic, refrigerated, and used within 3 or 4 days. (*see also* **pepitas, pumpkin pie,** *and* **vegetables**)

TEST KITCHEN SECRET

To bake fresh pumpkin, purchase a small cooking pumpkin (not a jack-o'-lantern) that weighs about 4 pounds. Wash it and cut in half crosswise. Place the halves, cut side down, in a small roasting pan or on a jellyroll pan, and bake at 325° for 45 minutes or until fork tender; cool 10 minutes, then peel, and discard or roast the seeds. Puree the pulp in a food processor or mash thoroughly. LYDA JONES

pumpkin pie A baked single-crust custard pie with a filling of pureed pumpkin, sugar, eggs, milk, and spices. Pumpkin pie is traditionally served at Thanksgiving.

pumpkin seeds (*see* **pepitas**)

punch A hot or cold drink blended from various ingredients including carbonated beverages, fruit juices, wine, and liquor. Sometimes sherbet, ice cream, and fruit are added. Punch is often made to serve a large crowd and is usually ladled from a large punch bowl into smaller punch cups. (*see also* **alcohol, beverage,** *and* **liquor**)

pungent A term used to describe an aroma or flavor that's sharp, biting, acrid, or bitter.

pupu (POO poo) The Hawaiian term for any hot or cold appetizer or hors d'oeurve. Pupu includes a variety of food items from macadamia nuts to barbecued meats. (*see also* **hors d'oeuvre**)

puree (pur RAY) A process of grinding or mashing food until it has a smooth texture. Pureeing can be accomplished by using a food processor, blender, or by forcing the food through a food mill or sieve. Pureed foods can be used as garnishes, side dishes, soups, or sauces.

quail (KWAYL) (*see* **wild game**)

quart A standard unit of measure that equals 32 fluid ounces. It's handy to know that four quarts equal one gallon. (*see also* **measuring** *and Metric Equivalents chart, page 572*)

quenelles (kuh NEHL) Small dumplings made of seasoned ground fish, chicken, veal, or game; they are gently poached in stock and served with a sauce or in soup.

quesadilla (keh sah DEE yah) A flour tortilla folded in half over some combination of cheese, meat, chicken, or refried beans. The filled and folded quesadilla is toasted, grilled, or fried and served with salsa or sour cream. (*see also* **tortilla**)

CHICKEN-AND-BRIE QUESADILLAS WITH CHIPOTLE SALSA

2 cups chopped plum tomato (about 8)	½ cup chopped fresh cilantro, divided
1 small onion, chopped	1 cup finely chopped cooked chicken
3 garlic cloves, minced	
3 tablespoons fresh lime juice	1 (4.5-ounce) can chopped green chiles, drained
2 teaspoons minced canned chipotle chiles in adobo sauce	8 (7-inch) flour tortillas
½ teaspoon salt	8 ounces Brie, trimmed and diced
5 green onions, minced and divided	

• Stir together first 6 ingredients, ¼ cup green onions, and ¼ cup cilantro. Let salsa stand 1 hour.

• Stir together remaining green onions, remaining ¼ cup cilantro, chicken, and green chiles.

• Arrange 4 tortillas on a large baking sheet coated with vegetable cooking spray. Top evenly with cheese, chicken mixture, and remaining tortillas, pressing down slightly.

• Bake at 425° for 8 to 10 minutes or until cheese melts. Cut into wedges, and serve immediately with salsa. Yield: 12 appetizer servings.

Note: Freeze remaining chipotle chiles in adobo sauce, if desired.

queso (KEH soh) A Spanish term for cheese.

quiche (KEESH) A French dish consisting of a pastry shell filled with savory egg custard and various ingredients such as onions, mushrooms, ham, or shellfish. The mixture is baked until set and served for brunch, lunch, or dinner; miniature quiches can be served as appetizers. The most well-known quiche is quiche Lorraine, flavored with cheese and bacon. Special quiche dishes like the one shown are available or you can make quiche in a regular pieplate. (*see also* **egg**)

quick bread A category of breads that doesn't require kneading or rising time because they're leavened with baking powder, baking soda, or eggs. Biscuits, muffins, popovers, and a variety of sweet and savory loaves are included in this category. (*see also* **biscuit, leavening agent, muffin, pancake, popover,** *and* **waffle**)

TIMESAVING TIP
To conveniently prepare hot, steaming quick breads for breakfast, mix dry and liquid ingredients separately the night before; place the liquid ingredients in the refrigerator, and then combine them the next morning, and bake.

quince (KWIHNC) A hard, round or pear-shaped fruit that looks and tastes like a cross between an apple and pear. The yellowish-white flesh is dry and tart, so much so that it's not very popular with Americans although it's very popular in Mediterranean countries. They're available from August through January in some supermarkets. Because they're so hard, quinces are mostly cooked in jams, jellies, and preserves.

Storage: Ripen quinces at room temperature and then refrigerate in plastic bags up to 2 weeks.

quinoa (KEEN wah) While a traditional part of South American cuisine, quinoa is relatively new to Americans. It's high in protein, vitamins, minerals, and unsaturated fat, but low in carbohydrates. The ivory-colored, mild-flavored grain tastes like couscous and cooks like rice although in about half the time. Serve it as a side dish to replace rice or add it to soups, salads, and even puddings. Quinoa can be found in health food stores and some supermarkets. (*see also* **grain**)

rabbit (*see* **wild game**)

rack of lamb A cut from the lamb's rib section that starts out as a rib roast containing rib bones. The rack can be left intact, cut into individual chops, or shaped into a circle to form a crown roast. (*see also* **lamb**)

raclette cheese (rah KLEHT) A firm cow's milk cheese from Switzerland with a mellow, nutty flavor; the cheese is often heated over an open fire and scraped off as it melts. Melted raclette is typically served with boiled potatoes, dark bread, and pickled vegetables. (*see also* **cheese**)

R

radicchio (rah DEE kee oh) A type of red Italian chicory with tender but firm leaves that have a bitter flavor. Radicchio adds interest to ordinary green salads. It can also be grilled, sautéed, or baked. **Storage:** Chill in a plastic bag up to a week. (*see also* **lettuce**)

radish The root of a plant in the mustard family that comes in various sizes, shapes, and colors. Besides round red radishes, there are thin white ones known as icicles, long carrotlike Japanese daikons, large black turniplike radishes, and slender red French breakfast radishes. Their flavors range from mild to peppery and their crisp textures make them ideal for tossing in salads, though they are often used as garnishes. Some, particularly the daikon, are used for cooking. Radishes are plentiful in most produce markets and supermarkets. **Storage:** Remove and discard their leaves and refrigerate radishes in a plastic bag up to a week. (*see also* **daikon**)

ragoût (ra GOO) A rich French stew of meat, poultry, or fish made with or without vegetables. The well-seasoned mixture can include wine.

MAPLE-GLAZED QUAIL WITH WHITE BEAN RAGOÛT

4 (4-ounce) dressed quail	¼ teaspoon salt
2 medium onions, diced	¼ teaspoon pepper
1 tablespoon vegetable oil	¼ teaspoon dried thyme
1 tablespoon sugar	3 tablespoons butter or
4 fresh mushrooms, sliced	margarine, melted
1 teaspoon white vinegar	White Bean Ragoût
⅓ cup fine, dry breadcrumbs	Maple Brown Sauce

• Remove breast and back bones from quail; set quail aside.
• Sauté onion in hot oil in a large skillet over low heat 10 minutes or until browned; add sugar and mushrooms, and cook until tender, stirring often. Stir in vinegar and next 4 ingredients. Spoon into quail cavities, and secure with wooden picks. Tuck wings under, and place breast side up in a buttered 2-quart casserole. Brush with melted butter.
• Bake at 350° for 25 minutes or until a meat thermometer inserted in stuffing registers 165°. Serve over a bed of White Bean Ragoût; drizzle with Maple Brown Sauce. Yield: 2 servings.

WHITE BEAN RAGOÛT

1 cup dried great Northern or	1 bay leaf
navy beans	3 tablespoons diced carrot
½ cup diced onion	2 cups beef broth

- Sort and wash beans; drain.
- Combine beans and water to cover in a large saucepan; bring to a boil, remove from heat, and let stand 1 hour. Drain beans, and return to pan. Add onion and remaining ingredients; bring to a boil. Cover, reduce heat, and simmer 2 hours or until beans are tender, stirring occasionally. Remove and discard bay leaf. Yield: 2 cups.

MAPLE BROWN SAUCE

1 teaspoon butter or margarine	½ cup beef broth
1 teaspoon all-purpose flour	1 tablespoon maple syrup

- Melt butter in a small heavy saucepan over low heat; whisk in flour until smooth. Cook 1 minute, whisking constantly.
- Whisk in broth; cook over medium heat 5 minutes or until thickened and bubbly, whisking constantly. Stir in maple syrup. Yield: ½ cup.

rainbow trout (*see* **trout**)

raisin (RAY zihn) A sweet dried grape that can be cooked in side dishes or baked goods or tossed into raw salads. There are several varieties available:
- **Dark seedless:** Made from Thompson seedless grapes that are dried for several weeks. Their sweet flavor makes them good for snacking.
- **Golden seedless:** From Thompson seedless grapes treated with sulphur dioxide to prevent darkening, plus they have a shorter drying time. They are moist and can be used for cooking or snacking.
- **Muscat:** Muscat grapes yield large, fat, dark, very sweet raisins favored by many bakers.
- **Zante:** Zante grapes produce tiny, dried currants often used in baked goods.
Storage: Store raisins in a covered container at room temperature for a month or refrigerated up to 6 months. (*see also* **currant, dried fruit,** *and* **grape**)

RAISIN SAUCE

2 cups raisins	1 tablespoon cornstarch
1½ cups water	1 tablespoon grated orange rind
Pinch of salt	3 tablespoons fresh orange juice
2 cups sugar	½ cup chopped walnuts or pecans

- Bring first 3 ingredients to a boil in a saucepan; reduce heat, and simmer 30 minutes. Combine sugar and next 3 ingredients; stir into raisin mixture. Return to a boil, stirring constantly. Boil, stirring constantly, 1 minute. Stir in walnuts. Yield: 2 cups.

ramekin (RAM ih kihn) A small, round ceramic baking dish that looks like a miniature soufflé dish and is used to serve desserts or savory dishes. Custard cups or individual soufflé dishes can be substituted for ramekins. A ramekin can also be a small cheese tart.

ramen (RAH mehn) Instant-style Japanese noodles in broth with small pieces of meat and vegetables. Dried ramen noodles sealed in packets with bits of dehydrated vegetables and broth are sold in most supermarkets.

LITE BITE
Regular ramen noodles are fried before they're dried, so make sure you purchase low-fat varieties if you're watching fat consumption.

rancid Term that describes a fat or fatty food with stale or tainted flavor caused by exposure to light, water, or heat. To prevent, store solid fats such as butter and lard in the refrigerator in original packages or a covered container; unopened, they will keep frozen up to 6 months. Keep unopened shortening in a cool, dry place indefinitely; once opened, store no longer than a year. Store oils in airtight containers away from light and heat. Nut oils go rancid quickly, so purchase in small quantities and store in refrigerator. Cool temperatures may make oils solid or cloudy; bring to room temperature, and they will become clear again. (*see also* **fats and oils**)

LITE BITE
Vitamins A and E can be lost if rancidity occurs.

rape (RAYP) A vegetable related to the cabbage and turnip families but with a pungent, bitter flavor that's popular in Italy where it's fried, steamed, or braised. Rape, also known as broccoli raab, is best known for the oil from its seeds. (*see also* **broccoli raab, canola oil,** *and* **rapeseed oil**)

rapeseed oil Oil low in saturated fat made from the seeds of the rape vegetable. It's used for cooking and sold as canola oil. (*see also* **canola oil** *and* **fats and oils**)

rare A degree of doneness that indicates meat with a deep red center that provides slight resistance and is spongy when pressed. Rare meat is typically cooked to 140°, but because of safety concerns, the USDA no longer recommends eating beef, veal, or lamb rare. These meats should be cooked to at least medium rare or 145°. (*see also* **beef**)

rasher An English term referring to a single thin slice of bacon or ham.

raspberry An intensely flavored red, black, or golden-colored berry made up of many tiny individual sections of fruit, each with its own seed, surrounding a central core. Its sweet, slightly acidic flavor makes raspberries suited for eating fresh with cream or for cooking in jams, tarts, pies, sauces, or other desserts. Fresh raspberries are available May through November, but they can also be purchased canned or frozen.

RESCUE for seedy sauce:
While raspberry seeds are tiny and edible, they can be annoying, so if pureeing for a sauce, strain the mixture through a sieve to remove the seeds.

Storage: Store in an airtight container in the refrigerator for 2 to 3 days, rinsing lightly just before serving. (*see also* **berry**)

ratatouille (ra tuh TOO ee) An earthy, vegetable dish that often includes eggplant, tomatoes, onions, red and green bell peppers, and zucchini simmered in olive oil and seasoned with herbs. The vegetables can be cooked together or separately and then combined, and served hot or cold.

RATATOUILLE

1 eggplant, cubed	2 garlic cloves, minced
1 large zucchini, cubed	2 (14½-ounce) cans fancy
2 medium yellow squash, cubed	tomato wedges, undrained
¼ cup olive oil	½ cup dry white wine
1 small green pepper, coarsely	⅓ cup small pitted ripe olives
chopped	1 teaspoon salt
1 small yellow bell pepper,	2 teaspoons dried Italian
coarsely chopped	seasoning
1 small red bell pepper, coarsely	1 bay leaf
chopped	¾ cup freshly grated Parmesan
1 medium onion, chopped	cheese (optional)

• Sauté first 3 ingredients in hot oil in a large Dutch oven over medium-high heat 6 to 8 minutes. Add peppers, onion, and garlic; sauté 8 minutes, stirring occasionally. Add tomatoes and next 5 ingredients; cover, reduce heat to medium, and simmer 15 minutes or until tender. Discard bay leaf.
• Transfer ratatouille to a large serving dish. Sprinkle with cheese, if desired. Serve with a slotted spoon. Yield: 10 servings.

rattlesnake A poisonous snake found in the United States that when cooked tastes like bland, chewy chicken. The meat can be cut into cubes and threaded on skewers for grilling; it's sometimes served at county fairs and festivals or as part of wild game banquets and feasts.

ravigote sauce (rah vee GOHT) The name for two different herb-flavored French sauces, one served cold and the other hot. The cold sauce is made from a vinaigrette mixed with capers, onions, and herbs, and is usually served with fish or shellfish. The hot version is made from a velouté sauce flavored with white wine, vinegar, and shallots, and served with poultry or fish. (*see also* **velouté sauce** *and* **vinaigrette**)

ravioli (rav ee OH lee) Small square or round pillows of pasta dough stuffed with meat, cheese, or vegetables. Prepare this Italian specialty by boiling, then baking with a cream, cheese, or tomato sauce. The Chinese use won tons to make ravioli, while the Jewish version is known as kreplach. (*see also* **kreplach, pasta,** *and* **won ton**)

> **TIMESAVING TIP**
> Commercially refrigerated and frozen ravioli offer great flavor and convenience, and cook in boiling water in minutes.

reamer A cone-shaped wooden utensil with a ridged surface that's used for extracting juice from fruit. (*see also* **juicer**)

reconstitute (ree CON stih toot) Adding water to a concentrated, condensed, or dehydrated food in order to restore it to its original strength. (*see also* **dried fruit** *and* **rehydrate**)

red beans Medium-sized red kidney beans that often play a role in Mexican and Southwestern cooking where they are typically served whole or as refried beans. Other parts of the country enjoy them in chili con carne; in Louisiana and other Southern locales, the beans go hand-in-hand with rice. (*see also* **beans, dried;** *and* **frijoles**)

SPICY RED BEANS AND RICE

2 pounds dried red kidney beans
5 bacon slices, chopped
1 pound smoked sausage, cut into ¼-inch-thick slices
½ pound salt pork, quartered
6 garlic cloves, minced
5 celery ribs, sliced
2 green bell peppers, chopped
1 large onion, chopped
2 (32-ounce) containers chicken broth
2 cups water
1 teaspoon salt
1 teaspoon ground red pepper
1 teaspoon black pepper
Hot cooked rice

• Place kidney beans in a Dutch oven. Cover with water 2 inches above beans, and let soak 8 hours. Drain beans; rinse thoroughly, and drain again.
• Sauté bacon in Dutch oven over medium-high heat 5 minutes. Add smoked sausage and salt pork; sauté 5 minutes or until sausage is golden brown. Add garlic and next 3 ingredients; sauté 5 minutes or until vegetables are tender.
• Stir in beans, broth, 2 cups water, and next 3 ingredients; bring to a boil. Boil 15 minutes; reduce heat, and simmer, stirring occasionally, 3 hours or until beans are tender. Remove salt pork before serving. Serve over rice. Yield: 2 quarts.

Note: For quick soaking, place kidney beans in a Dutch oven; cover with water 2 inches above beans, and bring to a boil. Boil 1 minute; cover, remove from heat, and let stand 1 hour. Drain and proceed with recipe.

Southernism

The date that New Orleans unofficially adopted Red Beans and Rice as a traditional Monday meal seems to elude food historians; however, red beans have been ingrained in the New Orleans landscape for at least 200 years. For some cooks, ham hocks, andouille sausage, or bacon are a must, while for others, pickled or salt pork makes a great pot of red beans. It's well known that red beans were beloved by Louis "Satchmo" Armstrong. In a letter to a fellow New Orleanian, Armstrong wrote, "It really shouldn't be any problem at all for you to figure out my favorite dish. We all were brought up eating the same thing, so I will tell you: Red Beans and Rice with Ham Hocks is my birthmark."

redeye gravy Gravy made from the drippings of fried country ham and coffee, which is added for a richer color and flavor. The gravy is cooked until slightly thickened and served with ham, grits, or biscuits, usually at breakfast. (*see also* **country ham**)

COUNTRY HAM WITH REDEYE GRAVY

6 thin slices uncooked country ham (about 1 pound)	**½ cup strongly brewed coffee**
	½ cup hot water
2 teaspoons brown sugar	**¼ teaspoon freshly ground pepper**

• Cut gashes in fat to keep ham from curling. Lightly grease a 10-inch cast-iron skillet, using fat cut from ham; heat over medium-high 1 minute. Reduce heat to medium; sauté ham, in batches, in skillet 3 to 4 minutes or until browned, turning several times. Remove ham from skillet; cover and keep warm.

• Add sugar and remaining 3 ingredients to skillet; bring to a boil. Boil 3 minutes or until slightly thickened and reduced to about ½ cup. Serve gravy over ham. Yield: 8 servings.

Southernism

There's no doubt Southerners are crazy for gravy, especially redeye gravy. To most Southerners, a classic breakfast means country ham with redeye gravy, eggs, grits, and homemade biscuits. A dose of strong black coffee, the recipe's key ingredient, will give folks a much-needed morning jolt, hence the name.

redfish A member of the drum family with reddish-orange skin, a black-spotted tail, and firm, ivory-colored flesh with a mild flavor. This is the lean fish that originally catapulted blackened dishes to popularity and has become much more scarce as a result. (*see also* **blackened** *and* **drum**)

red pepper A general name given to a variety of hot red chile peppers. Red peppers are usually dried and are available whole, flaked, or ground. (*see also* **cayenne pepper, chile pepper, hot sauce,** *and* **peppers**)

red potato Small, round red-skinned potatoes with white, waxy flesh that makes them good for boiling. This potato is referred to as a new potato because it's harvested while still young. (*see also* **potato** *and* **vegetables**)

red snapper (*see* **fish** *and* **snapper**)

reduce A process of boiling wine, stock, or sauce until, by evaporation, it's thickened and concentrated with more intense flavor. The mixture is sometimes referred to as a reduction.

red velvet cake A holiday layer cake traditionally made with chocolate or cocoa and red food coloring. The resulting reddish cake layers are frosted and filled with white cream cheese frosting to take on a stunning festive appearance. (*see also* **cake, frosting,** *and recipe on the following page*)

RED VELVET CAKE

½ cup butter or margarine, softened
1½ cups sugar
1 tablespoon white vinegar
1 teaspoon vanilla extract
3 large eggs
1 (1-ounce) bottle red liquid food coloring

2½ cups all-purpose flour
2 tablespoons cocoa
1 teaspoon baking soda
½ teaspoon salt
1 cup buttermilk
Cream Cheese Frosting

• Beat butter at medium speed with an electric mixer until fluffy; gradually add sugar, vinegar, and vanilla, beating well. Add eggs, 1 at a time, beating until blended after each addition. Add food coloring, beating until mixture is combined.
• Combine flour and next 3 ingredients; add to butter mixture alternately with buttermilk, beginning and ending with flour mixture. Beat at low speed until blended after each addition. Pour into 2 greased and floured 9-inch cakepans.
• Bake at 350° for 20 to 22 minutes or until a wooden pick inserted in center comes out clean. Cool in pans on wire racks 5 minutes; remove from pans, and cool on wire racks. Spread Cream Cheese Frosting between layers and on tops and sides of cake. Yield: 1 (2-layer) cake.

CREAM CHEESE FROSTING

1 (8-ounce) package cream cheese, softened
½ cup butter or margarine, softened

1 (16-ounce) package powdered sugar
1½ teaspoons vanilla extract
1 cup chopped pecans

• Beat cream cheese and butter until creamy; gradually add sugar and vanilla, beating well. Stir in pecans. Yield: 3 cups.

refried beans A popular Mexican side dish or filling of mashed and fried red beans, black beans, or pinto beans. The beans can be eaten plain or spread on tortillas. They're sold canned in most supermarkets. (*see also* **frijoles, pinto bean,** *and* **red beans**)

refrigerator cookie (*see* **cookie** *and* **icebox cookie**)

Reggiano Parmigiano (rej JYAH noh pahr muh ZHAH nah) An Italian hard grating cheese that's aged at least 2 years. (*see also* **cheese**)

rehydrate A process where water that was lost during a drying process is restored. Dried mushrooms and tomatoes are often rehydrated before they're used. (*see also* **dried fruit, dried tomato, mushroom,** *and* **reconstitute**)

relish A cooked or pickled sauce made of fruits or vegetables and used as a spicy, sweet, or savory condiment. Relishes can include pickle relish used for hot dogs, piccalilli, pickled vegetables, corn relish, or chutney. Relish mixtures can be made at home or purchased in jars from supermarkets. (*see also* **chutney, corn relish,** *and* **piccalilli**)

rémoulade (ray muh LAHD) A tangy French mayonnaise-based sauce flavored with mustard and herbs; some versions also include anchovies, capers, chopped gherkins. Rémoulade is served chilled with cold meats, fish, and shellfish.

RÉMOULADE SAUCE

1 cup mayonnaise	1 tablespoon chopped fresh
3 green onions, sliced	parsley
2 tablespoons Creole mustard	¼ teaspoon ground red pepper
2 garlic cloves, pressed	Garnish: sliced green onions

• Stir together first 6 ingredients until sauce is well blended. Chill until ready to serve. Garnish, if desired. Yield: about 1¼ cups.

render A process of separating animal fat from meat tissues by melting the fat over low heat. Once melted, the fat is strained and can be used for frying or flavoring; the remaining crisp bits of meat, called cracklings, are sometimes used like crumbled bacon and stirred into cornbread. (*see also* **cracklings**)

rennet (REN iht) A coagulating enzyme from a calf's stomach that aids in curdling milk for making cheese or for junket. Rennet can be purchased in tablet or powdered form. (*see also* **junket**)

Reuben sandwich (ROO behn) A sourdough rye bread sandwich heaped with layers of corned beef, Swiss cheese, and sauerkraut. Reubens are grilled in butter and can be served cold or hot.

Rhine wine A generic term used in North America to describe a medium-sweet white wine such as Chablis or Burgundy, and should not be confused with the Rhine Valley, a well-respected German wine-growing region producing dry to sweet white wine made from Riesling grapes. (*see also* **Johannisberg Riesling** *and* **wine**)

rhubarb A long, celery-like vegetable generally cooked and eaten as a fruit. Its long stalks or ribs range in color from red to pink, and they are too tart to be eaten raw. In fact, rhubarb is usually cooked with a generous amount of sugar to balance its tartness. After sweetening, it makes delicious sauces, jams, and desserts, and is referred to as "pieplant" because of its popularity as a pie filling. You will often find it teamed with strawberries, ginger, or oranges.

Storage: Rhubarb is highly perishable, so it should be refrigerated in a plastic bag up to 3 days. It can also be blanched and frozen in freezer containers up to 6 months.

TEST KITCHEN SECRET

The large green leaves on the tips of rhubarb stalks contain oxalic acid and can be toxic. Always trim and discard them. MARGARET MONROE DICKEY

RHUBARB CRUMBLE

1 cup uncooked regular oats	⅓ cup butter or margarine
⅔ cup firmly packed brown sugar	6 cups chopped rhubarb (1½
⅓ cup all-purpose flour	pounds)
½ teaspoon ground cinnamon	1 cup sugar

• Combine first 4 ingredients; cut in butter with a pastry blender until mixture is crumbly.
• Combine rhubarb and sugar; toss gently, and place in a greased 8- or 9-inch square baking dish. Top rhubarb mixture with oats mixture.
• Bake at 350° for 45 minutes or until lightly browned. Serve with ice cream, if desired. Yield: 8 servings.

rib The paired, curved bones that stiffen the body cavities of birds or animals and the meat that adheres to them. The rib sections from beef, lamb, and pork carcasses are often barbecued and basted with a tangy sauce. Individual stalks of celery and rhubarb are also referred to as ribs. (*see also* **spareribs**)

ribbon A term used to describe the consistency of an egg and sugar batter beaten until thick and pale. When the beater or whisk is lifted from the batter, the mixture should slowly drain back into the bowl and form a ribbonlike pattern.

rice The starchy seed of a semiaquatic grass of Asian origin that's a staple in the diets of much of the world's population. The major rice-producing states in our country are Arkansas, Louisiana, Mississippi, Missouri, Texas, and California. Rice has a mild, nutty, adaptable flavor and aroma that enables it to be eaten plain or paired with a variety of other ingredients.

There are thousands of varieties of rice, but they can basically be divided into three main categories, based on the size of the seed:

• **Long-grain rice** is four or five times as long as it is wide and cooks into fluffy grains that separate easily. Aromatic basmati and Texmati rice with their sweet, nutty taste and aroma fall into the long-grained category; these are ideal for using in pilafs. Della rice is a Southern-produced long-grain variety known for its popcornlike taste and aroma, while pecan rice is a Louisiana version enjoyed for its pecanlike flavor and scent. Jasmine rice, a favorite from Thailand, can be identified by its sweet floral scent.

• **Medium-grain rice** is two or three times longer than it is wide and cooks into relatively moist, tender grains that become stickier as it cools. This rice is often used in Spain for making paella.

• **Short-grain rice** is fat, almost round and has a high starch content that makes it moist, tender, and sticky when cooked; it's the rice of choice for Asian cuisines because it's easy to handle with chopsticks. Mochi is short-grain rice used in Japan to make rice cakes. Arborio rice is short-grain rice preferred by Italians for making risotto because it forms a creamy sauce as it cooks.

Southernism

Rice culture in the United States began in the the late 1600s in coastal South Carolina, where the subtropical climate and extensive system of estuaries offered perfect growing conditions. In 1700, more than 300 tons of Carolina Gold rice were exported out of Charleston, a venture that eventually made Lowcountry planters wealthy beyond compare and established the variety as one of the world's finest. The demise of slavery ended the rice culture in South Carolina because the fields were not suitable for mechanical harvesting. Today, Arkansas, Louisiana, Mississippi, Missouri, Texas, and California are the major rice-growing states.

Rice can be further divided into two other broad categories—white and brown. Brown rice has only the outer hull removed, leaving the bran intact, making it more nutritious than white rice. It takes longer to cook, is chewier, and nuttier-tasting than white rice. There's a quick-cooking version of brown rice that has been (*continued on the following page*)

♡ LITE BITE

Rice bran is the outer layer of the rice kernel. It's high in insoluble fiber and may be effective in lowering cholesterol. Rice is high in carbohydrates and low in sodium and fat. It's also a good source of iron and many B vitamins.

partially cooked, then dehydrated. White rice has the husk, bran, and germ removed; it's sometimes referred to as polished rice. There are also several other forms of white rice: Converted or parboiled white rice has been soaked, pressure-steamed, and dried; this procedure adds some of the nutrients from the bran and germ back to the kernel. Sometimes converted rice takes on a slightly yellow cast. It requires longer cooking than regular white rice. Instant or quick-cooking white rice has been fully or partially cooked before being dehydrated; it takes just minutes to cook, but lacks in flavor and texture.

TIMESAVING TIP

Instant rice cooks in 5 minutes. Basmati rice cooks in just 12 minutes and has an appealing aroma, taste, and texture. Another way to save time is by cooking up a large batch of rice and storing it in an airtight container in the refrigerator up to a week; just reheat or microwave briefly until heated through.

RESCUE for a pan with stuck-on rice:

Let it soak in warm water for at least 30 minutes, then scrape it with a metal or plastic spatula. If necessary, heat the pan of water over low heat to help loosen the rice.

Several other rice products are also available at the supermarket. Rice flour is finely ground white or brown rice and can be used as a thickener and for baking. Wild rice isn't actually rice, but a marsh grass, and requires an extended cooking time; it can, however, be combined with white or brown rice for serving.

Storage: Store rice in an airtight container in a cool, dark, dry place. White rice will keep almost indefinitely, but brown rice is more perishable and will keep 6 months, unless refrigerated, and then it will keep longer. (*see also* **Arborio rice, basmati, jasmine rice, mochi, paella, risotto, Texmati rice,** *and* **wild rice**)

EASY OVEN RICE

1 (10½-ounce) can French onion soup, undiluted
¼ cup butter or margarine, melted
1 (4½-ounce) jar sliced mushrooms

1 (8-ounce) can sliced water chestnuts
1 cup uncooked long-grain rice

• Combine soup and butter; stir well. Drain mushrooms and water chestnuts, reserving liquid. Add enough water to reserved liquid to measure 1⅓ cups.

• Add mushrooms, water chestnuts, reserved liquid, and rice to soup mixture; stir well. Pour into a lightly greased 11- x 7-inch baking dish.

• Cover and bake at 350° for 1 hour and 10 minutes or until liquid is absorbed and rice is tender. Yield: 6 side-dish servings.

READER TIP

"We eat a lot of rice, so I purchased a rice cooker. This way I get perfect rice every time, no matter how much I cook. It steams from 2 to 24 cups of rice at a time in a pan that sits inside the cooker. I usually put the rice and water in the cooker when I start a meal and it's done by the time we eat." W.G., EUFAULA, AL

rice bran oil Unsaturated oil extracted from the rice bran during the polishing process. This oil lowers "bad" cholesterol, or LDLs. It can be found in Asian markets and health food stores. Buy in small quantities because this oil quickly becomes stale and turns rancid.
Storage: Store in a cool, dark place.

rice flour Regular rice flour is a fine, powdery flour made from milled, ground regular white or brown rice. It's too tender for cakes and breads, but is great for shortbread. Mochi rice is also ground and used as a thickener in Asian cooking. (*see also* **mochi** *and* **rice**)

rice-flour noodles Very thin, long translucent white noodles made from finely ground rice and water and used in Asian cooking. Also known as rice sticks or rice vermicelli, these noodles quickly puff into a tangle of crispy strands when deep-fried. The noodles can also be soaked and used in soups or stir-fries. Rice-flour noodles can be found in Asian markets and some supermarkets, and are sold in coiled nests or in stick form. (*see also* **Asian noodle** *and* **noodle**)

rice paper An edible, thin, almost translucent small sheet made from water and rice flour or the pithy root of the rice paper shrub. The sheets are used as wrappers for foods to be eaten as is or deep-fried; it's also a wrapper for Vietnamese and Thai spring rolls. Rice paper can be purchased in Asian markets and some supermarkets. (*see also* **spring roll**)

rice pudding This creamy, custardlike dessert is made with milk, sugar, eggs, and rice, and often flavored with cinnamon or nutmeg. Raisins or currants are sometimes stirred into rice pudding.

CREAMY RICE PUDDING

1 quart milk	½ cup sugar
1 cup uncooked regular rice	½ cup half-and-half
½ teaspoon salt	1 teaspoon ground cinnamon
1½ teaspoons vanilla extract	1 cup raisins
4 egg yolks, beaten	

• Combine first 4 ingredients in a medium saucepan. Cover and cook over low heat about 40 minutes or until rice is tender, stirring occasionally.
• Combine egg yolks and next 3 ingredients in a small bowl. Gradually stir about one-fourth of hot mixture into yolk mixture; add yolk mixture to remaining hot mixture. Cook over low heat, stirring constantly, until mixture reaches 160° and is thickened and bubbly (about 3 minutes). Stir in raisins. Serve warm or chilled. Yield: 10 servings.

ricer A tool that looks like a large garlic press, but is used to mash cooked foods such as potatoes, carrots, or turnips. The food is placed in a hopper and pushed through by a plunger; when it exits the tiny holes, it resembles grains of rice. Ricers can be purchased at kitchen supply stores.

rice sticks (*see* **rice-flour noodles**)

rice vinegar Chinese and Japanese vinegar made from fermented rice wine and is usually milder than most Western vinegars. Chinese versions are generally white, pale amber, or black; the lighter ones are used for sweet-and-sour and seafood dishes, and the black is a table condiment. Japanese rice vinegar is mellow and almost sweet and used for sushi and salads. Both can be found in Asian markets and some supermarkets. (*see also* **vinegar**)

rice wine Several variations exist: Mirin is a sweet wine used exclusively for cooking, and sake is a traditional Japanese beverage, but can also be used for cooking. Dry sherry can substitute for either. (*see also* **mirin** *and* **sake**)

ricotta cheese A fresh, moist Italian cheese made from the whey remaining after mozzarella and provolone cheeses have been made; milk is often added. Ricotta is white, slightly grainy and sweet, and can be used in savory dishes such as lasagna and manicotti, or sweet desserts such as cheese-cake or cannoli. (*see also* **cannoli, cheese, lasagna, manicotti,** *and* **whey**)

Riesling (*see* **Johannisberg Riesling**)

rigatoni (rihg ah TOH nee) Large, grooved tubes of Italian pasta.

rind The rather thick skin or outer coating of foods such as melons, citrus fruit, some vegetables, some cheeses, and country hams. Some cheese rinds are soft and edible. Citrus rinds consist of both the colored zest and the white pith; the rinds can be cooked and candied. Melon rinds, particularly those of watermelons, can be cooked and pickled. Ham rind is usually removed before cooking, but can be added to soups and stews for additional flavor. (*see also* **peel** *and* **zest**)

Rioja (ree OH ha) A region in Spain known for its sturdy dry red wines. (*see also* **wine**)

ripen When foods, particularly fruits, have reached their peak of flavor and texture. Ripeness is often indicated by a change in color, a more prominent aroma or scent, a softer texture, and a sweeter taste.

risotto A rice dish prepared by sautéing short-grain Italian Arborio rice in butter and then gradually stirring in boiling stock. The mixture is patiently simmered and stirred until the starch in the rice dissolves and forms a creamy sauce that complements the chewy rice. Risottos can be flavored with chicken, shellfish, sausage, vegetables, cheese, white wine, and herbs, and served as a side dish or main course. (*see also* **Arborio rice** *and* **rice**)

BROCCOLI RISOTTO WITH PARMESAN

6½ cups chicken broth
1 medium onion, chopped
2 tablespoons olive oil
1½ cups uncooked Arborio rice
1 (16-ounce) package broccoli florets
1 cup shredded Parmesan cheese
¼ teaspoon salt
¼ teaspoon pepper
Shredded Parmesan cheese

- Bring broth to a boil in a saucepan; remove from heat, and keep warm.
- Sauté chopped onion in hot oil in a saucepan over medium-high heat until tender.
- Add rice; cook, stirring constantly, 2 minutes. Reduce heat to medium; add ¾ cup broth, and cook, stirring constantly, until absorbed.
- Repeat procedure with 4½ cups hot broth, ¾ cup at a time. Add broccoli and remaining 1¼ cups hot broth, ½ cup at a time.
- Cook, stirring constantly, until liquid is absorbed and rice is creamy. (Cooking time is about 30 minutes.) Stir in 1 cup cheese, salt, and pepper. Serve with additional cheese. Yield: 8 servings.

roast To cook food in an uncovered pan in the oven with dry heat or on a spit over an open fire, giving it a crusty, browned exterior and a juicy interior. This method of cooking is usually reserved for tender cuts of meat or poultry; tougher cuts require moist cooking methods. Vegetables such as whole potatoes, sweet potatoes, beets, and tomatoes lightly coated with olive oil also roast nicely. This term also refers to a large piece of meat, such as a rib roast or pork roast, cooked by the roasting method. (*see also* **beef, lamb, pork, poultry,** *and* **veal**)

rock candy A hard candy made by allowing a concentrated sugar syrup mixture to evaporate and crystallize around a small wooden stick or piece of string. Rock candy can be made at home or purchased in candy shops, and is sometimes used to sweeten tea or coffee. (*see also* **candy** *and* **sugar syrup**)

rocket (*see* **arugula** *and* **lettuce**)

rockfish One of the largest families of fish found in the Pacific Ocean. This low-fat, firm-fleshed fish generally has black or olive to bright orange or crimson skin with yellow fins, and is sometimes spotted or striped. Significant varieties include bocaccio, ocean perch, orange rockfish, yellowtail, and striped bass; they're suitable for most cooking methods. (*see also* **fish**)

rock salt (*see* **salt**)

Rocky Mountain oyster Also called mountain oysters or prairie oysters, these are the testicles of a lamb, calf, or boar. They have little flavor, but are considered a delicacy in Italy and France, and are usually sautéed, deep-fried, braised, or poached.

rocky road A combination of chocolate, miniature marshmallows, and nuts that can be incorporated into candy, brownies, ice cream, or pies.

ROCKY ROAD FUDGE BROWNIES

1 (19.8-ounce) package brownie mix	⅓ cup milk
1 cup chopped pecans	½ cup butter or margarine
3 cups miniature marshmallows	1 (16-ounce) package powdered sugar, sifted
2 (1-ounce) squares unsweetened chocolate	½ teaspoon vanilla extract

• Prepare brownie mix according to package directions; stir in pecans. Spoon batter into a greased 13- x 9-inch baking pan.
• Bake at 350° for 25 minutes. Remove from oven, and immediately sprinkle miniature marshmallows over hot brownies.
• Combine chocolate, ⅓ cup milk, and butter in a heavy saucepan. Cook over low heat until chocolate and butter melt, stirring often.
• Remove from heat. Transfer to a medium mixing bowl. Add powdered sugar and vanilla; beat at low speed with an electric mixer until smooth. (If frosting is too stiff for spreading, add milk, 1 tablespoon at a time, stirring until smooth.) Spread over brownies. Cool in pan on a wire rack. Cover and chill 1 hour or up to 24 hours before cutting into bars. Yield: 2 dozen.

roe (ROH) The eggs of female fish and the milt or reproductive glands of male fish. Roe is considered a delicacy. It's usually removed from the fish and fried, sautéed, or poached. The most desirable roe comes from carp, herring, mackerel, and shad, but the roe from flounder, mullet, perch, salmon, and sturgeon is also eaten. If salted, the roe is transformed into caviar. (*see also* **caviar** *and* **she-crab soup**)

Southernism

She-crab soup, the hallmark of Charleston cuisine, was so named because it included the crab roe. Restrictions on harvesting eggs today ensure a steady crop of crabs, so no restaurants serve the soup with roe today.

roll A small, individual serving of yeast bread that can be made in various flavors and shapes.

ROLL VARIATIONS

Cloverleaf Rolls: *Lightly grease muffin pans. Shape dough into 1-inch balls; place 3 dough balls into each muffin cup. Cover and let rise until doubled in bulk. Bake.*

Easy Pan Rolls: *Lightly grease 1 or 2 (9-inch) cakepans. Shape dough into 1½-inch balls in pan, leaving ½-inch space between them. Cover and let rise until doubled in bulk. Bake.*

Bow Ties: *Roll dough into several long ropes about ½ inch in diameter. Cut ropes into 8-inch strips. Carefully tie each dough strip into a knot. Place bow ties on a lightly greased baking sheet. Cover and let rise until doubled in bulk. Bake.*

Fan Tans: *Roll dough into a large rectangle about ¼ inch thick. Spread softened butter over dough. Cut dough lengthwise into 1-inch strips. Stack 5 or 6 strips, buttered side up, on top of one another. Cut each stacked section, and place sections, cut side down, into lightly greased muffin pans. Cover and let rise until doubled in bulk. Bake.*

Crescents: *Roll dough into a 12 inch circle (about ¼ inch thick) on a lightly floured surface. (Reserve excess dough for other uses.) Spread softened butter over dough. Cut into 12 wedges; roll each wedge tightly, beginning at wide end. Seal points, and place rolls, point side down, on a greased baking sheet, curving into a half-moon shape. Cover and let rise until doubled in bulk. Bake.*

Parker House: *Roll dough to ¼-inch thickness; cut with a 2½-inch round cutter. Brush tops with melted butter. Make an off-center crease in each round, using the dull edge of a knife. Fold each round along crease with larger half on top. Place folded rolls in rows 2 inches apart on greased baking sheets. Cover and let rise until doubled in bulk. Brush again with melted butter. Bake.*

rolling out A process of using a rolling pin to flatten dough into a thin, flat, even layer. *(see also* **baking tools***)*

rolling pin *(see* **baking tools***)*

romaine lettuce (roh MAYN) *(see* **lettuce***)*

room temperature When a recipe specifies that a food be held at room temperature it's generally thought to be 72°. However, if red wine is to be served at room temperature, it should be slightly cooler at 60° to 68°. (*see also* **temperature**)

root beer When created in the mid-1800s by Philadelphia pharmacist Charles Hires, root beer was a low-alcohol, effervescent beverage made by fermenting yeast and sugar with various roots and herbs such as sassafras, sarsaparillas, ginger, and wintergreen. Today's nonalcoholic version is a sweetened carbonated beverage flavored with various root and herb extracts.

Roquefort cheese (ROHK fuhrt) A semisoft, blue-veined cheese aged in caves near the village of Roquefort in southwestern France. It has a creamy white interior with blue veins and a sharp, peppery aroma and salty flavor. It appears as any other blue cheese except for the identifying red sheep appearing on its foil-wrapped cylinder. Only salad dressings made with true Roquefort cheese can be labeled Roquefort dressing. (*see also* **cheese**)

CREAMY ROQUEFORT DRESSING

1 (8-ounce) container sour cream	2 teaspoons lemon juice
4 ounces Roquefort cheese, crumbled	¼ teaspoon dry mustard
	⅛ teaspoon pepper
	4 drops of hot sauce

• Combine all ingredients, stirring with a wire whisk until blended. Cover and chill thoroughly. Serve over salad greens. Yield: 1½ cups.

rose hip The ripe, reddish-orange tart-flavored berry of the rose. It's usually available dried and ground and can be used in making syrups, tea, wine, jams, and jellies. Rose hips are an excellent source of vitamin C and are often ground into powder and compressed into vitamin tablets. However, once rose hips are dried and pulverized, the vitamin C content can vary. Find them in health food stores and some pharmacies.

rosemary (*see* **herbs**)

rosette (roh ZEHT) A decorative roselike design made from icing or whipped cream with a piping bag fitted with a star-shaped tip. This term also refers to a deep-fried pastry made by dipping the end of a rosette iron into a thin batter and then into deep, hot oil; when crisp and brown the rosette is removed from the iron and dusted with powdered sugar or cinnamon-sugar and served as a dessert. A rosette iron is a long metal rod with a heatproof handle and a decorative butterfly, heart, star, or flower shape on the other end.

rose water An extract of rose petals that has an intense aromatic flavor used in some Asian and Middle Eastern pastries and confections.

rosé wine (*see* **blush wine**)

rotary beater A kitchen tool with two beaters connected to a gear-driven wheel with a hand crank and a hand grip. Two hands are required for operation—one to hold the tool and one to crank the wheel. Though wire whisks are often used as a modern replacement, the beater is still a good way to whip cream, beat egg whites, or mix thin batters. (*see also* **mixer**)

rotelle (roh TELL ay) Also called wagon wheels, this small, round Italian pasta is shaped like a wheel with spokes. (*see also* **pasta**)

rotini (roh TEE nee) Short spirals of pasta. (*see also* **pasta**)

rotisserie (roh TIHS uh ree) A cooking unit that slowly rotates food impaled on a spit in front of or over a heat source. Most rotisseries are motorized. This process allows heat to circulate evenly around meat or poultry while it self-bastes with its own juices.

roulade (roo LAHD) A French term for a slice of meat, poultry, or fish rolled around a stuffing of breadcrumbs, cheese, or vegetables, and secured with a wooden pick. Modern menus often use this term to refer to a rolled package, even without the breadcrumb or cheese filling. Some roulades are browned before baking or braising. A roulade is also a soufflélike cake baked in a jellyroll pan, spread with a sweet or savory filling, and rolled up, jelly-roll fashion.

round The hind leg section of beef that produces cuts of meat that vary in tenderness, but are generally flavorful. These cuts include the top round roast, eye-of-round roast, bottom round roast, and round steak. (*see also* **beef**)

roux (ROO) A cooked mixture of flour and fat that thickens and adds distinctive taste to many dishes made by Louisiana Cajuns and Creoles. The color and flavor of the roux is determined by how long it cooks. In general, a blond or medium-brown roux is used in sauces or gravies for dark, heavy beef or wild game dishes; it adds a toasted nutty flavor. A dark brown or black roux is used in sauces and gravies for sweet, light meats, such as pork, veal, fish, and shellfish, and gumbo. (*see also* **Cajun cooking, Creole cooking, gumbo,** *and recipe on the following page*)

> **TEST KITCHEN SECRET**
>
> *When making a roux, use a heavy saucepan or skillet and a wooden spoon for stirring. And be patient because a roux can take as long as 20 to 40 minutes to perfect. The darker the color, the more flavorful it is, but the less thickening power it has.* Vie Warshaw

CHICKEN AND SAUSAGE GUMBO

1 pound hot smoked link sausage
such as andouille, cut into
¼-inch slices
4 skinned chicken breast halves
¼ to ⅓ cup vegetable oil
½ cup all-purpose flour
1 cup chopped onion
1 green bell pepper, chopped
½ cup sliced celery
3 garlic cloves, minced
7 cups hot water
2 teaspoons Creole seasoning
1 tablespoon Worcestershire
sauce
½ teaspoon dried thyme
1 teaspoon hot sauce
2 bay leaves
½ cup sliced green onions
6 cups hot cooked rice
Gumbo filé (optional)

• Cook sausage in a Dutch oven over medium heat until browned. Remove sausage, reserving drippings. Set sausage aside. Cook chicken in drippings until browned. Remove chicken, reserving drippings.

• Measure drippings, adding enough oil to measure ½ cup. Add oil mixture to Dutch oven; place over medium heat until hot. Add flour, and cook, stirring constantly, until roux is chocolate-colored, 20 to 30 minutes.

• Add chopped onion and next 3 ingredients to roux; cook until vegetables are tender, stirring often. Remove from heat; slowly add hot water, stirring constantly. Bring mixture

Southernism

At the heart of every gumbo is a dark, silky roux. The smooth, rich mahogany mixture imparts a smoky, nutty flavor essential to this earthy soup. You'll need flour, oil, and patience to get it to the dark caramel color that adds the most flavor. It'll take from 20 to 40 minutes to make a roux, depending on your pot, oil, and temperature. Don't try to rush the process—if the roux burns, throw it out and start again. It isn't worth saving.

to a boil. Add chicken, Creole seasoning, and next 4 ingredients to Dutch oven; reduce heat, and simmer, uncovered, 1 hour, stirring occasionally.

• Remove chicken from Dutch oven; set aside to cool. Add sausage to Dutch oven; cook, uncovered, 30 more minutes. Stir in green onions; cook, uncovered, 30 more minutes.

• Bone chicken; coarsely shred. Add chicken to gumbo; cook until mixture is thoroughly heated. Discard bay leaves. Serve gumbo over rice with gumbo filé, if desired. Yield: 9 cups.

royal icing A decorative icing traditionally made with powdered sugar, egg whites, a few drops of lemon juice, and food coloring. It hardens as it dries, and is often used for fine-line piping on cookies and cakes. Recipes for royal icing now substitute meringue powder in place of raw egg whites. (*see also* **cake decorating, decorator's icing, food coloring, icing,** *and* **meringue powder**)

ROYAL ICING

1 (16-ounce) package powdered	3 tablespoons meringue powder
sugar	6 to 8 tablespoons warm water

- Beat all ingredients at low speed with an electric mixer until blended.
- Beat at high speed 4 to 5 minutes or until stiff peaks form. If icing is too stiff, add additional water, ¼ teaspoon at a time, until desired consistency. Yield: about 3 cups.

Note: Royal Icing dries rapidly. Work quickly, keeping extra icing covered tightly at all times. Find meringue powder at crafts stores and cake decorating stores.

rub (*see* **dry rub**)

rugelach (RUHG uh luhkh) Small crescent-shaped cookies made with cream cheese dough rolled around various fillings, such as nuts, raisins, or jam. They are traditionally served during Hanukkah.

rum (RUHM) A liquor distilled from the fermented juice, molasses, or syrup of sugar cane. Most rum comes from the Caribbean and ranges in color from light to dark amber. (*see also* **liquor** *and* **Puerto Rican rum**)

rumaki (ruh MAH kee) A hot appetizer or hors d'oeuvre made of a slice of water chestnut and a piece of chicken liver that's wrapped in bacon, skewered with a wooden pick, and typically marinated in a soy sauce mixture before it's grilled or broiled. (*see also* **appetizer** *and* **hors d'oeuvre**)

rusk (RUHSK) A thick or thin slice of yeast bread that has been baked until dry and crisp. In France, it's biscotte; in Italy, it's biscotti; and in Germany, it's zwieback. Plain or flavored rusks can be purchased in supermarkets or coffee shops. (*see also* **biscotti** *and* **zwieback**)

Russian dressing This American salad dressing is made from mayonnaise, chili sauce, pimiento, chives, and various herbs. It's thought that perhaps the first versions of this dressing also included caviar, thus the title.

rutabaga (ROO tuh bay guh) A large, round root vegetable that looks similar to an overgrown turnip and thus is sometimes called a yellow turnip. It has thin, pale yellow skin with a purple blush, and a slightly sweet, firm flesh that becomes golden-colored when cooked. Rutabagas are delicious peeled and cooked as a turnip, in a small amount of water, sometimes with a little added sugar, salt, or herbs. They are available fresh or canned.

Storage: Store in a plastic bag in the refrigerator up to a month. (*see also* **vegetables** *and recipe on the following page*)

LITE BITE
Rutabagas contain a fair amount of vitamin C and calcium. They're low in calories, fat, and sodium, and contain no cholesterol.

GREEK-ROASTED RUTABAGA

1 large rutabaga, peeled and cut into 2-inch pieces*	1 tablespoon lemon juice
	1 teaspoon Greek seasoning
¼ cup olive oil	½ teaspoon salt
1 tablespoon dried oregano	⅛ teaspoon pepper

• Toss together all ingredients, and spread into a lightly greased 15- x 10-inch jellyroll pan.

• Bake at 450° for 25 minutes; stir mixture, and bake 25 more minutes. Yield: 6 to 8 servings.

Q **Why do rutabagas have a waxy coating on the outside?**

A They are coated with clear paraffin which helps hold in moisture; it's harmless and comes off when the rutabaga is peeled.

* Substitute 10 medium potatoes, cut into chunks, for rutabaga, if desired. Bake at 450° for 10 minutes; stir and bake 30 more minutes.

rye A cereal grass similar to wheat that produces dark brown kernels that can be milled into flour for bread baking or used to make whiskey. Light or dark rye flour is available; the light is sifted and contains less bran than the dark. Cracked rye is coarsely ground unpolished rye kernels and can be cooked as a breakfast cereal or added to pilafs. Rye berries are unpolished whole rye kernels that can be cooked in casseroles, soups, and stuffings. (*see also* **grain**)

sabayon (sah bah YAWN) The French term for a foamy, stirred custard sauce made from eggs, sugar, and wine. In Italy, it's known as zabaglione. (*see also* **zabaglione**)

saccharin (SAK uh rihn) An artificial sweetener that's about 300 to 500 times sweeter than sugar yet lower in calories but tends to leave a bitter aftertaste, especially when heated. For years, saccharin carried a health warning on the label, but scientists recently declared it safe for consumption.

Sachertorte (SAH kuhr tohrt) An Austrian cake made of rich, dense chocolate cake layers spread with apricot jam and coated with a poured chocolate glaze; it's often served with unsweetened whipped cream. The cake was created in 1832 by the chef of Vienna's Sacher Hotel. In many cases the cake has the word "Sacher" inscribed on top.

SACHERTORTE

4 (1-ounce) squares semisweet chocolate	½ cup all-purpose flour
	⅔ cup apricot preserves or jam
⅓ cup butter	Bittersweet Glaze
4 egg yolks	Unsweetened whipped cream
½ cup sugar	(optional)
5 egg whites	

- Place chocolate and butter in top of a double boiler; bring water to a boil. Reduce heat to low; cook until chocolate melts. Remove from heat.
- Beat egg yolks until thick and pale. Gradually add sugar to egg yolks, beating continuously at medium speed with an electric mixer. Add chocolate mixture, beating just until blended.
- Beat egg whites at high speed until stiff peaks form; fold into chocolate mixture. Gently fold in flour. Pour batter into a greased and floured 9-inch round cakepan.
- Bake at 350° for 24 to 25 minutes or until a wooden pick inserted in center comes out clean. Cool in pan on a wire rack 10 minutes; remove from pan, and cool completely on wire rack.
- Carefully split cake in half horizontally to make 2 layers. Rub preserves through a sieve. Spread preserves between layers and on top of cake. Let stand 20 minutes. Pour Bittersweet Glaze over cake to cover completely. Serve with whipped cream, if desired. Yield: 10 servings.

BITTERSWEET GLAZE

⅔ cup whipping cream
2 tablespoons light corn syrup
6 ounces bittersweet chocolate, finely chopped
1 teaspoon vanilla extract

- Combine whipping cream and corn syrup in a saucepan; bring to a simmer over medium heat. Remove from heat, and add chocolate. Let stand 1 minute. Stir gently until chocolate melts completely. Stir in vanilla. Cool completely. Yield: 1 cup.

safflower oil (*see* fats and oils)

saffron (SAF ruhn) A spice that's the dried yellow-orange stigma of a crocus flower, which must be gathered by hand, hence the spice's exorbitant price. Saffron has a slightly bitter taste and a strong, pungent aroma, and adds flavor and a yellow tint to dishes. Fortunately, a little saffron goes a long way, and even though it's used sparsely, it's a critical ingredient in dishes such as paella. Saffron can be stored in a cool, dark place up to 6 months. (*see also* paella *and* spice)

sage (*see* herbs)

sake (SAH kee) A Japanese wine made from fermented rice. Though it can be served hot or cold, it's traditionally served warm (100° to 105°) in small porcelain cups; it's considered the national alcoholic drink of Japan. (*see also* mirin *and* rice wine)

salad A salad can be a single food item such as lettuce or salad greens or a mix of different foods. It's generally accompanied or bound by a dressing such as mayonnaise or vinaigrette. Some salads accompany a meal while more substantial meat or seafood salads may serve as an entrée. Others include fresh or frozen fruit salads, gelatin salads, pasta, rice, and grain salads, vegetable salads, and tossed salads. (*see also* **chef's salad, lettuce,** *and* **vinaigrette**)

TEST KITCHEN SECRET

Dressing clings better to dry leaves of lettuce, offering better flavor. If you're making salad for company, wash and spin your greens in the morning. Then wrap them in paper towels and store in a zip-top plastic bag, and chill until ready to use. They'll keep this way for about 3 days. JAMES SCHEND

salad dressing An accompaniment for salad that's typically based on a vinaigrette, mayonnaise, or other emulsified product. (*see also* **dressing, mayonnaise,** *and* **vinaigrette**)

LITE BITE

Try using reduced-fat dressings to cut calories. Most are very tasty.

salad spinner A kitchen tool that uses centrifugal force to remove water from freshly washed salad greens. The greens are placed in a perforated basket inside a container fitted with a lid and handle. As the handle is turned, the inner basket spins rapidly, forcing moisture out through the outer container. (*see also* **lettuce**)

TEST KITCHEN SECRET

It's easier to use a salad spinner if you place it in the corner of your sink. This increases your leverage by lowering the height of the crank and helps stabilize the spinner. VANESSA McNEIL

salamander (SAL uh man duhr) A small overhead broiler or kitchen tool with a heavy iron head attached to a metal shaft with a wooden handle; both can be heated to quickly brown foods or to quickly caramelize a top surface layer of sugar as in crème brûlée. (*see also* **crème brûlée**)

salami (suh LAH mee) A type of cured, air-dried Italian sausage composed of lean beef, pork, garlic, and spices, and often either red or white wine. Among the best known salamis are Genoa (rich, garlicky, and studded with white peppercorns), cotto (studded with black peppercorns), nonpork kosher salami (cooked and semi-soft), and pepperoni, (highly seasoned with black and red pepper). As long as the casing is uncut, salami can be stored for several years. Once cut, it should be wrapped in plastic wrap and refrigerated up to 2 weeks. (*see also* **sausage**)

Salisbury steak (SAWLZ beh ree) A ground beef patty seasoned with onion and parsley, then fried or broiled, and served with gravy made from pan drippings. It's named after its creator, Dr. J.H. Salisbury.

SALISBURY STEAK

1 (10¾-ounce) can golden mushroom soup, undiluted and divided	1 large egg, beaten
	1½ cups sliced fresh mushrooms
1½ pounds ground beef	⅓ cup beef broth
½ cup finely chopped onion	¼ cup Worcestershire sauce
¼ cup Italian-seasoned breadcrumbs	¼ teaspoon pepper

• Combine ¼ cup soup, beef, and next 3 ingredients; stir well. Shape mixture into 6 (½-inch-thick) patties.
• Brown patties in a large skillet over medium-high heat. Remove patties, discarding half of pan drippings. Cook mushrooms in remaining drippings in skillet over medium-high heat, stirring constantly, until tender. Combine remaining soup, beef broth, Worcestershire sauce, and pepper; add to mushroom mixture. Return patties to skillet; bring to a boil. Cover, reduce heat, and simmer 20 minutes. Yield: 6 servings.

Sally Lunn Delicate, slightly sweet yeast bread. Some say it was created by baker Sally Lunn in the eighteenth century in Bath, England, to be served with afternoon tea. This cakelike bread eventually became a Southern favorite after it was brought to America by the English colonists.

salmon (SAM uhn) A large family of fish found in the northern Atlantic and Pacific oceans. Principal varieties include:
• **Chinook or king salmon,** the finest and most expensive from Pacific waters; it can range up to 120 pounds, has a high-fat, soft flesh that's off-white to bright red.
• **Coho or silver salmon,** also is from the Pacific, but is firmer, lighter in color, and lower in fat than chinook.
• **Sockeye or red salmon,** a Pacific salmon used for canning, is moderately fat and has firm, deep red flesh.
• **Pink or humpback salmon** is the smallest, most delicately flavored of the Pacific varieties. It's also pink, low in fat, and sometimes used for canning.
• **Chum or dog salmon** has the palest color and the lowest fat content of all Pacific salmon.
• **Atlantic salmon** has a high-fat, oily flesh that's pink to red or orange.

Salmon is sold whole, in fillets, or steaks. It's also available canned or smoked and can be served as a main course, in salads, or as a spread or dip.
Storage: Cook fresh salmon the day it's caught or within 24 hours of purchase. It should be wrapped in plastic wrap or placed in a zip-top plastic bag and refrigerated until time to cook. (*see also* **fish** *and recipe on the following page*)

CARAMELIZED MAPLE-AND-GARLIC-GLAZED SALMON

1 (2½-pound) salmon fillet,
    cut into 6 pieces
1 teaspoon salt
2 tablespoons butter or margarine

⅓ cup maple syrup, divided
1 teaspoon granulated garlic
1 tablespoon chopped fresh
    chives

• Sprinkle salmon evenly with salt.

• Melt butter in a large skillet over medium heat. Add salmon, skin side up; cook 2 minutes.

• Place salmon, skin side down, on a lightly greased rack in a broiler pan. Brush salmon with half of syrup.

♡ **LITE BITE**

Eating salmon may reduce the risk of heart disease due to its high amount of polyunsaturated omega-3 fatty acids.

• Broil 5 inches from heat 5 to 7 minutes or until syrup caramelizes. Brush salmon with remaining syrup; sprinkle with garlic and chives. Yield: 6 servings.

salmonella (sal muh NEHL uh) A type of bacteria that causes about half the cases of food poisoning and enters the human system through contaminated water, raw or undercooked poultry, raw or undercooked eggs, raw milk, and raw or undercooked meats. Avoid cross-contamination by keeping counter, cutting boards, and knives clean. (*see also* **food safety**)

salsa (SAHL sah) This term usually refers to a Mexican sauce made from tomatoes flavored with cilantro, chiles, and onions. However, contemporary chefs have begun to think of salsa as any type of hot or cold chunky mixture that might include herbs, spices, fruits, vegetables, or beans.

♡ **LITE BITE**

Serve salsa with meat, poultry, or fish to add flavor without lots of fat and calories.

FRESH TOMATO SALSA

3 plum tomatoes, peeled, seeded,
    and diced
2 tablespoons chopped fresh
    cilantro
1 tablespoon minced onion

1 to 2 teaspoons minced jalapeño
    pepper
1 teaspoon fresh lime juice
⅛ teaspoon salt

• Combine all ingredients in a small bowl. Yield: 1½ cups.

salsify (SAL sih fee) A long, slender, parsnip-shaped root vegetable. Salsify, also known as oyster plant or oyster vegetable because some think its taste resembles a delicately flavored oyster, can be boiled, steamed, or added to soups and stews; it's available from June through late February.

Storage: Store salsify in a plastic bag in the refrigerator up to a week. After peeling salsify, store it in a mixture of lemon juice and water to prevent darkening.

salt A white granular substance made of sodium chloride and used to season and intensify the natural flavor of foods. In addition, salt serves the purpose of controlling yeast growth in bread dough and helps in preserving foods such as ham and fish. Most salt comes from salt mines, which are usually deposits left by dried salt lakes. There are several forms of salt:

- **Table salt,** used for cooking and as a condiment, is fine-grained household salt and contains additives to keep it from clumping. Most table salt is iodized or fortified with iodine to help prevent goiter.

- **Kosher salt** is coarser than table salt and contains no additives. It's sometimes sprinkled over pretzels.

- **Pickling or canning salt** is finer ground than table salt and is used to make brines for pickles. It contains no additives so it won't cloud pickling liquids.

- **Rock salt** is nonedible, unrefined salt and contains more minerals and impurities. It's used for freezing homemade ice cream and to make a bed on which to serve baked oysters and clams.

- **Sea salt** is made from seawater; it comes fine or coarse-grained.

- **Gray salt** comes from the Brittany coast; it's slightly moist and chunky in texture and retains minerals found in seawater (iron, magnesium, calcium, potassium, manganese, zinc, and iodine), which add flavor and echo the mineral content of the human body.

- **Seasoned salt,** such as celery salt or garlic salt, is regular salt combined with other flavoring ingredients.

- **Salt substitutes** contain little or no sodium.

saltimbocca (sahl tihm BOH kuh) An Italian specialty made of veal scallops topped with thin slices of prosciutto; it's sometimes rolled up and secured with wooden picks before being sautéed in butter and braised in wine. (*see also* **ham** *and* **Parma ham**)

salt pork A fat layer of pork that comes from the sides and belly of the hog and is cured in salt; it's used mainly as a cooking fat or as a flavoring and seasoning agent. Salt pork shouldn't be confused with fatback, which is unsalted. (*see also* **fatback**)

Southernism

We tend to think of salt pork as a seasoning agent. But the New Dixie Cookbook, *dated 1895, states: "Wash a piece of salt pork, the leg is best, put over the fire in cold water to cover and boil slowly three hours, allowing twenty minutes to the pound..." The meat in question was not what we call salt pork, but ham. That explains why so many older recipes called for actually eating rations of salt pork. Of course, it was a fact of life that when times were hard, pioneers would often slice and fry salt pork and serve it with sweet potatoes and turnip greens. And Texas cowpokes were known to carry salt pork with them on the trail.*

salt-rising bread Popular in the days before yeast was readily available, salt-rising bread is leavened by a fermented mixture of flour, cornmeal, water, and salt. The bread has a smooth texture and a tangy taste and aroma.

sangría (san GREE uh) A refreshing Spanish beverage made of red wine, fruit juice, lemon and orange slices, sugar, and soda water; sometimes liqueurs and brandy or other ingredients are added. If made with white wine, it's known as sangría blanco; both are served cold over ice.

GARDEN SANGRÍA

1 gallon dry white wine
2 cups brandy
1 cup orange liqueur
4 oranges, sliced
1 bunch fresh mint leaves
1 (1-liter) bottle club soda
  or ginger ale, chilled
1 quart whole strawberries
2 lemons, thinly sliced
2 limes, thinly sliced

• Combine first 5 ingredients in a large container; cover and chill 8 hours.
• Add club soda and remaining ingredients just before serving. Serve over ice. Yield: 1½ gallons.

sapsago cheese (sap SAY goh) A hard, cone-shaped Swiss cheese made from cow's milk. It has a sharp, pungent flavor and light green color that comes from a special variety of clover added to the curd. Sapsago is used for grating and can be added to many different dishes from salads to pasta. (*see also* **cheese**)

sardine (sahr DEEN) A generic name given to small saltwater fish in the herring family that have a strong flavor and soft bones. Sardines are usually salted, smoked, and canned in oil, tomato sauce, or mustard sauce. They get their name from the island of Sardinia in the Mediterranean, where the fish canning industry began. (*see also* **fish**)

LITE BITE
Sardines are one of the best nondairy sources of calcium.

sashimi (sah SHEE mee) A Japanese dish of sliced raw fish served with condiments such as soy sauce, daikon, wasabi, or ginger. Sashimi is usually the first course in a Japanese meal. (*see also* **daikon, ginger, soy sauce, sushi,** *and* **wasabi**)

sassafras (SAS uh fras) An aromatic member of the laurel family, the sassafras tree produces leaves that can be dried and used to make filé powder and sassafras tea. The root bark is dried and used as a flavoring in root beer. (*see also* **filé powder** *and* **root beer**)

satay (sah TAY) A Southeast Asian dish of skewered meat, fish, or poultry that's grilled or broiled. Satay can be eaten as an appetizer or main dish, and is typically served with a spicy peanut sauce

sauce A flavorful liquid intended to enhance the flavor and texture of food. Sauces can be used on appetizers, main dishes, vegetables, and desserts, and can be thick or thin, hot or cold. There are hundreds of different sauce variations, but all can basically be classified into five "mother" sauces: béchamel (basic white sauces based on a roux of butter, flour, and liquid); velouté (a roux-based sauce made with butter, flour, and light-colored chicken, veal, or fish stock); espagnole (a roux-based sauce made with butter, flour, and a rich brown meat stock); hollandaise and mayonnaise (made from an emulsion of fat and egg); and tomato-based sauces. Vinaigrettes (made from a combination of oil, vinegar, and seasonings) are included by some chefs for a sixth type.

> ### TEST KITCHEN SECRET
>
> *Always cook sauces over low to medium heat, and cook only for the length of time specified in the recipe. High heat and lengthy cooking cause some sauces to curdle or break down.* REBECCA KRACKE GORDON

RESCUE for a lumpy sauce:
A wire whisk is a valuable tool when making sauces. If you constantly stir with a whisk, the chances of lumping are greatly decreased. However, if lumps do form, quickly beat the sauce with the whisk or a hand-held immersion blender until it's smooth. If all else fails, press the sauce through a wire-mesh strainer with the back of a spoon to remove the lumps.

(*see also* **béchamel sauce, brown sauce, hollandaise sauce, mayonnaise, mother sauces, velouté sauce, vinaigrette,** *and* **white sauce**)

saucepan (*see* **cookware**)

sauerbraten (SOW uhr brah tihn) A German-style beef roast marinated in a sour-and-sweet marinade before it's browned and simmered in the same marinade for several hours. Sauerbraten is usually accompanied with dumplings, boiled potatoes, or noodles.

sauerkraut (SOW uhr krowt) A vegetable dish or condiment made of shredded, crisp white cabbage fermented in salt and sometimes flavored with caraway seeds and juniper berries. Although it's considered of German origin, sauerkraut was actually discovered by Chinese laborers building the Great Wall of China over 2,000 years ago; they survived on a mixture of sour cabbage in rice wine. The dish was eventually brought to Europe where the

Q: Is it possible to make homemade sauerkraut?

A: It's possible, but not always feasible. Multiple layers of chopped or shredded cabbage must be salted and tightly compressed in a large crock, and left to ferment for weeks, during which time the mixture produces a strong, and to some, an unpleasant odor. After fermentation, the mixture must be packed and sealed in sterilized jars and processed in a boiling water bath. It's much more practical to purchase jars or cans of commercially prepared sauerkraut.

Germans adopted it as a favorite. It's sold in jars and cans in supermarkets; it can also be found fresh in some delicatessens. Sauerkraut is a popular topping for hot dogs; it also can be braised with roast pork and sausages. To make it less salty, place in a colander and rinse with cold water. **Storage:** If refrigerated in its own juice in a glass jar or plastic container, sauerkraut will last for a month or longer.

sausage (SAW sihj) Sausage was originally concocted as a means of using and preserving every last scrap of animal trimmings after a hog butchering. The meat proved so flavorful and popular that today there is almost an endless number of sausages that can be used in a variety of ways to appeal to a multitude of tastes. Basically, all sausages are mixtures of chopped or ground meat and fat mixed with salt and other seasonings, preservatives, and sometimes fillers of cereal, soybean flour, or dried milk solids; it's the unique blend of these various ingredients that gives each type of sausage its personality. This mixture is usually packed into casings for links, although country-style sausage in bulk meat is formed into patties or rolls that can be sliced and cooked. Sausage meat is usually pork-based, but it can also come from any meat, fish, poultry, shellfish, or wild game. Sausage, as a whole, is traditionally high in fat; however, there are many lower fat versions available as well as vegetarian sausages made or flavored with vegetables and/or

TEST KITCHEN SECRET

Fresh sausages are delicious slowly pan-fried or poached in a little water and then grilled or sautéed to give them a crisp, brown surface. Other types of sausages can be cooked slowly on a griddle, pan-fried, broiled, or grilled. Margaret Monroe Dickey

LITE BITE
Choose a more healthful alternative with reduced-fat ground pork sausage or low-fat smoked sausage. Vegetarian sausages are also flavorful and low in fat.

bean curd. The flavor of sausages can range from mild to hot and spicy, and sausages can be cooked, cured, smoked, dried, or left uncooked and sold fresh. Most can be grouped by the processing method used:

• **Fresh or uncooked sausages** are made from fresh meat and are not cooked, cured, or smoked; they must be cooked thoroughly before eating. They include bratwurst, chorizo, Italian, Polish kielbasa, and pork sausage.

bratwurst

• **Uncooked and smoked sausages** are made with fresh or cured meat that has been smoked, but not cooked; they must be cooked thoroughly before eating. They include kielbasa, mettwurst, smoked country-style, and smoked pork sausage.

kielbasa

• **Cooked sausages** are usually made from fresh meat cured during processing and are fully cooked; most are ready to eat, though some should be heated before serving. They include andouille, blood sausage, precooked bockwurst, precooked bratwurst, braunschweiger, and liver sausage.

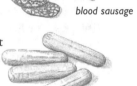

blood sausage

• **Cooked and smoked sausages** are made from fresh meat that has been cured, smoked, and fully cooked; these can be eaten cold or hot. They include beef salami, bologna, cotto salami, frankfurters, kielbasa, and knackwurst.

knackwurst

• **Dry and semidry sausages** are made from fresh meat that has been cured and air-dried up to 6 months during processing and is ready to eat; it's sometimes smoked. Most dry sausages are salamis, while semidry are summer sausages, and include Genoa, cervelat, hard salami, and pepperoni.

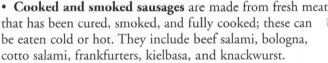

hard salami

Storage: Wrap sausage in plastic wrap and store in the refrigerator. Fresh sausage will keep several days as will uncooked and smoked sausage. Cooked sausage keeps 5 or 6 days; cooked and smoked keeps a week after opening; dry and semidry sausage keeps several weeks after opening. All but dry and semidry can be frozen up to 2 months. Freezing dry and semidry sausages leads to a loss of quality. (*see also* **andouille, bologna, bratwurst, braunschweiger, chorizo, frankfurter, Italian sausage, kielbasa, knackwurst, pepperoni,** *and* **salami**)

sauté (saw TAY) A basic French cooking method where food is cooked quickly, usually over medium or medium-high heat, in a small amount of hot fat or oil in a skillet or sauté pan. During sautéing, food is tossed or stirred in the pan so that the outside is evenly cooked without overcooking the inside.

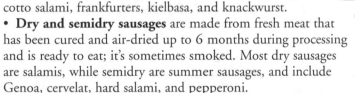

LITE BITE

To cut fat and calories, coat food with vegetable cooking spray and sauté in a nonstick skillet. Note that it's best to spray the food rather than the skillet since repeated sprayings will eventually render it no longer nonstick.

sauté pan A wide frying pan with straight sides that are a little higher than those of a regular skillet. Sauté pans can be purchased in different sizes, but the 2½- to 4-quart sizes are the most useful. Some of the pans have a high, angled handle on one side and a loop handle on the other so the pan can be easily lifted.

Sauternes (soh TERN) A sweet white wine from the Sauternes district of France's Bordeaux region. Sauternes are typically consumed as an after-dinner or dessert wine, but they also team nicely with rich appetizers. The wine is made from overly ripe, sugary grapes, resulting in a very sweet, fruity, intense, buttery, golden wine. Sauterne (without the "s") refers to inexpensive, medium-sweet California white wine. (*see also* **wine**)

Sauvignon Blanc (SOH vihn yohn BLAHNGK) Widely cultivated in France and California, this grape produces white wine known for its acidity, grassy or herbaceous aroma, and semisweet character. (*see also* **wine**)

savarin (SAV uh rihn) A rich French yeast cake baked in a ring mold, soaked with rum syrup, and filled with pastry cream, crème chantilly, or fresh fruit. When made with raisins it's called a "baba." (*see also* **baba** *and* **chantilly**)

savory (SAY vuh ree) This term describes a food that's piquant and full-flavored rather than sweet. Savory is also an herb that's a member of the mint family. Summer savory has a milder flavor than winter savory, which has a bitter, pungent flavor similar to a cross between thyme and mint; both complement dried beans, lentils, meat dishes, poultry, and tomatoes. (*see also* **herbs**)

savoy cabbage (*see* **cabbage**)

Sazerac (SAZ uh rak) A cocktail drink made of whiskey, sugar syrup, bitters, and Pernod. The cocktail is commonly associated with the Sazerac Coffee House in New Orleans. However, the Fairmont Hotel also claims ownership of the famous cocktail, the namesake of its legendary Sazerac Restaurant and Bar. (*see also* **bitters** *and* **Pernod**)

Southernism

New Orleans lore has it that Antoine Peychaud, a Creole immigrant, created the first Sazerac in his French Quarter pharmacy in the 1830s by mixing brandy, absinthe, and a dash of his secret bitters. The popularity of the cocktail quickly spread throughout the city's coffee houses (which was the term for drinking establishments in mid-1800s).

scald (SKAWLD) A process whereby a liquid such as milk is heated to just below the boiling point.

Because milk scorches and boils over easily, recipes that require hot milk specify scalding as a safeguard against overcooking. You'll know it has reached the scalding point when tiny bubbles begin to appear around the edge of the saucepan. MARY ALLEN PERRY

scale The process of removing the scales from a fish, usually by scraping the fish with a dull knife or a special tool called a fish scaler. This term also refers to a kitchen scale, a device used to weigh ingredients or food items. There are several types of kitchen scales available, but the most common are the spring scale, which weighs items placed in a pan or bowl on top and depresses a spring; the balance scale, which has a pan for ingredients on one side and weights on a platform on the other; and the beam balance scale, which uses weights that slide along two bars.

scallion (SKAL yuhn) A young, immature onion, sometimes referred to as a spring onion or green onion. (*see* **onion**)

scallop (SKAHL uhp) A popular bivalve mollusk similar to the oyster and clam that's found in saltwater regions. Scallops propel themselves through the water with a large muscle that opens and closes their shells; this muscle, which is firm, sweet, and low in fat, is usually the only portion of this shellfish that's eaten. There are two broad groups of scallops: Bay scallops are generally found on the East Coast. They're very tiny, about ½ inch in diameter, and sweet and succulent. They are similar to the even smaller calico scallops that are harvested from deeper waters in the Gulf of Mexico and along the eastern coast of Florida. Sea scallops are larger, usually about 1½ inches in diameter, and not as tender. The color of scallops should be creamy white, pale beige, or creamy pink; if they're stark white, it's a sign they've been soaked in water to increase their weight or that they are not true scallops, and have possibly been cut from large pieces of fish fillets.

Storage: Scallops should be firm, free of excess cloudy liquid, and smell sweet. If spoiled, they have a strong sulfur odor. Refrigerate fresh scallops in their own liquid in a closed container up to 2 days.

READER TIP

"If you ever have the chance to find fresh scallops still in their shells, grab them! Their taste is superior, and they're easy to shuck. Just slide a knife into the crack between the shells to open, then run the knife around the scallop meat to remove it, and peel and discard the tough tissue off the side of the scallop."

J.R., Atlantic Beach, FL

Scallops can be fried, sautéed, grilled, steamed, poached, or baked, but however you choose to prepare them, watch the cooking time carefully. They cook in just a few minutes, and if left on the heat too long, they quickly turn rubbery and dry. LYDA JONES

scalloped To cook food, usually potatoes, by layering it with cream or a sauce in a casserole and topping with breadcrumbs or cheese. This term also refers to the process of forming a raised, decorative rim on a pie pastry. (*see also* **crimp**)

WINTER HERB GARDEN SCALLOPED POTATOES

6 small russet potatoes
2 tablespoons butter or margarine
¼ cup chopped purple onion
3 tablespoons chopped dried tomato
2 garlic cloves, minced
2 tablespoons all-purpose flour
2 cups whipping cream
½ cup milk
½ (8-ounce) package cream cheese, softened

2 tablespoons chopped fresh chives
2 tablespoons chopped fresh parsley
1 teaspoon chopped fresh rosemary
1 teaspoon salt
¼ teaspoon pepper
½ cup grated Asiago cheese
½ cup shredded Parmesan cheese

• Peel potatoes, and cut into ⅛-inch-thick slices. Set aside.
• Melt butter in a large skillet over medium heat.
• Add onion, tomato, and garlic; sauté until tender.
• Add flour, stirring until blended. Gradually add whipping cream, milk, and cream cheese, stirring until smooth.
• Stir in chives and next 4 ingredients; cook, stirring constantly, 3 minutes.
• Combine potato and cream sauce in a lightly greased 11- x 7-inch baking dish.
• Bake, covered, at 375° for 1 hour. Sprinkle with Asiago and Parmesan cheeses; bake, uncovered, 15 more minutes or until potato is tender. Yield: 6 to 8 servings.

scaloppine (skah luh PEE nee) An Italian term that describes a thin scallop or slice of meat, usually veal or pork, prepared by dredging it in flour and sautéing in butter or olive oil; it's typically served with a wine or a tomato-based sauce. (*see also* **veal**)

scampi (SKAM pee) An Italian term for the tail portion of a small lobster or prawn. In the United States, we think of scampi as large shrimp cooked in garlic, butter, white wine, and herbs. (*see also* **prawn** *and* **shrimp**)

scant A measuring term that indicates an amount that's slightly less than full, such as a scant teaspoonful. (*see also* **measuring**)

schnapps (SHNAHPS) Colorless liqueur distilled from grains or potatoes and flavored with peach or peppermint. Schnapps can be consumed alone as a cordial or as an after-dinner drink, used to flavor other drinks, or incorporated as an ingredient in some dessert recipes. (*see also* **liqueur**)

schnitzel (SHNIHT suhl) A German term for "cutlet" that describes a thin scallop or slice of meat, typically veal, that's dipped in egg, then breaded, and fried.

VEAL SCHNITZEL

1 pound veal cutlets	¾ cup butter
2 large eggs	5 ounces Gruyère cheese, thinly
1 teaspoon salt	sliced
¾ teaspoon coarsely ground	3 tablespoons chopped fresh
pepper	parsley
½ cup all-purpose flour	Garnishes: lemon slices, fresh
1½ cups soft breadcrumbs	parsley sprigs
(homemade)	

• Place veal between 2 sheets of heavy-duty plastic wrap; flatten to ⅛-inch thickness, using a meat mallet or rolling pin.

• Combine eggs, salt, and pepper; beat well. Dredge cutlets in flour; dip in egg mixture, and coat with breadcrumbs.

• Melt half of butter in a large skillet over medium heat; add half of cutlets, and cook 4 to 5 minutes. Turn cutlets; top with half of cheese. Cover and cook 3 more minutes. Repeat procedure with remaining butter, veal, and cheese. Sprinkle with chopped parsley; garnish, if desired. Yield: 4 servings.

scone (SKOHN) A traditional Scottish quick bread originally made with Scotch oats, cooked on a griddle, and cut into triangles. Modern versions are similar to rich biscuits and are usually made with flour and baked in the oven; they might be cut into rounds, squares, triangles, or diamond shapes, and can be savory or sweet. (*see also* **quick bread** *and* **tea time**)

Q When should scones be served?

A Scones are typically served with butter or jam at breakfast or afternoon tea, though they're so delicious, you might want to eat one for a snack.

scoop A kitchen tool used in professional kitchens for measuring, portioning, filling, and forming. Home cooks have traditionally served up ice cream with scoops, and are beginning to use them for other timesaving purposes, such as filling muffin pans with batter.

TEST KITCHEN SECRET

There are many different sized scoops available in large department stores, kitchen shops, and restaurant supply stores. Volumes range from 1- and 2-tablespoon scoops to ¼- and ½-cup scoops. We find all sizes handy in our kitchens. MARGARET MONROE DICKEY

TIMESAVING TIP

An ice cream scoop is a handy tool. Save time by using scoops to portion muffin batter, cookie dough, meatball mixtures, and salads such as chicken, tuna, or potato.

score To make shallow cuts in the surface of foods such as meat or fish for decorative purposes or to help flatten a piece of meat, such as flank steak. It also allows marinades or seasonings to more easily penetrate meats. Cutting through tough meat fibers can tenderize tougher cuts of meat. Scoring the outer fat layer of a whole ham allows the fat to drain off and gives it a prettier appearance. Sometimes breads are scored or slashed before baking; this gives them an attractive appearance, but it also provides a place for gases to escape as the bread rises. (*see also* **slash**)

Scotch Whiskey distilled in Scotland from mash made of sprouted barley that has been dried over peat fires and aged for at least 3 years in oak or sherry casks. (*see also* **liquor** *and* **whiskey**)

Scotch bonnet chile A short, cone-shaped fresh chile, sometimes referred to as a habanero chile, with a pale yellow-green, orange, or red color, and a very hot, smoky flavor. (*see also* **peppers**)

scrape To rub the surface of a food in order to remove its outer coating. For example, carrots are often scraped before eaten.

scrapple A Pennsylvania Dutch dish made from finely chopped "scraps" of pork simmered with cornmeal mush and flavored with sage. The scrapple mixture is packed in a loafpan and cooled, then sliced and fried in fat, and served hot for breakfast. (*see also* **mush**)

screwdriver A cocktail drink of orange juice and vodka served over ice. (*see also* **vodka**)

scuppernong (SKUHP uhr nawng) (*see* **grape**)

sea bass A name given to various saltwater fish such as the white sea bass, which is actually a member of the drum family, and the giant sea bass, which is related to the grouper family. However, black sea bass and striped bass are true bass, and are sold whole, in steaks, or fillets. Their flesh is lean to moderately fat; they can be baked, broiled, or sautéed. (*see also* **fish**)

sear A cooking process where meat is browned quickly on all sides over high heat in a skillet, under a broiler, or in a very hot oven. Searing is usually done to give it a richer, more complex flavor before it's braised. Some sources claim searing seals in the meat's juices.

sea salt (*see* **salt**)

season This term describes the process of preparing the surface of cookware, particularly cast iron, to prevent sticking. (*see also* **cast-iron cookware**)

seasoning Enhancing or improving a food's flavor by adding salt, pepper, herbs, or spices. Other commonly used seasonings include vinegars and condiments, such as Worcestershire sauce, soy sauce, and mustard.

seaweed A primitive sea plant belonging to the algae family and popularly used in Japanese cooking, especially in soups and sushi. Seaweed is also used as a flavoring or as a stabilizer and thickener in a wide variety of commercially processed foods such as ice cream, pudding, soups, and syrups. Seaweed is sold in most health food stores and Asian markets. The most common types are:
• **Kelp:** Sold in wide, dark strips and is popular simmered in soups as a salt substitute or in beans as a thickening agent.
• **Dulse:** (DUHLS) Coarse, red seaweed that's dried and eaten as is or fried or toasted. It has a salty, tangy flavor and is used in seafood chowders, fish cakes, salads, and sometimes as a bacon substitute.
• **Nori:** (NOH ree) Dark green, purple, or black paper-thin sheets with a salty flavor and is used most often to make sushi.
• **Wakame:** (WAH kah meh) Dark green strips with a mild flavor and is sometimes added to Japanese soups or salads.
• **Hijki:** (hee GEE kee) Spaghetti-like green-black strips with strong flavor and is added to salads or stir-fries for extra crunch.
• **Agar-agar:** Long strands or sticks that can be soaked and eaten in soups like noodles, but primarily is used as a gelatin-like thickener.

sec (SEHK) A French term that means "dry" and is used to describe non-bubbly, nonsweet wines. However, when the term is used in reference to champagne, it has another meaning; it indicates medium-sweet champagne. The driest champagne is referred to as extra brut. (*see also* **brut** *and* **dry**)

section A segment of citrus fruit that has been removed from the peel and membrane. This term also refers to the process of separating segments of citrus fruit from the membrane with a knife. (*see also* **orange**)

sediment Grainy deposit made of tannins and pigments that settles to the bottom of some wines. The wine should be poured so that the sediment stays in the bottle. The best way to accomplish this is to let the sediment settle completely before pouring or decanting. (*see also* **decant**)

seeding The process of removing seeds from fruits and vegetables.

seitan (SAY tan) A protein-rich meat substitute made of concentrated wheat gluten; it has a firm, chewy texture and bland flavor. Seitan is used in many vegetarian dishes and can be found in the refrigerator or freezer section of health food stores and some large supermarkets.

seize When melted chocolate comes into contact with a small amount of moisture or liquid, particles of cocoa solids will start clumping together and cause the chocolate to harden or "seize." However, a large amount of liquid will actually prevent seizing. As a rule of thumb, when adding liquid to melted chocolate, there must be at least 1 tablespoon of liquid for every 2 ounces of chocolate to avoid seizing. (*see also* **chocolate**)

self-rising flour (*see* **flour**)

seltzer (SELT suhr) A naturally effervescent mineral water named for the German village of Nieder Selters. Man-made seltzer, also known as soda water or club soda, is flavorless water with induced carbonation. Seltzer can be consumed alone or used as a mixer for alcoholic or soda fountain drinks.

Sémillon (say mee YOHN) A white grape grown in France and California that produces dry white wines that are usually best mixed with other wines, such as Sauvignon Blanc. It's most often used in making French Sauternes and dessert wines. (*see also* **Sauternes** *and* **wine**)

semisweet chocolate (*see* **chocolate**)

semolina (seh muh LEE nuh) Grainy, pale yellow durum wheat flour that's high in protein and gluten and often used for making pasta. (*see also* **gluten, pasta,** *and* **wheat**)

Senate bean soup A bean soup often served in the United States Senate dining room; it's made from white beans cooked with smoked ham hocks, potatoes, and onion.

serrano chile (seh RRAH noh) A short, tapered chile with a green or orange-yellow color, thick flesh, and very hot flavor. It's found fresh in Mexican markets and some supermarkets; it's also available canned, pickled, or packed in oil. Serrano chiles are especially tasty in guacamole and salsa. (*see also* **peppers**)

serrated edge The cutting edge of a knife with a series of tiny teeth that saw the food. This type knife is good for slicing items that have a hard exterior and a soft interior such as bread and some cakes. (*see also* **knife**)

sesame oil (SEHS uh mee) Obtained from sesame seeds and comes in two intensities. The first is light in color and flavor and good for everything from salad dressings to sautéing. The second is darker, has a much stronger flavor, and is used sparingly in Asian dishes. Due to its intense flavor and low smoke point, sesame oil is often paired with a bland, more heat-stable oil. (*see also* **fats and oils**)

sesame seed (SEHS uh mee) Tiny, flat seeds with a nutty, slightly sweet flavor that were brought to America by African slaves who referred to them as "benne seeds." They became popular in Southern cooking and are often used in baked goods such as breads, pastries, cakes, and cookies as well as in salads and other savory dishes.

They are also used by Middle Easterners to make tahini, a paste that flavors other dishes. Sesame seeds can be purchased in small quantities in supermarkets or in bulk in Middle Eastern and Asian markets and health food stores. **Storage:** Sesame seeds tend to go rancid quickly because of their high oil content, so it's best to refrigerate them up to 6 months or freeze up to a year. (*see also* **benne seed wafers** *and* **tahini**)

set Certain foods need time to set or firm up before serving. This is usually done by allowing the food to stand at room temperature or by chilling it in the refrigerator. For example, custards, lasagna, and some frostings are better after they have set. And all gelatin mixtures require time to thicken or congeal before they're served. (*see also* **congeal** *and* **gelatin**)

seven-minute frosting Fluffy meringue frosting made by beating egg whites, sugar, and corn syrup together in the top of a double boiler until stiff peaks form. This frosting gets its name because the beating process usually takes about seven minutes.

SEVEN-MINUTE FROSTING

1½ cups sugar	1 tablespoon light corn syrup
5 tablespoons cold water	Dash of salt
2 egg whites	1 teaspoon vanilla extract

• Combine first 5 ingredients in top of a large double boiler. Beat at low speed with a handheld electric mixer 30 seconds or just until blended.
• Place over boiling water; beat constantly at high speed 7 minutes or until stiff peaks form. Remove from heat. Add vanilla; beat 2 minutes or until frosting is thick enough to spread. Yield: 4¼ cups.

seven & seven A cocktail beverage made of 7UP soda and Seagram's 7-Crown blended whiskey.

seven-spice powder A spice blend used in Japanese cooking; it usually consists of ground anise, sesame seeds, flax seeds, rapeseeds, poppy seeds, nori, and dried citrus peel. (*see also* **anise, poppy seed, rape, seaweed,** *and* **sesame seed**)

seviche (seh VEE chee) Also called ceviche, this Latin American appetizer consists of very fresh, raw saltwater fish marinated in lime or other citrus juice, which has the effect of "cooking" the fish. (The fish is not technically cooked, however, so the health risks are the same as for eating raw fish.) Onions, tomatoes, chiles, and cilantro are often added to the marinade.

shad (*see* **herring**)

shallot (SHAL uht) A petite member of the onion family shaped like garlic with a head made up of several cloves covered in a thin, papery, reddish-brown to yellow-brown skin. Shallots have a mild, delicate flavor and can be used in the same way as onions. **Storage:** Store shallots in a cool, dry place up to a month. (*see also* **onion**)

shank The front leg of beef, veal, lamb, or pork, also known as the foreshank or arm. This section of meat, though very flavorful, is typically some of the toughest meat on the animal, and requires long, slow cooking such as braising to make it tender. (*see also* **beef, lamb, pork,** *and* **veal**)

shark A type of saltwater fish that ranges in taste, color, and texture according to the variety. For example, the dogfish and blacktip sharks have white, mild-tasting meat, while the mako shark, similar to swordfish, is firmer with a stronger flavor. Shark can be broiled, grilled, baked, poached, and fried. Because it has a firm flesh, shark is good for cutting into cubes and threading onto kabobs; it can also be simmered in soups or cooked and chilled and added to salads. (*see also* **fish**)

sharpening steel A long, pointed, thin rod made of high-carbon steel used to sharpen knives. To use a sharpening steel, draw knives across the steel rod at a 20-degree angle for about 5 to 10 times on both sides of the blade. Dull knife blades need to be resharpened on a sharpening stone or whetstone before being honed on a sharpening steel rod. (*see also* **knife** *and* **whetstone**)

she-crab soup A creamy soup popular in South Carolina that's made from the crabmeat and roe (the eggs) of fresh blue crabs and flavored with sherry. She-crab soup is a seasonal specialty because fresh crab roe is only produced in the spring. Our recipe at right simulates traditional she-crab soup but omits the roe, as most restaurants do today, to ensure that a steady crop of crabs remains. (*see also* **roe**)

Southernism

She-crab soup is a Lowcountry (eastern South Carolina and Georgia) hallmark. Sherry is used as a garnish; simply pour a few tablespoons onto the creamy, thick soup. You need "real" sherry, not the cooking sherry you find at the grocery store.

PLANTATION CRAB SOUP

1 quart heavy whipping cream
⅛ teaspoon salt
⅛ teaspoon pepper
¼ cup unsalted butter
⅓ cup all-purpose flour
2 cups Homemade Fish Stock or
    bottled clam juice

2 tablespoons lemon juice
1 teaspoon ground nutmeg
½ pound fresh lump crabmeat,
    drained
Garnish: chopped parsley
Sherry

• Combine first 3 ingredients in a heavy saucepan; bring to a boil over medium heat. Reduce heat, and simmer, uncovered, 1 hour. Set aside.
• Melt butter in a large heavy saucepan over low heat; add flour, stirring until smooth. Cook 1 minute, stirring constantly. Gradually add Homemade Fish Stock; cook over medium heat until thickened. Stir in cream mixture, and cook until thoroughly heated. Add lemon juice, nutmeg, and crabmeat. Garnish, if desired. Spoon sherry over soup. Yield: 5½ cups.

HOMEMADE FISH STOCK

1 pound mild fish bones
1 quart water

1 bunch fresh parsley stems
1 medium onion, thinly sliced

• Combine all ingredients in a large saucepan. Bring to a boil; cover, reduce heat, and simmer 2 hours. Pour mixture through a wire-mesh strainer, discarding bones, parsley, and onion. Yield: 2½ cups.

shell The hard outer hull or covering of nuts, shellfish, eggs, or peas. This term also refers to the process of removing the hull or shell. (*see also* **shuck**)

shellfish A saltwater animal that has a shell of some sort, but no fins, skull, or backbone. All are moderately lean and rich in minerals. There are two main types of shellfish:
• **Crustaceans** are more animated and scurry or swim about; they're recognized by their pincers and antennae. They include crabs, crawfish, lobsters, and shrimp.
• **Mollusks** include bivalves that have hinged shells and include clams, mussels, oysters, and scallops. Univalves or gastropods, which have one shell such as abalone and snails, also fall into this category. Even though squid and octopus don't have shells, they are also classified as mollusks because of the delicate bones within their bodies. (*see also* **clam, crab, crawfish, lobster, mussel, shrimp, snail, squid, octopus,** *and* **oyster**)

shepherd's pie An old English main dish of ground meat, traditionally lamb or mutton, vegetables, and gravy. The mixture is placed in a casserole and topped with mashed potatoes and baked. Modern versions of shepherd's pie sometimes use ground beef. (*see recipe on the following page*)

SHEPHERD'S PIE

1 (22-ounce) package frozen
    mashed potatoes
1 pound ground beef
1 onion, chopped
½ cup frozen sliced carrot,
    thawed
2 tablespoons all-purpose flour

2 teaspoons salt, divided
½ teaspoon pepper, divided
1 cup beef broth
1 large egg, lightly beaten
½ cup (2 ounces) shredded
    Cheddar cheese
Garnish: chopped fresh parsley

• Cook potatoes according to package directions; set aside.
• Cook beef and onion in a large skillet over medium-high heat 5 to 6 minutes, stirring until beef crumbles and is no longer pink. Drain and return to skillet; add carrot.
• Stir in flour, 1 teaspoon salt, and ¼ teaspoon pepper.
• Add broth, and cook, stirring constantly, 3 minutes or until slightly thickened. Spoon mixture into a lightly greased 11- x 7-inch baking dish.
• Stir together potatoes, egg, remaining 1 teaspoon salt, and remaining ¼ teaspoon pepper. Spoon over beef mixture.
• Bake at 350° for 25 minutes. Sprinkle with cheese, and bake 5 more minutes. Garnish, if desired. Yield: 6 servings.

sherbet (SHER biht) A smooth, frozen mixture of sweetened fruit juice and water, though some versions include milk or other dairy products, wine, liqueur, egg whites, or gelatin. Sherbet is richer than an ice, but softer and lighter than ice cream because it's made with less milk fat. However, sherbet is usually sweeter than ice cream so it can contain about the same number of calories. (*see also* **ice cream** *and* **sorbet**)

THREE-INGREDIENT ORANGE SHERBET

Try any (or all) of the variations, and pick your favorite flavor.

1 (15½-ounce) can crushed
    pineapple, undrained
1 (2-liter) bottle orange soft
    drink, chilled

1 (14-ounce) can sweetened
    condensed milk
Garnish: orange rind strips

• Stir together first 3 ingredients in a large bowl, and pour into freezer container of a 5-quart electric freezer. Freeze mixture according to manufacturer's instructions.
• Pack electric freezer with additional ice and rock salt, and let sherbet stand 1 hour before serving. Scoop sherbet into bowls, and garnish, if desired. Yield: about 3 quarts.

Three-Ingredient Blackberry Sherbet: Substitute frozen blackberries for crushed pineapple and grape soft drink for orange soft drink.

Three-Ingredient Peach Sherbet: Substitute frozen peaches for crushed pineapple and peach soft drink for orange soft drink.

Three-Ingredient Strawberry Sherbet: Substitute 1 (16-ounce) package frozen sliced strawberries for crushed pineapple and strawberry soft drink for orange soft drink.

sherry Fortified wine made principally in Spain that ranges in color from pale gold to dark brown, and in flavor from bone dry to very sweet. Finos are considered dry and light, while olorosos are sweet, dark, and fuller flavored. Sherry can be consumed as an apéritif or as an after-dinner drink. Dry sherries are usually served chilled and sweet sherries are served at room temperature. (*see also* **apéritif, cooking wine, fino,** *and* **fortified wine**)

shiitake (shee TAH kay) (*see* **mushroom**)

Shirley Temple A nonalcoholic beverage that's popular with children; it's made from grenadine syrup, ginger ale, and garnished with a maraschino cherry. The drink was originally created for children who wanted to have a "cocktail" with adults.

shirred eggs (SHERD) Eggs covered with a small amount of milk or cream, sprinkled with breadcrumbs, and baked in ramekins or custard cups until the whites are firm. (*see also* **egg**)

shish kabob (SHIHSH kuh bob) A grilled or broiled skewer threaded with chunks of meat, poultry, shellfish, firm fish, vegetables, or fruits. The meat, usually lamb or beef, is sometimes marinated before being threaded on the skewer. (*see also* **brochette, kabob,** *and* **skewer**)

shoestring potatoes Short slender French fries. (*see also* **French fries**)

shoofly pie A rich, molasses-based custard pie thought to have originated in Pennsylvania Dutch country. There are two different versions of how this pie got its name. The first is that the pie was originally made to attract flies away from other foods; the second declares that the pie was so sweet that flies had to be constantly chased away.

short A term used to describe pastry that contains a high proportion of shortening, margarine, butter, or cooking oil to flour. Baked goods that are short are tender, rich, flaky, and crisp.

shortbread A tender, rich, short pastry of Scottish origin originally associated with Christmas and Hogmanay or New Year's Eve. Made from butter, flour, and sugar, shortbread dough was traditionally formed into a circle and cut into pie-shaped wedges called petticoat tails. Another way of making shortbread is to press the dough into a round, shallow, carved, earthenware mold. After baking, the large shortbread cookie is turned out of the mold and cut into wedges. (*see* **short** *and recipe on the following page*)

SCOTTISH SHORTBREAD

A basic blend of butter, sugar, and flour results in a taste far more than the sum of its parts. Good shortbread needs careful handling and precise baking.

1 pound unsalted butter, softened	**4 cups all-purpose flour**
1 cup sugar	**½ cup cornstarch**
2 teaspoons vanilla extract	**¼ teaspoon salt**

• Beat butter at medium speed with an electric mixer until creamy; gradually add sugar, beating well. Stir in vanilla.

• Combine flour, cornstarch, and salt; gradually add to butter mixture, beating at low speed after each addition. (Mixture will be stiff.) Turn dough out onto a lightly floured surface; knead lightly 8 to 10 times.

• Press dough into an ungreased 15- x 10-inch jellyroll pan. Prick dough at 1-inch intervals with a fork, and score (cut) into 2½- x 1-inch bars. Cover and chill at least 2 hours.

• Bake at 325° for 35 minutes. Cool in pan on a wire rack 5 minutes; cut shortbread into bars. Cool completely before removing from pan. Store in an airtight container at room temperature up to 1 week, or freeze up to 3 months. Yield: 5 dozen.

shortcake A dessert made from a large, rich, sweet biscuit that's split in half and filled with fresh strawberries or other fruit, and whipped cream. Sometimes short-cake is made with slices of angel food cake or sponge cake instead of biscuits.

TIMESAVING TIP

A shortcut for shortcake is easy when you combine 1 (16-ounce) container strawberries, sliced, and ¼ cup sugar; cover and set aside. Brush 9 large frozen biscuits with 3 tablespoons of melted butter. Combine 3 tablespoons sugar and 1 teaspoon ground cinnamon; sprinkle over biscuits. Bake biscuits according to package directions. Serve with strawberry mixture and whipped cream. Serve immediately to eight happy friends.

STREUSEL STRAWBERRY SHORTCAKE

3 cups biscuit mix	**¼ cup butter or margarine**
⅔ cup milk	**2 cups whipping cream**
¼ cup butter or margarine, melted	**½ cup sugar**
½ cup firmly packed brown sugar	**2 (16-ounce) containers fresh**
½ cup chopped pecans	**strawberries, sliced**

• Stir together first 3 ingredients until a soft dough forms. Divide dough in half, and press into 2 greased 8-inch round cakepans.

• Combine sugar and nuts; cut in ¼ cup butter with a fork until crumbly. Sprinkle evenly over dough.

• Bake at 400° for 15 to 20 minutes or until a wooden pick inserted in center comes out clean. Cool in pans on wire racks 10 minutes. Remove from pans, and cool completely on wire racks.

• Beat cream at medium speed with an electric mixer until foamy; gradually add ½ cup sugar, beating at high speed until stiff peaks form.

• Place 1 cake layer on a large serving plate. Layer with half each of strawberries and whipped cream; top with remaining cake layer. Layer with remaining strawberries and whipped cream. Yield: 8 servings.

shortening (*see* **fats and oils**)

shred To cut, tear, or grate foods, such as cheese, into long, narrow strips. Shredding is done on the largest holes of a box grater or with a shredding disc in a food processor. Grating, on the other hand, means to reduce foods to tiny particles using the smallest holes on a grater.

shrimp A small crustacean with a long tail and 10 legs; its tender, sweet meat has made it the most popular shellfish in the United States. Though there are hundreds of species of shrimp, only a few varieties appear in our markets; two of the main ones are Gulf shrimp from the Gulf of Mexico and black-striped tiger shrimp from Asian waters. Shrimp are available in many different colors, from light gray to pink to brown (though they all turn pink during cooking), and vary in size from colossal to miniature. Small and medium shrimp are good in salads and casseroles, while large and jumbo shrimp are ideal stuffed, grilled, or in entrées for entertaining. When purchasing shrimp, remember 1 pound of raw, unpeeled shrimp equals 8 to 9 ounces cooked, peeled shrimp. So purchase a pound of shrimp for every two to three servings. Shrimp are usually sold headless, but if they are whole, twist off the heads, being sure to remove (continued on the following page)

TEST KITCHEN SECRET

To peel shrimp, pull off the head, if it's still on. Then pull off the legs on the inside curve of the shrimp and peel off the shell, beginning at the top by running your thumb under the section of the shell located between the legs. The tail shell may be left on the shrimp for show, if desired. Using a small knife or shrimp deveiner, make a slit down the back of the shrimp, and remove the sand vein.

JAN MOON

TIMESAVING TIP

A shrimp butler is a timesaving tool if you clean lots of shrimp at a time. We were skeptical at first because it deveins shrimp one at a time. When we deveined 5 pounds in 10 minutes, it made us believers. Simply place headless shrimp (any size) in the hopper —one at a time—and turn the handle. The butler splits the shell and removes the vein in one motion, and clean, shell-on shrimp exit the machine. The shells peel right off because they're already cut. For more information visit **www.shellmaster.net** or call 407-324-3101.

all parts of the head region. Shrimp are also sold shelled, raw or cooked, and fresh or frozen. They can be prepared in a variety of ways, including boiling, frying, and grilling. Fresh shrimp cook very quickly in about 2 minutes in boiling water. As soon as they turn evenly pink, they're done. Pour the shrimp and water into a colander and drain.

LITE BITE

Shrimp are low in fat and calories and good sources of niacin, potassium, and iron. Although high in cholesterol and sodium, shrimp contain no saturated fat, which is believed to be the culprit for high blood cholesterol.

Storage: Fresh shrimp should smell like the sea with no hint of ammonia.

Q Do I need to devein shrimp?

A Deveining shrimp is mostly an aesthetic choice rather than a necessity. The black sand vein line that runs down the back of a shrimp is its intestinal tract. In small shrimp, it's really not noticeable, but in larger shrimp, the vein is unappealing and can add a gritty, muddy taste. While there's no harm in eating cooked shrimp that haven't been deveined, some people prefer to remove the vein. It's an easy process, particularly with a special deveining tool, which looks like a knife tapered sharply like a bird's beak. However, a knife can be used; just slit the shrimp lengthwise down its back, and pull away the vein with the tip of the knife.

Store shrimp in the refrigerator, and use within a day or two after purchasing. Shrimp may be frozen raw in the shell or cooked and peeled for longer storage. (*see also* **devein, prawn, scampi,** *and* **shellfish**)

shrimp boil (*see* **crab boil**)

shuck The process of removing oysters, clams, or mussels from their shells, or peeling the husks and silks from ears of corn. This term also refers to removing peanuts, peas, or beans from their shells. (*see also* **clam, mussel,** *and* **oyster**)

sideboard A piece of furniture used as a serving table in a dining room; it sometimes has several narrow drawers for storing flatware or silver serving pieces.

side dish A starch or vegetable dish that typically accompanies the main dish or entrée.

sieve (SIHV) A bowl-shaped fine wire-mesh strainer used to strain liquid or solids from food. A sieve can also be used to separate lumps or larger particles of food from smaller ones or to puree soft foods, that are pushed through the sieve with the back of a large spoon. (*see also* **colander, strain,** *and* **strainer**)

sift Passing dry ingredients such as flour, powdered sugar, and baking powder through a fine-mesh sifter, sieve, or strainer to remove lumps, to blend ingredients, and to incorporate air, which makes the ingredients lighter. Sifters are usually made of stainless steel or heavy-weight plastic and employ a rotary crank to work ingredients through the mesh. Unless *Southern Living* recipes specify that the ingredient should be sifted, you don't need to do so. (*see also* **flour**)

Q **Do I have to wash my sifter each time I use it?**

A As long as no lumps get trapped in the sifter, it can be turned upside down over a trash can and tapped or shaken to remove any traces of ingredients. If food gets trapped in the tiny holes, soak the sifter in hot, soapy water and scrub with a vegetable brush. Dishwasher-safe sifters can save on cleanup time.

simmer Cooking food gently in liquid over low heat just below a boil so that tiny bubbles gently break the surface. Simmering is the ideal temperature for many soups and sauces; a gentle simmer is used when braising or poaching meat or fish. (*see also* **boil, braise,** *and* **poach**)

simple syrup (*see* **sugar syrup**)

sizzling rice soup A broth-based Chinese soup featuring chicken or pork and sometimes shrimp, along with a variety of vegetables. Deep-fried rice patties, placed in each soup bowl, sizzle and pop when the hot soup is added.

skate A kite-shaped saltwater fish, also called a "ray," that has a firm, white flesh with a mild, sweet flavor. Fresh skate often has an ammonia-like odor, which is removed by soaking in lemon juice and water before it's poached, baked, or fried. (*see also* **fish**)

skewer (SKYOO uhr) A long, thin pointed metal rod or wooden stick used to thread small chunks of meat and/or vegetables to be grilled for shish kabobs. Skewers that are square or flat are best because they hold food securely as it's moved during grilling. (*see also* **kabob** *and* **shish kabob**)

skillet (*see* **cookware**)

skim Removing the top layer from the surface of a liquid, such as cream from milk or scum, foam, or fat from a soup or stock. When skimming, use a large spoon or a metal skimmer that has a long handle with a shallow mesh or perforated bowl. Skimmers are also used to lift foods out of hot liquids.

LITE BITE
Chill cooked soup or stock to allow the surface fat to harden. This enables more fat to be skimmed.

skirt steak A cut of beef from the flank section, which lies between the abdomen and chest cavity. Skirt steak is a long, flat piece of meat that has a tough, stringy texture, but is flavorful and tender if cooked correctly. It can be grilled or braised, and is best known as the steak used to make fajitas. (*see also* **beef** *and* **fajitas**)

slab A term that describes a large, thick slice of food, such as bread, bacon, spareribs, or cheese.

slash A shallow cut made in the surface of food, such as bread dough or whole fish, to allow steam to escape as it cooks. (*see also* **score**)

slaw (*see* **coleslaw**)

slice Cutting food into uniformly thick pieces, as in bread or meat. Slicing vegetables, such as zucchini, allows them to have a larger cooking surface area.

sliver Foods, such as almonds, cheese, and meat, that have been cut into long, narrow strips. Cake or pie can also be cut into tiny wedges called slivers.

sloppy Joe A casual sandwich that holds a mixture of ground beef flavored with ketchup, onions, and green peppers. Most sloppy Joes are served on hamburger buns.

slow cooker An electrical appliance that allows a meal to be cooked while you're away from home. Most slow cookers are made of thick stoneware, and the slow cooker bowl or crock is surrounded by an enclosed heating system. The low temperature gently simmers food for hours unattended. Slow cookers range in size from 1 to 6 quarts, and some models have a removable stoneware liner that's dishwasher-safe. (*see also* **Crock-Pot**™)

> **TEST KITCHEN SECRET**
>
> *If your slow cooker recipe calls for cooking on low and you want to speed it up by cooking on high, remember that one hour on high equals 2 hours on low. The low setting is best used for all-day cooking.* VIE WARSHAW

TIMESAVING TIP
Instead of using the conventional cooktop or oven for long-cooking dishes, use a slow cooker. They're excellent for making stews and braised dishes and they'll cook on their own without as much attention.

slump A cobblerlike dessert of cooked fruit baked with a biscuit or dumpling on top. Popular in the eighteenth and nineteenth centuries, slumps were often served with cream. (*see also* **grunt**)

slurry A mixture of flour or cornstarch and a cold liquid that's stirred into a boiling liquid mixture to thicken it.

smelt Small, 4- to 7-inch-long silvery fish that are rich, oily, and mild-flavored. Smelt are sold canned or fresh. If fresh, they are typically floured, fried, and eaten whole—head, body, and bones. (*see also* **fish**)

Smithfield ham A country-cured ham from Smithfield, Virginia, considered by many to be the premier country ham. These hams come from hogs raised on a diet of acorns, hickory nuts, and peanuts, and are dry-cured, seasoned, smoked, and aged a minimum of 6 to 12 months. Their lean, dark meat is rich, salty, and dry; they can be served raw, but are usually baked or boiled. Before cooking a Smithfield ham, soak it in water for 12 to 24 hours to remove excess saltiness. (*see also* **country ham** *and* **ham**)

smoked salmon Fresh salmon that has been cured by either hot smoking (smoked 6 to 12 hours at 120° to 180°) or cold smoking (smoked from a day to 3 weeks at 70° to 90°). Indian-cured salmon has been brined and cold-smoked up to 2 weeks, and results in a type of salmon jerky. Kippered salmon is a chunk, steak, or fillet that has been mildly brined and hot smoked. Lox, which has been brined and cold smoked, is usually slightly salty, although sugar is sometimes added to cut the saltiness. Often, the origin of the salmon is added to the name, such as Nova Scotia or Irish smoked salmon; these products are usually cold-smoked. (*see also* **fish** *and* **salmon**)

smoke point The temperature at which a fat or oil begins to break down and starts to smoke and impart unpleasant flavors. The higher the smoke point, the better suited a fat is for frying.

Approximate smoke points for most fats are: Butter (350°); vegetable shortening (356° to 370°); lard (361° to 401°); olive oil (375° to 410°); corn oil (410°); canola oil (435°); peanut oil (450°); safflower oil (450°); soybean oil (450°); and vegetable oil (441° to 450°). In general, remember that safflower, peanut, canola, and corn oils have a high smoke point; extra-virgin olive oil has a low smoke point. (*see also* **fats and oils**)

TEST KITCHEN SECRET

Because Southerners fry a lot, they should select oils such as peanut oil with a high smoke point. It's also important to be cautious when heating or reheating an oil to a high temperature; once it reaches the smoke point, it can quickly burst into flames. VANESSA McNEIL

Q **Can I reuse fat or oil after deep-frying with it?**

A Reusing fats and exposing them to air reduces their smoke points, but when properly cared for, oil can be reused at least once. Cool hot oil and pour through a sieve or several thicknesses of cheesecloth into a clean, dry glass or heavy plastic container; cover and refrigerate. Discard oil if the color darkens or if foaming occurs when adding food.

smoothie A thickened, chilled beverage, similar to a milk shake, made by pureeing fruit with yogurt, milk, or ice cream. Sometimes a protein or vitamin-fortified dry mix is added to a smoothie mixture.

EASY PINEAPPLE SMOOTHIE

½ cup chopped fresh or canned
  pineapple
1 frozen raspberry-flavored juice
  pop or ¼ cup grape juice
3 tablespoons sugar
¼ teaspoon vanilla extract

1 teaspoon pink lemonade
  drink mix
1 cup orange juice
1 cup ice cubes
Vanilla ice cream (optional)

• Process first 7 ingredients and, if desired, ice cream in a blender until smooth, stopping to scrape down sides. Freeze 5 minutes. Yield: 1 serving.

s'mores A campfire or cookout favorite made by layering graham crackers with hot, toasted marshmallows and squares of milk chocolate.

smorgasbord (SMOHR guhs bohrd) A Swedish term that refers to a buffet table that offers a wide selection of foods such as appetizers, salads, hot and cold meats, meatballs, open-faced sandwiches, vegetables, cheeses, breads, and desserts. (*see also* **Swedish meatballs**)

smother A method of cooking where a food is completely or almost completely covered with another food, sauce, or liquid while it's baked or braised. For example, country-fried steak is often smothered in gravy.

snail A small, soft-bodied mollusk with a spiral shell that's usually known by the French name "escargot." Snails can be purchased canned, frozen, or fresh in some gourmet or specialty markets. They are usually boiled before being baked or broiled in the shell and served with seasoned butter. (*see also* **escargot**)

snap beans (*see* **beans, fresh;** *and* **green bean**)

snapper A saltwater fish found in U.S. waters from the Gulf of Mexico to the coast of North Carolina. There are many different species of snapper, but the most popular is red snapper, named because of its reddish-pink skin and red eyes. Snapper is a firm-textured, low-fat fish, and is sold whole and as steaks or fillets. (*see also* **fish**)

snickerdoodle (SNIHK uhr doo dl) A round cookie with a crackly, crisp surface and a chewy inside. Snickerdoodles are sometimes flavored with nutmeg and rolled in a mixture of sugar and cinnamon before being baked.

snifter A footed glass with a large balloon-shaped bowl that's larger at the bottom and tapered toward the top. Because brandy is usually served in a snifter glass, it's often referred to as a brandy snifter. (*see also* **brandy** *and* **wine glasses**)

snip Cutting soft food or herbs with kitchen shears or scissors into small pieces using quick, short strokes. Snip tomatoes right in the can or herbs in a small cup.

snow crab (*see* **crab**)

snow pea A bean with a bright green, almost translucent flat pod that's thin and crisp. Snow peas are sweet and tender enough to be eaten raw or cooked whole, though it's best to pinch off the tip ends and remove any strings just before using. When raw, the peas can be served with dip or tossed into salads. Also known as Chinese snow peas, they are often added to stir-fried dishes. Snow peas look similar to sugar snap peas, which have fatter pods.

Storage: Once picked, the sugar in peas quickly converts to starch, so cook them soon. You can refrigerate them in a plastic bag for a day or so before they begin to loose flavor. (*see also* **pea** *and* **sugar snap pea**)

TEST KITCHEN SECRET

Snow peas are easy to prepare. They can be dropped into boiling water and cooked about 30 seconds, or they can be steamed over boiling water in less than a minute. They can also be stir-fried by themselves or tossed into a stir-fried recipe; add them at the last minute, and cook just until they turn bright green. REBECCA KRACKE GORDON

soba (SOH buh) Japanese noodles made from buckwheat flour. Soba noodles are thin, flat, and have a grayish-brown color. (*see also* **Asian noodle** *and* **noodle**)

soda A slang name, used mostly in the Northeast and Midwest, for a non-alcoholic, carbonated drink. Soda also describes a soda fountain drink made with ice cream and carbonated water. This term also refers to the chemical leavening agent, baking soda. (*see also* **baking soda**)

Southernism

While soda may apply to carbonated beverages in the Northeast and Midwest, many Southerners tend to call carbonated beverages "Coke." With Coca-Cola originating in Atlanta, you'll hear many Southerners ask, "Would you like a Coke?" If you reply that you do, most Southerners will then ask, "What kind?"

READER TIP

"When making sherbet or ice cream punches, I make sure the soda is thoroughly chilled and add it at the last minute so it won't warm up the rest of the punch or melt the sherbet." W.W., Newton, MS

soda bread A quick bread leavened with a mixture of baking soda and an acid ingredient, such as buttermilk. (*see also* **Irish soda bread**)

soda water (*see* **seltzer**)

sofrito (soh FREE toh) A Spanish sauce made by sautéing annatto seeds in rendered pork fat. After the seeds are removed, chopped onions, green peppers, garlic, pork and various herbs are added to the now red-colored oil and simmered until thick and tender. The Italian version is called soffrito; it's a similar mixture but sautéed in olive oil. (*see also* **annatto**)

soft ball stage (*see* **candy**)

soft crack stage (*see* **candy**)

soft-shell crab (*see* **crab**)

sole A saltwater flatfish related to the flounder family with a white underside and brown to gray top skin; the flesh is lean, pearly white, and mild-flavored. The best known type of sole is Dover sole, which is harvested in coastal waters from Denmark to the Mediterranean Sea. True Dover sole is imported frozen; much of what is sold in the United States as sole is actually flounder. Sole can be prepared in a variety of ways including poaching, steaming, baking, and broiling. (*see also* **dauphine** *and* **fish**)

sop (SOP) An old Southern term for using biscuits, cornbread, or rolls to soak up and eat gravy, sorghum, molasses, honey, or any meat or cooking juices on the plate.

Southernism

Former Georgia Gov. Zell Miller grew up sopping sorghum and claims it takes a special touch. He even writes about it in his autobiography.

sopa (SOH pah) A Portuguese and Spanish term for soup. "Sopa seca" is a dish based on rice, vermicelli, or dry tortilla strips that have been combined with tomatoes, onions, garlic, and broth, and cooked until all the liquid is absorbed, thereby becoming a "dry soup."

sopaipilla (soh pi PEE yuh) A crisp, deep-fried Mexican dessert pastry that's puffy with a hollow center. Sopaipillas are usually served with honey or a cinnamon-flavored syrup.

sorbet (sor BAY) A refreshing frozen dessert similar to sherbet, except it's usually a bit softer; it doesn't contain milk, eggs, or gelatin. Sorbets are usually smoother than ices or granitas. (*see also* **granita, ice, sherbet,** *and recipe on the following page*)

PEACH SORBET

Feel free to use either fresh or frozen sliced peaches in this sorbet.

3 cups water
1 cup sugar
1 (16-ounce) package frozen peach slices, thawed

¼ cup lemon juice
¾ cup fresh orange juice
¼ teaspoon almond extract

• Bring water and sugar to a boil in a medium saucepan, stirring often; reduce heat, and simmer 5 minutes, stirring occasionally. Cool; cover and chill.
• Process peach slices and lemon juice in a blender or food processor until smooth, stopping to scrape down sides.
• Combine sugar mixture, peach mixture, orange juice, and almond extract; pour into freezer container of a 4-quart hand-turned or electric freezer.
• Freeze according to manufacturer's instructions.
• Pack freezer with additional ice and rock salt, and let stand 1 hour before serving. Yield: 7 cups.

sorghum (SOR guhm) A cereal grass mostly used in the United States as animal feed, except for the sweet juice that's extracted from the stalks and boiled down to make sorghum syrup. Sorghum syrup has a medium brown color and a sweet flavor similar to molasses; it's used as table syrup and for sweetening and flavoring baked goods. (*see also* **molasses**)

Southernism

The making of sorghum is a fall ritual across the southern Appalachians. In olden times, sorghum mills used a grinding apparatus usually powered by a mule to transform cane into juice, and then the juice was boiled into the syrup that eventually became sorghum. In many rural areas, this ritual boiling of sorghum turned into a community gathering complete with food, gossip, and plenty of fiddle playing. Today, across the region, the annual sorghum making becomes the backdrop for arts and crafts festivals complete with hayrides and other harvest fun.

sorrel (SOR uhl) A hardy herb that can also be eaten as a salad green; its leaves are smooth, arrow-shaped, and bright green. Sorrel has a sour, citrus-like flavor, and can be used raw in salads or cooked as a flavoring for soups and sauces. (*see also* **herbs**)

soufflé (soo FLAY) A French term for a puffy creation leavened with stiffly beaten egg whites and stabilized by a

TEST KITCHEN SECRET

Baked soufflés are delicate and need to be tested carefully for doneness. Try to prevent moving the dish or sudden drafts of cold air. They're done when a knife inserted halfway between the center and the edge comes out clean. If you remove a soufflé from the oven too early, it will collapse. VIE WARSHAW

white sauce thickened with egg yolks. A soufflé can be sweet or savory; while most are served hot, some are served cold. Hot soufflés are more fragile than those that are chilled or frozen because the hot air trapped in the soufflé begins to escape as soon as the dish is removed from the oven. Sweet dessert soufflés may be baked, chilled, or frozen; chilled or frozen ones are often mousse-type mixtures held firm with gelatin. Whether sweet or savory, most baked soufflés are prepared in classic ovenproof soufflé dishes, which are round and have straight sides that allow the light egg mixtures to climb and rise. (*see also* **egg, mousse,** *and recipe on the following page*)

RESCUE for a fallen soufflé:
First, check to see if the mixture is undercooked; if so, then return it to the oven to finish cooking. To hide cracks, top a savory soufflé with grated cheese or finely chopped herbs, or dust a dessert one with powdered sugar.

Steps to great soufflés:
• Preheat oven and assemble your soufflé dish with a foil collar before beginning recipe preparation.
• Be sure your mixing bowl and beaters are grease free. If any fat is present, egg whites won't whip to their maximum volume.
• Separate eggs while cold (it's easiest), but for best volume, let the whites come to room temperature before beating them.
• Beat egg whites until stiff, but not dry. Overbeaten egg whites may cause a soufflé to collapse.
• Be ready to fold the rest of the ingredients together as soon as you beat the egg whites. Stir a small amount of beaten whites into soufflé mixture to lighten it; then gently and quickly fold in remaining whites, being careful not to deflate mixture.

TEST KITCHEN SECRET

When beating egg whites for a soufflé, beat them until stiff, but not dry. They're ready if they no longer slip when the bowl is tilted. MARY ALLEN PERRY

Q Why do some soufflé recipes call for adding a collar to the soufflé dish, and how do you make one?

A Use a collar on a soufflé dish when the dish is three-fourths full or more; this gives the mixture more room to expand plus provides extra support as it rises or sets. To make a collar, measure the circumference of the top of the dish and add 3 inches. Fold a 12-inch-wide piece of foil lengthwise into thirds. If making a sweet soufflé, lightly butter and sprinkle one side of the foil with sugar; if making a savory soufflé, sprinkle the buttered foil with fine, dry breadcrumbs. Attach the collar, buttered side in, around the outside of the dish so that the foil extends about 2 inches above the dish; overlap the ends of the foil and secure with string or tape. Fill the soufflé dish, and bake or chill according to the recipe, then carefully remove collar.

CLASSIC CHEESE SOUFFLÉ

Bake this savory soufflé in a very hot oven to encourage its initial puff; then reduce the heat to cook it through and produce its golden cap.

2 tablespoons butter or margarine	⅛ teaspoon hot sauce
¼ cup all-purpose flour	1 cup milk
½ teaspoon salt	1½ cups (6 ounces) shredded sharp
¼ teaspoon pepper	Cheddar cheese
¼ teaspoon dry mustard	6 large eggs, separated

• Lightly butter a 2-quart soufflé dish. Cut a piece of aluminum foil long enough to circle the dish, allowing a 1-inch overlap. Fold foil lengthwise into thirds, and lightly butter 1 side. Wrap foil, buttered side against dish, so it extends 3 inches above the rim. Securely attach foil with string. Set aside.

• Melt 2 tablespoons butter in a heavy saucepan over low heat; add flour and next 4 ingredients, stirring until smooth. Cook 1 minute, stirring constantly. Gradually add milk; cook over medium heat, stirring constantly, until thickened and bubbly. Add cheese, stirring until melted. Cool slightly.

• Beat egg yolks until thick and pale. Gradually stir about one-fourth of hot cheese mixture into yolks; add to remaining hot mixture.

• Beat egg whites at high speed with an electric mixer until stiff but not dry; fold into cheese mixture. Pour into prepared soufflé dish. Bake at 475° for 10 minutes. Reduce heat to 400°, and bake 15 more minutes or until puffed and golden. Remove collar, and serve immediately. Yield: 6 servings.

TIMESAVING TIP

Unbaked soufflé mixtures can be spooned into individual baking dishes or custard cups and frozen up to a week. These smaller soufflés can be baked either all at once or one at a time at a later date. This trick doesn't work with larger soufflés. In addition, petite soufflés don't require foil collars.

Individual Cheese Soufflés: Spoon cheese mixture into 6 buttered 10-ounce soufflé dishes or custard cups. Bake at 350° for 15 to 20 minutes or until puffed and golden. **Note:** You can freeze Individual Cheese Soufflés before baking. Use freezer-to-oven dishes. Cover with plastic wrap, and freeze. To bake, place frozen soufflés on a baking sheet; bake at 350° for 40 minutes or until golden.

soul food Traditional African-American cuisine, long popular in the South, believed to have been named due to its comforting, soul-satisfying flavors. Some dishes commonly thought of as soul foods are yams, collard greens, black-eyed peas, cornbread, and ham hocks.

Southernism

Chef Leah Chase of New Orleans says it best, "All food is soul food, it just depends on where your soul resides." She grew up with the comfort of foods such as crisp, juicy fried pork chops, tender collard greens, fried okra, pickled beets, and hot cornbread. And she and others before her have shared their love of and talents for this ordinary fare that brings extraordinary satisfaction.

soup Any combination of vegetables, meat, poultry, shellfish, fish, or fruits cooked in a liquid. Soups can be hot or cold, sweet or savory, thick or thin, and served as an appetizer, main course, or dessert. Soups served as the main course tend to be chunkier and meatier, such as chilies and gumbos.

Lighter, more delicate cream and brothlike soups are served as appetizers; they should be served in smaller amounts to stimulate the appetite. A cold, sweet fruit soup might be garnished with whipped cream and served as a dessert.

Storage: Many meat and vegetable soups (but not cream soups) take on a richer taste if refrigerated for a day to give the flavors time to blend and develop; this makes them ideal for make-ahead. To freeze, package soups in pint or quart plastic freezer containers or heavy-duty zip-top freezer bags; label with recipe name, date, and amount, and freeze up to 3 months. Frozen soups can be thawed in the refrigerator and slowly reheated in a saucepan over low heat. (*see also* **skim**)

> ## TEST KITCHEN SECRET
>
> *Use a bulb baster to remove fat from the surface of broth or soup. Or, wrap an ice cube in damp cheesecloth and skim it over the surface of a soup; the fat will congeal on contact and then is easily removed. Another easy way to remove fat from a soup is to cover and refrigerate it overnight until the fat solidifies on the surface; then just lift off the fat.* JAN MOON

TIMESAVING TIP
To speed prep time, use canned broth. To save chopping time, use a food processor to chop and slice vegetables. Or, to save even more time use precut, frozen, or canned vegetables.

QUICK VEGETABLE SOUP

This version of vegetable soup may fast become one of your favorites because it tastes great. It's easy, too. You probably have the ingredients on hand to get started. Don't miss the beefy variation. You can add leftover chopped cooked roast beef, too.

1 (14½-ounce) can stewed tomatoes, undrained	2 cups water
1 (8-ounce) can tomato sauce	1½ teaspoons beef bouillon granules
1 (10-ounce) package frozen mixed vegetables	⅛ teaspoon freshly ground pepper

• Combine all ingredients in a Dutch oven. Bring to a boil; cover, reduce heat, and simmer 20 minutes, stirring occasionally. Yield: 7 cups.

Quick Vegetable-Beef Soup: Brown 1 pound ground chuck in a large skillet, stirring until it crumbles and is no longer pink. Drain. Add to soup, and bring to a simmer.

RESCUE for a too salty soup:
If you've added too much salt to a soup, simply drop in a peeled, raw potato and cook a few minutes. Then remove the potato before serving the soup.

sour A sharp, tart taste, usually due to an acidic ingredient such as lemon juice or vinegar. A "sour" is also a type of cocktail drink made of liquor, sugar, and citrus juice shaken with cracked ice and served with an orange slice and a maraschino cherry. This term might also be used to describe something that has fermented, spoiled, or become rancid.

sour cream A smooth, thick dairy product made of cream that has been deliberately soured by the addition of a bacterial culture. Sour cream comes in low-fat and nonfat versions and has a pleasingly tangy-tart flavor. It can serve as a condiment or be incorporated into recipes for cakes,

TEST KITCHEN SECRET

Sour cream will curdle and separate if exposed very long to high heat, so when adding it to cooked sauces or other hot mixtures, first bring it to room temperature and then add it slowly, near the end of cooking. Make sure you're cooking over low heat, and unless flour has been mixed into the sour cream, don't allow it to simmer or boil. VANESSA MCNEIL

cookies, and breads. Sour cream is used in sauces and salad dressings or as a topping for baked potatoes.
Storage: Always check the container for the sell-by date; it can be stored in the refrigerator up to a week after this date. (*see also* **cream**)

LITE BITE

For a lower calorie, lower fat substitute for sour cream, use fat-free or light sour cream, or replace it with an equal amount of plain yogurt.

sourdough A bread leavened with fermented starter, which gives it a slightly sour, tangy flavor. San Francisco is known for its sourdough breads. (*see also* **starter**)

SOURDOUGH STARTER

Sourdough Starter is a tangy yeast mixture used for bread making. It will last indefinitely if you keep "feeding" it with equal amounts of flour and water as well as a tiny bit of sugar.

1 (¼-ounce) envelope active dry yeast	1 teaspoon salt
½ cup warm water (105° to 115°)	2 cups warm water (100° to 110°)
2 cups all-purpose flour	Starter Food
3 tablespoons sugar	

• Combine yeast and ½ cup warm water in a 1-cup liquid measuring cup; let stand 5 minutes.
• Combine flour, sugar, and salt in a medium-size nonmetal bowl, and stir well. Gradually stir in 2 cups warm water. Add yeast mixture, and mix well.

- Cover starter loosely with plastic wrap or cheesecloth; let stand in a warm place (85°) 72 hours, stirring 2 or 3 times daily. Place fermented mixture in refrigerator, and stir once a day. Use within 11 days.
- To use, remove sourdough starter from refrigerator; let stand at room temperature at least 1 hour. Stir starter well, and measure amount of starter needed. Replenish remaining starter with Starter Food, and return to refrigerator; use starter within 2 to 14 days, stirring daily.
- When Sourdough Starter is used again, repeat procedure for using starter and replenishing with Starter Food. Yield: 3 cups.

STARTER FOOD

1 cup all-purpose flour   1 teaspoon sugar
1 cup water

- Stir all ingredients into remaining Sourdough Starter.

COUNTRY CRUST SOURDOUGH

2 (¼-ounce) envelopes active   2 teaspoons salt
   dry yeast   2 large eggs, beaten
1¼ cups warm water (100° to 110°)   5½ to 6 cups unbleached
1 cup Sourdough Starter   all-purpose flour
   (at room temperature)   Vegetable oil
¼ cup vegetable oil   Butter or margarine, melted
¼ cup sugar

- Combine yeast and warm water in a 2-cup liquid measuring cup; let stand 5 minutes.
- Combine yeast mixture, Sourdough Starter, ¼ cup oil, sugar, salt, eggs, and 3 cups flour in a nonmetal bowl. Gradually stir in enough remaining flour to make a soft dough.
- Turn dough out onto a floured surface, and knead until smooth and elastic (8 to 10 minutes). Place in a well-greased bowl, turning to grease top. Cover and let rise in a warm place, (85°), free from drafts, 1 to 1½ hours or until doubled in bulk.
- Punch dough down, and divide in half; place on a floured surface. Roll each half into an 18- x 9-inch rectangle. Tightly roll up dough, starting at narrow edge; pinch seam and ends together to seal. Place loaves, seam side down, in 2 greased 9- x 5-inch loafpans. Brush tops with oil. Cover and let rise in a warm place, free from drafts, about 1 hour or until doubled in bulk. Bake at 375° for 30 to 35 minutes or until loaves sound hollow when tapped. Remove loaves from pans; brush with butter. Yield: 2 loaves.

Southern Comfort A potent, 100-proof peach-flavored bourbon
liqueur produced in St. Louis, Missouri. (*see also* **bourbon** *and* **proof**)

soybean A nutritious legume, low in carbohydrates and high in protein, and used to make a variety of products, including tofu, soy sauce, tamari, miso, soy flour, soybean oil, and soy milk. The soy pods are tan to black and are covered with a fine tawny to gray fuzz. Soybeans range from pea to cherry size, and can be red, yellow, green, brown, or black; they have a bland flavor and can be cooked like any other dried bean and used in soups, stews, and casseroles. The beans can also be sprouted to make bean sprouts and used in salads or cooked as a vegetable. Fresh soybeans are available for purchase in Asian markets and some health food stores. The dried beans and a variety of soybean products can be found in most supermarkets and health food stores. (*see also* **beans, dried; beans, fresh; bean sprouts; miso; soy sauce; tamari;** *and* **tofu**)

LITE BITE

Soy products may help lower cholesterol and promote healthy hearts.

soybean oil (*see* **fats and oils**)

soy flour A finely ground, light beige flour made from soybeans. Soy flour is high in protein and low in carbohydrates, but is usually mixed with other flours rather then used alone. It can be purchased at health food stores.

soy milk A pale yellow milk made from pressed, ground, cooked soybeans. It's higher in protein than cow's milk and makes an excellent substitute for those allergic to milk. Soy milk is sold plain, sweetened, or flavored, and is also used as the basis for tofu.

soy sauce A rich, salty-flavored sauce often used in Asian cooking to flavor soups, sauces, marinades, meat, fish, and vegetables. Soy sauce is made from fermented soybean meal and wheat or barley, and can range in color from light, which is a thinner sauce, to dark brown, which is richer and has molasses added; low-sodium soy sauce is also available.
Storage: Soy sauce will keep indefinitely at room temperature.

spaetzle (SHPEHT sluh) Tiny German noodles or dumplings made from flour, eggs, water or milk, salt, and sometimes nutmeg. The dough for the noodles is rolled out and cut into slivers, or rubbed through a colander or special sieve with large holes. The noodles are usually dropped into boiling water or broth and cooked; they can be added to soups or other dishes. In Germany, spaetzle is served as a side dish much like potatoes or rice.

spaghetti (spuh GEHT ee) Long, thin, solid strands of pasta made from semolina and water. Spaghetti is thicker than spaghettini and vermicelli and is often served with a tomato-based meat sauce and sprinkled with Parmesan cheese. (*see also* **pasta, semolina,** *and* **vermicelli**)

SPAGHETTI WITH MEATBALLS

Looking for a make-ahead spaghetti? You can shape the meatballs and freeze them in zip-top bags. Just thaw them in the refrigerator when ready to proceed.

½ cup chopped onion
2 tablespoons butter or
    margarine, melted
1 (28-ounce) can tomatoes,
    undrained and chopped
1 (6-ounce) can tomato paste
1 tablespoon chopped fresh
    parsley
¼ teaspoon pepper

¼ teaspoon dried oregano
1 pound ground beef
2 tablespoons grated onion
½ teaspoon salt
¼ teaspoon pepper
2 tablespoons vegetable oil
½ (16-ounce) package dried
    spaghetti

• Sauté onion in butter in a large skillet. Add tomatoes and next 4 ingredients. Cook over medium heat 20 minutes, stirring occasionally.
• Combine ground beef and next 3 ingredients; mix well. Shape into 1½-inch meatballs. Cook in a large skillet in hot oil over medium heat until no longer pink; drain. Add meatballs to sauce; cook over low heat 15 minutes.
• Cook spaghetti according to package directions; drain. Serve sauce over spaghetti. Yield: 4 main-dish servings.

spaghetti squash A type of winter squash with a flesh that separates into yellow-gold spaghetti-like strands that can be dressed with a sauce and served as a combination vegetable and pasta substitute. The strands can also be served in casseroles or as a salad ingredient. (*see also* **squash**)

spanakopita (span uh KOH pih tuh) A Greek pie that has a top and bottom crust made from phyllo dough and is filled with sautéed spinach and onions mixed with eggs and feta cheese. (*see also* **phyllo**)

Spanish olive (*see* **olive**)

Spanish onion (*see* **onion**)

spareribs A long, narrow, fatty cut of meat that includes the lower portion of the ribs and breastbone of a hog. They're typically marinated or rubbed with seasoning and then baked or grilled with barbecue sauce. When shopping for ribs, it's helpful to know there are several types available:
• **Spareribs** come from the belly or side of the hog, have the least amount of meat, and are less tender than other ribs. Plan on a minimum of 1 pound per person.
• **Back ribs** are cut from the blade and center section of the loin and are meatier, with meat between the bones. Allow at least 1 pound per person.
• **Country-style ribs** are cut from the rib end of the loin and are the meatiest of all pork ribs. They usually yield enough meat to be eaten with a knife and fork; plan on one-half to 1 pound per person. (*see also* **pork, rib,** *and recipe on the following page*)

CHIPOTLE GRILLED PORK RIBS

¼ cup butter or margarine
1 medium-size sweet onion, chopped
1 garlic clove, minced
1 jalapeño pepper, seeded and chopped
1 cup ketchup
¼ cup red wine vinegar
¼ cup chipotle peppers in adobo sauce
1 tablespoon Worcestershire sauce
2½ to 3 pounds pork back ribs
1½ teaspoons salt

• Melt butter in a saucepan over medium-high heat. Add onion, garlic, and jalapeño pepper, and sauté 2 to 3 minutes or until tender. Stir in ketchup and next 3 ingredients; bring to a boil. Reduce heat, and simmer 20 minutes. Reserve ½ cup sauce for dipping, if desired.

• Cut pork ribs into 2 sections, and sprinkle evenly with salt. Brush both sides of ribs with sauce.

• Prepare a hot fire by piling charcoal on 1 side of grill, leaving other side empty. (For gas grills, light only 1 side.) Coat food rack with cooking spray, and place on grill. Arrange food over empty side (unlit side of gas grill), and grill, covered with grill lid, 2 hours, turning and basting every 30 minutes. Yield: 3 servings.

TEST KITCHEN SECRET

" For easier serving, cut spareribs apart into serving-size portions before they're cooked. If you ask the butcher, he will usually do this for you. To get them really tender, try precooking ribs by baking them once to render fat; then bake them again with barbecue sauce, or place them on a hot grill and brush with sauce. " JAMES SCHEND

sparkling wine (*see* **champagne**)

spatula (SPA che luh) A handy, versatile kitchen utensil used for many different chores. Spatulas can be made of wood, metal, rubber, or plastic; rigid wooden spatulas are good for scraping the sides of pots and turning foods; plastic or rubber spatulas are suited for stirring ingredients in curved bowls and for folding mixtures together. Metal spatulas, which come in both long and short sizes, are ideal for spreading frosting over cakes. (*see also* **baking tools**)

spearmint An herb that's a member of the mint family; it has soft, bright green leaves and a flavor and aroma that's slightly milder than peppermint. Spearmint is used as a flavoring, a garnish, and in herb teas. (*see also* **herbs**)

spice A large group of aromatic seasonings that are made from bark, roots, seeds, buds, berries, or stems of various plants and trees. Spices are typically sold dried, either whole or ground; ground spices are convenient to use, but loose their aroma and flavor more quickly, so they should be purchased in small quantities. Whole spices can usually be ground as needed.

Storage: Store ground spices in airtight containers (glass containers with tight lids work best) in a cool, dark, dry place for about 1 year; if properly stored, whole spices will usually keep up to 5 years. Our Test Kitchens staff stores seldom-used spices in the freezer in moisture-proof containers. Moisture, heat, and light are a spice's worst enemies. (*see also specific spices*)

TIMESAVING TIP
Arrange spices in a cabinet or rack in alphabetical order. This way you can always put your hand on what you need right away, and see what's missing.

MOST COMMONLY USED SPICES:

Allspice: The pea-size berries of an evergreen tree that belongs to the myrtle tree family. The dried brown berries taste like a blend of cloves, cinnamon, and nutmeg. They are used most often when canning, pickling, or poaching and in cider, cookies, cakes, and pies. They can be purchased whole or ground.

Cardamom: This ground pungent, sweet spice comes from the pod of a plant in the ginger family. It has an exotic, aromatic flavor that hints of licorice and is used in pastries, cookies, cakes, coffee, and hot spiced wine. (*see also* **cardamom**)

Celery Seed: Comes from the seeds of wild celery called lovage. It has a strong flavor and should be used sparingly in making pickles, soups, salads, and meat dishes. (*see also* **celery seed**)

Chili Powder: A hot and spicy, but slightly sweet powdered seasoning mixture made from a blend of chile peppers, cumin, salt, allspice, garlic, oregano, cloves, and coriander. It's a major ingredient in many Mexican dishes.

Cinnamon: This sweet, mildly pungent spice comes from the dried bark of a tree in the laurel family. It's available in stick form or ground and can be used in making pickles, baked fruit, spice cakes, or sprinkled with sugar on toast; the sticks make excellent stirrers for beverages. (*see also* **cinnamon**)

Cloves: Shaped like miniature nails, these dried buds of the tropical evergreen clove tree have a strong, sweet, almost hot flavor. Sold whole or ground, cloves can be used in pickling, to garnish hams, for making mincemeat, fruitcake, gingerbread, or spice cake.

Cumin: These aromatic, nutty-flavored seeds come from the dried fruit of a plant in the parsley family. It's available in seed or ground form and is often an ingredient in Middle Eastern, Asian, and Mediterranean recipes; it might also be used to make curries, chili powder, and liqueur.

Curry Powder: A pulverized blend of exotic aromatic spices that varies according to hotness. Turmeric is a primary ingredient in curry, and it gives some curried dishes their characteristic yellow color. Curry powder is widely used in Indian cooking as well as in egg dishes, fruit dishes, marinades, sauces, salad dressings, dips, and spreads. (*see also* **curry powder**)

Ginger: Dried ground, crystallized, and candied ginger comes from fresh gingerroot. Its warm, spicy-sweet flavor is often added to marinades, chutney, gingerbread, and Asian dishes. Crystallized and candied ginger are often used in candies and desserts. (*see also* **ginger**) (*continued on the following page*)

Mace: This spice tastes hot and spicy-sweet, like nutmeg, but more delicate. That's because it's made from the weblike covering of the nutmeg shell. Use it to flavor cakes, fruit dishes, custards, breads, and pastries. (*see also* **mace**)

Mustard: Made from the tiny brown or white seeds of plants in the mustard family, this pungent spice can be purchased whole or ground. It's used in making pickles, relishes, coleslaw, corned and boiled beef, deviled eggs, salad dressings, cheese dishes, and sauces. (*see also* **mustard**)

Nutmeg: This dried, oval-shaped seed comes from the tropical evergreen nutmeg tree and is sold whole or ground. The warm, spicy, slightly sweet flavor is excellent in eggnog, rice pudding, cakes, breads, and custards. (*see also* **nutmeg**)

Paprika: This powder is used as a seasoning and as a garnish; it's made from ground, dried capsicum peppers, and the flavor can range from mild to pungent to hot. It's often used in fish dishes, eggs, and stews; it's also an ingredient in sausages, spice mixes, and rubs. (*see also* **paprika**)

Peppercorns: Although they are tiny, these berries of the pepper plant can have a powerful, pungent flavor. Black and white peppercorns can be used whole or ground, while the green ones are generally packed in water or brine or dehydrated and are less pungent. Use peppercorns in sauces, dressings, or for grinding and general seasoning. (*see also* **peppercorn**)

Pickling Spice: A pungent, spicy blend of a variety of whole spices used in making pickles, chutneys, vinegars, or spiced fruits. (*see also* **pickling spice**)

Red Pepper: Made from the dried fruit of the capsicum pepper plant, red pepper is available ground or in flakes. Its hot, pungent flavor makes it ideal for seasoning sausage, dried beans, chowders, gumbos, pizza sauce, deviled eggs, and cheese straws. (*see also* **red pepper**)

Saffron: Known as the most expensive spice because it comes from the stigmas of saffron crocus flowers, which must be hand-picked and dried. Fortunately, a little of this pungent, aromatic, pleasantly bitter spice goes a long way; it's an expected ingredient in risotto, paella, and bouillabaisse, and can also be used in sauces, seafood, and baked goods. (*see also* **saffron**)

Turmeric: Made from the dried, ground root of a tropical plant in the ginger family, turmeric has a musky odor and a slightly bitter flavor. It's best known for its intense yellow-orange color. It's used to add both flavor and color to egg dishes, pickles, chowchow, rice dishes, chicken dishes, salad dressings, and dips. (*see also* **turmeric**)

TEST KITCHEN SECRET

Ground spices may cloud liquid mixtures, so use whole spices tied in cheesecloth or placed in a metal tea ball for beverages and pickles. Remember you can use white pepper instead of black pepper if you don't want the specks to show. JAMES SCHEND

Q How do I grind whole spices?

A Place about 1 tablespoon of the spice in an electric spice grinder or a clean, small, never-before-used-for-coffee mill. Grind to a fine powder and use immediately. You can also grind spices using a mortar and pestle, meat mallet, or rolling pin. Special nutmeg grinders or pepper mills can be used to grind some spices.

spinach (SPIHN ihch) A vegetable with dark green, spear-shaped leaves that are curled or smooth and attached to thin stems. The leaves have a slightly bitter flavor and can be served cooked, as in Florentine dishes or spanakopita, or served raw in salads. Spinach is usually very gritty because it grows on short stems close to the ground, so make sure it's thoroughly washed or buy it washed. Spinach is also available canned and frozen.

TIMESAVING TIP
Buy washed baby spinach, which has tender stems that do not need to be removed. A 10-ounce package is equal to 1 pound of fresh spinach.

Storage: If unwashed, wash in cold water and pat dry. Chill the leaves in a plastic bag lined with damp paper towels up to 3 days. (*see also* **Florentine, à la; greens;** *and* **spanakopita**)

SPINACH BLACK BEAN LASAGNA

2 large eggs, lightly beaten
1 (15-ounce) container ricotta
   cheese
1 (10-ounce) package frozen
   chopped spinach, thawed and
   well drained
¼ cup chopped fresh cilantro
½ teaspoon salt
4 cups (16 ounces) shredded
   Monterey Jack cheese with
   peppers, divided

2 (16-ounce) cans black beans,
   rinsed and drained
1 (2-pound, 13-ounce) jar pasta
   sauce
½ teaspoon ground cumin
9 precooked lasagna noodles
Garnish: chopped fresh cilantro

• Stir together first 5 ingredients and 1 cup Monterey Jack cheese; set aside.
• Mash beans with a potato masher or fork in a large bowl; stir in pasta sauce and cumin. Spread one-third of bean mixture in a lightly greased 13- x 9-inch baking dish.
• Layer with 3 noodles, half of spinach mixture, and 1 cup Monterey Jack cheese; repeat layers once. Spread with one-third bean mixture; top with remaining 3 noodles and remaining bean mixture. Bake, covered, at 350° for 1 hour; uncover and top with remaining Monterey Jack cheese. Bake 5 more minutes or until cheese melts. Garnish, if desired. Yield: 6 servings.

spiny lobster (*see* **lobster**)

split A small bottle of wine that's one-fourth the size of a regular bottle and contains approximately 6 ounces. (*see also* **wine bottles**)

split pea (*see* **field pea**)

sponge cake Light, airy cake similar to angel food cake in that it doesn't contain shortening and is leavened by beaten egg whites that are folded into the batter. However, sponge cakes are richer than angel food cakes because they contain egg yolks and sometimes baking powder. Sponge cakes can be flavored with a variety of ingredients, from citrus to chocolate. (*see also* **cake** *and* **génoise**)

VANILLA SPONGE CAKE

Enjoy generous slices of healthy sponge cake topped with scoops of frozen yogurt or sliced fresh strawberries for an easy and guilt-free dessert.

1 cup sifted cake flour	10 egg whites
½ cup sugar	1 teaspoon cream of tartar
4 egg yolks	½ teaspoon salt
1 teaspoon vanilla extract	¾ cup sugar

• Sift flour and ½ cup sugar together 3 times; set aside. Beat egg yolks at high speed with an electric mixer 4 minutes or until thick and pale. Add vanilla; beat at medium speed 5 more minutes or until mixture is thick. Set aside.

• Beat egg whites in a large mixing bowl at high speed until foamy. Add cream of tartar and salt; beat until soft peaks form. Add ¾ cup sugar, 2 tablespoons at a time, beating until stiff peaks form.

• Sprinkle one-fourth flour mixture over egg whites; gently fold in. Repeat procedure with remaining flour, adding one-fourth of mixture at a time.

• Gently fold beaten egg yolks into egg white mixture. Pour batter into an ungreased 10-inch tube pan.

• Bake at 350° for 45 to 50 minutes or until cake springs back when lightly touched. Invert pan carefully. Cool in pan 40 minutes. Loosen cake from sides of pan, using a narrow metal spatula; remove from pan. Yield: 14 servings.

spoon A metal, plastic, or wooden utensil used for eating, stirring, or serving. Spoons have a round or oval bowl attached to a handle. All cooks need a variety of spoons in order to make cooking easier. The selection might include:

• **Slotted spoons:** essential for removing solid foods from liquids.

• **Wooden spoons:** sturdy, don't scratch bowls or pans, don't add a metallic taste to foods, and their handles stay cool. They will, however, eventually warp, crack, or split.

• **Large metal spoons:** handy for stirring large quantities and for transferring food from one container to another.

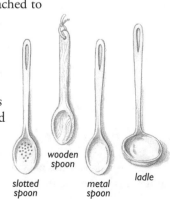

wooden spoon

slotted spoon

metal spoon

ladle

- **Ladles:** a type of spoon that's necessary for serving soups and sauces.
- **Measuring spoons:** crucial for accurately measuring ingredients.
- **Common flatware spoons:** includes the teaspoon, soup spoon, iced tea spoon, and serving spoons.
- **Dressing spoons:** special long-handled spoons, often found in antique stores, that give neat and easy access to stuffing in a turkey.

spoonbread A pudding made from cornmeal, eggs, butter, and milk, and sometimes enlivened with baking powder and a dash of sugar baked in a casserole dish and served as a side dish.

Southernism

This Southern soufflé may take its name from suppon or suppawn, an Indian porridge, and perhaps the name stuck because this comfort food is best eaten with a spoon. Spoonbread is an any-meal kind of food: Thomas Jefferson, for instance, ate it for breakfast, lunch, and dinner. According to Southern food author, John Egerton, spoonbread is "the ultimate, glorified ideal" of cornbread. An essential Southern savory, "a properly prepared spoonbread," Egerton writes, "can be taken as testimony to the perfectibility of humankind."

OLD-FASHIONED SPOONBREAD

1 quart milk	4 large eggs, lightly beaten
1 cup white cornmeal	¼ cup sugar
¼ cup butter or margarine	2 teaspoons salt

- Heat milk in a small saucepan over low heat 10 to 12 minutes or until almost boiling; stir in cornmeal. Cook over low heat, stirring occasionally, 5 minutes or until thickened; stir in butter. Remove from heat, and beat with a wooden spoon 1 minute.
- Stir one-fourth of hot mixture into eggs; add to remaining hot mixture, stirring constantly. Stir in sugar and salt. Pour into a greased 2-quart baking dish. Bake spoonbread at 350° for 1 hour. Yield: 6 servings.

springerle (SPRING uhr lee) An embossed German Christmas cookie that's flavored with anise. The embossed designs are imprinted on the uncooked dough by either a special carved wooden rolling pin or by carved molds that the dough is pressed in. After imprinting, the cookies sit at room temperature overnight to dry so the designs will remain as the cookies bake. (*see also* **anise, cookie,** *and* **cookie mold**)

springform pan (*see* **baking dishes and pans**)

spring roll A smaller, more delicate type of egg roll that's wrapped in a thin, rice paper wrapper. (*see also* **egg roll** *and* **rice paper**)

sprinkle To scatter drops of liquid or small amounts of dry ingredients over the surface of a food. The term also refers to colored grains of sugar or chocolate used to decorate ice cream, cookies, or pastries.

spritz (SPRIHTS) Small, rich, buttery Scandinavian cookies formed into decorative shapes when the dough is forced through a cookie press or pastry bag. Sometimes the dough is tinted with food coloring or sprinkled with colored sugar before it's baked. This term can also refer to quickly spraying a light mist of water or adding a bit of soda water to mixed drinks.

CHRISTMAS SPRITZ COOKIES

1 cup butter, softened	⅛ teaspoon salt
1 cup sugar	10 drops yellow liquid food
2 large eggs	coloring
2 teaspoons vanilla extract	Red and green decorator candies
2½ cups all-purpose flour	

• Beat butter at medium speed with an electric mixer until creamy; gradually add sugar, beating well. Add eggs and vanilla, beating until blended.
• Combine flour and salt; add to butter mixture, beating at low speed until blended. Add food coloring, beating until blended.
• Use a cookie gun with a bar-shaped disc, and shape dough into 1½-inch cookies following manufacturer's instructions; or shape dough into 1-inch balls, and flatten to ¼-inch thickness with a flat-bottomed glass. Place on greased baking sheets; sprinkle with candies. Bake at 375° for 8 minutes or until edges are lightly browned. Transfer to wire racks to cool. Yield: 8 dozen.

spritzer (SPRIHT suhr) A refreshing cocktail drink typically made of wine and soda water.

sprouts Seeds or beans that have budded into edible shoots. Fresh sprouts make a crunchy addition to sandwiches and salads. Several types of sprouts are available in supermarkets:
• **Alfalfa sprouts** are tiny, green and white shoots from alfalfa seeds; they have a mild, nutty taste.
• **Bean sprouts** are pale, creamy white crunchy shoots from mung beans and have a nutty flavor.
• **Lentil sprouts** are delicate, tender brown and green sprouts from lentils; they have a mild, nutty taste.
• **Radish sprouts** have tender, leafy green tops and come from radish seeds; they have a peppery taste.
• **Wheat sprouts** are tender, brown and green shoots from wheat berries; they have a sweet, nutty taste.
Storage: Store sprouts in a plastic bag in the refrigerator for 2 to 4 days. Be aware that raw sprouts sometimes carry salmonella and E. coli bacteria, so to limit your risk to bacterial exposure, cook all sprouts before eating.

spumante (spoo MAHN tay) An Italian term for sparkling wine, the best known of which originates from the northern Italian town of Asti. (*see also* **champagne**)

spumoni (spoo MOH nee) A layered Italian dessert usually consisting of ice cream, rum-flavored whipped cream, and candied fruit or nuts.

spun sugar Starts with a sugar syrup mixture that has been cooked to the hard crack stage; then a fork or whisk is dipped into the mixture to draw out fine, golden strands of the hardened sugar. The strands are used to decorate desserts and pastries, such as croquembouche. (*see also* **candy** *and* **croquembouche**)

squab (SKWAHB) (*see also* **pigeon** *and* **poultry**)

squash (SKWAHSH) A group of vegetables that are members of the gourd family and generally divided into two categories—summer squash and winter squash. Summer squash are at their peak during summer months and are best eaten while young and tender. Their flesh has a high water content and mild flavor that doesn't require long cooking. They should be stored in plastic bags in the crisper drawer of the refrigerator up to 3 days. Some of the most common types of summer squash are:

• **Crookneck squash** have a bright yellow color and are about the same size of a zucchini, but with a thin, curved neck. They can be sautéed, baked, or boiled.

• **Pattypan squash** are pale green, yellow, or white and are about 4 inches in diameter; they are round with scalloped edges. They can be sautéed or hollowed out and filled and baked.

• **Zucchini squash** are usually green, but sometimes yellow, and look similar to a cucumber but are longer and thinner. They can be battered and deep-fried, sautéed, steamed, or baked.

> **TEST KITCHEN SECRET**
>
> *When selecting yellow squash, be sure to look at the stem; it can indicate the quality of the squash. If the stem is hard, dry, shriveled, or dark, the squash is not fresh.* LYDA JONES

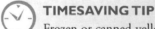 **TIMESAVING TIP**
Frozen or canned yellow crookneck squash or zucchini is ideal for adding to soups.

Winter squash are generally available year-round, but are best in fall and winter months; they are allowed to mature until their flesh is thick and their shells are hard, and therefore require longer cooking. Whole winter squash can be kept for months in a cool, dark place; if cut, they can be refrigerated up to a week. Several of the more commonly available winter squashes are:

> **READER TIP**
> *"I like to use butternut squash in place of pumpkin in pie, soups, and risotto. It has a sweeter flavor and is less watery."* S.J., Monroe, LA

• **Acorn squash** are acorn-shaped and about 6 inches in diameter; they have dark green, ribbed shells and orange flesh, and can be halved, stuffed, and baked. (*continued on the following page*)

- **Butternut squash** are large and long with a round bulb at one end. They have beige skin and orange flesh and are good for baking and puréeing.
- **Hubbard squash** are large and irregularly shaped with a gray-green or dark green bumpy shell and yellow-orange flesh. They can be pureed or baked into pies.
- **Spaghetti squash** are about the size of a football and have a creamy yellow skin. They can be baked whole, then halved, and the flesh forms long, thin strands that can be served like spaghetti.
- **Turban squash** are round with a topknot and a colorful shell with streaks of orange, yellow, and green. They can be baked, steamed, or simmered. (*see also* **acorn squash, chayote, hubbard squash, pattypan squash, spaghetti squash,** *and* **vegetables**)

squash blossoms The flowers of both winter and summer squashes; be sure to pick blossoms that are fresh with closed buds, making sure they are chemical-free. Squash blossoms can be added to salads, stuffed with soft cheese, or battered and fried. (*see also* **flowers, edible**)

squid (SKWIHD) Also called calamari, squid is a member of the cephalopod family and found mostly in Atlantic and Mediterranean waters. While squid's popularity has grown in recent years, it has always been a favorite in Mediterranean and Asian cuisines. Sold fresh or frozen, squid have a small, tubelike, white body that contains an ink sac and a translucent spine topped with a head and 10 tentacles. Squid can be stuffed, baked, boiled, deep-fried, stir-fried, or used in seafood salads; the Japanese use it in sushi. Squid can be purchased fresh or frozen.
Storage: Fresh squid is highly perishable so it should be refrigerated on a bed of ice for no more than 2 days before cooked. (*see also* **calamari**)

stale A term that describes food, especially breads, cereals, or crackers that have lost their original freshness and flavor, but are not necessarily spoiled.

Q **Why does bread get stale so fast, especially when I store it in the refrigerator?**

A Bread is porous, which causes it to quickly dehydrate in the refrigerator. It's best to freeze bread or keep it at room temperature. To freeze, seal tightly in freezer plastic wrap or zip-top freezer bags, and freeze up to 1 month.

star anise A star-shaped, eight-pointed, dark brown pod from a Chinese evergreen tree related to the magnolia. Each anise pod contains eight seeds that are bitterer than regular anise seeds. Star anise is used in Asian cooking to flavor teas; Westerners use it to flavor liqueurs and baked goods. It can be found whole in Asian markets and some supermarkets and is ground for an ingredient in Chinese five-spice powder. (*see also* **five-spice powder** *and* **liqueur**)

starch A term that describes thickening agents such as flour, cornstarch, tapioca, and arrowroot. This term also refers to a digestible carbohydrate that comes from many types of plants, especially vegetables and grains such as rice, pasta, or potatoes. (*see also* **arrowroot, carbohydrates, cornstarch, flour,** *and* **tapioca**)

star fruit (*see* **carambola**)

starter A special leavening made from a mixture of yeast, flour, water, and sugar. The mixture is covered with plastic wrap or cheesecloth, and stays at room temperature until it ferments. The starter is then refrigerated and used to help leaven sourdough bread, biscuits, coffee cakes, and pancakes. (*see also* **sourdough** *and* **yeast**)

Getting Started:
• Mix and store the starter in glass, stoneware, or plastic. Metal can cause a chemical reaction with the starter.
• Place the starter in a bowl large enough to allow it to double in volume as it ferments.
• Never cover the container too tightly. The yeast needs air to live and the gas from the fermentation process needs to escape. Punch a small hole in the plastic wrap cover or leave the lid ajar.
• If a clear liquid forms on top of the mixture, just stir it back in.
• Allow the starter to come to room temperature before using it.

> ### TEST KITCHEN SECRET
> *"When making sourdough starter, use active dry yeast instead of quick-rising yeast. Remember to store the starter in the refrigerator in a glass jar covered with cheesecloth instead of a metal lid, and always bring it to room temperature before adding to recipes."* Rebecca Kracke Gordon

steak au poivre (oh PWAHV rh) A French dish featuring beef steak that's generously covered with crushed peppercorns and then broiled or sautéed. The dish might be finished with a topping of butter or a sauce made from pan drippings; sometimes it's flamed with brandy. (*see also* **flambé**)

steak fries Large, flat, or wedge-shaped French fries. (*see also* **French fries**)

steak tartare A mixture of ground or finely chopped lean, high-quality, raw beef and onions, capers, parsley, and seasoning; sometimes the mixture is shaped into a mound with an indentation in the top where a raw egg or egg yolk is added. The mixture is typically served as an appetizer spread on bread or crackers. We no longer recommend making this dish because of the possible bacterial contamination in raw meat and eggs.

steamed pudding A sweet, dense breadlike dessert usually made by steaming batter in a covered decorative steamed pudding mold on a rack over boiling water in a covered pot. The batter typically includes breadcrumbs, spices, and dried fruit; when unmolded, it retains its decorative shape. Steamed pudding is customarily served warm, flamed with rum or brandy, and accompanied with hard sauce. (*see also* **hard sauce, plum pudding,** *and* **steamed pudding mold**)

steamed pudding mold A special mold with decorative sides and a lid that clamps shut used in making steamed pudding. Most steamed pudding molds have a central tube like a pound cake pan, so heat is easily distributed, allowing the pudding to cook more evenly. (*see also* **steamed pudding**)

RESCUE if you don't have a steamed pudding mold: Substitute any heavy heat-proof bowl of similar size, greasing it well to keep the pudding from sticking; then seal the top with a double layer of heavy-duty aluminum foil.

steaming A moist-heat cooking method in which heat is transferred by steam to the food being cooked. The food is usually placed on a rack or in a metal or bamboo steamer basket over boiling water in a covered pan; sometimes food can be steamed by placing it directly in a very small amount of simmering liquid in a covered pan. Steaming is an excellent way to cook vegetables and delicate foods, such as fish, because it's gentler than boiling or poaching, and does a good job of retaining the food's flavor, shape, texture, and nutrients. (*see also* **vegetables**)

Q How do I set up my cookware to steam vegetables?

A It can be done several ways. You could place a set of Chinese bamboo racks in a large wok, or you could use a collapsible, inexpensive metal steamer basket. You could even improvise a steamer basket by placing a metal colander on top of a wire rack or custard cups in a pot with a tight-fitting lid. Once this is done, add a few inches of water to the pot, making sure that it doesn't rise about the level of the steamer rack or the bottom of the basket. Bring the water to a boil; then reduce the heat to a simmer. Place the food on the rack or in the basket, cover, and begin timing.

steel (*see* **sharpening steel**)

steep To extract flavor from dry ingredients, such as tea leaves or ground coffee, by soaking in hot liquid. (*see also* **infusion** *and* **tea**)

Sterno The brand name of a canned solid fuel often used to heat chafing dishes and to keep foods warm while entertaining.

stew A dish made from meat, poultry, or fish plus vegetables and seasoning that's cooked in liquid for a long time until the meat and vegetables are tender. Stew is usually thicker and more substantial than soup and is typically served as a main course. Stews are economical to prepare because they are often made with foods that require long cooking for tenderness, such as root vegetables and tougher cuts of meat. This term also refers to the process of cooking a food in liquid for a long time, usually in a covered pot.

sticky bun Made from sweet yeast roll dough that's arranged in a pan that has been coated with cinnamon and sugar or another sugary mixture; as the rolls bake, the mixture in the bottom of the pan caramelizes and becomes sticky. The rolls typically have to be pulled apart for serving.

CARAMEL STICKY BUNS

1 (16-ounce) package hot roll mix	3 tablespoons butter, softened
1½ cups Caramel Sauce (following page)	¼ cup sugar
1 cup chopped pecans, toasted	2 teaspoons ground cinnamon

- Prepare roll dough according to package directions. Let stand 5 minutes.
- Pour Caramel Sauce into a lightly greased 13- x 9-inch pan or into 2 lightly greased 8-inch square pans. Sprinkle with pecans.
- Roll dough into a 15- x 10-inch rectangle. Spread with butter; sprinkle with sugar and cinnamon.
- Roll up, starting at a long edge. Cut into 1-inch-thick slices. Arrange slices, cut side down, over Caramel Sauce.
- Cover and let rise in a warm place (85°), free from drafts, 30 minutes or until doubled in bulk.
- Bake at 375° for 16 minutes. Let stand on a wire rack 5 minutes. Invert onto a serving dish. Yield: 15 buns.

Note: Buns may be frozen before rising. Remove from freezer, and let thaw at room temperature; continue as directed above.

CARAMEL SAUCE

2 cups whipping cream	2 cups sugar
¼ cup butter	½ cup water
½ teaspoon baking soda	2 teaspoons lemon juice

• Cook first 3 ingredients in a Dutch oven over medium heat, stirring occasionally, until butter melts; remove mixture from heat.

• Bring sugar, water, and lemon juice to a boil in a Dutch oven over high heat, stirring occasionally, 8 minutes or until mixture begins to brown. Reduce heat to medium, and cook, stirring occasionally, 5 minutes or until caramel colored. Pour sugar mixture gradually into whipping cream mixture. Remove from heat; let stand 1 minute. Whisk until smooth.

• Cook over medium-low heat, stirring occasionally, until a candy thermometer registers 230° (thread stage); cool. Yield: 2½ cups.

stir The process of mixing ingredients with a spoon or other utensil to combine them. It's a good idea to stir foods often during cooking to prevent sticking and to help them cook evenly.

stir-fry The process of cooking that employs the Asian technique of rapidly frying small pieces of food in a small amount of oil over high heat. A wok is the perfect pan for stir-frying because it provides a larger cooking surface and prevents the food from flying out of the pan as it's stirred. Most stir-fired dishes result in food that's crisp-tender, more nutritious, and attractive.

TEST KITCHEN SECRET

When stir-frying, prepare the ingredients before you begin. Add oil to the wok, then lift and tilt the pan to distribute it over the bottom; preheat the oil about 1 minute. As you add the food, try not to overload the wok; if too much is added at once, the wok cools and the food will stew rather than fry. JAMES SCHEND

Q What can I use for stir-frying if I don't have a wok?

A A large, deep cast-iron skillet or heavy sauté pan makes a good substitute.

CHICKEN-VEGETABLE STIR-FRY

4 skinned and boned chicken breast halves	¼ cup soy sauce
1 medium-size sweet onion	1 to 2 tablespoons chili-garlic paste
1 green bell pepper	2 tablespoons cornstarch
1 red bell pepper	1 tablespoon brown sugar
3 carrots	1 tablespoon grated fresh ginger
3 green onions	2 tablespoons dark sesame oil
1 (10½-ounce) can chicken broth, undiluted	Hot cooked rice

• Cut chicken into ¼-inch-thick strips; cut onion in half, and cut halves into slices. Cut bell peppers into ¼-inch-thick strips, and cut carrots and green onions diagonally into slices. Set aside.
• Whisk together broth and next 5 ingredients until smooth. Heat oil in a wok at medium-high heat 2 minutes. Add chicken; stir-fry 3 minutes or until browned. Add vegetables; stir-fry 3 minutes. Add broth mixture; stir-fry 1 minute or until thickened. Serve over rice. Yield: 4 to 6 servings.

stock The liquid that's the result of simmering meat, poultry, fish, seafood, or vegetables with seasonings in water for several hours. Stock is a homemade broth, while broth is thought of as a canned, store-bought product. When refrigerated, stocks often gel; they can be used as a flavorful base for soups and sauces. A brown stock is made by browning bones and vegetables before they're simmered; this gives richer flavor and color. Seafood, fish, or vegetable stocks are excellent soup bases. (*see also* **she-crab soup**)

TIMESAVING TIP

Freeze stock in muffin pans or ice cube trays; once frozen, pop them out and store in a zip-top freezer bag. When making a sauce or soup, add some frozen stock to a hot pan and heat until melted. Also, the leftover carcasses of whole roasted chickens or turkey can be used to make stock; freeze them if you don't have time to make it right away.

TEST KITCHEN SECRET

"*Make stocks in a narrow, deep stockpot to prevent excessive evaporation during cooking, and remember to start with cold water covering the ingredients.*" MARGARET MONROE DICKEY

BEEF STOCK

5 pounds beef bones	8 fresh parsley sprigs
2 large carrots, quartered	4 fresh thyme sprigs
3 large onions, quartered	½ teaspoon black peppercorns
2 celery ribs, quartered	2 bay leaves
4 quarts cold water, divided	3 garlic cloves, crushed
¼ cup tomato paste	

• Place first 4 ingredients in a large roasting pan; roast, uncovered, at 500° for 45 minutes to 1 hour or until well browned, turning occasionally.
• Transfer bones and vegetables to a stockpot. Add 2 cups water to roasting pan; bring to a boil over medium-high heat, stirring to loosen bits that cling to bottom of pan; pour into stockpot. Add remaining 3½ quarts water and tomato paste. Tie parsley, thyme, and remaining ingredients in a cheesecloth bundle. Add to stockpot. Bring to a simmer; simmer, partially covered, 6 hours. Skim fat and foam off top of stock after first 10 minutes of simmering.
• Line a large wire-mesh strainer with a double layer of cheesecloth; place over a large bowl. Use a ladle to strain stock. Discard solids. (Using a ladle and avoiding sediment in bottom of pot prevents cloudiness.) Cool stock slightly.
• Cover and chill; discard solidified fat from top of stock. Store stock in refrigerator up to 3 days or freeze up to 3 months. Yield: 8 cups.

stollen (STOH luhn) A German yeast bread filled with dried fruits, shaped into a large, folded oval loaf, and topped with powdered sugar icing. Stollen is traditionally served on Christmas morning.

stone crab A type of crab found in coastal waters from North Carolina to Mexico, but harvested commercially only in South Florida. Fishermen twist off the claws and throw the crabs back to grow new ones; since freezing or icing can cause the crabmeat to stick to the inside of the shell, the claws are cooked immediately, often while still on the boat, and sold precooked. (*see also* **crab**)

stone-ground flour A flour produced by grinding grain between two slowly moving stones that crush the grain without separating the germ from the bran. The coarse flour spoils faster than regular flour and should be bought in smaller quantities. (*see also* **flour**)

stoneware Strong, hard, glazed pottery fired at very high temperatures and is nonporous and chip-resistant. Stoneware can serve as bakeware, cookware, and dinnerware; it's also safe to use in the microwave oven.

stout (STOWT) Dark British ale or beer made with roasted malt; it has a higher hops content than regular beer and a strong, bittersweet flavor. (*see also* **ale, beer, hops,** *and* **malt**)

straight up Term to describe a cocktail drink served without ice.

strain A process of pouring liquid or dry foods through a sieve, mesh strainer, or cheesecloth to separate liquids from solids or to remove unwanted particles. This term also refers to pressing soft food through the holes of a sieve, which results in a pureed texture; this is often done when making homemade baby foods. (*see also* **cheesecloth, colander, sieve,** *and* **strainer**)

strainer Also called a sieve, a strainer is a kitchen utensil with a perforated or mesh container used to strain liquids or to sift dry ingredients such as flour or powdered sugar. Strainers are available in different sizes and shapes and mesh densities. Some strainers are bowl-shaped and some are cone-shaped. They can be made of various materials, such as plastic or stainless steel. Some have strong handles and frames with hooks that allow them to rest on top of pots or bowls. (*see also* **sieve** *and* **strain**)

strata A make-ahead casserole usually made with layers of bread and cheese; other ingredients, such as poultry and seafood, can be added. It's soaked with an egg and milk mixture that's poured over the layers.

VEGETABLE-CHEESE STRATA

¾ diced onion
½ cup diced green onions
1 (8-ounce) package sliced fresh
  mushrooms
2 tablespoons olive oil
1 red bell pepper, cut into thin
  strips
1 green bell pepper, cut into thin
  strips
5 cups 1-inch Italian bread cubes
  (about 1 loaf)

1½ cups (6 ounces) shredded
  Cheddar cheese
½ cup shredded Parmesan cheese
6 large eggs
1¾ cups milk
1 tablespoon Dijon mustard
½ teaspoon salt
½ teaspoon pepper
¼ teaspoon hot sauce

• Sauté first 3 ingredients in hot oil in a skillet until tender; stir in bell pepper. Cook, stirring often, 10 minutes or until liquid evaporates.

• Spread 2½ cups bread cubes in a lightly greased 11- x 7-inch baking dish. Top with half of vegetable mixture, and sprinkle with ¾ cup Cheddar cheese and ¼ cup Parmesan cheese. Repeat layers.

• Whisk together eggs and remaining 5 ingredients; pour over strata. Cover and chill 8 hours.

• Remove from refrigerator; let stand at room temperature 15 minutes.

• Bake, uncovered, at 350° for 45 minutes or until set. Yield: 6 servings.

TEST KITCHEN SECRET

We often include stratas in our brunch entertaining stories because these egg-based casseroles can be made ahead and stored in the refrigerator overnight. You just pop them in the oven and bake that morning. Guests love them! VANESSA MCNEIL

strawberries Romanoff A French dessert made by soaking strawberries in orange liqueur and topping them with whipped cream.

strawberry A red, juicy, cone-shaped berry that's mildly sweet and has tiny, edible seeds on the outside of its skin. A member of the rose family, strawberries have grown wild for centuries and are now commercially produced in California and Florida. They're available year-round with their peak season from April to June. Canned and frozen strawberries are also available, as are preserves, jams, jellies, and syrups.

Storage: Store strawberries in a moisture-proof container in the refrigerator for 3 to 4 days. (*see also* **berry** *and* **hull**)

TIMESAVING TIP

For a quick, fresh strawberry sauce, hull and halve berries; process in a food processor until almost smooth. Mix in a little powdered sugar and season with a teaspoon of lemon juice.

TEST KITCHEN SECRET

Don't wash or hull berries until you're ready to use them. Rinse before removing the stems, because once hulled, strawberries absorb water like a sponge. A gadget called a strawberry huller or a small sharp knife is handy for removing caps. REBECCA KRACKE GORDON

streusel (STROO zuhl) A crumbly topping made of flour, sugar, butter, and sometimes nuts and spices. Streusel mixtures are typically sprinkled on coffee cakes, sweet breads, pies, and muffins before they're baked.

string bean (*see* **beans, fresh;** *and* **green bean**)

string cheese Mozzarella-style cheese manufactured from cow's milk and shaped into ropes that can be pulled apart and eaten. (*see also* **cheese**)

striped bass An Atlantic coastal fish that migrates from the sea to spawn in freshwater streams during autumn months; its size varies greatly, but smaller striped bass tend to have a better flavor. Striped bass has a moderately fat, firm-textured flesh with a mild, sweet flavor; it can be broiled, grilled, poached, or steamed. (*see also* **fish**)

strip steak A flavorful, tender beef steak cut from the top loin muscle in the short loin section. It's sometimes known as a New York strip, Kansas City strip, or Delmonico steak. (*see also* **beef**)

stroganoff (STRAW guh noff) A main dish of tender beef, onions, and sliced mushrooms that are sautéed in butter, combined with a sour cream sauce, and served over hot noodles. Stroganoff can be made with different cuts of beef, but the tenderloin or top loin is preferred. (*see also* **beef**)

BEEF STROGANOFF

1½ cups all-purpose flour	1 small onion, chopped
1½ teaspoons salt	2 garlic cloves, minced
½ teaspoon pepper	½ cup dry white wine
2 pounds sirloin steak, cut into 1-inch cubes	3 cups beef broth
	2 tablespoons tomato paste
1½ cups butter or margarine, melted	2½ cups sour cream
	7½ cups hot cooked noodles
3 cups sliced fresh mushrooms	

• Combine first 3 ingredients in a large zip-top plastic bag; add steak. Seal bag, and shake until meat is coated.

Q **Why does stroganoff sauce sometimes look curdled?**

A If this happens, it's because the stroganoff mixture was cooked too long or at too high a temperature after the sour cream was added. Just cook and stir briefly (about 1 minute) after adding the sour cream.

• Brown meat in butter in a large skillet, stirring occasionally. Remove meat from skillet; cover and keep warm. Add mushrooms, onion, and garlic to drippings in skillet; cook, stirring constantly, until tender. Remove from pan; keep warm.

• Add wine to skillet; cook over high heat, deglazing skillet by scraping particles that cling to bottom. Cook until wine is reduced by half.

• Add broth and tomato paste, stirring until smooth. Cook over medium heat, stirring constantly, until thickened. Add meat and mushroom mixture; cook until thoroughly heated. Stir in sour cream, and cook just until mixture is hot, stirring constantly. Serve over noodles. Yield: 10 servings.

stromboli (strohm BOW lee) A sandwich, similar to a calzone, made of pizza dough that's wrapped over a filling, such as mozzarella cheese and pepperoni, and baked. (*see also* **calzone**)

strudel (STROO duhl) A long, rectangular European pastry made with many layers of very thin dough rolled around a sweet or savory filling, and baked until crisp. The paper-thin dough resembles phyllo, which is often substituted when making homemade strudel.

AUTUMN-APPLE STRUDEL

1 cup hot water	2 cups chopped pecans, toasted
½ cup golden raisins	12 frozen phyllo pastry sheets,
6 large Granny Smith apples,	thawed
peeled and each cut into	¾ cup butter or margarine,
8 wedges	melted
2 cups sugar, divided	Powdered sugar
2 tablespoons grated orange rind	1 cup whipping cream
1 tablespoon vanilla extract	¼ cup sifted powdered sugar
¼ cup butter or margarine	2 tablespoons apple brandy or
1 (7¼-ounce) package butter	apple cider
cookies, finely crumbled	⅛ teaspoon ground nutmeg

• Pour 1 cup hot water over raisins; let stand 20 minutes. Drain; set aside.
• Stir together apple wedges, 1 cup sugar, orange rind, and vanilla.
• Melt ¼ cup butter in a large skillet over medium-high heat; add apple mixture, and cook, stirring occasionally, 15 to 20 minutes or until mixture thickens. Remove from heat; stir in raisins. Cool.
• Stir together cookie crumbs, remaining 1 cup sugar, and pecans. Set aside.
• Unfold phyllo, and cover with a damp towel to prevent it from drying out.
• Stack 4 sheets on a flat surface covered with wax paper, brushing each sheet with melted butter. Sprinkle with one-third of crumb mixture. Repeat procedure twice with remaining phyllo, butter, and crumb mixture. Top with apple mixture, leaving a 2-inch border around edges. Fold in short sides 2 inches. Roll up, starting at long side. Place seam side down on a greased baking sheet. Cut ¼-inch-deep slits, 1 inch apart, across top. Brush strudel with melted butter. Bake at 375° for 25 minutes or until golden. Cool 10 minutes. Dust with powdered sugar.
• Beat whipping cream at medium speed with an electric mixer until foamy; gradually add ¼ cup powdered sugar, beating until soft peaks form. Stir in brandy and nutmeg. Serve with warm strudel. Yield: 10 servings.
Note: For cookies, we used Pepperidge Farm Chessmen Butter Cookies.

stud The process of inserting seasonings, spices, or nuts into the surface of a food. For example, whole cloves are often used to stud hams, while lamb or pork roasts are sometimes studded with garlic cloves.

stuffing A seasoned mixture, often called dressing in the South, that's used to fill the cavity of poultry, fish, vegetables, or fruits. The classic example of a stuffed food is the holiday turkey, but any food with a natural or hollowed out cavity can be filled with stuffing. In the case of turkey or poultry, it's safer and faster to bake stuffing alongside the bird, rather than inside it. However, stuffing baked inside the bird is always moister and more delicious. Popular stuffing mixtures are made of bread, cornbread, rice, vegetables, oysters, pork, or fruit. (*see also* **cornbread dressing**)

TEST KITCHEN SECRET

"When stuffing food, especially poultry, it's OK to prepare the stuffing mixture ahead, but don't add it to the bird until just before cooking. If stuffed in advance and allowed to stand, even if refrigerated, harmful bacteria may develop that may not be destroyed during cooking. And make sure the stuffing cooks to 165°; if it isn't done, and the bird is, then transfer the stuffing to a baking dish and bake until it tests done. The easiest way to test the temperature is with an instant-read thermometer." MARGARET MONROE DICKEY

Q Is there really any difference between stuffing and dressing?

A There's no difference other than stuffing is often thought of as being baked inside a turkey or other food rather than around the outside or in a separate pan, as is dressing.

RESCUE for leftover stuffing mixture:
If all the stuffing doesn't fit in a turkey or chicken, place the leftover stuffing in a casserole and bake with the bird during the last 30 or 45 minutes of cooking.

---

sturgeon (STER juhn) A large fish found in the waters of the Pacific Northwest and southern Atlantic; it migrates from saltwater to spawn in rivers, sometimes growing to gargantuan size. Its high-fat flesh is white, rich, very firm, and delicately flavored. Sturgeon can be grilled, broiled, sautéed, or baked but is usually smoked or pickled. Sturgeon roe is a great delicacy because it's considered to be the true, premium caviar. (*see also* **caviar** *and* **fish**)

submarine sandwich (*see* **hero sandwich**)

substitutions (*see Handy Substitutions chart on page 566*)

succotash (SUHK uh tash) A vegetable dish made by cooking lima beans, corn kernels, and sometimes red and green bell peppers together.

Southernism

Succotash is an Indian word meaning "broken into bits." This simple dish of indigenous corn and lima beans was introduced to settlers by the Algonkian and Powhatan tribes of the southern United States. The recipe was adopted by African slaves and is a staple of traditional soul food cookery.

sucralose A sugar substitute derived from table sugar (sucrose) that tastes much like sugar. It contains no calories and can be used in baking. It's marketed under the name Splenda. (*see also* **sucrose** *and Sugar Substitute Guide on page 565*)

sucrose (SOO krohs) A sugar that comes from sugarcane, sugar beets, maple sap, and/or sorghum. It's sweeter than glucose, but not as sweet as fructose, and is typically known as table sugar. (*see also* **fructose, glucose, sorghum, sugar,** *and* **sugarcane**)

suet (SOO iht) The solid white fat found around the kidneys and loins of cattle, sheep, and other animals; it was often an ingredient in traditional British recipes for pastry, steamed or boiled puddings, stuffing, and mincemeat to add richness. (*see also* **plum pudding**)

sugar A crystalline sweetener that's a carbohydrate and known as sucrose. It's made primarily from sugar beets and sugarcane, but can also be made from maple sap and sorghum. Besides its sweetening value, sugar adds tenderness to doughs, stability to meringue mixtures, a golden surface to baked goods, and can contribute to the preservation of some foods. Many different forms of sugar are available:

• **Granulated sugar** is all-purpose sugar than can be used in most types of cooking.
• **Superfine sugar** or castor sugar is granulated sugar that has been pulverized into fine, uniform crystals that readily dissolve in liquid.

TEST KITCHEN SECRET

You can make your own superfine sugar by processing granulated sugar in a blender or food processor fitted with a metal blade. It takes about 30 seconds of pulsing or blending. LYDA JONES

• **Powdered sugar,** confectioners' sugar, or icing sugar, is granulated sugar that has been ground to a fine powder. It usually carries an "X" designation on the label to indicate the degree of fineness; 10X sugar is finer than XXXX sugar, which is finer than XX. It dissolves almost instantly and is used to make frostings and for dusting on cookies and cakes.
• **Brown sugar** is granulated sugar that has been combined with molasses. Light brown sugar has a more delicate flavor, while dark brown is more intense. Brownulated sugar is granulated crystals, while liquid brown sugar is also available. Use brown sugar to make chewy cookies and cakes.
(*continued on the following page.*)

- **Raw sugar** is unprocessed sugar that typically contains impurities; only processed or cleaned raw sugar is available in the United States. Turbinado is raw sugar that has been washed with steam.
- **Less common sugars** are: coarse sugar, which comes in large granules and is used to decorate baked goods; colored sugar that has been dyed for decorative purposes; date sugar is made from dried dates; jaggery is made from palm tree sap or sugar cane; maple sugar is made by boiling maple sap until almost dry; piloncillo sugar is unrefined Mexican sugar; and rock sugar comes in large crystals and has been cooked until it begins to caramelize.

Storage: Store sugar in a cool, dry place. Put brown sugar and powdered sugar in heavy plastic bags or airtight containers. Brown sugar can also be stored in an airtight container in the refrigerator. If properly stored, sugar will keep indefinitely. (*see also* **brown sugar, corn syrup, glucose, jaggery, powdered sugar, spun sugar, sugar beet, sugarcane, turbinado sugar,** *and Sugar Substitute Guide on page 565*)

sugar beet A type of beet with white flesh and white, yellow, or black skin; it has an extremely high sugar content and is used to make table sugar.

sugarcane A type of thick grass that grows 12 to 15 feet high in tropical and subtropical areas. The stalks of grass are cut, pressed for juice, which has an extremely high sugar content, and processed to produce molasses and table sugar. (*see also* **molasses** *and* **sugar**)

sugar free/sugarless A food labeling term approved by the FDA to designate when food contains no sweeteners or less than ½ gram sugar per serving size; it may, however, contain sugar alcohols, even though they also provide calories.

LITE BITE
"Sugar free" does not necessarily mean reduced or low calorie.

sugar plum A small candy often made with dried cherries or dried apricots and fondant. (*see also* **fondant**)

sugar snap pea A sweet pea that's a cross between an English pea and a snow pea. Also called a sugar pea, this bright green, crisp pod and tender pea seeds are both edible. Sugar snaps are available during spring and fall months, and can be served raw or briefly cooked. (*see also* **pea, snow pea,** *and* **sweet green pea**)

DILLED PEAS AND POTATOES VINAIGRETTE

Served warm or cold, these peas and potatoes put a new spin on side dish options.

8 small red potatoes (1½ pounds)	2 tablespoons minced fresh dill
1 pound sugar snap peas*	½ teaspoon salt
½ cup olive oil	½ teaspoon freshly ground pepper
6 tablespoons white wine vinegar	6 green onions, chopped

• Cook potatoes in a Dutch oven in boiling water to cover 25 to 30 minutes or until tender; drain. Thinly slice.

• Cook snap peas in boiling water 2 minutes or until crisp-tender; drain. Plunge peas into ice water to stop the cooking process; drain.

• Whisk together oil and next 4 ingredients in a large bowl. Add sliced potato, snap peas, and onions, tossing gently to coat. Cover and chill 2 hours, or serve immediately. Yield: 6 to 8 servings.

* Substitute 1 (16-ounce) package frozen sugar snap peas for fresh, if desired.

sugar substitute A powder, liquid, or tablet that simulates the sweetness of natural sugar. Some sugar substitutes are referred to as low-calorie sweeteners because they still contain calories, even though they are almost negligible. Aspartame, saccharin, sucralose, and acesulfame-K are common sugar substitutes. Aspartame, made from amino acids, can sometimes lose its sweetness, especially when cooked; saccharin sometimes leaves an aftertaste; and sucralose and acesulfame-K can be used in cooking. (*see also* **aspartame, saccharin, sucralose,** *and the Sugar Substitute Guide on page 565*)

> **Q Isn't it possible to replace sugar with these sugar substitutes?**
>
> **A** Sugar substitutes have more sweetening power than sugar, so you will find that you need less than the exact sugar equivalent. This can be a problem when you need the bulk that sugar provides, as in baked goods. We suggest you use saccharin-based sweeteners for up to half but not all the sugar, and add a little fruit juice to hide saccharin's aftertaste.

sugar syrup A syrup, also called simple syrup, made from sugar and water that's heated gently until the sugar is dissolved. Sugar syrups have a variety of uses, from glazing cakes and breads, to poaching fruits, to mint juleps; they're also the basis for making some frostings and candies. Sugar syrups can be flavored with herbs, extracts, juices, and liqueurs, and used to sweeten beverages such as tea. **Storage:** Sugar syrups can be stored at room temperature up to 1 week or chilled up to 6 months. (*see also* **candy**)

> **TEST KITCHEN SECRET**
>
> *"To make a simple sugar syrup, combine water and sugar in a saucepan—for a thin syrup, use 3 parts water to 1 part sugar; for a medium syrup, use 2 parts water and 1 part sugar; for a heavy syrup, use equal parts sugar and water. Then cook over low heat, stirring gently, until the sugar dissolves; continue simmering an additional minute, then remove from the heat, and let cool."* JAN MOON

sukiyaki (soo kee YAH kee) A Japanese dish that consists of stir-fried beef, a variety of vegetables, noodles, an egg or tofu, and is flavored with soy sauce. It was originally created as an easy, complete meal to cook and serve at the table. (*see also* **soy sauce, stir-fry,** *and* **tofu**)

summer coating Also known as bark or candy coating or confectionery coating, this mixture of sugar, vegetable fat, flavoring, and coloring is used as a coating for candy. While some summer coatings do contain cocoa powder, they do not contain cocoa butter. It firms back up after melting more readily than chocolate, so it's sometimes used for dipping candies.

summer pudding A classic British dessert of sweetened, cooked fresh berries and red currants that are pressed in a bread-lined casserole dish, topped with additional bread, covered, and refrigerated overnight. When unmolded, the dessert is served with whipped cream. (*see also* **currant**)

summer sausage (*see* **sausage**)

sunchoke (*see* **Jerusalem artichoke**)

sundae An ice cream dessert made from scoops of ice cream topped with one or more sweet sauces such as hot fudge or caramel sauce. Sundaes are typically garnished with whipped cream and chopped nuts or fruit.

sun-dried tomatoes (*see* **dried tomato**)

sunfish A variety of freshwater fish common in North America that includes the bluegill, largemouth and smallmouth bass, rock bass, spotted bass, and crappie. The fish have vivid skin colors and a sweet flavor.

sunflower seed oil (*see* **fats and oils**)

sunflower seeds These seeds are harvested from sunflowers grown primarily in Russia, California, Minnesota, and North Dakota. Their hard, black-and-white striped shells must be removed before the tan, oval kernels can be eaten. The seeds are sold dried or toasted, either in or out of the shell, as well as plain or salted. They can be eaten as a snack, used in salads, or added to a variety of baked goods.

Storage: Store seeds in an airtight container in the refrigerator or freezer; if roasted, they will keep up to 4 months, and if raw, up to a year.

TEST KITCHEN SECRET

When shelled sunflower seeds are mixed with baking soda, a chemical reaction occurs that sometimes causes baked goods to take on a blue or greenish cast. It's OK to eat, but not so attractive. LYDA JONES

superfine sugar (*see* **sugar**)

surimi (su REE mee) A processed food made from mild, white-fleshed fish; it's colored and flavored to resemble various types of shellfish, such as crabmeat.

sushi (SOO shee) A Japanese specialty of rice seasoned with sweet rice vinegar and served with ingredients such as raw fish, pickles, vegetables, and tofu. The rice mixtures are sometimes rolled and wrapped in thin sheets of nori or seaweed, and cut into slices. Sushi can be an appetizer, snack, or entrée; it's often served with soy sauce for dipping. (*see also* **sashimi** *and* **seaweed**)

swamp cabbage (*see* **hearts of palm**)

sweating To cook food, usually vegetables, over low heat in a covered pan just until they soften and release moisture. Sweating brings out flavor and juices, but should be done without browning the food.

Swedish meatballs Made of ground meat, onions, breadcrumbs, egg, and seasonings, these meatballs are shaped into balls, browned, and served in a brown sauce made from pan drippings and cream. (*see also* **smorgasbord**)

sweet-and-sour A type of dish in which a sweet element, such as sugar or fruit, is balanced against a sour one, such as vinegar. These flavors are often incorporated into a sauce or dressing and served with meat, seafood, or vegetables. For example, Chinese sweet-and-sour dishes might feature shrimp, chicken, or pork, while Germans are partial to sweet-and-sour cabbage and sauerbraten roasts. (*see also* **sauerbraten**)

sweetbreads The thymus glands of calves, lambs, or young hogs. There are two glands—one is an elongated gland taken from the throat, and the second is a rounder gland taken from near the heart. Both have subtle, rich flavor and delicate texture, though sweetbreads from milk-fed veal or young calves are considered the best. They're highly perishable and should be prepared the day of purchase. Before cooking, soak them in water to which a small amount of lemon juice or vinegar is added; afterwards, they are blanched, and often breaded, fried, and sauced. (*see also* **variety meats**)

sweetened condensed milk Milk made from a mixture of cow's milk and sugar that's heated to evaporate about 60 percent of the water, leaving a condensed, sweet mixture often used to make desserts. Sweetened condensed milk is not to be confused with evaporated milk, which is made from unsweetened milk. A nonfat version is available. (*see also* **evaporated milk** *and* **milk**)

Q Is it safe to cook an unopened can of sweetened condensed milk in boiling water?

A No! The cans have been known to explode and cause burns. Instead, pour 1 (14-ounce) can sweetened condensed milk into a 1-quart slow cooker. Cook, covered, 6 or 7 hours or until the milk is the color of peanut butter, whisking every 30 minutes. Another method is to pour the milk into an 8-inch glass pieplate and cover with aluminum foil. Place the pieplate inside a 2-quart shallow casserole dish, and fill dish with 1 inch of hot water. Bake at 425° for 1 hour and 20 minutes or until the milk is thick and caramel-colored.

sweet green pea Also known as English peas, garden peas, or green peas, these tiny, young peas are glossy, crunchy, and sweet when picked and served fresh. Unfortunately, canned and frozen sweet green peas are no match for the fresh, but when seasoned and topped with butter, they still make a nice addition to most meals. (*see also* **pea**)

sweetmeat A piece of candy, candied fruit, nut, or pastry.

sweet potato There are several varieties of sweet potato, but the two that are most popular are a darker-skinned variety and a pale variety. The darker-skinned variety is sometimes referred to as a yam, although true yams are not related to the sweet potato. What is marketed in the United States as "yams" are really a variety of sweet potato grown in the South. A true yam is a starchy edible root and is generally imported from the Caribbean. It's rough and scaly and very low in beta carotene.

Q **What's the difference between a sweet potato and a yam?**

A In the South, moist, dark-fleshed sweet potatoes are often called yams, and to add to the confusion, canned sweet potatoes are frequently labeled as yams. However, true yams are not sold that often in the United States, though they can sometimes be found in Latin American markets.

"Yams," as most of us perceive them, are actually sweet potatoes with a vivid orange color, soft moist consistency when cooked, and a sweeter flavor than yams. Other varieties of sweet potatoes are lighter skinned and have a firmer, drier texture when cooked. Fresh sweet potatoes are generally thought of as a fall crop, though they are available year-round; canned and frozen sweet potatoes are also available. Try them baked, boiled, candied, fried, or sautéed; they can be peeled and sliced, cut into chunks for glazing or pureed for pies.

TIMESAVING TIP

Canned sweet potatoes may be substituted for fresh. Three medium-size sweet potatoes are roughly equivalent to 1 (16-ounce) can sweet potatoes or 2 cups cooked and mashed.

Storage: Store sweet potatoes in a cool (around 55°), dry, dark place (do not refrigerate). Under perfect conditions they can be stored for 3 to 4 weeks. (*see also* **vegetables** *and* **yam**)

Southernism

No Southern Thanksgiving dinner would be complete without the sweet potato in some form. This beloved tuber survived the devastation of the Civil War because it grows underground. George Washington Carver is largely credited with encouraging the use of sweet potatoes after the war with a series of reports he wrote from Tuskegee Institute in Tuskegee, Alabama. Sweet potato pie is a distinctly Southern, 1800s recipe; we like our sweet potatoes mashed with butter, sugar, and vanilla extract, and our casseroles are often so sweet they could be called desserts. Many casseroles bear the hallmark golden-brown marshmallows as a topping. As times change, so does this Southern staple. Today, roasted sweet potatoes are popular on many menus at home and in restaurants.

SWEET POTATO PIE

2 pounds sweet potatoes, peeled and sliced	1 teaspoon ground nutmeg
½ cup butter or margarine	1 teaspoon vanilla extract
3 large eggs	1 teaspoon lemon extract
1 cup sugar	1 (12-ounce) package frozen deep-dish piecrusts, thawed
½ cup sweetened condensed milk	Garnishes: whipped cream, grated
½ cup evaporated milk	nutmeg

• Cook sweet potato in boiling water to cover 30 minutes or until tender; drain.

• Beat sweet potato and butter at medium speed with an electric mixer until smooth. Add eggs and next 6 ingredients, beating well. Pour mixture evenly into each piecrust.

• Bake at 350° on lower oven rack for 45 to 50 minutes or until set. Garnish, if desired. Yield: 2 (9-inch) pies.

TEST KITCHEN SECRET

Cook sweet potatoes with the skins on. When fork-tender, drain and submerge in cold water. The peels will be easier to remove. VIE WARSHAW

TIMESAVING TIP

Whole sweet potatoes can be microwaved just as regular potatoes. Scrub 2 medium-size sweet potatoes and prick several times with a fork; arrange on a layer of paper towels in the microwave oven. Microwave, uncovered, at HIGH for 7 to 8 minutes or until done, turning and rearranging the potatoes after 3 minutes. Let stand 5 minutes before serving.

Swiss chard (*see* chard)

Swiss cheese
A generic term for a creamy, pale yellow cow's milk cheese that has a firm, smooth texture with large holes and a nutty flavor. There are many types of Swiss cheese available; some of the more familiar include:

• **Emmentaler** is a firm-textured cheese with a sweet, nutlike flavor, and is thought of as Switzerland Swiss cheese; it's used in fondue.

• **Gruyère** is a firm-bodied cheese with a rich, sweet, nutty flavor that's sharper than regular Swiss cheese and has few holes; it's often used in fondue or to top French onion soup.

• **Jarlsberg** is a smooth, firm-textured Norwegian Swiss cheese with small holes and a mellow, nutty flavor; it's an all-purpose cheese.

• **American-made or domestic Swiss** cheeses are smooth-textured with a mild flavor and large holes. (*see also* **cheese**)

Swiss steak
A thick piece of beef round or sirloin steak that has been tenderized by pounding. It's coated with flour and browned on both sides, then smothered with broth, seasonings, and sometimes chopped tomatoes, onions, carrots, and celery, and then braised or baked until tender. (*see also* **smother** *and recipe on the following page*)

SWISS STEAK MONTEREY

⅓ cup all-purpose flour
½ teaspoon garlic salt
¼ teaspoon pepper
2 pounds cubed round or
   sirloin steak

3 tablespoons vegetable oil
2 (8-ounce) cans tomato sauce
1 (1.3-ounce) envelope dry onion
   soup mix
1 (8-ounce) container sour cream

• Combine first 3 ingredients. Dredge cubed steak in flour mixture.
• Brown steak, in batches, in hot oil in a Dutch oven. Return all steak to pan. Stir in tomato sauce and soup mix; bring to a boil. Cover, reduce heat, and simmer 15 minutes. Remove steak, reserving liquid in pan; keep warm.
• Stir sour cream into tomato mixture; simmer, stirring constantly, until heated. (Do not boil.) Serve over steak. Yield: 6 to 8 servings.

swordfish A very large saltwater sport fish with a dorsal fin and an upper jawbone that projects to a bladelike point. Found in waters throughout the world, swordfish can weigh several hundred pounds and are difficult to catch, which makes them one of the more pricey fish on the market. Their meat varies from off white to orange and is mild-flavored, moderately fat, firm, and dense. Enjoy swordfish by sautéing, broiling, baking, or poaching. (*see also* **fish**)

syllabub (SIHL uh buhb) An old English drink of thick, frothy, light eggnog made by beating milk or cream with wine or ale, sugar, and spices. Many Charleston cooks still make this recipe for holiday parties. The recipe has survived in many community cookbooks, especially those in coastal areas settled by the English.

syrup A liquid usually made from maple sap, cane sugar, corn, molasses, sorghum, or a simple solution of sugar and liquid. Fruit-flavored syrups can be used atop pancakes and waffles, and chocolate-flavored syrup serves as a topping for ice cream and desserts.
Storage: An unopened bottle of syrup keeps up to a year in a cool, dry place. However, take notice of mold or bubbles on the syrup's surface; this is a sign of spoilage, and the syrup should be discarded. (*see also* **cane syrup, corn syrup,** *and* **sugar syrup**)

Szechuan (SEHCH wahn) (*see* **Chinese cuisine**)

Tabasco pepper (tuh BAS koh) (*see* **peppers**)

Tabasco® sauce (*see* **hot sauce**)

tabbouleh (tuh BOO luh) A Middle Eastern dish of bulghur wheat mixed with chopped tomatoes and onions. Tabbouleh is traditionally flavored with parsley and mint and dressed with olive oil and lemon juice. It's typically served cold as a side dish or salad. (*see also* **bulghur**)

table d'hôte (tah buhl DOHT) Like the French term "prix fixe," this term also indicates a menu that offers a complete meal for a set price rather than à la carte. (*see also* **prix fixe**)

tablespoon A measure of volume in the United States system that equals 3 teaspoons or 0.50 fluid ounces. This term also refers to a spoon with a large, slightly pointed bowl used to serve foods at the table.

taco (TAH koh) A type of Mexican "sandwich" made with small folded corn or flour tortillas, that are crisp (deep-fried) or soft. The taco shells are spread with beef, pork, chicken, chorizo sausage, or refried beans, and topped with chopped tomatoes, shredded lettuce, grated cheese, chopped onions, guacamole, sour cream, and salsa. (*see also* **refried beans, salsa,** *and* **tortilla**)

> **TIMESAVING TIP**
> The quickest way to soften tortillas is to wrap them in paper towels, cover, and microwave on MEDIUM (50% power) for 1 to 2 minutes or until they are soft and pliable. They can also be heated in a skillet or wrapped in foil and heated in a conventional oven at 325° for 10 minutes.

taffy (TAF ee) A soft, chewy candy made with cooked sugar, butter, and flavoring; the mixture is pulled repeatedly into long ropes and twisted as it cools, giving it a shiny opaque color. Saltwater taffy, made popular in the late 1800s in Atlantic City, was given its name because a small amount of saltwater was added to the mixture.

tahini (tah HEE nee) A thick paste made from crushed sesame seeds and used in Middle Eastern cooking as a flavoring for dishes such as hummus. It can be purchased in Middle Eastern food stores or in some supermarkets. (*see also* **falafel, hummus,** *and* **sesame seed**)

tailgate picnic An outdoor meal served from the rear or tailgate of a vehicle, usually before or after a sporting event. The menus of some tailgate picnics offer simple, cold finger foods, but others are elaborate, festive affairs, complete with cocktails and grilling.

takeout Food that is ordered from a restaurant or deli but taken home to eat. Some people refer to takeout as "carry out" or "to-go" food. Most take-out foods must be picked up at the restaurant, but some is actually delivered to your home.

> **TIMESAVING TIP**
> Busy work schedules can make at-home entertaining a daunting task. One way to make it easier is to order part of your meal as take-out food. If arranged in your own serving dishes, your guests will never know. It'll be your secret!

T

tamale (tuh MAH lee) A popular Mexican dish of chopped, chili-flavored meat that's coated with masa dough, wrapped in a softened corn husk, and steamed until the masa is cooked; to eat, just peel back the corn husk. Sometimes tamales are sweet; these usually have a fruit-filled center.

HOT TAMALES

½ (8-ounce) package corn husks or about 9 whole dried corn husks (we tested with Don Enrique)
¾ cup yellow cornmeal
½ cup plus 1 tablespoon chili powder
3 tablespoons onion powder
1 tablespoon garlic powder
2 tablespoons ground cumin
1 tablespoon ground red pepper
4 teaspoons salt
1 teaspoon black pepper
3 pounds ground beef
1 (8-ounce) can tomato sauce
¾ cup water
1 large egg
Tamale Sauce

• Place whole corn husks in a large bowl (each husk should contain several layers); cover with hot water. Let stand 1 to 2 hours or until softened. Remove any silks; wash husks well. Drain well; pat dry.
• Combine cornmeal and next 11 ingredients; stir well. Roll meat mixture into 24 (4-inch-long) logs. Separate layers of corn husks. Place 1 log in center of 1 layer of corn husk; wrap husk tightly around meat. Twist ends of husks; tie securely with narrow strips of softened corn husk or pieces of string. Cut off long ends of husks, if necessary. (You may not need all of the corn husk layers.)
• Layer tamales in a large Dutch oven. Pour Tamale Sauce over tamales; bring to a boil. Reduce heat; simmer, uncovered, 1½ hours, rearranging tamales every 30 minutes. Yield: 8 to 12 servings.

TAMALE SAUCE

1 (6-ounce) can tomato paste
¼ cup chili powder
2 tablespoons onion powder
1 tablespoon salt
1 tablespoon ground cumin
2 teaspoons garlic powder
9 cups water

• Combine all ingredients in a large bowl, stirring until smooth. Yield: 9¼ cups.

tamari (tuh MAH ree) A Japanese sauce made from soybeans; it's similar to soy sauce, but thicker and darker, and it has a mellower flavor. (*see also* **soybean** *and* **soy sauce**)

tamarillo (tam uh RIHL oh) A small oval fruit, sometimes called a tree tomato, that's native to South America and is also grown in New Zealand. Tamarillos have a tough, smooth skin that can be red, purple, amber, or yellow. The tart, pink flesh contains small black seeds similar to tomato seeds. Tamarillos can be eaten fresh, but often they're sweetened with sugar and cooked. Tamarillos are still somewhat hard to find, but they're in season from May through October and available in some specialty produce markets.
Storage: Ripe tamarillos can be refrigerated in plastic bags up to 10 days.

tamarind (TAM uh rihnd) Also known as an Indian date, the tamarind is a fruit of a tree grown in Asia, northern Africa, and India. Its long, dark pods contain small seeds and a sweet-and-sour pulp that's dried and used as a flavoring, much like lemon juice. Tamarind is frequently used in Indian and Middle Eastern cuisines as well as in Worcestershire sauce, chutneys, and many soft drinks. Some cooks are beginning to use tamarind to flavor sorbets or salad dressings, and as a tenderizer in marinades. Fresh tamarind pods may be difficult to find, but tamarind paste, syrup, or frozen tamarind pulp can be purchased in Indian, Asian, or Middle Eastern markets.

tandoori (tan DUR ee) A term that describes foods cooked in a rounded-top tandoori oven made of brick and clay and used to bake foods over direct heat from a smoky fire. The heat in such ovens is very intense and can cook a chicken on a skewer or Indian bread in less than 5 minutes.

tangelo (tan JEHL oh) A small- to medium-sized sweet, tart citrus fruit that's a cross between a mandarin orange or tangerine and a grapefruit. Tangelos have light to deep orange skins that peel easily, and pale yellow to deep orange flesh with few seeds. (*see also* **citrus fruit, mandarin orange,** *and* **tangerine**)

tangerine A small- to medium-sized citrus fruit, named after the city of Tangier, Morocco; it's a member of the mandarin orange family. Tangerines have thick, rough, but very easy-to-peel skins; their sweet flesh contains seeds. (*see also* **citrus fruit** *and* **mandarin orange**)

tangy A term that describes a pleasantly tart flavor.

tannin (TAN ihn) A chemical compound found in the stems and seeds of grapes that imparts an astringent, pucker quality to wines that usually diminishes as the wine ages and mellows. Tannin is also an astringent substance found in tea. (*see also* **tea** *and* **wine**)

tapas (TAH pahs) Appetizers popularly served throughout Spain. Tapas can be served hot or cold and are usually accompanied with cocktails or sherry. They can make up an entire meal or be served as a snack. They can range from simple olives, ham, and cheese to more complex creations of omelets, stuffed peppers, and miniature sandwiches. (*see also* **appetizer**)

tapenade (TA puh nahd) A thick, French paste made of capers, anchovies, black olives, garlic, olive oil, and lemon juice. Tapenade is typically used as a condiment, garnish, or sauce.

tapioca (tap ee OH kuh) A starch extracted from the root of the cassava plant and used to thicken cooked dishes. Tapioca can be purchased in several forms but the most common type is quick-cooking tapioca; it's used as a thickener for soups, and in fruit fillings and puddings. Old-fashioned pearl tapioca is used mostly in making pudding. It must be soaked prior to cooking. Tapioca flour, much like cornstarch, is used to thicken soups, gravies, and fruit fillings. **Storage:** Store in a cool, dry place up to 2 years. (*see also* **cassava** *and* **cornstarch**)

TEST KITCHEN SECRET

If you don't have tapioca, substitute an equal amount of flour. After adding tapioca to a hot liquid, avoid letting it boil; this could make it stringy. Instead, remove the mixture from the heat while it's still a little thin so the tapioca can thicken as it cools. Also, don't stir tapioca mixtures too much because this could make them gelatinous. MARY ALLEN PERRY

taro root (TAHR oh) The starchy, potato-like root of the taro plant used in Asian and Polynesian cooking; it has brown skin, gray-white flesh, and an acidic flavor. However, taro takes on a nutlike flavor when cooked. Also called dasheen, taro root can be used in the same way as potatoes.

tarragon (TEHR uh guhn) (*see* **herbs**)

tart A shallow pastry crust with a sweet or savory filling that ranges from bite size to individual to full size. This term also describes a sharp acidic or sour flavor.

HONEY-PECAN TART

1 cup sugar	2½ cups pecan halves, coarsely
¼ cup water	chopped
1 cup whipping cream	1 (15-ounce) package refrigerated
¼ cup unsalted butter, cut into	piecrusts
small pieces	2 teaspoons sugar, divided
¼ cup honey	½ (4-ounce) package bittersweet
½ teaspoon salt	chocolate, chopped

- Bring 1 cup sugar and ¼ cup water to a boil in a medium-size heavy saucepan, stirring until sugar dissolves. Cover and boil over medium-high heat, without stirring, 8 minutes or until golden, swirling pan occasionally.
- Remove from heat, and gradually stir in whipping cream (mixture will bubble with addition of cream).
- Add butter, honey, and salt, stirring until smooth. Stir in pecans; simmer over medium heat, stirring occasionally, 5 minutes. Remove from heat; cool completely.
- Unfold 1 piecrust on a lightly floured surface; roll into an 11-inch circle. Fit into a 9-inch removable bottom tart pan. Trim edges. Freeze crust 30 minutes.
- Spread pecan mixture into crust. Unfold remaining piecrust, and roll into a 10-inch circle. Place crust over mixture, pressing into bottom crust to seal; trim edges. Sprinkle with 1 teaspoon sugar. Freeze 30 minutes.
- Bake at 400° for 30 minutes. Cool on a wire rack.
- Place chocolate in a small heavy-duty zip-top plastic bag; seal. Submerge in hot water until chocolate melts. Snip a tiny hole in 1 corner of bag; drizzle chocolate over tart. Sprinkle with remaining 1 teaspoon sugar. Yield: 1 (9-inch) tart.

tartare (*see* **steak tartare**)

tartar sauce (TAHR tuhr) A mayonnaise-based sauce that contains finely chopped pickles, capers, onions, olives, and lemon juice or vinegar. Tartar sauce is traditionally served with fried fish, but it's also a tasty accompaniment with broiled, baked, or poached fish. It can be purchased in most supermarkets, but it can be prepared easily at home. (*see also* **mayonnaise**)

tarte Tatin (tart tah TAN) A French upside-down apple tart made by arranging sliced apples in a buttered and sugared pan or baking dish, and topping it with pastry dough. The sugar beneath the sliced apples caramelizes during baking, and when the tart is inverted, forms the top.

tasso (TAH soh) Cajun sausage made from cured pork or beef richly seasoned with red pepper, garlic, filé powder, and other herbs and spices, then smoked for several days to give it a smoky, tangy flavor. Tasso is often used to season beans, eggs, and pasta dishes. Outside of Cajun country, tasso can be difficult to find; the easiest way to purchase it is through mail order at **comeaux.com** or call 1-800-323-2492. (*see also* **Cajun cooking, filé powder,** *and* **sausage**)

tea An aromatic beverage made by infusing water with the cured leaves of an evergreen shrub native to China. Tea is one of the world's oldest and most popular drinks. The English enjoy their tea so much that they developed afternoon tea and high tea as occasions where tea can be enjoyed each day. Tea is generally named for its leaf type, size, or region of origin.

There are three main types of tea:

• **Black tea** comes from leaves that have been fermented before being heated and dried. It's the strongest, richest, and most mellow of teas. Orange pekoe tea contains black tea leaves that are smaller than medium-size pekoe tea leaves. Darjeeling is an example of black tea.

• **Green tea** is a popular Asian tea that has recently grown in favor with Westerners due to claims that it benefits health. Its leaves have been steamed and dried, but not fermented. It produces a greenish-yellow liquid that has a slightly bitter, astringent flavor. Gunpowder is an example of green tea.

• **Oolong tea** is made from leaves that are partially fermented and has a rich, mellow flavor that falls between black tea and green tea. Formosa Oolong is an example of this type of tea.

Q Should I purchase loose tea or tea bags?

A It depends. Although tea bags are convenient, tea aficionados maintain that loose tea is fresher and allows the leaves to circulate in hot water to fully release their essence. If you choose this route, the best solution is to spoon loose tea into the bottom of a pot, or use a strainer or a pot that comes with its own infuser. Another good idea is to purchase a metal-mesh tea ball that can be filled with loose tea. On the other hand, health enthusiasts maintain tea bags are the wisest choice for a healthy cup of tea because the leaves are pulverized, thereby exposing more surface area so that the tea's healing compounds can be released. It's up to you!

There are also specialty teas flavored with floral, fruit, or spice additions. Blended teas are commercial brands made from a blend of black teas, such as English Breakfast. Instant tea is made from brewed tea that has been dehydrated and granulated. And then there are the ever-popular herb or tisane teas; they aren't true teas because they're made with herbs, flowers, and spices, and therefore, contain no caffeine. True tea contains caffeine. Tea can be sweetened, flavored with lemon or mint, served with cream, and enjoyed hot or cold over ice.

LITE BITE

A good reason to drink tea is for its beneficial antioxidants, but be sure to select real tea leaves as opposed to herbal tea.

Storage: Store each type of tea in its own airtight container at room temperature. If properly stored, tea can last up to 2 years. (*see also* **green tea, high tea, iced tea, pekoe tea, tea time,** *and* **tisane**)

RESCUE for cloudy tea:
First, avoid placing hot tea in the refrigerator. Let it cool to room temperature and then chill. To clear up cloudy tea, add a little boiling water.

tea biscuit A term used by the British to describe any type of cookie or cracker served with afternoon tea.

teaspoon A unit of measure in the United States system that equals 0.17 fluid ounces. This term also refers to a small spoon with a slightly pointed bowl that's used to stir tea or coffee. An iced tea spoon has a longer handle and is used for stirring iced tea. (*see also* **measuring**)

tea time The British have traditionally set aside two times each day to enjoy tea. The first is afternoon tea, where a light meal or refreshments can be served; this might include bread and butter, cucumber or other delicate sandwiches, cookies, scones, and Devonshire or clotted cream served along with a pot of hot tea. The second is high tea, which is a substantial late afternoon or early evening meal; meat or fish, biscuits and jam, cakes and pastries, and a pot of hot tea might be offered. (*see also* **clotted cream, high tea,** *and* **tea**)

temper The process of gradually bringing something to the proper temperature or texture by mixing, stirring, heating, or cooling. For example, slowly stirring a little hot liquid into eggs or other foods in order to gradually raise their temperature without causing them to curdle. When chocolate is melted for dipping or molding, it must also be tempered; this process of melting and cooling to the correct temperature stabilizes cocoa butter crystals so the chocolate will be shiny, smooth, and unblemished by bloom.

temperature The degree of heat in a food or dish, refrigerator or freezer, room, or oven as measured on the graduated scale of a thermometer. Cooks should be aware of some key temperatures for different stages of cooking. Among them:
• Freezers should be set to about 0°, while refrigerators should be between 35° and 40°.
• Lukewarm liquid is considered to be 95°, while hot liquid is 100° to 110°; water boils at 212°.
• A cool room is 65°; a warm room ranges from 70° to 75°.
• A low or slow oven measures 180° to 200°; a moderate oven measures 350° to 375°; and a hot oven measures 475° to 500°. (*see also* **high altitude**)

T

temple orange A medium-sized orange that's a cross between a tangerine and an orange. Temple oranges have rough, thick, loose skin, and sweet, tart flesh with many seeds. (*see also* **orange**)

tempura (tehm POOR uh) A Japanese dish consisting of pieces of seafood or vegetables dipped in a very light batter and deep-fried. Tempura is often served with a soy sauce-based dipping sauce. (*see also* **soy sauce**)

tenderizer (*see* **meat tenderizer** *and* **papain**)

tenderloin A flavorful and very tender muscle that runs through the beef short loin or pork loin sections; it can be served whole or cut into filet mignon or pork medaillons. It's one of the most prized cuts of beef or pork. Generally, the beef tenderloin is larger and more costly than pork. Not as familiar, but still prized cuts, are the tenderloins that come from other animals such as chicken, lamb, and venison. (*see also* **beef** *and* **pork**)

GRILLED PORK TENDERLOIN WITH MOLASSES SAUCE

½ cup molasses	1 small onion, chopped
2 tablespoons chopped fresh	2 garlic cloves, chopped
rosemary	1 tablespoon olive oil
2 tablespoons Dijon mustard	1 cup dry white wine
1 tablespoon olive oil	1 cup chicken broth
½ teaspoon salt	1 teaspoon cornstarch
½ teaspoon freshly ground pepper	1 tablespoon water
2 (¾-pound) pork tenderloins	½ teaspoon salt

• Stir together first 6 ingredients. Set aside half of mixture; cover and chill.
• Place pork in a dish or heavy-duty zip-top plastic bag; pour remaining molasses mixture over pork. Cover or seal; chill 8 hours, turning occasionally.
• Remove pork from marinade, discarding marinade. Grill, covered with grill lid, over medium heat (300° to 350°) about 25 minutes or until a meat thermometer inserted into thickest portion registers 160°, turning occasionally.
• Sauté onion and garlic in 1 tablespoon hot oil in a saucepan until tender. Add wine and broth; cook over medium-high heat, stirring occasionally, until mixture is reduced by three-fourths.
• Stir in reserved molasses mixture; simmer 5 minutes. Pour through a wire-mesh strainer into a bowl, discarding onion and garlic; return to pan.
• Stir together cornstarch and water. Stir into wine mixture. Bring to a boil over medium heat, stirring constantly, 1 minute. Stir in ½ teaspoon salt. Serve with sliced pork. Yield: 6 servings.

tequila (tuh KEE luh) Liquor made in Mexico from the fermented juice of the agave plant and named after Tequila, Mexico. Tequila has a high alcohol content; it ranges in color from white to golden. It's used as the basis of the popular margarita cocktail. (*see also* **margarita**)

teriyaki (tehr uh YAH kee) A Japanese entrée that has been marinated and grilled with teriyaki sauce, which is composed of soy sauce, sake or sherry, sugar, ginger, and seasonings. Teriyaki sauce is sweeter than soy sauce and adds a glaze to food as it cooks. (*see also* **soy sauce**)

terrine (teh REEN) A term that refers to both a special earthenware, enameled iron, or glass heat-proof cooking and serving dish, and the mixture that's cooked in it. A terrine typically holds a highly seasoned pâté-type mixture made of coarsely ground meats, fish, shellfish, poultry, and/or vegetables; the mixture is baked without a crust in a terrine dish lined with pork fat and served hot or cold. (*see also* **pâté**)

Tetrazzini (teh trah ZEE nee) Named after opera singer Luisa Tetrazzini, this main dish combines cooked spaghetti and chicken or turkey with a rich sherry-Parmesan cheese cream sauce; sometimes other ingredients such as mushrooms and almonds are included. The mixture is sprinkled with breadcrumbs and Parmesan cheese, and baked until bubbly and golden.

CHICKEN TETRAZZINI

3 cups chopped cooked chicken
1 cup shredded Parmesan cheese, divided
1 (10¾-ounce) can cream of mushroom soup, undiluted*
1 (10-ounce) container refrigerated Alfredo sauce*
1 (3½-ounce) can sliced mushrooms, drained
½ cup slivered almonds, toasted
½ cup chicken broth
¼ cup dry sherry
¼ teaspoon freshly ground pepper
7 ounces vermicelli, cooked

• Stir together chicken, ½ cup Parmesan cheese, and next 7 ingredients; stir in pasta. Spoon mixture into 6 lightly greased 6-ounce baking dishes or an 11- x 7-inch baking dish. Sprinkle with remaining ½ cup Parmesan cheese.
• Bake at 350° for 25 minutes or until thoroughly heated. Yield: 6 servings.

* Substitute reduced-sodium, reduced-fat cream of mushroom soup and light Alfredo sauce, if desired.

Texmati rice An aromatic white or brown rice grown in the United States that's a cross between long-grain rice and basmati rice. It has a sweet, nutty taste and aroma. (*see also* **basmati** *and* **rice**)

Tex-Mex (TEHKS mehks) A term used to describe the foods based on the combined cultures of Texas and Mexico. Tex-Mex foods include a variety of dishes; some of the best known are burritos, nachos, and tacos.

Thai coffee A coffee drink that consists of strong, chicory-tinged coffee, sweetened condensed milk, and ice. It's an excellent complement to Thai food, which is often very spicy. (*see also* **chicory**)

T

Thai curry paste A paste of aromatic herbs, spices, and vegetables used in Thai cuisine as a spicy-hot flavoring. Yellow curry paste is the mildest, while red curry can vary in heat intensity; green curry paste is the hottest. (*see also* **curry**)

thawing A process, also referred to as defrosting, where frozen food is allowed to return to room temperature.
Thawing tips:
• Never thaw any kind of meat, seafood, or poultry under warm water or at room temperature. Thaw them only in the refrigerator to keep bacteria from multiplying.
• A whole frozen turkey will take 2 to 5 days to fully thaw; plan on 3 to 4 hours defrosting time per pound.
• Count on large pieces of meat (over 4 pounds) taking 4 to 7 hours per pound to defrost.
• Steaks and chops will take 8 to 14 hours or overnight. A whole chicken can require 12 to 16 hours to thaw.
• Smaller pieces of meat, fish, or chicken can be placed in a zip-top plastic bag and placed in cold water, changing the water often; this will generally decrease the thawing time, but the food will lose more of its juices and be drier when cooked.
• Meat, fish, or chicken can also be thawed in a microwave oven on MEDIUM LOW (30% power), but it will lose some of its moisture and must be carefully monitored.
• Vegetables can be thawed at room temperature or by cooking them in a small amount of boiling water. (*see also* **food safety**)

thermometer Every kitchen should contain these basic thermometers:
• Either a **probe-type** meat thermometer, which is inserted into meat (not touching fat or bone) before it's put into the oven, and left there until the proper temperature is reached. Or, an **instant-read** thermometer, which can be substituted for a probe-type thermometer; it's accurate and gives a reading in seconds and can be used to test different sections of the same piece of food; it's also convenient for grilled foods.
• A **candy** or **deep-fat frying** thermometer is used when cooking candy, some frostings, and sugar syrups, and when frying foods in a large quantity of oil or shortening. This type thermometer is marked with the stages of candy making; most also have markings for frying temperatures.
   Other helpful thermometers include an **oven** thermometer that's calibrated to match oven temperatures, so that you can determine if your oven is heating properly. **Refrigerator** or **freezer** thermometers verify if proper chilling is taking place. And a **microwave** thermometer can be left in foods during cooking in the microwave oven. Thermometers help eliminate guesswork by accurately measuring the doneness of food.

thickening agent An ingredient used to give a thicker consistency to a mixture such as a sauce, gravy, pudding, or soup. There are several agents used for this purpose; the most common include flour, cornstarch, arrowroot, gelatin, egg yolk, and tapioca. To prepare flour and cornstarch for thickening, gradually stir cold liquid into them, or combine

them with the cold liquid in a screw-top jar and shake thoroughly. Then stir the mixture into the food that needs thickening; keep stirring to prevent lumping. Most flour and cornstarch mixtures must return to a boil and boil 1 minute to complete thickening. Gelatin must be softened, dissolved, and allowed to firm up (boiling gelatin destroys its firming ability). (*see also* **arrowroot, cornstarch, flour, gelatin,** *and* **tapioca**)

thin A process of diluting mixtures by adding more liquid. This term also describes a product that's watery or lacks body.

Thousand Island dressing A salad dressing or sandwich spread made from mayonnaise, chili sauce, and finely chopped pickles, green peppers, olives, and hard-cooked eggs. (*see also* **dressing** *and* **salad dressing**)

thread stage (*see* **candy**)

thyme (TIME) An herb with tiny gray-green leaves that have a strong, slightly lemon-mint flavor and aroma. Thyme can be used fresh, dried, or ground. (*see also* **herbs**)

Tia Maria (tee uh muh REE uh) A dark brown, rum-based Jamaican liqueur that has a strong coffee flavor. (*see also* **liqueur**)

tiger lily buds The light-golden dried buds of the tiger lily that's native to China and Japan but also grown in North America. The buds have a delicate, musky-sweet flavor and are sometimes used as a garnish or added to Chinese stir-fry dishes. They must be soaked in water before using. They're sold in Asian markets. (*see also* **stir-fry**)

tilapia (tuh LAH pee uh) A freshwater fish native to Africa, but increasingly is farm-raised in the United States and other countries. Tilapia generally has gray skin, lean white flesh, a firm texture, and a sweet, mild flavor. It's suitable for almost any cooking method. (*see also* **fish**)

tilefish A saltwater fish found in the Atlantic Ocean from the Mid-Atlantic States to New England. Tilefish has multicolored skin with distinctive yellow dots and low-fat, firm flesh. (*see also* **fish**)

timbale (TIHM buhl) A custard mixture that includes meat, vegetables or cheese and is baked in individual molds; timbales can also be made of pastry, rice, or potato. This term also refers to the timbale mold itself, usually round and tapers toward the bottom to facilitate unmolding. Another type of timbale is made by dipping a specially shaped iron into a batter, then frying; the resulting shell is filled with a sweet or savory mixture.

tipsy pudding A British dessert similar to trifle that gets its name from layers of wine-soaked sponge cake and whipped cream or custard. Sometimes tipsy pudding is garnished with almonds. (*see also* **trifle**)

tiramisù (tih ruh mee SOO) A rich Italian dessert made with layers of ladyfingers or sponge cake soaked in brandy and espresso and sweetened mascarpone cheese custard cream. Tiramisù is often garnished with whipped cream and shaved chocolate. (*see also* **cheese** *and* **ladyfinger**)

TIRAMISÙ

⅔ cup sugar
3 cups whipping cream, divided
2 large eggs
2 egg yolks
1 tablespoon all-purpose flour
½ vanilla bean, split
1 (16-ounce) package mascarpone cheese
¾ cup brewed espresso
3 tablespoons Marsala
2 (3-ounce) packages ladyfingers
3 tablespoons powdered sugar
1 tablespoon cocoa

• Stir together sugar, 2 cups cream, and next 4 ingredients in a heavy saucepan. Cook over medium heat, stirring constantly, 20 minutes or until thickened; cool. Discard vanilla bean. Whisk in mascarpone cheese.
• Stir together espresso and Marsala. Dip each ladyfinger in coffee mixture; place in a 13- x 9-inch dish. Pour mascarpone mixture over ladyfingers.
• Beat remaining 1 cup whipping cream at high speed with an electric mixer until foamy; gradually add powdered sugar, beating until soft peaks form. Spoon over mascarpone mixture, and sprinkle with cocoa. Cover and chill 2 hours. Yield: 10 servings.
Note: Prepare espresso by stirring together 1 cup hot water and ½ cup ground espresso coffee. Let stand 5 minutes; pour through a strainer lined with a coffee filter into a cup, discarding grounds. Yield: ¾ cup.

tisane (tih ZAN) Also known as herb tea, tisane is made by steeping any mixture of herbs, flowers, and spices in boiling water. It's usually consumed hot for its purported medicinal or calming and rejuvenating qualities. A wide selection of tisanes is available at most supermarkets. (*see also* **herbs** *and* **tea**)

toast The process of browning, crisping, or drying a food by exposing it to heat; coconut, nuts, and seeds are sometimes toasted. This term also refers to a slice of bread toasted in a toaster, under a broiler, or on a grill; toasting gives the bread a pleasant flavor and crisp texture. (*see also* **French toast**)

toddy (TOD ee) A warming drink made of whiskey, rum, or brandy, sugar, spices, lemon, and very hot water.

toffee (TAWF ee) This firm, but stick-to-your-teeth, candy is made with brown sugar or molasses, water or cream, and lots of butter. Sometimes toffee is topped with chocolate and sprinkled with chopped nuts.

PECAN TOFFEE

1½ cups chopped pecans, divided
1 cup sugar
1 cup butter, softened
⅓ cup water
5 (1.55-ounce) milk chocolate bars, broken into small pieces

• Line a 15- x 10-inch jellyroll pan with heavy-duty aluminum foil; lightly grease foil. Sprinkle foil with 1 cup pecans to within 1 inch of edges.
• Bring sugar, butter, and ⅓ cup water to a boil in a large heavy saucepan over medium heat, stirring constantly. Cook over medium-high heat, stirring constantly, 12 minutes or until a candy thermometer registers 310° (hard crack stage). Pour hot mixture over pecans; sprinkle with chocolate, and let stand 30 seconds. Sprinkle with remaining pecans. Chill 30 minutes.
• Break up toffee using a mallet or rolling pin. Store in an airtight container. Yield: 1¾ pounds.

tofu Also known as soybean curd, bean curd, or Chinese cheese, custard-like tofu is made from curdled soy milk, which is extracted from ground, cooked soybeans. Tofu has a slightly nutty, bland flavor, and the ability to take on the flavor of the foods with which it's cooked. Its texture is smooth and creamy. Tofu is available in several different degrees of firmness, depending on how much whey has been pressed out. It's sold in blocks packaged in water or vacuum-packed in most supermarkets. Tofu is used in a variety of Asian dishes including soups, stir-fries, and salads. It's healthful, easily digested, low in calories, and high in calcium and protein. **Storage:** Tofu is very perishable and should be refrigerated no more than a week. If packaged in water, drain it and cover again with fresh water. In fact, all tofu should be stored covered with water that should be changed daily. It can be frozen up to 3 months. (*see also* **bean curd** *and* **soybean**)

> **Q What does it mean when a recipe calls for drained and pressed tofu?**
>
> A Pressing out liquid gives the tofu a firmer texture and allows it to absorb more flavors. It can be drained, covered with paper towels and pressed, and stored overnight in the refrigerator. But the quickest way is to place it in a clean cloth dish towel or cheesecloth, twist the ends, and firmly wring out the moisture. The tofu will be pressed and crumbled in one step.

Toll House cookie The original chocolate chip cookie. It was created in the 1930s at the Toll House Restaurant outside Whitman, Massachusetts, and is still popular today.

tomalley (TOM al ee) The green-colored liver of a lobster; it's considered a delicacy and is often used to add flavor to sauces.

tomatillo (tohm ah TEE oh) Resembling a small green tomato partially wrapped in a wrinkled parchmentlike husk, tomatillos are an essential ingredient in Mexican and Tex-Mex foods, especially green salsa. They have a firm, crisp, pale yellow flesh and a tart, acidic, lemony, herbal flavor. Although tomatillos are not related to the tomato, they are sometimes called Mexican green tomatoes and are sold in Latin-American markets and some supermarkets. Most recipes call for tomatillos to be either poached in gently simmering water or roasted in a skillet; they're eaten raw in guacamole, salads, and sandwiches. **Storage:** Purchase those with dry, tight-fitting husks for longest shelf life, and keep in a plastic bag in the refrigerator up to 2 weeks. (*see also* **salsa; Tex-Mex;** *and* **verde, salsa**).

tomato (tuh MAY toh) Although it's typically used as a vegetable, the tomato is a fleshy fruit of a vine plant native to South America. The early Spanish thought that tomatoes were poisonous, while the French claimed the fruit had aphrodisiac powers and actually referred to it as a love apple. After finally gaining acceptance in the United States in the 1900s, the fruit has now achieved the status of being one of America's favorite foods. Today, there are many varieties of tomatoes available. Among them are the:

- **Beefsteak** tomato, which is large, bright red, and delicious both raw and cooked.
- **Globe** tomatoes are medium-sized, firm, and juicy; they can be served raw or cooked.
- **Plum** tomatoes, also called **Italian Roma**

Southernism

One of the most beloved Southern rites of summer is eating the first tomato sandwich. This delicacy requires white bread, though some have converted to whole wheat in the interest of health—slathered with mayonnaise (you'll find passionate discussion about which brand is best), sprinkled with salt and pepper, and consumed over the kitchen sink to catch the drips.

TEST KITCHEN SECRET

To peel a large number of tomatoes, cut a small X at the base of each and drop into a pot of boiling water just until the skins begin to loosen (about 10 to 15 seconds). Remove the tomatoes with a sieve, tongs, or long fork, and hold under cold running water. The peels practically slip off! LYDA JONES

tomatoes, are egg-shaped, red or yellow, thick and meaty with small seeds, have little juice, and a mild, rich flavor. They are especially good for canning and in sauces.

beefsteak

plum

cherry

pear

• **Cherry** tomatoes are about an inch in diameter and can be red or yellow. They are popular for eating in salads or for using as a garnish. They can also be sautéed with herbs for a side dish.
• **Pear** tomatoes or **grape** tomatoes are slightly smaller than cherry tomatoes and have red or yellow skin and a mild, sweet flavor.
• **Green** tomatoes have a firm texture, mild flavor, and are excellent fried, broiled, or added to relishes.

Fresh tomatoes are available year-round, but are at their peak from June through September. The most prized tomatoes are vine-ripened on tomato plants, though they can also be purchased from roadside stands and some produce markets. There's no comparison between these and the tomatoes that have been commercially grown, picked green, and artificially ripened; these never come close in texture, aroma, or taste. Other popular tomato products that are available include dried tomatoes, canned tomatoes, tomato paste, tomato puree, and tomato sauce.
Storage: If fresh tomatoes need to ripen, store them at room temperature in a brown paper bag with an apple for several days. Once ripened, tomatoes can be stored at room temperature up to 3 days. To keep them from getting overripe, they can be refrigerated, but it significantly reduces the quality of their flavor and texture. Freezing and canning yield goods results, but only if you will be using them in a cooked mixture. (*see also* **beefsteak tomato, dried tomato, tomato juice, tomato paste,** *and* **tomato sauce**)

TEST KITCHEN SECRET

"*When tomatoes are out of season, consider using Roma or plum tomatoes. They offer quality flavor and texture, even during the winter months. John Floyd, the editor of* Southern Living, *recommends adding a squeeze of lemon juice to tomatoes out of season to increase their acidity and flavor.*" MARGARET MONROE DICKEY

READER TIP
"*An easy way to seed a tomato is to cut it in half crosswise; then take each half in your hand and gently squeeze, removing the seeds with your fingers or a spoon.*" J.W., Charlottesville, VA

tomato juice A tangy, slightly sweet, thick liquid obtained by blending the pulp and juice of a tomato. (*see also* **tomato**)

tomato paste Thick paste made from tomatoes that have been cooked, strained, and reduced to a rich concentrate. Tomato paste is often used to add flavor and to thicken soups and sauces. The paste is available in cans and tubes, and can be found in most supermarkets. (*see also* **tomato**)

tomato sauce One of the five French mother sauces; a slightly thinned tomato purée, which is sometimes seasoned with herbs, onions, or peppers, and used as a base for other sauces, as a flavoring for soups, or as a topping for meat loaf. (*see also* **mother sauces** *and* **tomato**)

Tom Collins (*see* **collins**)

tonic water (TAHN ik) Water that has been infused with carbon dioxide to create effervescence; it's also flavored with fruit extracts, sugar, and a small amount of quinine, which is a bitter alkaloid. Tonic water is typically used as a mixer when making cocktails such as gin and tonic.

torta (TOHR tuh) An Italian term that means tart, pie, or cake. In Spanish, it means cake, loaf, or sandwich. Sometimes Mexicans use this term to describe a dish composed of savory pudding sandwiched between stacked tortillas. (*see also* **tortilla**)

torte (TOHRT) German for a rich cake made with ground nuts or breadcrumbs instead of flour. Some tortes are made in a single layer, while others are multilayered and filled with whipped cream, jam, or buttercream. Occasionally, a tart is referred to as a torte. (*see also* **linzertorte** *and* **Sachertorte**)

TIMESAVING TIP

A quick way to decorate a cake-type torte is to place a paper doily on top of the cake, and then dust or sift powdered sugar or cocoa powder over the top. Carefully lift the doily straight up and off the cake.

tortellini (tohr tl EE nee) Italian for a type of pasta shaped into small circles, folded over a cheese or meat stuffing, and wrapped around a finger into a circle. The pasta is typically either poached and served separately or served in a broth or sauce. Tortellini can be purchased dry or frozen. (*see also* **pasta**)

CREAMY TOMATO PESTO DIP WITH TORTELLINI

4 quarts water
1 (9-ounce) package refrigerated
  mushroom tortellini
1 (9-ounce) package refrigerated
  spinach tortellini
1 (9-ounce) package refrigerated
  tomato tortellini
12 dried tomatoes
1 (8-ounce) package cream
  cheese, softened
1 (7-ounce) jar roasted sweet red
  peppers, drained

½ cup shredded Parmesan cheese
2 garlic cloves, minced
6 fresh basil leaves
2 tablespoons olive oil
1 tablespoon lemon juice
¾ teaspoon salt
¼ teaspoon dried crushed red
  pepper
Green and ripe olives (optional)

• Bring 4 quarts water to a boil in a stockpot.
• Add pasta, and cook over medium-high heat 5 minutes. Rinse with cold water. Drain; chill, if desired.
• Place dried tomatoes in a bowl, and cover with boiling water. Let stand 20 minutes. Drain.
• Process tomatoes, cream cheese, and next 8 ingredients in a food processor or blender until smooth, stopping to scrape down sides. Spoon pesto into a large bowl, and sprinkle with olives, if desired. Serve with tortellini. Yield: 20 appetizer servings.

tortilla (tohr TEE yuh) Flat, thin, round, unleavened Mexican bread made from either corn flour (masa) or wheat flour. Tortillas are patted out by hand or pressed in a tortilla press, and baked on a griddle or in a skillet. They are the basis of countless classic Mexican dishes such as tacos, enchiladas, and burritos. Both corn and flour tortillas are sold prepackaged in the refrigerated section of most supermarkets. (see also **burrito, chalupa, masa, taco, Tex-Mex,** and **tortilla press**)

Q Is there a real difference between corn and flour tortillas?

A Corn tortillas are made from ground corn flour called masa; they have a coarser texture and are smaller than flour tortillas. Flour tortillas, made from wheat flour, are whiter, have a smoother texture and are larger than corn tortillas.

TEST KITCHEN SECRET

To heat corn or flour tortillas, wrap them in aluminum foil or put them in a clay tortilla warmer, and heat at 325° for 10 minutes. They can also be heated in the microwave oven; place up to 4 in an unsealed, heavy-duty zip-top plastic bag, and microwave at HIGH for 30 to 45 seconds or until thoroughly heated. JAMES SCHEND

RESCUE for leftover tortillas:

Don't throw away leftover tortillas; cut into triangles or thin strips, and fry or bake them to top a salad or soup, or sprinkle them over your favorite casserole.

tortilla press A metal utensil used to flatten tortilla dough into tortillas. The press has two hinged disks; the top disk is lowered over the ball of dough resting on the lower disk. (*see also* **tortilla**)

tortoni (tohr TOH nee) An Italian frozen dessert made with whipped cream or ice cream. Tortoni is flavored with rum or sherry and topped with macaroon crumbs or ground almonds. Sometimes known as biscuit tortoni, this dessert is typically served in small paper cups. (*see also* **macaroon**)

toss To lightly mix ingredients by turning them over several times with two large spoons or your hands. For example, salads greens are often tossed with salad dressing.

tostada (toh STAH duh) A crisp-fried tortilla topped with refried beans, shredded chicken or beef, and garnished with lettuce, cheese, tomatoes, sour cream, guacamole, and salsa. You'll enjoy the meatless version that follows. (*see also* **tortilla**)

CHICKPEA-CHIPOTLE TOSTADAS

Vegetable oil
12 corn tortillas
1 medium onion, chopped
½ red bell pepper, chopped
2 garlic cloves, chopped
1 tablespoon olive oil
1½ (15-ounce) cans chickpeas, rinsed and drained
1 cup chicken broth
2 tablespoons chopped fresh cilantro
2 chipotle peppers in adobo sauce, minced*
½ teaspoon salt
2 tablespoons fresh lime juice
1 (8-ounce) container sour cream
½ cup salsa verde or green chile sauce*
½ head iceberg lettuce, shredded
6 plum tomatoes, chopped
5 ounces reduced-fat feta cheese, crumbled

• Pour vegetable oil to a depth of 2 inches into a large skillet. Heat to 375°. Fry tortillas, 1 at a time, over medium-high heat 30 seconds on each side or until crisp and lightly browned. Drain and keep warm.
• Sauté onion, bell pepper, and garlic in hot olive oil in a large skillet over medium-high heat 5 minutes or until tender. Add chickpeas and next 4 ingredients; bring to a boil. Reduce heat, and simmer 5 minutes.
• Process chickpea mixture in a food processor or with a hand blender until smooth. Return mixture to skillet. Simmer, stirring occasionally, until very thick. Stir in lime juice; cook 2 to 3 minutes.
• Stir together sour cream and salsa. Spread chickpea mixture evenly over tortillas. Top evenly with lettuce and tomato. Drizzle with sour cream mixture, and sprinkle with cheese. Serve immediately. Yield: 6 servings.

*Substitute 2 canned jalapeño peppers and 2 drops of liquid smoke for chipotle peppers, and substitute ½ cup regular salsa for salsa verde, if desired.

tournedo (TOOR nih doh) Thick slices from a beef tenderloin that are lean, tender, flavorful, and smaller than a filet mignon. Sometimes tournedos are wrapped in bacon prior to grilling or broiling; they are often sautéed in butter and served on a crouton or round piece of fried bread and topped with mushroom sauce. (*see also* **beef, filet mignon,** *and* **tenderloin**)

tree ear mushroom (*see* **mushroom**)

trichinella (TRIK in el la) A type of parasite that can be ingested through undercooked meat, especially pork. Today, virtually all pork is free of trichinella, but it's still recommended that it be cooked to 160°. (*see also* **food safety** *and* **pork**)

trifle (TRY fuhl) A layered English dessert typically served from a deep trifle dish and made of sponge cake, pound cake, ladyfingers, or cookies soaked in liqueur or sherry. This is topped with layers of jam or fruit and a layer of custard. Trifle is usually crowned with whipped cream and garnished with fruit, nuts, or grated chocolate.

> **TIMESAVING TIP**
> Shortcut versions of trifle rely on frozen whipped topping or whipped cream, packaged pudding mixes, and a variety of fruits or sweets with or without liqueurs.

BANANA PUDDING TRIFLE

1⅓ cups sugar	¼ cup bourbon
¾ cup all-purpose flour	2 tablespoons rum
½ teaspoon salt	6 ripe bananas, sliced
4 cups milk	6 (1.4-ounce) English toffee
8 egg yolks	candy bars, crushed
1 tablespoon vanilla extract	2 cups whipping cream
1 (12-ounce) package vanilla	2 tablespoons powdered sugar
wafers	

• Combine first 3 ingredients in a large heavy saucepan; whisk in milk. Bring to a boil over medium heat, whisking constantly. Remove from heat.
• Beat egg yolks until thick and pale. Gradually stir one-fourth of hot mixture into yolks; add to remaining hot mixture, stirring constantly. Cook, stirring constantly, 1 minute. Stir in vanilla.
• Layer one-third of wafers in a 16-cup trifle bowl or 4-quart baking dish. Combine bourbon and rum; brush over wafers. Top with one-third of banana. Spoon one-third of custard over banana, and sprinkle with ⅓ cup crushed candy bar. Repeat layers twice.
• Beat cream at medium speed with an electric mixer until foamy; gradually add powdered sugar, beating until soft peaks form. Spread whipped cream over trifle, and sprinkle with remaining crushed candy bar. Cover and chill 3 hours. Yield: 10 to 12 servings.

tripe (TRYP) The lining of beef stomachs, though pork and lamb tripe are also occasionally available. There are multiple stomach chambers and several kinds of tripe, all of which are tough and require long simmering. Fresh tripe has been cleaned and parboiled before it's packaged; canned and pickled tripe is also available. Tripe has little flavor, and when simmered, develops a gelatinous quality. (*see also* **variety meats**)

Triple Sec (TRIH pl sehk) Clear, strong, orange liqueur used to make cocktails. (*see also* **liqueur**)

triticale (triht ih KAY lee) A hybrid wheat and rye cereal grain with a full, nutty flavor. Triticale is available in whole berries, flakes, and flour, and can be found in health food stores and some supermarkets. The berries can be cooked and used in casseroles or pilaf. The flour is low in gluten, so it's usually combined with wheat flour if used for bread making. (*see also* **grain**)

trivet (TRIHV iht) A flat, short-legged object placed under a hot dish to protect the surface of a table.

trout (TROWT) A large group of fish that are related to the salmon family and found primarily in freshwater lakes and streams, though they are sometimes farm-raised. Trout generally have a firm white, orange, or pink flesh with a medium- to high-fat content. There are many different species, but some of the most common are rainbow trout, brook or speckled trout, steelhead trout, and brown trout. They can be purchased fresh or frozen, whole, or in fillets. They can be pan-fried, poached, baked, grilled, or broiled. Canned, smoked, and kippered trout are also available in some supermarkets. (*see also* **fish**)

Southernism

The Appalachian Mountains are famous for their cold, clear trout steams. In fact, this region has become known for its emerging aquaculture businesses that raise trout to ship worldwide. For information on where to buy this farm-raised delicacy, visit **www.ustfa.org** *or call 1-304-728-2189.*

truffle (TRUHF uhl) A rich, French candy made of melted chocolate, butter or cream, sugar, and various flavorings such as liqueur, coffee, and nuts. After the mixture cools, it's rolled into balls and coated with cocoa powder, chocolate sprinkles, or sugar; some are dipped into melted white or dark chocolate for a hard coating. Another type of truffle is an edible fungus that's grown underground near oak trees and is highly prized for its earthy aroma and delicate flavor. These truffles are round, irregularly shaped, and have thick, rough, wrinkled skin. The main varieties are the dark brown or black truffle of France and the white truffle of Italy; they are rare and expensive. Canned truffles, truffle paste, sometimes frozen truffles, and truffle oil are available in gourmet specialty stores. Used sparingly, dark truffles can be thinly sliced and added to pâtés, omelets, risottos, and sauces; white truffles are usually grated over cooked pasta, polenta, or risotto.

CHOCOLATE-PRALINE TRUFFLES

3 (4-ounce) semisweet chocolate
   bars, broken into pieces
¼ cup whipping cream

3 tablespoons butter, cut up
2 tablespoons almond liqueur
Praline Pecans

• Microwave chocolate and whipping cream in a 2-quart microwave safe bowl at MEDIUM (50% power) 3½ minutes.
• Whisk until chocolate melts and mixture is smooth. (If chocolate doesn't melt completely, microwave and whisk at 15-second intervals until melted.) Whisk in butter and liqueur; let stand 20 minutes.
• Beat at medium speed with an electric mixer 4 minutes or until mixture forms soft peaks. (Do not overbeat.) Cover and chill at least 4 hours.
• Shape mixture into 1-inch balls; roll in Praline Pecans. Cover and chill up to 1 week, or freeze up to 1 month. Yield: about 2 dozen.

TEST KITCHEN SECRET

Some older truffle candy recipes call for using raw egg yolks to give the candies a creamy texture. This actually isn't necessary because butter and whipping cream make them very smooth. However, if you want to use an older recipe, be sure to add an egg substitute rather than raw eggs. LYDA JONES

Note: We used Ghirardelli semisweet chocolate bars. Substitute 2 cups (12 ounces) Hershey's semisweet chocolate morsels for semisweet chocolate bars, if desired.

PRALINE PECANS

1½ cups chopped pecans
¼ cup firmly packed light brown
   sugar

2 tablespoons whipping cream

• Stir together all ingredients; spread in a lightly buttered 9-inch round cakepan.
• Bake at 350° for 20 minutes or until coating appears slightly crystallized, stirring once. Remove from oven; stir and cool. Store in an airtight container. Yield: about 1½ cups.

Praline Almonds: Substitute 1½ cups chopped sliced blanched almonds for pecans. Bake at 350° for 15 minutes, stirring once. Yield: about 1½ cups.

truss (TRUHS) To tie poultry or meat with twine or secure with skewers or pins in order to preserve shape and to improve appearance during cooking. A long trussing needle can be used if the bird or meat is to be secured with twine. (*see also* **poultry**)

tube pan (*see* **baking dishes and pans**)

tulipe (too LEEP) A thin, crisp French wafer cookie that forms a ruffled cuplike shape when it's placed in a cup mold such as a muffin tin or custard cup while still warm. Tulipe cups can be used as edible containers for ice cream, berries, and other desserts.

tuna (TOO nuh) A large saltwater fish that's a member of the mackerel family. Tuna generally have a tender, firm-textured, rich-flavored flesh that's moderate to high in fat. The main varieties of tuna are: Albacore, the mildest tuna and the only type that can be called "white," is the most expensive canned tuna. Yellowfin tuna has a light flesh and a slightly stronger flavor than albacore. Bluefin tuna has a darker flesh and a stronger flavor as it matures. Bonito tuna is the strongest flavored of all tunas. Many Japanese recipes use dried bonito or dashi. Fresh tuna is plentiful during spring, summer, and early fall, but frozen and canned tuna is available year-round. Canned tuna is also available packed in water or oil.

Storage: Store fresh tuna in a plastic bag, and place on a bed of crushed ice and refrigerate up to 24 hours. (*see also* **dashi** *and* **fish**)

turbinado sugar (tur bih NAH doh) Raw sugar that has been steam-cleaned, leaving coarse, blond crystals that have a delicate molasses flavor. (*see also* **sugar**)

turbot (TER boh) A flatfish found in waters off Iceland to the Mediterranean; it has a firm, lean, white flesh and mild flavor. Many think turbot rivals the quality of Dover sole, but true turbot is usually imported frozen to the United States. It can be poached, baked, broiled, or fried. (*see also* **fish**)

tureen (too REEN) A large, covered ceramic container with handles and a notched lid for a ladle. Soup or stew is served from a tureen at the dining table.

turkey A principal USDA-recognized poultry that's especially popular during the holiday season but also served year-round. A typical-sized roast turkey offers a plentiful amount of both white and dark meat; most range in size from 5 to 20 pounds. If you want just white meat, buy turkey breasts. Dark meat fans can find turkey drumsticks and wings sold separately. Some whole turkeys have built-in plastic thermometers that pop up when the turkey is done. Self-basting turkeys have been injected with butter, vegetable oil, or saline solution. Smoked turkey and canned boned turkey also are available. Other forms of turkey found in the supermarket include tenderloins, cutlets, ground turkey, luncheon meats, and sausages.

Storage: Fresh turkeys should be stored in the coldest part of your refrigerator up to 2 days. Frozen whole turkeys can be stored up to a year in the freezer. If they have been purchased frozen, turkeys do not need to be rewrapped before being frozen again. However, fresh and frozen turkey and turkey pieces need to be rewrapped in freezer wrap or placed in freezer bags before being frozen up to 6 months. Always chill leftover turkey meat, stuffing or dressing, and gravy separately. You can keep cooked turkey in the refrigerator up to 2 days. Leftover meat can also be frozen. (*continued on the following page*)

BUYING GUIDE

The following amounts should allow ample turkey for Thanksgiving plus leftovers to enjoy later.

TYPE OF TURKEY	SERVINGS PER POUND
Whole, up to 12 pounds*	1 pound per person
Whole, over 12 pounds	¾ pound per person
Bone-in Breast	½ pound per person
Boneless Breast or Roll	⅓ pound per person

*For prestuffed turkeys, add an extra ¼ pound per person.

RESCUE for cooks with turkey questions: Contact the USDA Meat and Poultry Hotline at 1-800-535-4555, the Butterball Turkey Hotline at 1-800-BUTTERBALL or **butterball.com**, or visit the National Turkey Federation at **eatturkey.com**

Carving a Turkey

Let the cooked turkey "rest," covered with aluminum foil, 10 to 15 minutes before carving. Make sure you have a sharp knife so you can produce pretty slices. Carve the bird, breast side up, on a cutting board in the kitchen or on a serving platter at the table.

Uncover the turkey, remove stuffing, and transfer to a serving bowl. Grasp the end of a drumstick, and pull it away from the body. Cut through the skin and meat between the thigh and body (illustration 1); bend the leg away from bird to expose leg joint. Slice through joint, and remove the leg.

Cut through joint that separates the thigh and drumstick. Slice dark meat from leg and thigh rather than placing them whole on the serving platter.

Q **What is the best way to thaw a frozen turkey?**

A The best way to let a turkey thaw is in the refrigerator—and this may take several days depending on the weight of the bird. Thawing in the refrigerator instead of at room temperature is the safest method to use because it reduces the risk of bacterial growth. Leave the turkey in its original wrapper, place it in a pan to catch any juices, and refrigerate until it's thawed. Allow 2 to 4 days for thawing. A 4- to 12-pound bird will take 1 to 2 days to thaw; a 12- to 20-pound bird will take 2 to 3 days; and a 20- to 24-pound turkey will take up to 4 days to thaw. Once thawed, a turkey should be cooked immediately.

To carve the breast meat, steady the bird with a carving fork, and make a deep horizontal cut just above the wing. Beginning at the outer top edge of breast, cut thin slices from the top down to the horizontal cut (illustration 2). If the wing tips were twisted under the turkey before roasting, carve the whole turkey without removing the wings; otherwise, remove them by cutting through the joints where the wings and backbone meet. Save the carcass to make broth for soup; it can be stored in the freezer up to 4 months. (*see also* **poultry** *and* **stuffing**)

Turkish coffee Strong coffee served in small cups; it's ground as fine as flour, combined with sugar and water in a long-handled, lipped coffee pot called an "ibrik," and boiled three times before it's served. (*see also* **coffee**)

turmeric (TUR muh rihk) A bright yellow powdery spice, sometimes referred to as Indian saffron, produced from the root of a tropical plant related to ginger. Turmeric has a strong, bitter flavor and is used to add color and flavor to Indian and Middle Eastern dishes. Turmeric is usually an ingredient in curry preparations; it's also a main ingredient in mustard because it contributes to the bright yellow color. (*see also* **spice**)

READER TIP

"Saffron is so expensive that I sometimes substitute turmeric, especially when color is more important than flavor. Just a pinch of turmeric adds the same color to food as saffron." A.L., Little Rock, AR

turnip A round root vegetable with white skin, a purple-tinged top, and creamy white flesh. Young turnips have a mild, crisp, sweet flavor, but as they age, they develop a stronger flavor and coarser texture. The roots should be washed and peeled, and can then be boiled and mashed, or roasted and pureed; they can also be cubed and tossed with butter or used raw in salads. Turnip greens, the leafy top of the vegetable, have a slightly bitter flavor and can be cooked in a variety of ways, including boiling, sautéing, steaming, and stir-frying. Turnips are generally available year-round, but are best during cold weather months.

Storage: Turnips can be refrigerated in a plastic bag for 1 to 2 weeks. Wash fresh greens in cold water, and pat dry; place them in a plastic bag lined with moist paper towels, and store in the refrigerator up to 3 days. (*see also* **greens** *and* **pot liquor**)

TEST KITCHEN SECRET

To avoid an off-taste when cooking turnip greens, use a stainless steel pan; aluminum pans turn the greens a dark color and impart a metallic taste. Adding a teaspoon of sugar, a bit of wine, or cooking in chicken broth imparts a pleasant flavor and minimizes any bitterness. MARGARET MONROE DICKEY

Southernism

In the South, turnip greens are popular soul food. They're typically boiled, often with a piece of ham hock or salt pork for flavoring. Contemporary recipes call for a shorter cooking time and may add a splash of wine. Whatever your flavoring choices, don't pass up the cooking liquid or "pot likker"—it's almost as good as the greens.

---

turnover A round or square piece of pastry dough that's folded in half over a sweet or savory filling; when folded, the dough forms a semicircle or triangle. Turnovers can be baked or deep-fried. They can range in size

TIMESAVING TIP

In a hurry for a turnover? Use refrigerated pie pastry dough. It's already rolled out; just cut into shapes, and fill with several spoonfuls of canned pie filling.

from small to large, and can be served as an appetizer, entrée, or dessert.

turtle A type of reptile that lives in fresh water (called terrapin), saltwater (the sea or green turtle), or on land (called tortoise), and has a shell covering its body. For culinary purposes, those turtles from fresh or brackish water are considered to have the best meat and are eaten the most often; these include snapping turtles, soft-shell turtles, and diamond-back turtles. Turtle meat is sometimes pounded and served like steak, but by far the most outstanding dish is turtle soup. Turtle meat can be difficult to come by; it's sometimes found canned or frozen in specialty food stores. That's why, more often than not, mock turtle soup is served rather than the real thing. On a sweeter note, Southerners love turtle candies made with peanuts or pecans smothered in caramel and dipped in milk chocolate.

turtle beans (*see* **beans, dried;** *and* **black beans**)

tutti-frutti (TOO tee FROO tee) A term used to describe either an ice cream or a dessert composed of a variety of mixed candied fruits. This term also refers to a fruity flavoring used in candy and gum.

Twelfth-Night cake
A rich British spice cake traditionally served on January 6, the twelfth day after Christmas. The cake is typically made with candied fruits, almonds, and almond paste.

twice-baked A term that refers to a food product that's baked, then reworked, and baked a second time such as twice-baked potatoes, biscotti, or zwieback. In twice-baked potatoes, the potato is baked until tender, then the pulp is removed, mashed, seasoned, and piled into the shell to bake a second time. In making biscotti or zwieback, the dough is baked in a loaf, and then cut into slices, and baked again. (*see also* **biscotti, potato,** *and* **zwieback**)

READER TIP
"When I make twice-baked potatoes, I've found it helpful to use a grapefruit spoon to scoop the pulp from the baked potatoes; it makes a clean cut and removes the pulp without tearing the skins." C.B., Greensburg, KY

BACON-STUFFED POTATOES

4 large baking potatoes, baked	1 cup (4 ounces) shredded
½ cup butter or margarine	Cheddar cheese
½ cup whipping cream	1 tablespoon grated onion
6 slices bacon, cooked and	1½ teaspoons salt
crumbled	Paprika

• Cut a 1-inch-wide strip from top of each baked potato. Carefully scoop out pulp, leaving shells intact.
• Mash potato pulp with butter and whipping cream; stir in bacon and next 3 ingredients. Spoon evenly into shells, and place on a baking sheet. Sprinkle with paprika.
• Bake at 425° for 15 minutes. Yield: 4 servings.

Tyler pie A rich pie or tart named for President John Tyler. The pie, sometimes called Tyler pudding pie, is made with brown sugar, butter, cream, and eggs, and is sometimes topped with grated nutmeg or coconut.

tzimmes (TSEHM mehs) A Jewish casserole of sweet stew traditionally served on Rosh Hashanah or Passover. Tzimmes may include various root vegetables, dried or fresh fruit, and beef brisket, and is usually sweetened with honey and cinnamon.

udon (oo DOHN) Flat, ribbonlike Japanese wheat noodles, sold dried, fresh, or pre-cooked in some Asian markets. (*see also* **Asian noodle**)

ugli fruit (UHG lee) A large citrus fruit thought to be a cross between a grapefruit and a tangerine. Grown in Jamaica, it has a very thick, yellow-green loose skin, yellow-orange flesh, and a flavor reminiscent of mandarin oranges, honey, and pineapple. They're hard to find, but are sometimes available from winter to spring, and are usually eaten raw. (*see also* **citrus fruit**)

unbleached flour Wheat flour that has not been treated with a whitening agent; use it interchangeably with all-purpose flour. (*see also* **flour**)

United States Department of Agriculture (USDA) The

United States Department of Agriculture (USDA) is a department of the executive branch of the federal government; one of its main responsibilities is to make sure that foods are safe, wholesome, and accurately labeled. The USDA provides food inspection and grading procedures as well as other services for food producers and consumers.

TEST KITCHEN SECRET

We stay current with the latest food safety recommendations of the USDA and suggest that you should, too. Visit **www.fsis.usda.gov** *or call* 1-800-535-4555 *for more information.* LYDA JONES

Universal Product Code (UPC) A code consisting of numbers

and linear symbols printed on packaged items to identify the product, manufacturer, distributor, contents, and price. The code can be scanned directly into a cash register for sales and inventory purposes.

unleavened bread Unleavened bread, made without a leavening agent, is typically dry and hard. Familiar kinds of unleavened breads include water crackers, tortillas and Jewish matzo. Jews observe "The Feast of Unleavened Bread," which occurs immediately after Passover. (*see also* **matzo** *and* **tortilla**)

unmold To remove food from a container or mold in which it was cooked or congealed. For example, salads or desserts containing gelatin might be unmolded from a pan or shaped mold just as cooked cakes, muffins, and breads are unmolded from their baking pans. Fragile items are easier to unmold if the pan is coated with cooking spray.

TEST KITCHEN SECRET

Removing a congealed salad from a mold can be tricky. To make it easier, spray the mold with cooking spray before filling. To unmold, run a spatula around edges of the mold to let air underneath. Next, wet a dish towel with hot water, and wring out the excess. Wrap towel around the bottom and sides of mold, and let it stand 1 minute (not too long or the salad will start to melt). Invert a serving plate over the salad and carefully flip the mold and plate over, and lift off the mold. JAN MOON

upside-down cake Similar to a tarte tatin, an upside-down cake is made by sprinkling butter and brown sugar in a cake pan, and then topping with decoratively arranged fruit over which cake batter is poured. As the cake bakes, the sugar and butter melt and glaze the fruit. To serve, the cake is inverted and removed from the pan, and the glazed fruit becomes the topping of the cake. The most well known upside-down cake is made with pineapple, but other types of fruit could be used. (*see also* **pineapple** *and* **tarte Tatin**)

Southernism

The ideal upside-down cake is baked in the truest of Southern utensils, the cast-iron skillet. A well-seasoned skillet won't allow the sugary topping of the cake to stick, and its thick sides invite even cooking of the cake batter.

Valencia orange (vuh LEHN she uh) A sweet, juicy, almost seedless orange with thin, deep golden skin that's difficult to peel. Valencias can be eaten out of hand or squeezed for juice. (*see also* **orange**)

vanilla (vuh NIHL uh) A flavoring that comes from the long, slender bean or pod of an orchid plant. Vanilla comes in the following forms:
• Vanilla **extract** is made by chopping vanilla beans, soaking them in a mixture of alcohol and water, and then aging the solution. To be classified as "pure," the extract must contain 13.35 ounces of vanilla beans per gallon and be at least 35 percent alcohol. The extract is brown and very fragrant.
• **Imitation** vanilla is made from an artificial form of vanillin (the primary flavor component in the vanilla bean). It's sweeter and less aromatic than a pure extract and can have a bitter aftertaste. It's an inexpensive substitute for vanilla extract.
• Vanilla **flavoring** refers to a blend of pure vanilla extract and imitation vanilla. Its price and quality fall between that of vanilla extract and imitation vanilla.
• Vanilla **beans** can be purchased in bulk or individually; they are dark brown, shriveled, and about the size of a pencil; after use, they can usually be rinsed, dried, and stored for reuse.
Storage: Vanilla extract, imitation vanilla, and vanilla flavoring can be kept in a cool, dark place up to a year. Vanilla beans can be stored in an airtight container up to 6 months. (*see also* **extracts, flavoring,** *and* **vanilla bean**)

VANILLA EXTRACT

6 vanilla beans, divided	1 cup sugar
1 quart vodka	½ cup water

• Cut each of 3 vanilla beans into 4 pieces; split each piece lengthwise. Place in a 1½-quart bottle; add vodka.
• Cover tightly, and shake vigorously. Let stand in a cool, dry place 3 weeks, shaking bottle every 2 days.

• Line a funnel with a coffee filter; pour mixture through funnel into a bowl, discarding beans.

• Cook sugar and water in a small saucepan over medium-high heat, stirring occasionally, 2 to 3 minutes or until sugar dissolves. Remove from heat; cool completely. Add to vodka mixture.

• Cut remaining 3 vanilla beans into pieces. Fill small decorative bottles with 1 vanilla bean piece and extract; cover tightly, and let stand in a cool, dry place 1 month. Yield: 4½ cups.

vanilla bean The dried, cured podlike fruit of a tropical orchid plant. The moist, pliable pods contain many tiny black seeds, which, along with the pod, are used for flavoring. To use the whole bean, cut it in half lengthwise, scrape out the seeds, and add them, with the pod, to the dish you are preparing. Strain the vanilla bean before serving the flavored food.
Storage: Keep beans in an airtight container in a cool, dark place up to 6 months. (*see* **vanilla**)

vanilla sugar (*see Test Kitchen Secret under* **vanilla**)

varietal wine (vuh RY ih tl) A labeling term that describes wines made from one primary grape or a blend of grapes. American varietal wines tend to be named after the variety of grape from which they are made, while European wines tend to be named for the region or location from which they are made. (*see also* **wine**)

variety meats A term that describes the edible organs and extremities of beef, veal, lamb, and pork. Variety meats include the brains, pig's feet, chitterlings (hog intestines), heart, kidneys, liver, sweetbreads (thymus glands), tongue, testicles, and tripe (stomach wall). (*see also* **chitterlings, kidney, liver, sweetbreads,** *and* **tripe**)

veal Meat from calves that are from 1 to 3 months old. Veal has a mild flavor that makes it suitable for recipes that include high-flavored sauces, rich seasonings, and spicy coatings. Veal requires careful cooking because its lack of fat can cause it to become tough and dry. Veal roasts and shanks respond best to slow cooking by moist heat methods. Covering veal at least part of the time during cooking is recommended to maximize tenderness. Veal cuts such as chops, cutlets, and scallops, however, are best when quickly pan-fried.

Selecting: Veal is usually very lean, has no marbling, and little external fat. Good veal is pale pink; in fact, the redder the meat, the older the veal. Bones should be porous and red. Any visible fat should be very pale. You may find prime and choice veal at the supermarket. Prime veal, the highest quality, has usually been milk-fed. Choice veal has usually been grain-fed.

VEAL CUTS

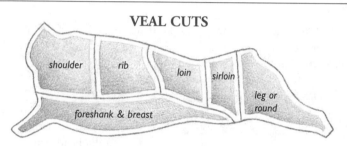

Veal is first divided into wholesale cuts from which smaller pieces of meat are carved for sale in supermarkets. The cuts closely resemble those of beef, but they're smaller in scale. Nearly all veal cuts are naturally tender because it comes from such a young animal.

- **Shoulder:** The source of shoulder, arm, and blade roasts for roasting, braising, or stewing as well as for cubed stewing veal. Boneless shoulder roasts are also available.

- **Rib:** Is sold as whole rib roast for roasting and is also cut into individual chops for grilling, broiling, or braising.

- **Loin:** Yields whole loin roast for roasting or individual loin chops for grilling, broiling, or braising.

- **Sirloin:** Is sold as sirloin roasts for roasting or sirloin steaks for braising, pan-frying, or broiling.

- **Leg or Round:** The source of veal cutlets and scallops for rapid sautéing, rump roasts for roasting, or round steaks for braising or pan-frying. It's also the source for boneless leg of veal.

Foreshank and breast: The foreshank is cut crosswise into thick, round, bone-in shanks used in traditional osso buco. The breast is the source of boned whole breast roast and boned rolled breast for stuffing, roasting, and braising.

loin chops

sirloin steak

shoulder roast

rib roast

shanks

Storage: Remove veal from its wrapping, and rewrap it in wax paper. Veal can be stored in the refrigerator up to 2 days or frozen 6 to 9 months. (*see also* **Oscar; osso buco; parmigiana, à la; piccata; scaloppine; schnitzel;** *and* **veal Oscar**)

TIMETABLE FOR ROASTING VEAL

CUT	APPROXIMATE WEIGHT IN POUNDS	APPROXIMATE TOTAL COOKING TIMES IN MINUTES PER POUND AT 325° (160° INTERNAL TEMPERATURE)
Rib roast	3 to 5	25 to 30
Loin	3 to 4	34 to 36
Sirloin	6 to 8	25 to 30
Boneless shoulder or rump	3 to 6	30 to 35

veal Oscar (OS kuhr) Named in honor of Sweden's King Oscar II, who was partial to this dish made of sautéed veal cutlets topped with asparagus, crabmeat, and béarnaise sauce. (*see also* **béarnaise sauce, cutlet, Oscar,** *and* **veal**)

veau (VOH) The French term for veal.

vegetable cooking spray Canned oil that has been packed under pressure, is dispersed by a propellant, and used to grease pots, pans, baking dishes, and grill racks. Most cooking sprays are mixtures of soybean or canola oil, lecithin, water, and a propellant. Some also contain flour, which is convenient for use on cake pans, but not for sautéing. Olive oil cooking spray is also available; it's ideal for sautéing onions and peppers but is not recommended for using with baked goods because it burns at lower temperatures plus it adds a distinct olive oil flavor. (*see also* **fats and oils** *and* **sauté**)

TEST KITCHEN SECRET

Never aim cooking spray toward an open flame or gas grill or burner; remove grill racks, and spray before starting the fire. Because cooking spray contains a propellant, the flame could travel back up the stream of spray and cause serious injuries or damage. JAN MOON

LITE BITE

When you're watching your fat intake, cooking spray is the best choice for lightly greasing a pan. We go by the guideline that 3 sprays is roughly equivalent to 1 teaspoon shortening. Here's how their content compares:

TYPE FAT	CALORIES	CHOLESTEROL	FAT GRAMS
3 sprays cooking spray	6	0	negligible
1 teaspoon shortening	38	0	4.3

vegetable oil (*see* **fats and oils**)

vegetable peeler A knifelike kitchen utensil that usually has a swivel blade designed to thinly peel the outer skins of vegetables. Blades may be vertical or horizontal.

vegetables The edible portion of a plant, which might include the leaves, stalks, roots, tubers, and flowers, that are used primarily as a side dish, but sometimes as a main dish or salad. Vegetables contain mostly water and are generally high in vitamins.

Storage: For maximum flavor and nutritive value, use fresh vegetables within one to two days of purchase. Store most vegetables dry and unwashed. Wash most vegetables just before using. Too much moisture causes vegetables to deteriorate rapidly.

To prevent flavor and odor penetration and to minimize water loss, store different types of produce (except potatoes, tomatoes, and onions) in closed plastic bags in the refrigerator.

Store potatoes and onions in a cool, dry, well-ventilated place such as a pantry out of direct sunlight. Don't, however, store potatoes and onions together as they tend to hasten spoilage of each other. Store tomatoes at room temperature in a basket or on a windowsill out of direct sunlight.

To prevent wilting and flavor change, rinse leafy green vegetables under cool water, and drain thoroughly. Wrap in paper towels, place in zip-top plastic bags, and refrigerate.

Corn, beans, and peas lose sweetness as their natural sugar turns to starch during storage. Store these vegetables dry and unwashed in plastic bags in the refrigerator, and use as soon as possible.

It's a good idea to check vegetables daily for spoilage no matter where they're stored (pantry, refrigerator, or simply at room temperature). If one piece shows signs of spoilage such as mold, oozing, or sliminess, it can quickly ruin the whole lot. If you detect spoilage, discard those vegetable pieces. Once cut, vegetables should be stored in the refrigerator in plastic bags.

To freeze, start with just-harvested vegetables at their peak and prepare amounts to fill only a few containers at a time. Discard any damaged produce. Wash and drain the vegetables; then peel or shell if needed, and cut into desired size pieces for freezing.

For the best quality frozen product, most vegetables should be blanched before canning. Blanching is heating or scalding vegetables in boiling water for a short period of time to inactivate natural enzymes that cause loss of flavor, color, and texture. Blanching heightens the flavor of vegetables, sets the color, helps retain nutrients, and destroys surface microorganisms.

Blanching times vary for different vegetables, usually 2 to 4 minutes depending on the size pieces. Overblanching causes a loss of color, flavor, and nutrients, while underblanching stimulates rather than inactivates damaging enzymes. For blanching, bring 1 gallon of water to a boil for every pound of prepared vegetables. (Use 2 gallons of water per pound of leafy green vegetables.) Place vegetables in a blanching basket, and submerge in boiling water. Cover and begin timing when water returns to a boil. Then remove basket from boiling water and immediately plunge into ice water for the same length of time you blanched the vegetables.

Cooling vegetables immediately and thoroughly after blanching is essential to halt the cooking process. Drain vegetables well before packing to eliminate extra moisture, which can cause a noticeable loss of quality during freezing.

After blanching, freeze vegetables in a dry pack or a tray pack. For a dry pack, place cooled vegetables in freezer containers, leaving ½ inch headspace, and freeze.

In a tray pack, freeze vegetables individually so they remain loose in the frozen package. Simply spread vegetables in a single layer on a shallow tray or baking sheet, and freeze until firm. Begin checking vegetables every 10 minutes after 1 hour. Package the individually frozen vegetables, leaving no headspace; seal and freeze.

When cooking frozen vegetables, you get the best tasting results if you cook them in their frozen state. Leafy greens and corn on the cob are two exceptions that cook more evenly if allowed to partially thaw.

To prepare vegetables for cooking, brush off loose dirt before washing vegetables. Use a stiff vegetable brush to remove dirt from the more durable vegetables such as sunchokes that tend to harbor dirt. A sinkful of lukewarm water is recommended for removing sand and grit from vegetables such as artichokes, zucchini, spinach, and leeks.

Peel vegetables when a recipe specifies. Many vegetables such as small eggplant, summer squash, and potatoes don't have to be peeled. Leaving the skin on is optional and can help retain nutrients. Some vegetables discolor quickly once they're peeled or sliced. To prevent discoloration, briefly dip vegetables in a solution of 1 tablespoon lemon juice to 1 cup water.

Cook most vegetables as briefly as possible in as little liquid as possible to retain nutrients, color, and texture. The microwave oven is perfect for cooking fresh vegetables because you need only a scant amount of water.

Q Are baby vegetables like regular vegetables, but smaller?

A Some baby vegetables are just regular vegetables that are harvested early, but some are special varieties that have been bred to be small. Prepackaged baby carrots are actually trimmed to their small size.

In turn, the vegetables cook quickly, retaining good color and nutrients. Steaming fresh vegetables in a steamer basket over boiling water preserves more vitamins than cooking in boiling water. Be sure the boiling water level does not touch the basket.

There are some vegetables such as artichokes, large green beans, cabbage, and some greens that you'll want to cook uncovered in a large pot of boiling water. The boiling activity will soften tough vegetable fibers.

Sautéing and stir-frying are quick, easy, and ideal for many vegetables. Stirring vegetables in a small amount of hot fat over medium to medium-high heat preserves color, texture, and nutrients. When stir-frying, it's often recommended that you cut vegetables on the diagonal; this is to expose the most surface area for quick cooking.

Braising (cooking slowly, covered, in a flavorful liquid) is a recommended cooking method for many root vegetables as well as cabbage and brussels sprouts. These vegetables will absorb the flavor of the braising liquid during long, slow cooking.

Roasting enhances the natural sweetness of many vegetables. This dry heat cooking with no added liquid preserves nutrients and concentrates flavor. You can roast any number of vegetables by this simple method: Cut similarly textured vegetables to the same size pieces. Prepare to roast only enough vegetable pieces to create a single layer in a roasting pan. Drizzle vegetables with 1 to 2 tablespoons of olive oil, and sprinkle with salt and pepper. Roast at 450° or 500° for 6 to 8 minutes, stirring once. Some vegetables such as potatoes will take much longer to cook. Roasted vegetables are simple to prepare and versatile. You can match them with many entrées and casseroles.

For some vegetables, the degree of doneness is a matter of personal preference. We often give a range in cooking time for foods including asparagus, green beans, snow peas, and peppers, because some like their vegetables crisp-tender and some very tender. Some vegetables such as onions and cabbage benefit from long cooking times. They gain a natural sweetness that can't be rushed.

If you're cooking vegetables to serve crisp-tender and cold, a recipe may instruct you to plunge the cooked vegetable into ice water immediately after cooking. This sudden change in temperature "shocks" the vegetable and stops the cooking process. (*see also* **blanch, boil, braise, roast, steaming,** *specific vegetables, and Cooking Fresh Vegetables chart page 570*)

velouté sauce (veh loo TAY) One of the five French mother sauces; it's made by thickening a white sauce with veal, chicken, or fish stock. Velouté sauce is sometimes called "blond sauce." (*see also* **mother sauces** *and* **sauce**)

venison (VEHN uh suhn) Meat from the deer family. Venison is typically a dark red color with little marbling; it has a firm, dense, smooth texture, mild aroma, and a sweet, herbal, nutty flavor. Freshly killed deer should be cleaned, skinned, and chilled immediately. If aged in a meat locker, the meat becomes more tender and the flavor improves. When dressing the deer, trim as much of the fat as possible, leaving a thin covering to keep the meat from drying out during cooking. Make sure the sinew (tendon) has been removed and that the meat has been carefully boned. Also remove the fell (the white membrane separating the muscles).

READER TIP

"If you're ever in doubt of how the deer was handled, you can always marinate it to help reduce any strong flavor." C.S., Duncanville, TX

Venison loin can be cut into cubes for kabobs, the hindquarter into steaks, and pieces can be made into sausage or ground for burgers or chili.

Storage: Venison should be placed in plastic bags and wrapped in freezer paper for freezing. It has a storage life similar to beef. (*see* **wild game** *and beef storage chart page 37*)

MUSHROOM-CRUSTED VENISON LOIN

A chicken and mushroom pâté comprises the tender and tasty "crust" around this venison loin that's a specialty of Chef David Everett's at Ford's Colony in Williamsburg, Virginia.

1 (3¼-ounce) package fresh shiitake mushrooms
1 (8-ounce) package fresh crimini mushrooms
¼ cup olive oil
1 teaspoon sea or table salt
½ teaspoon pepper
1 pound skinned and boned chicken breast halves
¼ cup loosely packed fresh parsley
¼ cup loosely packed fresh chervil
1 (20-ounce) boneless venison loin *

• Wash mushrooms thoroughly; remove and discard stems.
• Pour oil into a large skillet; add mushrooms, salt, and pepper. Cover and cook until mushrooms are tender. Drain and set mushrooms aside.
• Position knife blade in a food processor; add chicken, and process until finely chopped, stopping occasionally to scrape down sides. Add mushrooms, parsley, and chervil; process until mixture is thoroughly blended, stopping occasionally to scrape down sides.
• Cut 2 sheets of heavy-duty plastic wrap long enough to fit around venison loin. Place chicken mixture on 1 sheet, and top with remaining sheet. Roll mixture to about ¼-inch thickness, covering entire sheet. Remove top layer of plastic wrap.
• Place venison in center of chicken mixture. Using plastic wrap to lift chicken mixture, cover entire venison with chicken mixture; remove plastic wrap, and place venison, seam side down, on a greased baking sheet.
• Bake at 350° for 40 minutes or until a meat thermometer registers at least 150° (medium-rare). Yield: 8 servings.

*1 (20-ounce) beef tenderloin, trimmed, may be substituted. Bake as directed.

vent To allow the circulation of air or the escape of a liquid or gas.

Veracruz (ver ah KROOZ) Mexican dishes of fish or shellfish cooked in a sauce of tomatoes, chiles, onions, and garlic, and flavored with oregano and lime juice. Many Veracruz dishes are served over rice.

verbena (ver BEE nuh) (*see* **herbs**)

verde, salsa (VAIR day) A lively salsa made of tomatillos, onion, jalapeño pepper, and lime juice; it's typically served with chips, seafood, or chicken. (*see also* **tomatillo**)

vermicelli (ver mih CHEHL ee) Long, very thin strands of pasta that are much thinner than spaghetti strands. Vermicelli is made from wheat flour or, in the case of Asian pasta, from rice flour. (*see also* **pasta** *and* **spaghetti**)

vermouth (ver MOOTH) White wine that's flavored with herbs and spices, and fortified. Dry vermouth contains 2 to 4 percent sugar and can be served as an apéritif; it's also an ingredient in martini cocktails. Sweet vermouth contains 14 percent sugar and can also be served as an apéritif; it's also an ingredient in a Manhattan cocktail. (*see also* **apéritif, fortified wine, Manhattan,** *and* **martini**)

Véronique (vay roh NEEK) A term that indicates a dish, such as sole Véronique, that has been garnished with white seedless grapes. (*see also* **sole**)

vichyssoise (vih shee SWAZ) Rich, creamy French soup made from leeks and potatoes. Vichyssoise is served cold and garnished with chopped chives. (*see also* **leek** *and* **potato**)

Vidalia onion A large, pale yellow onion with a sweet, juicy white flesh. To be called a Vidalia, the onion must be grown within a designated area around Vidalia, Georgia. (*see also* **onion**)

Southernism

The Vidalia onion took root in Toombs County, Georgia, when a farmer named Mose Coleman discovered in the spring of 1931 that the onions he had planted were not hot, but sweet. The onions were popular and sold so quickly that by the 1970s, they had become a major crop in the area. Georgia's state legislature gave Vidalia onions legal status by limiting their production to 20 counties.

BAKED VIDALIA ONIONS

4 large Vidalia onions	¼ teaspoon freshly ground pepper
¼ cup butter, cut into pieces	1 cup shredded Parmesan cheese
1 teaspoon salt	

- Peel onions, leaving root ends intact. Cut each onion into eighths, cutting to, but not through, root ends.
- Place each onion on a lightly greased 12-inch square of aluminum foil.
- Press cut butter evenly into onions; sprinkle with salt, pepper, and cheese.
- Wrap onions in foil, and arrange in a 13- x 9-inch pan.
- Bake onions at 400° for 1 hour. Yield: 4 servings.

Viennese coffee (vee uh NEEZ) Strong, hot coffee sweetened to taste, topped with whipped cream, and served in a tall glass. (*see also* **coffee**)

vin (VAN) The French term for wine.

vinaigrette (vihn uh GREHT) A temporary emulsion of oil and vinegar generally used to dress salad greens and vegetable dishes. A simple vinaigrette consists of 3 parts oil to 1 part vinegar, with salt, pepper, and herbs added for seasoning. (*see also* **dressing** *and* **vinegar**)

> **TIMESAVING TIP**
> Bottled vinaigrette makes a quick and easy marinade; the vinegar helps tenderize meat and adds a tangy flavor.

PECAN VINAIGRETTE

¼ cup white wine vinegar
2 tablespoons Dijon mustard
2 garlic cloves
½ teaspoon salt
½ teaspoon pepper
2 tablespoons dry sherry (optional)
1 cup olive oil
¼ cup chopped pecans, toasted

- Process first 5 ingredients and, if desired, sherry in a blender until smooth, stopping to scrape down sides. Turn blender on high; gradually add oil in a slow, steady stream until thickened. Stir in pecans. Yield: 1¼ cups.

vinegar (VIHN ih ger) A weak solution of acetic acid made from fermented cider, wine, or beer. The first vinegars were probably French wines that had soured. Today, vinegar is made from a variety of red and white wines; sherry vinegar, which originated in Spain, is also available. In addition to wine vinegars, there are many other types of vinegar based on fruits and grains. They include:
- **Cider vinegar,** made from apple juice, and the most popular form of vinegar. It has a pale, golden brown color with a strong aroma and faint apple flavor.
- **Distilled** or **white vinegar,** made from grain alcohol. It's colorless, but has a strong aroma and flavor.
- **Rice vinegar,** often used in Asian cooking, is made from rice wine or sake; it has a tangy, slightly sweet flavor, and is clear to pale gold. (*continued on the following page*)

> **TEST KITCHEN SECRET**
> *The acid content of vinegar makes it a great preservative. When used to prepare pickles or other home-canned recipes, look for vinegar that's labeled 5% acidity.* VIE WARSHAW

- **Malt vinegar,** a mild vinegar made from malted barley.
- **Balsamic vinegar,** made from the juice of a very sweet white grape; it's dark brown with a delicate, sweet flavor that comes from being aged in wooden barrels for several years; this extended process makes it more expensive. Light-colored balsamic is also available in some markets.
- **Flavored herb** and **fruit vinegars** are made by steeping fresh herbs, such as dill and tarragon, or fruits, such as raspberries and blueberries, in vinegar. **Storage:** Because it's acidic, vinegar doesn't have to be refrigerated; its shelf life is almost indefinite. Even a color change or the development of sediment doesn't usually affect the flavor of vinegar. (*see also* **balsamic vinegar, cider vinegar, malt vinegar,** *and* **rice vinegar**)

vinegar pepper sauce A splash of this condiment made of mild chile peppers pickled in a vinegar brine adds a tangy flavor to collard greens or turnip greens. Called pickapepper sauce, it's about as popular as ketchup on Southern tables. (*see also* **hot sauce**)

vinegar pie A sweet pie made from a mixture of eggs, sugar, small amounts of flour and vinegar, and nutmeg.

vintage (VIHN tihj) A term that describes a grape harvest from a specific year and the wines made from that harvest.

vintner A wine merchant or producer who actually blends and sells wine.

violet, crystallized (*see* **crystallized flowers** *and* **flowers, edible**)

Virginia ham (*see* **country ham, ham,** *and* **Smithfield ham**)

vitamin Nutrients necessary to maintain health and proper body functions. Vitamins can be categorized as fat-soluble (vitamins A, D, E, and K) or water soluble (B vitamins and vitamin C).

vodka (VOD kuh) A clear, colorless, odorless, and practically tasteless liquor made from potatoes, corn, wheat, or rye. Vodka is usually 80 to 100 proof and is an important ingredient in cocktails such as the screwdriver, bloody Mary, and vodka martini. When served plain or straight, vodka is best ice cold. (*see also* **bloody Mary, liquor, martini,** *and* **screwdriver**)

vol-au-vent (vawl oh VAHN) A light, puff pastry shell that looks like a pot with a lid; it can be small, individual size, or larger. The shell is often filled with a savory mixture, such as chicken and vegetables in cream sauce, and can be served as an appetizer or entrée. Before serving, the pastry "lid" is placed on top of the filling. (*see also* **puff pastry**)

volume The measurement used most often for measuring liquids; it's usually measured in teaspoons, tablespoons, cups, pints, gallons, fluid ounces, and bushels. (*see also* **measuring** *and* **metric measure**)

Vouvray (voo VRAY) White wine produced in the village of Vouvray in the French Loire Valley. Vouvray is typically made from Chenin Blanc grapes and can be dry, semisweet, sweet, or sparkling. (*see also* **Chenin Blanc** *and* **wine**)

wafer A thin, crisp cookie or cracker that's either sweet or savory. (*see also* **benne seed wafers**)

waffle (WAHF uhl) Thin, slightly crisp, but moist quick bread with a honeycomb-patterned surface; it's made from a batter much like pancakes. The surface makes waffles perfect for holding syrup; sometimes they're also served with fresh fruit or other toppings. Waffles are created in a special kitchen appliance called a waffle iron; the irons can be electric or designed for cooktop cooking. Electric waffle irons cook both sides of the waffle at once, but the cooktop versions must be turned over once to cook the second side. Frozen waffles are also available in supermarkets. (*see also* **pancake** *and* **quick bread**)

> **TIMESAVING TIP**
> Try frozen waffles; they're not as good as fresh, but if toasted in a toaster or baked in the oven, they're close!

Q **What's a Belgian waffle?**
A These waffles are thick and cakelike with extradeep indentations and require a special waffle iron. Belgian waffles may be served with syrup, fruit, ice cream, or whipped cream.

TEST KITCHEN SECRET

It might take some time to prepare enough waffles for your family, so you'll want to keep the cooked ones warm and crisp until serving time. The best way is to place them on a rack on a baking sheet, and put in a 250° to 300° oven until you're finished. JAN MOON

RESCUE for sticking waffles:
If possible, use a waffle iron with a clean, nonstick surface. After it preheats, lightly coat the grids with oil or vegetable cooking spray.

Waldorf salad (WAWL dorf) The original Waldorf salad contained only apples, celery, and mayonnaise, and was created at the Waldorf-Astoria Hotel in New York in the 1890s; modern versions often include chopped nuts. The salad is typically served on a bed of lettuce. (*see recipe on the following page*)

READER TIP
"My family loves Waldorf salad, so to make it special, I vary the type and color of apples. Sometimes I use several types in the same salad." A.J., Ashland, VA

CLASSIC WALDORF SALAD

2 tablespoons orange juice
3 large tart red apples, unpeeled
and diced
½ cup diced celery
½ cup sour cream

½ cup raisins
¼ cup chopped pecans or walnuts
1½ teaspoons sugar
Lettuce leaves (optional)

• Sprinkle orange juice over apples; toss gently and drain. Combine apples, celery, and next 4 ingredients; stir well. Cover and chill. Serve on lettuce leaves, if desired. Yield: 6 servings.

walla walla A sweet, juicy onion grown in and around Walla Walla, Washington. It's available June through August.
Storage: High sugar content makes the Walla Walla fragile, so store in a cool, dry place only 2 to 3 weeks. (*see also* **onion**)

walnut The fruit of the walnut tree, which grows in Asia, Europe, and North America. The two most popular varieties are the English walnut and the black walnut. The mild-flavored English walnut is the most widely available; it has a large, round, light brown, slightly wrinkled shell that cracks easily. Inside the English walnut are two distinct lobes of plump, crisp nutmeat.

TEST KITCHEN SECRET

To crack an English walnut, place it on the flat bottom end and, holding by the seam, tap the pointed end with a hammer; it should break open and expose the walnut halves. JAMES SCHEND

The North American black walnut has a much more intense flavor; it has a very hard, thick, rough, black shell. Black walnuts are difficult to shell and are smaller than English walnuts.
Storage: If unshelled, walnuts can be stored in a cool, dry place up to 3 months. Once shelled, the nutmeat can be refrigerated in an airtight container up to 6 months or frozen up to a year. (*see also* **English walnut** *and* **nuts**)

walnut oil A nutty-flavored oil from pressed walnuts. High in polyunsaturated fat, walnut oil can be used in dressings, sauces, and baked goods. However, walnut oil is expensive; it's frequently used in bottled salad dressings where it's combined with less flavorful oils. To guard against rancidity, walnut oil should be stored in the refrigerator or in a cool, dark place up to 3 months. (*see also* **fats and oils**)

wasabi (WAH sah bee) Made from the root of a Japanese plant, wasabi is used to make a green-colored, pungent-flavored, pastelike condiment that's often served with sushi and sashimi. Wasabi can be purchased in Asian markets in powder or paste form. Wasabi tastes similar to horseradish and is sometimes referred to as Japanese horseradish. (*see also* **sashimi** *and* **sushi**)

wassail (WAHS uhl) An English holiday drink made of spiced wine or ale sweetened with sugar and spices. Nonalcoholic versions are typically based on fruit juices. Wassail is traditionally served in a punch bowl and garnished with small roasted apples.

PINEAPPLE WASSAIL

4 cups unsweetened pineapple
 juice
1 (12-ounce) can apricot nectar
2 cups apple cider
1 cup orange juice
1 teaspoon whole cloves
3 (6-inch) cinnamon sticks,
 broken

• Bring all ingredients to a boil in a Dutch oven; reduce heat, and simmer 20 minutes. Pour through a strainer; discard spices. Serve hot. Yield: 2 quarts.

water A colorless liquid that has many uses as a beverage and in cooking. Many different bottled waters are sold, including:
• **Sparkling water,** a natural or artificial carbonated water; it can be flavored or sweetened.
• **Tonic water,** a carbonated beverage flavored with quinine; it has a slightly bitter flavor.
• **Mineral water,** a carbonated or noncarbonated water with a high mineral content and can taste slightly metallic.
• **Seltzer** or **soda water,** an artificially carbonated water without added minerals or salts. It can also be flavored or sweetened.
• **Distilled water,** a pure bottled water with a flat flavor.
• **Club soda,** an artificially carbonated water with added minerals and mineral salts and is often mixed with alcohol to make cocktails.

water bath Sometimes called a bain-marie, a water bath is created by placing a baking dish or pan holding food inside a larger pan and then pouring boiling water into the larger pan. The water, which should reach about halfway up the sides of the dish containing the food, helps insulate the food from the harsh, direct heat of the oven and provides gentle, moist, even cooking. This technique is designed to cook delicate foods such as custards, mousses, and cheesecakes without curdling. A water bath can also be used to keep sauces warm. Special water bath or bain-marie pans can be purchased, but you can also fashion your own using different-sized pans. (*see also* **bain-marie, boiling water bath,** *and* **custard**)

water biscuit A simple, plain, crisp cracker that's often served with cheese and wine because it doesn't possess any distracting flavors.

water chestnut The edible tuber of a water plant native to Southeast Asia; they have brownish-black skin, white to ivory flesh, crisp texture, and a slightly sweet, nutty flavor. Water chestnuts are widely used in Asian cooking and are valued for the crunch they add to stir-fried dishes. They are available fresh in most Asian markets, but can also be purchased whole or sliced in cans in most supermarkets.

Storage: Fresh water chestnuts should be refrigerated in a plastic bag up to a week. Once canned water chestnuts are opened, they can be placed in a plastic container, covered with water, and refrigerated up to 10 days. (*see also* **stir-fry**)

watercress (*see* **lettuce**)

watermelon A type of melon with sweet, crisp, juicy meat. There are many different varieties and sizes of watermelon, but the most popular is the large, elongated, oval-shaped melon with a variegated, striped, or two-tone green rind. The meat can range from deep pink to red, and some are even yellow or cream-colored. They usually have flat, black seeds, but seedless varieties are also available. Regular watermelons typically weigh 15 to 35 pounds, but they may be much smaller or larger, depending on the variety.

Storage: If possible, store whole watermelon in the refrigerator up to a week; if it's too large, keep in a cool, dark place. Cut melon should be tightly wrapped, refrigerated, and used within a day or so. (*see also* **melon**)

TEST KITCHEN SECRET

To make a watermelon basket, cut a thin slice off the bottom of the melon so that it sits flat. Then mark a line lengthwise around the top one-third of the melon, and mark a 2-inch-wide strip across the top for handle. Cut out and remove the large sections to form the basket. Remove the melon meat, leaving a 1-inch shell. Use a melon baller to cut the meat, or cut it into cubes. If desired, cut a zigzag pattern on the edge of the melon using a sharp knife. MARY ALLEN PERRY

♡ **LITE BITE**
Watermelon has the highest amount of lycopene of all fruits and vegetables. Lycopene is an antioxidant that is believed to reduce the risk of heart disease and some cancers.

WATERMELON SORBET

4 cups water
2 cups sugar
8 cups seeded, chopped
   watermelon

1 (12-ounce) can frozen pink
   lemonade concentrate,
   thawed and undiluted

• Bring 4 cups water and sugar just to a boil in a medium saucepan over high heat, stirring until sugar dissolves. Remove from heat. Cool.

- Process sugar syrup and watermelon in batches in a blender until smooth. Stir in lemonade concentrate. Cover and chill 2 hours. Pour mixture into freezer container of a 1-gallon electric freezer. Freeze according to manufacturer's instructions. Yield: 2½ quarts.

wax bean (*see* **beans, fresh;** *and* **green bean**)

wax paper Thin, semitransparent paper that has been coated on both sides with wax. Because it's waterproof, wax paper is often used to line cakepans and to cover foods for storage.

RESCUE for messy microwave:
Before microwaving food, place a sheet of wax paper on the floor or glass tray of microwave for easy cleanup.

TEST KITCHEN SECRET

We use wax paper all the time in the Test Kitchens. It's great for placing under the edges of a cake to protect the platter during frosting. We also roll out pastry dough between sheets of wax paper; just wet the back of the bottom sheet and seal it to the countertop to keep it from slipping. JAN MOON

wedding cookies (*see* **Mexican wedding cookies**)

well-and-tree platter A serving platter that has a depressed design of a tree with branches; it's designed to allow meat juices to drain away.

well done A degree of doneness (170°) that indicates meat has no redness and is brown throughout; it should be firm and spring back when pressed. (*see also* **beef, medium rare, medium well,** *and* **rare**)

Welsh rarebit A British dish of melted Cheddar cheese with beer that's served over toast. Welsh rarebit can be served as a main course or for high tea; it's called "golden buck" when topped with a poached egg.

wheat A type of cereal grass grown worldwide; it contains large amounts of gluten, which is necessary for bread making. There are three major types of wheat: hard wheat, soft wheat, and durum wheat. Hard wheat is high in protein and produces gluten-rich flour that makes it particularly suitable for yeast breads. Soft wheat is lower in protein, lower in gluten, and therefore better suited for making biscuits and cakes. Durum wheat is high in gluten, but is mostly ground to make semolina, the basis for pasta. The actual wheat kernel is made of bran, germ, and endosperm. The bran is sold separately and used to add flavor and fiber to baked goods. Nutritious wheat germ is sold toasted and natural and used to add nutrients to foods and to make wheat germ oil. The endosperm is the primary source of many wheat flours. Other available forms of wheat include: wheat berries (the whole kernel), cracked wheat (the berry broken into pieces), (*continued on the following page*) bulghur (precooked and dried cracked wheat), and farina (coarse particles milled from the endosperm); these may be cooked as cereals, served in pilafs, or added to breads or other dishes. Most wheat products can be purchased in health food stores and some supermarkets.

Storage: Whole or cracked wheat can be stored in an airtight container in a cool, dry place up to 6 months or frozen up to a year. Wheat bran can be stored in an airtight container in a cool, dry place up to a month, refrigerated for 3 months, or frozen up to a year. Wheat germ has a high-oil content and is very perishable, so keep it in the refrigerator up to 3 months. (*see also* **bran, bulghur, farina, flour, grain,** *and* **semolina**)

whetstone (HWEHT stohn) A block of hard stone made of carborundum on which knives are periodically honed to maintain a sharp edge. This is done by lubricating the stone with oil or water; then, with slight pressure, draw the blade of the knife across the whetstone at about a 20-degree angle for 5 or 6 times on each side. If the whetstone has a fine-grained side and a coarse-grained side, always hone the knife on the coarser side first, and finish on the finer side. To maintain a sharp knife blade, a sharpening steel can also be used. (*see also* **knife** *and* **sharpening steel**)

whey (HWAY) When milk coagulates during cheese making, it separates into solid curds and a watery liquid called whey. The whey can be used to make whey cheese, such as ricotta. (*see also* **cheese** *and* **curd**)

whip To beat foods such as heavy cream or egg whites for meringue using a wire whisk, rotary beater, or an electric mixer to incorporate air into the mixture to increase the volume. (*see also* **cream, meringue, mixer, rotary beater,** *and* **whisk**)

> **TEST KITCHEN SECRET**
>
> *When you whip heavy cream or egg whites, use a large, deep bowl. The larger the bowl, the easier it is to incorporate air, plus a deep bowl contains the mixture and prevents splattering. Also, make sure the bowl and whip are free of all oil and fat residue; otherwise the cream or egg whites won't whip as high.* VANESSA MCNEIL

whipping cream (*see* **cream**)

whisk (HWIHSK) (*see* **baking tools**)

whiskey (HWIHSK ee) A distilled alcoholic beverage made from a fermented mash of grains such as corn, rye, and barley. The character and quality of whiskey is determined by the processing of the grain, the water used, and the aging. Among the more popular whiskeys are bourbon, rye, and Scotch. (*see also* **bourbon, Irish whiskey, liquor, rye,** *and* **Scotch**)

whiskey sour (*see* **sour**)

white bean A generic term used for a variety of ivory-white dried beans. White beans generally fall into one of four categories: marrow beans, great Northern beans, navy beans, or pea beans. (*see also* **beans, dried; great Northern beans; navy bean;** *and* **pea bean**)

white chocolate (*see* **chocolate**)

white pepper (*see* **peppercorn**)

white Riesling (*see* **Johannisberg Riesling** *and* **wine**)

white Russian A cocktail beverage made of vodka, coffee liqueur such as Kahlúa, and cream, and served over ice. If no cream is added, it becomes a black Russian. (*see also* **Kahlúa**)

white sapote (sah PO tee) A small round fruit that grows wild in Central America; it has a pale yellow-green skin and sweet, juicy flesh that tastes similar to a pear. It's usually cooked into jam or eaten fresh, out of hand.
Storage: White sapotes should ripen at room temperature; once ripe, keep in the refrigerator up to 5 days.

white sauce A basic sauce, sometimes called cream sauce, made with butter, flour, and milk, cream, or stock. White sauce is made by stirring together flour with melted butter, and then adding the liquid; it's cooked and stirred until it becomes thick and bubbly. There are two types of white sauce: béchamel (uses milk), and velouté (uses light stock); both are French mother sauces. White sauce can be served with vegetables, poultry, fish, and meat, and used as the base for other sauce mixtures and in casseroles. (*see also* **béchamel sauce, cream sauce, mother sauces,** *and* **velouté sauce**)

> **TEST KITCHEN SECRET**
>
> *For a smooth white sauce, stir the flour into the melted butter, and then add all the liquid at once, stirring well with a wire whisk. Heat the mixture until it starts to bubble and thicken, stirring constantly.* JAN MOON

READER TIP
"White sauce is one basic recipe I've memorized because I use it so often. It's easy to vary the color and flavor by stirring in cheese or herbs or other ingredients." G.M., Garland, TX

white Zinfandel (*see* **wine** *and* **Zinfandel**)

whiting A saltwater fish found in the Atlantic Ocean from New England to Virginia. Sometimes called "silver hake" or "silver perch," whiting is a member of the cod family and has a low-fat, firm, delicate flavored flesh. It can be salted, smoked, poached, broiled, pan-fried, or baked. (*see also* **fish**)

whole wheat flour (*see* **flour** *and* **wheat**)

wiener (WEE nuhr) (*see* **frankfurter**)

Wiener schnitzel (VEE nuhr SHNIHT suhl) A well-known Viennese dish that actually originated in France. It features a veal cutlet pounded until very thin, and then coated with flour, dipped in egg, and coated with breadcrumbs; it's sautéed briefly, just until cooked through. Wiener schnitzel is usually served with lemon slices and sometimes hard-cooked eggs, capers, and anchovies. (*see also* **veal**)

wild game A wild animal hunted for food. From the founding of Jamestown to the Civil War, game was an important part of the daily diet. This was especially true for many Southerners who lived in small towns or rural areas. In fact, game played such an important role in the history of Southern food that hunters and cooks developed and perfected excellent recipes using the meat. Some of the recipes have been modernized, but close versions still occasionally show up on Southern tables today. Wild game covers a wide range of animals, but they can be broken down into two main categories:

• **Game birds,** which include ducks, doves, geese, grouse, partridges, quail, and wild turkeys.
• **Game mammals,** which include bison, bear, deer, muskrats, rabbits, raccoons, squirrels, and wild boar. Game hunting is tightly regulated; certain animals can be hunted for personal use only in season. Any game sold in supermarkets, specialty stores, or by mail order has been raised on a game farm. For example, rabbits, buffalo, venison, ducks, geese, and quail are sometimes farm-raised and can occasionally be purchased.

> **TEST KITCHEN SECRET**
>
> *To keep quail and doves moist, brush them with cooking oil or place bacon slices on their breasts before cooking. Also, cooking them covered with moist heat not only keeps them tender, it makes them more flavorful.* VIE WARSHAW

READER TIP
"We've found that a marinade of bottled vinaigrette salad dressing helps mellow the strong flavor found in some game." J.S., Asheville, NC

wild rice Wild rice is the grain of a marsh grass grown in the United States and Canada. The long, black grains have a nutty flavor and chewy texture. Wild rice is expensive and requires up to an hour to cook. Before using, it should be washed in cold water. **Storage:** Wild rice keeps indefinitely if stored in a cool, dry place or in the refrigerator. (*see also* **rice**)

> **TEST KITCHEN SECRET**
>
> *To stretch expensive wild rice, try combining it with a little long-grain white rice or brown rice. It teams especially well with brown rice because they require about the same amount of cooking time.* VANESSA MCNEIL

WILD RICE-CHICKEN SALAD

2 (6.2-ounce) packages long-grain and wild rice mix
2 (6-ounce) jars marinated artichoke quarters, undrained
4 cups chopped cooked chicken
1 medium-size red bell pepper, chopped

2 celery ribs, thinly sliced
5 green onions, chopped
1 (2.25-ounce) can sliced ripe olives, drained
1 cup mayonnaise
1½ teaspoons curry powder
Leaf lettuce

• Cook rice mix according to package directions.

• Drain artichoke quarters, reserving ½ cup liquid. Stir together rice, artichoke, chicken, and next 4 ingredients.

• Stir together artichoke liquid, mayonnaise, and curry powder; toss with rice mixture. Cover and chill 8 hours. Serve on leaf lettuce. Yield: 8 servings.

wine The fermented juice of freshly gathered ripe grapes, wine has a rich history and is produced around the world in many different styles from different types of grapes. However, all wines can be classified under four broad categories: natural still, sparkling, fortified, and aromatic. Natural still wines include red, white, and rosé or blush. They can be dry, semisweet, or sweet. Sparkling wines include French champagnes as well as effervescent wines made in other parts of the world. Fortified wines, such as sherry and port, have been strengthened by the addition of brandy or liqueur. Aromatic wines such as vermouth have been flavored by the addition of other ingredients such as herbs or spices.

Always pay attention to a wine's name because it usually tells you a lot about that wine. For example, the name might tell you:

• If it's a varietal wine and named for the grapes that are used to make it. Zinfandel, Chardonnay, and Riesling are all varietal wines. If produced in the United States, at least 75 percent of the wine must come from the type grape for which it's named. Most European wines are named after the regions in which they are produced, but as a rule, each region makes its wines from a predominant type of grape. (*continued on the following page*)

(continued on the following page)

TEST KITCHEN SECRET

When cooking with wine, add it while the dish is still cooking briskly so the alcohol will have a chance to cook off. Also, add full-bodied red wine to hearty dishes such as stews and dry white wine to mild-flavored seafood and poultry dishes. Keep in mind that adding red wine will sometimes cause a dish to turn slightly pink, so only add it when this coloring won't be offensive. JAMES SCHEND

READER TIP

"I've found white wines are best served just out of the refrigerator or slightly warmer; the sweeter the wine, the cooler it can be. Light, young red wines taste best between 55° and 60°, while full-bodied reds can be 60° to 65°. Remember that you can start with the wine being a little too cold because it will warm up as the meal begins." R.B., Atlanta, GA

- If it's a proprietary wine and blended in a way characteristic of a specific winery.
- If it's an American-made, generic wine, such as Hearty Burgundy or Mountain Chablis, there won't be any information about grape content. The vintage also appears on a wine label; this tells you the date the grapes were harvested. A nonvintage wine is a blend of wines produced in different years.

Some of the more common varietal types of wine include:
- *Cabernet Sauvignon,* a deep, rich ruby-red wine with peppery, berry, and vanilla qualities from oak aging. It's a full-bodied, intense wine and pairs well with beef, poultry, pasta, and game meats.
- *Champagne* and *sparkling wine,* a wine made by a specific process and results in fine bubbles of carbon dioxide. Dry champagne or sparkling wine may be labeled brut (very dry), sec (sweet), or demi-sec (even sweeter).
- *Chardonnay,* a popular white wine grape; it's generally a deep golden color and is aged in oak barrels. Usually dry, Chardonnay has buttery, fruity, vanilla, and toasty flavors. It pairs well with a host of entrées.
- *Gewürztraminer* (guh VURTZ tra meen er), is a fruity, highly aromatic, crisp, spicy white wine that's available in varying degrees of sweetness. The drier versions complement fish and poultry, while the sweeter varieties are perfect for spritzers and make good dessert wines.

Q **How do you pair wine with food?**

A In general, a hearty red wine pairs well with a hearty roast beef, while a more delicate white is better with fish. But, depending on the effects of sauces and seasonings, this rule of thumb can vary. For example, a grilled fish that's highly seasoned might go nicely with a light fruity red Pinot Noir. Also, try to match the level of sweetness; a dry tart wine would taste sour if served with a sweet dessert. So, always consider the complete dish before you select a wine. Ask your local wine merchant to help you.

- *Merlot,* a ruby-red wine that's softer than Cabernet. Its flavor hints of berry, black cherry, plum, spices, and tobacco. It pairs well with poultry and lamb.
- *Pinot Noir,* a delicate red wine with a complex flavor that hints of spicy cherries and earthiness. It pairs well with beef and ham.
- *Riesling,* a crisp, floral white wine from Germany. Dry Rieslings can be served with light appetizers or seafood, and sweeter versions go well with spicy foods.
- *Sauvignon Blanc,* a dry white wine that's lighter in color and body and hints of citrus and herbs more than Chardonnay. It pairs nicely with seafood or tomato-sauced dishes.
- *Zinfandel,* a popular California red wine with a flavor of berries, cherries, and spices. It teams well with roasted or grilled red meats, stews, and game. White Zinfandel is made by letting the crushed grapes have only brief contact with their skins, resulting in "blush" wine with a light, fruit flavor.

Storage: If you plan to drink wine within a few days or weeks, it may be stored in a cool, dark pantry, but for longer storage, keep the bottles in a controlled constant temperature of 50° to 55°. They should be placed on their sides, in a wine rack to keep their corks moist and swollen so no air can come in contact with the wine. (*see also* **brut, Cabernet Sauvignon, Chablis, champagne, Chardonnay, cooking wine, demi-sec, fortified wine, Johannisberg Riesling, Merlot, Pinot Noir, Sauvignon Blanc, sec, varietal wine,** *and* **Zinfandel**)

wine bottles The bottle used for natural still or sparkling wines; the standard size holds 750 milliliters or 25.6 ounces. A split holds one-fourth of a standard bottle or 6.5 ounces. A magnum is equivalent to two standard bottles or 1.5 liters. Methuselas hold the equivalent of eight standard bottles, and a Nebuchadnezzar equals 20 standard bottles.

Q **Is there a proper way to open wine?**

A Wine should be opened gently, using an opener that will enable you to extract the cork cleanly; several types of corkscrews are available. Be sure to wipe off the rim of the bottle before serving or decanting the wine. If serving from the bottle, twist the bottle as you pour to prevent dripping.

wine glasses Red wine glasses have larger bowls than white wine glasses. This allows more room for swirling so that you can enjoy the big bouquet that's the trademark of fine red wine. Ideally, a wine glass should be thin, and the rim should not be any thicker than the glass itself. Champagne and sparkling wines are best in tall, slender glasses called flutes, which help to conserve their signature effervescence. (*see also* **bouquet**)

white wine glass

red wine glass

champagne flute

wine vinegar (*see* **vinegar**)

wintergreen An evergreen plant native to eastern North America; its leaves produce a pungent oil that's used to flavor a variety of products including candy and gum.

winter squash (*see* **squash**)

wok (WAHK) A cooking pan with a rounded bottom and curved sides that diffuses heat and makes it easy to toss or stir-fry ingredients. Woks usually have two handles, a domed lid, and comes with a ring-shaped stand for use on a gas cooktop. Special flat-bottomed woks are also available for electric ranges. (*see also* **stir-fry**)

won ton (WAHN tahn) A small Chinese dumpling made of paper-thin dough filled with minced meats, seafood, poultry, or vegetables. Won tons can be boiled, steamed, or deep-fried, and are eaten as appetizers or as dumplings in soup.

won ton soup A Chinese soup consisting of chicken broth and won ton dumplings, flavored with soy sauce, and garnished with green onions, pork or chicken, and vegetables. (*see also* **soy sauce** *and* **won ton**)

wood ear mushroom (*see* **mushroom**)

Worcestershire sauce (WOOS tuhr shuhr) A thin condiment sauce developed in India by British Colonials and first bottled in Worcester, England. It's a mixture of soy sauce, tamarind, garlic, onions, molasses, lime, anchovies, vinegar, and other various seasonings. Worcestershire sauce has a distinct piquant flavor that's useful in seasoning meats, gravies, and soups; it's also a flavoring in Bloody Mary cocktails. In recent years, a light or "white" Worcestershire sauce has been developed for use when it's undesirable to add a dark sauce to a light-colored mixture. (*see also* **bloody Mary, condiment,** *and* **tamarind**)

wurst (WUHRST) The German term for sausage (*see also* **sausage**)

yam A thick, starchy tuber popular in South America and Central America, the West Indies, and parts of Asia and Africa. Although similar, the yam is not related to sweet potatoes. The yam has off-white to dark brown skin and flesh that varies from off-white or yellow to purple or pink. Although yams contain more sugar and moisture than sweet potatoes, they don't taste as sweet and are not as high in nutrients. Yams are sold in some Latin-American markets and can be used in the same ways as sweet potatoes. **Storage:** Yams can be stored in a cool, dark, dry place up to 2 weeks; do not refrigerate. (*see also* **sweet potato**)

yard-long bean A thin legume that looks like a green bean but grows up to 3 feet long. Yard-long beans also taste similar to green beans, though not as sweet. They can be found in Asian markets and some supermarkets. They are typically cut into smaller pieces and sautéed. (*see also* **legume**)

yarrow (YAR oh) A dark green, aromatic English herb with downy stems and compact flowers. Yarrow has a slightly bitter, peppery flavor, and is occasionally used to flavor salads, soups, egg dishes, and tisane (herb) teas. (*see also* **herbs** *and* **tisane**)

yeast (YEEST) A living microorganism that converts sugar or starch into carbon dioxide gas and ethyl alcohol; it enables bread to rise and is crucial in making beer. There are two types of commercially produced yeast: baker's and brewer's. Baker's yeast is used as a leavening agent in baked goods. There are three types:
• *Active dry yeast* comes in the form of dried granules that are inactive until mixed with a warm (100° to 110°) liquid. It's available as either regular or

quick-rising, which is also known as rapid-rise yeast. Quick-rising yeast makes dough rise faster than regular yeast; it doesn't have to be dissolved separately and can be combined with other dry ingredients to which warm liquid is added. Active yeasts are sold in small, sealed packages or jars.

• *Compressed fresh yeast* comes in the form of tiny compressed cakes that are moist and very perishable and will keep under refrigeration for only about 10 days. While it can also be frozen, compressed yeast must be used as soon as it has defrosted. This type of yeast is not nearly as convenient as active dry yeast, and therefore, is not used as often.

• *Yeast starters* are composed of a batter of flour, water, sugar, and airborne or baker's yeast. After the mixture ferments, a portion is removed and used as the base and leavener for bread. If fed a mixture of flour, water, and sugar, the starter can be kept alive for years. Generally, 2 cups of foamy starter can be substituted for each package of yeast called for in a recipe.

Brewer's yeast is nonleavening, grown on hops, and used to make beer. Because it's high in B vitamins, it's also sold in health stores as a nutritional supplement. **Storage:** Store packets of active dry yeast in a cool, dry place; it should stay

Q **What is the rapid-mix method of bread making?**

A It's mixing the yeast with some of the dry ingredients before adding the liquids. This eliminates the need to dissolve the yeast. When using this method, the liquid should be 120° to 130° when you add it to the dry ingredients unless otherwise specified.

fresh until the expiration date stamped on the package. Jars of dry yeast should be stored in a cool, dry place until opened, and then they should be refrigerated and used before the expiration date on the jar. Compressed yeast cakes can be refrigerated for about 10 days or frozen for several months. Yeast starter can be refrigerated and kept as long as it's replenished every 2 weeks. (*see also* **breads, yeast; sourdough;** *and* **starter**)

yellow cake A basic cake made from a batter containing egg yolks; it goes well with any flavor of frosting. (*see also* **cake**)

yellow crookneck squash A type of summer squash with a long, slender neck and bulbous body. It has a pale to deep yellow skin, creamy yellow flesh, and mild, delicate flavor. It can be steamed, grilled, sautéed, or fried. **Storage:** Refrigerate yellow squash in a plastic bag up to 5 days, longer if garden-fresh. (*see also* **squash, vegetables,** *and recipe on the following page*)

GRILLED YELLOW SQUASH AND TOMATOES

¼ cup sugar
1 teaspoon salt
½ teaspoon freshly ground pepper
⅓ cup olive oil
¼ cup balsamic vinegar
6 small yellow squash, cut in half lengthwise

6 plum tomatoes, cut in half lengthwise
¼ cup chopped fresh chives (optional)
¼ cup chopped fresh basil (optional)

• Whisk together first 5 ingredients until blended. Place squash in a large heavy-duty zip-top plastic bag. Pour marinade over squash. Seal bag, and chill 2 hours, turning bag occasionally. Remove squash from marinade, reserving marinade.
• Cook reserved marinade in a small saucepan over medium-high heat 5 to 7 minutes or until reduced to ½ cup.
• Grill squash, covered with grill lid, over medium-high heat (350° to 400°) 5 to 6 minutes on each side or until squash is crisp-tender.
• Add tomato halves to grill, and grill 2 minutes on each side. Sprinkle with chives and basil, if desired. Serve with marinade. Yield: 6 to 8 servings.

yogurt (YOH gert) A thick, tart, soft custardlike dairy product made from milk that has been fermented and coagulated by friendly bacteria. There are a variety of commercially produced yogurts on the market, including plain yogurt, yogurt with fruit on the bottom, yogurt with fruit mixed throughout, artificially sweetened yogurt, flavored yogurt (has sugar and either artificial flavoring or natural fruit flavoring added), yogurt drinks, and frozen yogurt. It's also available low fat or fat free, and though typically made from cow's milk, it can also be made from goat's milk, sheep's milk, or soy milk. Yogurt is a good source of B vitamins, protein, and calcium, and is more easily digestible than fresh milk; it's also believed that it helps keep the digestive tract in healthy condition. Yogurt can be eaten straight from the carton, used as a salad dressing, as a topping for sweet or savory dishes, or added to dips, sauce, or soups.

TEST KITCHEN SECRET

Cooking with yogurt can cause it to become thin and watery. For best results, bring the yogurt to room temperature before heating, and slowly add it to hot food toward the end of cooking, without stirring too much. Stirring a tablespoon of flour into a cup of plain yogurt before it's cooked will help prevent curdling. MARY ALLEN PERRY

LITE BITE

Yogurt is a good source of B vitamins, protein, and calcium, and is much more digestible than fresh milk. It's also said to keep the intestinal system populated with good bacteria and, therefore, in healthy condition. These benefits, however, are thought to be lost when yogurt is frozen, which destroys most of the beneficial bacteria.

Storage: Refrigerate yogurt as soon as possible after purchase. It will stay at peak flavor for about 10 days after the expiration date on the carton.

yogurt, frozen A soft, frozen dessert similar to ice cream, but made from sweetened yogurt. Sometimes fruit and natural or artificial flavorings are added to frozen yogurt; low-fat and nonfat versions are available.

yolk The yellow portion of an egg; it contains all the fat and slightly less than half of the egg's protein. The 5 grams of fat in a large egg yolk are about 1.6 grams of saturated fat and 2.6 grams unsaturated fat. The remaining portion of the yolk does contain some cholesterol. All of the egg's vitamins A, D, and E are found in the yolk. (*see also* **egg**)

Yorkshire pudding (YORK sheer) A British breadlike dish often served with roast beef. Made with eggs, flour, milk, and beef drippings, it's a cross between a popover and a soufflé. Yorkshire pudding is usually prepared in the same pan the roast was cooked in or in a shallow baking dish or muffin tins. It bakes until puffy, crisp, and golden brown, but must be served immediately or, like a soufflé, it will deflate. (*see also* **popover, pudding,** *and* **soufflé**)

STANDING RIB ROAST WITH YORKSHIRE PUDDING

1 (6-pound) standing rib roast	1 teaspoon freshly ground pepper
1 teaspoon kosher salt	Yorkshire Pudding

• Sprinkle roast with salt and pepper. Place roast, fat side up, on a lightly greased rack in an aluminum foil-lined roasting pan.
• Bake at 350° for 2 hours or until a meat thermometer inserted into thickest portion registers 145° (medium rare) or to desired degree of doneness.
• Transfer roast to a serving platter, reserving ½ cup drippings for Yorkshire Pudding; keep warm. Serve roast with Yorkshire Pudding. Yield: 8 servings.

YORKSHIRE PUDDING

1 cup all-purpose flour	1 cup milk
¼ teaspoon salt	½ cup reserved beef drippings
2 large eggs	

• One hour before the roast is done, whisk together first 4 ingredients; cover and chill 30 minutes.
• Spoon 1 tablespoon reserved drippings into each of 8 muffin cups. Heat drippings at 400° for 6 minutes; spoon batter evenly into muffin cups.
• Bake at 400° for 30 minutes or until golden. Yield: 8 servings.
Note: Bake pudding in a 13- x 9-inch baking dish, if desired. Heat beef drippings in a baking dish as directed; add batter, and bake as directed.

yucca (YUHK uh) (*see* **cassava**)

Yukon gold potato A type of potato developed in Canada in the 1960s and 1970s; it has yellow flesh that gives the illusion that it's pre-buttered. The Yukon can be baked, boiled, sautéed, or fried. (*see also* **potato**)

yule log (YOOL) (*see* **bûche de Noël**)

zabaglione (zah bahl YOH nay) Also called "sabayon" in France, zabaglione is an Italian foamy dessert custard made by whisking together egg yolks, wine (usually Marsala), and sugar in the top of a double boiler. Zabaglione is usually made just before serving; it's typically served by itself or as a sauce over cake, fruit, ice cream, or pastry. (*see also* **sabayon**)

zest (ZEHST) The colored, outermost layer of citrus rind that's rich in aromatic oils and removed with a citrus zester. Zest adds flavor to desserts and baked goods as well as to raw or cooked savory dishes. (*see also* **citrus zester**)

TEST KITCHEN SECRET

Before you zest fruit, be sure to scrub it well to remove any wax or chemicals; then pull a zester across or down the fruit's rind, or rub the fruit against a fine grater (be careful to only remove the colored skin and not the white pith, which tends to be very bitter). Never juice the fruit before zesting because this will make zesting much more difficult. LYDA JONES

Zinfandel (ZIHN fuhn dehl) A red wine grape with spicy, berry flavors that's used to make red wines ranging from light and fruity to rich and bold. White Zinfandel is a blush wine made by allowing the grapes only brief contact with their skins before they are removed. (*see also* **wine**)

zip-top bag Plastic bags with a leak-proof seal used for food storage. Other handy uses for these bags are:
- To hold crackers or cookies to be crushed with a rolling pin.
- To hold flour, batter, or crumbs for coating foods.
- To hold food while it marinates.
- To make an improvised pastry or piping bag.
- To freeze liquid ingredients (there are also special freezer zip-top bags).
- To toss salad with dressing.

After filling a zip-top bag, close it almost all the way, and then mash out as much of the remaining air as you can before sealing.

TEST KITCHEN SECRET

To make filling a zip-top bag easier, place the open bag in a bowl, and fold the top sides of the bag over the edges of the bowl. This will hold the sides of the bag up and help keep the top open. VIE WARSHAW

ziti (ZEE tee) Long, thin, slightly curved tubes of pasta used in Italian cooking. (*see also* **pasta**)

zombie (ZAHM bee) A strong, potent cocktail drink made of several types of rum, curaçao, Pernod, two or three different fruit juices, orgeat syrup, and grenadine, and served in a large goblet over crushed ice. Zombie drinks are usually garnished with slices of pineapple and a maraschino cherry. (*see also* **curaçao, grenadine, orgeat,** *and* **Pernod**)

zucchini (zoo KEE nee) A popular summer squash shaped like a thin cucumber; its skin can vary from dark to light green and sometimes has yellow markings. The zucchini has creamy white-green flesh, a mild flavor, and is available year-round in supermarkets, with its peak during late spring and summer. Zucchini can be steamed, grilled, sautéed, deep-fried, or baked.
Storage: Refrigerate zucchini in a plastic bag up to 5 days, longer if garden-fresh. (*see also* **squash** *and* **vegetables**)

ZUCCHINI-AND-CORN SKILLET

3 small zucchini	1 teaspoon salt
1 tablespoon butter or margarine	¾ teaspoon lemon pepper
1 tablespoon vegetable oil	½ cup (2 ounces) shredded
1 to 2 garlic cloves, minced	mozzarella cheese
1 (15½-ounce) can whole kernel corn, drained*	2 tablespoons chopped fresh basil
1 (2-ounce) jar diced pimiento, drained	

• Cut each zucchini lengthwise into quarters. Thinly slice quarters.
• Melt butter with vegetable oil in a large skillet over medium-high heat; add zucchini and garlic, and sauté 3 to 4 minutes.
• Add corn and next 3 ingredients; cook, stirring often, 2 to 3 minutes or until zucchini is tender. Sprinkle with cheese and basil; heat until cheese melts. Yield: 6 servings.

*Substitute 2 cups fresh corn kernels (about 4 ears), if desired.

zwieback (ZWY bak) A rusk bread made from slightly sweetened yeast dough that has been baked, sliced, and then baked again to make it very crisp and dry. Zwieback can be purchased in most supermarkets. (*see also* **rusk** *and* **twice-baked**)

TEST KITCHEN SECRET

Zwieback can be crushed and used instead of cookie crumbs when making dessert crusts for pies and cheesecakes. Zwieback crusts have a crisp texture and are not as sweet as cookie crumbs. REBECCA KRACKE GORDON

EQUIVALENT WEIGHTS and YIELDS

FOOD	WEIGHT OR COUNT	YIELD
Apples	1 pound (3 medium)	3 cups sliced
Bacon	8 slices cooked	½ cup crumbled
Bananas	1 pound (3 medium)	2½ cups sliced or about 2 cups mashed
Bread	1 pound	12 to 16 slices
	1½ slices	1 cup soft crumbs
Butter or margarine	1 pound	2 cups (4 sticks)
	¼-pound stick	½ cup (1 stick)
Cabbage	1 pound head	4½ cups shredded
Candied fruit or peels	½ pound	1¼ cups chopped
Carrots	1 pound	3 cups shredded
Cheese		
American or Cheddar	1 pound	about 4 cups shredded
cottage	1 pound	2 cups
cream	3-ounce package	6 tablespoons
Chocolate morsels	6-ounce package	1 cup
Cocoa	16-ounce can	5 cups
Coconut,		
flaked or shredded	1 pound	5 cups
Coffee	1 pound	80 tablespoons (40 cups brewed)
Corn	2 medium ears	1 cup kernels
Cornmeal	1 pound	3 cups
Crab, in shell	1 pound	¾ to 1 cup flaked
Crackers		
chocolate wafers	19 wafers	1 cup crumbs
graham crackers	14 squares	1 cup fine crumbs
saltine crackers	28 crackers	1 cup finely crushed
vanilla wafers	22 wafers	1 cup finely crushed
Cream, whipping	1 cup (½ pint)	2 cups whipped
Dates, pitted	1 pound	3 cups chopped
	8-ounce package	1½ cups chopped
Eggs	5 large	1 cup
whites	8 to 11	1 cup
yolks	12 to 14	1 cup
Flour, all-purpose	1 pound	3½ cups unsifted
cake	1 pound	4¾ to 5 cups sifted
whole wheat	1 pound	3½ cups unsifted
Green pepper	1 large	1 cup diced
Lemon	1 medium	2 to 3 tablespoons juice; 2 teaspoons grated rind
Lettuce	1-pound head	6¼ cups torn
Lime	1 medium	1½ to 2 tablespoons juice; 1½ teaspoons grated rind
Macaroni	4 ounces dry (1 cup)	2 cups cooked
Marshmallows		
large	10	1 cup
miniature	10	1 large marshmallow
	½ pound	4½ cups
Milk, evaporated	5-ounce can	about ⅔ cup
	12-ounce can	1½ cups
sweetened condensed	14-ounce can	1¼ cups
Mushrooms	3 cups raw (8 ounces)	1 cup sliced, cooked
Nuts, almonds	1 pound	1¾ cups nutmeats
	1 pound shelled	3½ cups
peanuts	1 pound	2¼ cups nutmeats
	1 pound shelled	3 cups

Equivalent Weights and Yields *(continued)*

FOOD	WEIGHT OR COUNT	YIELD
Nuts *(continued)*		
pecans	1 pound	2¼ cups nutmeats
	1 pound shelled	4 cups
walnuts	1 pound	1⅔ cups nutmeats
	1 pound shelled	4 cups
Oats, quick cooking	1 cup	1¾ cups cooked
Onion	1 medium	½ cup chopped
Orange	1 medium	½ cup juice; 2 tablespoons grated rind
Peaches	2 medium	1 cup sliced
Pears	2 medium	1 cup sliced
Potatoes, white	3 medium	2 cups cubed cooked or 1¾ cups mashed
sweet	3 medium	3 cups sliced
Raisins, seedless	1 pound	3 cups
Rice, long grain	1 cup	3 to 4 cups cooked
precooked	1 cup	2 cups cooked
Shrimp, raw, unpeeled	1 pound	8 to 9 ounces cooked, peeled, deveined
Spaghetti	7 ounces	about 4 cups cooked
Strawberries	1 quart	4 cups sliced
Sugar, brown	1 pound	2⅓ cups firmly packed
powdered	1 pound	3½ cups unsifted
granulated white	1 pound	2 cups

SUGAR SUBSTITUTE GUIDE*

SUGAR SUBSTITUTE DESCRIPTION	AMOUNT EQUAL TO ½ CUP SUGAR

The following sugar substitutes are measured like sugar, so when you use them in recipes to replace sugar, you can use the same amount of substitute as you would use of sugar.

DiabetiSweet: Contains a combination of acesulfame-K and isomalt; no aftertaste; looks like sugar; heat stable	½ cup
Equal Spoonful: Contains aspartame; no aftertaste; loses some sweetness in high heat	½ cup
Splenda: Contains sucralose, a modified sugar molecule that's not absorbed by the body; no aftertaste; extremely heat stable; also available in packets	½ cup
Sugar Twin: Contains saccharin; some aftertaste; heat stable	½ cup

These sugar substitutes are in more concentrated form, so you do not use as much of these as you would use of sugar in order to get the same sweetness.

Equal for Recipes: Contains aspartame; no aftertaste; the bulk form of Equal packets; loses some sweetness in high heat	3½ teaspoons
Equal Packets: Contains aspartame; no aftertaste; same as Equal for Recipes, but in packets; loses some sweetness in high heat	12 packets
Sweet 'N Low: Contains saccharin; some aftertaste; available in bulk form or in packets; heat stable	1 tablespoon or 12 packets
Sweet One: Contains acesulfame-K; no aftertaste; heat stable	12 packets

Liquid sugar substitutes blend easily with other ingredients and work well in sauces and marinades.

Sweet 'N Low: Contains saccharin; some aftertaste; heat stable	1 tablespoon
Sweet-10: Contains saccharin; some aftertaste; heat stable	1 tablespoon

*This is not an inclusive list and is not meant as an endorsement of any particular product.

HANDY SUBSTITUTIONS

INGREDIENT	SUBSTITUTION
BAKING PRODUCTS	
Arrowroot, 1½ teaspoons	• 1 tablespoon all-purpose flour • 1½ teaspoons cornstarch
Baking powder, 1 teaspoon	• ½ teaspoon cream of tartar plus ¼ teaspoon baking soda
Chocolate	
semisweet, 1 ounce	• 1 ounce unsweetened chocolate plus 1 tablespoon sugar
unsweetened, 1 ounce or square	• 3 tablespoons cocoa plus 1 tablespoon fat
chips, semisweet, 1 ounce	• 1 ounce square semisweet chocolate
chips, semisweet, 6-ounce package, melted	• 2 ounces unsweetened chocolate, 2 tablespoons shortening plus ½ cup sugar
Cocoa, ¼ cup	• 1 ounce unsweetened chocolate (decrease fat in recipe by ½ tablespoon)
Coconut	
flaked, 1 tablespoon	• 1½ tablespoons grated fresh coconut
cream, 1 cup	• 1 cup whipping cream
milk, 1 cup	• 1 cup whole or reduced-fat milk
Corn syrup, light, 1 cup	• 1 cup sugar plus ¼ cup water • 1 cup honey
Cornstarch, 1 tablespoon	• 2 tablespoons all-purpose flour or granular tapioca
Flour	
all-purpose, 1 tablespoon	• 1½ teaspoons cornstarch, potato starch, or rice starch • 1 tablespoon rice flour or corn flour • 1½ tablespoons whole wheat flour • ½ tablespoon whole wheat flour plus ½ tablespoon all-purpose flour
all-purpose, 1 cup sifted Note: Specialty flours added to yeast bread will result in a reduced volume and a heavier product.	• 1 cup plus 2 tablespoons sifted cake flour • 1 cup minus 2 tablespoons all-purpose flour (unsifted) • 1½ cups breadcrumbs • 1 cup rolled oats • ⅓ cup cornmeal or soybean flour plus ⅔ cup all-purpose flour • ¾ cup whole wheat flour or bran flour plus ¼ cup all-purpose flour • 1 cup rye or rice flour • ¼ cup soybean flour plus ¾ cup all-purpose flour
cake, 1 cup sifted	• 1 cup minus 2 tablespoons all-purpose flour
self-rising, 1 cup	• 1 cup all-purpose flour, 1 teaspoon baking powder plus ½ teaspoon salt
Marshmallows	
cream, 7-ounce jar	• 16-ounce package marshmallows, melted, plus 3½ tablespoons light corn syrup
miniature, 1 cup	• 10 large
Pecans, chopped, 1 cup	• 1 cup regular oats, toasted (in baked products)
Shortening	
melted, 1 cup	• 1 cup cooking oil (do not use cooking oil if recipe does not call for melted shortening)
solid, 1 cup (used in baking)	• 1 cup minus 2 tablespoons lard • 1⅛ cups butter or margarine (decrease salt called for in recipe by ½ teaspoon)

INGREDIENT	SUBSTITUTION
Sugar	
brown, 1 cup firmly packed	• 1 cup granulated white sugar
maple, ½ cup	• 1 cup maple syrup
powdered, 1 cup	• 1 cup sugar plus 1 tablespoon cornstarch (processed in food processor)
granulated white, 1 teaspoon	• ⅛ teaspoon noncaloric sweetener solution or follow manufacturer's directions
granulated white, 1 cup	• 1 cup corn syrup (decrease liquid called for in recipe by ¼ cup) • 1 cup firmly packed brown sugar • 1 cup honey (decrease liquid called for in recipe by ¼ cup)
Tapioca, granular, 1 tablespoon	• 1½ teaspoons cornstarch • 1 tablespoon all-purpose flour
Yeast, active dry, 1 (¼-ounce) package	• 1 tablespoon active dry yeast

DAIRY PRODUCTS

Butter, 1 cup	• ⅞ to 1 cup shortening or lard plus ½ teaspoon salt • 1 cup margarine (2 sticks; do not substitute whipped or low-fat margarine)
Cream	
heavy (30% to 40% fat), 1 cup	• ¾ cup milk plus ⅓ cup butter or margarine (for cooking and baking; will not whip)
light (15% to 20% fat), 1 cup	• ¾ cup milk plus 3 tablespoons butter or margarine (for cooking and baking) • 1 cup evaporated milk, undiluted
half-and-half, 1 cup	• ⅞ cup milk plus ½ tablespoon butter or margarine (for cooking and baking) • 1 cup evaporated milk, undiluted
whipped	• 1 (13-ounce) can evaporated milk (chilled 12 hours). Add 1 teaspoon lemon juice. Whip until stiff.
Egg	
1 large	• 2 egg yolks (for custard and cream fillings) • 2 egg yolks plus 1 tablespoon water (for cookies) • ¼ cup egg substitute
2 large	• 3 small eggs
1 egg white (2 tablespoons)	• 2 tablespoons egg substitute • 2 teaspoons sifted, dry egg white powder plus 2 tablespoons warm water
1 egg yolk (1½ tablespoons)	• 2 tablespoons sifted dry egg yolk powder plus 2 teaspoons water • 1½ tablespoons thawed frozen egg yolk
Milk	
buttermilk, 1 cup	• 1 tablespoon vinegar or lemon juice plus whole milk to make 1 cup (let stand 10 minutes) • 1 cup plain yogurt • 1 cup whole milk plus 1¾ teaspoons cream of tartar
fat free, 1 cup	• 4 to 5 tablespoons nonfat dry milk powder plus enough water to make 1 cup • ½ cup evaporated skim milk plus ½ cup water
whole, 1 cup	• 4 to 5 tablespoons nonfat dry milk powder plus enough water to make 1 cup • ½ cup evaporated milk plus ½ cup water
sweetened condensed, 1 (14-ounce) can (about 1¼ cups)	• Heat the following ingredients until sugar and butter dissolve: ⅓ cup plus 2 tablespoons evaporated milk, 1 cup sugar, 3 tablespoons butter or margarine

INGREDIENT | SUBSTITUTION

Milk *(continued)*

sweetened condensed, 1 cup
- Heat the following ingredients until sugar and butter dissolve: ⅓ cup evaporated milk, ¾ cup sugar, 2 tablespoons butter or margarine
- Add 1 cup plus 2 tablespoons nonfat dry milk powder to ½ cup warm water. Mix well. Add ¾ cup sugar, and stir until smooth.

Sour cream, 1 cup
- 1 cup plain yogurt plus 3 tablespoons melted butter
- 1 cup plain yogurt plus 1 tablespoon cornstarch
- 1 tablespoon lemon juice plus evaporated milk to equal 1 cup

Yogurt, 1 cup (plain)
- 1 cup buttermilk

FRUIT AND VEGETABLE PRODUCTS

Lemon

1 medium
- 2 to 3 tablespoons juice plus 2 teaspoons grated rind

juice, 1 teaspoon
- ½ teaspoon vinegar

peel, dried, 1 teaspoon
- 2 teaspoons freshly grated lemon rind
- ½ teaspoon lemon extract

Orange

1 medium
- ½ cup juice plus 2 tablespoons grated rind

peel, dried, 1 tablespoon
- 1½ teaspoons orange extract

Mushrooms, 1 pound fresh
- 1 (8-ounce) can sliced mushrooms, drained
- 3 ounces dried mushrooms, rehydrated

Onion, chopped, 1 medium
- 1 tablespoon dried minced onion
- 1 tablespoon onion powder

Pepper

red or green bell, chopped, 3 tablespoons
- 1 tablespoon dried sweet red or green pepper flakes

red bell, chopped, 3 tablespoons
- 2 tablespoons chopped pimiento

Shallots, chopped, 3 tablespoons
- 2 tablespoons chopped onion plus 1 tablespoon chopped garlic

Tomatoes

fresh, chopped, 2 cups
- 1 (16-ounce) can (may need to drain)

juice, 1 cup
- ½ cup tomato sauce plus ½ cup water

Tomato sauce, 2 cups
- ¾ cup tomato paste plus 1 cup water

MISCELLANEOUS

Broth, beef or chicken

canned broth, 1 cup
- 1 bouillon cube dissolved in 1 cup boiling water
- 1 teaspoon powdered broth base dissolved in 1 cup boiling water

powdered broth base, 1 teaspoon
- 1 bouillon cube

powdered broth base, 1 teaspoon dissolved in 1 cup water
- 1 cup canned or homemade broth
- 1 bouillon cube dissolved in 1 cup boiling water

Chili sauce, 1 cup
- 1 cup tomato sauce, ¼ cup brown sugar, 2 tablespoons vinegar, ¼ teaspoon cinnamon, dash of ground cloves plus dash of ground allspice

Gelatin, flavored, 3-ounce package
- 1 tablespoon unflavored gelatin plus 2 cups fruit juice

Honey, 1 cup
- 1¼ cups sugar plus ¼ cup water

Handy Substitutions *(continued)*

INGREDIENT	SUBSTITUTION
Ketchup, 1 cup	• 1 cup tomato sauce, ½ cup sugar plus 2 tablespoons vinegar (for cooking)
Macaroni, uncooked, 2 cups (4 cups cooked)	• 8 ounces spaghetti, uncooked • 4 cups fine egg noodles, uncooked
Mayonnaise, 1 cup (for salads and dressings)	• ½ cup plain yogurt plus ½ cup mayonnaise • 1 cup sour cream • 1 cup cottage cheese pureed in a blender
Rice, uncooked, 1 cup regular (3 cups cooked)	• 1 cup uncooked converted rice • 1 cup uncooked brown rice or wild rice
Vinegar, balsamic, ½ cup	• ½ cup red wine vinegar (some flavor difference)

SEASONING PRODUCTS

INGREDIENT	SUBSTITUTION
Allspice, ground, 1 teaspoon	• ½ teaspoon ground cinnamon plus ½ teaspoon ground cloves
Apple pie spice, 1 teaspoon	• ½ teaspoon ground cinnamon, ¼ teaspoon ground nutmeg plus ⅛ teaspoon ground cardamom
Bay leaf, 1 whole	• ¼ teaspoon crushed bay leaf
Beau Monde seasoning, 1 teaspoon	• 1 teaspoon seasoning salt or seasoned salt • ½ teaspoon salt
Chives, chopped, 1 tablespoon	• 1 tablespoon chopped green onion tops
Dillweed, fresh or dried, 3 heads	• 1 tablespoon dill seed
Garlic 1 small clove garlic salt, 1 teaspoon	• ⅛ teaspoon garlic powder or minced dried garlic • ⅛ teaspoon garlic powder plus ⅞ teaspoon salt
Ginger crystallized, 1 tablespoon fresh, grated, 1 tablespoon ground, ⅛ teaspoon	• ⅛ teaspoon ground ginger • ⅛ teaspoon ground ginger • 1 tablespoon crystallized ginger rinsed in water to remove sugar, and finely cut • 1 tablespoon grated fresh ginger
Herbs, fresh, chopped, 1 tablespoon	• 1 teaspoon dried herbs or ¼ teaspoon ground herbs
Horseradish, fresh, grated, 1 tablespoon	• 2 tablespoons prepared horseradish
Mustard, dried, 1 teaspoon	• 1 tablespoon prepared mustard
Onion powder, 1 tablespoon	• 1 medium onion, chopped • 1 tablespoon dried minced onion
Parsley, dried, 1 teaspoon	• 1 tablespoon fresh parsley, chopped
Pimiento, chopped, 2 tablespoons	• rehydrate 1 tablespoon dried sweet red pepper flakes • 2 to 3 tablespoons chopped fresh red bell pepper
Pumpkin pie spice, 1 teaspoon	• ½ teaspoon ground cinnamon, ¼ teaspoon ground ginger, ⅛ teaspoon ground allspice plus ⅛ teaspoon ground nutmeg
Spearmint or peppermint, dried, 1 tablespoon	• 3 tablespoons chopped fresh mint
Vanilla bean, 1 (1 inch)	• 1 teaspoon vanilla extract
Worcestershire sauce, 1 teaspoon	• 1 teaspoon bottled steak sauce

COOKING FRESH VEGETABLES

VEGETABLE	SERVINGS	PREPARATION	COOKING INSTRUCTIONS (ADD SALT, IF DESIRED)
Asparagus	3 to 4 per pound	Snap off tough ends. Remove scales, if desired.	*To boil:* Cook, covered, in small amount of boiling water 4 to 6 minutes or until crisp-tender. *To steam:* Cook, covered, on a rack above boiling water 6 to 8 minutes.
Beans, green	4 per pound	Wash; trim ends, and remove strings. Cut into 1½-inch pieces.	Cook, covered, in small amount of boiling water 12 to15 minutes.
Beans, lima	2 per pound unshelled, 4 per pound shelled	Shell and wash.	Cook, covered, in small amount of boiling water 20 minutes.
Beets	3 to 4 per pound	Leave root and 1 inch of stem; scrub with vegetable brush.	Cook, covered, in boiling water 35 to 40 minutes. Remove peel.
Broccoli	3 to 4 per pound	Remove outer leaves and tough ends of lower stalks. Wash; cut into spears or florets.	*To boil:* Cook, covered, in small amount of boiling water 8 to 10 minutes. *To steam:* Cook, covered, on a rack above boiling water 10 to 15 minutes.
Brussels sprouts	4 per pound	Wash; remove discolored leaves. Cut off stem ends; slash bottom with an X.	Cook, covered, in small amount of boiling water 8 to 10 minutes.
Cabbage	4 per pound	Remove outer leaves; wash. Shred or cut into wedges.	Cook, covered, in small amount of boiling water 5 to 7 minutes (shredded) or 10 to 15 minutes (wedges).
Carrots	4 per pound	Scrape; remove ends, and rinse. Leave tiny carrots whole; slice large carrots, or cut into strips.	Cook, covered, in small amount of boiling water 8 to 10 minutes (slices) or 12 to15 minutes (strips).
Cauliflower	4 per medium head	Remove outer leaves and stalk. Wash. Leave whole, or break into florets.	Cook, covered, in small amount of boiling water 10 to 12 minutes (whole) or 8 to 10 minutes (florets).
Corn	4 per 4 large ears	Remove husks and silks. Leave corn on cob, or cut off tips of kernels, and scrape cob with dull edge of knife.	Cook, covered, in boiling water 10 minutes (on cob) or in small amount of boiling water 6 to 8 minutes (cut).
Eggplant	2 to 3 per pound	Wash and peel, if desired. Cut into cubes, or cut crosswise into slices.	*To boil:* Cook, covered, in small amount of boiling water 8 to 10 minutes. *To sauté:* Cook in small amount of butter or vegetable oil 5 to 8 minutes.
Greens	3 to 4 per pound	Remove stems; wash thoroughly. Tear into bite-size pieces.	Cook, covered, in 1 to 1½ inches boiling water 5 to 8 minutes (spinach); 10 to 20 minutes (Swiss chard); 30 to 45 minutes (collards, turnip greens, mustard, kale).

Cooking Fresh Vegetables *(continued)*

VEGETABLE	SERVINGS	PREPARATION	COOKING INSTRUCTIONS (ADD SALT, IF DESIRED)
Leeks	3 per pound	Remove root, tough outer leaves, and tops, leaving 2 inches of dark leaves. Wash thoroughly. Slice, if desired.	Cook, covered, in small amount of boiling water 12 to 15 minutes (whole) or 10 to 12 minutes (sliced).
Mushrooms	4 per pound	Wipe with damp paper towels, or wash gently and pat dry. Cut off tips of stems. Slice, if desired.	Sauté in butter 5 minutes.
Okra	4 per pound	Wash and pat dry. Trim ends.	Cook, covered, in small amount of boiling water 5 to 10 minutes.
Parsnips	4 per pound	Scrape; cut off ends. Slice or cut into strips.	Cook, covered, in small amount of boiling water 15 to 20 minutes.
Peas, black-eyed	2 per pound unshelled, 4 per pound shelled	Shell and wash.	Cook, covered, in small amount of boiling water 15 to 20 minutes. or until tender.
Peas, green	2 per pound unshelled, 4 per pound shelled	Shell and wash.	Cook, covered, in small amount of boiling water 10 to 12 minutes.
Potatoes, all-purpose or new	3 to 4 per pound	Scrub potatoes; peel, if desired. Leave whole, or slice or cut into chunks.	Cook, covered, in small amount of boiling water 30 to 40 minutes (whole) or 15 to 20 minutes (slices, chunks, or new potatoes).
Potatoes, baking	2 to 3 per pound	Scrub potatoes; rub skins with vegetable oil.	Bake at 400° for 1 hour or until done.
Potatoes, sweet	2 to 3 per pound	Scrub potatoes; leave whole to bake, or slice or cut into chunks to boil.	Bake at 375° for 1 hour or until done. *To boil:* Cook in boiling water to cover 20 to 30 minutes.
Pumpkin	4½ to 5 cups cooked, mashed pumpkin per 1 (5-pound) pumpkin	Slice in half crosswise. Remove seeds.	Place cut side down on baking pan. Bake at 325° for 45 minutes or until tender. Cool; peel and mash.
Rutabagas	2 to 3 per pound	Wash; peel and slice or cube.	Cook, covered, in boiling water 15 to 20 minutes. Mash, if desired.
Squash, summer	3 to 4 per pound	Wash; trim ends. Slice or dice.	*To boil:* Cook, covered, in small amount of boiling water 8 to 10 minutes (slices) or 15 minutes (whole). *To steam:* Cook, covered, on a rack over boiling water 10 to 12 minutes (sliced or diced).
Squash, winter (acorn, butternut, hubbard)	2 per pound	Rinse; cut in half, and remove seeds.	*To boil:* Cook, covered, in boiling water 20 to 25 minutes. *To bake:* Place cut side down in shallow baking dish; add ½ inch water. Bake, uncovered, at 375° for 30 minutes. Turn and season or fill; bake 20 to 30 minutes or until tender.
Turnips	3 per pound	Wash; peel and slice or cube.	Cook, covered, in boiling water to cover 15 to 20 minutes or until tender.

METRIC EQUIVALENTS

Recipes in this cookbook use the standard United States method for measuring liquid and dry or solid ingredients (teaspoons, tablespoons, and cups). The following charts are provided to help cooks outside the U.S. successfully use these recipes. All equivalents are approximate.

METRIC EQUIVALENTS FOR DIFFERENT TYPES OF INGREDIENTS

A standard cup measure of a dry or solid ingredient will vary in weight depending on the type of ingredient. A standard cup of liquid is the same volume for any type of liquid. Use the following chart when converting standard cup measures to grams (weight) or milliliters (volume).

STANDARD CUP	FINE POWDER (ex. flour)	GRAIN (ex. rice)	GRANULAR (ex. sugar)	LIQUID SOLIDS (ex. butter)	LIQUID (ex. milk)
1	140 g	150 g	190 g	200 g	240 ml
¾	105 g	113 g	143 g	150 g	180 ml
⅔	93 g	100 g	125 g	133 g	160 ml
½	70 g	75 g	95 g	100 g	120 ml
⅓	47 g	50 g	63 g	67 g	80 ml
¼	35 g	38 g	48 g	50 g	60 ml
⅛	18 g	19 g	24 g	25 g	30 ml

USEFUL EQUIVALENTS FOR DRY INGREDIENTS BY WEIGHT

(To convert ounces to grams, multiply the number of ounces by 30.)

1 oz	=	¹⁄₁₆ lb	=	30 g
4 oz	=	¼ lb	=	120 g
8 oz	=	½ lb	=	240 g
12 oz	=	¾ lb	=	360 g
16 oz	=	1 lb	=	480 g

USEFUL EQUIVALENTS FOR LENGTH

(To convert inches to centimeters, multiply the number of inches by 2.5.)

1 in			=	2.5 cm	
6 in	=	½ ft	=	15 cm	
12 in	=	1 ft	=	30 cm	
36 in	=	3 ft = 1 yd	=	90 cm	
40 in			=	100 cm	= 1 m

USEFUL EQUIVALENTS FOR COOKING/OVEN TEMPERATURES

	FAHRENHEIT	CELSIUS	GAS MARK
Freeze Water	32° F	0° C	
Room Temperature	68° F	20° C	
Boil Water	212° F	100° C	
Bake	325° F	160° C	3
	350° F	180° C	4
	375° F	190° C	5
	400° F	200° C	6
	425° F	220° C	7
	450° F	230° C	8
Broil			Grill

USEFUL EQUIVALENTS FOR LIQUID INGREDIENTS BY VOLUME

¼ tsp				=	1 ml
½ tsp				=	2 ml
1 tsp				=	5 ml
3 tsp = 1 tbls			= ½ fl oz	=	15 ml
	2 tbls	= ⅛ cup	= 1 fl oz	=	30 ml
	4 tbls	= ¼ cup	= 2 fl oz	=	60 ml
	5⅓ tbls	= ⅓ cup	= 3 fl oz	=	80 ml
	8 tbls	= ½ cup	= 4 fl oz	=	120 ml
	10⅔ tbls	= ⅔ cup	= 5 fl oz	=	160 ml
	12 tbls	= ¾ cup	= 6 fl oz	=	180 ml
	16 tbls	= 1 cup	= 8 fl oz	=	240 ml
1 pt		= 2 cups	= 16 fl oz	=	480 ml
1 qt		= 4 cups	= 32 fl oz	=	960 ml
			33 fl oz	=	1000 ml
				=	1 liter

RECIPE INDEX

CHART INDEX